AF285466

## Text smart

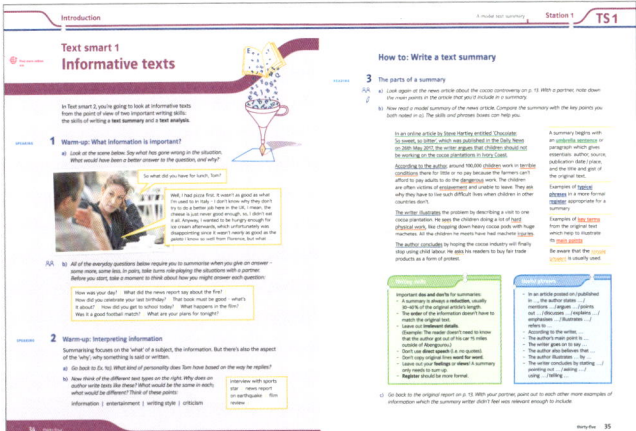

Auf den *Text smart*-Seiten lernst du, wie du mit verschiedenen Textsorten umgehst (z. B. Sachtexten, argumentativen Texten oder auch einem Kurzfilm) und sie im Anschluss für deine eigenen Arbeiten nutzen kannst.

## Across cul...

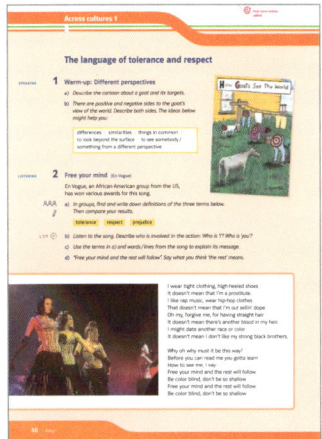

Hier kannst du Themen und Begegnungssituationen in der englischsprachigen Welt mit deinem Alltag vergleichen.

## Diff pool

## Skills

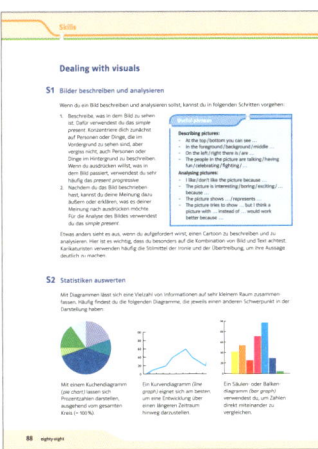

## Grammar, Vocabulary

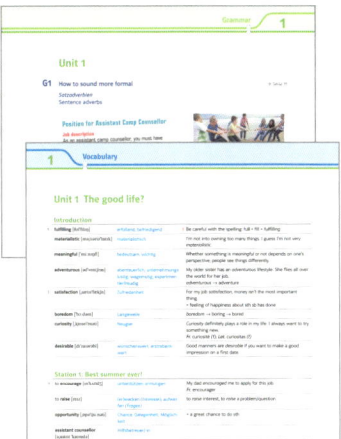

Im hinteren Buchteil stehen dir hilfreiche Anhänge zur Verfügung. Achte auf die Verweise in den Units, die dir sagen, in welchem Anhang du nachschlagen kannst.

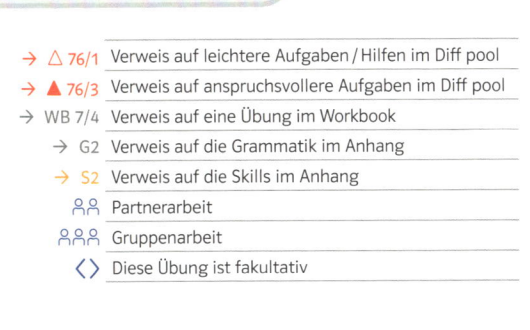

| | |
|---|---|
| → △ 76/1 Verweis auf leichtere Aufgaben / Hilfen im Diff pool | ⬳ Schreiben (geschlossen / einfach) |
| → ▲ 76/3 Verweis auf anspruchsvollere Aufgaben im Diff pool | ⬳ Schreiben (offen / kreativ) |
| → WB 7/4 Verweis auf eine Übung im Workbook | ⬔ Hier entsteht ein Produkt für dein Portfolio. |
| → G2 Verweis auf die Grammatik im Anhang | S1/14 ⊙ Verweis auf die Schüler-CDs im Workbook (Audio) |
| → S2 Verweis auf die Skills im Anhang | L1/19 ⊙ Verweis auf die Lehrer-CDs (Audio) |
| ⛌ Partnerarbeit | ⬒ Verweis auf die Lehrer-DVD (Film) |
| ⛌ Gruppenarbeit | ⊕ Code auf www.klett.de eingeben und Zusatzmaterial nutzen |
| ⟨⟩ Diese Übung ist fakultativ | ⛭ Übungen, die die Unit task besonders vorbereiten |
| | 🇬🇧 🇺🇸 Across cultures |

**Green Line 6 G9** für Klasse 10 an Gymnasien

**Herausgeber:** Prof. Harald Weisshaar, Bisingen

**Autorinnen und Autoren:** Jennifer Baer-Engel, Göppingen; Carolyn Jones, Beckenham
sowie Cornelia Kaminski, Fulda; Elise Köhler-Davidson, Exeter

**Beratung:** Paul Dennis, Lahnstein; Cornelia Kaminski, Fulda; Nilgül Karabulut, Aachen; Hartmut Klose, Seevetal;
Antje Körber, Merseburg; Jörg Nieswand, Berlin; Jörg Schulze, Dresden sowie Dr. Jan Kulok, Ostfildern

**1. Auflage**          1   8  7  6  5  4   |   26   25   24   23   22

Alle Drucke dieser Auflage sind unverändert und können im Unterricht nebeneinander verwendet werden.
Die letzte Zahl bezeichnet das Jahr des Druckes.

**Redaktion:** Michael Mattison; Martina Reckart; Lektorat editoria: Cornelia Schaller, Fellbach
**Herstellung:** Anita Bauch; Anne Leibbrand

**Gestaltung:** Petra Michel, Essen
**Umschlaggestaltung:** know idea, Freiburg; Koma Amok, Stuttgart
**Illustrationen:** Peer Kramer, Düsseldorf; jani lunablau, Barcelona
sowie Christian Dekelver, Weinstadt (Karten)
**Satz:** Satzkiste GmbH, Stuttgart
**Reproduktion:** Schwaben-Repro, Stuttgart
**Druck:** Mohn Media Mohndruck GmbH, Gütersloh

Printed in Germany
ISBN 978-3-12-854260-7 (fester Einband)
ISBN 978-3-12-854261-4 (flexibler Einband)

# Green Line 6 G9

von
Jennifer Baer-Engel
Carolyn Jones
Cornelia Kaminski
Elise Köhler-Davidson

herausgegeben von
Harald Weisshaar

Ernst Klett Verlag
Stuttgart · Leipzig

# Inhalt

# Inhalt

Die in diesem Band aufbereiteten Inhalte stellen ein Angebot dar, sie sind nicht obligatorisch durchzunehmen. Maßgeblich für die Auswahl der Texte und Aufgaben ist der Lehrplan Ihres Bundeslandes bzw. Ihr schulinternes Curriculum.

# Unit 1
# The good life?

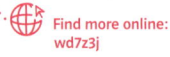

Find more online:
wd7z3j

---

SPEAKING

## 1 Thinking about priorities in life → WB 2/1

→ S1 **a)** *First, describe what you see in the photo above.*

**b)** *Now imagine what kind of lives the two people might have, and what their priorities in life might be. Explain what makes you think so.*

**c)** *Describe the photos on p. 199 at the back of your book. Explain whether the photo above or one of the other two comes closer to your 'good life'.*

> **Word bank**
>
> to (not) make enough money to afford … |
> to (not) worry … | to (not) have a boring /
> fulfilling / fun / materialistic / meaningful /
> an adventurous / … life | to have the right /
> wrong priorities | to (not) accept other
> people's priorities / lifestyles / …

LISTENING

## 2 ⟨ The good life in songs ⟩ → WB 2/2

L 1/1–2 ⊙ **a)** *Listen to the two songs on the next page. Say which one you spontaneously like better, and why.*

**b)** *Read the lyrics. Point out the references about what makes a 'champagne' or a 'good' life.*

**c)** 1. Can you see yourself in **both** songs? Explain.
 2. Discuss if it's fair to say that one lifestyle is 'better' than the other.

**Champagne Life** (by Ne-Yo, 2010)

Oh got an addiction for life and this living.
Like every day's my birthday, know what I'm getting.
Reserved for top notch, that's where I'm sitting.
Me and my friends and, found six Miss Independents.
And my attitude's so chill and so breezy.
In my designer suit I make this look easy.
Sexy baby, don't you dare act like you don't see me,
Baby I know you see me.

It's all about them fast car nights and them big bold days.
Living this champagne life, everything's OK.
Let's toast it up, oh, let's toast it up, oh.
Said we play all night, and we play all day.
Living this champagne life, everything's OK
Let's toast it up, oh, baby let's toast it up.

**The Good Life** (by Thirsty Merc, 2015)

Some of us spend all our time
Chasing dreams of dollar signs
But I got riches of a different kind
Love is my fortune.
'Cause all the bucks don't make much sense
If they don't bring you happiness
Love's a picture so immense
It's bigger than Ben Hur.

I'm no billionaire, no VIP, no diamonds on my shoes
But I'm living, living the good life,
   living, living the good life
I got everything I ever need as long as I got you
We'll be living, living the good life,
   living, living the good life …

PEAKING

**3  Thinking about the job world: Statistics on work patterns**

→ S2

**a)** *In groups of 4–5, look at the two charts about work patterns in the UK. Point out the main facts that you learn.*

→ △ 76/1

**b)  1.** Explain how the following ideas could play a role in the statistics:

job satisfaction | boredom | curiosity

**2.** Discuss whether it's desirable to stay in a job for more or less than two years.

**c)** *Your turn: Complete these sentences with ideas about yourself (4–6 lines):*

**1.** In 10 years' time, I'll have / be / do …
**2.** My idea of success / a good life is / isn't …,

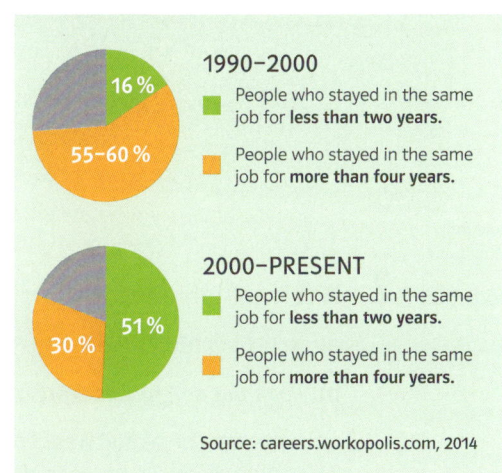

**1990–2000**

16 %
■ People who stayed in the same job for **less than two years.**

55–60 %
■ People who stayed in the same job for **more than four years.**

**2000–PRESENT**

51 %
■ People who stayed in the same job for **less than two years.**

30 %
■ People who stayed in the same job for **more than four years.**

Source: careers.workopolis.com, 2014

# Best summer ever!

READING    **1**   **A look at an informal job advert**

**a)** *Read text A, a flyer for a summer job. In your own words, say what job it advertises.*

**b)** *How successful is the advert in encouraging people to apply? Evaluate it according to these criteria: raising interest | concrete information | fun*
*Then exchange your ideas with a partner and say if you would apply for the job or not.*

**A**

**Action Summer UK** are offering a **FANTASTIC** opportunity to 15–17 year olds just like you! Come and join us as an assistant counsellor in one of our summer camps!

You'll help the senior counsellors to lead children in activities such as sports, arts and outdoor adventures – we have something for everyone, no matter what you're passionate about! You'll become more confident and develop endless new skills.

Experiences as a camp counsellor are some of the BEST a teenager can have – just read our counsellors' testimonials to see what we mean! It's the greatest way to spend a summer. Head for **www.actionsummer.org.uk** now for a complete job description.

**B**

### ACTION SUMMER UK
### Position for Assistant Camp Counsellor

**Job description:** As an assistant camp counsellor, you are supposed to set a good example at all times for the younger children. In your role, you are supposed to support and motivate the children in all their activities, so you should have an outgoing personality. You will also need to be spontaneous in dealing with unexpected situations. And, of course, you are expected to be a team player.

**A counsellor's job will / can include all of these areas of responsibility:**
1. supporting senior counsellors during sports and other activities
2. preparing and serving food in the cafeteria
3. organising evening entertainment
4. helping with chores (washing clothes, etc.)

**You are expected to:**
– take part in Orientation Day for counsellors
– be available for at least two weeks in August
– be between 15 and 17 years of age

Please e-mail your CV with an application letter to Martha Ross: **ross@actionsummeruk.ac.uk**

READING    **2**   **A formal job description: The bigger picture**

**a)** *Now read text B, the full job description. Name the main qualifications that are required.*

→ △ 76/2   **b)** *Point out differences there are between texts A and B.*

**c)** *What kind of person would be a successful applicant for this job? Consider the following criteria as you justify your ideas:*

specific experience | qualifications and skills | personal characteristics

STENING

## 3 It's such a cliché! → WB 3/3–4

Two friends, Ella and Ryan, are talking about the summer job in the advert.

L1/3 ⊙

**a)** *Listen and sum up their attitudes towards work in general. Think of the phrases on the right and these two points as you listen:*

→ S7

– what's useful / enjoyable at the job
– gender

**b)** *Listen again. Explain why working as a camp counsellor might be a good option for Ella this summer.*

**c)** *Comment on Ella's and Ryan's views on gender stereotypes.*

> **Useful phrases**
>
> Employers like / don't like:
> reliable / responsible / focused applicants | all-rounders | applicants who only think of … | people who stand out / don't stand out from the crowd | applicants with lots of strengths / few weaknesses
>
> It's a cliché / stereotype to think of men / women in jobs that require …

READING

## 4 What careers do girls and boys prefer?

**a)** *Read this extract from a news report and sum up the main message. Say if the report surprises you or not, and why.*

Gender stereotyping is still an issue when boys and girls consider career options, research shows. Millions of pounds have been spent trying to persuade more girls to choose science and engineering, and to persuade boys to read more. But a report today says that, in the end, boys and girls choose traditional career paths. The survey of 500 14- to 16-year-olds studying for their GCSEs shows that, when asked about their career ideas, girls listed healthcare (22 percent), education (11 percent) and fashion (10 percent) as their three favourite options. With the boys, a career in IT was the favourite (16 percent) followed by engineering (12 percent) and healthcare (10 percent).

Source: The Independent Online

Female construction workers: still not typical, report shows

**b)** *Conduct a class survey:*
1. Ask the people in your class what their career ideas and plans are. Put your results on a wall display.
2. Now compare your classroom results with the news report.

→ △ 77/3

**c)** *Look at the professions below. Discuss which are considered to be typical male or female jobs, or either. Justify your opinions.*

**Examples:**
A: Any job which involves … is expected to be a female job because women are expected to be good with / at … In my opinion … / If you look more closely …
B: So many people still think men / women are supposed to be … That's why people always associate jobs like a / an … with men / women. When I look around, the reality is …

architect | business executive | dancer | doctor | engineer | fashion designer | firefighter | model | musician | nurse | pilot | reporter | sales assistant | teacher | web designer

VOCABULARY  **5** **Expressing expectations** → Fact page, p. 200

→ △ 77/4, 78/5

*Write some sentences about one of the jobs in Ex. 4c), or another job.*
*Use **be expected to** and **be supposed to + infinitive**. Take turns to read out your sentences and guess which jobs you're describing.*

Examples:
For this job you**'re supposed to be** good with people and **are** also **expected to have** …
This person **is expected to have** a perfect body and he**'s** / she**'s supposed to be** …

READING  **6** **The importance of a CV** → WB 3/5

a) *For a job application, a CV is a must. Read the one on the right, which Ella has written for the camp counsellor job you read about on p. 8. Say why you think a CV is so important.*

b) *CVs are written for a particular job. Check what Ella has emphasised in her CV. Does she meet the expectations? Give examples and say if you would give her the job.*

**Curriculum Vitae**

**Personal details:**
Name:     Ella Lewis
Address:     21 Redhatch Road
         Brighton  BN1 35H
Tel:     06383  8372634
E-mail:     ellal@smail.co.uk
Nationality:     British
Date of birth:     26.04.2002

**Education:**
2013 – (2018)     Dunstan Comprehensive School
         Will take GCSEs in 10 subjects
2006 – 2013:     Whiteleaf Primary School

**Work experience:**
2016 –     Children's party organiser

**Personal profile:**
I am a hard-working and reliable person. I enjoy meeting new people and have good communication skills. Also, I work well in a team. I like working with children because it gives me the chance to show my people skills. My main hobby is swimming and I have won several local competitions.

References available on request.

WRITING  **7** **Your turn: A personal profile for your CV** → WB 4/6

→ △ 78/6
→ S6

*Go back to text B on p. 8. Choose **one** of the four areas of responsibility for the job. For your own CV, write a personal profile. Emphasise the skills, qualifications and strengths that would be important for your area of responsibility.*

**Tip**

In more formal texts like CVs or application letters, it's common (but not required) to use **long forms**, not short forms:
I'm … → **I am** …
I've had … → **I have had** …

**Across cultures**

In some countries, applicants are expected to include a **photo** with their **CV** – but *not* in the UK or US. And in some countries, you needn't even state your full name, age or gender.

What are the pros and cons of an employer seeing your photo or knowing your name, gender or age?

READING

## 8 The application letter

**a)** *Read Ella's application letter below. What are the differences between a letter to a friend and a formal letter like this one? Make a grid and fill in the different criteria.*

→ S5

→ △ 78/7

**b)** *Say how well Ella 'sells herself' when she emphasises what she could bring to the job.*

Action Summer UK
20–22 Larksdale Rise
Chester CH3 2BD

21 Redhatch Road
Brighton BN1 35H

6th May 2017

Application for position as Assistant Summer Camp Counsellor

Dear Ms Ross,

With reference to your online advertisement, I am writing to apply for a position as an Assistant Summer Camp Counsellor.

As you will see from my CV, I am 15 years old and preparing for my GCSE exams. I enjoy working with children very much; **hopefully**, I will be a teacher one day. **Therefore**, I am very interested in the opportunity you offer. **Moreover**, as I have had a Saturday job for the last year as a children's party organiser, I already have a lot of experience in leading games and activities and in encouraging children of all ages to take part. **Personally**, I enjoy sports activities the most.
At a summer camp with a lake, **surely** a counsellor with good swimming skills could be a useful addition to your team. **Additionally**, I have good canoeing skills.

Thank you for considering my application. I am available for an interview any evening or weekend. I look forward to hearing from you soon.

Yours sincerely,
*Ella Lewis*
Ella Lewis

Att. CV

Put your **address** and the **date** here.

Put the **address** of the person or company you're writing to here.

Show what the letter is about in an underlined **heading**.

In the 1st paragraph, say **why** you are writing, **where** you saw the ad, **which** job you're applying for.

In the 2nd paragraph, talk about your **background** and **experience** (your age; what you hope to do in the future; description of work experience / skills). Also, refer to your **CV** here.

Use a friendly **ending** and a standard **final sentence**.

Print your **name** under your **signature** and say if there is an **attachment** to your e-mail (or an enclosure to your letter).

LANGUAGE

## 9 Improve your style: How to sound more formal → G1 → WB 4/7, 5/8–9

**a)** *Read the letter again. Decide which words in **bold** are **linking adverbs** and which are **commenting**. Make a grid with those words.*

**b)** *Now add these adverbs to your grid from a):*

furthermore | however | in fact | luckily | nevertheless | unfortunately

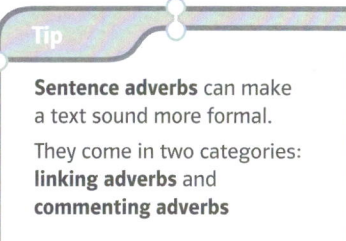

**Tip**

**Sentence adverbs** can make a text sound more formal.

They come in two categories: **linking adverbs** and **commenting adverbs**

**c)** *Link these sentences or begin new sentences with **sentence adverbs** on this page.*

1. I have well-developed computer skills.
2. I am free in the last week of July.
3. I love music and love to sing.
4. I don't have any cooking experience.
5. My French isn't too bad.
6. I am definitely a team player.

a) I'm able to visit France quite often.
b) I don't play an instrument.
c) I can help with IT issues if you need me.
d) I am very interested in learning!
e) I don't mind working independently.
f) I can be available for all of August.

**WRITING**  **10**   **Your turn: Apply for a job of your choice in the UK** → WB 5/10

→ S12

**a)** *Go online and find an advert for a summer or weekend job in the UK you'd find interesting. Here are some ideas you might like to research, or perhaps you have other ideas:*

lifeguard **|** assistant at a tourist information centre **|** waiter

**b)** *Write a CV and/or an application letter for the job you chose.*

**MEDIATION**   **11**   **A male au pair's testimonial**

→ S10

On a camping holiday with your family in Bavaria, you meet some English teenagers. One evening, you're discussing travelling abroad on au pair exchanges. You mention you've heard of male au pairs, but the others don't believe it: "It's a girl's thing." So you find this testimonial below and decide to write about the topic of male au pairs on your social media. You do it in English so your international friends can read it too.

**a)** *Give your opinion on male au pairs. Then read the testimonial below.*

Mein Name ist Timo und ich werde versuchen, meine Zeit in Neuseeland so gut wie möglich zu beschreiben. Nach meinem Abitur habe ich mich dazu entschlossen, als Au Pair nach Neuseeland zu gehen, da ich nach der langen Zeit des Lernens Lust hatte, ein fernes und exotisches Land kennenzulernen.

Zuerst war ich ein bisschen skeptisch, ob ich als Junge überhaupt eine Chance haben würde, als Au Pair in eine Gastfamilie aufgenommen zu werden. Schon nach einem Monat hat sich aber eine Gastfamilie gemeldet, die mich gerne aufnehmen und mich um ihren 4-jährigen Jungen kümmern lassen wollte.

Ich lebe hier in Waikato ziemlich genau auf halbem Wege zwischen Auckland und Hamilton in der größten Agrarregion. Mit meinem Gastbruder bin ich viel in Spielparks unterwegs oder wir besuchen Freunde, bauen Höhlen, fahren Fahrrad oder springen auf dem Trampolin.

Außerdem habe ich ihm Schreiben beigebracht und sogar Klavierunterricht gegeben, nachdem meine Gasteltern für mich ein kleines Klavier gekauft haben, da ich unheimlich gerne Klavier spiele.

Das ist nur ein Beleg dafür, wie viel Glück ich mit ihnen hatte und wie großzügig sie waren. Der Junge ist wie ein kleiner Bruder für mich geworden und es wird mir schwer fallen, ihn hier zu lassen, wenn ich wieder zurück nach Deutschland muss.

Ich war auch für Hausarbeiten verantwortlich wie „Saubermachen", die Haustiere füttern und pflegen, wobei ich einen Tag in der Woche hatte, an dem ich das ganze Haus geputzt habe, was mir aber keine Probleme bereitet hat. Alles in allem habe ich mich hier sehr wohl gefühlt. Meiner Meinung nach gibt es wirklich keinen Grund, warum man nicht als Au Pair nach Neuseeland gehen sollte. Hier passt einfach alles!

– Timo S.

**Mit meinem Gastbruder**

Source: AIFS Educational Travel

**b)** *Write a blog post that sums up Timo's experience and what he had to do as an au pair.*

→ S12 **‹c›** *Internet research: Find out about formal qualifications you need to be an au pair.*

L 1/6 ⊙  # The cocoa controversy

SPEAKING **12** **Pre-reading: What do the pictures say?**

*There's a controversy surrounding cocoa from Africa. Describe the pictures below. What hints do they give you about the controversy? Exchange ideas, and then turn to p. 14.*

## Chocolate: So sweet, so bitter

**by Steve Hartley** | Abengourou / Ivory Coast | 26 May 2017

As the main ingredient for the chocolate many Europeans and Americans eat in massive quantities, as well as a main ingredient for many cosmetics, cocoa is one of Ivory Coast's most important exports. The chocolate industry there is worth around £60 billion a year and the country provides about 35% of the world's cocoa. These facts make it difficult to understand why 40% of the population lives below the poverty line and why child labour is such an issue there. In Ivory Coast, about 100,000 children are doing the dangerous and physically difficult work of harvesting cocoa beans. Most of them are sent by their families; they are paid very little and forced to live in terrible conditions on the cocoa plantations. And some children are paid nothing at all; they are slaves. Some farmers claim they have no other way of surviving because they themselves earn less than £2 a day; they can't pay adult workers or provide them with healthcare while keeping their prices low enough to compete. These are the reasons that are given to justify child labour and child slaves.

I came wanting to see for myself what life is like for the young workers at a large cocoa plantation. As I got out of my car about 15 miles outside Abengourou, I felt the sun burning on my skin. I noticed four children walking along a muddy path towards some trees; they could hardly carry all the heavy tools and equipment. They arrived feeling exhausted – and had yet to start their day's work. Slowly, they climbed the largest of the trees and I watched them chop down heavy yellow cocoa pods with their huge machetes, which seemed nearly as big as they were. All of them had scars on their legs from machete injuries.

Then I found Abdoulaye sitting alone. His job was to cut the pods open to get the cocoa beans, again with a machete. "My mother sent me here," he said. "I'm the oldest of five children and I have to work so they can eat. I haven't seen them for two years now and I've never been to school." Abdoulaye said he's heard that children in other countries enjoy chocolate, which he has never tasted, and doesn't understand why his own life is so hard.

As I drove away, I saw three girls carry heavy containers full of cocoa beans and I saw them dump the contents onto a large truck before they walked back for more. I left hoping the cocoa industry would finally wake up and give these children their childhoods back. We've all heard of fair trade products – let's keep buying them and make our message clear.

READING

## 13 Understanding the issues

→ S3  **a)** *Read the first paragraph of the news report on p. 13. Then:*

1. Sum up the general problem.
2. Explain the importance of these statistics:  £60 billion  |  35%  |  40%  |  £2  |  100,000

**b)** *Now read the rest of the report. Sum up its main message. Then describe the different jobs the children do in front of the reporter.*

**c)** *Your reaction: Point out lines in the text which you feel are emotionally powerful.*

**d)** *Is this the kind of report that could inspire people to help others? If yes, how? Explain.*

LANGUAGE

## 14 Present participle or infinitive after verbs of perception + object  → G2  → WB 6/11–12

**a)** *Look at these sentences and find more examples like them in the second half of the text.*

| I **felt** | **the sun** | **burning** | on my skin. |
| I **watched** | **them** | **chop down** | cocoa pods. |

**b)** *Find the rule: When do we use a **participle** or an **infinitive** after **verbs of perception** + **object**?*

→ △ 79/8
→ ▲ 79/9  **c)** *Look at the picture of a school's fair trade market. Write sentences about the actions. Use a **participle** or **infinitive** after phrases like **I saw / noticed / watched …**  |  **He felt …***

LANGUAGE

## 15 Present participle after verbs of rest and motion  → G3  → WB 7/13

**a)** *Look at this phrase and find two more examples on p. 13 (2nd half of text):*

I **came** want**ing** …

→ △ 79/10  **b)** *Complete the sentences in the text about student protesters who want to help to end child labour.*

Example:
We **arrived** feel**ing** really excited.

We  **1**  (arrive – feel) ✔ really excited. Sam was late, but when the march started, he  **2**  (run in – wave) a really cool flag. Then we all  **3**  (walk along – shout) "Down with child labour!" In the park, we  **4**  (stay – sing) songs for nearly an hour. At the beginning, we  **5**  (come – hope) some people would be there. At the end we  **6**  (leave – know) a lot of people had really listened! I  **7**  (catch myself – think) how great it feels to try and change things. Everyone can do something!

SPEAKING

## 16 Social commitment → WB 7/14

For some people, the 'good life' involves helping others, one's community, or maybe the environment. Some make a career out of it; others help as volunteers in their free time.

→ S1

**a)** *Get together in groups of six. Each group member chooses **one** of the photos of volunteer activity below. Describe your photo to the others. Take turns.*

A

B

C

D

E

F

**b)** *In your group, discuss what makes people help other people. Why can it be important for individuals as well as for a community in general?*

**c)** *Discuss how the following motivations can play a role in actively showing social commitment:*

- having a guilty conscience
- helping for selfish reasons
- really wanting to do something good / helpful

> **Across cultures**
>
> In the UK and the US, job applicants but also applicants to student exchanges and universities are often expected to show examples of **social commitment** on their **CVs**.

SPEAKING

## 17 Your turn: Your involvement → WB 8/15

**a)** *In your groups, talk about people you might know who show social commitment. Describe who they are and what they do.*

**b)** *Are you involved in your local community? If yes, describe what you do and what made you want to get involved. If not, what could you imagine doing: an activity from Ex. 16, or something different? Talk about it briefly in your groups and then write about it (6–8 lines).*

> **Useful phrases**
>
> - I'd like to volunteer my time at a youth / religious / … centre
> - Providing services for the elderly / the homeless / the disabled / people who need … is how I'd like to show social commitment.
> - I'd like to do volunteer work during a gap year / I'd like to …

L 1/8

# I do remember how it feels ...

*What's the best way to survive a first job? Read some teenagers' tips for other young people:*

**The Words-of-Wisdom Wall** | **"Job stuff you want to know now. NOT later."**

Learn from Nathan, Cassie and many other **Words-of-Wisdom** members!

My first job, which I was very happy to get at first, was with a family friend. He's a carpenter and I worked for him on Saturdays. I really jumped at the chance to earn my own money for the first time! The problem was that it was winter when I started. So not only was it super cold, but stacking all the wood outside was exhausting. My friends found much easier jobs in shops that sell cool clothes or computer games, so they still had the energy to have fun after work. Not me! One shouldn't be jealous, I know; but I did feel that way. So my advice is to look around at different job options, don't just take the first easy option. It might not be so easy after all!
– Marlon

@Marlon: I'm one of those kids who works in a cool clothes shop. I know the work day never goes by fast enough for some people, but time does go by quickly when you work in a shop which is full of young people! Another big benefit is that we don't have to pay as much for the clothes we buy for ourselves. It was paradise at first; all the clothes! Never before had I spent so much money on clothes. But before you start to get jealous, listen to this: The result was that I didn't have any money left over for my holiday that year, which was my original reason to earn some money! So no matter what your job is, here are my words of wisdom to everybody: Don't spend all your money on things you don't need, or you'll be very sorry!
– Cassie

@Cassie: Oh, I do remember how it feels to end up with less money than you expected! Hardly had I arrived on my first day at the bike shop when they gave me about a thousand forms to sign. Of course, I signed without reading them because they looked soooooo boring. I thought I knew exactly how much my pay would be – I even knew the exact date I would finally be able to buy the bike that I wanted! But I was wrong. You always get less than you think because they take out money for taxes. I was shocked when I received my first wages. And so I complained. My boss, who could have been very angry, patiently went through all the forms with me. I felt really stupid. But it was a lesson that I had to learn, and I did learn it.
– Nathan

My first Saturday job was at a huge café which was always incredibly busy. I used to work for eight hours, with no break. Exhausting! Nobody ever told me to go outside for some fresh air or something to eat. And stupid 16-year old me: I was too shy to ask! Rarely was the café quiet, so I just kept on working! The boss, who never sat down herself, didn't even notice. Top tip: the law says you're supposed to take breaks, so make sure you do!
– Lucy

**READING** **18** **Understanding the posts** → WB 9/16

→ S3 **a)** *Sum up the problem each of the young people experienced in their first job. Then give the reasons for their problems.*

**b)** *Comment on which 'words of wisdom' you think sound the most helpful.*

**LANGUAGE** **19** **Revision: Defining relative clauses** → G4

**a)** *Look at the sentences from the text. Explain when you use the relative pronouns* **who**, **which** *or* **that**.

1. My friends found much easier jobs in shops **that** sell cool clothes.
2. I'm one of those kids **who** works in a cool clothes shop.
3. Time does go by quickly when you work in a shop **which** is full of young people.
4. I would finally be able to buy the bike **that** I wanted.

 **b)** *Read about somebody else's experiences at a first job. Use the phrases to complete the text with* **defining relative clauses**. *Decide where you can leave out the relative pronoun. If you can leave it out, put it in brackets.*

**Example:** I was part of a student team **who / that** organised social activities.

| realised it | organised social activities | I worked in | he showed me | never joined in |

| they gave me | we like doing | I designed |

In my first job, I was part of a student team `1` at a summer school. The office `2` was very noisy and fun, but there was one quiet boy `3` . I decided he was far too serious for me! The first job `4` was to design some posters for a theme party, but, of course, I was so busy joking around that the posters `5` were full of mistakes. The quiet boy, Mark, was the only person `6` and he helped me to correct things before anyone noticed. I liked the friendship `7` and Mark and I are still friends now! There are a lot of things `8` together, especially stuff on our smartphones.

**LANGUAGE** **20** **Find the rule: Non-defining relative clauses** → G4

**a)** *Explain the different function of the relative clause in each sentence:*

1. **Defining relative clause:** That's the boss who patiently went through all the forms with Nathan.
2. **Non-defining relative clause:** Nathan's boss, who could have been very angry, patiently went through all the forms with him.

> **Tip**
>
> In non-defining relative clauses …
> – you use **who** for people and **which** for things. You never use **that**.
> – you always need a **comma** to separate the main clause from the relative clause.

**b)** *Find three more* **non-defining relative clauses** *in the text on p. 16.*

LANGUAGE   **21   Defining or non-defining relative clauses?** → WB 9/17

*After reading the Words-of-Wisdom Wall, a young boss who employs a lot of young people decided to post a comment herself. Write the text in your exercise book. Decide which sentences have **defining** or **non-defining relative clauses**. Put in commas where you need them.*

> It was interesting to read your posts which I really enjoyed. Maybe I could add a few memories about young people who have worked for me. I once employed a young man that was a real know-it-all. Dan who was very confident never listened to my advice. He always said he already knew how to do things – and then continued to do things wrong! Then there was Amy. She was the girl who spent several hours a day texting her friends. This was the same girl that complained about how everyone else was so lazy. Hm. Oh, and I'll never forget Sean who worked for me briefly. He was the guy that at his interview had said he was 'passionate' about helping customers but then strangely disappeared every time a customer arrived!
> – Emma

LANGUAGE   **22   Career Day**

*Read this information from a leaflet for students at the Career Day. Combine the two sentences. Use **non-defining relative clauses** with extra information.*

**Example:**  Career Day will take place in Hall A, **which** is on the first floor.

1.  Career Day will take place in Hall A. It is on the first floor. ✔
2.  For a Career Day information leaflet, please go to one of our assistants. They'll be in yellow T-shirts.
3.  Local universities will explain how to apply for different courses. They have information desks in the hall.
4.  The 'Allegro' café will serve hot food from 12:00 to 2:00. It is near the main entrance.
5.  There will be a presentation with useful advice by an interview expert. It will be limited to 25 visitors.
6.  Local employers can answer your questions about career options. They will be waiting to meet you.

LANGUAGE   **23   Make the text more interesting**

→ △ 80/11
→ ▲ 80/12

*Use **non-defining relative clauses** to add the extra information to the text below.*

In 2016, a teenage inventor from London became the youngest person ever to win an investment on Dragons' Den. Arminder Singh Dhillon was only eleven when he thought of his idea. He called his product 'Boot Buddy'. Arminder presented his idea with the support of his family. He showed the Dragons his model. The Dragons liked Arminder's invention so much that they offered him £20,000 to start his business.

Arminder: Proud of his idea

1.  which is a popular TV show about new business ideas
2.  who is still only a teenager
3.  which he invented to save time when he cleaned his football boots
4.  who appeared with him on the show
5.  which was made up of a water bottle, a plastic knife and a toothbrush
6.  which does the job in five minutes

LNGUAGE

## 24  How to: Use inversion for emphasis  → G5  → WB 10/18

→ ⚠ 80/13, 81/14

a) *Look at the example in the tip box below. Then find four examples in the text on p. 16 that also show inversion. Write them down.*

b) *Now invert the sentences below in a similar way. Use the word or phrase in **bold** to start with.*

**Example:  1.**  I have **never** felt so nervous.  → **Never have I** felt so nervous.

1.  I have **never** felt so nervous. ✔
2.  He had **hardly** finished lunch when he heard the fire alarm.
3.  I **only** realised how much I liked art **when** I went to Italy.
4.  She had **no sooner** arrived than the film started.
5.  He **not only** got a new office, but he got more money too!
6.  We **rarely** have time to just sit and do nothing.

> **Tip**
>
> You can make your language more interesting or dramatic by changing the emphasis of a sentence. With **inversion**, you bring adverbial phrases from the back of a sentence to the front, for more attention.
>
> **Example:**
> He did**n't** smile or greet us **once**!
> → **Not once did he** smile or greet us!

LANGUAGE

## 25  How to: Use *do / does / did* for emphasis  → G6  → WB 10/19, 11/20

Sometimes, **do**, **does** or **did** is added for extra emphasis, especially in conversation. Often – but not always – somebody has just said something which you see differently.

*Read the dialogue on the right between two colleagues. Then complete Ivy's lines to emphasise that she doesn't agree. Use **do**, **does** or **did** where necessary. Follow the example.*

**Example:**
A:  So you don't like action films?
B:  No, I **do** like action films. I just don't like the new one.

Kim:  The boss's new assistant never says hello to anyone except to the important people.
Ivy:  Oh that's not true. She **1**. She says hello to me and I'm not important.
Kim:  And she's got no sense of style. Her skirts are too short and they don't suit her at all.
Ivy:  Oh Kim, what are you talking about?! They **2**. I think she looks great in them.
Kim:  She gave a presentation yesterday; it didn't go well.
Ivy:  Who told you that?! I was there and I can tell you it **3**.
Kim:  I hope you don't think I'm jealous of her.
Ivy:  Well, really, I **4** that, Kim.

WRITING

## 26  ⟨ Your turn:  First day surprise! ⟩

a) *What could happen that would give you a nice surprise on your first day at work?*

→ S5–6

b) *Write a post for an online forum called 'First day surprise!' Remember to add **non-defining relative clauses** with more interesting information. (Also, you could try to use **inversion** or sentences with **do/does/did** to add emphasis.)*

c) *Do a gallery walk and read all the posts. Then, in groups, decide which was the best description. Give reasons for your choices.*

# Making a good impression

In an interview situation, you really want to make a good impression. So how do you do that?

## 1 Criteria for a good impression

**a)** *Before you watch, exchange ideas on the importance of the following criteria at a job interview:*

knowledge | personality | dress code | body language | register

DVD 5/3

**b)** *Now watch the film. Take notes about each candidate's performance, based on the criteria in a). Then answer these questions:*

1. Describe what the job is for and what kind of skills the person should have.

2. Rate the candidates; explain your ideas.
3. Discuss who you would give the job to.

Saanvi

Phil

Courtney

## 2 Useful techniques

**a)** *Think of why, in an interview, you might need to take these actions:*

buy time | change the topic | emphasise positive things

**b)** *Watch again. What was wrong about how the candidates dealt with these questions?*

1. "What makes you want to work in advertising?"
2. "How would you describe your strengths?"
3. "What's your biggest weakness?"

→ S8

**c)** *In pairs, take turns asking and answering 'tricky' / difficult / awkward questions like the ones you see in the useful phrases box.*

→ △ 81/15

**d)** *Role play: Act out scenes from the film. Find ways to improve on the candidates' responses where necessary.*

> **Useful phrases**
>
> **What the interviewer can say:**
> – What is your biggest strength / weakness?
> – How would your friends describe you?
> – Where do you see yourself 10 years from now?
>
> **What the candidate can say:**
> – That's a good / an interesting question. Let me see … / Let me think for a moment …
> – I've been told I'm good at …
> – I like to think that … is my biggest strength.

## Job interviews for a summer camp

Take part in job interviews for positions at Action Summer UK's camp.

---

### Step 1

#### Get to know the jobs → WB 12/22

*In groups of four, take turns to talk about each of the four counsellor jobs below. Mention what skills you think would be helpful for that job according to the expectations that are listed:*

A **sports & activity organiser** is expected to:
- teach sports skills to the children
- organise sports matches
- make sure they have the right equipment

A **cafeteria helper** is expected to:
- help prepare meals for and with the children
- do the food shopping for meals
- organise food for events

An **entertainments organiser** is expected to:
- organise a programme of social activities
- think of fun ideas for competitions
- organise theme parties

A **big sister / brother** is expected to:
- live with a group of children in a tent
- help with chores
- help them with their problems

---

### Step 2

#### Choose a job → WB 12/23

*Go back to the profile you wrote for yourself as part of Ex. 7 on p. 10. Based on what you wrote, decide which of the jobs above would be best for you.*

---

### Step 3

#### Form expert groups → WB 13/24

*Sit in groups with other students who are applying for **the same** job. Decide on how you could answer these interview questions.*

1. What made you decide to apply?
2. What would you bring to the job?
3. How would you describe your strengths?
4. What's your biggest weakness?

→ Vocabulary (pp. 8–11) → Social commitment (p. 15) → Making a good impression (p. 20)

---

### Step 4

#### Form mixed groups to practise → WB 13/25

*Form new mixed groups of four and take turns being interviewer and applicant.*
***Interviewers:*** *Ask questions for the different jobs as in Step 3.* **Applicants:** *Give answers that focus on your strengths. Give each other feedback on how well you did.*

---

### Step 5

#### Fish bowl: Conduct interviews with applicants and panels → WB 13/26

1. You need **four** groups of interviewers to form 'interview panels' of 2–3 people. Each panel represents a job from Step 1, so each member of each panel was an expert for the same job in Step 3.
2. Each other student in class will take turns to apply for the job that he / she became an expert on in Step 3.
3. **Inside** the fish bowl: The first interview panel interviews its first applicant, then another, and so on.
4. **Outside** the fish bowl: The rest of the class watches, in a circle, as the panel interviews each applicant one by one.
5. After the first panel is finished, it's the next panel's turn, with new applicants.

S1/6–11
L1/11–16

# The Giver

*In a future world, Jonas is a member of a community whose lives are completely regulated. When young people reach the age of twelve, they go through the special ceremony called 'Assignment': The Elders announce to them the jobs they will do for the rest of their lives. Jonas is now a 'Twelve' and about to find out his destiny at Assignment.*

SPEAKING

**1  Before you read**

*The Elders' business is to match professions to young people. Think of criteria you think could play a role in assigning the right job to the right person.*

The first speech at the ceremony was made by the Chief Elder, the leader of the community who was elected every ten years. The speech was much the same each
5 year: recollection of the time of childhood and the period of preparation, the coming responsibilities of adult life, the extreme importance of Assignment, the seriousness of training to come.
10    "This is the time," she began, looking directly at them, "when we acknowledge differences. You have spent all your years till now learning to fit in, to standardize your behavior. But today we honor your
15 differences. They have determined your futures."
    She began to describe this year's group and its variety of personalities, though she singled no one out by name. She mentioned
20 that there was one with singular skills at caretaking, another with unusual scientific skills. Jonas shifted in his seat, trying to recognize each reference as one of his groupmates. He heard nothing that he
25 recognized as himself, Jonas.
    Eighteen, Fiona, on his left, was called. Jonas knew she must be nervous, but Fiona was a calm female. She had been sitting, serenely, throughout the ceremony.

The photos featured on these pages are stills from the 2014 film adaptation of *The Giver*. (In the film, Jonas is sixteen, not twelve.)

Even the applause, though enthusiastic, 30 seemed serene when Fiona was given the important assignment of Caretaker of the Old. It was perfect for such a sensitive, gentle girl, and her smile was satisfied when she took her seat beside him again. 35
    Jonas prepared himself to walk to the stage when the applause ended and the Chief Elder picked up the next folder and looked down to the group to call forward the next new Twelve. Jonas took a deep breath and smoothed his 40 hair with his hand.
    "Twenty," he heard a voice say clearly. "Pierre."
    She *skipped* me, Jonas thought. Had he heard wrong? No. There was a sudden stir 45 in the crowd and he knew that the entire community realized that the Chief Elder had moved from Eighteen to Twenty, leaving a gap. On his right, Pierre, with a startled look, rose from his seat and moved to the stage. 50

A mistake. She had made a mistake. But Jonas knew, even as he had the thought, that she hadn't. The Chief Elder made no mistakes, not at the Ceremony of Twelve.

55 *Much later, after all the other Twelves had been given their Assignments, the Chief Elder finally turned to Jonas.*

"Jonas," she said, looking down at him. "I apologize to you in particular. I caused you
60 anguish."

"I accept your apology," Jonas replied in a shaky voice.

"Please come to the stage now."

Earlier that day, alone in his own dwelling,
65 he had practised the kind of self-confident walk that he hoped he could make to the stage when his turn came. All of that was forgotten now. He simply forced himself to stand, to move his feet that felt heavy and clumsy, to go forward, up the steps and across the platform 70 until he stood at her side.

Reassuringly, she placed her arm across his shoulders.

"Jonas has not been assigned," she informed the crowd, and his heart sank. 75 Then she went on, "Jonas has been *selected*."

He blinked. What did that mean? He felt a collective, questioning stir from the audience. They too were puzzled.

In a firm, commanding voice she 80 announced, "Jonas has been selected to be our next Receiver of Memory."

READING → S3

## 2 The story so far

**a)** *Outline the information given in the text about how the Elders arrive at their decisions.*

**b)** *Which adjectives can you use to describe how Jonas feels as he realises that he's being treated differently from everyone else?*

Alone in his sleepingroom, prepared for bed, Jonas opened his folder at last. Some of the other Twelves, he had noticed, had been given folders thick with printed pages.  He
5 imagined Benjamin, the scientific male in his group, beginning to read pages of rules and instructions with great pleasure. He pictured Fiona smiling her gentle smile as she bent over the lists of duties and methods that she would
10 be required to learn in the coming days. But his own folder was startlingly empty. Inside there was only a single printed sheet. He read it twice.

```
          JONAS
   RECEIVER OF MEMORY

1. Go immediately at the end of
   school hours each day to the
   Annex behind the House of the
   Old and present yourself to
   the attendant.

2. Go immediately to your dwelling
   at the conclusion of Training
   Hours each day.

3. From this moment you are
   exempted from rules governing
   rudeness. You may ask any
   question of any citizen and
   you will receive answers.

4. Do not discuss your training
   with any other member of the
   community, including parents
   and Elders.

5. From this moment you are
   prohibited from dream-telling.

6. Except for illness or injury
   unrelated to your training, do
   not apply for any medication.

7. You are not permitted to apply
   for release.

8. You may lie.
```

**3** **The community**

**a)** *Explain what the rules on Jonas' sheet tell us about the community he lives in.*

**b)** *Think of more rules which could be important to the community.*

*A few days later, Jonas goes for his first training session as the 'Receiver of Memory' and meets The Giver, who will pass on to Jonas his special ability.*

In his mind, Jonas had questions. A thousand. A million questions. As many questions as
5 there were books on the walls. But he did not ask one, not yet.

The man sighed, seeming to put his thoughts in order. Then he spoke again. "Simply stated," he said, "although it's not
10 really simple at all, my job is to transmit to you all the memories I have within me. Memories of the past."

"Sir," Jonas started slowy, "I would be very interested to hear the story of your life, and
15 to listen to your memories. I apologize for interrupting," he added quickly.

The man waved his hand impatiently. "No apologies in this room. We haven't time."

"Well," Jonas went on, uncomfortably
20 aware that he might be interrupting again, "I am really interested, I don't mean that I'm not. But I don't exactly understand why it's so important. I could do some adult job in the community, and in my free time I could come
25 and listen to the stories from your childhood. I'd like that. Actually," he added, "I've done that already, in the House of the Old. The Old like to tell about their childhoods, and it's always fun to listen."
30 The man shook his head. "No, no," he said. "I'm not being clear. It's not my past, not my childhood that I must transmit to you."

He leaned back, resting his head against the back of the chair. "It's the memories of the
35 whole world," he said with a sigh. "Before you, before me, before the previous Receiver, and generations before him."

Jonas frowned. "The whole world?" he asked. "I don't understand. Do you mean not
40 just us? Not just the community? Do you mean

Elsewhere too?" he tried, in his mind, to grasp the concept. "I'm sorry, sir. I don't understand exactly. Maybe I'm not smart enough. I don't know what you mean when you say 'the whole world' or 'generations before him'. I thought 45 there was only us. I thought there was only now."

"There's much more. There's all that goes beyond – all that is Elsewhere – and all that goes back. I received all of those when I was 50 selected. And here in this room, all alone, I re-experience them again and again. It is how wisdom comes. And how we shape our future."

He rested for a moment, breathing deeply. "I am so *weighted* with them," he said, finally. 55 "It's as if …" The man paused, seeming to search his mind for the right words of description. "It's like going downhill through deep snow on a sled," he said, finally. "At first, it's exhilarating: the speed; the sharp, clear air; 60 but then the snow builds upon the runners, and you slow, you have to keep going, and … –"

He shook his head suddenly, and peered at Jonas. "That meant nothing to you, did it?" he asked. 65

Jonas was confused. "I didn't understand it, sir."

"Of course you didn't. You don't know what snow is, do you?"

Jonas shook his head. 70

"Or a sled? Runners?"

"No, sir," Jonas said.

"Downhill? The term means nothing to you?"

"Nothing, sir." 75

"Well, it's a place to start. I'd been wondering how to begin."

READING

## 4 The Receiver of Memory

→ S3 **a)** *Sum up the job description of the Receiver of Memory.*

**b)** *Explain why it's difficult for The Giver to make Jonas understand what he does and how he feels.*

*Over the weeks, The Giver passes on many experiences to Jonas, including what it's like on a sled in the snow.*

"Why don't we have snow, and sleds, and hills?" he asked. "And when did we, in the
5 past? Did my parents have sleds when they were young? Did you?"

The old man shrugged and gave a short laugh. "No," he told Jonas. "It's a very distant memory. That's why it was so exhausting –
10 I had to pull it forward from many generations back. It was given to me when I was a new Receiver, and the previous Receiver had to pull it through a long time period too."

"But what happened to those things?
15 Snow, and the rest of it?"

"Climate Control. Snow made growing food difficult, limited the agricultural periods. And unpredictable weather made transportation almost impossible at times. It
20 wasn't a practical thing, so it became useless when we went to Sameness.

"And hills too," he added. "They made it difficult, limited the agricultural periods. And they made the transportation of goods
25 difficult: trucks; buses. Slowed them down. So …" He waved his hand, as if a gesture had caused hills to disappear. "Sameness," he concluded.

Jonas frowned. "I wish we had those things,
30 still. Just now and then."

The old man smiled. "So do I," he said. "But that choice is not ours."

*Slowly, Jonas starts to realise that he no longer sees the world only in black-and-white, like
35 everybody else in the community.*

Days went by, and weeks. Jonas learned, through the memories, the names of colors; and now he began to see them all, in his ordinary life (though he knew it was ordinary
40 no longer, and would never be again). But they didn't last. There would be a flash of green – the landscaped lawn around the Central Plaza; a bush on the riverbank. The bright orange of pumpkins from the agricultural fields beyond the community boundary – seen in an instant, 45 the flash of brilliant color, but gone again, returning to their flat and colorless shade.

The Giver told him that it would be a very long time before he had the colors to keep.

"But I want them!" Jonas said angrily. 50
"It isn't fair that nothing has color!"

"Not fair?" The Giver looked at Jonas curiously. "Explain what you mean."

"Well …" Jonas had to stop and think it through. "If everything's the same, then there 55 aren't any choices! I want to wake up in the morning and *decide* things! A blue tunic or a red one?"

He looked down at himself, at the colorless fabric of his clothing. "But it's all the same, 60 always."

"Yes, I know about Gabriel."

"Well, he's right at the age where he's learning so much. He grabs toys when we hold them in front of him – my father says he's learning small-muscle control. He's really cute." 75

The Giver nodded.

"But now that I can see colors, at least sometimes, I was just thinking: What if we could hold up things that were bright red, or bright yellow, and he could choose? Instead of the Sameness." 80

"He might make wrong choices."

"Oh." Jonas was silent for a minute. "Oh, I see what you mean. It wouldn't matter for a newchild's toy. But later it *does* matter, doesn't it? We don't dare to let people make choices of their own." 85

"Not safe?" The Giver suggested. 90

"Definitely not safe," Jonas was sure. "What if they were allowed to choose their own mate? And chose *wrong*?"

"Or what if," he went on, almost laughing at the absurdity, "they chose their own *jobs*?" 95

"Frightening, isn't it?" The Giver said.

Jonas chuckled. "Very frightening. I can't even imagine it. We really have to protect people from wrong choices."

"It's safer." 100

"Yes," Jonas agreed. "Much safer."

by Lois Lowry (abridged and adapted)

Then he laughed a little. "I know it's not important, what you wear. It doesn't matter. But –

"It's the choosing that's important, isn't it?" 65 The Giver asked him.

Jonas nodded. "My little brother –" he began, and then corrected himself. "No, that's inaccurate. He's not my brother, not really. But this newchild that my family takes care of – his 70 name's Gabriel?"

---

## 5   Understanding the key message

In the last of the extracts, Jonas makes the following statement:

"If everything's the same, then there aren't any choices. I want to wake up in the morning and *decide* things!"

a) *Describe how The Giver leads Jonas to change his opinion on choices and Sameness.*

→ ▲ 81/16   b) *Explain how the concept of Sameness is the key idea in the story. Include an explanation of what you think the leaders of the community – the Elders – are so afraid of. The word bank can help you.*

**Word bank**

- practical / useless | right / wrong | fair / unfair | safe / dangerous
- choice | control | danger
- to control | to make a right / wrong choice

READING

## 6 A film and literature genre: Dystopia

**a)** *Read the skills box below. Can you think why dystopian stories are often extremely popular in books and films?*

> ### Reading skills
>
> A **utopia** is an imaginary, ideal society where everybody lives in peace and harmony. In a **dystopia**, society **seems** like a utopia at first, but turns out to be the opposite. The action is often set in a sad, frightening future. Typically, dystopian stories show how totalitarian states do terrible things to their people, e.g. forcing them to live in a certain way, spying on them constantly, and even programming their bodies to function in a desirable way.
> Famous examples of dystopian literature are *1984* (by George Orwell) and *The Hunger Games Trilogy* (by Suzanne Collins).

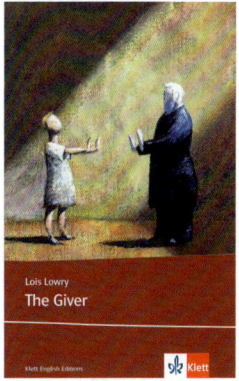

Lois Lowry
The Giver

**b)** *Point out lines and scenes that show how* The Giver *is a dystopian story.*

‹**c)**› *Your turn: Tell the class about a dystopian book / film that you like.*

SPEAKING

## 7 Imagine …

A world like the one Jonas lives in – with no books, no music, no art, no colour – is surely a big contrast to your world.

*Make a list of things you do every day. Give your list to your partner, who is a member of Jonas' community. Let him / her comment on these things from the community's perspective. Then switch roles and do the same.*

SPEAKING

## 8 Memories

**a)** *Comment on the community's decision to allow only one person to hold past memories.*

→  81/17   **b)** *Explain how memories help countries, communities and individuals to make good decisions about the present and the future.*

**c)** *Describe one of your own memories which has helped you to make a decision.*

SPEAKING

## 9 ‹ Role play › → WB 14/27

**a)** *With your partner, think about some event in the past (on a class trip / at school / at a party). It can be a funny, dangerous, emotional, or sad situation. Now think about pro and con arguments for eliminating these memories. Would it be good or bad not to have those memories any more?*

→ S8   **b)** *Perform a role play: Partner A agrees to eliminate memories and partner B is against it.*

LISTENING

## 1 In the bookshop

L 1/18 ⊚ **a)** *Listen to a dialogue between two friends, Grace and Bryan. Sum up in 2–3 sentences what they're talking about.*

✎ **b)** *Take notes about their different personalities. Say what you think might be the right professions for them. Give reasons for your opinion.*

ᕮᕮ **c)** *Who can you identify with more – Grace or Bryan? With a partner, talk about your own plans for the future. What's important / not so important for you?*

LANGUAGE

## 2 Additionally, I'd like to show ... → WB 17/1

✎ **a)** *Decide which* **linking adverbs** *fit in these sentences. Sometimes more than one answer is possible.*

additionally    furthermore    however    in fact    moreover    nevertheless    therefore

Example: **1.** I have a lot of different skills. **Therefore**, I feel that I should share what I have.

1. I have a lot of different skills. I feel that I should share what I have. ✔
2. I enjoyed working at a kids' summer camp. I think it's the best experience you can have.
3. I'm enthusiastic, reliable and creative. I love challenges and meeting new people.
4. I realise the position doesn't pay anything. I'd like to do it for the experience.
5. I can come in for an interview if that works for you. I can send references.
6. I've done a lot of volunteering. I'd like to work for an NGO[1] later.

**b)** *Finish these sentences with your own ideas.*

1. I'm waiting for the results of my final exams. In fact, …    2. I've applied for a work and travel programme. Furthermore, …    3. I have to find a room to rent near the university. Therefore, … 4. It's very difficult to get a position there. However, …

LANGUAGE

## 3 I won't sit waiting for you any longer → WB 17/2

✎ **a)** *Complete the sentences with a* **verb of rest or motion** *and the* **present participle**.

Today is the last day of our holidays and what did we do all summer? I ⬚**1** (come – hope) for a good time but every morning you ⬚**2** (sit – watch) TV. Luckily, you turned it off before lunch, but then you ⬚**3** (sit – listen) to the radio. Whenever we met your friends in town, you ⬚**4** (stand – chat) to them and you didn't even introduce me. When the weather was good, we went to the beach, but you ⬚**5** (lie – stare) into space with earphones on. I ⬚**6** (arrive – hope) we'd have a nice time together. And I ⬚**7** (stay – think) it could only get better. But now I've had enough. I'm not going to ⬚**8** (sit – cry) about it any longer. Goodbye!

**b)** *Imagine it's the first day at your new job. Make five sentences to describe your day. Use a verb and a present participle from the boxes below.*

arrive | catch myself | come | lay | leave | sit | stand | walk

feeling | looking | reading | smiling | waiting | watching | wondering | worrying

**1** NGO = non-governmental organisation [ˌnɒŋɡʌvnˈmentl ɔːɡnaɪˈzeɪʃn] Nichtregierungsorganisation

## 4 Unfortunately, your application . . .

a) *In this letter below, the head of Human Resources[1] at a big advertising company writes to an applicant suggesting ways of improving his application. Complete the letter with* **commenting adverbs**. *Sometimes more than one answer is possible.*

| certainly | luckily | obviously | personally | surely | unfortunately |

Dear Mr Thompson,

**1** , you weren't paying attention when I explained how to fill out the application so I will explain it again. You **2** know the difference between 'personal details' and 'personal profile'. Please correct these sections accordingly[2]. The profile should **3** tell us why you are suitable[3] for the position. So if you think you are suitable, explain how. **4** , I would not include 'watching videos online' and 'hanging out with friends' as your hobbies. **5** for you, we want to give you the chance to improve your application. **6** , the deadline[4] is in three days so you must act quickly.

Sincerely,
*Anita Fowler*
Head of Human Resources

b) *Decide which of these commenting adverbs you could also use for the letter in a).*

| clearly | happily | honestly | hopefully | of course | probably |

c) *Add a commenting adverb to these sentences.*

**Example: 1.** Look at her long list of qualifications. **Surely**, she's the best applicant we've had.

1. Look at her long list of qualifications. She's the best applicant we've had. ✔
2. I don't think all the information in your CV is true.
3. All of the candidates we invited are going to come in for interviews.
4. Our pay is comparable to similar companies in the area.
5. She has applied for other jobs and is waiting for the best offer.
6. He accepted a position with our main competitor[5].

## 5 It's all about jobs

a) *For each word write down the first job or profession that comes to your mind.*

adventurous | all-rounder | commitment | exhausted | hard-working | helper | organiser | people skills | physical | responsibility

b) *Compare your list with a partner's. Explain your choices.*

c) *Choose two of the jobs or professions you listed in a) that you could imagine working in. Then add other words that describe them.*

1 **Human Resources** [ˌhjuːmən rɪˈzɔːsɪz] Personalabteilung | 2 **accordingly** [əˈkɔːdɪŋli] entsprechend | 3 **suitable** [ˈsuːtəbl] geeignet | 4 **deadline** [ˈdedlaɪn] Abgabetermin | 5 **competitor** [kəmˈpetɪtə] Konkurrent/-in

LANGUAGE

## 6 Doesn't he notice me getting desperate? → WB 18/3

a) *Complete the sentences with the **present participle** or the **infinitive** of the verb.*

As I was standing outside the gym door, I heard our coach
**1** (shout) at the team. Again. Now I knew that this was
the day, and I felt my decision **2** (become) even more
firm[1]. It was the right thing to do. How many times had
I heard him **3** (offend[2]) us and **4** (scream) at us over
the years? – Too many times. Did he notice me **5** (get)
more and more desperate at every practice? In my head, I
listened to my family **6** (cheer) me on and I knew where
my priorities were. I'd leave the team although I had
good chances of making a career out of basketball. He
just wasn't the kind of coach I wanted to play for. When
I opened the door, I saw the coach **7** (look) angrily at
me and **8** (point) in my direction. This wasn't going to
make it any easier.

b) *Complete the sentences with your own ideas.*

1. I felt the pressure …   2. We heard the crowd …   3. The class listened to the teacher …
4. I saw my classmates …   5. My best friend watched me …   6. …

LANGUAGE

## 7 But I did do everything that was asked for! → WB 18/4

*Write a reply to each of these sentences. Use **do** or **did** for emphasis.*

**Example:** 1. So they don't have a suitable position available? – Yes, they **do** have one.
I just don't know if I want it.

1. So they don't have a suitable position available? ✔
2. If they haven't replied yet, then you probably didn't write a very good application letter.
3. You just don't have the qualifications we're looking for.
4. You mean you didn't name one single weakness when they asked?
5. I don't know why you didn't consider engineering. In my opinion it would be perfect for you.
6. Wait, you don't have any references available?

WRITING

## 8 What's the good life?

a) *Describe the cartoon, then analyse it. What's the cartoonist making fun of?*

b) *Write a short text about what 'the good life' means to you. You can use one of these sentences or your own to start with:*

Life is too short to … | A good life starts with … | … is the key to a good life.

**1 firm** [fɜːm] fest; sicher |
**2 to offend** [əˈfend] beleidigen

NGUAGE

## 9 I'm a woman who …

*Use a **relative pronoun** to combine the two sentences.*

Example: 1. I'm a woman **who** has always had different interests than other women.

1. I'm a woman. I have always had different interests than other women. ✔
2. In Year 6 I had a great teacher. He encouraged me to stand out from the others.
3. Once I met a firefighter. He was very passionate about his job.
4. I chose a profession. It was typically just for men.
5. I joined a new team. It was full of only men.
6. People are meaningful to me. They don't expect me to justify my choices.

NGUAGE

## 10 A good life? → WB 19/5

a) *Decide which **relative pronoun** you need to complete the sentences.*

Dave Chappelle, **1** (who / whose) parents were both teachers, is a stand-up comedian and actor. He was born in Washington, D.C., in 1973. His first film appearance was in Mel Brooks' movie *Robin Hood: Men in Tights*[1], **2** (whose / which) was in movie theaters in 1993. Chapelle, **3** (who / whose) mother was a minister[2], converted[3] to Islam in 1998. He continued to act throughout the 1990s, mostly in comedies. In 2003 he started *Chapelle's Show*, **4** (who / which) was a comedy television series. After two seasons[4] of the show, **5** (that / which) was very successful, he suddenly left it. Chapelle, **6** (which / who) said his ego needed to quiet down, went to South Africa to take a much-needed break from the negative sides of being famous. He has since returned to the comedy scene in the US, where he can be seen both on TV and live on stage.

b) *Write a short biography about one of your favourite celebrities. Did they ever give up their celebrity status?*

NGUAGE

## 11 Never will you regret[5] working with us!

a) *Here are some guidelines for volunteers working in a refugee camp. Use **inversion** to rewrite the sentences.*

Example: 1. **Never** are you supposed to get involved in an argument between residents.

1. You're **never** supposed to get involved in an argument between residents. ✔
2. You'll only be allowed to work with the children **after** you've received proper training.
3. You should **never** provide medical help. That's a doctor's job.
4. Refugees **not only** need food and a place to sleep, they also need emotional support.
5. You'll **never** have experienced satisfaction like this **before**.
6. The residents will **rarely** be here longer than three months before they move to other refugee homes.

b) *Choose from these adverbs or adverb phrases to write four sentences with inversion.*

hardly    never    never before    no sooner    not for one moment

not only    no way    only then    rarely

**1 tights** [taɪts] Strumpfhose | **2 minister** [ˈmɪnɪstə] Pfarrer/-in | **3 to convert** [kənˈvɜːt] konvertieren |
**4 season** [ˈsiːzn] Staffel | **5 to regret** [rɪˈgret] bedauern

LANGUAGE

**12** **Let's talk about my boss!** → WB 19/6

**a)** *Have a look at the sentences below and decide if you need a **defining** or **non-defining relative clause**.*

1. My boss is a great guy.
   a) My boss is a great guy who is passionate about his job.
   b) My boss is a great guy, who is passionate about his job.
2. He is married and has one son.
   a) His son who is 20 will be starting university in September.
   b) His son, who is 20, will be starting university in September.

3. He also has two daughters.
   a) The daughter who lives in New York is a model.
   b) The daughter, who lives in New York, is a model.
4. He and his wife have three houses.
   a) They spend most of their time in their house in Florida which is the biggest one.
   b) They spend most of their time in their house in Florida, which is the biggest one.

**b)** *Write two sentences that go with the sentences below – one with a **defining** and one with a **non-defining relative clause**.*

Example: I'm passionate about shoes.
   a) The green shoes I bought yesterday go perfectly with my new green dress.
   b) Shoes, which are really a girl's best friend, can be very expensive.

1. My best friend has bought a new tablet.    2. I could talk for hours about my dream jobs.
3. Our favourite holiday destination is Spain.    4. All of her films are really popular.

VOCABULARY

**13** **Future perspectives**

**a)** *Choose the correct verb in each sentence.*

1. At some schools you're (encouraged / required) to participate in social projects as part of the school curriculum[1].
2. A lot of employers look for people who (were involved in / were never involved in) groups and teams during their time at school.
3. A lot of young people have a hard time (determining / assigning) what they want to do for the rest of their lives.
4. Parents shouldn't (force / regulate) their children's lives too much because young people need to learn to take on responsibilities on their own.
5. Instead, parents should (provide / limit) support and advice.
6. It's also very important that parents (respect / select) their children's choices, no matter what career path they choose.

**b)** *Write sentences with the verbs you didn't use in a).*

**c)** *Change these verbs into nouns by adding the suffixes **-ment**, **-ation** or **-ion**.*

Example: be involved = involvement

| assign | determine | encourage | limit | regulate | require | select |

1 **school curriculum** [ˌskuːl kəˈrɪkjələm] Lehrplan

## 14 Can consumer habits[1] change the world?

DIATION

**a)** *Which of the aspects below are important to you when you buy a product? Do the same criteria apply to all the different things you buy, e.g. clothes, cosmetics, food? Discuss these questions with your partner.*

price | quality | organic[2] origin | country of production | appearance | brand

**b)** *One of your friends has joined a volunteer group that wants to inform people about child labour and the advantages of fair trade. He / She asks you to collect information about fair trade chocolate from Ivory Coast. You find this article on the internet and write down the key points for the group's website in English. The annotations below can help you.*

### „Kinder"-Schokolade – Ist da drin was draufsteht?

Viele Erwachsene in Deutschland kennen weder die Farbe der Kakaobohne noch wissen sie, wie Kakao eigentlich wächst. Anders ist das bei den Kindern aus der Elfenbeinküste. Sie kennen die Frucht sehr gut. Die Elfenbeinküste ist der größte Kakaoproduzent[3] der Welt. Jeder vierte Einwohner lebt vom Kakaoanbau. Trotzdem liegt die Armutsrate[4] in der Elfenbeinküste laut Statistik bei 43 Prozent. Die Kleinbauern haben ein durchschnittliches Tageseinkommen[5] von gerade einmal 50 US-Cent pro Kopf. Das veranlasst viele Familien, die eigenen Kinder in die harte Arbeit mit einzubinden.

„Wer Kinderarbeit bekämpfen will, muss die Bauern aus der Armut holen", sagt eine ivorische Gewerkschafterin, die als kleines Mädchen oft selbst nicht zur Schule gehen konnte, weil sie ihren Eltern bei der Ernte helfen musste. Offiziell regelt der Staat, wie viel die Bauern beim Verkauf ihrer Bohnen mindestens bezahlt bekommen. Doch in der Region sind Zwischenhändler[6] am Werk, die ihnen weit weniger bezahlen als vorgeschrieben. Da die Bauern mangels Fahrzeugen keine Möglichkeit haben, ihre Ernte selbst an den Hafen zu bringen, sind sie den Machenschaften dieser Händler ausgeliefert.

Ein einzelner Kakaobauer kann das System und die multinationalen Konzerne nicht bezwingen – der Verbraucher jedoch schon! Denn „faire Schokolade" ist längst keine Utopie mehr:

Selbst im Discounter gehört sie längst zum Standardsortiment. Dass der Kauf von Fairtrade-Produkten durchaus Wirkung auf die Menschen in den Anbaugebieten hat, zeigt das Dorf Tiemokokro. Noch vor einigen Jahren passten in die Schlaglöcher der Dorfstraßen ganze Kühe. Das hat sich inzwischen geändert. Besonders stolz sind die Dorfältesten auf ihre neue Schule. In einem Land, in dem laut Schätzungen knapp die Hälfte der Bevölkerung Analphabeten sind, keine Selbstverständlichkeit. Errichtet werden konnte sie aus Geldern der Fairtrade-Kooperative. So sind es oft die kleinen Entscheidungen im Alltag, die das Leben der Bauern und Kinder in anderen Teilen der Erde retten können.

Source: earthlink e.V. (abridged)

**c)** *In small groups, discuss how consumer habits can change the world.*

**1 consumer habits (pl)** [kənˈsjuːmə ˌhæbɪts] Konsumverhalten | **2 organic** [ɔːˈgænɪk] biologisch; Bio- | **3 cocoa producer** [ˈkəʊkəʊ prəˌdjuːsə] | **4 poverty rate** [ˈpɒvəti ˌreɪt] | **5 daily income** [ˌdeɪli ˈɪnkʌm] | **6 middlemen** [ˈmɪdlmen]

Find more online:
96pk5a

## Text smart 1
# Informative texts

In Text smart 1, you're going to look at informative texts from the point of view of two important writing skills: the skills of writing a **text summary** and a **text analysis**.

SPEAKING

## 1 Warm-up: What information is important?

**a)** *Look at the scene below. Say what has gone wrong in the situation. What would have been a better answer to the question, and why?*

> So what did you have for lunch, Tom?

> Well, I had pizza first. It wasn't as good as what I'm used to in Italy – I don't know why they don't try to do a better job here in the UK; I mean, the cheese is just never good enough, so, I didn't eat it all. Anyway, I wanted to be hungry enough for ice cream afterwards, which unfortunately was disappointing since it wasn't *nearly* as good as the *gelato* I know so well from Florence, but what …

**b)** *All of the everyday questions below require you to summarise when you give an answer – some more, some less. In pairs, take turns role-playing the situations with a partner. Before you start, take a moment to think about how you might answer each question:*

> How was your day? | What did the news report say about the fire? |
> How did you celebrate your last birthday? | That book must be good – what's it about? | How did you get to school today? | What happens in the film? |
> Was it a good football match? | What are your plans for tonight?

SPEAKING

## 2 Warm-up: Interpreting information

Summarising focuses on the 'what' of a subject, the information. But there's also the aspect of the 'why'; why something is said or written.

**a)** *Go back to Ex. 1a). What kind of personality does Tom have based on the way he replies?*

**b)** *Now think of the different text types on the right. Why does an author write texts like these? What would be the same in each; what would be different? Think of these points:*

information | entertainment | writing style | criticism

> interview with sports star | news report on earthquake | film review |

# How to: Write a text summary

**READING**

## 3 The parts of a summary

a) *Look again at the news article about the cocoa controversy on p. 13. With a partner, note down the main points in the article that you'd include in a summary.*

b) *Now read a model summary of the news article. Compare the summary with the key points you both noted in a). The skills and phrases boxes can help you.*

In an online article by Steve Hartley entitled 'Chocolate: So sweet, so bitter', which was published in the Daily News on 26th May 2017, the writer argues that children should not be working on the cocoa plantations in Ivory Coast.

> A summary begins with an **umbrella sentence** or paragraph which gives essentials: author, source, publication date / place, and the title and gist of the original text.

According to the author, around 100,000 children work in terrible conditions there for little or no pay because the farmers can't afford to pay adults to do the dangerous work. The children are often victims of enslavement and unable to leave. They ask why they have to live such difficult lives when children in other countries don't.

> Examples of **typical phrases** in a more formal **register** appropriate for a summary

The writer illustrates the problem by describing a visit to one cocoa plantation. He sees the children doing a lot of hard physical work, like chopping down heavy cocoa pods with huge machetes. All the children he meets have had machete injuries.

> Examples of **key terms** from the original text which help to illustrate its **main points**

The author concludes by hoping the cocoa industry will finally stop using child labour. He asks his readers to buy fair trade products as a form of protest.

> Be aware that the **simple present** is usually used.

### Writing skills

Important **dos and don'ts** for summaries:
- A summary is always a **reduction**, usually 30–40 % of the original article's length.
- The **order** of the information doesn't have to match the original text.
- Leave out **irrelevant details**.
  (Example: The reader doesn't need to know that the author got out of his car 15 miles outside of Abengourou.)
- Don't use **direct speech** (i.e. no quotes).
- Don't copy original lines **word for word**.
- Leave out your **feelings** or **views**! A summary only needs to sum up.
- **Register** should be more formal.

### Useful phrases

- In an article posted on / published in …, the author states … / mentions … / argues … / points out … / discusses … / explains … / emphasises … / illustrates … / refers to …
- According to the writer, …
- The author's main point is …
- The writer goes on to say …
- The author also believes that …
- The author illustrates … by …
- The writer concludes by stating … / pointing out … / asking … / using … / telling …

c) *Go back to the original report on p. 13. With your partner, point out to each other more examples of information which the summary writer didn't feel was relevant enough to include.*

WRITING

## 4   Your turn: Your checklist for summary writing

→ △ 82/1

*Write a personal checklist of things to do – or **not** to do – when you plan and write a summary. The information on p. 35 gives you the input you need, but you can also include tips of your own. Maybe there's something you feel you need to pay special attention to. Then exchange checklists with a partner for peer-editing.*

> **Tip**
>
> A checklist should be **simple**. It only needs to feature **categories** and **key terms**, not full sentences.

READING

## 5   Differences in summary quality

a) *Below, a student has written an **unsuccessful** summary of 'Chocolate: So sweet, so bitter'. As you read it, note down what you find is wrong for a summary. Refer to your checklist.*

> In the article, the writer said that cocoa is the main ingredient for the chocolate many Europeans and Americans eat in massive quantities. He also tells us that chocolate is a main ingredient for many cosmetics and that the chocolate industry is worth about £60 billion a year in Ivory Coast. He says that he doesn't understand why 40% of the population lives below the poverty line or why so many children work on the cocoa plantations. To be honest, I don't understand it either!!! But whatever. Anyway, he suggested that a possible reason is that farmers don't make enough money to employ adult workers or give them healthcare. But he didn't seem to be convinced that this was a good enough reason to employ children. And you know what? I'm not convinced either! Not at all. I mean, would you be? I'm glad that this journalist has got his priorities in life right. He sees what the REAL problems are. Good job!
>
> The writer went to a cocoa plantation 15 miles from the Ivory Coast town of Abengourou to meet the children who worked there. It was a really hot day and the sun was burning on his skin. The children he met were tired and injured. They could hardly carry all the heavy tools and equipment. They arrived feeling exhausted – and had yet to start their day's work. Slowly, they climbed the largest of the trees and the writer watched them chop down heavy yellow cocoa pods with their huge machetes, which seemed nearly as big as they were. All of them had scars on their legs from machete injuries. One boy, Abdoulaye, told him, "I'm the oldest of five children and I have to work so they can eat. I haven't seen them for two years now and I've never been to school." Abdoulaye has never tasted chocolate and doesn't understand why his life is so much harder than that of children in other countries.
>
> The writer wants the cocoa industry to change its ways and so he asked us to support the children by buying fair trade products, which I will definitely do. "Let's keep buying them and make our message clear," he says. Yes, let's do that!

b) *Now look at the points below. With a partner, exchange ideas about the summary's quality for each point. Use your notes from a).*

| personal views | irrelevant information | copying original lines word for word |

| summary length | use of tenses | use of direct speech / quotes | register |

READING   **6** **From oral to written summaries** → WB 20/1

→ S3

a) *Before you can do written summary work, you need to understand the content. Read the text below. Then work together to sum up the report's main message, orally.*

## Sleep scientists' wake-up call for a later school day

**by Jonathan Webb** | Science reporter, BBC News, Bradford | 8 September 2015

**A**s they prepare a major study to test the idea, UK scientists have said that starting school at 10:00 could have huge benefits for teenagers. Research suggests that society pays too little attention to our 'body clock' – and teenagers in particular have a late-running biological rhythm. This means an early start can cause sleep deprivation, which can then affect learning and health.

A sleep expert made the argument at the British Science Festival in Bradford.

Dr Paul Kelley said that teens lose up to two hours of sleep per day, which is "a huge society issue". He and colleagues from Oxford are leading a project called Teensleep, which is currently recruiting 100 schools from around the UK to take part in a test.

Our body clock is a daily cycle which drives the regular rise and fall of certain genes as well as the ebb and flow of our cognitive performance, our metabolism and so on.

For much of our lives – and especially in our teen years – there is a mismatch between this rhythm and the typical working day. In fact, Dr Kelley said, the body clock of most people between age 10 and 55 is not well-suited to rising early. "Most people wake up to alarms because they don't naturally wake up at the time when they have to get up and go to work. So we've got a sleep-deprived society – it's just that this age group of 14- to 24-year-olds is more deprived than any other group."

Dr Kelley and his colleagues, including well-known Oxford sleep researcher Prof Russell Foster, argue that school days should start at 10:00 and university at 11:00, to better match the rhythms of teenagers and young adults. "All the evidence points to the same thing," Dr Kelley told BBC News. "There are no negative outcomes for moving the school day later."

Source: BBC Online
(abridged and adapted)

b) *Now each of you writes an umbrella sentence and a first paragraph for a summary. Peer-edit each other's results: What works well? What can be improved, and how?*

c) *Write the rest of the summary. Follow the model on p. 35 and your checklist from Ex. 4.*

d) *Your turn: As a teenager yourself, give your opinion on the report's message about teens and sleep.*

# How to: Write a text analysis

READING

## 7 Text analysis: Comparing two examples

Two students have analysed the report on p. 37 based on how **well-written**, how **convincing** and how **interesting** it is for a general audience of all ages.

*Read the students' results below. Exchange ideas with your partner on which analysis is a real modern text based on the criteria mentioned above, and why you think so.*

→ △ 82/2

**A**

Jonathan Webb of the BBC presents an interesting subject: that teenagers need more sleep. I can totally relate to that! But I can't relate to every aspect of how this article was written. The author's style is objective, and he does a good job of presenting basic facts together with quotes from experts. However, he doesn't always do a good job of presenting the topic clearly. For example, he makes the mistake of using pretty language ('ebb and flow') or using terms that are too big and scientific ('cognitive', 'metabolism'). Huh? Who wants to read stuff like that?! I don't! In the end, the writer does his job, but using simpler terms would make the content more interesting and easier to read.

**B**

The report by Jonathan Webb of the BBC aims to inform the reader about sleep deprivation as a general problem for society.

First, the writer offers plenty of facts without getting lost in detail. Also, the writer quotes experts in the field, and it's interesting for the reader to learn what solutions the experts suggest. This mix of facts and expert views creates an objective impression which is convincing.

From a language point of view, the writer uses scientific terms like 'cognitive performance' or 'metabolism', but he also uses terms like 'body clock' which everybody can understand.

Overall, the writer presents a healthy balance of information that is relevant, objective and easy to follow.

WRITING

## 8 Building blocks of an analysis → WB 21/2

a) *Read the skills box below. Which points match your ideas from Ex. 7? Which don't?*

> **Writing skills**
>
> For a **successful analysis**, consider these points:
> - A text analysis always involves examining **particular aspects** of a text: e. g. why it was written ('author's intention'); how objective he / she is; how interesting the style is; how convincing an argument is; and so on.
> - **Structure:** Make sure that you feature an introduction and conclusion, and that you introduce new ideas in new paragraphs.
>
> - **Don't confuse analysing with commenting!** When you analyse, you explain and examine, with examples from the text to justify your assessment. But when you comment, you're expressing your opinion in an open discussion, not always based on particular criteria.
> - Like a summary, an analysis needs a more **formal register** with typical **set phrases**.

b) *Work with a partner to make a checklist for a successful text analysis. Include useful phrases.*

c) *Compare your results in class. Edit your checklist to include other classmates' helpful ideas.*

d) *If you analysed the text on p. 13, what would you focus on? Give reasons.*

## 9 Text summary and analysis: Show what you know!

### Option A: Write a summary

→ △ 82/3
→ S6

*Read the text below and write a summary of it.*

### Option B: Write an analysis

*Read the text below and write an analysis of it. Consider the criteria on the right when deciding what to focus on in your analysis.*

> level of interest for the reader | objectivity | how well the message is communicated | the writer's intention

---

## Teens and tech: What happens when students give up smartphones?

Erin Cotter | Thursday 23 April 2015

A recent report by Childwise found that children aged five to 16 spend an average of six and a half hours a day in front of a screen, more than twice as much as they did 20 years ago. Debate about the effects of the culture on young people – sexting, bullying, mental health and cyber addiction – has never been livelier. While many young people recognise the problem, they don't question their choices. "Gaming and social media are so much a part of their lives that they haven't really thought about it," says Sally Llewellyn, a teacher at Capital City Academy (CCA) in London.

So what happens when you ask a group of tech-loving teens to switch off for a week? The Disconnect project did that with a group of 15-year-olds from CCA. Over several weeks, we discussed their gaming and social media habits and then challenged them to go offline for a week.

"At first the students were against it," says Llewellyn. "But the more they considered it, the more interesting the idea of disconnecting became. Once we started looking at what they'd done the previous week, and how much time they'd spent on their smartphones and games, they were horrified."

Girls were on their phones from the moment they woke up until they went to bed – they even slept with them by their side. Boys used social media less, but they spent up to six hours a day gaming.

One student, Abdi, was worried about how he would fill his time. "After a week you'd just start repeating what you did the day before. If I wasn't gaming, I'd probably watch a movie or something, and I'd hate to watch the same movie twice."

Was it hard? Yes. But impossible? No. Most who took up the challenge found it less difficult than they expected, which suggests that the relationship they have with their devices is less addictive than compulsive.

More importantly, all of them said they got something out of it. "I watched TV with my friends," says one. "I read a book. I can't remember the last time I did that," adds another. "I got my homework in on time and hung out much more with my family." They also reported going to bed earlier – lack of sleep being a related and growing area of concern.

Source: The Guardian Online (abridged and adapted)

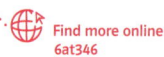Find more online:
6at346

# The language of tolerance and respect

SPEAKING

**1** **Warm-up: Different perspectives**

a) *Describe the cartoon about a goat and its targets.*

b) *There are positive and negative sides to the goat's view of the world. Describe both sides. The ideas below might help you:*

> differences | similarities | things in common | to look beyond the surface | to see somebody / something from a different perspective

LISTENING

**2** **Free your mind** (En Vogue)

En Vogue, an African-American group from the US, has won various awards for this song.

a) *In groups, find and write down definitions of the three terms below. Then compare your results.*

tolerance    respect    prejudice

L2/1

b) *Listen to the song. Describe who is involved in the action: Who is 'I'? Who is 'you'?*

c) *Use the terms in a) and words / lines from the song to explain its message.*

d) *"Free your mind and the rest will follow". Say what you think 'the rest' means.*

I wear tight clothing, high-heeled shoes
It doesn't mean that I'm a prostitute.
I like rap music, wear hip-hop clothes
That doesn't mean that I'm out sellin' dope.
Oh my, forgive me, for having straight hair
It doesn't mean there's another blood in my heir.
I might date another race or color
It doesn't mean I don't like my strong black brothers.

Why oh why must it be this way?
Before you can read me you gotta learn
How to see me, I say:
Free your mind and the rest will follow
Be color blind, don't be so shallow
Free your mind and the rest will follow
Be color blind, don't be so shallow

## 3 Everyday people, everyday situations

*Divide up into groups. Each group works with **one** of the photos below:*

1. Make a list of possible reactions the people in your photo may face in public situations like these.
2. Discuss reasons for those reactions.
3. Explain how you think the people in the photos *themselves* would react to others' reactions and comments. What might they say?
4. Share your ideas with the class.

### Word bank

to look different / to behave differently / to have a different lifestyle (from the mainstream) | to be prejudiced against sb (based on race / gender / sexual orientation / religion / differences / stereotypes / clichés) | to provoke others (un)willingly | to (not) accept diversity

### Tip

In discussion, everyone is entitled to their opinion, popular or not. Just remember the phrases for arguing a point **politely**. → S8

**A** A father, covered in tattoos, and his daughter at a street fair

**B** Women in niqabs in a European pedestrian zone

**C** A gay couple sharing a kiss in the park

## 4 Showing respect through language

Here and on the following pages, learn more about how to communicate respectfully.

L 2/2–4

→ S7 **a)** *Listen. Then sum up the action in each scene.*

**b)** *Get into groups of three. As you listen again, take notes on **one** of the three points below. Give examples of phrases / dialogue that show how your point is featured. The phrases on the right can help you.*

- judging a book by its cover
- respecting others' privacy
- assuming others share your opinion

### Useful phrases

- I don't think it's fair / acceptable / appropriate to …
- Could you please show more respect for …?
- It's hard to judge if you don't know …
- I like to treat others / strangers / people from different … as I like to be treated myself.
- See … from his / her / their point of view.

**c)** *Your turn: How would you react to the not-so tolerant comments from the scenes you heard?*

**d)** *With a partner, talk about other possible reactions to the situations.*

**e)** *Think back to the positive aspects of the cartoon on p. 40. If every person applied it in everyday life, how would there be less prejudice?*

# Is that what you really think?

## 5 Scene 1

**a)** *Pre-viewing: Describe what you see in stills A and B below. What storyline ideas seem possible?*

A

Mark and two friends

B

Dan and Liam

DVD 5/4

**b)** *Watch the first scene of the film (until 02:00). Then:*

1. Describe the action in stills A and B above. Which of your storyline ideas from a) match what really happens?
2. Identify the different topics the characters bring up.

**c)** *Sum up Dan's and Liam's opinions on being gay. Mention key statements.*

**d)** *What do you think could happen next?*

> **Word bank**
>
> – same-sex / gay / lesbian / straight
> – to come out
> – to have one's coming out
> – different ways to live one's life

## 6 Scene 2

**a)** *Now watch until 02:28. What has happened to cause Dan's surprise?*

**b)** *Describe how Dan feels. Use the adjectives below if you think they fit:*

> angry | curious | disappointed |
> disgusted | happy | interested |
> left out | shocked | surprised

**c)** *Do you think Dan will want to talk to Liam about what he saw? If yes, what could he say? With a partner, collect phrases you think Dan could use to bring up the subject.*

**VIEWING**

## 7 Scene 3

**a)** *Now watch the film to the end. Say what you think of the ending and why.*

**b)** *Look at these key statements from Scene 3. Who says them? Explain why each statement is important. Say which emotions are expressed in each.*

We'll still be hanging out as much as before – if you want. **|** I thought we were best mates. **|** I didn't mean it. I wouldn't have said it if I'd known … **|** But is that what you really think?

**c)** *Say how much tolerance and respect you feel Liam and Dan have in their friendship.*

**‹d)›** *How could the story go on? Write an additional scene (or just ideas for it) in script format.*

**VOCABULARY**

## 8 Acting and reacting in sensitive situations → WB 22/1

**a)** *Look at the problematic situations below. For each one, write down how one could / should / shouldn't react to what you hear or see. The phrases in the box can help you. Exchange ideas with a partner.*

> **Useful phrases**
>
> Don't take this the wrong way, but … **|** I hope it doesn't hurt your feelings when I say … **|** I wouldn't be a friend if I didn't tell you … **|** I'm sorry but I need to ask you to … **|** Do you really think it's appropriate to …?

1. On the bus, somebody is talking on their phone and using loud, vulgar language.
2. You don't want your friend to embarrass him- / herself at the big party on Saturday with an awful outfit.
3. A classmate likes your new outfit, but is surprised you were able to afford it. "Much nicer than your normal stuff! Didn't think you had that kind of money."
4. A friend is spreading horrible rumours about somebody you like and respect.

**b)** *With your partner, think of how the other side may react to what you say in a). But you must reckon with both positive **and** negative reactions!*

> **Useful phrases**
>
> I apologise if it offends you to see / hear … **|** Well, you've got your opinion / view / …, I've got mine. **|** Sorry, but do you know the whole situation / story / …? **|** Maybe I shouldn't have mentioned … **|** I'm glad you mentioned …

**→ S8 ‹c)›** *Role play: Take turns acting out scenes in a) and b). Peer evaluation: Say what worked or didn't work so well.*

# Unit 2
# California dreaming

Find more online:
k3us73

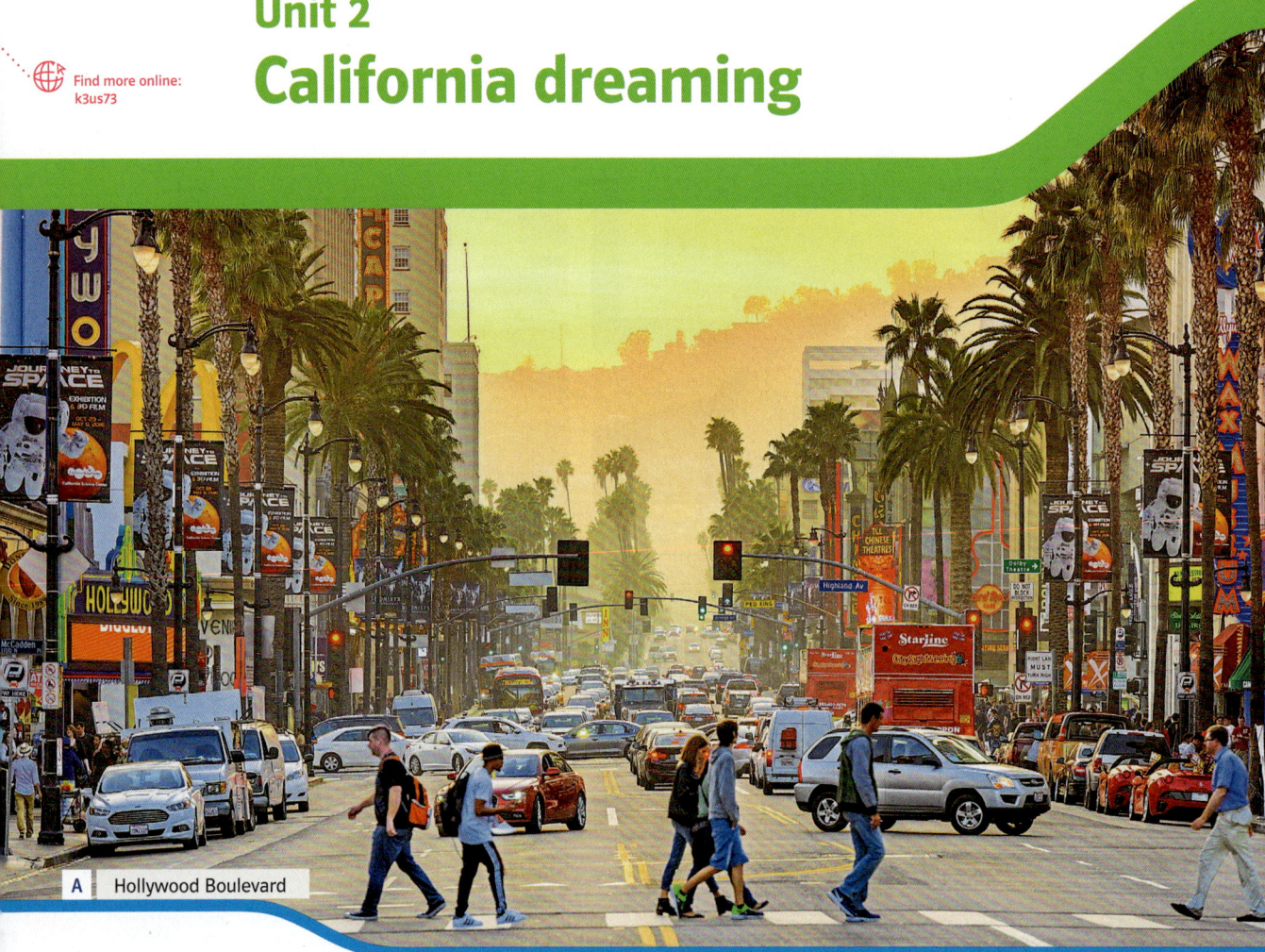

A  Hollywood Boulevard

SPEAKING

**1** **Warm-up: Your ideas about California**

a) *What comes to your mind first when you think of California? Collect your ideas in a grid. These categories can help you:*

people | climate | nature | entertainment | lifestyle

→ S1  b) *Now describe the pictures above. When you think of the ideas you collected in a), what pictures would you use to complete your impression of California?*

WRITING

**2** **Imagine yourself in the scene** → WB 23/1

→ △ 83/1  *Choose one of the roles below. Then write a short text about what you're doing in the picture and what you feel (see, hear, smell).*

a young actor walking along Hollywood Boulevard | a farm worker on the field | a tourist driving across Bixby Bridge | a Google employee at work | a skateboarder at Venice Skatepark

B Bixby Bridge, Big Sur

C At Venice Skatepark

D Farm workers in Salinas

E A lounge at Google headquarters, Silicon Valley

SPEAKING

## 3 Quotations about California

Think – pair – share: Read the quotations below and think about what they say about California. Share your ideas in small groups and then in class.

> Whatever starts in California unfortunately has a tendency to spread.
> Jimmy Carter, US President 1977–1981

> I live in the Mexican part of L.A.; it's called L.A.
> Bobby Slayton, actor

> I'm goin' to California / To find my pot of gold
> from: Pink, *Gone to California*

> There is science, logic, reason; and then there is California.
> Edward Abbey, writer

> To think that a boy from Austria could grow up to become Governor of California; that's the American Dream.
> Arnold Schwarzenegger, actor

> As one went to Europe to see the past, so one must visit Southern California to observe the future!
> Alison Lurie, writer

L 2/5

# Hollywood hopes

In his blog Alex, an aspiring young actor, writes about his life in Hollywood:

Have you ever thought of trying your luck out here? It isn't easy. DO NOT expect to just stroll in and get an acting job because it doesn't work that way. By the time you read
5 this, maybe I'll have gotten my first small role in a movie, after years of no glitz and no glamor. – Let me tell you about a typical week in Hollywood.

Okay, so on Monday morning I think,
10 "Wow! You're living in the place where dreams come true! And very soon you'll be living *your* dream!" Then I get ready for work. I entertain tourists while they're waiting for their bus tours. It's just a day job to keep my head above
15 water while I'm waiting for my big break. It's not exactly glamorous work, but it's a good opportunity to showcase my talents. And in L.A. you never know who's watching you, right? Today could just be my lucky day.

Then on Tuesday, maybe there'll be a cattle 20 call. They're open auditions that anyone can go to – and usually 'anyone' does. So they can be a bit of a nightmare. Sometimes you can wait in line for hours with all these other wannabes, then by the time it's your turn, 25 they'll already have filled all the roles! When that happens, you just have to pack up your stuff and wait for the next opportunity. It's best to chalk these interviews up to experience and not give up. 30

Okay, so now it's Wednesday. There's a movie premiere tonight on Hollywood Boulevard and I'll be going to it. It starts at 8:00 but I'm meeting my buddy there at 6:00 to set up. It isn't much, but I do online movie reviews. I 35 even interview some of the stars – for a couple of minutes anyway. It gets my face out on the internet, maybe causes a small stir.

So that brings me to Thursday – my favorite day. On Thursdays I like to visit my buddy Dave. 40 He owns an RV park just outside L.A. where they often shoot movie scenes. Today they're filming a scene with an exploding trailer for an action movie. Dave is a great guy. He always lets me know when they need 'extras'. Of 45 course, I don't get paid much for the work, but at least I get to meet the stars.

Well, I guess I only made it to Thursday, but that's what my life in L.A. is all about. Making it to the next day. I haven't become a 50 star yet. But I know it's going to happen one day very soon!

READING

## 1 Living in Hollywood

→ S3   a) *Outline what efforts Alex makes to pursue his dream in Hollywood.*

b) *Analyse Alex's character. Choose three of the character traits below and find examples in the text that show Alex has them.*

confident   determined   hard-working   optimistic   outgoing

passionate   patient   persistent   realistic   relaxed   smart

c) *With a partner talk about character traits you have that would make you (not) suitable for Hollywood. Give reasons.*

ABULARY

## 2 Expressing the same idea differently → WB 24/2

→ △ 83/2

a) *Find words or phrases in the text that go with the definitions below. (They're in the same order as the words / phrases appear in the text.)*

> trying to be successful at something | walk in a relaxed way | just be able to survive | show what you're really good at | a person who is trying to become famous, usually without success | learn from something negative that has happened to you | produce a lot of interest or excitement

b) *Choose three of the words / phrases you found in a) and use them to write a short paragraph (4–5 sentences).*

ANGUAGE

## 3 Simple present and present progressive with future meaning → G7

*Find the rule: Look at these sentences. Think about when you use the **simple present** and the **present progressive** to talk about the future.*

1. The movie premiere **starts** at 8:00, but I'**m interviewing** some of the stars before that.
2. The next bus **leaves** in five minutes. I can't miss it because at 3:00 I'**m meeting** a director who is looking for young talents.
3. Training **ends** at 6:00 tonight, then I'**m picking** up my best friend to go to the movies.

ANGUAGE

## 4 We're meeting at the premiere tonight → WB 24/3, 25/4

a) *Read the dialogue. Decide if you need the **simple present** or the **present progressive**.*

A: The premiere **1** (start) at 8:00 tonight.
B: But we **2** (meet) at 8:00, aren't we? Then that's too late!
A: No, we **3** (not meet) at 8:00. I **4** (come) to your apartment at 6:30. We talked about it, remember?
B: But my acting lesson **5** (not finish) until 6:00 normally, so I don't know if I'll be home by then.

A: Well, I **6** (pick up) Susan on the way so we'll just wait for you.
B: But Susan **7** (only leave) work at 6:00, so how will that work?
A: It's all arranged. I **8** (pick) her up at the café where she works. Stop worrying!
B: I just want everything to work out. Lots of important people **9** (come) to the premiere!

b) *Compare schedules with a partner. Use the **simple present** and the **present progressive** to talk about the future.*

> Example: A: School **ends** at 11:00 on Friday. Let's go downtown together!
> B: I'**m** already **doing** something with Tina. But …

STENING

## 5 In line for a cattle call

L 2/6

a) *Alex, Sarah and Ninja are all standing in line at an open audition when they start a conversation. Listen and sum up in 2–3 sentences what they're talking about.*

→ S7

b) *Make a grid for the three young actors. Then listen again and take notes about what you learn about their personalities.*

c) *Say who you think might be most successful in Hollywood. Justify your opinion.*

LANGUAGE

**6** **Find the rule: Two more future forms** → G8–9

**a))** *Look at the examples of the **future progressive** and the **future perfect** and explain how they're formed. Then say how you use them differently to talk about the future.*

1. My friends keep telling me that I **won't be going** to any more auditions in five years' time. They say I'**ll be traveling** the world to present my new movie.
2. By the time I get to the premiere, they'**ll** already **have interviewed** all the stars. – Stop worrying! I'm sure they **won't** even **have started**.

**b)** *Find more examples for the two future forms in the text on p. 46.*

LANGUAGE

**7** **What will Alex be doing at different times tomorrow?**

*Alex hasn't had his big break yet, but he's found an agent to help him pursue his dream. Tomorrow Alex has a busy day. Look at his planner and say what he'll be doing at the different times.*

**Start like this:** From 9:00 to 10:00 Alex will be entertaining the tourists. At 10:15 …

9:00–10:00 entertain tourists ✔
10:15 meet with agent
11:00–12:30 practice for audition at 2 p.m.
12:45 lunch
1:15 catch train to audition
1:30 arrive at audition; wait backstage
2:00 try luck at audition
3:00–6:30 work in day job again
8:00 interview stars at movie premiere

LANGUAGE

**8** **By this time next year …**

→ ▲ 83/3

*In order to motivate herself, Sarah imagines what she'll have achieved by this time next year. Use the phrases to make sentences with the **future perfect**.*

**Example:** By this time next year I'**ll have made** my dreams come true. I …

make dreams come true ✔ | stop going to auditions | get first big role | earn enough money to buy own apartment | meet all the stars in Hollywood | change name to something more memorable | be nominated for first award

LANGUAGE

**9** **Looking into your future** → WB 25/5

**a)** *Use the future progressive **(I'll be doing)** and the future perfect **(I'll have done)** to write five sentences about your future. The phrases in the box can help you to get started.*

**Examples:** When I'm 20 years old, I'**ll be studying** to become an actor. / By 2040, I'**ll have started** my own business.

**b)** *With a partner, ask each other questions about your future.*

**Start like this:** **Will** you **have traveled** to Australia in ten years' time? – Yes, I will. / No, I won't. But I'**ll have been** to many other countries. I'**ll** …

**Useful phrases**

By the time I'm 25 … | In 50 years' time … | By 2040 … | Before I move out … | If you visit me in ten years … | By the time I finish school … | When I'm 20 years old … | At this time next year … | By next September … | …

MEDIATION  **10** **A German pioneer in Hollywood: Carl Laemmle** → WB 26/6

→ S10

*You told your exchange partner from California that one of the founders of the American film industry was German. He / She is really excited and asks you to write a guest post on his / her 'Hollywood blog'. Read the article and write a post about Carl Laemmle's life.*

# Carl Laemmle

Es klingt nach einem Drehbuch zu einem echten Hollywood-Blockbuster: ein Mann aus Baden-Württemberg, der zu einem der Begründer der amerikanischen Filmindustrie wird.

Carl Laemmle wurde am 17. Januar 1867 in der Nähe von Ulm geboren. Er machte eine Ausbildung zum Kaufmann, bevor er mit 17 Jahren nach Amerika auswanderte. In New York verdiente er seinen Lebensunterhalt als Laufbursche, bevor es ihn nach Chicago zog, wo einer seiner Brüder lebte.

Gleich zu Beginn des 20. Jahrhunderts machte sich Laemmle in Chicago selbstständig und erstand ein 5-Cent-Filmtheater, ein sogenanntes Nickelodeon. Nur ein Jahr später gründete er einen Filmverleih und innerhalb kürzester Zeit gehörten ihm 50 Kinos in Chicago. Im Jahr 1908 war Laemmles Firma bereits der größte Filmverleih der USA. Zwei Jahre danach gründete er seine erste eigene Filmproduktion, die „Independent Motion Picture Company". Laemmle setzte dabei als erster Produzent in der amerikanischen Filmindustrie auf Stars, und er nannte die Schauspieler, die in seinen Produktionen mitwirkten, im Vorspann – die Konkurrenz tat dies nicht. Kurze Zeit später zog es ihn an die Westküste.

Im sonnigen Kalifornien waren die Löhne niedriger und das Wetter besser als anderswo. Dadurch konnten mehr Drehtage in kürzerer Zeit bewältigt werden. Laemmle kaufte in einer einsamen Gegend bei Los Angeles eine Hühnerfarm und errichtete die Universal City Studios – heute ist die Gegend unter dem Namen „Hollywood" bekannt. Seine Firma wurde zur größten Filmfirma Amerikas und produzierte Filme wie „Der Glöckner von Notre Dame" und „Das Phantom der Oper". Auch die weltberühmte „Frankenstein"-Verfilmung mit Boris Karloff – die erste Tonfilmversion überhaupt – stammte aus dem Hause Laemmle. Insgesamt produzierte Carl Laemmle mehr als 9.400 Filme. Seine Erfolgstory endete erst 1936, als er infolge der Weltwirtschaftskrise seine Firma verkaufen musste.

Source: Bremerhaven.de (abridged)

READING  **11** **A star on the Walk of Fame** → WB 26/7–8

*Read about the Walk of Fame, a popular tourist destination in Hollywood. Can you think of reasons why it might be important for celebrities to have their own star there?*

### Across cultures

The **Hollywood Walk of Fame** comprises more than 2,500 stars along Hollywood Boulevard and Vine Street. With these stars, actors, musicians, directors, producers, bands, theater groups or others are honored for their contributions to the entertainment business. Anyone, including fans, can nominate a person for a star on the Walk of Fame, as long as the nominee approves the nomination. Each June, about 20 celebrities are selected to receive their stars. Apart from real-life people, fictional characters can be nominated too. In 1978, in honor of his 50th anniversary, Mickey Mouse became the first animated character to receive a star.

L 2/8 ◎ **A golden state?**

SPEAKING
**12** **Before you read**

ᯖ *California's official nickname is 'the Golden State'. What do you associate with this term? Collect ideas with a partner.*

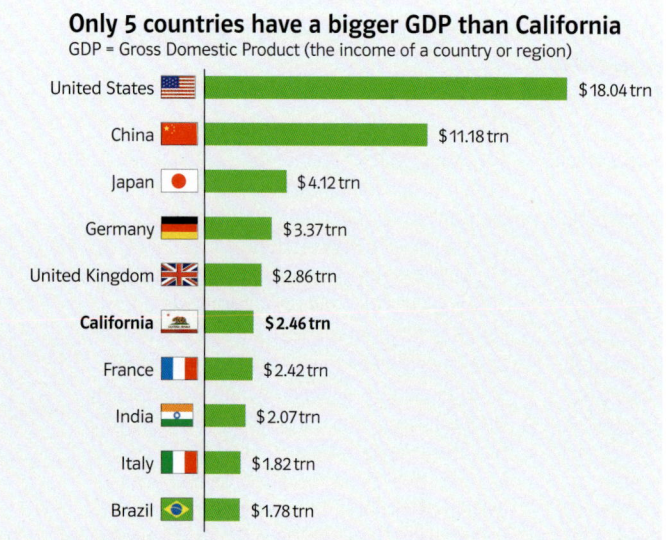

**Only 5 countries have a bigger GDP than California**
GDP = Gross Domestic Product (the income of a country or region)

| | |
|---|---|
| United States 🇺🇸 | $18.04 trn |
| China 🇨🇳 | $11.18 trn |
| Japan 🇯🇵 | $4.12 trn |
| Germany 🇩🇪 | $3.37 trn |
| United Kingdom 🇬🇧 | $2.86 trn |
| **California** 🏴 | **$2.46 trn** |
| France 🇫🇷 | $2.42 trn |
| India 🇮🇳 | $2.07 trn |
| Italy 🇮🇹 | $1.82 trn |
| Brazil 🇧🇷 | $1.78 trn |

Sources: Bureau of Economic Analysis; CIA World Factbook (2015)

In the 16th and 17th centuries, European explorers on the American continent searched for El Dorado ('the golden one' in Spanish), a city which was said to be made of gold. They
5 never found it (it probably never existed), but the name still refers to any place where great wealth can be found very quickly.

In 1855, the Californian town of Mud Springs changed its name to El Dorado for a
10 very good reason. During the California Gold Rush, it had become a center in the search for the precious yellow metal. Mud Springs boomed and the town decided it needed a more attractive name. And what name could
15 be better than El Dorado? By the 1880s, most of the gold had gone, but the spirit of that rush has remained throughout the Golden State.

Although California's sunny climate is a big attraction for many, the state's strong
20 economy is what really attracts millions of people. Silicon Valley in Northern California, for example, is home to many of the world's largest technology companies: Apple, Facebook, Google, eBay, Netflix and many others. Each of these began as a small start-
25 up company – often just one or two people and a good idea. For example, the first Apple computers were made in a bedroom, and Google began as a student project. In the 1990s, internet start-ups became a kind of
30 'California Gold Rush 2.0', and millions of dollars were spent on starting new web businesses. People thought this would go on forever, but in 2001 the 'dot-com bubble' burst, and millions of dollars were lost. A new boom,
35 however, has made technology one of the leading industries in California and worldwide.

Agriculture has long been another California success story. The state's climate is ideal for growing fruit and vegetables,
40 and great fortunes have been made from this. However, the good times may not last forever. Growing fruit and vegetables needs a lot of water, and water shortages are one of California's biggest problems. The drought
45 which started in 2011 has caused particularly serious problems for farmers, who are now being urged to use new cultivation techniques to save water.

The success of California's industries also
50 attracts workers from other parts of the US and from Latin America – especially Mexico – who often do jobs such as picking fruit, cleaning homes, working in restaurants, etc. Many of the Hispanic workers cross the border
55 illegally and there are Californians who think the US-Mexican border should be guarded more effectively. In their opinion, it's just one short step from illegal immigration to more serious crimes. Other Californians, however,
60 say that without these illegal immigrants, who often do the hard jobs no Americans want to do, many farms and businesses would have to close down.

READING

## 13 Understanding the text

→ S2-3

a) *Sum up what you've learned about California's success story from the diagram and the text.*

b) *Think back to the ideas you collected in Ex. 12. Now that you've read the text, would you say that California is a 'golden state'? If so, justify your opinion with examples from the text. If you don't, say what else you'd expect from a 'golden state'.*

c) *The idea of building a wall along the Mexican border is a topic of much controversy in American society. What might the consequences of trying to stop illegal immigration this way be?*

LANGUAGE

## 14 Revision: Using *the*, *a / an* or no article → G10 → WB 27/9

*Read the text about Silicon Valley. Decide if you need **the**, **a / an** or **no article (–)**.*

Surprisingly enough, Silicon Valley is *not* 1 valley and, of course, it is *not* made of 2 silicon. It's 3 area of around 15,000 km² south of San Francisco in 4 Northern California, and it's famous for having 5 large number of tech companies. The first of these produced 6 microprocessors and 'silicon chips' that were needed for computers, and that's where Silicon Valley got its name from. Although it's famous for 7 companies like Facebook or Google, Silicon Valley is also home to hundreds of other companies which produce 8 components and software for electronic devices that are used by hundreds of millions of 9 people every day. For example, you may never have heard of Cisco Systems or Oracle, but there is probably some of their technology inside 10 devices in your home.

Today, the term 'Silicon Valley' is often used for 11 Californian tech industry in general. A sentence like 'Silicon Valley earns billions of 12 dollars for 13 US economy' would probably refer to tech companies based both around San Francisco as well as in other parts of 14 state.

LANGUAGE

## 15 Abstract nouns: Article or no article? → G10 → WB 27/10

→ △ 84/4
→ ▲ 84/5

a) *Find the rule: Explain why the definite article **(the)** is used in the second sentence but not in the first.*

1. **Industry** plays a major role in California's economy.   2. Technology, agriculture, tourism and entertainment are **the industries** which California is most famous for.

b) *Now use the words in **bold** to write new sentences with the definite article.*

1. **Income** is the amount of money you earn from work and other sources.   2. **Success** is what many people look for when they come to California.   3. **Jobs** in Silicon Valley are very popular with young people.   4. **Technology** is important for all kinds of businesses.   5. **Drought** is a big problem for California's agricultural industry.   6. "**Climate** is what we expect, weather is what we get." (Mark Twain)

c) *Explain how the nouns in a) and b) are different from other nouns.*

LISTENING

## 16 My kind of company!

L 2/9

a) *Listen to different people talking about their jobs in Silicon Valley. Take notes about the pros and cons of working in California's tech industry.*

→ S7

b) *Listen again. What is said about prospects for young entrepreneurs in Silicon Valley?*

c) *Can you imagine giving up school and starting a career in Silicon Valley? Discuss with a partner.*

MEDIATION **17** **Where is the German Silicon Valley?** → WB 28/11–12

→ S10

**a)** *In an online forum there is a discussion going on about the uniqueness of Silicon Valley. You'd like to offer an example of an innovative entrepreneur from Germany. Read this article and write a short summary in English for the forum.*

Ob Pullover, Hose oder T-Shirt, immer mehr Menschen kaufen ihre Kleidung im Internet. Was nicht gefällt oder nicht passt, wird auf Kosten des Händlers zurückgeschickt. In Deutschland sind das durchschnittlich 40 Prozent der bestellten Waren.

Ob und wie man das ändern könnte, darüber grübelte Sebastian Schulze, Gründer des IT-Unternehmens UPcload, schon während seines Studiums. „Dann sind wir irgendwann darauf gekommen, dass es doch ganz cool wäre, wenn man die Körpermaße einer Person mit einer Webcam erfassen könnte," erzählt Schulze. Sein Unternehmen könne das größte Problem im Onlinehandel lösen, „nämlich dass Menschen, die online Kleidung kaufen möchten, nicht wissen, was ihre passende Größe ist."

Schulze war 22 Jahre alt, als er 2010 mit seinem Partner Asaf Moses in Berlin sein Unternehmen gründete. Sein Studium hatte er gerade beendet, Berufserfahrung hatte er keine. Schulze sagt, er habe während seines Studiums drei Praktika gemacht. „Danach habe ich gedacht, dass ich lieber in der ersten Reihe stehen und Verantwortung tragen will: Wenn ich schon viel arbeite, dann für eine eigene Sache."

Vor allem in Berlin tue sich laut Sebastian Schulze einiges, was IT-Start-ups angeht. Mehr Fördermittel und Kapital kämen in die Stadt, man spüre eine große Euphorie. Die Finanzierung ist neben der brillanten Idee der wichtigste Punkt für ein junges Unternehmen. Was in den USA häufig passiert, dass nämlich ein reicher Nachbar dem Gründer von nebenan Geld leiht, weil ihm dessen Geschäftsidee gefällt, gibt es in Deutschland nicht. In den ersten vier Jahren fließen durchschnittlich 700.000 Euro in ein IT-Start-up.

Source: Deutsche Welle (abridged)

→ △ 84/6 **‹b›** *Do you have an idea for your own start-up company? In small groups, collect ideas in a placemat and decide on what kind of company you'd like to start (it needn't have to do with IT!). Prepare a 3-minute talk and present your business idea to the class.*

READING **18** **Trendsetting California** → Fact page, p. 201

*California hasn't only attracted millions of people, it has also exported many trends and innovations. Read the information in the box. Then think about your own lifestyle and say which of these innovations are part of your life.*

### Across cultures

In 1873, **jeans** were invented by Jacob Davis and Levi Strauss in San Francisco. Originally, they were used as work pants for miners and factory workers. Later they became a symbol of youth rebellion and a fashion statement.

In the 1950s, a group of surfers in Santa Monica attached roller skate wheels to wooden boards to enable them to surf when the waves were flat. This new sport became known as 'landsurfing' or **skateboarding**.

Venice, a well-known Los Angeles beach community, is said to be one of the world's trendsetting hotspots: it was here that **fitness** first became popular with the muscle-packed beach bodybuilders in the 1970s, and it was also here that the **inline skating** craze was born in the 1990s.

LANGUAGE **19** **My life as a farm worker**

In spite of the state's strong economy, not all the people who come to California find their personal success there. This is how one young farm worker describes her life:

In the 1980s, my father came from Mexico to California to pick strawberries and grapes. He worked hard, learned English and made good money. After four years, he returned to Mexico and he found a good job with a Mexican company that exports agricultural products to the US. My family were very happy when I went to California too, but it's very different today. Most employers only pay the minimum wage, and they make you work as many hours as they like. That's illegal, of course, but nobody really cares. The second problem is that it's seasonal work. In the winter I only work 15 to 20 hours a week. That doesn't even pay my rent. So it's not an easy life. The government doesn't care about people like us and the local community aren't always very friendly to immigrants. I'm not sorry I came. I've found good friends and my English has gotten a lot better. But I don't think I'm going to save any money. Maybe one day I can find a better-paid job.

✎ **a)** *Collective nouns are nouns like 'team' or 'company' that refer to groups of people. Look at the text again and write down the sentences with collective nouns from the text.*

**b)** *Collective nouns can be followed by the singular or plural form of the verb. While in **American English** collective nouns are usually used with a singular verb, in **British English** they can be used with either a singular or plural verb. Which form you choose depends on whether you want to talk more about the group as one unit or about individual members of the group. Compare these sentences:*

1. *Adriana's family **is** from Mexico. (The sentence refers to the family as one unit.)*
2. *Adriana's family **are** worried about her. (Individual members of the family are worried.)*

SPEAKING **20** **Interpreting diagrams: Ethnic diversity in California**

Because of constant migration, the make-up of California's population has changed significantly during the last decades.

→ S2 **a)** *Look at the line graph. Point out what it tells you about the state's population today and what it might be like in the future. What can you say about the point on the graph where the blue and red lines cross? Check the skills file at the back of your book (pp. 88–89) if you need help.*

**Future population, cultural shift**

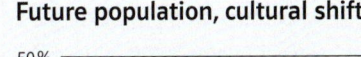
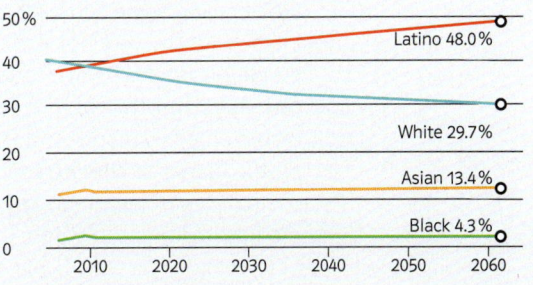

Sources: California Department of Finance; U.S. Census Bureau

→ △ 85/7 **b)** *Comment on what you think will be the consequences of these shifts in California's society.*

L 2/10 ⊙   # Should we be worried?

On its show today, L.A. Talk Radio KABC is speaking to helicopter pilot and firefighter Mario Ramirez about his work.

KABC:   Our guest on the show today is CAL FIRE pilot Mario Ramirez. Welcome to the show, Mario, and thanks for taking the time to talk to us. I'm sure you
5   must be busy right now.

Mario:   Hi, thanks. Yes, it's wildfire season again, and this is always a very busy time for us. Just this morning, we had to go out to three different incidents.

10  KABC:   Dropping water onto fires from helicopters?

Mario:   Yes, that's right. But this morning, we were forced to use tanker planes too. They can carry a lot more water.

15  KABC:   Should we be worried? It sounds like half of California is burning.

Mario:   Well, that would be exaggerating. But we're facing some serious problems because of the very hot and dry
20   conditions that we have today. A few years ago, the wildfire season lasted only five months. Today it's seven, thanks to climate change, and the number of larger wildfires has
25   increased dramatically too.

KABC:   Sounds as if you're very busy in the dry season, but what happens when it does finally rain?

Mario:   Well, that's when we're expected to coordinate with the other emergency   30 services. When you suddenly get a lot of rain after a long dry period, you get floods. Sometimes the only way to rescue people is by helicopter.

KABC:   And there are mudslides too. They're   35 said to go hand in hand with wildfires, aren't they?

Mario:   Yes, that's another major problem. People love to build nice homes on a beautiful hillside with a view, but   40 then you get a lot of rain followed by a mudslide, followed by collapsed houses half-covered in mud.

KABC:   Yes. The fires destroy the trees, so there is nothing to hold the soil in place   45 when the rain comes, is there?

Mario:   You know your stuff! Should I get my boss to interview you for a job?

KABC:   Ha ha! No, thanks. For that kind of job you need to be willing to risk your life.   50 I'm not that brave.

Mario:   You were right about the trees, of course, but it isn't just fire that's causing this problem. People aren't supposed to cut down trees but they do it anyway,   55 especially farmers. They argue that letting them die of dehydration will cause disease and bugs that will then spread to other healthy trees and lead to new problems.   60

KABC:   Mario, I'm going to have to stop you there but many thanks for sharing your experiences with us.

READING   **21**   **Understanding the interview**

→ S3   a)   *Outline the environmental problems Mario and his colleagues have to deal with.*

b)   *Explain how the different environmental problems are connected.*

**22** **Using different English verbs for the same German verb** → G11

**a)** *Look at these two groups of sentences. For each group, find a German verb you could use to translate all the examples.*

> **Shall** / **Should** we go to Yosemite National Park next weekend?
> Firefighters **are supposed to** / **are expected to** help the public in emergencies.
> Californians **are supposed to** / **are said to** be laid-back, even in dangerous situations.
> You **are to** leave your house immediately if there's any risk of a mudslide.
> I think we **should** / **ought to** leave the house; it's not safe here.

> We **had to** / **were forced to** leave the park because there were wildfires.
> In national parks, tourists **must** / **are required to** / **are obliged to** stay on the marked paths.

**b)** *Find more sentences with the verbs from a) in the text on p. 54 and translate them into German.*

**23** **What are people supposed to do?** → WB 29/13–14

**a)** *Use the verbs below to complete the text. Sometimes more than one answer is possible.*

> be expected to     be to     should     be forced to     be supposed to     be required to
>
> be said to     ought to     have to

Anybody who wants to avoid earthquakes **1** think about moving away from California. On average, there are around ten earthquakes every day. Most of them are very light, but it's not unusual to feel a slight movement and to see small cracks in the walls of buildings.

California's biggest earthquake in recorded history was in San Francisco in 1906. It killed more than 3,000 people and destroyed much of the city. It **2** have been the most important earthquake in modern times because it provided so much information about the causes of earthquakes and about how to make sure buildings survive them. Today architects in California **3** design new buildings which will remain standing in all but the worst earthquakes.

So what **4** you **5** do if there's an earthquake? If you're indoors, stay there. Keep away from the walls and try to get under a desk or table. If you're outdoors, stay away from buildings and trees. If you're driving, you **6** stop immediately but stay in the car until the earthquake stops. If you're

at home and you need help, remember that the emergency services **7** visit the worst affected areas first, so you may **8** wait for hours or even days for help. First check for the smell of gas; then check for damage to your building immediately. If you can smell gas or if there are serious cracks, everybody **9** leave the building. Remember that there may be aftershocks – small earthquakes which follow the main one.

**b)** *Can you think of any other natural hazards? Collect ideas with a partner. Say what people might be supposed to do when they're affected by these hazards.*

LANGUAGE

**24** **Brown is said to be the new green!**

→ ▲ 85/8

**a)** *Use the verbs below to rewrite these sentences from a website about California's environment. Sometimes more than one answer is possible.*

be to    be expected to    ought to    be said to

be supposed to    be required to

**Example:** 1. California **is supposed to / said to** have the best
              weather in the US.

1. People say that California has the best weather in the US. ✔
2. As a visitor to California, you must respect the environment
   at all times.
3. You shouldn't have barbecues in dry areas, or waste water.
4. When you visit one of the national parks, you need to be careful with wild animals.
5. When there's a drought, Californians have to stop using water for their gardens and
   outdoor swimming pools.
6. People in California should follow the water conservation rules, but many of them
   don't want to give up their lifestyle.

**b)** *Each of you writes three sentences about California with the verbs in a). Leave a gap where the verb is supposed to be. Then exchange your sentences. Your partner has to guess the right verb.*

SPEAKING

**25** ‹ **Interpreting diagrams: Cause and effect** › → WB 30/15

**a)** *Los Angeles is said to be a 'multi-hazard city'. Look at the diagram and explain how the different problems are connected with each other. Keep in mind what you've learned from the text on p. 54.*

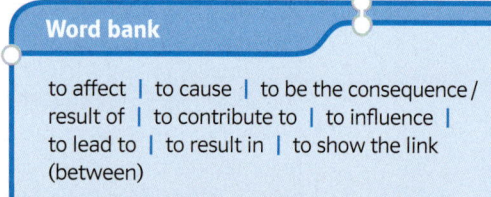

**Word bank**

to affect | to cause | to be the consequence /
result of | to contribute to | to influence |
to lead to | to result in | to show the link
(between)

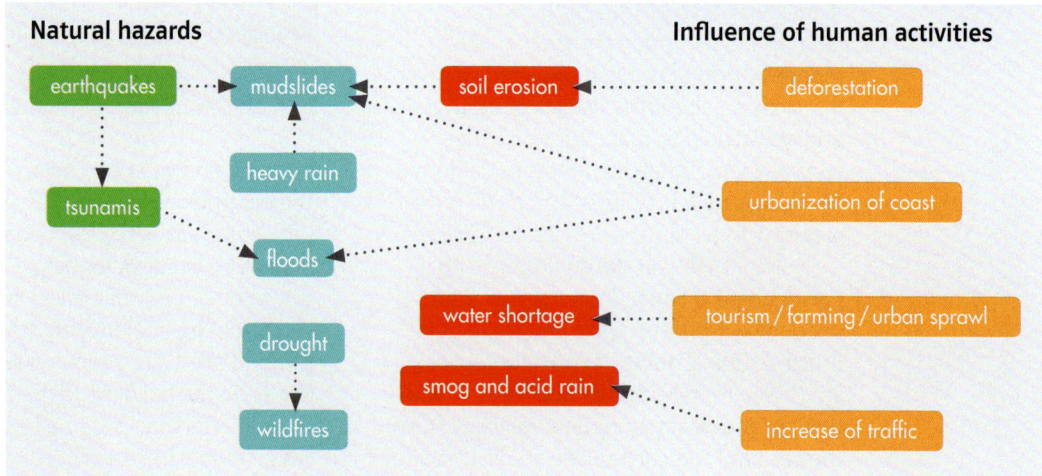

**b)** *Think back on the interview with Mario Ramirez (p. 54). How could a diagram like this help to support his explanations?*

**READING**     **26**     **Healthy eating in sports stadiums**

**a)** *Read the information in the box and comment on the idea of healthy eating in sports stadiums.*

**⟨b)⟩** *Role play: You're convinced that this idea should be adopted in your football stadium.*
*There are only food stalls with fast food like burgers, chips, etc. Write and act out a dialogue*
*with the owner of one of these food stalls.*

---

**Across cultures**

**Healthy eating** combined with a better understanding of environmental
issues is a worldwide trend that has also found its followers in California.
As with many other trends, however, Californians have taken the whole
thing a step further by combining healthy eating with a popular American
activity – baseball! Just below the scoreboard in the Giants' stadium in
San Francisco there is a large garden. The fruits and vegetables grown
there – from artichokes to zucchini – are used by two bistros at the
stadium to prepare fresh and healthy dishes for the ballgame spectators.
In addition, once a week groups of students visit the garden to learn
about gardening, nutrition and cooking.

---

**SPEAKING**     **27**     **Looking back: Your ideas about California**

→ △ 85/9

*Think – pair – share: Go back to the Introduction pages and your first impressions of California.*
*Has your picture of California changed after you've looked at it from different perspectives?*
*If so, in what ways? If it hasn't changed, how does the new information fit your first impressions?*
*Share your ideas in small groups and then in class.*

---

**SPEAKING**     **28**     **How to: Give a group presentation** → WB 30–32/16–19

L 2/12

**a)** *Listen to a presentation about*
*Californian symbols, both*
*positive and negative.*
*Take notes about the structure*
*of the presentation.*

**b)** *Now listen to the presentation*
*again. Write down useful*
*phrases for the following*
*elements:*

introduction | smooth
transitions | conclusion

**c)** *Read the information in the*
*skills box. Then comment*
*on how effective you find*
*the presentation in a).*
*What would you do the same*
*way / differently? Give reasons.*

**Speaking skills**

These steps can help you with your next **group presentation**:
1. **Research** information about your topic and decide on a
   clear structure.
2. Decide **who does what** in your group. The speaker who
   takes on the first part will introduce your topic and give
   a short conclusion at the end. You can also agree on one
   person who will take questions from the audience.
3. Each of you makes notes about his / her part. Don't
   forget to think of a **smooth transition** from your part to
   the next.
4. **Practise** your presentation. If one of your partners
   wants to use a **visual** for his / her part, you can help
   him / her by putting the right slide / showing your group
   poster. Agree on a **signal** for the right timing.
5. Give your presentation. Remember that **you're 'on'**, even
   when you aren't speaking! Listen and show interest
   in what the others are saying. If you look bored, your
   audience will get bored too.

# What's important for a handout?

A handout is a good way of helping listeners to follow the structure of a presentation and to understand the most important points. This page will give you some useful tips to prepare an effective handout for your next presentation.

## 1 Handout tips

*When you make a handout, keep in mind that people who weren't at your presentation should be able to understand the main ideas from your handout. Read the tips on the right. Can you add further tips from your own experience?*

> ### Presentation skills
>
> 1. Your handout should follow the same **structure** as your presentation. Include a short outline of your main points; keep your sub-points short and simple.
> 2. Don't use too many different fonts or unnecessary pictures or clip arts; **you don't want to distract** your audience. However, it's a good idea to include a chart, graph or picture that is central to your topic.
> 3. Make sure you give a **short summary / conclusion**.
> 4. Give the **sources** you used for your presentation.

## 2 Example handouts

**a)** *Look at these example handouts. Use the criteria you collected in Ex. 1 to make notes about what was done well and what could be improved.*

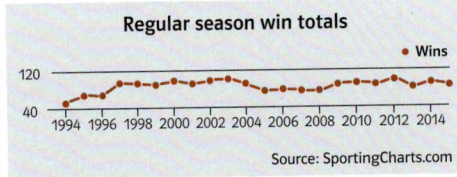

⚾ ⚾ ⚾ **SAN FRANCISCO GIANTS**

1. A **great** baseball team
   a) Have won the **most games** of any team in the history of American baseball.
   b) They have played in the World Series **20 times**.
2. History
3. Famous players
   a) Jackie **Robinson** #42
   b) Orlando **Cepeda** #30

Conclusion: One of the **best** teams ever!

**Regular season win totals**
• Wins
120
40
1994 1996 1998 2000 2002 2004 2006 2008 2010 2012 2014
Source: SportingCharts.com

Sources: Wikipedia; San Francisco Giants official website

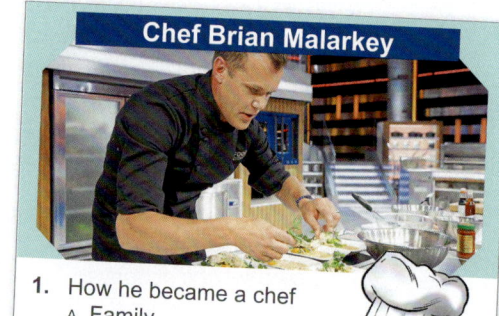

**Chef Brian Malarkey**

1. How he became a chef
   A. Family
   B. School
   C. Training
2. How he became a famous celebrity chef
   A. TV (Top Chef, Top Chef Masters, The Real Housewives of Orange County, The Taste)
   B. magazines
3. How he learned from his mistakes
4. How he cooks now
   A. "less pizzazz, more substance"
   B. "back to the craft"
   C. no deep fryer, no freezer

**b)** *Have a look at your notes about the group presentation on p. 57, Ex. 28 again. Then write a handout for it.*

# My star for the Walk of Fame

Your class wants to nominate one person for the Walk of Fame. In order to choose a candidate, you're going to prepare group presentations with which you try to convince your class selection committee that your group's candidate deserves a star.

## Step 1

### Choose a person to nominate → WB 33/20

*In groups of five, each of you chooses one person. This person doesn't need to be an American, and he / she doesn't need to be an entertainer. You can also choose someone from the world of science, politics or sports, for example.*

## Step 2

### Write a short profile → WB 33/21

*Collect information for a short profile of your nominee. Think about these questions:*

- How did he / she make his / her dream come true?
- What obstacles did he / she have to overcome?
- Why does he / she deserve a star on the Walk of Fame?

*Make your profile interesting and enjoyable to listen to since you'll have to convince your group.*

## Step 3

### Present your nominee in your groups → WB 33/22

*In your groups, present your nominees to each other. In this same group, agree on one Walk of Fame candidate that you're going to present to the class.*

## Step 4

### Prepare your group presentations → WB 34/23

*Before you present your group's nominee to the class, divide up the profile into logical parts and add more information where necessary. Don't forget to make an effective handout.*

→ How to: Give a group presentation (p. 57)  → What's important for a handout? (p. 58)

## Step 5

### Your class selection committee → WB 34/24

*After the presentations, one member of each group becomes the delegate to your class selection committee. The committee's task is to choose a nominee for the Walk of Fame based on the presentations and handouts. Then, in a fish bowl, the rest of you form a circle around the committee and listen to their arguments for and against each candidate. After they've made their decision, evaluate their decision-making process.*

# Famous

## 1 Before you read

*What first comes to your mind when you think about being famous? Share your ideas with a partner.*

It started with a camera and a coffee shop.

No, that's not right. Any psychologist will tell you it started way before that. Like, when my brother Alex became seriously ill around
5   the age of three, and five years later when my parents divorced, and all that psychological gobbledygook.

But that camera, a black Nikon P90 with a 24x zoom lens, a fourteenth-birthday present
10  from my father, was the charm that changed everything. It was the bridge I crossed from being a typical, everyday eighth grader to someone completely different.

An atypical eighth grader. A slightly
15  almost-famous eighth grader. Not that it was my plan. It just happened.

The day was gray, wet, and chilly. The coffee shop was called Cafazine, and it provided two of life's greatest pleasures –
20  coffee and gossip. After a quick scan of the headlines, I turned my attention to a tall woman in front of me holding the hand of a little boy. She was wearing a long gray raincoat, wide-brimmed hat, and sunglasses,
25  and suddenly I recognized her – it was Tatiana

Frazee, the supermodel! I'd seen enough pictures of her in magazines and on TV to know. Besides, why would anyone *not* famous wear a hat and big sunglasses inside on a cloudy day?                                        30

Her son, Connor, was pointing at a large brownie with chocolate chips inside the glass counter.

"I want that, Mommy!" he whined.

"Not before dinner," Tatiana answered.     35

"But I want it!" Conner persisted.

"I said no," Tatiana repeated.

"Yes!" The boy pulled at the gloved hand.

"No," Tatiana replied icily.

By now they had reached the counter.     40

"What would you like, ma'am?" the young man by the cash register asked. As the supermodel turned away from her son to answer, Conner suddenly yanked her hand as hard as he could.                                      45

Tatiana Frazee lost her balance and toppled forward, banging her perfect chin on a display of CDs, sending them crashing.

To this day I don't know what compelled me to yank the camera from my pocket and     50
slide the shutter into quick-shot mode just in time to catch Tatiana as she wheeled around and slapped Conner on the cheek.

The next shots caught Tatiana glaring at me with a mixture of horror and fury. An     55
instant later she scooped Conner up under her arm and ran out of the shop.

A photo agent friend of my dad's sold the shots to a tabloid and to a website that specialized in celebrities' most embarrassing     60
moments. A few weeks later I received a check for what seemed like a fortune to a fourteen-year-old. Just for taking some pictures.

*After more of her photos have been published, there's an article about Jamie in the* New York     65
Weekly. *On their way to school one day, Jamie talks about it with her boyfriend, Nasim.*

"You're famous," Nasim said. It was the first time anyone ever told me that, and I had to
70 admit that it felt good. Right up there with "You're pretty" or "You're smart." No, even *better* than "You're smart."

"Thank you," I replied.

"How many people do we know who have
75 been profiled in a major magazine? New York City's youngest paparazzo ever? I believe the correct answer would be one."

I grabbed his arm to stop him and we kissed in the middle of the crowded sidewalk.
80 "Thank you," I said, our faces close. "Only, for the six hundred and seventy-fifth time, I am not a paparazzo. I am a celebrity photographer."

Nasim rolled his eyes, and we started to
85 hurry again, our shoulders now and then bumping. "There is no difference."

"There's a big difference," I insisted. "I may take pictures of celebrities, but I don't stalk or harass them or try to get them to punch me so
90 that I can sue them for assault."

Nasim changed the subject.

*Jamie receives an invitation to spend one week hanging out with teen superstar Willow Twine, photographing her and documenting*
95 *her life. On day seven of her week in L.A., however, she wakes up and realizes that her camera is gone.*

I know it sounds like a cliché, but I feel naked without my camera. Or even worse than
100 naked, since these days who cares if you're naked? The camera represents who I am. It's my identity. With it, I'm a sixteen-year-old celebrity photographer. (And maybe something of a celebrity myself?) Without it,
105 who am I?

What am I?

The answers to these questions will have to wait. Right now I just need to find my Nikon. I try to remember last night. Not that it should
110 be difficult; it's just that out here, day and night, and day after day, blend together into a sort of nonstop repetition of the same thing over and over again. Last night was a party. But even on nights when there's no 'official' party

there's a loose semiparty atmosphere. People
115 come and go, appear and disappear – Willow's friends, security guard, personal assistant, therapist, masseur, agents, magazine photographer (me!), pool guy, gardeners, cook – in an unending parade.
120

As best as I can remember, I had my camera with me early this morning when I came upstairs to find a place to sleep. Before that I'd gone out to the guesthouse – where I'd been 'assigned' when I first arrived earlier
125 this week – but the door was locked, so I'd wandered back to the main house and found this room. Normally I would have put the camera on a night table or dresser, but since there is no furniture in the room, I left it on the
130 floor beside the mattress, and close to the wall so I wouldn't accidentally step on it if I got up in the middle of the night, or day, or whatever.

So where is it? I check the bathroom. Not there either. I walk barefoot out into the
135 hallway, then downstairs and out across the grassy lawn. I head toward the pool, where Zach, the house boy, and Daphne, the house techie, are straightening up from last night's frolic.
140

"Either of you see a camera?" I ask.

"Think I saw one on the kitchen counter," Zach says.

The kitchen counter? That's weird. I don't recall even being in the kitchen last night.
145 I was mostly out around the pool.

Passing through the French doors, the aroma of fresh-brewed coffee is in the air, and there on the marble kitchen counter, where I swear I wouldn't – couldn't – have left it, is my
150 Nikon.

"Buenos dìas, Miss Jamie. You like some breakfast?" Maria, the Mexican cook, hands me the mug of coffee she knows I crave.

The camera rests on the marble counter
155 beside me while I sip my coffee. Now that it's back in my sight, my anxiety has gone. I didn't take many shots at the party last night. Willow asked me not to. Does that sound crazy? After all, I'm here on assignment, right? Document a
160 week in Willow's life, they said.

But 'they' are Willow's management, and 'they' have made it clear that my assignment is

to show the world the Willow Twine 'they' want
165 to see – the sweet, girlish pop star (her true
age, twenty-one, is a more closely guarded
secret than the president's personal cell phone
number).

All I'd taken the previous night were a few
170 innocent party shots. I had intentionally not
taken the shots that editors everywhere would
have paid a lot of money for. As a result, this
morning I'm in no rush to review what's in
the camera's memory. I wonder if I can really
175 make this idea of staying here in California
work. It's not *that* crazy, is it? I've earned the
trust of Willow Twine, one of the biggest stars
in Hollywood. She's already introduced me to
a bunch of her actor friends and has promised
180 to hook me up with even more. If I stay, I
have a chance to become the Annie Leibovitz
of the L.A. young actor scene. I could grow
with them. I could be their favourite go-to
photographer for decades to come.

185 But what about Nasim? My insides clench
and my heart beats wildly when I think of him
and the fight we had before I left New York. I
would so hate to lose him, but I know what my
father would say: You're young, you can't let a
190 guy influence the direction of your career.

I pick up the camera, turn the viewer on,
and have a look at the previous day's shots.
Willow holding the red shoes she bought me
for the party. Willow hanging out by the pool
195 with her best friend, Anne-Marie. Willow and
Anne-Marie trying on clothes for the party.
I get to the last shot I remember taking the
night before – Willow in a pink dress by the
pool, welcoming guests. But the camera's
200 counter indicates that there are six more
shots. How weird is this? I think. First I wake
up and my camera isn't where I'm certain I left
it. And now I discover I took pictures I don't
remember taking.

205 I flip to the first one … and freeze. I am
staring at a shot I definitely don't remember
taking. And for good reason. I didn't take it.

But that hardly matters now. I've stopped
breathing. My heart is thudding. Goose bumps
210 race up my arms, and it might be imagination,
but I think I can feel tiny beads of cold sweat
seep out of my pores.

In my camera is a shot that changes
everything.

**Stop and think:**

What do you think the picture on Jamie's
camera shows? Collect ideas with a partner.

*After finding the mysterious shot on her* 215
*camera, Jamie hides in a bathroom and has an*
*imaginary conversation with Carla Harris, her*
*photo agent.*

I'm sitting in the pink bathroom in Willow's
mansion – a digital gold mine in my hands – 220
hearing voices in my head.

Me: "Can I really do this? Destroy Willow's
career in order to advance mine?"

Carla: "Darling, are you crazy? This is your
ticket. Everything you've dreamed of since 225
day one. People would kill for this kind of
opportunity. You think if it was the other way
around – if Willow Twine needed to wreck your
career to advance her own – she'd hesitate for
a second?" 230

"But Willow and I are friends."

"Oh, please! You've known her for exactly
one week."

"You don't know. You haven't been out here
with us." 235

"My dear, they were calling me an old-
timer in this business back when you were still
in Pampers. I've seen and heard it all. Believe
me, I know."

by Todd Strasser (abridged and adapted)

→ △ 86/10

**READING**

## 2 Understanding the story

a) *Sum up each part of the story in 2–3 sentences. Then find a heading for each part.*

b) *What adjectives would you use to describe Jamie's character? Give examples from the text to support your ideas.*

**READING**

## 3 Two words, same meaning?

→ S3

a) *Jamie insists she is a 'celebrity photographer', not a 'paparazzo'. Explain the difference between these two words from Jamie's point of view.*

b) *Read the first part of the story again when Jamie takes embarrassing photos of Tatiana Frazee. Comment on her definitions of 'celebrity photographer' and 'paparazzo' in a). Would you agree with her that she is **not** a paparazzo?*

c) *After the incident at the coffee shop, Tatiana Frazee sends a message to her best friend. Think about how she must have felt when she realised that Jamie had taken photos of her embarrassing moment. Then write Tatiana's message to her friend.*

**PEAKING**

## 4 A role play: Jamie's dilemma

a) *While Jamie is sitting in the bathroom in Willow's house, she's talking out loud about her dilemma. In her head Carla, her photo agent, is trying to persuade her to sell the photos, while Nasim, her boyfriend, is trying to talk her out of it. In groups of three, write a short role play. Then act it out in class.*

b) *After what you've heard in your role plays, how would you decide if you were in Jamie's shoes? Write her a message with your advice.*

c) *At the end, Carla's voice in Jamie's head says: "I've seen and heard it all. Believe me, I know." Explain the meaning of this statement.*

**PEAKING**

## 5 At what price fame ...? → WB 35/25

a) *Look at some key lines from the story below. Then compare the lives of Jamie and Willow. In what ways are they different; in what ways are they the same?*

> The camera represents who I am. It's my identity. With it, I'm a sixteen-year-old celebrity photographer. (And maybe something of a celebrity myself?) Without it, who am I? What am I? (lines 101–106)

> But 'they' are Willow's management, and 'they' have made it clear that my assignment is to show the world the Willow Twine 'they' want to see – the sweet, girlish pop star. (lines 162–165)

b) *Look at the words below. What would or wouldn't you give up to become famous? Explain why.*

anonymity    appearance    family    friends    home    identity    normality

personality    school    security    values

LISTENING

## 1 From Tinseltown[1] to Techtown

L 2/14 ⊙ **a)** *Listen to a journalist interviewing Jack Jonston, who was a Hollywood actor before he started his new career. Sum up what they're talking about in 2–3 sentences.*

**b)** *Listen again and take notes about the following topics:*

why Jack ended his career in Hollywood | how he thinks his tech career is continuing his acting career

**c)** *Write the beginnings of two news articles about Jack's decision to leave Hollywood – one for a tabloid[2] and one for a serious newspaper. In what ways would they be different?*

LANGUAGE

## 2 A major event

**a)** *Choose the correct tense to talk about the future:* **simple present** *or* **present progressive**.

> Dear Mom and Dad,
> I want to tell you about a very important decision I've made: My new life **1** (start) at 3:30 a.m. tomorrow! That's when my bus to L.A. **2** (leave). I didn't buy a return ticket because I **3** (stay) out there until I've made it. Don't worry – I **4** (plan) on coming home again – but only after I've got my first movie role. Planes to L.A. **5** (fly) every day out of Omaha, but please don't come to visit until I tell you it's OK. Tina **6** (go) with me and our first audition **7** (take place) on Friday at 10:00. We heard that the directors **8** (not arrive) until 11:00 or 12:00, but we **9** (not take) any chances, and our plan is to be there at 6:00. I'm sorry I didn't tell you this in person, but I'm too nervous!
> Love, Janey

**b)** *Write a letter to inform your parents or a friend about a major decision in your life. Use the* **simple present** *and the* **present progressive** *to talk about the future.*

LANGUAGE

## 3 Hollywood Dream Factory

**a)** *Put in* **relative pronouns** *only where necessary.*

1. Every year thousands of people ▮▮ have big hopes and dreams move to L.A.
2. Although we think of aspiring actors first, there are also writers, directors, producers, musicians, comedians and others ▮▮ want to chase their dreams in Hollywood.
3. The professions ▮▮ they choose depend on their skills and talents.
4. The age ▮▮ they are when they start their career is also an important factor.
5. People ▮▮ are under 30 have a better chance of becoming famous.
6. And young people ▮▮ parents are already in the business have even better chances.
7. But the competition ▮▮ they face is still hard.
8. There are only about 70,000 people in the US ▮▮ main income is from acting.

**b)** *Look at the sentences with a relative pronoun in a). Rewrite them in a way you don't need the relative pronoun any more.*

**Example:** 1. Every year thousands of people with big hopes and dreams move to L.A.

---

**1 Tinseltown** [ˈtɪnslˌtaʊn] Hollywood *(umgangssprachlich)* | **2 tabloid** [ˈtæblɔɪd] Boulevard-/Klatschzeitung

BULARY

## 4 It's the perfect opportunity!

a) *Match the adjectives and the nouns to make suitable **phrases** for the sentences below.*

> aspiring | golden | logical | memorable |
> relaxed | seasonal | southern | worldwide

> work | recognition[1] | opportunity | event |
> solution | border | atmosphere | actor

1. Like millions of others, Kirk Douglas was also once an …
2. Is it really necessary to spend billions of tax dollars to protect the … of the US?
3. Many companies in Silicon Valley emphasize a … in the workplace[2].
4. Getting honored with a star on the Walk of Fame was a …
5. I couldn't miss the chance to work with him. It was a …
6. One of the final steps to real success is when your brand achieves …
7. The … to my family's problems was to risk crossing the border in search of …

b) *In small groups, take turns to act out the verbs from Unit 2 below (you're allowed to use sounds, but you mustn't speak). The others need to guess which verb you chose.*

> approve | burst | close down | explode | guard | increase | observe | pack up |
> photograph | remain | set up | shoot (a film) | showcase (one's talents) | stroll | urge

GUAGE

## 5 Are hamburgers healthy?

a) *Look at these sentences and explain the difference between the nouns in A and B.*

1. A: I'm looking for **a job** and applied at a fast-food place. – B: Did you get **the job**?
2. A: **Food** in California is expensive, isn't it? – B: Yes, but **the food** I buy is also very healthy.

b) *Decide where you need **the**, **a / an** or **no article (–)**.*

Surprisingly enough, `1` hamburgers can be healthy too. `2` hamburgers at In-N-Out Burgers of California are made with `3` freshest ingredients. Usually it's all of `4` extras that people put on them that are unhealthy. Did you know that `5` ketchup has lots of `6` sugar in it? One tablespoon has almost as much as `7` chocolate chip cookie. Some people call `8` sugar the worst ingredient in `9` modern food. However, our bodies do need `10` healthy kind of sugar like `11` sugar you get from fruit, but not added sugar. So next time you go to `12` hamburger stand, think about ordering `13` extra slice of tomato instead of `14` ketchup.

c) *Write two sentences for each of these abstract nouns, one with an article and one without. Then translate the sentences into German. How is the use of the definite article before an abstract noun different in German?*

> anonymity    effort    glamor    politics    risk

**1 recognition** [ˌrekəgˈnɪʃn] Anerkennung | **2 workplace** [ˈwɜːkpleɪs] Arbeitsplatz

LANGUAGE

## 6 Welcome to the studios!

a) *What did people say to the new employee on his first day on the job? Use the **future progressive** to complete the sentences.*

1. Welcome to the studios! I expect you ▮▮▮ (come) to the meeting at 9:00, right?
2. Hi there! In an hour we ▮▮▮ (set up) to shoot a new ad. Please be there!
3. I'm from Human Resources[1]. We ▮▮▮ (observe) you closely for the next six weeks. Relax!
4. I'm Sue. Next week the boss ▮▮▮ (nominate) employees for a workshop. Interested?
5. Hey man! Lots of people ▮▮▮ (urge) you to work long hours. Don't listen to them!
6. This is Sheila. She ▮▮▮ (take) photos of the new employees for the studio website.

b) *Complete these sentences with your own ideas. Use the **future progressive**.*

Example: 1. While you're still going to school, I**'ll be going** to auditions in Hollywood.

1. While you're still going to school … 2. When you read this letter … 3. This time tomorrow my friends and I … 4. I can't believe her luck. Next month …

LANGUAGE

## 7 Talking about future plans → WB 38/1

a) *Grant owns a start-up company in Silicon Valley. Look at his schedule. Say what **will be happening** or what **will have happened** at a certain time in the future.*

Start like this: At 8:00 Grant will be … / By 1:00 he'll have …

| | |
|---|---|
| 7:00–8:30 | breakfast with Phil |
| 9:00–10:00 | Young Inventors – meeting at Hilton Hotel |
| 11:00–1:00 | read new applications, choose applicant for new position |
| 1:30 | phone interview, reporter will send questions by 10:00 |
| 5:30 | dinner with Joy, buy flowers on the way to restaurant |

b) *Imagine you have your own tech company in Silicon Valley. Make a schedule for new inventions you plan for the future. Then use the **future progressive** and the **future perfect** to talk about these plans.*

Examples: 1. 2028–2030: research use of robots in homes
→ In 2029 we**'ll be researching** the use of robots in homes.
2. 2031: launch[2] new robot onto the market
→ By 2031 we**'ll have launched** a new robot onto the market.

LANGUAGE

## 8 Planning your business career → WB 39/2

*Choose from these words to rewrite the sentences. Sometimes more than one answer is correct.*

might    be to    should    must    be said to    need to    have to    be supposed to

1. I was required to pay $400 for the course materials. 2. You ought to look at alternative study programs. 3. He is expected to pay back the student loan[3]. 4. Some of the students may have the chance to receive a scholarship[4]. 5. People say that the company is one of the best in town. 6. If you want to be successful in business, you need to be persistent. 7. We are expected to find our own crowdfunding. 8. You must call her in the morning about your application.

1 **Human Resources** [ˌhjuːmən rɪˈzɔːsɪz] Personalabteilung | 2 **to launch** [lɔːnʃ] einführen | 3 **loan** [ləʊn] Darlehen; Kredit | 4 **scholarship** [ˈskɒləʃɪp] Stipendium

## 9 Tourism in California

**a)** *Complete the **conditional sentences** with the correct verb forms.*

If people had to name California's major industries, one of them **1** (definitely – be) tourism, in which national parks play a big role. But if the parks **2** (aim) to preserve[1] nature for future generations, won't it be difficult to remain a multi-billion dollar industry? In 2014 almost four million people visited Yosemite and spent more than $ 400 million in the park and in surrounding[2] communities. Thousands of people would lose their jobs if the park **3** (not attract) so many tourists. However, the numbers of visitors have left scars on Yosemite and all the other national parks. Many people don't realize it, but if hikers don't stay on the marked paths, they **4** (might destroy) vegetation. If the number of cars in the parks **5** (continue) to rise, air pollution will get worse. Some people believe that if cars **6** (be) banned in the parks, this would greatly improve the situation.

Since they were created, people in the US have been proud of their national parks. If park officials and politicians[3] hadn't worked together at the very beginning, the parks **7** (never succeed). Today they're still working on ways of balancing[4] preservation[5] and protection with enjoyment and education. Other voices remind officials that the parks have always been changing. So, for example, if there weren't forces such as wind and erosion, many of the spectacular sights in the parks **8** (not exist). But how do you find the middle road between loving a park to death and protecting it?

If we just preserve the parks, **9** (the state – still earn) money from tourism?

**b)** *What do you think about the role of national parks as a multi-billion dollar industry? Write a post for an online forum where there's a discussion between nature lovers and businesspeople.*

## 10 Showcase your talents!

**a)** *In groups of three, choose one of these reality shows from American TV and find out more about it on the internet.*

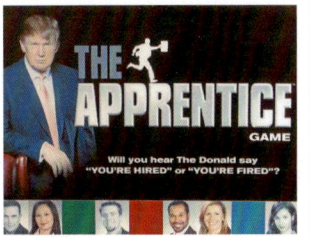
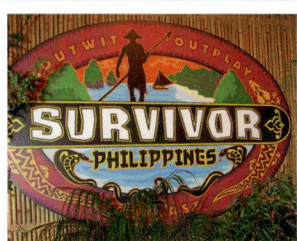

**b)** *Collect arguments to support this statement: "Our show is the best place to showcase your talents."*

**c)** *Form new groups with one 'expert' for each reality show. Discuss which of the three shows is best to showcase your talents.*

**d)** *In class, discuss the pros and cons of reality shows for showcasing your talents and achieving success.*

**1 to preserve** [prɪˈzɜːv] schützen | **2 surrounding** [səˈraʊndɪŋ] umgebend; umliegend | **3 politician** [ˌpɒlɪˈtɪʃn] Politiker/-in | **4 to balance** [ˈbæləns] ausgleichen; ins Gleichgewicht bringen | **5 preservation** [ˌprezəˈveɪʃn] Erhaltung; Bewahrung

## Text smart 2
# Argumentative texts

Find more online:
4q5p5c

To argue a point in a serious way, the **letter to the editor** and the **argumentative essay** are frequently-used formats. Both of these formats often play a role in written exams too.

SPEAKING

**1 Warm-up: Reasons to speak out**

**a)** *Read the news excerpt below. Say what your first reaction is, and why.*

### Harsh media criticism of talent show

by Nisha Kumani | 19 May 2018 | London

The jury of the popular British TV show 'Be The Star You Are' (BTSYA) finds itself under media attack once again. Jury insults and harsh criticism caused contestant Lara Maldini to break down in tears and collapse on stage during last night's show. The audience booed the jury as Maldini had to be …

**b)** *Stories like the one above can provoke strong reader reactions, whether positive or negative. Look at the criteria below. Say which ones would be the appropriate style for a reaction on* **social media** *and for a reaction in* **letter form** *to a newspaper. Say why.*

formal | informal | objective | factual | emotional | well-structured | funny | interesting

**c)** *Your turn: What kind of story or topic could provoke you enough to want to speak out in written form, e.g. in a letter to a news source? Look at the examples on the right for ideas.*

an unfair film or TV review | a provocative advert or report | a negative / one-sided article about your favourite celebrity

READING

**2 Responding to a written text in written form**

**a)** *Now read excerpts from two* **letters to the editor** *on the news story above. Then:*
1. Sum up the message of each text. 2. Say which point of view you agree with, and why.

One of the most entertaining and popular TV formats is the talent show with a star jury. It's a fact that millions of viewers watch shows like BTSYA each week. Most of these shows, however, are harshly criticised by the media and parent groups. This bashing of a popular form of entertainment must stop. First of all, I'm 17 and I've been enjoying shows like BTSYA since …

I really wonder how many more of these horrible insults people are prepared to tolerate. Young people like myself (I'm 18) are trying to show their talent, but the juries only seem to be interested in bad jokes, insults and how good *they* look on TV. For several reasons, it's time we bring back a certain level of quality to TV. First, it's obvious that the jury has absolutely no …

**b)** *Discuss in class how each letter could go on, and with which arguments.*

# How to: Write a letter to the editor

*Letter to the editor:*

I would like to address the different letters you have received about your report from 19 May on the Lara Maldini scandal. Basically, I get the feeling that the juries of shows like BTSYA are told to be either extremely positive or extremely negative, but rarely honest. The young contestants need constructive feedback, but they don't get it. Therefore, it is time to do away with juries in order to save the talent shows.

First, I do not want to hear nasty insults like the ones that Peter Dolan threw at Maldini and at so many candidates before her. Although some may find this entertaining, it can really break a young person's spirit and do real damage, as psychologists have often said.

My point is that talent – or lack of it – can be described without four-letter words and insults.

Next, if juries are not able to give constructive feedback, then they should not have the job in the first place. In my opinion, all a talent show needs is a host, an audience, and viewers who vote for their favourites. They don't need a jury.

Some might say "It's all just for fun; let it go." But I am convinced that it is not funny when people get hurt. This is why I say that the TV producers need to feel how angry some of us are. If enough people let them know, the message will hopefully get through and cruel, nasty juries may soon be a thing of the past.

*Shane Eaton (Radford, Oxfordshire)*

**READING**

## 3 Understanding the text

→ △ 86/1 *Read the letter above which a teenager wrote about the 'Be The Star You Are' show. Then:*
1. Sum up the main points the writer makes.   2. Say if you agree or not, and why.

**WRITING**

## 4 A model letter to the editor: Structure and language

a) *Read the two boxes and also the text elements below them. In the letter above, find examples of the different elements and write them in your exercise book.*

**Writing skills**

Points to consider in a **letter to the editor**:
- Show that **your opinion** is the right one.
- **Counter arguments** can help to support your own arguments.
- You can use personal pronouns (*I, my, me*), but be **serious** and **formal** in tone.
- **Paragraphs** should be clearly structured, e.g. with adverbs like *first, next,* etc.
- Shorter letters are often **reader-friendly**.

**Useful phrases**

**Phrases for your arguments:**
In my opinion, … | As far as I know, … | I am convinced that … | Because of … | My point is that … | The fact / truth is that … | It is obvious that …
**Introducing counter arguments:**
Although … | Some might say that … | Don't let anyone tell you that … | It is a typical mistake to say / think / claim …

argument / counter argument     the main issue     linking words to structure paragraphs / ideas

supporting facts / information     suggestions     conclusion     no short forms

b) *Work with a partner. What other arguments and counter arguments can you think of for Shane's letter?*

WRITING

→ △ 86/2

## 5 Using the correct register for a more formal context → WB 40/1

*Letter to the editor:*

Your report about BTSYA yesterday was total crap. Who gave you the right to criticise shows for young people?!?! I'm 17 and I bet if YOU were 17, you'd like BTSYA too! But that's the problem: You're some stupid old idiot who has no idea what young people wanna see! So Lara Maldini cried on TV and collapsed – who the hell cares?!

The stupid cow had NO TALENT and she deserved to hear that her voice was crap. Why do you feel so sorry for her after she'd been so nasty to ALL the other contestants on the show?!?! Oh, you didn't know that? Well then, get the FULL STORY next time and stop writing such rubbish!!!

*Stella Fox, London*

*Identify the problems in this short letter to the editor which a newspaper wasn't able to publish. Rewrite it so that the letter would be acceptable for a newspaper context.*

### Examples:
– You're some stupid old idiot who has no idea what young people …
  → **Better:** I would like to ask if you really know what young people …
– Well then, get the FULL STORY next time …
  → **Better:** I suggest trying to learn the full story next time …

LANGUAGE

## 6 Sequence adverbs

*After the 'BTSYA' show in London, there was an attack on jury member Peter Dolan. An audience member saw it and told the police about it. Read her short written statement for the police. Fill in the missing **sequence adverbs** in a logical way.*

The show had just ended when strange things started to happen in the audience. **1** , the man next to me said, "That nasty Peter Dolan can't just insult Lara like that! I'm going to hit him in the face right now!" **2** , the woman on the other side of me said, "No, you aren't, because I'm gonna hit YOU first!" **3** the man could say anything, she jumped over me and hit him in the nose. **4** , their friends started to hit each other, and **5** almost everybody else in the audience started shouting things like "Lara, we love you!" or "Lara, you loser!" It was chaos, with bloody noses everywhere. I tried and tried to get away, and **6** I was able to. **7** the police arrived, everyone slowly calmed down.

after

after that

before

finally

first

next

then

WRITING

## 7 How to begin properly

a) *Look at the letter on p. 69 again. What arguments would you offer if you replied to it?*

b) *Write the introduction paragraph of your own reply to the letter on p. 69. Make sure you use the right style and register.*

c) *In pairs, swap introductions. Peer-edit each other's work.*

# How to: Write an argumentative essay

Nick Shaw, a writer for the student website at his school in Leeds, has written an essay on an issue he feels strongly about.

## The media are failing young people with unrealistic images of the sexes

Everywhere one looks in the media – in adverts, on TV, at the cinema – young men and women are confronted with images of what they are expected to look and be like. Unfortunately, these images are unrealistic and full of clichés. If this does not stop, it may do serious damage to many young people, as the following arguments will show.

First, I would like to begin with body types. Basically, the media present us with only one acceptable body type for each sex: A woman is expected to be skinny and sporty, look like a model, and have a big chest too. A man is also expected to look like a model and be tall, muscular and sporty. On the one hand, one could see this as the media's way of encouraging us to be sportier and healthier. Obviously, there is nothing wrong with that. But on the other hand, it is completely irresponsible to only present perfect images. The fact is that perfect-looking people are the exception, not the rule. As a result, more and more young people are risking their health with steroid use, plastic surgery and extreme diets. I am convinced that if the media presented more normal body types, young people would not risk their health to try to be 'perfect'.

Secondly, I must harshly criticise the image of success in the media. For the most part, we are told that success is an attractive white man in a suit. Although it is true that most high-level businesspeople are men in suits, there are reasons to criticise this one-sided image: One, young people like myself are more likely to look up to the young sweatshirt-and-jeans billionaires of Silicon Valley than to men in suits; times are changing. Two, even if an advert or a film must show someone in a suit, why not a woman? Successful women do exist. Three, success is not just about material things like an expensive suit or car. And four, success is not only for white people; other ethnic groups want – and find – success too. Therefore, it is clear that the media's image of success is outdated, wrong, negative and unrealistic.

To sum up, the media focus too much on unrealistic ideas of perfection and success when they present us with their new films, shows and products. My suggestion would be for the media to present more realism and more variety so that young people have more real role models to choose from.

– Nick Shaw (staff writer, Year 11)

Leave your comments for Nick here.

READING

## 8 Understanding the text

→ S3 **a)** *Read the essay on the previous page. Summarise the author's main point.*

→ △ 87/3 **b)** *Discuss your attitude to the issue and to this particular essay. Justify your views.*

WRITING

## 9 How to structure an argumentative essay

**a)** *There are two main formats for an **argumentative essay**:*
 – *In a **persuasive essay**, the author argues for only **one** view: his / her own.*
 – *In a **neutral essay**, the writer presents the reader with a **balance** of different views to consider. Say what essay format has been used on the previous page, and how you know.*

 **b)** *Read about the elements of argumentative essays below. Then show that you understand how the essay on p. 71 works by writing an outline for it with a partner. Your outline should name each section of the essay and also **briefly** summarise what each part is about. Copy your finished outline into your folder.*

Examples: – The intro is from lines xx to xx. It presents … Key words / ideas are …
 – Paragraph xx introduces a pro argument. Important facts are …

---

### Writing skills

Both persuasive and neutral essays require a **formal**, **serious style**. Here are some typical elements of **both** formats:

1. An **introduction** presents your **main point**. It can also include:
 questions you promise to answer | a short explanation of why the topic is relevant.
2. The main body of an essay must include **arguments** and **counter arguments**; the reader must see that the writer has looked at the topic from *different* sides. Arguments are introduced in paragraphs. Two structures are typical:
 a) one side's arguments first, and then counter arguments *(pro-pro-pro; con-con-con)*
 b) argument and counter argument in the *same* paragraph, then a new paragraph for another argument and counter argument, etc. *(pro-con; pro-con; pro-con)*.
3. **Quotations** (e.g. from experts) and **facts** which support arguments can also be helpful.
4. A **conclusion** restates the main question, or, shows that you are right.

---

**c)** *Go back to the essay and pick out words and phrases that you would use to present arguments and counter arguments. Add these to your folder.*

WRITING

## 10 More practice: Structuring an argumentative essay → WB 41/2

 **a)** *In groups, discuss your opinions on the essay headline below:*
→ △ 87/4

"Our constant use of social media is stopping us from making real friends in real life"

**b)** *Work together to list arguments for and against the subject. Think of examples and facts that could support different arguments from different points of view.*

**c)** *Decide on **one** standpoint for your group and make a list of supporting points. Then write a structured outline of an essay based on the model essay and on the skills box above. For your outline, you must choose between the neutral and the persuasive essay format.*

WRITING

## 11   Options: What do you think?

**a)** *Select **one** of the controversial topics below. Write a draft for a letter to the editor **or** an argumentative essay with reasons for or against the issue that is being discussed.*

→ S6

*Letter to the editor:*
16 year-old-drivers in the UK? No thanks. The UK already has enough problems with its 17-year-old drivers, as the high accident rate reveals. Also, just look at how many traffic accidents all the young drivers in the USA cause, where it is possible to drive at 16 or even younger; the facts speak for themselves. I am quite sure that the UK has enough problems as it is. 16-year-old drivers would be unsafe at *any* speed; keep them away from the wheel until they're 17.

*Pippa Lee, York*

### Angry flight attendants slam airline's decision to force female cabin crew to wear high heels

by Tom Campbell | 7 June 2018 | London

An e-mail sent out to all female flight attendants last week required that heels must be worn by all female crew members at all times, whether on short- or long-distance flights. Angry women have expressed outrage and plan to continue protesting until the decision is done away with and they will be able to get back to their …

*Letter to the editor:*
In your article 'No shirt, no shoes, no service!', I completely agree with places like Spain or Thailand for issuing fines of $ 250 or more to tasteless young tourists. If young men think it is fine to walk into a restaurant or a clothing store with no shirt on, far from the beach, then they certainly deserve to pay a big fine. In fact, I would welcome such fines everywhere here in Florida too, where the 'no shirt' tourist crowd is a big problem in our city's streets.
  First, it's a fact that not everybody enjoys seeing …

**b)** *Peer-editing: Once you're finished with your letter or essay, pair up with a classmate who has also finished his/her text on the same topic and in the same format. Peer-edit each other's texts.*

Find more online:
3wv4pq

# Having a voice

Having a voice is a key aspect of democracy and participation in society. There are many different ways that people can make their voices heard; you're going to look at some of them on these pages, including concrete examples at Thomas Tallis School in Greenwich, London.

READING

**1 A questionnaire** → WB 42/1

*Do the questionnaire below. Choose the **one** sentence in each set of questions that best describes your attitude towards each point.*

## How far would YOU go to have a voice? Take the test and find out!

**1** a) If I were on a student council, I'd want to lead it and make change happen!

b) I'd like to be on a student council, but I wouldn't want to lead it.

c) It's enough for me to have a good student council. I don't need to be on it.

d) Who needs a student council? What a waste of time! How boring.

**2** a) Why vote in elections? I'm just one person – how can my vote make any difference?

b) I can't believe that some people never vote in elections. What losers!

c) People have fought for our right to vote. It's disrespectful not to vote if you have the opportunity.

d) If you don't understand the issues, it's best to leave it to others to vote.

**3** a) I admire political activists who do dangerous protest stunts, like climbing skyscrapers to hang up protest banners.

b) People are crazy and stupid to do dangerous protest stunts. It doesn't change anything – and it's illegal too!

c) Protest is OK, but why be so dramatic with stunts? There are other ways to make your point.

d) I can totally imagine doing a dangerous protest stunt, to draw attention to an issue I really believe in.

**4** a) I would sign somebody else's petition, but start one myself? No thanks.

b) Yes, I would volunteer my time to collect signatures on the street for a petition.

c) I can imagine starting my own petition about something I feel strongly about.

d) I would never waste my time on petitions. Don't bother me with stuff like that.

**5** a) I respect people who do their bit for the local community. Perhaps I should do more myself.

b) Charity is great, but it should begin with your friends and family, not strangers.

c) I want to get more involved in global issues. The world around me really means something to me.

d) I'm always so busy, a million things to do. I don't have time to 'have a voice'!

**6** a) Considering things like child labour and animal protection when we buy clothes is a way to make a statement.

b) I love it when protesters spray-paint people in fur coats. They deserve it! How can people be so cruel to animals?!

c) Clothes are just clothes. They have nothing to do with politics so why waste a thought on them?

d) I wouldn't wear fur myself – but if others do, that's fine. Having a voice doesn't mean you can dictate lifestyles.

PEAKING

## 2 Discuss your results → WB 42/2

*Now see what results you get below. Say if you agree with yours or not, and why.*

■ **Mostly reds:** You consider it very important to have a voice! You express your voice and like to persuade others to join you. You would go far – too far perhaps? – to stand up for your beliefs.

■ **Mostly yellows:** You see how important it is to get involved. It's just that you prefer other people to take the lead. Maybe you haven't yet found an issue you feel really passionate about?

■ **Mostly greens:** You're happy to sit back and let other people do the work. Maybe you don't believe you could make a difference, but don't forget that being involved can bring rewards!

■ **Mostly blues:** You live in a bubble and haven't got a political bone in your body! Wider issues don't really interest you. But your voice and your actions are valuable. Don't just run and hide!

VIEWING

## 3 The Student Council at TTS

Now learn about having a voice at TTS …

DVD 5/5

**a)** *Watch until 03:25. Sum up what you learn about the Student Council and what they do.*

> **Word bank**
>
> discussion / to discuss  |  to feel strongly about sth  |  to nominate sb  |  participation / to participate  |  representative / to represent

A

**b)** *Watch again and point out the details you found the most interesting. Explain why.*

VIEWING

## 4 Student Voice at TTS

**a)** *Watch the rest of the film. Sum up why the members are in Student Voice and how they're making a difference.*

**b)** *Now compare and contrast the Student Council and the Student Voice.*

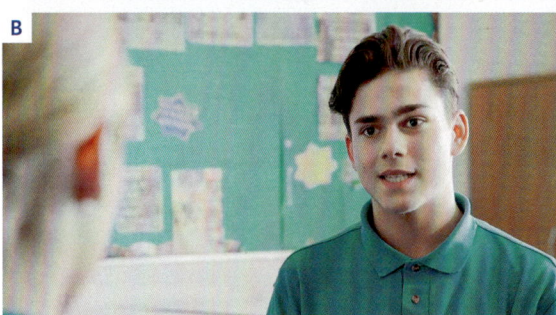

B

PEAKING

## 5 Your turn: Having a voice at your school

**a)** *Compare what you've seen at TTS with your own experiences at school.*

→ S8

**b)** *In small groups, try to find agreement on the top three things you'd change / improve at your school. Present your ideas.*

C

## Legende

Diese Symbole und Erklärungen zeigen dir,
wie du mit den Hilfen, Aufgaben und Aktivitäten
auf den *Diff pool*-Seiten arbeiten kannst.

△ Hilfe zur Unit-Aufgabe | oder eine
leichtere Variante der Unit-Aufgabe |
oder eine zusätzliche Aufgabe

▲ eine zusätzliche Herausforderung

# Unit 1

△ **1 Thinking about the job world** → Help with Introduction, p. 7/3b)

*This list of reasons for and against changing jobs can help you with Ex. 3b):*

- You learn a lot at a new job; you also learn to deal with new situations again and again.
- Having a long-term job[1] means security – that can be important in a person's life.
- Leaving jobs often means you never feel at home at a job – you're always on the move.
- You lose friends; it isn't always easy to stay in touch with colleagues from your old job.
- You meet new people, make new friends.
- Changing jobs often means moving. That's expensive, annoying[2], costs time.
- New people bring new ideas: There's more innovation in a company.
- You satisfy[3] your curiosity.
- The longer you hold a job, the harder it is to get fired[4].

△ **2 A formal job description** → Help with Station 1, p. 8/2b)

*These words and phrases can help you talk about the differences
between the two texts:*

## Word bank

describes job in detail | mentions tasks | gives a list of responsibilities |
says what the person is expected to do | gives information on what the
application should contain | gets a lot of people interested in the job |
names the benefits | explains what others say about the job

**1 long-term job** [ˌlɒŋtɜːm ˈdʒɒb] langfristiger Arbeitsplatz | **2 annoying** [əˈnɔɪɪŋ] nervig | **3 to satisfy** [ˈsætɪsfaɪ]
befriedigen | **4 to get fired** [ˌget ˈfaɪəd] entlassen werden

## 3 What careers do girls and boys prefer? → Instead of Station 1, p. 9/4c)

a) *Look at the different job criteria below. Discuss which ones you think are important for choosing a career.*

b) *What sort of jobs could you describe with these criteria? Describe different jobs and whether you would apply for them or not.*

- requires more physical[1] / more emotional strength
- can be done full-time / part-time
- is a dream job for little girls / little boys
- matches male / female way of thinking
- is what boys / girls are more interested in
- has lots of male / female role models[2] in real life / in film / on TV
- requires communication / language / organisation / creative skills

## 4 Expressing expectations → Instead of Station 1, p. 10/5

*Talk about the jobs in the box with your partner. What do you think is expected of each of them? Does your partner agree? Use **be expected to / be supposed to + infinitive** in your sentences.*

**Example:**
A: I believe as a doctor you**'re expected to be** good at …
B: I agree, but you**'re** also **supposed to have** … And teachers **are expected to be** …
A: Hm, I think they**'re** …

architect | business executive | dancer | doctor | engineer | fashion designer | firefighter | model | musician | nurse | pilot | reporter | sales assistant | teacher | web designer

be able to work long hours | be attractive | be creative | be good at listening to people | be good at maths / sciences | be great at explaining things | be in good physical shape[3] | enjoy being with children | not get nervous easily | have a good memory | have good communication skills | like working with machines / computers | like being in front of a camera / an audience

**1 physical** ['fɪzɪkl] körperlich | **2 role model** ['rəʊl ˌmɒdl] Vorbild | **3 shape** [ʃeɪp] *hier:* Verfassung

## 5 When I was young … → After Station 1, p. 10/5

Tim's great-grandfather grew up a long time ago – and he likes to tell his great-grandchildren how hard everything was back then! Use the information in the box to write down what Great-grandad Arthur tells his family.

**Start like this:**
When we were young, we **were supposed to** … | My parents were very, very strict. I **was** always **expected to** … | All children **were supposed to** … For example, my sisters …

> help on the farm before and after school | walk to school every day | bring wood to school in winter, to stay warm | be very quiet during lessons | respect our teacher | do homework after helping on the farm after school | help with the chores | eat what is on the table even when you don't like it | be thankful for food | do what parents tell us to do | never disagree with parents | go to bed straight after dinner | look after the smaller children | be home before it gets dark

## 6 A personal profile for your CV → Help with Station 1, p. 10/7

Use the information in the grid below to find ideas for your own profile.

|  | Sports | Cafeteria | Entertainment | Chores |
|---|---|---|---|---|
| Qualifications | – coach of a local sports team<br>– member of swim team | – weekend job in a pizza place / cafe | – member of Drama Club / of a band / dancing group | – do garden work for neighbours<br>– wash my own clothes |
| Strengths | – good with kids / at teaching | – calm<br>– friendly<br>– reliable | – not nervous in front of people<br>– strong nerves[1] | – hard-working<br>– don't mind getting dirty! |
| Skills | – great at swimming / football | – good at preparing / serving food | – good at singing / dancing / acting / motivating people | – good with my hands |

## 7 The application letter → Help with Station 1, p. 11/8b)

Look at the grid from Ex. 6. Which of the qualifications, strengths and skills does Ella say she has? Copy the grid and complete it with information about Ella.

**1 strong nerves** [ˌstrɒŋ ˈnɜːvz] gute Nerven

## 8  Verbs of perception: Present participle or infinitive? → After Station 2, p. 14/14c)

*Lisa can't believe all the things that happen in the flats across the street. In the list below you see what happened in just 20 minutes! Use the information to write sentences about her neighbours. Use* **verbs of perception** *like 'see', 'notice', 'listen to', 'hear'. Which activities need a* **participle construction***, which need an* **infinitive***?*

**Start like this:**  I **heard** one man …

1. man – sing non-stop[1] – in an awful voice
2. woman – drop two bags of rubbish out the window!
3. man – clean the flat with no clothes on!
4. woman – hide expensive shopping bags before husband gets home
5. two men – shout at and hit each other non-stop
6. woman – play the piano very nicely
7. man – try to stop a fire in his kitchen
8. two police officers – break down[2] a door to a flat

## 9  You're a crime witness → After Station 2, p. 14/14c)

*You came home late at night and saw someone breaking into your neighbour's flat.
Then you told the police about it. Write about what you heard, saw, noticed, watched. Did you see all of the action, or just parts of it? Here are some ideas:*

> stranger  |  carry big travel bag  |  walk close to the house  |  look up at windows  |  open garden gate[3]  |  turn round and look up and down street  |  walk very quietly to back of house  |  glass – break  |  someone – switch on torch  |  walk slowly around house  |  come out through front door  |  run down street

## 10  A winter's dream → After Station 2, p. 14/15b)

*Complete the following sentences with a* **participle** *or* **infinitive***. Use the verbs below.*

Lily was walking through the woods when she saw children 【1】 . She carefully walked across the lake 【2】 . Suddenly she felt the 【3】 . She stood still 【4】 . The children came towards her 【5】 . Lily could hear the 【6】 . She turned round and watched the 【7】 . She felt water 【8】 . The children stood 【9】 . Lily heard them 【10】 , but couldn't understand. She watched them 【11】 to the side of the lake. Lily felt water 【12】 . Then she woke up!

| | |
|---|---|
| skate on the frozen[4] lake | wave her arms |
| ice – move below her feet | |
| wonder what to do | shout and laugh |
| ice – break | hole in the ice – get bigger |
| get into her shoes | stare at her |
| say something | run back | cover her body |

---

**1 non-stop** [ˌnɒnˈstɒp] pausenlos; ununterbrochen  |  **2 to break down** [breɪk ˈdaʊn] *hier:* einschlagen  |
**3 gate** [geɪt] Tor  |  **4 frozen** [ˈfrəʊzn] gefroren

△ **11 A blind date?** → After Station 3, p. 18/23

*Rewrite the following text with **defining** and **non-defining** relative clauses.*

Yesterday I saw Jason (he's Sarah's new boyfriend). He walked into the new café in King Street (it sells fair trade coffee and cake). And guess what – he was holding hands with a pretty girl (it wasn't Sarah). So I followed them inside (that was difficult because I didn't want Jason to see me). I pretended to be interested in the chocolate bars (they have them on the counter[1]). I looked into a mirror (it was hanging behind the counter) and saw Jason (he was sitting at a table with the girl). I thought that Sarah (she gets so jealous!) might be really angry. I first thought of taking a photo (I could send it to Sarah). But I realised that I'd left my phone (it was a present for my birthday) at home. So I walked up to them and said hello. Jason (he was surprised) smiled at me and said: "Hi Rebecca! This is Naomi, she goes to the School for the Blind[2]. I work for it on Friday afternoons. She forgot her cane[3] at home, so I said I'd help her to find her way to the café. It belongs to her parents."

▲ **12 Awesome inventions** → After Station 3, p. 18/23

*Here are some more inventions that were presented on the show Dragons' Den. What can you do with them? Find out more and then write a short text. Use **defining** and **non-defining** relative clauses. Then 'sell' one or more of the inventions to your classmates!*

One remote control[4] for everything! Looks like a magic wand[5]: the **Kymera Wand**

A new frozen[6] dessert for people with food allergies: from **Worthenshaws** (name later changed to **Kirsty's**)

An interactive toy for small children: the **iTeddy**

△ **13 How to use inversion for emphasis** → Instead of Station 3, p. 19/24b

*Look at Ex. 24a) on p. 19. Use inversion to rewrite the sentences below in a similar way. Use the word or phrase in **bold** to start with.*

Example: 1. I have **never** felt so nervous. → **Never have I** felt so nervous.

1. I have **never** felt so nervous. → Never have I … ✔
2. He had **hardly** finished lunch when he heard the fire alarm. → Hardly had …
3. I **only** realised how much I liked art **when** I went to Italy. → Only when … did I …
4. She had **no sooner** arrived than the film started. → No sooner had …
5. He **not only** got a new office, but he got more money too! → Not only did he …
6. We **rarely** have time to just sit and do nothing. → Rarely do we …

1 **counter** [ˈkaʊntə] Tresen; Theke | 2 **for the blind** [blaɪnd] für Sehbehinderte | 3 **cane** [keɪn] Stock | 4 **remote control** [rɪˌməʊt kənˈtrəʊl] Fernbedienung | 5 **magic wand** [ˌmædʒɪk ˈwɒnd] Zauberstab | 6 **frozen** [ˈfrəʊzn] gefroren

△ **14** **A year in Cameroon[1]** → After Station 3, p. 19/24b)

🖊 Anthony's first job was as a volunteer for a non-profit organisation[2] in Cameroon. Use *inversion* to rewrite what he posted about it on the 'Words-of-Wisdom Wall'.

1. I did**n't only** work as a volunteer for a non-profit organisation, I also worked for a football club. → Not only …
2. Some of the children had **never** seen a white person **before**. → Never before …
3. I've **rarely** had time to think about my future plans since Cameroon. → Rarely …
4. But I **never** regretted[3] my decision to spend time in Africa. → Never …
5. I did**n't** think **for one moment** about giving up. → Not for one moment …
6. "There's **no way** he'll want to stay there when the rainy season starts!" my friends thought. → No way will …
7. I do**n't only** want to tell people about the hard living conditions in Cameroon, I also want to tell them what a beautiful country it is. → Not only …

△ **15** **Acting out a scene from the film** → Help with Skills, p. 20/2d)

The following ideas can help you write a different dialogue for Saanvi, Phil and Courtney.

**Saanvi:** I'm very passionate about advertising; if I wasn't so nervous, it would be more obvious! | Sorry, but I get so nervous at job interviews! | I can be calm under pressure, believe me; if you invite me back, I won't be as nervous.

**Phil:** I believe it's important to improve yourself, which is why I'm taking extra writing lessons to improve my style. | I might sound a bit too self-confident, but I'll show you I'm the right candidate, just give me a chance. | I've been told I learn quickly.

**Courtney:** Sorry my bus / underground was late; it won't happen again. | Sorry about my phone; I'm a bit nervous and forgot to turn it off. | I'm interested in new products and how they're sold. | I'm good with people / I've been told I'm a good listener.

▲ **16** **How language helps to tell the story** → After Story, p. 26/5b)

✏ On p. 26, line 70, babies are described as 'newchildren'. Find other examples of words used by the community which you find unusual. Explain how their language might affect the way members of the community see the world.

△ **17** **Memories** → Help with Story, p. 27/8b)

Some memories are very important for the world. Look at these memories and think of where we'd be without them. The useful phrases in the box can help you.

World Wars I & II | the atomic bomb[4] | nuclear disasters like Fukushima in 2011

**Useful phrases**

The death of … / destruction[5] of … / disaster in … has taught us to: talk to and listen to each other more | be more careful with … | show more respect to … | stop … before it can start | look for different kinds of … / different ways to …

---

**1 Cameroon** [ˌkæməˈruːn] Kamerun | **2 non-profit organisation** [ˌnɒnprɒfɪt ɔːɡnaɪˈzeɪʃn] gemeinnützige Organisation | **3 to regret** [rɪˈɡret] bereuen | **4 atomic bomb** [əˌtɒmɪk ˈbɒm] Atombombe | **5 destruction** [dɪˈstrʌkʃn] Zerstörung

# Text smart 1

△ **1 Your checklist for summary writing** → Help with Station 1, p. 36/4

✎ *Copy the grid and add more information for your own checklist on summary writing.*

| | Dos | Don'ts |
|---|---|---|
| Length | ✔ Always remember that a summary is reduction | ✘ Don't write too much! 30–40 per cent of original length is enough |
| Contents | ✔ Change order of information if necessary | ✘ No direct speech, no quotes <br> ✘ … |
| Language | ✔ … | ✘ Don't use the same style you use when you talk to your friends. |

△ **2 Compare two examples of an analysis** → Help with Station 2, p. 38/7

*These aspects of texts can help you judge which analysis is more successful:*

A **well-written analysis** … is easy to understand | doesn't contain too many long / very short sentences | is written in more formal, serious language | is well-structured in paragraphs for different ideas and arguments

A **convincing analysis** … presents arguments | contains facts and figures | includes quotes to support the arguments | makes sense to the reader | convinces with factual language, information, and sometimes quotes from experts, but not with emotional language and feelings

An **interesting analysis** … focuses on what would interest the reader, and not just the writer him-/ herself! | presents clear examples | contains humour / suspense / surprise to grab / keep the reader's attention | avoids boring style

△ **3 Finding and using key words** → Help with Options, p. 39/9

*It's a good idea to think of key words and ideas **before** you write a summary / an analysis:*

> **Word bank**
>
> **problems for children / teens:** time | bullying | cyber addiction | lack of sleep | relationship with devices / smartphones is addictive / compulsive
>
> **switching off is:** not impossible | difficult | hard | a challenge
>
> **social media:** 'Disconnect' project | switch off | go offline | addictive
>
> **changes before / after:** more time to read / watch TV / do homework / hang out with friends, family

# Unit 2

## 1 Imagine yourself in the scene → Help with Introduction, p. 44/2

*Match the sentences below to the photos on pp. 44–45. Then choose one of the photos and use the sentence as a starting point for your text about the people and the scene.*

1. I can see the waves crashing against the rocks in the distance. 2. I can feel the sun shining on my back. 3. I enjoy walking along the busy streets. 4. The fields in front of me seem to go on forever. 5. I can hear my colleagues chatting and laughing.

## 2 Expressing the same idea differently → Instead of Station 1, p. 47/2a)

*Match the definitions on the left with the words / phrases from the text on p. 46.*

cause a stir | stroll | chalk something up to experience | a wannabe | aspiring | keep your head above water | showcase your talents

trying to be successful at something | walk in a relaxed way | just be able to survive | show what you're really good at | a person who is trying to become famous, usually without success | learn from something negative that has happened to you | produce a lot of interest or excitement

## 3 Using different future forms → After Station 1, p. 48/8

*Complete the text with **different future forms** – they might be forms you already know or forms you've just learned in Station 1.*

"Hurry now," Jason's mom shouted. "The train **1** (leave) at 10:15, and we **2** (pick up) Cecy on the way, remember?" Jason came running down the stairs. His mom was already in the car, waiting impatiently. "The plane **3** (take off) at 2 p.m. – if Jason doesn't catch the train, he **4** (miss) the plane too. Let's just hope he **5** (be able to) manage without us," she thought. Jason jumped in. "Let's go," he said. "Isn't this just great? At 10 o'clock this evening Cecy and I **6** (sit) in a café and **7** (plan) activities for the summer camp." "Well that sounds fun, but I'm sure that by the time you get back in two months you **8** (do) a lot more work and **9** (spend) less time in a café than you imagine now. Working in a summer camp for kids with special needs isn't easy at all. Did you pack the information the organization sent you?" "Oh no. I forgot. But it doesn't matter. Cecy **10** (remember) to bring it, I'm sure." "And she **11** (think) of

informing the camp team of your arrival time too, right?" "I think so," Jason answered. "I think they **12** (meet) us at the airport. Don't worry, mom. When you hear from me next, I'm sure we **13** (have) the time of our lives, and you **14** (stop) worrying right after my first phone call." "Actually, I've already stopped," his mom thought. "I'm sure Cecy **15** (do) my job for the next few weeks."

### 4 Some facts about the Academy Awards[1] → After Station 2, p. 51/15

*Decide whether you need **the**, **a / an** or **no article (–)**.*

California wouldn't be the same without **1** tech industry, or Hollywood without **2** film industry. Making films has always been **3** big business in L.A.: **4** most people love **5** good movies. That's why so many new films are produced in Hollywood each year. But it's hard to achieve **6** success, and it's not easy to explain **7** success of films like *La La Land* or *Titanic*, which both won **8** number of Academy Awards. A film can win **9** award in many different categories: for best actor or actress, costume design, screenplay[2] or best original score (music). However, most often **10** films are remembered not for **11** money they earned – although **12** money is of course very important – but for **13** fantastic performances of all **14** artists involved. Not all of them are actors: Edith Head won eight Oscars, all for **15** costume design, and Dennis Murren won nine for **16** visual effects in his films.

### 5 The Golden Raspberry Awards[3] → After Station 2, p. 51/15

*Everyone in the film industry wants to win an Oscar – and often nominees have prepared a speech long before Oscar night just in case they win. Nobody wants a Golden Raspberry Award, though, which is the award for particularly bad movies and performances. Choose one of the winners of a 'Razzie Award' below and write a short speech in which you explain why you deserve an Oscar instead.*

Halle Berry, for worst actress in *Catwoman* (2011) |
Bill Condon, for worst director in *Breaking Dawn – The Twilight Saga Part 2* (2013) |
Jesse Eisenberg, for worst supporting actor in *Batman versus Superman* (2017)

### 6 Your own start-up → Help with Station 2, p. 52/17b)

*Think about a new business idea that you find interesting and present it to the class.*
*Use these questions as a structure for your presentation:*

1. What gets on your (or others') nerves every day that could be improved with a good business idea? Think of your daily routine (school, homework, free time …).
2. What money, talents, equipment or help would you need for your business? Who could you ask for advice? How long will it take to turn the idea into the end product?
3. How would you like to sell your product or idea, to whom and where? At what price?
4. Where do you see your business in one year – five years – ten years? And yourself?

---

**1 Academy Award** [əˌkædəmi əˈwɔːd] Oscar *(Filmpreis der Motion Picture Academy)* | **2 screenplay** [ˈskriːnpleɪ] Drehbuch | **3 Golden Raspberry Award** [ˌɡəʊldn ˈrɑːzbri əˌwɔːd] Goldene Himbeere

△ **7 California's changing population** → Help with Station 2, p. 53/20b)

*Here are some possible consequences of California's changing population. Discuss with a partner: Which consequences are likely to happen, which are not? Give reasons.*

**1.** Spanish will become the official language in California.   **2.** The Californian government will spend more money on the education of Latino children.   **3.** White people will leave California and move to states with a white majority.   **4.** There'll be more TV and radio channels[1] in Spanish.   **5.** Politicians who are against Mexican immigrants will lose elections in California.   **6.** Latinos and whites will mix – there'll be no separate groups by 2060.

▲ **8 You're supposed to …** → After Station 3, p. 56/24

*Read the text. Choose from the verbs below to rewrite the underlined parts. Then think of a suitable translation into German.*

| should | be expected to | must | be supposed to | ought to | be required to | be said to |

If you go to California, <u>do visit its fantastic national parks</u>. Some of them are world-famous, like Yosemite or Redwood – <u>people say that the biggest trees on earth grow there</u>. But <u>make sure you don't leave</u> the trail if you hike in the park because you could easily get lost! If you do get lost, <u>rangers will have to search for you</u>, and they don't like putting in extra time for tourists who <u>have been told to stay on the</u> <u>path</u>. If you decide to camp in the park, <u>put all your food into a plastic bag</u> and hang it on a tree at night. Hungry bears love eating leftovers from your picnic in the park. <u>Some people say that they search</u> for food in the tents too! Although <u>tourists are told to read</u> about all the risks before entering the park, rangers <u>have to go out every day</u> to save those who aren't careful enough.

△ **9 Talking about California** → Help with Station 3, p. 57/27

*These phrases can help you talk about your ideas about California:*

Before we talked about California in class I thought / believed that … │ I'd heard a lot about California / I'd seen films that are set in California and thought that … │ I knew that California is said to be …, but … │ Everything I'd heard about California seemed … │ What I found very interesting is … │ I didn't know that … │ However, after we'd read / learned about … I realized that … │ I now think that … │ Nevertheless, I still believe …

**1 channel** ['tʃænl] Programm

△ **10** **What kind of a person is Jamie?** → Instead of Story, p. 63/2b)

*From this list of adjectives, choose the ones that you think describe Jamie best. Work with a partner to choose one from each group. Then compare your list of adjectives with a different partner's and again choose five adjectives from your two lists. With a third partner, narrow your choice down to three adjectives. Give reasons for your choice.*

| 1 | honest | jealous | optimistic | ambitious¹ | relaxed |
|---|--------|---------|------------|-----------|---------|
| 2 | angry | confident | embarrassed | smart | emotional |
| 3 | irresponsible | open | polite | quiet | rude |
| 4 | active | lonely | rich | famous | outgoing |
| 5 | persistent | generous | friendly | curious | reliable |
| 6 | unsure | violent | cold | realistic | clever |
| 7 | mean | sensitive | dominant | boastful² | passionate |
| 8 | open-minded³ | unfriendly | patient | happy | determined |

## Text smart 2

△ **1** **A model letter to the editor** → Help with Station 1, p. 69/3

*You can use these phrases to discuss the letter on p. 69 from your point of view:*

> **Useful phrases**
>
> – I agree / disagree when the writer says / states / claims that …
> – I accept / can't accept the idea that … because I (don't) feel / (don't) believe …
>
> – I share / support the author's view when he says …, but I disagree when he claims …
> – Because of this …, / Therefore …, / For this reason, … I agree / disagree with …

△ **2** **Phrases for a more formal register** → Help with Station 1, p. 70/5

*The letter and its phrases below can give you ideas on how to improve the letter on p. 70:*

> *I am writing to complain about* how you reported on Peter Dolan and the 'BTSYA' show in yesterday's newspaper. *I am sorry to say that* there is much to complain about. *First, I must point out that* your report was *totally* one-sided. You focused on the negative aspects, but not on what makes the show a success. *Additionally,* it was clear that the writer was not aware of the complete story: Nobody in the jury likes Lara Maldini, so it was no surprise that they criticised her. *I realise that* it is not possible to include all the details in stories like this, but *I do feel that* your readers deserve to read a *balanced* report. – Ken West, Dover

**1 ambitious** [æmˈbɪʃəs] ehrgeizig | **2 boastful** [ˈbəʊstfl] angeberisch | **3 open-minded** [ˌəʊpnˈmaɪndɪd] offen; aufgeschlossen

△ **3** **What the media show and don't show** → Help with Station 2, p. 72/8b)

*The photo on the left was used in an ice cream advert; the one on the right wasn't.*
*Think about reasons why. This could help you with your discussion about the media.*

△ **4** **Structuring an argumentative essay** → Help with Station 2, p. 72/10

✎ *Go through the aspects in the box below and sort them. Which ones would help*
*with arguments **for** or **against** social media? Use the ideas for your essay.*

> keep in touch with people | exchange ideas | (not) reliable as a source
> of information | entertainment | requires (a lot of) time | meet new
> people | feel less lonely | can't live without it | cyberbullying |
> real emotions | learn (too much) about the private lives of others |
> age limits | what is real, what isn't? | dangers of chatting with strangers

# Dealing with visuals

## S1 Bilder beschreiben und analysieren

Wenn du ein Bild beschreiben und analysieren sollst, kannst du in folgenden Schritten vorgehen:

1. Beschreibe, was in dem Bild zu sehen ist. Dafür verwendest du das *simple present*. Konzentriere dich zunächst auf Personen oder Dinge, die im Vordergrund zu sehen sind, aber vergiss nicht, auch Personen oder Dinge im Hintergrund zu beschreiben. Wenn du ausdrücken willst, was in dem Bild passiert, verwendest du sehr häufig das *present progressive*.
2. Nachdem du das Bild beschrieben hast, kannst du deine Meinung dazu äußern oder erklären, was es deiner Meinung nach ausdrücken möchte. Für die Analyse des Bildes verwendest du das *simple present*.

> **Useful phrases**
>
> **Describing pictures:**
> – At the top / bottom you can see …
> – In the foreground / background / middle …
> – On the left / right there is / are …
> – The people in the picture are talking / having fun / celebrating / fighting / …
>
> **Analysing pictures:**
> – I like / don't like the picture because …
> – The picture is interesting / boring / exciting / … because …
> – The picture shows … / represents …
> – The picture tries to show … but I think a picture with … instead of … would work better because …

Etwas anders sieht es aus, wenn du aufgefordert wirst, einen Cartoon zu beschreiben und zu analysieren. Hier ist es wichtig, dass du besonders auf die Kombination von Bild und Text achtest. Karikaturisten verwenden häufig die Stilmittel der Ironie und der Übertreibung, um ihre Aussage deutlich zu machen.

## S2 Statistiken auswerten

Mit Diagrammen lässt sich eine Vielzahl von Informationen auf sehr kleinem Raum zusammenfassen. Häufig findest du die folgenden Diagramme, die jeweils einen anderen Schwerpunkt in der Darstellung haben:

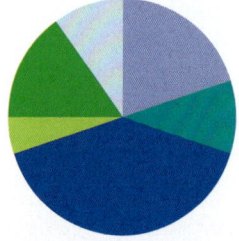

Mit einem Kuchendiagramm (*pie chart*) lassen sich Prozentzahlen darstellen, ausgehend vom gesamten Kreis (= 100 %).

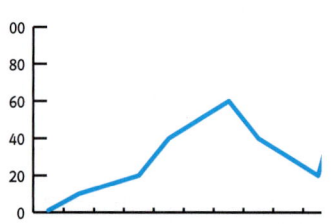

Ein Kurvendiagramm (*line graph*) eignet sich am besten, um eine Entwicklung über einen längeren Zeitraum hinweg darzustellen.

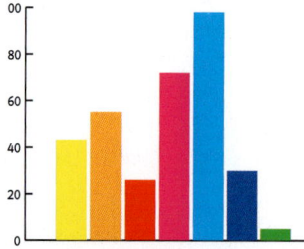

Ein Säulen- oder Balkendiagramm (*bar graph*) verwendest du, um Zahlen direkt miteinander zu vergleichen.

Wenn du die Auswertung eines Diagramms präsentieren sollst, hilft es dir, schrittweise vorzugehen:

1. Sage zunächst, um welche Art von Diagramm es sich handelt und was es darstellt. Vergiss nicht, die Quelle und das Jahr der Veröffentlichung zu nennen.
2. Beschreibe, was du aus dem Diagramm ablesen kannst.
3. Fasse die wichtigsten Aussagen des Diagramms in 1–2 Sätzen zusammen.

**Useful phrases**

- The table / bar graph / line graph / pie chart / … was published by … in …
- It's about … / deals with … / …
- The (next) largest group of … | The majority / minority of … | Half of … | Most of … | 30 percent of the people …
- The number of … goes up / grows by … / drops / goes down / doesn't change.
- The numbers / figures show / suggest that …
- We can draw the conclusion that …

# Text skills

## S3 Schnelllesetechniken

| Skimming („den Rahm abschöpfen") | Scanning („maschinell durchsuchen") |
| --- | --- |
| Wenn du danach gefragt wirst, worum es in einem Text geht, solltest du nur das Wichtigste (*gist*) zusammenfassen. Hierzu überfliegst du den Text und achtest darauf, ob bestimmte Wörter (*key words*) oder Personen häufiger vorkommen. Auch die Überschrift oder Bilder können dir helfen einzuschätzen, was wichtig ist und was nicht. Diese Art des Schnelllesens nennt man auch *skimming*. | Wenn du nach bestimmten Einzelheiten (*details*) gefragt wirst, solltest du den Text überfliegen, um die Stellen mit den wichtigen Informationen zu finden. Dabei suchst du gezielt nach passenden Stichwörtern (*key words*). Sie zeigen dir an, welche Teile du genauer lesen solltest, um die gesuchten Informationen zu erhalten. Diese Art des Überfliegens nennt man auch *scanning*. |

## S4 Wichtige Merkmale von Texten erkennen

### Story

Wenn du eine Geschichte genauer liest oder analysierst, solltest du nicht nur über die Handlung (*plot*) selbst nachdenken, sondern auch darüber, wie die Geschichte erzählt wird. Zu den wichtigsten Erzähltechniken (*narrative techniques*) gehören:

| Atmosphere / Mood | Bestimmte Wörter und Beschreibungen schaffen in einer Geschichte eine gewisse Stimmung (*atmosphere* oder *mood*). Stimmung entsteht z. B. dadurch, dass die fünf Sinne (*five senses*) angesprochen werden: Wenn man liest, was die Figuren sehen, hören, riechen, schmecken oder fühlen, ist es leichter, sich in sie hineinzuversetzen. |
| --- | --- |

| Climax | Der Höhepunkt *(climax)* ist der Hauptwendepunkt in einer Geschichte, an dem die Spannung am höchsten ist. Die Hauptfigur befindet sich oft in einer schwierigen Situation und macht Veränderungen durch, sie wird z. B. stärker oder selbstbewusster. Siehe auch *turning point*. |
|---|---|
| Flashback | Eine Rückblende *(flashback)* erzählt Ereignisse, die vor einem bestimmten Zeitpunkt in der Geschichte stattgefunden haben. So wird z. B. die Erinnerung einer Figur an etwas Vergangenes beschrieben. |
| Narrative perspective | Die Wirkung, die eine Geschichte auf den Leser hat, wird stark von der Erzählperspektive *(narrative perspective)* beeinflusst. Die häufigsten Erzählperspektiven sind:<br><br>**Ich-Erzähler *(first-person narrator)***<br>Der Ich-Erzähler erzählt aus seiner eigenen Perspektive und oft (aber nicht immer) ist er die Hauptfigur der Geschichte. Der Leser und der Ich-Erzähler erleben die Geschichte sozusagen „gemeinsam".<br><br>**Er- / Sie-Erzähler *(third-person narrator)***<br>Dieser Erzähler erzählt die Geschichte „von außen". Die Perspektive ist nicht die der Hauptfigur. |
| Suspense | Spannung *(suspense)* ist eine wichtige Erzähltechnik, um den Leser in die Geschichte hineinzuziehen. Spannung kann direkt in den ersten Zeilen oder aber langsam im Verlauf der Geschichte aufgebaut werden. Sie wird z. B. durch starke, dramatische Sprache oder durch das Zurückhalten von Informationen erzeugt. |
| Turning point | Ein Wendepunkt *(turning point)* ist der Teil einer Geschichte, in dem eine Figur eine wichtige Entscheidung treffen muss. Diese Entscheidung beeinflusst den weiteren Verlauf der Geschichte. Siehe auch *climax*. |

### Graphic novel

In einem Comicroman *(graphic novel)* wird eine Geschichte nicht nur mit Worten, sondern vor allem mit Bildern erzählt. Es ist deshalb wichtig, dass du nicht nur auf die Sprechblasen *(speech bubbles)* und die Bildtexte *(captions)* achtest, sondern auch auf die Gestaltung und Anordnung der einzelnen Bilder *(panels)*.

### Poetry

Beim Verständnis von Gedichten geht es nicht darum, die „richtige" Bedeutung zu finden – dasselbe Gedicht kann von verschiedenen Menschen ganz unterschiedlich verstanden werden. Wichtig ist aber, dass du deine Interpretation am Text belegen kannst. Dazu ist es hilfreich, auch formale Merkmale zu untersuchen und mit dem Inhalt in Verbindung zu bringen.

| Rhyme scheme | Gedichte, die sich reimen, folgen immer einem bestimmten Reimschema *(rhyme scheme)*. Typische Reimschemata sind: **AABB** und **ABAB** sowie **ABCB**. Es gibt aber auch Gedichte, die sich nicht reimen, sogenannte *free verse poems*. |
|---|---|

| Rhythm / Stress | Ein Gedicht funktioniert nur mit dem richtigen Rhythmus (rhythm). Er bestimmt, welche Stelle in jeder Zeile betont wird. Die Betonung (stress) liegt dann immer an der gleichen Stelle. Bei Gedichten, die sich nicht reimen, ist es wichtig, dass du selbst entscheidest, wo die Betonung liegt oder wo eine Pause gemacht werden sollte. |
| --- | --- |
| Symbol / Simile / Metaphor | In Gedichten spielen Symbole eine wichtige Rolle. Ein **Symbol** (symbol) steht stellvertretend für etwas anderes, z. B. für ein Gefühl, eine Idee oder eine Handlung. So ist das Herz ein Symbol für die Liebe. Bei einem **Vergleich** (simile) werden Dinge oder Personen mit etwas anderem verglichen, um auszudrücken, dass sie die gleichen Eigenschaften besitzen. Dabei wird like oder as verwendet, z. B. happy as a rainbow. Eine **Metapher** (metaphor) ist ein verkürzter Vergleich ohne like oder as, z. B. I'll be the light to guide you. |

### Drama

Theaterstücke sind in Akte (acts) und Szenen (scenes) unterteilt. Es gibt in der Regel keinen Erzähler, der die Figuren genauer beschreibt. Stattdessen wird die Handlung direkt durch die gesprochene Sprache und durch die Darstellung der Figuren vermittelt. Deshalb ist es bei der Interpretation von Theaterstücken besonders wichtig, neben dem Text auch auf die Sprechweise, Gestik und Mimik zu achten. So kannst du Rückschlüsse auf Charaktereigenschaften, Gedanken und Gefühle der Figuren ziehen.

| Characters | Die Figuren (characters) stellen oft klassische Typen oder Rollen dar. Auf der einen Seite gibt es einen Helden (good guy), dem ein Bösewicht (bad guy) gegenübersteht. |
| --- | --- |
| Language | In Theaterstücken wird die Handlung durch gesprochene Sprache vermittelt. Die Figuren sprechen in Dialogen miteinander. |
| Stage directions | Alles, was nicht durch gesprochene Sprache vermittelt werden kann, wird in Regieanweisungen (stage directions) vorgegeben. Hier werden auch Angaben zu Requisiten (props), Bühnenbild und Licht gemacht. Wenn man ein Theaterstück liest, können die Regieanweisungen wichtige Hinweise z. B. auf die Stimmung der Szene und die Gefühle der Figuren geben. Sieht man das Theaterstück auf der Bühne, wird die Handlung und Stimmung des Stückes durch Körpersprache, Bewegungen, Bühnenbild, Licht, usw. getragen. |

### Film

Wenn du einen Film beschreibst, kommt es darauf an, wo und zu welcher Zeit er spielt (setting), sowie auf die Besetzung der Rollen (cast), den Schauplatz (location) und die Handlung (plot). Ein Film erzählt eine Geschichte mit Worten, aber auch mit Bildern, Geräuschen, Licht, Farben und Musik. Diese audiovisuellen Effekte (audio-visual effects) schaffen eine ganz bestimmte Atmosphäre und verstärken damit die Wirkung des Gesehenen. So wird z. B. eine Actionszene meist mit schneller, lauter Musik unterlegt, eine romantische Szene eher mit ruhiger, leiser Musik. Die Kameraeinstellungen (shots) beeinflussen, wie wir Szenen wahrnehmen. Sie sind nicht zufällig gewählt, sondern werden gezielt eingesetzt, um die Wirkung einer Szene zu unterstreichen.

# Writing skills

## S5 Textsorten und ihre Besonderheiten

Hier sind einige der wichtigsten Textsorten, die dir im Unterricht immer wieder begegnen werden:

| | |
|---|---|
| **Print ads** | Werbeanzeigen sprechen den Leser direkt an und verwenden eine emotionale Sprache, um ihn vom Kauf eines Produkts zu überzeugen. Wichtige Elemente sind der *eye-catcher* (ein Bild und / oder ein Text), ein ansprechender Slogan, weitere Textelemente *(ad copy)*, 1–2 Fotos des Produkts sowie Kontaktinformationen bzw. Angaben, wo das Geschäft oder die Firma zu finden ist. |
| **Argumentative texts** | Bei argumentativen Texten wird zwischen zwei wesentlichen Textsorten unterschieden, dem *letter to the editor* und dem *argumentative essay*. In einem *letter to the editor* äußerst du deine Meinung zu einem Thema und unterstreichst diese mithilfe von Fakten und Beispielen. Bei einem *argumentative essay* kommt es darauf an, ein kontroverses Thema aus verschiedenen Blickwinkeln zu beleuchten, d.h. du bist aufgefordert, Argumente und Gegenargumente zu präsentieren. |
| **Blog post** | Ein Blog ist eine Art Online-Tagebuch, in dem regelmäßig Beiträge veröffentlicht werden. Meist sind Blog-Einträge aus der Ich-Perspektive geschrieben und drücken den persönlichen Standpunkt des Bloggers aus. |
| **Dialogue / Film script** | Wenn du einen Dialog schreibst, z.B. für eine Filmszene, denke daran, dass du ihn kurz hältst und echte mündliche Sprache verwendest, also z.B. *short forms*, *question tags*, verstärkende Ausdrücke, usw. Achte bei den *stage directions* für ein Film- oder Theaterskript darauf, dass du nur das angibst, was man auch sehen oder darstellen kann. Gedanken kann man nicht sehen, aber du kannst in den *stage directions* Hinweise auf die Gefühle einer Person geben, z.B. durch Anweisungen für Mimik und Gestik. |
| **Diary entry** | Ein Tagebucheintrag erzählt und kommentiert Ereignisse aus der ganz persönlichen Sicht einer Person und ist normalerweise nicht für andere Leser bestimmt. Verwende ausdrucksstarke Adjektive und Adverbien, um die Gedanken und Gefühle dieser Person zu beschreiben. |
| **E-mail / Letter** | Achte auf die richtige Anrede für den Adressaten, z.B. *Dear …*, Gruß-formeln am Schluss, z.B. *Yours / Love / Best wishes*, und beachte die Höflichkeitsregeln. Bei formellen E-Mails oder Briefen verwendet man eher die Langformen, z.B. *I am* statt *I'm*. Denke bei einem Brief an die Angabe der Empfänger- und Absenderadresse und an das Datum. |

| News report | Konzentriere dich bei einem Tatsachenbericht auf die Fakten und spare deine persönliche Meinung aus. Achte außerdem auf eine sachliche Sprache und vermeide emotionale Ausdrücke. Die Schlagzeile *(headline)* sollte direkt auf das Thema des Artikels hinweisen und außerdem das Interesse des Lesers wecken. Beachte, dass in Zeitungsberichten häufig Passivformen verwendet werden. |
|---|---|
| Review / Online rating | Eine Rezension hilft dem Leser zu entscheiden, ob es sich lohnt, einen bestimmten Film anzuschauen oder ein bestimmtes Buch zu lesen. Zuerst beschreibst du kurz die wichtigsten Details, dann folgt deine Bewertung, die du mit guten Argumenten belegen solltest. Achte darauf, dass du bei deiner Bewertung fair bleibst. |
| Story | Wenn du deine eigene Geschichte schreibst, schmücke sie aus und gestalte sie sprachlich abwechslungsreich. Meistens sind Geschichten im *simple past* geschrieben. Wenn du eine Geschichte vervollständigen sollst, muss dein Teil zum vorgegebenen Text passen. Vermeide also inhaltliche Widersprüche. Außerdem sollten sich Erzählperspektive und Erzählzeit im Verlauf der Geschichte nicht ändern. |
| Summary | Bei einer *summary* kommt es darauf an, die wichtigsten Informationen aus einem Ausgangstext zusammenzufassen. Achte darauf, dass deine *summary* nicht länger ist als 30–40 % des Ausgangstextes. |
| Text analysis | In einer Textanalyse beurteilst du die Qualität eines Ausgangstextes. Dabei solltest du verschiedene Aspekte beleuchten: Warum hat der Autor den Text geschrieben? Wie objektiv ist er? Wie gut oder schlecht bringt er dem Leser seine Ideen nahe? Wie interessant ist der Text geschrieben? usw. |

## S6 Einen eigenen Text schreiben

### 1. Die Planung deines Textes

Nimm dir für diese Phase ausreichend Zeit. Lies die Aufgabenstellung genau durch und überlege, für wen dein Text bestimmt ist (Adressat) und welche Textsorte verlangt wird (Bericht, Zusammenfassung, Kommentar, usw.). Vor dem Schreiben erstellst du am besten eine Gliederung, indem du kurz notierst, wie dein Text aufgebaut sein soll.

Ein guter Text besteht normalerweise aus den folgenden drei Teilen:

**Einleitung *(introduction)*:** Hier erfährt der Leser, worum es in deinem Text geht. Du kannst auch eine Fragestellung einführen, die in deinem Text erörtert werden soll.

**Hauptteil *(main part)*:** Der Hauptteil ist in mehrere Abschnitte gegliedert und beinhaltet die Details (Fakten, Argumente, Beispiele, usw.) zu deinem Thema.

**Schluss *(conclusion)*:** Deinen Text solltest du mit einem geeigneten Schlussteil beenden. Dies kann eine Zusammenfassung von dem sein, was du im Hauptteil geschrieben hast, oder eine persönliche Äußerung.

## 2. Der erste Entwurf

Auf der Grundlage deiner Planung kannst du einen ersten Entwurf schreiben. Denke daran, dass du für jede neue Idee einen eigenen Abschnitt beginnst.

## 3. Die Überarbeitung

Nachdem du den ersten Entwurf erstellt hast, ist es wichtig, dass du oder einer deiner Mitschüler den Text noch einmal kritisch durchliest. Am hilfreichsten ist es, wenn du den Text mehrmals liest, jedes Mal mit einem anderen Schwerpunkt. Dabei kann dir eine Checkliste helfen (siehe rechts).

Überarbeite anschließend die kritischen Stellen. Wenn du Feedback von einem Mitschüler bekommen hast *(peer-editing)*, sieh es dir genau an und entscheide, was davon du für deinen Text übernehmen möchtest. Wenn du von einem Mitschüler gebeten wirst, seinen Text zu lesen, achte darauf, dass du bei deiner Kritik fair bleibst.

**Inhalt:**
- Sind alle wesentlichen Punkte enthalten?
- Gibt es keine inhaltlichen Fehler?
- Ist der Text logisch aufgebaut und hat eine klare Struktur?
- Passt die Sprachebene *(register)* zur Textsorte?

**Rechtschreibung:**
- Sind die Wörter richtig geschrieben?
- Stimmt die Zeichensetzung?
- Ist der Text einheitlich im *British* oder *American English* geschrieben?

**Grammatik:**
- Stimmen die Zeitformen?
- Ist die Formenbildung richtig (z. B. Adjektive, Adverbien, usw.)?

# Listening skills

## S7 Hörverstehen üben

Beim Englisch lernen hilft es, möglichst viele authentische Texte anzuhören, z. B. Nachrichten in Radio und Fernsehen, Podcasts oder Hörbücher. Dabei ist es nicht schlimm, wenn du nicht jedes Wort verstehst. Dir wird außerdem auffallen, wie unterschiedlich die Aussprache des Englischen je nach Herkunft des Sprechers sein kann. So gibt es neben den Unterschieden zwischen dem britischen, amerikanischen oder australischen Englisch z. B. auch innerhalb Großbritanniens verschiedene Dialekte oder regionale Akzente. Aber auch hier ist es nicht schlimm, wenn du nicht alles verstehst. Selbst ein Engländer aus London könnte Schwierigkeiten haben, einen Schotten aus Glasgow auf Anhieb zu verstehen.

Analog zum Leseverstehen (→ S3) können dir beim Hörverstehen die beiden folgenden Techniken helfen:

| Listening for gist | Listening for detail |
|---|---|
| Versuche, das Wichtigste *(gist)* in einem Hörtext zu erkennen und kurz zusammenzufassen. Achte dabei besonders auf Wörter *(key words)* und Themen, die mehrmals vorkommen und vermutlich eine wichtige Rolle spielen. | Versuche gezielt, dem Text bestimmte Einzelinformationen *(details)* zu entnehmen. Achte dabei besonders auf Wörter, die du bei der Beantwortung der Fragestellung erwartest, und die passenden Informationen dazu. |

# Speaking skills

## S8 Gespräche führen

Die folgenden Schritte können dir helfen, ein erfolgreiches Gespräch zu führen:

1. Beginne das Gespräch freundlich, z. B. mit etwas, was euch beide verbindet (der Ort, die Situation, usw.).
2. Halte das Gespräch am Laufen. Es ist wichtig, deinem Gesprächspartner das Gefühl zu geben, dass er einbezogen wird. Dazu dienen *feedback phrases*, Nachfragen und *question tags*, wie du anhand des folgenden Beispiels sehen kannst:

   *Then we went to the new shoe shop in town, you know. And there were these amazing trainers – I showed you a photo, didn't I? Guess what Linda said when she saw them!*

   Wenn du etwas nicht verstehst, frage höflich nach *(What was that you mentioned about …? / Sorry, I didn't catch what you just said about …)*. Wenn du etwas nicht sagen kannst, weil dir der nötige Wortschatz fehlt, versuche es zu umschreiben oder bitte deinen Gesprächspartner um Hilfe.
3. Beende das Gespräch so freundlich, wie du es angefangen hast, und verabschiede dich. Vergiss nicht, dich zu bedanken, wenn du um Hilfe gebeten hast.

In vielen Situationen des täglichen Lebens – im Klassenzimmer, mit Freunden, in der Familie – hast du es in Diskussionen mit unterschiedlichen Meinungen zu tun. Umso wichtiger ist es, bei Meinungsverschiedenheiten höflich zu bleiben und Kompromisse zu finden. Die *useful phrases* können dir helfen, typische Diskussionssituationen zu meistern.

### Tip

Lass dich nicht verunsichern, wenn du beim Sprechen ins Stocken gerätst. In der gesprochenen Sprache ist es normal, dass Pausen, unvollständige Sätze, Wiederholungen oder Füllwörter vorkommen: *Well, I – I really don't know. It's – er, maybe you want to …?*

### Useful phrases

I agree with you but … | It's true that …, but … | I admit that …, but … | But don't forget … | I'm afraid I don't agree with … | In my opinion … | Surely you have to admit that … | You might think differently if … | I think it's wrong to say … because … | I can relate to both sides but …

## S9 Eine Präsentation vorbereiten und halten

Ob in der Schule oder später im Beruf, die Fähigkeit, eine gut vorbereitete und klar strukturierte Präsentation zu halten, spielt eine wichtige Rolle. Die folgenden Schritte können dir bei der Vorbereitung und Durchführung deiner Präsentation helfen:

1. Recherchiere Informationen zu deinem Thema und strukturiere sie, indem du z. B. eine Gliederung anlegst.
2. Überlege dir, mit welchem Material du deine Präsentation unterstützen willst. Gestalte dein Poster / deine Folie / dein Handout.
3. Bereite deine Präsentation vor, indem du nummerierte Karteikarten *(prompt cards)* anlegst, auf denen du dir die wichtigsten Punkte in Stichworten notierst.
4. Übe deine Präsentation zu Hause vor dem Spiegel oder vor einem kleinen Publikum (Eltern, Großeltern, Freunde). Stoppe die Zeit, die du brauchst, damit du bei deiner Präsentation nicht in Zeitnot gerätst.
5. Wenn du deine Präsentation hältst, achte darauf, dass du die Aufmerksamkeit aller Zuhörer hast. Dann erkläre kurz, worüber du sprechen wirst und wie deine Präsentation aufgebaut ist. Sprich langsam und möglichst frei. Verwende deine *prompt cards* nur als Hilfestellung. Beende deine Präsentation mit einer kurzen Zusammenfassung der wichtigsten Punkte. Bedanke dich fürs Zuhören und frage nach, ob deine Zuhörer Fragen haben.

### Useful phrases

- My presentation is about … | Today I'll talk about … | First I'd like to talk about … Then …
- Here's a new word. It's … in German.
- On my poster you can see … | The mind map shows … | I've prepared a handout for you.
- That's the end of my presentation. Do you have any questions?
- Thanks for listening.

# Mediation skills

## S10 Bearbeitung von *Mediation*-Aufgaben

*Mediation* ist die Übertragung wichtiger Informationen aus einem gesprochenen oder geschriebenen Text in eine andere Sprache, z. B. aus dem Englischen ins Deutsche oder umgekehrt. Das machst du, wenn du einen Text für jemanden zusammenfassen sollst, der die Sprache des Ausgangstextes nicht versteht. Gelegentlich kann es auch sein, dass du dolmetschen musst, also zwischen Gesprächspartnern vermittelst, die nicht dieselbe Sprache sprechen. Ganz wichtig: Es geht bei der *mediation* niemals um eine wörtliche Übersetzung *(translation)*!

Lies dir die Mediation-Aufgabe gut durch und beachte besonders folgende Punkte:

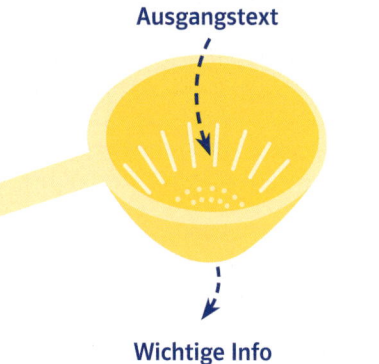

**Adressat:**
Für wen ist die Information bestimmt?
--→ Je nachdem, wer die Person ist und wie viel sie schon weiß, sprichst du sie unterschiedlich an.

**Ausgangstext**

**Zweck:**
Wozu benötigt die Person die Information?
--→ Du musst nur die Informationen wiedergeben, die für den Adressaten in der jeweiligen Situation wichtig sind. Alles andere kannst du weglassen. Es kann aber auch vorkommen, dass du Dinge zusätzlich erklären musst.

**Wichtige Info**

Einen schriftlichen Ausgangstext kannst du in Ruhe durchlesen und die wichtigsten Informationen auswählen. Dabei helfen dir die Lesetechniken, die unter *Text skills* beschrieben werden (→ S3). Formuliere die entsprechenden Inhalte so, dass der Adressat sie gut verstehen kann.

> **Tip**
>
> Achte bei einer schriftlichen *mediation* darauf, dass dein Text nicht länger als ca. 30–40 % des Ausgangstextes ist, ähnlich wie bei einer *summary*.

Bei einer Dolmetschaufgabe wird eine echte mündliche Gesprächssituation simuliert. Deshalb musst du schneller reagieren, um möglichst viel von dem sinngemäß wiederzugeben, was die Gesprächspartner zueinander sagen. Nicht ganz einfach ist es, wenn du Durchsagen am Flughafen oder am Bahnhof aus dem Englischen ins Deutsche übertragen sollst, da sie oft unbekannte Wörter enthalten und durch die Hintergrundgeräusche schwer zu verstehen sind. Hier kann es dir helfen, dich auf die Namen von Personen oder Orten, Zahlen, Zeitangaben oder auf andere wichtige Schlüsselwörter *(key words)* zu konzentrieren.

## S11 Paraphrasieren

Wenn du wichtige Informationen aus einer Sprache in die andere übertragen willst, kann es vorkommen, dass dir ein Wort nicht einfällt, vor allem in Gesprächssituationen, wenn alles sehr schnell gehen muss. Bleibe ganz ruhig und versuche, das Wort zu umschreiben *(paraphrasing)*.

> **Useful phrases**
>
> - It's somebody / a person who …
> - It's something that you use to …
> - It's a place that / where …
> - It's the same as … / the opposite of …

Wenn du Zeit brauchst, um das richtige Wort oder eine Umschreibung dafür zu finden, kannst du dir mit folgenden *phrases* behelfen: *Just a second … / Let me think …*

# Study skills

## S12 Im Internet recherchieren

Das Internet bietet eine Fülle von Informationen, die in der Regel frei zugänglich sind. Die folgenden Tipps können dir dabei helfen, genau die Informationen zu finden, die du für eine Präsentation oder für die Erstellung eines Textes brauchst:

1. Überlege dir gute Stichwörter, die du in eine Suchmaschine eingeben kannst. Wenn du z. B. eine Übersicht über das amerikanische Schulsystem suchst, kannst du als Stichwort *US school system* eingeben. Je mehr Stichwörter du eingibst, desto genauer sind deine Ergebnisse.
2. Wenn du eine Webseite mit interessanten Informationen gefunden hast, achte darauf, wer die Webseite erstellt hat. Sind die Informationen zuverlässig (Online-Lexikon, seriöse Zeitung, usw.) oder handelt es sich eher um persönliche Meinungen (Forum, Blog, usw.)?
3. Kopiere nicht einfach ganze Artikel aus dem Internet. Mache dir Notizen zu den wichtigsten Informationen und gebe sie anschließend in deinen eigenen Worten wieder.
4. Ordne dein Material und suche gezielt weiter, falls du zusätzliche Informationen brauchst.

## S13 Umgang mit neuen Wörtern

Die folgenden Tipps können dir dabei helfen, unbekannte Wörter in einem Text zu verstehen:

### Ähnlichkeit mit Wörtern, die du schon kennst
Oft haben verwandte Wörter den gleichen Stamm, aber andere Präfixe oder Suffixe. Wenn du z. B. *usual* schon kennst, wirst du *unusual* sicher verstehen. Englische Wörter haben oft keine Suffixe, aber es gibt sie in verschiedenen Wortarten. Wenn du das Wort *guide* als Nomen kennst, kannst du dir bestimmt denken, was das Verb *to guide* oder die Zusammensetzung *travel guide* bedeutet.

### Ähnlichkeit mit Wörtern, die du aus einer anderen Sprache kennst
Viele englische Wörter gibt es genauso oder ähnlich auch im Deutschen, z. B. *computer* oder *hobby*. Manchmal hilft dir auch ein Wort, das du aus einer anderen Sprache kennst, ein englisches Wort zu verstehen, z. B. weil es ähnlich geschrieben wird oder ähnlich klingt.

**Tip**

Nicht alle Wörter, die im Deutschen und Englischen ähnlich sind, haben dieselbe Bedeutung. Achte daher auf **false friends**, z. B. *to become* = „werden" (nicht „bekommen"); *brand* = „Marke" (nicht „Feuer").

### Verstehen der Wörter im Zusammenhang
Manchmal kannst du dir anhand eines Bildes oder einer Überschrift denken, was ein Wort in einem Text bedeutet. Und wenn du alle Wörter in einem Satz verstehst außer einem, kann dieses oft nur eine bestimmte Bedeutung haben. Was bedeutet z. B. *ridiculous* in folgendem Satz: *That's the silliest thing I've ever heard. It's **ridiculous**!*

## S14  Mit dem Wörterbuch arbeiten

Wenn du die Bedeutung eines Wortes nachschlagen willst, dann benutzt du am besten ein zweisprachiges Wörterbuch (Englisch-Deutsch bzw. Deutsch-Englisch beim Erstellen von eigenen Texten oder *Mediation*-Aufgaben). Wenn du zusätzliche Informationen zu einem englischen Wort brauchst, z.B. einen Beispielsatz oder eine Definition, dann bietet sich ein einsprachiges Wörterbuch an.

### Zweisprachige Wörterbücher
Die Leitwörter *(running heads)* oben auf der Seite helfen dir, schnell zu finden, was du suchst. Links steht das erste Stichwort, rechts das letzte Stichwort auf der Seite.

Hier findest du das Stichwort *(headword)*. Die Stichwörter sind alphabetisch geordnet.

Die Lautschrift zeigt dir, wie das Wort ausgesprochen und betont wird.

Diese Ziffern zeigen an, dass ein Stichwort unterschiedliche Bedeutungen hat.

Die kursiv gedruckten Hinweise helfen dir, die für deinen Text passende Bedeutung zu finden.

Einem Stichwort sind häufig Redewendungen und typische *phrases* zugeordnet.

Die römischen Ziffern machen deutlich, dass ein Stichwort unterschiedlichen Wortarten angehört.

Unregelmäßige Verb-, Plural- und Steigerungsformen stehen oft in Klammern.

**pay** [peɪ] **I.** *n no pl (wages)* Lohn *m*; *(salary)* Gehalt *nt*; *of a civil servant* Bezüge *pl*; *of a soldier* Sold *m* **II.** *vt* <paid, paid> ❶ *(give)* [be]zahlen; ~ **out** etw [aus]zahlen; **to ~ cash/dollars/money** [in] bar/in Dollar/Geld [be]zahlen; **to ~ dividends** *investment* Dividenden ausschütten; *firm* Dividenden ausbezahlen; *(fig)* sich auszahlen ❷ *(give money for/to, settle)* bezahlen; **to ~ one's dues** *(debts)* seine Schulden bezahlen; *(fig: obligations)* seine Schuldigkeit tun; *into account* einzahlen (auf + *akk*) ❸ *(fig: suffer the consequences)* **to ~ the price** [for sth] [für etw *akk*] bezahlen ❹ *(bestow)* **to ~ attention** Acht geben *akk*; **to ~** [sb] **a compliment** [jdm] ein Kompliment machen ▶ PHRASES: **to ~ one's way** finanziell unabhängig sein **III.** *vi* <paid, paid> ❶ *(give money)* [be]zahlen ❷ *(be worthwhile)* sich auszahlen; *(be profitable)* rentabel sein; ▪ **it ~s to do sth** es lohnt sich, etw zu tun ❸ *(fig: suffer)* ▪ **to ~** [for sth] [für etw *akk*] bezahlen; **to ~ with one's life** mit dem Leben bezahlen ◆ **pay back** *vt* ❶ *(give back)* zurückzahlen; *debts* bezahlen; *money* zurückgeben ❷ *(fig: for revenge)* ▪ **to ~ sb back for sth** jdm etw heimzahlen ◆ **pay down** *vt* an-

### Einsprachige Wörterbücher
Ein einsprachiges Wörterbuch erklärt die Bedeutung eines englischen Wortes auf Englisch. Da manche Wörter mehrere Bedeutungen haben, ist es wichtig, alle Einträge und Beispielsätze zu einem Wort zu lesen und mit deinem englischen Text zu vergleichen, um die richtige Bedeutung herauszufinden.

Das Wörterbuch hilft dir auch, die passende Verbindung mit anderen Wörtern zu finden. Das ist nützlich, wenn du selbst einen englischen Text schreiben willst und nach passenden Formulierungen suchst.

**pay**
*verb* [peɪ] PAST TENSE AND PAST PARTICIPLE **paid**

**BUY**
to give money to someone because you are buying something from them, or because you owe them money:
*Helen **paid** for the tickets.*
*Did you **pay** the telephone bill?*
*You can **pay** by cash or credit card.*

**WORK**
to give someone money for the work that they do:
*She gets **paid** twice a month.*
*People work for them because they **pay** well.*

→ **pay attention**
to look at or listen to someone or something carefully:
*I missed what she was saying because I **wasn't paying attention**.*

In diesem Grammatik-Anhang findest du ausführliche Erklärungen zu allen grammatischen Themen, die in *Green Line 6* behandelt werden. Die Grammatikkapitel (G) helfen dir, die Grammatik zu verstehen, einzelne Punkte nachzuholen oder bestimmte Regeln für Hausaufgaben und die Vorbereitung von Tests und Klassenarbeiten nachzuschlagen.

Regeln sind mit einem blauen Punkt (**o**) gekennzeichnet. Ein Ausrufezeichen (**!**) bedeutet, dass du hier besonders aufpassen musst. Die englische Zusammenfassung der wichtigsten Regeln findest du in der **English summary**. Mit **Test yourself** überprüfst du, ob du alles verstanden hast.
Die Lösungen hierzu findest du ab Seite 198.

## Grammatical terms

| | English term | Deutsche Bezeichnung |
|------|-------------|----------------------|
| G1 | Sentence adverbs | *Satzadverbien* |
| G2 | Present participle or infinitive after verbs of perception + object | *Das Partizip Präsens oder der Infinitiv nach Verben der Wahrnehmung + Objekt* |
| G3 | Present participle after verbs of rest and motion | *Das Partizip Präsens nach Verben der Ruhe und der Bewegung* |
| G4 | Defining and non-defining relative clauses | *Notwendige und nicht-notwendige Relativsätze* |
| G5 | Inversion of the verb for emphasis after certain adverbs | *Hervorhebung durch Inversion des Verbs nach bestimmten Adverbien* |
| G6 | Emphatic do / does / did | *Hervorhebung mit do / does / did* |
| G7 | The simple present and present progressive with future meaning | *Das Präsens mit Futurbedeutung* |
| G8 | The future progressive | *Die Verlaufsform des Futurs* |
| G9 | The future perfect | *Das Futur II* |
| G10 | The definite and the indefinite article | *Der bestimmte und der unbestimmte Artikel* |
| G11 | English equivalents for the German verbs *sollen* and *müssen* | *Englische Entsprechungen für die deutschen Verben „sollen" und „müssen"* |

# Unit 1

**G1**  **How to sound more formal**  → Seite 11

*Satzadverbien*
Sentence adverbs

## Position for Assistant Camp Counsellor

**Job description**
As an assistant camp counsellor, you must have good communication skills and you must enjoy working with children. **Furthermore**, you must be hard-working, fit and healthy. As assistant camp counsellor, **of course** you are also expected to be friendly and outgoing. **However**, you are also expected to set a good example at all times.

**Training**
We think it is important that all camp counsellors receive good training. **Therefore**, all successful applicants will be required to go to an Orientation Day when we will **happily** answer all your questions.

*Satzadverbien sind Adverbien, die sich auf die Aussage des ganzen Satzes beziehen. Zu ihnen gehören sowohl* **linking adverbs** *(satzverknüpfende Adverbien) als auch* **commenting adverbs** *(kommentierende Adverbien).*

- **Linking adverbs** *verbinden die Gedanken zweier Sätze und stellen eine logische Beziehung her. Sie können u.a. eine* **zusätzliche Information** *(moreover, furthermore, additionally), einen* **gegensätzlichen Gedanken** *(however, nevertheless), eine* **Erläuterung** *(in fact) oder eine* **Schlussfolgerung** *(therefore) einleiten.*
  *Adverbien dieser Art stehen meist* **am Satzanfang**.

- **Commenting adverbs** *leiten den folgenden Gedanken ein und kommentieren diesen zugleich. Sie drücken aus, was der Sprecher über den Inhalt des Satzes denkt. Zu diesen Adverbien gehören u.a. of course, happily, hopefully, luckily, fortunately, unfortunately, surely, certainly, probably, personally.*
  *Adverbien dieser Art stehen meistens* **am Satzanfang**, *treten aber mitunter auch als Nachgedanke am* **Satzende** *oder auch in der* **Binnenstellung** *auf, z.B.:*
  - **Hopefully**, they'll offer me the job.
  - They'll offer me the job, **hopefully**.
  - I'll **certainly** be disappointed if they don't offer me the job.

### English summary

**Linking adverbs** connect sentences logically. They usually appear in front position. They can be used to add on information, make a contrast, give an explanation or draw a conclusion.

Camp counselling is a fun and flexible job. **Moreover**, it's a great experience.

**Commenting adverbs** add information about the speaker's opinion of events. They can often be found in front position, sometimes in mid-position, and sometimes in end position.

Being a camp counsellor is **probably** one of the most challenging jobs you can have.

**Test yourself**  *After working as assistant camp counsellors, this is what some of the teenagers posted online. Complete their testimonials with these **sentence adverbs**: personally, in fact, hopefully, moreover, nevertheless, probably.*

1. Being a camp counsellor gives you an opportunity to lead groups, take on responsibility and to build your self-confidence. 🟨, it looks great on your CV.  – Tom
2. 🟨, I think that working as an assistant camp counsellor at a summer camp is the best experience any teenager can have.  – Jane
3. It was really hard work. 🟨, it was 🟨 the hardest job I've ever had to do!  – Brian
4. Spending 24 hours a day with a group of active young kids can be exhausting. 🟨, I wouldn't have missed the experience for the world.  – Sarah
5. You don't have to be crazy to work as a camp counsellor, but it helps! It was the most amazing job I've ever had and I had a fantastic time. 🟨 I can go back for more next year!  – Marco

## G2 I watched the kids …

→ Seiten 13–14

*Das Partizip Präsens oder der Infinitiv nach Verben der Wahrnehmung + Objekt*
Present participle or infinitive after verbs of perception + object

I **watched** the kids **harvesting** the cocoa pods.
= I watched the kids while they were doing it.

I **watched** the kids **harvest** the cocoa pods.
= I watched the complete action

*Nach einem **Verb der Wahrnehmung** (z. B. feel, hear, notice, see, smell und watch) **und einem direkten Objekt** kann a) das **present participle** oder b) der **Infinitiv** (ohne to) stehen. Ob man ein present participle oder einen infinitive verwendet, hängt davon ab, wie viel von einer Tätigkeit man wahrgenommen hat. Im Deutschen wird diese Konstruktion meist mit einem Nebensatz mit „wie" wiedergegeben.*

**a)** *Das* present participle *nach einem Verb der Wahrnehmung + Objekt*

| | Verb der Wahrnehmung | Direktes Objekt | Present participle | |
|---|---|---|---|---|
| I | watched | them | harvesting | the cocoa pods. |
| *Ich sah zu, wie sie gerade die Kakaoschoten ernteten.* | | | | |

○ *Das* present participle *nach einem Verb der Wahrnehmung und einem direkten Objekt drückt aus, dass ein Geschehen gerade abläuft oder ablief. Es wird besonders dann verwendet, wenn nur **ein Teil des gesamten Geschehens** wahrgenommen wird.*

**b)** *Der* infinitive *nach einem Verb der Wahrnehmung + Objekt*

| | Verb der Wahrnehmung | Direktes Objekt | Infinitiv ohne to | |
|---|---|---|---|---|
| I | watched | them | harvest | the cocoa pods. |
| *Ich sah zu, wie sie die Kakaoschoten ernteten.* | | | | |

○ *Der* infinitive *nach einem Verb der Wahrnehmung und einem direkten Objekt drückt aus, dass ein Geschehen **von Anfang bis Ende** wahrgenommen wurde. Diese Konstruktion steht besonders dann, wenn zwei oder mehrere Handlungen aufeinander folgen, z. B.* I watched the kids climb the tree and chop down the pods.

○ **English summary** ○───────────────────────────

After verbs of perception (hear, see, watch, feel etc.) and a direct object it is possible to use a present participle or an infinitive (without *to*).

| | |
|---|---|
| You use the **present participle** when you see, feel or hear only part of the action. | I **felt** the sun **burning** on my skin. |
| You use the **infinitive** when you see the complete action from beginning to end. | I **watched** three girls **carry** heavy containers full of beans to a lorry, **dump** the contents, then **walk** back for more. |

**Test yourself**   *A girl is talking about a lazy colleague. Complete what she says with the **present participle** or the **infinitive** form of the verbs in brackets.*

1. He always arrives really late for work and then he leaves early. Yesterday I saw him (arrive) at 9:30, (hang) his jacket on the chair, then (leave) again.
2. He prefers magazines to company reports. Today I noticed him (read) a car magazine.
3. And he makes a lot of personal phone calls. This morning I was walking past his office when I heard him (tell) somebody all about his last holiday.
4. He also takes other people's equipment without asking. Yesterday I watched him (pick up) a pen from his colleague's desk, quickly (put) it into his pocket and then (walk away).
5. Our boss isn't happy with him. As I was walking past her office today, I could hear her (shout) at him.

### G3   They arrived feeling exhausted

→ Seiten 13–14

*Das Partizip Präsens nach Verben der Ruhe und der Bewegung*
Present participle after verbs of rest and motion

> The children **arrived carrying** heavy tools and equipment.

> I **stood watching** them.

*Nach **Verben der Bewegung** wie arrive, leave, come, go, run, walk und **Verben der Ruhe** wie sit, stand, lie, stay, remain sowie nach anderen Verben wie find und catch (erwischen) + Objekt wird im Englischen häufig das **present participle** gebraucht.*

○ *Das **present participle** steht nach einem **Verb der Bewegung oder der Ruhe**, wenn zwei Handlungen mit dem gleichen Subjekt zur gleichen Zeit abliefen, z.B.:*
  – The children **arrived feeling** exhausted.   *(= Die Kinder fühlten sich erschöpft, als sie ankamen.)*
  – I **stood watching** them for a while.   *(= Ich stand da und schaute ihnen eine Weile zu.)*

○ *Das **present participle** steht auch nach **Verben wie find oder catch** + Objekt, z.B.:*
  – Later I **found** Abdoulaye **sitting** alone.
  – I **caught** him **crying**.

---

○ **English summary** ○

The **present participle** is often used after verbs of rest and motion and after verbs such as find / catch + object.

The man **came hoping** to see what life was like for the children.
He **found** himself **wishing** he could do something to help them.

---

**Test yourself**   *Read what happened to Julia at the beach yesterday and complete her blog.*

After a busy morning at work yesterday, I decided to spend my lunch break relaxing on the beach. But as I (lie – read) quietly, I soon (find – myself – wonder) if I had made the right choice. There weren't many people on the beach, just a few dog-walkers and two girls who were chatting quietly nearby as they (sit – eat) ice creams. Then suddenly a large dog (come – run) towards the two girls. He was barking loudly and the girls were scared. So they began to scream. When that didn't help, they threw stones. A moment later, the dog's owner (arrive – shout) angrily at the two girls. Then he (catch – me – watch) the drama, so he started shouting at me too! I (come – hope) for some peace on the beach. I (leave – think) the world had gone crazy!

## G4 The Words-of-Wisdom Wall

→ Seiten 16–18

*Notwendige und nicht-notwendige Relativsätze*
Defining and non-defining relative clauses

My first job was at a café **which was always incredibly busy**. Unfortunately, my boss was the kind of person **who never sat down herself**, so it was often difficult to take a break.

My first job, **which I was very happy to get at first**, was with a family friend. My boss, **who has his own business as a carpenter**, thought he was helping me out, but the work was really hard.

*Relativsätze sind Nebensätze, die ihr **Bezugswort** im Hauptsatz a) näher bestimmen (... a café which was always incredibly busy) oder b) zusätzlich beschreiben (My first job, which I was very happy to get at first, ...). Im Englischen nennt man diese zwei Arten von Relativsätzen* **defining** *und* **non-defining relative clauses**.

### a) Defining relative clauses

Cassie has a job in **a shop** **which / that sells cool clothes**.

She is **one of those kids** **who / that loves to wear the latest fashion trends**.

The problem is she keeps buying **things** **which / that she doesn't need**.

○ **Defining relative clauses** *bestimmen oder beschreiben ihr vorangestelltes **Bezugswort** näher. Sie legen fest, wer oder was gemeint ist. Welcher Laden? Welche Jugendliche? Welche Dinge? Ohne den Relativsatz wäre der Sinn des Hauptsatzes unvollständig, unklar oder sinnlos.*

○ *Relativsätze, die ihr Bezugswort näher bestimmen, stehen **ohne Komma**. Beim Sprechen macht man keine Pause.*

○ **Defining relative clauses** *werden durch Relativpronomen wie* **who** *oder* **that** *(bei Personen) und* **which** *oder* **that** *(bei Sachen) eingeleitet, wenn sie Subjekt im Relativsatz sind. Hat der Relativsatz ein eigenes Subjekt, können* who / which / that *auch weggelassen werden, z. B.* things **(which / that)** she doesn't need. *Diese Relativsätze nennt man* **contact clauses**.

## b) Non-defining relative clauses

> **Marlon**, who found his first job exhausting, wished he'd looked around for an easier job in a shop.

> **Cassie**, who works in a cool clothes shop, wishes she'd saved a bit more of her money for a holiday.

> **Lucy**, whose first job was at a huge café, wishes she had spoken to her boss about a break. **The café**, which was open all day, was always full, so she had to work non-stop.

- *Bei* non-defining relative clauses *ist das vorangestellte **Bezugswort bereits definiert**. Auch ohne den Relativsatz bleibt klar, wer oder was gemeint ist: Marlon, Cassie, Lucy und das Café, in dem Lucy arbeitet. Zu einer Verwechslung mit einer anderen Person oder mit einem anderen Café kann es nicht kommen. Die Relativsätze bestimmen daher ihr Bezugswort **nicht** näher. Sie enthalten lediglich eine zusätzliche oder ergänzende Information, die im Gegensatz zu den* defining relative clauses *ebenso gut in Klammern stehen oder gar entfallen könnte, ohne dass die Aussage im Hauptsatz verändert wird.*

- *Relativsätze, die nur Zusatzinformationen enthalten, werden vom Hauptsatz immer **durch Kommas abgetrennt**. Beim Sprechen wird eine Pause gemacht.*

- *Im Gegensatz zu* defining relative clauses *beginnen* non-defining relative clauses *immer mit einem Relativpronomen: Für Personen verwendet man* **who***; für Dinge verwendet man* **which***; und* **whose** *verwendet man für Personen oder Dinge. Das Relativpronomen* **that** *ist in einem* non-defining relative clause *nicht möglich.*

- *Das Relativpronomen* **which** *verwendet man außerdem, wenn der Relativsatz sich auf den ganzen Satz bezieht. Solche Relativsätze werden im Deutschen mit dem Pronomen* **was** *eingeleitet. Beim Sprechen wird eine Pause gemacht:*
  Marlon found a job with a family friend, **which** wasn't a good idea.
  *Marlon hat einen Job bei einem Freund der Familie gefunden,* **was** *keine gute Idee war.*

### English summary

There are two types of relative clause: **defining** and **non-defining**.

1. **Defining relative clauses** tell you which person or thing the speaker is talking about. **No comma** is used between the noun and the relative clause.

   Nathan is the guy **who / that** stupidly signed all the forms without reading them first.

2. **Non-defining relative clauses** are used after nouns that are definite already. They give extra information about a person or thing or about the main clause.
   You always need a **comma** to separate the main clause from the relative clause.

   Nathan, **who** stupidly signed all the forms without reading them, was shocked when he got his first wages. But his boss sat down with him and patiently explained everything, **which** was really nice of him.

**Test yourself** *Read Dan's comments about his Saturday job at a pet shop. Write the text in your exercise book. Decide if the sentences have **defining** or **non-defining relative clauses**. If you can leave the relative pronoun out, put it in brackets. Put in commas where necessary.*

> I was walking past the pet shop **which** I often do on my way into town when I noticed a job advert in the window. They were looking for a student **who** could help them on Saturdays. It seemed the perfect job for me, so I went in. The shop manager **who** was really busy quickly explained everything **that** I needed to know and then offered me the position. I liked the other people **who** worked there and I liked the job. But it was *hard*. When the shop was full of people **which** it usually was it was difficult to find time to take a break. And the money **that** I earned wasn't enough for the hours **which** I had to put in. – Dan

## G5  Not only was it super cold, but …

→ Seiten 16, 19

*Hervorhebung durch Inversion des Verbs nach bestimmten Adverbien*
**Inversion of the verb for emphasis after certain adverbs**

> *Negative (never, not only, …) und einschränkende (hardly, rarely, …) Adverbialbestimmungen treten meist im Inneren eines Satzes auf. Zur besonderen Betonung einer Aussage können sie jedoch auch am Satzanfang stehen. Tritt dieser Fall ein, wird eine **Inversion** von Subjekt und Verb ausgelöst (hier: it was → was it). Aus der Aussageform wird die **Frageform**.*

> **It was** not only super cold, but the work was exhausting too.
> Not only **was it** super cold, but the work was exhausting too.

○ *Negative und einschränkende Adverbialbestimmungen mit und ohne Inversion*

| Adverbiale Bestimmung | Gewöhnlicher Aussagesatz / Aussagesatz mit Inversion (Frageform) des Verbs |
|---|---|
| not only … but | He **not only** works hard, **but** he enjoys his life too. <br> **Not only** does he work hard, **but** he enjoys his life too. |
| rarely / never | I have rarely / never heard anything so stupid. <br> **Rarely / Never** have I heard anything so stupid. |
| hardly | She had hardly put the phone down when it rang again. <br> **Hardly** had she put the phone down when it rang again. |
| not for one moment | I didn't imagine **for one moment** that they would ever apologise. <br> **Not for one moment** did I imagine that they would ever apologise. |

○ *Wenn eine negative oder einschränkende Adverbialbestimmung zur besonderen Hervorhebung am Satzanfang steht, ändert sich die übliche Wortstellung. Subjekt und Verb stehen nicht mehr in der Aussageform, sondern in der **Frageform** umgesetzt, z. B.:*
he works → does he work; I have heard → have I heard; I imagined → did I imagine

❗ *Beachte auch die Besonderheiten bei den Adverbialbestimmungen in den folgenden Beispielen:*

| Adverbiale Bestimmung | Gewöhnlicher Aussagesatz / Aussagesatz mit Inversion des Verbs |
|---|---|
| never … before → Never before … | I **had** never spent so much money on clothes **before**. **Never before had** I spent so much money on clothes. |
| There's no way … → No way … | **There's no way that** we'**ll get** there on time. **No way will** we **get** there on time. |
| no sooner … than → No sooner … than | We had **no sooner** left the house **than** it started to rain. **No sooner had** we left the house **than** it started to rain. |
| only … when (she …) → Only when (she …) | She **only** realised that she'd lost her key **when she got home**. **Only when she got home did** she realise that she'd lost her key. |
| It was only then that … → Only then … | **It was only then that** she realised she had lost her key. **Only then did** she realise she had lost her key. |

○ **English summary** ○

If an adverb or adverb phrase with a negative or restrictive sense is placed at the beginning of the sentence for emphasis or dramatic effect, it must be followed by the inverted question form of the verb.

Never before **have I felt** so jealous.

Only then **did I realise** my mistake.

**Test yourself** *Read one person's view on the use of mobile phones in public places. Rewrite the text using **inversion** for emphasis.*

There is no way that people should be allowed to use mobile phones in public places. They not only make lots of noise, but they also force others to listen to their private conversations. Yesterday a woman on my bus talked non-stop. She had hardly finished one call when she started again. I have never heard such silly, unnecessary conversations! I was glad when she got off the bus. It was only then that I was able to read my book in peace.

## G6 I do remember how it feels ...

→ Seiten 16, 19

*Hervorhebung mit* do / does / did
*Emphatic* do / does / did

I know I shouldn't be jealous, but I **do** feel that way.

I never see you with a book, Tim. You only play videos!

That isn't true! I **do** read books, Dad. Just not today.

Please **do** have some more.

*In der Regel verwendest du* **do / does** *und* **did** *und den* **Infinitiv** *in Fragen und Verneinungen.* **Do / does / did** *können aber auch in bejahten Sätzen verwendet werden, wenn sie stärker betont werden sollen. Im Deutschen verwendest du hierfür oft Wörter wie „tatsächlich", „wirklich", „sehr" und „doch".*

○ do / does / did + ***Infinitiv*** *wird in einem bejahten Aussagesatz verwendet:*

**a) *zur Betonung einer Meinung oder eines Gefühls***

| genau | I **do understand** what you're trying to say. |
|-------|------------------------------------------------|
| *tatsächlich* | You're right. That sentence **does sound** strange. |
| *wirklich* | Oh yeah, I **did enjoy** the film. It was fantastic. |
| *so sehr* | I **do hope** that you'll be able to visit me next year. |

*Im Deutschen kannst du mit Wörtern wie „genau", „tatsächlich", „wirklich" und „so sehr" deine Meinung / Empfindung stärker zum Ausdruck bringen. Im Englischen verwendest du hierfür* do / does / did *und den Infinitiv des Vollverbs.*

**b)** *zur Betonung eines Gegensatzes (im Sinne von „doch")*

> Tom never takes the dog for a walk.
> – That isn't true. He **does take** him. Just not very often.

> You didn't do your homework yesterday.
> – That isn't true, Mum. I **did do** it.

> I know I said I didn't want to go to the party, but in the end I **did go**.

**c)** *um eine Aufforderung oder Bitte höflicher oder formeller auszudrücken*

> Please **do come** in, Mrs Delacruz. Nice to see you again.

> **Do have** a seat, I'll be right with you.

---

**English summary**

**Do, does** and **did** are sometimes used with the infinitive in positive sentences to emphasise a feeling, agreement or disagreement.
They can also be used in polite requests.

Your hair **does** look good today; nice!
You're right; Tom **did** mention plans for a party next weekend.
That's rubbish! She **does** love him.
**Do** tell me if you need anything, Mr Tate.

---

**Test yourself**  *Translate these sentences into English. Use **do / does / did** for emphasis.*

1. Das überrascht mich. Ich sehe doch ganz gut aus in Grau!
2. Ich hoffe so sehr, dass du den Job bekommst.
3. Also, du hast Tom gestern doch getroffen!
4. Du hast Recht. Die Milch schmeckt tatsächlich komisch.
5. Ich weiß genau, was du meinst, aber das stimmt nicht.
6. Sagen Sie doch Bescheid, wenn ich Ihnen mehr Kaffee bringen kann.
7. Sie hat so viel Gutes von dir gehört und möchte dich so gerne kennenlernen!
8. Guten Abend, schön, dass Sie kommen konnten! Kommen Sie doch bitte herein, die anderen sind schon da.
9. Mr Braxton, Sie wissen sehr wohl, dass man nie zu spät zu einem Vorstellungsgespräch kommen sollte, und trotzdem sind Sie zu spät gekommen.
10. Du hast dich auf der Party nicht wirklich amüsiert. – Doch, ich habe mich amüsiert. Ich musste nur früh weg.

# Unit 2

**G7** **It starts at 8:00 but we're meeting at 6:00** → Seiten 46–47

*Das Präsens mit Futurbedeutung*
The simple present and present progressive with future meaning

What time **does** the premiere **start**?

At 8:00, but I**'m meeting** my buddy there at 6:00 to set up.

*Neben dem* will future *und dem* going-to future *werden im Englischen häufig auch das* **simple present** (I do) *und das* **present progressive** (I'm doing) *verwendet, um über zukünftige Handlungen zu sprechen.*

○ *Das* simple present *verwendest du für zukünftige Handlungen, die durch* **Fahrpläne**, **Programme** *oder andere* **offizielle Vorgaben** *festgelegt sind. Solche Handlungen werden häufig mit Verben wie* arrive, leave, start, finish, open, close etc. *gebraucht, z.B.* The premiere starts at 8:00.

○ *Das* present progressive *verwendest du für zukünftige Handlungen, wenn es sich um* **Pläne** *oder* **Vereinbarungen** *handelt, die persönlich vereinbart wurden. Solche Handlungen werden häufig mit Verben wie* meet, come *und* go *gebraucht, z.B.* Alex is meeting his buddy at 6:00.

❶ *Das* present progressive *mit Futurbedeutung bietet eine Alternative zum* going-to future, *die von englischen Muttersprachlern häufig verwendet wird, z.B.* I'm meeting my friend at the premiere tonight. *statt* I'm going to meet my friend at the premiere tonight.

○ **English summary** ○

You use the **simple present** to talk about timetables, programmes, etc.

When **does** the train **leave**? – It **leaves** at 6:10.

You use the **present progressive** to talk about something that you've arranged to do in the future.

What **are** you **doing** this weekend? – I**'m working** on Saturday. On Sunday I**'m going** to the beach with some friends.

**Test yourself**   *Choose the **simple present** or the **present progressive** to complete the dialogue.*

Ella:   What  **1**  (you – do) tomorrow?

Mia:   I  **2**  (meet) my cousin at the new shopping mall. It  **3**  (open) tomorrow at 10:00.
Why don't you come with us?

Ella:   That sounds like a great idea. How  **4**  (you – get) there?

Mia:   By bus or by subway. I haven't decided yet. The bus is cheaper but it  **5**  (leave)
earlier and it  **6**  (take) a lot longer.

Ella:   I've got a better idea. My brother  **7**  (drive) into town tomorrow morning. I'm sure he
won't mind taking us with him. But let me ask him first what time he  **8**  (go).

## G8   What will Alex be doing by the time he's 30?

→ Seiten 46, 48

*Die Verlaufsform des Futurs*
The future progressive

**A**   By the time I'm 30, I**'ll be traveling** all over the world. But **will** I still **be writing** movie reviews when I'm rich and famous? Maybe. You never know!

**B**   I**'ll be seeing** Tom at the premiere tomorrow night.

Oh, I**'ll be going** to that too.
What time **will** you **be meeting up**?

---

*Das **future progressive** ist die Verlaufsform des Futurs. Mit dieser Zeitform beschreibst du:*
1. *Handlungen, die zu einem bestimmten Zeitpunkt **in der Zukunft gerade stattfinden** und **noch nicht beendet** sind (Bild A). Der Zeitpunkt wird häufig durch eine Zeitangabe wie at 9:30 tomorrow morning, by the time (+ simple present), in two weeks' time etc. festgelegt.*
2. *Handlungen, die **für die Zukunft fest vereinbart** worden sind (Bild B).*

○  *Das **future progressive** bildest du aus **will / won't be + present participle**.*

| *Aussage:* | Very soon Alex **will be living** his dream. |
|---|---|
| *Verneinung:* | He **won't be working** for the tour bus company any more. |
| *Entscheidungsfrage mit Kurzantwort:* | **Will** he still **be going** to cattle calls?<br>– No, he **won't**. |

⚠️ *Wenn du Handlungen beschreiben willst, die für die Zukunft fest vereinbart worden sind, kannst du das* future progressive *als Alternative zum* present progressive *mit Futurbedeutung oder zum* going-to future *verwenden, z. B.* I'll be seeing Tom at the premiere. / I'm seeing Tom at the premiere. / I'm going to see Tom at the premiere.

### English summary

| | |
|---|---|
| You use the **future progressive** to describe an unfinished action that will be taking place at a given time in the future. | Don't call me between 9 and 10 a.m. I**'ll be working**. |
| It is also used to describe or ask about an action which has been planned for the future. | I**'ll be going** to a cattle call on Tuesday. **Will** you **be going** too? |

**Test yourself** *Next week Alex has another busy week. Look at his plans and say what he'll be doing each day.*

> On Monday morning I'm meeting my agent. In the afternoon I've got a movie review to write for the internet. On Tuesday I'm going to an audition. On Wednesday I'll interview stars at a movie premiere on Hollywood Boulevard. On Thursday I'm going to visit my buddy Dave. And on Friday my parents are coming for the weekend so I'm picking them up from the airport.

**Start like this:** On Monday morning Alex will be meeting …

## G9  What will Alex have done by the time he's 30?

→ Seiten 46, 48

*Das Futur II*
**The future perfect**

By the time I'm 30, I**'ll have hit** the big time.

*Mit dem* **future perfect** *drückst du aus, dass eine Handlung oder ein Vorgang zu einem bestimmten Zeitpunkt in der Zukunft abgeschlossen sein wird. Dieser Zeitpunkt wird häufig durch eine Zeitangabe wie* by this time next year, by the time (+ simple present), in two weeks' time *etc. festgelegt.*

○ *Das* future perfect *bildest du aus* **will / won't have + past participle** *(3. Verbform).*

| Aussage: | By the time people read his blog, Alex **will have gotten** his first part in a movie, hopefully. |
|---|---|
| Verneinung: | The producers **won't have given** him a big part, surely. |
| Entscheidungsfrage mit Kurzantwort: | **Will** he **have given up** his day job by then? – No, he **won't**. |

❗ *Wie du bestimmt bemerkt hast, gelten für das* future progressive *und das* future perfect *dieselben signal phrases (z. B. by this time next week, by Friday etc.). Es ist wichtig, dass du auf den Kontext achtest, um zu entscheiden, welche Form des Futurs du verwenden musst.*

**English summary**

You use the **future perfect** for an action that will have been completed at a given time in the future.

By this time next year Alex hopes that he **will have gotten** his big break.

**Test yourself** *Alex tells his buddy Dave about his hopes for the future. Decide if you need the **future perfect** or the **future progressive** for the verbs in brackets.*

I really hope that by the time people read my blog I **1** (get) my big break and that I **2** (live) my dream. In six months' time, I'm sure I **3** (become) a star and the reporters **4** (want) to interview me. Then of course I'll be friendly and polite, but I'll tell them never to call me before 11:00 because I **5** (not get up) by then. I **6** (still – sleep).

## G10   California in the world
→ Seite 51

*Wiederholung: Der bestimmte und der unbestimmte Artikel*
Revision: The definite and the indefinite article

Every year people arrive in Hollywood looking for **fame**. But very few people actually achieve **the fame** they're looking for.

*Für den Gebrauch und das Weglassen des bestimmten Artikels **the** und des unbestimmten Artikels **a / an** gibt es im Englischen feste Regeln. Diese unterscheiden sich in einigen Fällen von der Verwendung des bestimmten und unbestimmten Artikels im Deutschen.*

1. *Der bestimmte Artikel* **the**

   ○ *Mit dem bestimmten Artikel stehen:*

| | |
|---|---|
| *Gebirge, Flüsse, Meere* | **the** Sierra Nevadas, **the** Colorado River, **the** Pacific Ocean |
| *Ländernamen im Plural* | **the** US, **the** UK, **the** Netherlands |
| *Adjektive im Superlativ* | **the** most famous, **the** most popular, **the** best (sights) |
| *Musikinstrumente* | I don't play **the** piano but I play **the** guitar. |

- **Ohne** den bestimmten Artikel stehen:

| Eigennamen von Bergen und Seen | Mount Whitney, Lake Tahoe |
|---|---|
| Namen von Straßen, Städten und Ländernamen im Singular | Hollywood Boulevard, Los Angeles, San Francisco, England, Germany |
| „die meisten" (ohne Einschränkung) | Most people like chocolate. (= fast alle Leute) |
| „die meisten" (mit Einschränkung) | Most of the people I know like chocolate. (= fast alle Leute, die ich kenne) |

- **Mit und ohne** den bestimmten Artikel stehen:

Konkrete Begriffe (Dinge, die du sehen, berühren und fühlen kannst) sowie abstrakte Begriffe (Dinge wie fun, success, fame, life, happiness, etc.)

| Wenn die genannten Begriffe im allgemeinen Sinne verwendet werden, stehen sie ohne den bestimmten Artikel: | Wenn die genannten Begriffe durch eine Ergänzung (oft einen Relativsatz oder of-phrase) näher bestimmt werden, stehen sie mit dem bestimmten Artikel: |
|---|---|
| During the 1850s many people came to California looking for gold. | By the 1880s most of **the** gold had gone. |
| Immigrants are important for California's economy. | It's **the** immigrants who often do the hard jobs no Americans want to do. |
| Each year thousands of people arrive in L.A. hoping for success. | But only very few people ever find **the** success they're looking for. |
| What does happiness mean to you? | There are no words to describe **the** happiness Alex felt when he got his first movie role. |

Mahlzeiten (breakfast, lunch, dinner) und Stoffbezeichnungen (milk, water, air)

| Ohne den bestimmten Artikel: | Mit dem bestimmten Artikel: |
|---|---|
| Let's have lunch at Arnie's. | **The** lunch I had there last week was delicious. |
| Water is a problem in California. | About 80 % of **the** water used in California is needed for agriculture. |

Institutionen (school, work, college, church, prison, hospital) und Verkehrsmittel (bus, train, plane)

| Ohne den bestimmten Artikel: | Mit dem bestimmten Artikel: |
|---|---|
| Alex didn't like school much. | He wasn't very happy at **the** school he went to. |
| We usually go into town by bus. | **The** bus into town leaves in five minutes. |

2. **Der unbestimmte Artikel** a / an

○ *Der unbestimmte Artikel steht **vor**:*

| | | |
|---|---|---|
| *Berufsbezeichnungen* | Jack is **a** vet. | *Jack ist Tierarzt.* |
| *Maßeinheiten (= pro / je)* | two euros **a** kilo | *zwei Euro **das** Kilo* |
| *Zeiteinheiten (= pro / je)* | three times **a** day / year | *dreimal **am** Tag / **im** Jahr* |
| *100 und 1000* | **a** hundred, **a** thousand | *hundert / tausend* |

○ *sowie **nach**:*

| | | |
|---|---|---|
| *half* | half **an** hour | *eine halbe Stunde* |
| *quite, kind of* | quite **a** / kind of **a** long way | *ein ziemlich langer Weg* |
| *such* | such **a** nice day | *so **ein** schöner Tag* |

○ *und in phrases wie:* in **a** hurry *(in Eile)*; for **a** long time *(lange Zeit)*; have **a** headache *(Kopfschmerzen haben)*.

○ **English summary** ○

You use the definite article *(the)* before:
1. nouns that refer to specific people or things;
2. names of rivers, seas, mountain chains, plural names of countries and musical instruments.

**The** sun is shining.
**the** Rhine, **the** Pacific Ocean, **the** Rockies, **the** US, **the** guitar

You do **not** use the definite article before:
1. an abstract noun;
2. names of mountains, lakes, towns, roads, countries and *most* when it means *almost all*.

Life is never boring in Hollywood.
Mt Whitney, Lake Ontario, Park Road
Most people like ice cream.

You use the indefinite article *(a / an)* before:
1. jobs, units of measurement, time, 100, 1000;
2. after *half, quite, kind of, such*;
3. and in certain expressions.

Mr. Summer is **a** pilot.
I've been waiting for half **an** hour.
I'm in **a** hurry.

**Test yourself** *Complete Alex's e-mail to his mother. Put in the **definite** or **indefinite article**. If **no article** is needed, write (–).*

Sorry I didn't send you an e-mail earlier, but I was tired after all ⟨1⟩ fun we had at ⟨2⟩ movie premiere last night. When I got up, it was already 10:30. Then after ⟨3⟩ breakfast, I had to learn all about ⟨4⟩ history of California for ⟨5⟩ test on Wednesday. That took about ⟨6⟩ hour and ⟨7⟩ half. And I haven't even started to learn about ⟨8⟩ economy or ⟨9⟩ different landscapes yet. No, I haven't gone back to ⟨10⟩ college. ⟨11⟩ test is for ⟨12⟩ job with ⟨13⟩ Tourist Office. If I pass, I'll soon be able to work as ⟨14⟩ tour guide two or three times ⟨15⟩ week in-between my auditions. But I've already heard it's pretty difficult and ⟨16⟩ most people have to take it at least twice, so I'm not very hopeful. I haven't found ⟨17⟩ fame as ⟨18⟩ actor yet. But I can honestly say that I've found ⟨19⟩ happiness. L.A. is such ⟨20⟩ fantastic city and I just love ⟨21⟩ excitement of living here. For me, it's simply ⟨22⟩ most exciting city in ⟨23⟩ US.

## G11 Should we be worried?

→ Seiten 54–56

*Englische Entsprechungen für die Verben „sollen" und „müssen"*
English equivalents for the German verbs *sollen* and *müssen*

The bus **was supposed to** be here ten minutes ago. I think we **should** call a taxi.

OMG! I **must** go now. I **have to** be at work at 9 and I **mustn't** be late again.

*Die deutschen Verben „sollen" und „müssen" werden im Englischen durch verschiedene Verben und Verbphrasen wiedergegeben.*

### a) Das Verb „sollen"

**shall / should / ought to / be to**

| | | |
|---|---|---|
| *Bitte um Anweisung / Rat* | shall (I / we) should | **Shall** I open the window? What **shall** we do? What **should** he / she / they do? |
| *Verpflichtung* | should | If you made a mistake, you **should** apologise. |
| *Meinung / Ratschlag* | should / ought to | I think we **should / ought to** care more about our environment. |
| *Anweisung / Befehl* | be to | If we hear the fire alarm, we **are to** leave the building immediately. |

❗ *Das Verb* shall *klingt sehr formal und wird von jungen Sprechern kaum noch verwendet (in den USA auch nur noch selten von erwachsenen Sprechern).*

**be supposed to / be expected to / be said to**

| | | |
|---|---|---|
| *Regel* | be supposed to | You**'re supposed to** call 911 only in an emergency. You **aren't supposed to** use it for general advice. |
| *Erwartung* | be supposed to / be expected to | Firefighters **are supposed to / are expected to** prevent fires, as well as put them out. |
| *Erwartung, die sich nicht erfüllt* | be supposed to | The Emergency Services **are supposed to** be on their way. But they haven't arrived yet. |
| *Gerücht / Behauptung* | be supposed to / be said to | Some fires **are supposed to / are said to** be good for the environment. |

### b) Das Verb „müssen"

**must / have to / need to**

| | | |
|---|---|---|
| *Notwendigkeit* | must / have to / need to | Firefighting is a dangerous job. You **must / have to / need to** be very brave to do that kind of work. |
| *keine Notwendigkeit* | needn't / don't have to / don't need to | But you **needn't / don't have to / don't need to** worry because you'll be given good training. |
| *schriftliche Anweisungen (Schilder; Vorschriften)* | must | Fire doors **must** be kept closed. Firefighters **must** wear protective clothing. |

❗ Must *und* have to *sind häufig austauschbar, aber es gibt einen wichtigen Unterschied:*
Must *weist auf ein persönliches Gefühl hin*; have to *auf eine auferlegte Pflicht oder eine Tatsache.*
I must tidy my room today. *(= Der Sprecher selbst hält es für wichtig.)*
I have to tidy my room every Saturday. *(= Es ist eine auferlegte Pflicht oder eine Tatsache.)*

**be required to / be forced to / be obliged to**

| | | |
|---|---|---|
| *Zwang* | be forced to | Firefighters **are** often **forced to** work long hours. |
| *Verpflichtung* | be required to / be obliged to | They**'re** also **required to / are obliged to** work on holidays and on weekends. |

○ **English summary** ○ ───────────────

The German verbs *sollen* and *müssen* can be expressed in English in different ways.

Equivalents for *sollen*: shall, should, ought to, be to, be supposed to, be expected to, be said to

Where **shall / should** we go for lunch?
If the door is locked, we **are to** wait outside.
You **were supposed to** be here half an hour ago.

Equivalents for *müssen*: must, have to, need to, be forced to, be required to, be obliged to, be supposed to, be to

I **must / need to / have to** water the plants today.
**Are** you **required to / obliged to** wear a school uniform?

**Test yourself**   a) *Complete these sentences with the correct verb for the German 'sollen'.*

1. If Mrs. Kent is late today, we ▮ wait for her in the hall.   2. Have you been to the new restaurant in West Street? It ▮ be very good.   3. The plane landed early. It ▮ land at 8:30.
4. If Lisa isn't feeling better soon, I think she ▮ see a doctor.   5. Are you hungry? ▮ I make us a sandwich?   6. We can take cell phones to school but we ▮ use them in class.

b) *Use a different verb for 'have to' in these sentences. Sometimes more than one answer is correct.*

1. We've got plenty of time. We **don't have to** hurry.   2. It's not going to rain today, so we **won't have to** take an umbrella.   3. There were no trains or buses to the village, so I **had to** take a taxi.   4. There's no food in the cupboard. I'**ll have to** go shopping today.   5. Sometimes we **have to** make difficult decisions. We have no choice.   6. **Do** firefighters **have to** rescue animals?

Im **Vocabulary** findest du alle wichtigen englischen Wörter und Redewendungen aus *Green Line* 6. Sie stehen in der Reihenfolge, in der sie im Buch vorkommen. Diese Wörter solltest du lernen und anwenden können. Andere nützliche Wörter (*Vocabulary for instructions and activities*), die du **nicht** auswendig lernen musst, findest du auf S.194–195

Auf das *Vocabulary* folgt das **Dictionary (English – German)**. Falls du ein Wort vergessen hast, kannst du in dieser alphabetischen Wortliste nachsehen.

Englische Begriffe wie *e-mail*, *cool* oder *cornflakes*, die du auch im Deutschen verwendest, stehen nicht im *Vocabulary*. Du kannst ihre Aussprache und Übersetzung aber im *Dictionary* nachschlagen. Das Gleiche gilt für Wörter, die auf Englisch und Deutsch fast gleich geschrieben und ausgesprochen werden, wie z.B. *park* oder *partner*.

In den drei Teilen von **Text smart** musst du nicht alle neuen Vokabeln auswendig lernen. Die Wörter und Ausdrücke, die im *Vocabulary* aufgelistet sind, sind die wichtigsten und sie solltest du lernen und anwenden können. Alle anderen neuen Wörter aus *Text smart* kannst du ebenfalls im *Dictionary* ab S.144 nachschlagen.

### Abkürzungen und Zeichen

| | | | | |
|---|---|---|---|---|
| *pl* | Mehrzahl (Plural) | | **!** | Achtung! |
| *sg* | Einzahl (Singular) | | ↔ | ist das Gegenteil von |
| *AE* | amerikanisch-englisches Wort | | → | ist verwandt mit |
| *coll/ugs* | umgangssprachlich | | = | entspricht |
| *liter* | literarisch | | ≠ | entspricht nicht |
| **5** | In dieser Übung kommen die Wörter vor. | | *Fr./Lat.* | verwandte Wörter in anderen Fremdsprachen |

### Englische Laute

**Konsonanten**

| | | | | |
|---|---|---|---|---|
| [b] | **b**ed | | [p] | **p**icture |
| [d] | **d**ay | | [r] | **r**ed |
| [ð] | **th**e | | [s] | **s**ix |
| [f] | **f**amily | | [ʃ] | **sh**e |
| [g] | **g**o | | [t] | **t**en |
| [ŋ] | morni**ng** | | [tʃ] | **ch**air |
| [h] | **h**ouse | | [v] | **v**ideo |
| [j] | **y**ou | | [w] | **w**e, **o**ne |
| [k] | **c**an, mil**k** | | [z] | ea**s**y |
| [l] | **l**etter | | [ʒ] | revi**s**ion |
| [m] | **m**an | | [dʒ] | pa**g**e |
| [n] | **n**o | | [θ] | **th**ank you |

**Vokale**

| | | | | |
|---|---|---|---|---|
| [ɑ:] | c**ar** | | [i] | happ**y** |
| [æ] | **a**pple | | [i:] | t**ea**cher |
| [e] | p**e**n | | [ɒ] | d**o**g |
| [ə] | **a**gain | | [ɔ:] | b**a**ll |
| [ɜ:] | g**ir**l | | [ʊ] | b**oo**k |
| [ʌ] | b**u**t | | [u] | Jan**u**ary |
| [ɪ] | **i**t | | [u:] | t**oo**, tw**o** |

**Doppellaute**

| | |
|---|---|
| [aɪ] | **I**, m**y** |
| [aʊ] | n**ow**, m**ou**se |
| [eɪ] | n**a**me, th**ey** |
| [eə] | th**ere**, p**air** |
| [ɪə] | h**ere**, id**ea** |
| [əʊ] | hell**o** |
| [ɔɪ] | b**oy** |
| [ʊə] | s**ure** |

| | |
|---|---|
| [:] | der vorangehende Laut ist lang, z.B. *you* [ju:] |
| [‿] | der Bindebogen zeigt, dass zwei Wörter in der Aussprache verbunden werden |
| ['] | die folgende Silbe trägt den Hauptakzent |
| [ˌ] | die folgende Silbe trägt den Nebenakzent |

Der Aussprachestandard in *Green Line* ist *British English*. Auch Wörter, die den Zusatz *AE* haben, werden entsprechend lautschriftlich dargestellt. Bei den Tonträgern und Filmsequenzen wird die jeweils passende Aussprache verwendet.

# Unit 1  The good life?

## Introduction

| | | | |
|---|---|---|---|
| 1 | **fulfilling** [fʊlˈfɪlɪŋ] | erfüllend; befriedigend | **!** Be careful with the spelling: fu**ll** + **f**ill = *fulfilling* |
| | **materialistic** [məˌtɪəriəˈlɪstɪk] | materialistisch | I'm not into owning too many things. I guess I'm not very *materialistic*. |
| | **meaningful** [ˈmiːnɪŋfl] | bedeutsam; wichtig | Whether something is *meaningful* or not depends on one's perspective; people see things differently. |
| | **adventurous** [ədˈventʃrəs] | abenteuerlich; unternehmungslustig; wagemutig; experimentierfreudig | My older sister has an *adventurous* lifestyle: She flies all over the world for her job. *adventurous* → adventure |
| 3 | **satisfaction** [ˌsætɪsˈfækʃn] | Zufriedenheit | For my job *satisfaction*, money isn't the most important thing. = feeling of happiness about sth sb has done |
| | **boredom** [ˈbɔːdəm] | Langeweile | *boredom* → boring → bored |
| | **curiosity** [ˌkjʊəriˈɒsəti] | Neugier | *Curiosity* definitely plays a role in my life: I always want to try something new. *Fr.* curiosité *(f)*; *Lat.* curiositas *(f)* |
| | **desirable** [dɪˈzaɪərəbl] | wünschenswert; erstrebenswert | Good manners are *desirable* if you want to make a good impression on a first date. |

## Station 1: Best summer ever!

| | | | |
|---|---|---|---|
| 1 | to **encourage** [ɪnˈkʌrɪdʒ] | unterstützen; ermutigen | My dad *encouraged* me to apply for this job. *Fr.* encourager |
| | to **raise** [reɪz] | (er)wecken *(Interesse)*; aufwerfen *(Fragen)* | to *raise* interest, to *raise* a problem/question |
| | **opportunity** [ˌɒpəˈtjuːnəti] | Chance; Gelegenheit; Möglichkeit | = a great chance to do sth |
| | **assistant counsellor** [əˌsɪstnt ˈkaʊnslə] | Hilfsbetreuer/-in | |
| | **senior counsellor** [ˌsiːniə ˈkaʊnslə] | leitender Betreuer/leitende Betreuerin; ranghohe/-r Minister/-in | *senior counsellor* ↔ assistant counsellor |
| | to **be passionate about sth** [bi ˈpæʃnət əˌbaʊt] | etw. leidenschaftlich gern tun; eine Leidenschaft für etw. haben; für etw. brennen | If you're *passionate about* sth, then you don't just like it, you love it! |
| | **testimonial** [ˌtestɪˈməʊniəl] | Erfahrungsbericht | Go online and read some of the people's *testimonials* about that company. *Lat.* testimonium *(nt)* |
| 2 | **qualification** [ˌkwɒlɪfɪˈkeɪʃn] | Qualifikation; Befähigung; Abschluss; Schulabschluss | What *qualifications* do you need for a job as a sales assistant? |
| | to **require** [rɪˈkwaɪə] | benötigen; erfordern | If you *require* sth, it's necessary for you to have it. *to require* = to need |

| | | | |
|---|---|---|---|
| **applicant** ['æplıkənt] | Bewerber/-in | In a letter of application, the *applicant* applies for a job. *applicant* → to apply → application |
| **position** [pə'zıʃn] | Stelle; Position | *position* = job |
| to **be supposed to** *(+ inf)* [bi sə'pəʊzd tə] | sollen | If you *are supposed to do sth*, you are expected to do it. |
| to **set a good example** [set ə ˌgʊd ˌıg'zɑːmpl] | ein Vorbild sein | Parents are supposed to *set a good example* for their children. |
| **at all times** [ˌət ˌɔːl 'taımz] | immer; jederzeit; stets | *at all times* = always |
| to **be expected to** *(+ inf)* [bi ık'spektıd tə] | sollen | When there's an accident, you*'re expected to* call the police. |
| to **be a team player** [ˌbi ə 'tiːm ˌpleıə] | gern im Team arbeiten | Some jobs can only be done by people who *are team players*. |
| **responsibility** [rıˌspɒnsə'bıləti] | Verantwortung; Aufgabe | That job includes a lot of interesting areas of *responsibility*. *responsibility* → responsible |
| **CV** *(Curriculum Vitae)* [ˌsiː'viː (kəˌrıkjələm 'viːtaı)] | Lebenslauf | A *CV* describes what jobs and activities you've done in your life so far, what exams you've passed, etc. *CV (BE)* = résumé *(AE)* |
| **application letter** [ˌæplı'keıʃn ˌletə] | Bewerbungsschreiben | If you want a job, you first have to send in an *application letter* and a CV. |
| 3 **gender** ['dʒendə] | Geschlecht | *gender* differences/roles |
| **employer** [ım'plɔıə] | Arbeitgeber/-in | The company my mum works for is one of the region's biggest *employers*. *employer* → to employ sb → employee |
| **focused** ['fəʊkəst] | zielgerichtet | Turning off your phone may help you to stay *focused* on your work. *focused* → focus → to focus (on) |
| **all-rounder** [ɔːl'raʊndə] | Alleskönner/-in; Multitalent | An *all-rounder* doesn't focus on just one special talent. |
| to **stand out (from)** [ˌstænd ˌ'aʊt] | sich abheben (von); herausragen (aus) | If you don't *stand out from* the hundreds of applicants, you won't get the job. |
| **weakness** ['wiːknəs] | Schwäche | *weakness* ↔ strength *weakness* → weak |
| **stereotype** ['sterıəʊtaıp] | Klischee; Stereotyp | A *stereotype* is an (often wrong) idea about what you expect a person to be like before you even know him/her. |
| 4 **gender stereotyping** ['dʒendə ˌsterıəʊtaıpıŋ] | geschlechtsspezifische Klischees | It's *gender stereotyping* to expect all women to be good in the kitchen and all men to love fast cars. |
| to **consider** [kən'sıdə] | betrachten; erwägen | In Britain people *consider* it bad manners to take sth without saying 'thank you'. = to regard sth as *Fr.* considérer |
| **engineering** [ˌendʒı'nıərıŋ] | Technik; Maschinenbau | *engineering* → engineer |
| **GCSE** *(= General Certificate of Secondary Education)* [ˌdʒiːsiːesˈiː (ˌdʒenrl səˈtıfıkət ˌəv ˌsekəndri ˌedʒʊ'keıʃn)] | *allg. Abschluss der weiterführenden Schulen in GB* | |
| to **list** [lıst] | auflisten; nennen | Please *list* all your strengths and weaknesses. |

| | | |
|---|---|---|
| **healthcare** [ˈhelθkeə] | Gesundheitsversorgung | I work in the *healthcare* industry. I'm a nurse. – Oh, me too! |
| **female** [ˈfiːmeɪl] | weiblich | |
| **construction worker** [kənˈstrʌkʃn ˌwɜːkə] | Bauarbeiter/-in | *Construction workers* build roads, buildings, bridges, etc. |
| **profession** [prəˈfeʃn] | Beruf | What *professions* pay the most? |
| **male** [meɪl] | männlich | *male* ↔ female |
| **to associate** [əˈsəʊʃieɪt] | assoziieren; verbinden | What do you *associate* with healthcare professions? |
| **(business) executive** [ˈbɪznɪs ɪɡˌzekjətɪv] | Geschäftsführer/-in; Manager/-in; gehobene Führungskraft | The *executives* all have their offices on the top floor of our building. |
| **firefighter** [ˈfaɪəˌfaɪtə] | Feuerwehrmann/-frau | A lot of young boys say they want to become *firefighters* one day. |
| **sales assistant** [ˈseɪlz ˌəˌsɪstnt] | Verkäufer/-in | |
| 6 **nationality** [ˌnæʃnˈæləti] | Nationalität; Staatsangehörigkeit | He was born in Pakistan, but he grew up in Britain; his *nationality* is British.<br>*nationality* → nation → national |
| **comprehensive school** [kɒmprɪˈhensɪv ˌskuːl] | Gesamtschule | |
| **organiser** [ˈɔːɡənaɪzə] | Organisator/-in | *organiser* → to organise → organisation |
| **hard-working** [ˌhɑːdˈwɜːkɪŋ] | fleißig | *hard-working* ↔ lazy |
| **people skills** *(pl)* [ˈpiːpl ˌskɪlz] | soziale Kompetenz | If you have good *people skills*, you communicate well and make people feel comfortable. |
| **reference** [ˈrefrns] | Referenz; Referenzschreiben | A *reference* is a letter written by sb who knows you and thinks you'd be able to do a job well. |
| **request** [rɪˈkwest] | Anfrage; Nachfrage | I'll send the company more information on *request*. |
| 7 **common** [ˈkɒmən] | üblich; verbreitet; gängig | |
| 8 **with reference to** [wɪð ˈrefrns tə] | bezugnehmend auf | **!** = a phrase typical only for formal letters<br>*with reference to* → to refer to sth |
| **hopefully** [ˈhəʊpfli] | hoffentlich | I really want this job, so *hopefully* I'll get it! |
| **therefore** [ˈðeəfɔː] | deshalb; deswegen; daher; somit | Miss Ellis, I'm sorry, but the quality of your work has been a problem, again. *Therefore*, I'm going to give your project to somebody else. |
| **moreover** [mɔːrˈəʊvə] | überdies; außerdem | |
| **addition** [əˈdɪʃn] | Zusatz; Ergänzung | Let's give her the job. – Yeah, she'd be a great *addition* to our team.<br>*addition* → to add |
| **(job) interview** [ˈdʒɒb ˌɪntəvjuː] | Vorstellungsgespräch | I applied for a job and now I've been invited for an *interview* on Thursday. |
| **Yours sincerely** [ˌjɔːz sɪnˈsɪəli] | Mit freundlichen Grüßen | This can be used at the end of a formal letter. |
| **signature** [ˈsɪɡnətʃə] | Unterschrift | Is THAT your *signature*?! Nobody can read it. Practise a bit before you sign your application!<br>*signature* → to sign<br>**Fr.** signature *(f)* |

| enclosure [ɪnˈkləʊʒə] | Anlage; Beilage | = sth you include with a letter |
|---|---|---|
| attachment [əˈtætʃmənt] | Anhang | = sth you attach to an e-mail |
| 9 furthermore [ˌfɜːðəˈmɔː] | überdies; außerdem | = a formal word you can use to introduce another point that helps your argument |
| unfortunately [ʌnˈfɔːtʃnətli] | leider; unglücklicherweise | *Unfortunately*, I can't come to your birthday party. Sorry! |
| nevertheless [ˌnevəðəˈles] | trotzdem; dennoch; nichts-destoweniger | |

## Frequently-used sentence adverbs

*Remember that commenting adverbs have to do with one's personal view; one uses them to comment. Linking adverbs, on the other hand, are for factual statements.*

| commenting | | linking | |
|---|---|---|---|
| actually | really | additionally | in general |
| definitely | seriously | after all | in the end |
| hopefully | surely | finally | moreover |
| luckily | typically | furthermore | nevertheless |
| normally | unfortunately | however | otherwise |
| originally | usually | in addition to | overall |
| personally | | in fact | therefore |

*Write four sentences using two commenting and two linking adverbs.*

## Station 2: The cocoa controversy

| cocoa [ˈkəʊkəʊ] | Kakao | There would be no chocolate without *cocoa*. |
|---|---|---|
| controversy [ˈkɒntrəvɜːsi] | Kontroverse; Auseinanderset-zung | to create/to cause *controversy*<br>= a public discussion that features very different and often emotional opinions |
| 12 quantity [ˈkwɒntɪti] | Menge; Quantität | Chocolate is sold in large *quantities* in Europe. |
| cosmetics *(pl)* [kɒzˈmetɪks] | Kosmetik | ! You can't use this noun in the singular. |
| to provide [prəˈvaɪd] | liefern; bereit stellen | They *provided* us with plenty of food every day.<br>1. to give sth that is needed; 2. to make available<br>*Lat.* providēre |
| poverty line [ˈpɒvəti ˌlaɪn] | Armutsgrenze | There are more and more people who live below the *poverty line*. |
| poverty [ˈpɒvəti] | Armut | *poverty* → poor |
| physical [ˈfɪzɪkl] | physisch; körperlich | Construction workers do hard *physical* work. |
| to harvest [ˈhɑːvɪst] | ernten | |
| bean [biːn] | Bohne | Harvesting cocoa *beans* is a difficult and dangerous job. |
| to force [fɔːs] | zwingen | If you *force* sb to do sth, you make them do it. |
| plantation [plænˈteɪʃn] | Plantage | In the southern states of the US, there used to be a lot of *plantations* which required the work of many, many slaves. |
| to justify [ˈdʒʌstɪfaɪ] | rechtfertigen | Can anything *justify* child labour? |

| | | |
|---|---|---|
| **exhausted** [ɪɡˈzɔːstɪd] | erschöpft | After running a marathon, they were *exhausted*. |
| to **chop** [tʃɒp] | hacken; klein schneiden | Please *chop* the vegetables for the soup. |
| **pod** [pɒd] | Hülse; Schote | |
| **machete** [məˈʃeti] | Machete; Buschmesser | = a very big knife<br>**!** Be careful with the pronunciation. |
| to **dump** [dʌmp] | abladen | |
| **onto** [ˈɒntə] | auf ... hinauf | They dumped the containers *onto* a large truck. |
| **trade** [treɪd] | Handel | Are these cocoa beans from fair *trade*? |
| 15 **march** [mɑːtʃ] | Marsch; Kundgebung | We're organising a protest *march* against child labour. |
| to **catch oneself doing sth** [kætʃ] | sich (selbst) dabei ertappen, wie ... | During lessons I *caught myself dreaming* of our next holiday. |
| 16 **commitment** [kəˈmɪtmənt] | Bindung; Verpflichtung; Engagement | Showing social *commitment* helps others, but it's meaningful for your own life as well. |
| **volunteer** [ˌvɒlənˈtɪə] | Freiwillige/-r; Ehrenamtliche/-r | She works as a *volunteer* at a hospital. |
| **selfish** [ˈselfɪʃ] | selbstsüchtig; egoistisch | Some people say it's *selfish* to do charity work only to make your CV look better. What do you think? |
| 17 **involvement** [ɪnˈvɒlvmənt] | Engagement; Beteiligung | How much *involvement* do you have time for: once or twice a week?<br>*involvement* → to be involved (in) |
| to **volunteer** [ˌvɒlənˈtɪə] | eine ehrenamtliche Tätigkeit übernehmen | I *volunteered* to help with our school's clothing drive.<br>*to volunteer* → volunteer *(n)* |
| **religious** [rɪˈlɪdʒəs] | religiös; gläubig | *Fr.* religieux/religieuse; *Lat.* religiosus |
| **the elderly** [ðiˈeldəli] | ältere Menschen; Senioren | = a more polite word for 'old' (when you speak about people) |
| **the homeless** [ðəˈhəʊmləs] | Obdachlose | *the homeless* → home |

## Adjectives as nouns

*You can use some adjectives as nouns by adding the definite article 'the'.*

One way to show social commitment is offering services for **the disabled**.
What does your community do for **the elderly**?
My aunt is member of a volunteer group that offers hot meals to **the homeless**.

Eine Möglichkeit, soziales Engagement zu zeigen, ist, Dienste für **Behinderte** anzubieten.
Was tut deine Gemeinde für **ältere Menschen**?
Meine Tante ist Mitglied einer Gruppe von Freiwilligen, die **Obdachlosen** warmes Essen anbietet.

the poor | the rich | the young

*Write sentences for the three other nouns.*

| | | |
|---|---|---|
| **the disabled** [ðə dɪˈseɪbld] | Behinderte | I can't decide if I want to volunteer my time for the homeless or *the disabled*; they all need help. |
| **volunteer** [ˌvɒlənˈtɪə] | freiwillig; ehrenamtlich | *volunteer* → to volunteer → volunteer *(n)* |
| **gap year** [ˈgæp ˌjɪə] | *ein Jahr Auszeit (zwischen Schule und Ausbildung/ Studium), das oft für einen freiwilligen ökologischen oder sozialen Dienst genutzt wird* | In many European countries it's now common to spend a *gap year* abroad. |

## Station 3: I do remember how it feels . . .

| | | |
|---|---|---|
| **wisdom** *(no pl)* [ˈwɪzdəm] | Weisheit; Klugheit | *Wisdom* comes with age and experience. |
| **carpenter** [ˈkɑːpntə] | Schreiner/-in; Zimmermann | Being a *carpenter* is great for me because I'm able to work with my hands. |
| **not only . . . but (also)** [nɒt ˌəʊnli bʌt ˈɔːlsəʊ] | nicht nur . . . sondern (auch) | *Not only* did I lose my passport in Australia, *but* I *also* lost my phone! Great holiday. |
| **to stack** [stæk] | stapeln | *Stacking* wood all day isn't my idea of job satisfaction! |
| **to go by** [ˌgəʊ ˈbaɪ] | vorbeigehen | School days never *go by* fast enough. |
| **left over** [left ˈəʊvə] | übrig | At the end of a month I never have any pocket money *left over*. |
| **pay** [peɪ] | Lohn; Gehalt | = the money a person receives for doing their job<br>*pay* → to pay |
| **tax** [tæks] | Steuer; Abgabe | Without *taxes* there would be no public schools, police or firefighters, for example. |
| **wage** [weɪdʒ] | Lohn | *wage* = pay |
| **patient** [ˈpeɪʃnt] | geduldig | *Fr.* patient/-e |
| **rarely** [ˈreəli] | selten | = not often |
| **top** [tɒp] | Spitzen-; oberster; bester | A *top* restaurant is a very good restaurant. |
| **law** [lɔː] | Gesetz; Recht | If you break the *law*, you may get into serious trouble.<br>*Fr.* loi *(f)* |
| 21 **know-it-all** [ˈnəʊɪtɔːl] | Besserwisser/-in | I can't believe you don't know what the capital of Australia is! Everyone knows it's Canberra. – Don't be such a *know-it-all*! |
| **brief** [briːf] | kurz | Has Mrs Chen told you about the new project yet? – No, I only saw her *briefly* this morning, there was no time. |
| 22 **to limit to** [ˈlɪmɪt tə] | limitieren auf; begrenzen auf; beschränken auf | The guided tour *is limited to* 15 people.<br>*to limit* → limit |
| 23 **investment** [ɪnˈvesmənt] | Einlage; Beteiligung; Investition | She's got a great business idea but needs an *investment* of £30.000 to get started. |
| **buddy** *(infml)* [ˈbʌdi] | Kumpel | *buddy* = mate |
| **to be made up of/from** [bi meɪd ˈʌp ˌəv/frəm] | zusammengesetzt sein aus; bestehen aus | What *is* this device *made up of*? |
| **toothbrush** [ˈtuːθbrʌʃ] | Zahnbürste | |
| 24 **no sooner** [nəʊ ˈsuːnə] | kaum | *No sooner* had I told him my secret than the whole school knew! What a friend. |

| 25 | **colleague** [ˈkɒliːɡ] | Kollege/Kollegin | I share my office with three *colleagues*. |
|---|---|---|---|
| | to **suit sb** [suːt] | (zu) jmdm. passen; jmdm. stehen | Which colour *suits me* better: black or grey? |

## Skills: Making a good impression

| 1 | **candidate** [ˈkændɪdət] | Bewerber/-in; Kandidat/-in | The ideal *candidate* should be able to take on responsibility, but also be a team player. *Fr.* candidat/-e *(m, f)* |
|---|---|---|---|
| 2 | to **emphasise** [ˈemfəsaɪz] | betonen | At job interviews, it's important to *emphasise* what you do well. |
| | **tricky** [ˈtrɪki] | schwierig; kompliziert | Be prepared for *tricky* questions at job interviews. *tricky* → trick |

## Unit task: Job interviews for a summer camp

| | **helper** [ˈhelpə] | Helfer/-in | *helper* → to help → help |
|---|---|---|---|

## Story: The Giver

| | **giver** [ˈɡɪvə] | Geber/-in; Spender/-in | *giver* → to give |
|---|---|---|---|
| | to **regulate** [ˈreɡjəleɪt] | regeln; regulieren | = to control sth by introducing rules |
| | **assignment** [əˈsaɪnmənt] | Aufgabe; Auftrag; Mission | Her boss is going to give her a tricky new *assignment*. = a piece of work that you must do for school or for a job |
| | **destiny** [ˈdestɪni] | Schicksal; Fügung; Vorsehung | *destiny* = fate *Fr.* destin *(m)* |
| 1 | to **assign** [əˈsaɪn] | zuordnen; übertragen | We're going to do group work, but don't divide up into groups yourselves: I'll *assign* you to your groups. *to assign* → assignment |
| | to **acknowledge** [əkˈnɒlɪdʒ] | anerkennen; einräumen | = to admit or accept that sth is true or that a situation exists |
| | to **fit in** [ˌfɪtˈɪn] | hineinpassen; sich einfügen | We've got a new neighbour who I think will really *fit in* well. |
| | to **standardize** *(AE)* [ˈstændədaɪz] | standardisieren; vereinheitlichen | How boring would it be if everyone's behavior *was standardized*? |
| | to **honor** *(AE)* [ˈɒnə] | ehren; würdigen; auszeichnen | In some cultures, it is very important to *honor* the elderly. *Fr.* honorer; *Lat.* honorare |
| | to **determine** [dɪˈtɜːmɪn] | bestimmen; ermitteln | How well one performs at work will *determine* how far one will go at that company. *to determine* = to influence strongly = to find out *Fr.* déterminer |
| | **throughout** [θruːˈaʊt] | während; überall in | ❗ Be careful with the spelling. |
| | **satisfied** [ˈsætɪsfaɪd] | zufrieden; befriedigt | He just got a text message and now he's got a very *satisfied* look on his face. Hm … *satisfied* → satisfaction |
| | **apology** [əˈpɒlədʒi] | Entschuldigung | After the argument she accepted her friend's *apology*. *apology* → to apologise |
| | to **select** [sɪˈlekt] | auswählen; aussuchen | = a more formal word for 'to choose' *Lat.* seligere: selectum |

| | | | |
|---|---|---|---|
| | **receiver** [rɪˈsiːvə] | Empfänger/-in; *hier:* Hüter/-in | *receiver → to receive* |
| 2 | **sheet** [ʃiːt] | Blatt | Write the facts on a *sheet* of paper. |
| 3 | **session** [ˈseʃn] | Sitzung; Stunde | |
| | **ability** [əˈbɪləti] | Fähigkeit | At the camp he showed his *abilities* as a leader. *ability → to be able* |
| | **to transmit** [trænzˈmɪt] | übertragen | |
| | **sir** [sɜː] | mein Herr *(Anrede)* | |
| | **impatient** [ɪmˈpeɪʃnt] | ungeduldig | *impatient ↔ patient* *Fr.* impatient/-e |
| 4 | **laugh** [lɑːf] | Lachen | *laugh → to laugh* |
| | **distant** [ˈdɪstnt] | entfernt; distanziert | Most of my memories from childhood are very *distant*, but some feel like it was yesterday. *distant → distance* |
| | **sameness** [ˈseɪmnəs] | Gleichheit; Gleichförmigkeit | *sameness → the same* |
| | **to slow down** [ˌsləʊ ˈdaʊn] | langsamer werden; bremsen | *Slow down*, please, there are children in the street. |
| | **ordinary** [ˈɔːdnri] | gewöhnlich; normal | I thought he was just an *ordinary* boy from school. I had no idea he was a famous actor. ! False friend: *ordinary* ≠ ordinär *Fr.* ordinaire |
| | **curious** [ˈkjʊəriəs] | neugierig | My little brother always tries to listen to my private conversations. He's very *curious*. *curious → curiosity* *Fr.* curieux/curieuse; *Lat.* curiosus |
| | **to make a choice** [ˌmeɪk ə ˈtʃɔɪs] | eine Wahl treffen | *to make a choice = to choose* |
| | **to matter** [ˈmætə] | von Bedeutung sein; etw. ausmachen | Some people say it doesn't *matter* how rich you are, it's what you do with your life that really *matters*. |
| | **to dare** [deə] | wagen | Nobody *dares* to go there. = Everybody is too frightened to go there. |
| | **mate** [meɪt] | Partner/-in | ! '*Mate*' is used as a biological term here. |
| 6 | **literature** [ˈlɪtrətʃə] | Literatur | |

> **Collocations: Jobs and life**
>
> | | |
> |---|---|
> | hard / difficult / exhausting / well-paid / traditional | job / profession |
> | fulfilling / adventurous / fun / boring | lifestyle / job / career |
> | materialistic / meaningful / desirable | life / lifestyle |
> | (un)qualified / (ir)responsible / (un)reliable / (un)focused | applicant / worker / candidate |
> | passionate / confident / hard-working / (im)patient / interested / independent | person / character |
> | outgoing / spontaneous / creative | personality |
> | specific / practical / useless | qualifications |
> | well-developed / good | skills |

## Jobs

**. . . in business / economy**
auditor
(business) executive
spokesperson

**. . . in education**
principal; head teacher
professor
teacher

**. . . in sales**
assistant
sales assistant
travel agent

**. . . in service**
attendant
(camp) counsellor
detective
firefighter
flight attendant
guard
guide
lifeguard
pilot
police officer
postman
private detective
waiter

**. . . in film / entertainment / media**
actor
advertiser
agent
director
DJ
extra
filmmaker
journalist; reporter
model
producer
publisher

**. . . in healthcare / care**
au pair
doctor
nurse

**. . . in farming / with animals**
farmer
vet

**. . . in official functions**
governor
historian
official
politician
president

**. . . in construction**
architect
construction worker
electrician
engineer
mechanic
miner
plumber

**. . . in science / technology / IT areas**
astronaut
IT manager
scientist
web designer

**. . . in creative areas**
artist
dancer
entertainer
(fashion/web) designer
musician
photographer
scriptwriter

*Students getting job information at a Job Fair*

**general terms**
businessman
employee
employer
entrepreneur
founder
worker

*What job would you like to do in the future? Write a short text.*

# Text smart 1  Informative texts

## Introduction

| | | | |
|---|---|---|---|
| 2 | **earthquake** ['ɜ:θkweɪk] | Erdbeben | *earthquake* → earth |
| | **review** [rɪ'vju:] | Kritik | After the first night of a new play, there are *reviews* in the newspapers. |
| | **criticism** ['krɪtɪsɪzm] | Kritik | *criticism* → critical |

## Station 1: How to: Write a text summary

| | | | |
|---|---|---|---|
| 3 | **entitled** [ɪn'taɪtld] | mit dem Titel | He read a novel *entitled* **Room**. *entitled* → title |
| | **around** [ə'raʊnd] | ungefähr; etwa | Only *around* 200 people were at the concert. |
| | **enslavement** [ɪn'sleɪvmənt] | Versklavung | *enslavement* → slave |
| | to **be unable to do sth** [bi ʌn'eɪbl tə] | unfähig sein, etw. zu tun; nicht in der Lage sein, etw. zu tun | On nice sunny days I'*m unable to focus* on my homework. *to be unable to* ↔ to be able to |
| | to **conclude** [kən'klu:d] | enden; schließen; schlussfolgern | *to conclude* → conclusion |
| 5 | **journalist** ['dʒɜ:nlɪst] | Journalist/-in | A *journalist* writes for a newspaper. |
| | **injured** ['ɪndʒəd] | verletzt | *injured* → injury |
| | **irrelevant** [ɪ'reləvnt] | irrelevant; nicht von Bedeutung | = not important |
| 6 | **study** ['stʌdi] | Studie; Untersuchung | Is there a *study* about how sleep influences your health? |
| | **in particular** [ˌɪn pə'tɪkjələ] | im besonderen | We should all pay more attention to our 'body clock', *in particular* teenagers. |
| | **biological** [ˌbaɪə'lɒdʒɪkl] | biologisch | *biological* → biology |
| | **deprivation** [ˌdeprɪ'veɪʃn] | Entbehrung; Entzug | Sleep *deprivation* is bad enough, but chocolate *deprivation*? To me, that's much worse! |
| | **currently** ['kʌrntli] | momentan | = now; at this moment in time |
| | to **recruit** [rɪ'kru:t] | rekrutieren; anwerben; einstellen | Soldiers *are recruited* to the army. |
| | **cycle** ['saɪkl] | Zyklus; Kreislauf | There are four seasons in the *cycle* of a year. |
| | **rise** [raɪz] | Anstieg; Zunahme | There's a *rise* in the world's population every year. |
| | **fall** [fɔ:l] | Abnahme | *fall* ↔ rise |
| | **gene** [dʒi:n] | Gen | Our *genes* determine our lives in many ways. |
| | **cognitive** ['kɒgnətɪv] | kognitiv | = referring to the mind |
| | **performance** [pə'fɔ:məns] | Leistung | Most people's cognitive *performance* is better in the morning than in the afternoon. |
| | **metabolism** [mə'tæblɪzm] | Stoffwechsel | |
| | **and so on** [ənd 'səʊˌɒn] | und so weiter | I love animals like dogs, cats, horses, rabbits, guinea pigs, *and so on*. |

| mismatch ['mɪsmætʃ] | Missverhältnis | I'm sorry, Ryan, but there's a *mismatch* between what you say and what you do. |
|---|---|---|
| well-suited (to doing sth) [ˌwel'su:tɪd] | geeignet (für/um zu); passend (für) | I hate the sight of blood. I'm not *well-suited* to being a doctor. |
| to **rise** [raɪz] | aufstehen | = a more formal way to say 'to get up' |
| deprived [dɪ'praɪvd] | beraubt; entzogen | *deprived* → deprivation |
| well-known [ˌwel'nəʊn] | (wohl) bekannt | My uncle is a *well-known* scientist. |
| researcher [rɪ'sɜːtʃə] | Forscher/-in | *researcher* → to research → research |
| evidence *(no pl)* ['evɪdns] | Beweis; Beleg; Beweismaterial | Is there any *evidence* he's a criminal?<br>*Fr.* évidence *(f)* |
| to **point to** ['pɔɪnt tə] | deuten auf; hindeuten auf; zeigen auf | Everything we know *points to* that result. |
| outcome ['aʊtkʌm] | Ergebnis; Resultat | *outcome* = result |

## Station 2: How to: Write a text analysis

| 7 | to **relate to** [rɪ'leɪt tə] | nachvollziehen; sich identifizieren mit; verstehen | I can't *relate to* the arguments in the text. I see it differently. |
|---|---|---|---|
| | objective [əb'dʒektɪv] | objektiv | = not influenced by any personal opinion |
| | scientific [ˌsaɪən'tɪfɪk] | wissenschaftlich; naturwissenschaftlich | *scientific* → science → scientist<br>*Fr.* scientifique |
| | to **aim to do sth** [eɪm] | anstreben; abzielen auf | What do you *aim to do* in life? |
| | plenty of ['plentɪˌəv] | eine Menge | *plenty of* food = lots of food |
| | to **quote** [kwəʊt] | zitieren | The journalist *quoted* an expert from the police.<br>*to quote* → quote |
| | balance ['bæləns] | Gleichgewicht | In the article he finds a good *balance* between scientific and normal language.<br>*Fr.* balance *(f)* |
| | relevant ['reləvnt] | relevant; von Bedeutung | *relevant* ↔ irrelevant |

# Across cultures 1  The language of tolerance and respect

| | tolerance ['tɒlrns] | Toleranz | *Fr.* tolérance *(f)* |
|---|---|---|---|
| 1 | **goat** [gəʊt] | Ziege | |
| | beyond [bi'ɒnd] | jenseits; über … hinaus | If you look just *beyond* the lake, you'll see our house. |
| 2 | to **free** [fri:] | befreien | I wish I could *free* those poor kids who have to work on cocoa plantations.<br>*to free* → free → freedom |
| | various ['veərɪəs] | verschieden; verschiedenartig | There are *various* options of how to do this task. |
| | prejudice ['predʒədɪs] | Vorurteil | = a negative opinion or feeling |

| | | | |
|---|---|---|---|
| 3 | mainstream ['meɪnstriːm] | Masse; Durchschnitt; Massen-; Durchschnitts- | I don't like what everybody else likes, that's boring. I'm not into the *mainstream*. |
| | to **be prejudiced against sb/sth** [bi 'predʒədɪst ə‚genst] | voreingenommen sein gegenüber jmdm./etw. | *to be prejudiced against* → prejudice |
| | **race** [reɪs] | Rasse | |
| | to **provoke** [prə'vəʊk] | provozieren; hervorrufen | The president's speech *provoked* a lot of protest. *Lat.* provocare |
| | **willingly** ['wɪlɪŋli] | gern; freiwillig | |
| | **unwillingly** [ʌn'wɪlɪŋli] | ungern; widerwillig | |
| | **diversity** [daɪ'vɜːsəti] | Vielfalt; Verschiedenheit | We speak of cultural *diversity* when people of different races, nationalities, languages, sexual orientations and religions live in the same community. |
| | **street fair** ['striːt feə] | Straßenfest | I love all the different kinds of food and music at *street fairs*. |
| | **pedestrian** [pɪ'destriən] | Fußgänger/-in; Fußgänger- | You won't find as many *pedestrian* zones in America as you can find in Europe. |
| | **kiss** [kɪs] | Kuss | When they said goodbye, she gave him a *kiss*. |
| 4 | **respectful** [rɪ'spektfl] | respektvoll | *respectful* → respect *(n)* → to respect *(v)* |
| | **privacy** ['prɪvəsi] | Privatsphäre | You want people to respect your *privacy*, so it's only fair to respect theirs. |
| | to **assume** [ə'sjuːm] | annehmen | You can't *assume* everybody shares your likes and dislikes. |
| | **acceptable** [ək'septəbl] | akzeptabel; annehmbar | *acceptable* → to accept *Fr.* acceptable |
| 5 | to **bring up** [‚brɪŋ 'ʌp] | zur Sprache bringen | During the class discussion their teacher *brought up* all the problems there were among the students. |
| | **same-sex** [‚seɪm'seks] | gleichgeschlechtlich | Many countries, including quite a few in Europe, do a lot for *same-sex* rights. Some do very little. |
| | **lesbian** ['lezbiən] | lesbisch; Lesbe | |
| | **straight** [streɪt] | heterosexuell | *straight* ↔ gay/lesbian |
| | to **come out** [‚kʌm 'aʊt] | sich outen | Her parents never really knew much about gays or lesbians, but when Lisa *came out* they had no problem with it at all. |
| 8 | **sensitive** ['sensɪtɪv] | sensibel; empfindsam; heikel | 1. If you're *sensitive*, you're aware of other people's feelings. 2. A *sensitive* person can get annoyed very easily if sb says the wrong thing. |
| | **problematic** [‚prɒblə'mætɪk] | problematisch; schwierig | *problematic* → problem *Fr.* problématique |
| | **vulgar** ['vʌlgə] | vulgär; gewöhnlich | He always tells really dirty jokes; he's so *vulgar*. *vulgar* = rude |
| | to **embarrass** [ɪm'bærəs] | in Verlegenheit bringen | *to embarrass* → embarrassing → embarrassed |
| | to **spread** [spred], **spread** [spred], **spread** [spred] | (sich) verbreiten | If sth *spreads*, it reaches a larger and larger area or more and more people. |
| | **horrible** ['hɒrəbl] | schrecklich; furchtbar | *horrible* = terrible = awful *horrible* → horror |

| | | |
|---|---|---|
| **rumour** [ˈruːmə] | Gerücht | There are *rumours* that she's left him. – Well, don't believe everything you hear.<br>= sth people say about sb that might not be true<br>*Fr.* rumeur *(f)* |
| to **take sth the wrong way** [ˌteɪkˌðə rɒŋ ˈweɪ] | etw. falsch auffassen; etw. in den falschen Hals bekommen | He *took* my joke *the wrong way.* |
| to **offend** [əˈfend] | beleidigen; verletzen | It really *offends* me when you make jokes about black people. My best friend is black, and anyway, it just isn't acceptable to talk like that, in my opinion. |

## Word families

| noun | adjective(s) | verb(s) | noun with prefix | adjective with prefix |
|---|---|---|---|---|
| tolerance | tolerant | to tolerate; to be tolerant; to show tolerance | intolerance | intolerant |
| respect | respectful | to respect; to show respect | disrespect | disrespectful |
| fairness | fair | to be fair | unfairness | unfair |
| embarrassment | embarrassed / embarrassing | to embarrass | | |
| offence | offensive | to offend | | |
| prejudice | | to show prejudice | | |
| | acceptable | to accept; to be acceptable | | |
| | appropriate | to be appropriate | | |
| racism | racist | to be racist | | |

# Unit 2  California dreaming

## Introduction

| | | |
|---|---|---|
| **skatepark** [ˈskeɪtpɑːk] | Skateboardanlage | *skatepark* → to skate → skates |
| **lounge** [laʊndʒ] | Lounge; Aufenthaltsraum | |
| **headquarters** *(pl)* [ˌhedˈkwɔːtəz] | Zentrale; Hauptsitz | Google *headquarters* are in Silicon Valley.<br>! Only used in the plural form. |
| 2 **skateboarder** [ˈskeɪtbɔːdə] | Skateboardfahrer/-in | *skateboarder* → skateboard → skateboarding |
| 3 **tendency** [ˈtendənsi] | Tendenz | For years, trends from California have had a *tendency* to spread quickly.<br>*Fr.* tendance *(f)* |
| **Mexican** [ˈmeksɪkn] | mexikanisch; Mexikanisch; aus Mexiko; Mexikaner/-in | *Mexicans* speak Spanish. |
| **pot** [pɒt] | Topf | We need new *pots* for our plants. |

| | | |
|---|---|---|
| **reason** ['riːzn] | Vernunft; Verstand | *reason* ↔ emotion<br>*Fr.* raison *(f)* |
| **governor** ['gʌvnə] | Gouverneur/-in | In the US each state has its own *governor*.<br>*governor* → government |
| to **observe** [əb'zɜːv] | beobachten; beachten; befolgen | Dolphins were *observed* near the coast yesterday.<br>*Fr.* observer |

## Station 1: Hollywood hopes

| | | |
|---|---|---|
| **aspiring** [ə'spaɪrɪŋ] | aufstrebend | = working hard to be successful |
| **luck** [lʌk] | Glück | He's going to try his *luck* in Hollywood. |
| to **stroll** [strəʊl] | schlendern; bummeln; spazieren | = to walk in a relaxed way |
| **that way** [ˌðæt 'weɪ] | so; auf diese Weise | Sorry, but it doesn't work *that way* in the entertainment business. |
| **glitz and glamor** *(AE) (no pl)* [ˌglɪts n̩ 'glæmə] | Glanz und Glamour | Many young actors in Hollywood hope for a life of *glitz and glamor*, but reality is often very different.<br>*glamor* → glamorous |
| to **keep one's head above water** [ˌkiːp wʌnz ˌhed əbʌv 'wɔːtə] | sich über Wasser halten | Entertaining tourists is just a job to *keep my head above water*. |
| to **showcase one's talent** [ˌʃəʊkeɪs wʌnz 'tælənt] | sein Talent unter Beweis stellen | The video *showcased their talent* as entertainers, but not as singers.<br>*to showcase* = to present |
| **lucky day** [ˌlʌki 'deɪ] | Glückstag | This is my *lucky day*: I've just found 100 dollars. |
| **cattle call** *(AE)* ['kætl ˌkɔːl] | Vorspielen; Vorsingen | *cattle call* = audition |
| **wannabe** *(infml)* ['wɒnəbi] | Möchtegern; Möchtegern- | You can find *wannabe* stars everywhere in Hollywood. |
| to **pack up** ['pæk ʌp] | zusammenpacken | = to put your things in a bag before you go away |
| to **chalk sth up to experience** [ˌtʃɔːk ʌp tə ɪk'spɪəriəns] | etw. als Erfahrung verbuchen | She's gone to at least 100 auditions so far and still hasn't gotten a role. She just *chalks it up to experience*. |
| **premiere** ['premieə] | Premiere; Uraufführung | ! Be careful with the pronunciation. |
| to **cause a stir** [ˌkɔːz ə 'stɜː] | für Aufsehen sorgen | She *caused a stir* when she fell down on the red carpet. |
| **RV park** *(AE)* [ˌɑːˈviː ˌpɑːk] | Campingplatz | |
| to **shoot** [ʃuːt] | drehen *(Film)* | At the school's Film Club we *shot* a film last year. |
| to **explode** [ɪk'spləʊd] | explodieren | In action films cars *explode* all the time. |
| **trailer** *(AE)* ['treɪlə] | Wohnwagen | In the US some people don't live in houses, they live in big *trailers*. |
| **extra** ['ekstrə] | Statist/-in; Komparse/Komparsin | As an *extra*, you can get a feeling for what life as an actor is like.<br>= a character in a film that doesn't speak<br>*extra* ↔ protagonist |
| **what it's all about** [ˌwɒt ɪts ˌɔːl ə'baʊt] | worum es geht | My grandpa always tells us *what life is all about*. |
| 1 **effort** ['efət] | Bemühung; Mühe | *Fr.* effort *(m)* |

| | | | |
|---|---|---|---|
| | to **pursue** [pəˈsjuː] | verfolgen | to *pursue* a dream/a goal<br>*to pursue sb/sth* = to follow sb/sth |
| | **persistent** [pəˈsɪstnt] | hartnäckig; ausdauernd; beharrlich | You have to be *persistent* in Hollywood, you can't give up too quickly. |
| | **relaxed** [rɪˈlækst] | entspannt; locker; gelassen | '*Relaxed*' is an adjective many people associate with California.<br>*relaxed* → to relax |
| | **suitable** [ˈsuːtəbl] | geeignet; passend | Why do you think you're *suitable* for the job? |
| 7 | **agent** [ˈeɪdʒnt] | Agent/-in | Every actor or singer needs an *agent*. |
| | to **catch** [kætʃ], **caught** [kɔːt], **caught** [kɔːt] | nehmen *(Zug, Bus)* | I need to *catch* the train at 1:15. |
| | **backstage** [ˌbækˈsteɪdʒ] | backstage; hinter der Bühne | If you have *backstage* tickets, there's a chance for you to meet the star personally. |
| 8 | **memorable** [ˈmemrəbl] | denkwürdig; unvergesslich | What a *memorable* moment it was when I took a selfie with my favorite star! |
| | to **nominate** [ˈnɒmɪneɪt] | nominieren; ernennen | = to suggest that sb should be chosen for an award |
| 10 | **founder** [ˈfaʊndə] | Gründer/-in | *founder* → to found |
| 11 | to **comprise** [kəmˈpraɪz] | umfassen; beinhalten; einschließen | The USA *comprises* 50 states.<br>*to comprise* = to include = to contain |
| | **producer** [prəˈdjuːsə] | Produzent/-in | To make a film, you need a director, actors, a *producer*, and lots of other people. |
| | **contribution** [ˌkɒntrɪˈbjuːʃn] | Beitrag; Beteiligung | What's your *contribution* to the party? Food, music? |
| | **as long as** [əz ˈlɒŋ əz] | solange | I'll lend you my car for your trip *as long as* you promise to drive carefully. |
| | **nominee** [ˌnɒmɪˈniː] | vorgeschlagener Kandidat/ vorgeschlagene Kandidatin | There are five *nominees* for the award. |
| | to **approve** [əˈpruːv] | anerkennen; gutheißen; genehmigen | My university application *has been approved*! |
| | **nomination** [ˌnɒmɪˈneɪʃn] | Nominierung; Ernennung | *nomination* → to nominate → nominee |
| | **in honor of** *(AE)* [ɪn ˈɒnər əv] | zu Ehren | |
| | **animated** [ˈænɪmeɪtɪd] | Zeichentrick- | *Animated* films are popular with people of all ages, not just with children. |

## Station 2: A golden state?

| | | | |
|---|---|---|---|
| | **golden** [ˈgəʊldn] | golden; Gold- | *golden* → gold |
| | **GDP** [ˌdʒiːdiːˈpiː] | BIP *(= Bruttoinlandsprodukt)* | The *GDP* (= *Gross Domestic Product*) refers to the total value of things and services produced in a country within a year. |
| | **income** [ˈɪnkʌm] | Einkommen | = the money you earn either from work or investments |
| | **explorer** [ɪkˈsplɔːrə] | Forscher/-in; Forschungsreisende/-r; Entdecker/-in | In the 16th century there were many Spanish *explorers* in North and South America.<br>*explorer* → to explore |
| | to **be said to** *(+ inf)* [bi ˈsed tə] | sollen; gelten als | French cooking *is said to* be the world's best, though many people would disagree. |

| to **exist** [ɪgˈzɪst] | existieren; bestehen | Do you think life after death *exists*?<br>*Fr.* exister |
| **wealth** [welθ] | Reichtum; Vermögen | *wealth* ↔ poverty<br>*wealth* → wealthy |
| **Californian** [ˌkælɪˈfɔːniən] | kalifornisch; Kalifornier/-in | |
| **Gold Rush** [ˈgəʊld ˌrʌʃ] | Goldrausch | The California *Gold Rush* took place in the 19th century. |
| **precious** [ˈpreʃəs] | wertvoll; kostbar | These old family photos are more *precious* to me than all the gold and silver in the world. |
| **metal** [ˈmetl] | Metall | *Fr.* métal *(m)*; *Lat.* metallum *(nt)* |
| to **boom** [buːm] | florieren; boomen | In 1855 Mud Springs *boomed* and changed its name to El Dorado. |
| to **remain** [rɪˈmeɪn] | bleiben | *to remain* = to stay |
| **sunny** [ˈsʌni] | sonnig | *sunny* → sun |
| **attraction** [əˈtrækʃn] | Anziehung; Anziehungskraft | California's climate is a big part of its *attraction* as a tourist destination. |
| **northern** [ˈnɔːðən] | nördlich; Nord- | *northern* – eastern – southern – western |
| **start-up company** [ˈstɑːtʌp ˌkʌmpəni] | Start-up (-Unternehmen); Unternehmensgründung | No place in the world is more famous for innovative *start-up companies* than California.<br>= a company that has been created based on a new idea |
| **dot-com bubble** [ˌdɒtkɒm ˈbʌbl] | Internetblase; Dotcom-Blase | |
| to **burst** [bɜːst], **burst** [bɜːst], **burst** [bɜːst] | bersten; platzen | The dot-com bubble *burst* in 2001. |
| **boom** [buːm] | wirtschaftlicher Aufschwung; Boom; Hochkonjunktur | California isn't the only US region to experience an IT *boom* over the years; the Seattle area is another.<br>*boom* → to boom |
| **leading** [ˈliːdɪŋ] | führend | *leading* → to lead → leader |
| **worldwide** [ˌwɜːldˈwaɪd] | weltweit | Technology is one of the leading industries *worldwide*. |
| **agriculture** [ˈægrɪkʌltʃə] | Landwirtschaft; Agrikultur | *agriculture* ↔ industry<br>*Lat.* ager *(m)* + cultura *(f)* |
| **fortune** [ˈfɔːtʃuːn] | Vermögen; Reichtum | My uncle made a *fortune* with buying and selling cars. |
| to **last** [lɑːst] | dauern; andauern; anhalten | Hot weather doesn't usually *last* very long. |
| **shortage** [ˈʃɔːtɪdʒ] | Knappheit; Mangel | If there's a *shortage* of sth, there isn't enough of it.<br>*shortage* → short |
| **drought** [draʊt] | Dürre; Trockenheit | ! 'Drought' rhymes with 'out'. |
| to **urge sb to do sth** [ɜːdʒ] | jmdn. zu etw. drängen | = to encourage sb very strongly to do sth |
| **cultivation** [ˌkʌltɪˈveɪʃn] | Anbau | The *cultivation* of fruit and vegetables needs a lot of water. |
| **Hispanic** [hɪˈspænɪk] | lateinamerikanisch; Latino/Latina; Hispano-Amerikaner/-in | He comes from Mexico, so he's *Hispanic*. |
| **border** [ˈbɔːdə] | Grenze | A large number of people cross the US-Mexican *border* illegally each year to try to start a better life in the US. |
| to **guard** [gɑːd] | bewachen | Many Americans feel the US-Mexican border isn't *guarded* well enough. |

| to **close down** [ˌkləʊz ˈdaʊn] | den Betrieb einstellen; schließen | A lot of mining companies have had to *close down* over the last several years. |
|---|---|---|
| 14 **silicon** [ˈsɪlɪkən] | Silizium | |
| **component** [kəmˈpəʊnənt] | Bestandteil; Komponente | Almost all companies in our town produce *components* for the car industry. |
| **device** [dɪˈvaɪs] | Gerät; Vorrichtung | A smartphone is an electronic *device*. |
| to **be based** [bi ˈbeɪst] | ansässig sein | Hundreds of companies *are based* in Silicon Valley. |
| 15 **agricultural** [ˌægrɪˈkʌltʃrl] | landwirtschaftlich | *agricultural* → agriculture |
| 16 **entrepreneur** [ˌɒntrəprəˈnɜː] | Unternehmer/-in | |
| 19 **strawberry** [ˈstrɔːbri] | Erdbeere | |
| **grape** [greɪp] | Traube | |
| to **export** [ɪkˈspɔːt] | exportieren; ausführen | *to export* → export<br>*Fr.* exporter |
| **minimum wage** [ˌmɪnɪməm ˈweɪdʒ] | Mindestlohn | Waiters in the US often only earn the *minimum wage*, which is why they depend on good tips to improve their income. |
| **seasonal** [ˈsiːznl] | saisonal; jahreszeitlich bedingt | Picking fruit is *seasonal* work. |
| **That doesn't pay my rent.** [ˌðət dʌznt ˌpeɪ maɪ ˈrent] | Davon kann ich meine Miete nicht bezahlen. | My dad's seasonal work *doesn't pay our rent*. |

---

### Collocations

**California**

agricultural / tech / entertainment industries
destroyed / protected nature / environment
healthy eating / food
illegal immigrants
immigration problems
sports / fitness craze
sporty / relaxed people
strong economy
sunny / hot / dry climate
technology / start-up companies
trendsetting hotspot / lifestyle / business

**Entertainment phrases**

aspiring actor; wannabe actor
glitz and glamor
to chalk sth up to experience
to find your pot of gold
to get a (big) role / a big break
to keep one's head above water
to live your dream; to make your dream come true
to shoot / film a scene
to showcase your talent
to try your luck
to wait for one's break / for a cattle call

*Write a dialogue between two friends: One sees only the positive aspects of California; the other sees the negative ones.*

| | | | |
|---|---|---|---|
| 20 | **decade** [ˈdekeɪd] | Jahrzehnt | = period of ten years<br>*Fr.* décade *(f)* |
| | **Latino** [ləˈtiːnəʊ] | lateinamerikanisch | In the US, there is a strong *Latino* influence in states like California, Arizona or Florida. |

## Station 3: Should we be worried?

| | | |
|---|---|---|
| **wildfire** [ˈwaɪldfaɪə] | Flächenbrand | OMG, that rumor about Ben is spreading like *wildfire*! |
| **incident** [ˈɪnsɪdnt] | Vorfall; Ereignis | Tell me about that horrible *incident* at school last week. |
| **tanker plane** [ˈtæŋkə ˌpleɪn] | Tankflugzeug | |
| **thanks to** [ˈθæŋks tə] | dank; wegen | Thank you for your help. *Thanks to* you we can go home earlier. |
| **climate change** [ˈklaɪmət ˌtʃeɪndʒ] | Klimawandel | A lot of people still don't believe in *climate change*. |
| to **increase** [ɪnˈkriːs] | zunehmen; wachsen | = to grow in size or number |
| to **coordinate** [kəʊˈɔːdɪneɪt] | koordinieren | |
| **emergency** [ɪˈmɜːdʒənsi] | Notfall; Notlage; Notfall- | That plane can't land, something's wrong with it – it's an *emergency*! |
| **flood** [flʌd] | Flut; Hochwasser; Überschwemmung | Too much rain can cause *floods*.<br>= a large amount of water (e.g. covering an area that is usually dry) |
| **mudslide** [ˈmʌdslaɪd] | Schlammlawine | *Mudslides* often come with floods.<br>*mudslide* → mud → muddy |
| **hillside** [ˈhɪlsaɪd] | Hang | Houses on a *hillside* with a nice view can be very expensive. |
| to **collapse** [kəˈlæps] | kollabieren; zusammenbrechen; einstürzen | = to fall down, to fall to the ground |
| to **be willing to do sth** [bi ˈwɪlɪŋ tə] | gewillt sein, etw. zu tun; bereit sein, etw. zu tun | How much *are* they *willing to* pay for the bike?<br>*to be willing to do sth* = to be prepared to do sth |
| to **cut down** [ˌkʌt ˈdaʊn] | fällen | To build the new neighborhood, they had to *cut down* a lot of trees. |
| **dehydration** [ˌdiːhaɪˈdreɪʃn] | Austrocknung | |
| **disease** [dɪˈziːz] | Krankheit | In refugee camps *diseases* spread quickly. |
| **bugs** *(pl)* [bʌgz] | Ungeziefer | We had to leave our holiday flat because there were *bugs* everywhere. |
| 22 **shall** [ʃæl] | sollen | **!** '*Shall*' is used in formal conversations. |
| to **be to** *(+ inf)* [ˈbi tə] | sollen | *to be to* = should |
| **ought to** *(+ inf)* [ˈɔːt tə] | sollen | *ought to* = should |
| to **be required to** *(+ inf)* [bi rɪˈkwaɪəd tə] | müssen | We*'re required to* clean the street in front of the house every week. |
| to **be obliged to** *(+ inf)* [bi əˈblaɪdʒd tə] | verpflichtet sein, etw. zu tun; müssen | Nurses *are obliged to* work on weekends. |
| 23 **on average** [ɒnˈævrɪdʒ] | durchschnittlich; im Durchschnitt | *On average* around 10,000 people visit the shopping center every day. |

| | | |
|---|---|---|
| **unusual** [ʌnˈjuːʒl] | ungewöhnlich | *unusual* ↔ usual |
| **slight** [slaɪt] | gering; leicht | A *slight* difference between two things is a very small one. |
| **crack** [kræk] | Riss; Spalt | Look, there's a new *crack* in that wall. How did that happen? |
| **recorded history** [rɪˌkɔːdɪd ˈhɪstri] | *hier:* Aufzeichnung | *Recorded history* shows that there haven't been any earthquakes here for the past 50 years. |
| **all but** [ˈɔːl bʌt] | alle bis auf | *All but* two of the students passed the exam. |
| **indoors** [ˌɪnˈdɔːz] | im Inneren | = inside, in a building |
| **outdoors** [ˌaʊtˈdɔːz] | im Freien | *outdoors* ↔ indoors |
| **smell** [smel] | Geruch; Duft; Gestank | Oh, what a terrible *smell*! <br> *smell* → to smell |
| **damage** [ˈdæmɪdʒ] | Schaden; Beschädigung | Natural disasters like earthquakes can cause a lot of *damage*. |
| **aftershock** [ˈɑːftəʃɒk] | Nachbeben | After the earthquake there were at least ten *aftershocks*. |
| 24 **conservation** [ˌkɒnsəˈveɪʃn] | Schutz; Erhaltung | The *conservation* of nature is one of our most important tasks. |
| 26 **eating** [ˈiːtɪŋ] | Essen; Ess- | A lot of people don't know what healthy *eating* means because they've never had healthy food. |
| 28 **smooth** [smuːð] | glatt; weich; geschmeidig | Feel this wood – it's really *smooth*. |
| **transition** [trænˈzɪʃn] | Übergang | *Transitions* in a presentation should be smooth. |

## True and false friends

*Many English words look like German words. But you have to be careful; there are different categories you need to be aware of:*

1. **True friends:** *These are words that look the same (often with very small differences in spelling) and have the same meaning, for example 'address', 'camera', 'camel', etc.*
2. **False friends:** *These are words that look the same but have a completely **different** meaning:*

| | | |
|---|---|---|
| to become = werden (≠ bekommen) | to grab = greifen (≠ graben) | sea = Meer (≠ See) |
| brave = mutig (≠ brav) | gym(nasium) = Turnhalle (≠ Gymnasium) | sensible = vernünftig (≠ sensibel) |
| chef = Koch (≠ Chef) | handy = handlich (≠ Handy) | to spend = ausgeben (≠ spenden) |
| chips = Pommes frites (≠ Chips) | map = Karte (≠ Mappe) | while = während (≠ weil) |
| director = Regisseur (≠ Direktor) | murder = Mord (≠ Mörder) | where = wo (≠ wer) |
| fabric = Stoff (≠ Fabrik) | photograph = Foto (≠ Fotograf) | to wink = zwinkern (≠ winken) |
| familiar = vertraut (≠ familiär) | plate = Teller (≠ Platte) | who = wer (≠ wo) |
| gift = Geschenk (≠ Gift) | receipt = Quittung, Beleg (≠ Rezept) | to wonder = sich fragen (≠ sich wundern) |

3. *Another category to be aware of: English words which have been taken into German, but used in ways that English speakers wouldn't understand:*
   Handy → mobile (phone) / cell (phone) → In English, 'handy' is an adjective which means *handlich, geschickt*. It isn't a noun.)
   Smoking → tuxedo → In English, 'smoking' refers only to *Rauchen*, not to clothing.

4. *Be careful! There are also German words which look like English ones but which don't exist in English at all!*
   Fitnessstudio → gym
   Mobbing → bullying
   Showmaster → TV host

## Skills: What's important for a handout?

| | | |
|---|---|---|
| **handout** ['hændaʊt] | Informationsblatt; Arbeitsblatt | = a piece of paper that gives important information (e.g. from a talk) |
| 2 **chef** [ʃef] | Koch; Küchenchef | ! False friend:<br>der Chef = the boss<br>der Koch = the *chef* |
| **training** ['treɪnɪŋ] | Ausbildung | The restaurant's chef received his *training* in different hotels. |
| **substance** ['sʌbstns] | Substanz; Gehalt | |
| **craft** [krɑːft] | Handwerk; Gewerbe | = traditional skill of making things by hand |
| **deep fryer** [ˌdiːp 'fraɪə] | Fritteuse | You can make chips in a *deep fryer*. |
| **freezer** ['friːzə] | Tiefkühlschrank | If you keep food in the *freezer*, it stays fresh. |

## Unit task: My star for the Walk of Fame

| | | |
|---|---|---|
| **selection** [sɪ'lekʃn] | Auswahl; Auswahl- | *selection* → to select |
| **politics** *(pl only)* ['pɒlətɪks] | Politik | ! 'Politics' is usually used with the singular form of the verb:<br>I think *politics* **is** important. |
| **obstacle** ['ɒbstəkl] | Hindernis | |
| to **overcome** [ˌəʊvə'kʌm] | überwinden | Sad experiences can be very difficult to *overcome*. |

## Story: Famous

| | | |
|---|---|---|
| 1 **tabloid** ['tæblɔɪd] | Boulevardzeitung | *Bild* is a German *tabloid*. |
| to **specialize in** *(AE)* ['speʃlaɪzˌɪn] | sich spezialisieren auf | My dad is a doctor, he *specializes in* heart diseases. |
| to **insist (on)** [ɪn'sɪstˌɒn] | insistieren; bestehen auf | Are you sure it's OK for us to stay in your apartment in New York? – Absolutely. I *insist*!<br>*Fr.* insister |
| to **stalk sb** [stɔːk] | jmdn. stalken; jmdm. nachstellen | Why do people *stalk* other people? That's so weird. |
| to **harass** ['hærəs; hə'ræs] | belästigen; drangsalieren | A lot of stars are *harassed* by their fans. |
| to **photograph** ['fəʊtəgrɑːf] | fotografieren | = to take a photo<br>*to photograph* → photographer |
| 5 **fame** [feɪm] | Ruhm | *fame* → famous |
| **anonymity** [ænə'nɪməti] | Anonymität | *Anonymity* is something famous people often miss most of all. |
| **normality** [nɔː'mæləti] | Normalität | *normality* → normal |

<table>
<tr><td></td><td>AE 🇺🇸</td><td>BE 🇬🇧</td></tr>
</table>

| | AE 🇺🇸 | BE 🇬🇧 |
|---|---|---|
| **Different spelling** | glamor, humor, neighbor<br>center, meter<br>to organize, to realize, to recognize<br>specialty, jewelry<br>to practice<br>traveling | glamour, humour, neighbour<br>centre, metre<br>to organise, to realise, to recognise<br>speciality, jewellery<br>to practise<br>travelling |
| **Different words** | apartment<br>grade<br>have/has gotten<br>highway, freeway<br>movie<br>period<br>RV park<br>soccer<br>store<br>subway<br>trailer<br>vacation | flat<br>class<br>have/has got<br>motorway<br>film<br>lesson<br>camping area<br>football<br>shop<br>underground<br>camper<br>holiday(s) |

# Text smart 2  Argumentative texts

## Introduction

| | | |
|---|---|---|
| **letter to the editor**<br>[ˌletə tʊ ðiˈedɪtə] | Leserbrief | *Letters to the editor* are reader reactions to news reports. |
| **editor** [ˈedɪtə] | Herausgeber/-in; Redakteur/-in | = 1. sb who works as the head of a newspaper or magazine;<br>= 2. sb who writes articles or checks other writers' articles |
| **argumentative essay**<br>[ɑːgjəˌmentətɪvˈeseɪ] | Erörterung | An *argumentative essay* needs to be convincing, but sorry, this essay isn't. |
| **frequent** [ˈfriːkwənt] | häufig | FAQs are *frequently*-asked questions. |
| 1 | **to speak out (about sth)**<br>[ˌspiːkˈaʊt] | seine Meinung (über etw.) deutlich vertreten; sich (zu etw.) äußern | Paul is always the first to *speak out about* things he thinks are wrong or unfair. |
| **insult** [ˈɪnsʌlt] | Beleidigung | Fair criticism is one thing, but there's nothing fair about a nasty *insult*. |
| **contestant** [kənˈtestnt] | Kandidat/-in | = sb who takes part in a competition, quiz, show, etc.<br>**!** Be careful with the word stress. |
| **to break down** [ˌbreɪkˈdaʊn] | zusammenbrechen | I've never seen dad so emotional, but he really *broke down* and cried after he heard about the accident. |
| **one-sided** [ˌwʌnˈsaɪdɪd] | einseitig | If an article features *one-sided* arguments, it isn't objective. |

| 2 | to **criticise** [ˈkrɪtɪsaɪz] | kritisieren | = to point out what is negative or bad about sth or sb<br>*to criticise* → criticism<br>*Fr.* critiquer |
|---|---|---|---|
| | to **tolerate** [ˈtɒlreɪt] | tolerieren; dulden | I can *tolerate* a lot, but I've really had enough of his insults.<br>*Fr.* tolérer |

## Station 1: How to: Write a letter to the editor

| 3 | **basically** [ˈbeɪsɪkli] | eigentlich; grundsätzlich; im Grunde genommen | You're *basically* right, but please consider my arguments too. |
|---|---|---|---|
| | **psychologist** [saɪˈkɒlədʒɪst] | Psychologe/Psychologin | *Psychologists* help people with their problems.<br>**!** Be careful with the pronunciation. |
| | **My point is …** [ˌmaɪ ˈpɔɪnt ɪz] | Was ich sagen will ist, … | *My point is* that talent shows don't need a jury. |
| | **host** [həʊst] | Gastgeber/-in; Talkmaster | In the US, many TV show *hosts* are bigger stars than their guests. |
| 4 | **as far as** [əz ˈfɑːr əz] | soweit | *As far as* I know, talent shows are still very popular, aren't they? |
| 5 | to **bet** [bet], **bet** [bet], **bet** [bet] | wetten | I *bet* you £10 that our team will win! |
| 6 | to **insult** [ɪnˈsʌlt] | beleidigen | = to say rude things about sb or to treat sb unfairly<br>*to insult* → insult<br>*Fr.* insulter |

## Station 2: How to: Write an argumentative essay

| | to **fail sb** [feɪl] | jmdn. hängenlassen; jmdn. im Stich lassen | |
|---|---|---|---|
| | **sex** [seks] | Geschlecht; Sexualität | |
| | to **be confronted with** [bi kənˈfrʌntɪd wɪð] | konfrontiert werden mit | On TV, we're often *confronted with* images which are difficult to look at.<br>= to face something that you have to deal with or react to |
| | to **present sb with sth** [prɪˈzent wɪð] | jmdm. etw. bieten | Adverts *present us with* a lot of things we don't need, but which we often want. |
| | **sporty** [ˈspɔːti] | sportlich | *sporty* → sport |
| | **chest** [tʃest] | Busen | |
| | **muscular** [ˈmʌskjələ] | muskulös | Football players often have very *muscular* legs. |
| | **irresponsible** [ˌɪrɪˈspɒnsəbl] | unverantwortlich; leichtsinning | He acted *irresponsibly* when he left the kids on their own.<br>*irresponsible* ↔ responsible |
| | **exception** [ɪkˈsepʃn] | Ausnahme | People with a perfect body are the *exception* and not the rule. |
| | **secondly** [ˈsekndli] | zweitens | First, I have to say that … And *secondly*, … |
| | **high-level** [ˌhaɪˈlevl] | Spitzen-; auf höchster Ebene | Wow, what a difference: In that suit, you look like a *high-level* businessman! |
| | to **look up to sb** [lʊk ˈʌp tə] | zu jmdm. aufschauen; jmdn. bewundern | Teenagers often *look up to* rock or film stars. |

| material [mə'tɪəriəl] | materiell | How many *material* things do we really need, and how many do we simply want? |
|---|---|---|
| **outdated** [ˌaʊt'deɪtɪd] | veraltet; überholt | I say his views are *outdated*, but he insists they're just traditional.<br>*outdated* = old-fashioned<br>*outdated* ↔ modern |
| **perfection** [pə'fekʃn] | Perfektion; Vollkommenheit | *perfection* → perfect |
| **realism** ['rɪəlɪzm] | Realismus; Realitätssinn | *realism* → real → realistic |
| **role model** ['rəʊl ˌmɒdl] | Vorbild | My *role model* is my older sister. |
| 10 to **stop sb from doing sth** ['stɒp frəm] | jmdn. davon abhalten, etw. zu tun | You can't *stop me from doing* what I want, so don't even try. |

## Across cultures 2  Having a voice

| to **have a voice** [ˌhæv ə 'vɔɪs] | ein Mitspracherecht haben | |
|---|---|---|
| **participation** [pɑːˌtɪsɪ'peɪʃn] | Mitwirkung; Beteiligung | *participation* → to participate |
| to **make one's voice heard** [ˌmeɪk wʌnz ˌvɔɪs 'hɜːd] | sich Gehör verschaffen | How can we *make our voices heard*? |
| 1 **student council** [ˌstjuːdnt 'kaʊnsl] | Schülerrat | The *Student Council* meets every Monday after school. |
| **vote** [vəʊt] | Abstimmung; Stimme; Wahl | A candidate has to earn my *vote*; then I might vote for him/her.<br>*vote* → to vote |
| to **make a difference (to sth)** [ˌmeɪk ə 'dɪfrəns] | etw. verändern | A lot of votes can *make a difference*. |
| to **admire** [əd'maɪə] | bewundern | Everyone *admires* a hero.<br>**Fr.** admirer; **Lat.** admirari |
| **activist** ['æktɪvɪst] | Aktivist/-in *(jmd. der sich für etw. engagiert)* | *activist* → active → activity |
| **banner** ['bænə] | Banner; Spruchband; Transparent | |
| to **make one's point** [ˌmeɪk wʌnz 'pɔɪnt] | seinen Standpunkt deutlich machen | You needn't shout to *make your point*. |
| to **believe in sb/sth** [bɪ'liːv ɪn] | an jmdn./etw. glauben | Betty *believes in* God. |
| **petition** [pə'tɪʃn] | Petition; Unterschriftenliste | Most students signed the *petition* for a new gym. |
| to **do one's bit** [ˌduː wʌnz 'bɪt] | seinen Teil beitragen | We all should *do our bit* to protect the environment. |
| **global** ['gləʊbl] | global; weltweit | A *global* problem is one that the whole world is confronted with. |
| **protection** [prə'tekʃn] | Schutz | *protection* → to protect |
| to **spray-paint** ['spreɪpeɪnt] | mit Farbe besprühen | The students were allowed to *spray-paint* the school's walls. |

| | | |
|---|---|---|
| **fur** [fɜː] | Fell; Pelz | *Fur* is the thick hair that covers the skin of many animals. |
| **coat** [kəʊt] | Mantel | |
| to **dictate** [dɪkˈteɪt] | diktieren; vorschreiben | Emma, you can't say you're tolerant and respectful of others' views when you always *dictate* YOUR views to everyone else. |
| 2 **belief** [bɪˈliːf] | Glaube; Überzeugung | *belief* → to believe (in) |
| **reward** [rɪˈwɔːd] | Belohnung; Preis | A *reward* of $100 has been offered to anybody who finds the stolen car. |
| to **take the lead** [ˌteɪk ðə ˈliːd] | die Führung übernehmen | My mum always *takes the lead* when we go hiking. |
| **bubble** [ˈbʌbl] | Blase | Can you make *bubbles* with chewing gum? |
| **bone** [bəʊn] | Knochen | Dogs love *bones*. |
| **valuable** [ˈvæljuəbl] | wertvoll | = sth that could be sold for a lot of money<br>*valuable* → value |
| 3 **representative** [ˌreprɪˈzentətɪv] | Repräsentant/-in; Stellvertreter/-in | *representative* → to represent |

## How words can start or end

*You already know a lot of words which can have prefixes and suffixes. Here is a new collection.*

### Adjectives

| | | | |
|---|---|---|---|
| dis- | honest, respectful, abled | desir(e), memor(y), suit, valu(e) | -able |
| im- | possible, patient | agricultur(e), glob(e), logic, season | -al |
| in- | direct, convenient, secure | grate, meaning, respect | -ful |
| ir- | regular, relevant, responsible | democrat, enthusiast | -ic |
| un- | able, comfortable, expected | biolog(y), hyster(y) | -ical |
| | | real, material | -istic |
| | | harm, home | -less |
| | | adventur(e), glamour | -ous |
| | | flirt, sport, trick | -y |

### Verbs

| | | | |
|---|---|---|---|
| dis- | appear, agree, obey | standard, symbol | -ise/ize |
| en- | courage | | |
| over- | come, hear | | |
| re- | build, read, tell, write | | |
| un- | wrap, pack | | |

*Find at least four more examples for adjectives and verbs with suffixes.*

In dieser alphabetischen Wortliste findest du das gesamte Vokabular von *Green Line* 1 bis 6.
Namen stehen in einer extra Liste am Ende des *Dictionary*.
Einträge, die aus mehreren Wörtern bestehen, kannst du meist unter verschiedenen
Stichwörtern nachschlagen. So ist z.B. *after all* unter *after* und unter *all* eingetragen.
Die Fundstellen stehen immer hinter dem jeweiligen Wort und zeigen dir an, wo es zum ersten Mal vorkommt, z. B.:
**to acknowledge** [ək'nɒlɪdʒ] anerkennen; einräumen **VI U1**, 22 kommt zum ersten Mal vor in Band 6, Unit 1, Seite 22
**to admire** [əd'maɪə] bewundern **VI AC2**, 74 kommt zum ersten Mal vor in Band 6, Across cultures 2, Seite 74
**U = Unit**, **AC = Across cultures**, **TS = Text smart**
Die mit * gekennzeichneten Verben sind unregelmäßig.
Die mit ° gekennzeichneten Vokabeln sind rezeptiv.
Die mit ⟨ ⟩ gekennzeichneten Vokabeln sind fakultativ.

# A

**a** [ə] ein/-e **I**
　**a bit** [ə 'bɪt] ein bisschen; ein wenig **II**
　**a couple of** [ə 'kʌpl̩ əv] ein paar **I**
　**a few** [ə 'fjuː] ein paar; wenige; einige **I**
　**a girl from Germany** [ə ˌɡɜːl frəm 'dʒɜːməni] ein Mädchen aus Deutschland **I**
　**a group of three** [ə ˌɡruːp əv 'θriː] eine Dreiergruppe **I**
　**a little** [ə 'lɪtl̩] ein wenig; etwas **I**
　**a lot** [ə 'lɒt] viel **I**
　**a lot of** [ə 'lɒt əv] viel/-e; eine Menge **I**
　**a total of** [ə 'təʊtl̩ əv] insgesamt **V**
　**a (day/week/year)** [ə 'deɪ/wiːk/jɪə] pro (Tag/Woche/Jahr) **IV**
　**a lot to learn** [ə ˌlɒt tə 'lɜːn] viel zu lernen **I**
**a.m.** [ˌeɪ'em] vormittags *(Uhrzeit)* **I**
**to abandon** [ə'bændən] aufgeben; zurücklassen **V**
**ability** [ə'bɪləti] Fähigkeit **VI U1**, 24
***to be able to** (do sth) [bi ˌ'eɪbl̩ tə] fähig sein zu; können; dürfen **II**
**aboard** [ə'bɔːd] an Bord **I**
**Aboriginal** [ˌæbə'rɪdʒɪnl̩] von australischen Ureinwohnern abstammend **V**
**about** [ə'baʊt] ungefähr; circa; etwa **I**
**about** [ə'baʊt] über; von **I**
　***to be about to** do sth [bi ə'baʊt tə] im Begriff sein, etw. zu tun **IV**
　**out and about** [ˌaʊt ən ə'baʊt] unterwegs **II**
　**What about …?** ['wɒt ˌəbaʊt] Wie wär's mit …?; Was ist mit …? **I**
　**What is … about?** [wɒt ɪz …ə'baʊt] Worum geht es in/im …? **I**
　**what it's all about** [wɒt ɪts ɔːl ə'baʊt] worum es geht **VI U2**, 46
**above** [ə'bʌv] oben **II**
**abridged** [ə'brɪdʒd] gekürzt °**VI U1**, 26
**abroad** [ə'brɔːd] im Ausland; ins Ausland **IV**
**abrupt** [ə'brʌpt] abrupt **V**
**absolutely** [ˌæbsə'luːtli] absolut; völlig **II**
**abstract** ['æbstrækt] abstrakt **V**
**absurdity** [əb'zɜːdəti] Absurdität ⟨**VI U1**, 26⟩
**accent** ['æksnt] Akzent **III**

**to accept** [ək'sept] akzeptieren; hinnehmen; annehmen **IV**
**acceptable** [ək'septəbl̩] akzeptabel; annehmbar **VI AC1**, 41
**accident** ['æksɪdnt] Unfall **II**
**accidentally** [ˌæksɪ'dentli] versehentlich; aus Versehen ⟨**VI U2**, 61⟩
**according to** [ə'kɔːdɪŋ tə] laut; gemäß **V**
**account settings** [ə'kaʊnt ˌsetɪŋz] Profileinstellungen **III**
**to achieve** [ə'tʃiːv] erreichen; erlangen **V**
**acid rain** [ˌæsɪd 'reɪn] saurer Regen ⟨**VI U2**, 56⟩
**to acknowledge** [ək'nɒlɪdʒ] anerkennen; einräumen **VI U1**, 22
**across** [ə'krɒs] auf der anderen Seite von; über; hinüber; herüber; quer durch **I**
　**Across** cultures [əˌkrɒs 'kʌltʃəz] Interkulturelles **I**
**to act** [ækt] spielen *(Theater)* **I**; sich verhalten; handeln **IV**
　**to act** like ['ækt laɪk] tun als ob **II**
　**to act out** [ækt 'aʊt] nachspielen **II**
　**acting** a scene [ˌæktɪŋ ə 'siːn] eine Theaterszene spielen **I**
**acting** ['æktɪŋ] Schauspielen **III**
**action** ['ækʃn] Handlung; Action; Aktion **I**
**active** ['æktɪv] aktiv **III**
**activist** ['æktɪvɪst] Aktivist/-in *(jmd. der sich für etw. engagiert)* **VI AC2**, 74
**activity** [æk'tɪvəti] Aktivität **II**
**actor** ['æktə] Schauspieler **II**
**actual** ['æktʃuəl] tatsächlich; wirklich; eigentlich **IV**
**ad** [əd'vɜːtɪsmənt] Anzeige; Werbespot **IV**
　**ad** copy ['æd ˌkɒpi] Werbetext **IV**
**AD** (= Anno Domini) [eɪ'diː] nach Christus **III**
film **adaptation** [ˌfɪlm ˌædæp'teɪʃn] Verfilmung °**VI U1**, 22
**adapted** [ə'dæptɪd] adaptiert; angepasst **V**
**to add** [æd] hinzufügen; ergänzen **V**
**addict** ['ædɪkt] Süchtige/-r; Abhängige/-r **IV**
**addiction** [ə'dɪkʃn] Sucht; Abhängigkeit ⟨**VI U1**, 7⟩
　cyber **addiction** ['saɪbər əˌdɪkʃn] Internetsucht; Internetabhängigkeit ⟨**VI TS1**, 39⟩
***to be addictive** [bi əˌ'dɪktɪv] süchtig machen ⟨**VI TS1**, 39⟩

**addition** [ə'dɪʃn] Zusatz; Ergänzung **VI U1**, 11
　in **addition** to [ɪn əˌ'dɪʃn tə] neben; daneben; darüber hinaus **V**
**additional** [ə'dɪʃnl̩] zusätzlich **II**
**address** [ə'dres] Adresse **I**
**to address** [ə'dres] ansprechen; sich wenden an **II**
**adjective** ['ædʒɪktɪv] Adjektiv; Eigenschaftswort **II**
**to admire** [əd'maɪə] bewundern **VI AC2**, 74
**to admit** [əd'mɪt] zugeben ⟨**VI U2**, 61⟩
**to adopt** [ə'dɒpt] übernehmen; annehmen; adoptieren ⟨**VI U2**, 57⟩
**adult** ['ædʌlt] Erwachsene/-r **II**
**to advance** [əd'vɑːns] vorantreiben ⟨**VI U2**, 62⟩
**advantage** [əd'vɑːntɪdʒ] Vorteil **V**
**adventure** [əd'ventʃə] Abenteuer **II**
**adventurous** [əd'ventʃrəs] abenteuerlich; unternehmungslustig; wagemutig; experimentierfreudig **VI U1**, 6
**adverb** ['ædvɜːb] Adverb **II**
**adverbial** clause [əd̩ˌvɜːbiəl 'klɔːz] Adverbialsatz **V**
**advert** ['ædvɜːt] Anzeige; Werbespot **III**
**to advertise** ['ædvətaɪz] Werbung machen; werben; anpreisen; inserieren **IV**
**advertisement** [əd'vɜːtɪsmənt] Anzeige; Werbespot **III**
**advertiser** ['ædvətaɪzə] Werbefachmann/-frau **IV**
**advertising** *(no pl)* ['ædvətaɪzɪŋ] Werbung; Reklame **IV**
**advice** [əd'vaɪs] Rat; Ratschlag **II**
**to affect** [ə'fekt] beeinflussen; beeinträchtigen; betreffen **V**
**to afford** [ə'fɔːd] sich leisten **III**
***to be afraid** (of) [bi ə'freɪd əv] (sich) fürchten; Angst haben (vor) **IV**
　I'm **afraid** … [ˌaɪm ə'freɪd] Leider … **IV**
**after** ['ɑːftə] nach *(zeitlich)* **I**; nachdem **V**
　**after** all [ˌɑːftər 'ɔːl] doch; schließlich; immerhin **I**
　**after** that [ˌɑːftə 'ðæt] danach **I**; nachdem **V**
**afternoon** [ˌɑːftə'nuːn] Nachmittag **I**
　this **afternoon** [ðɪs 'ɑːftənuːn] heute Nachmittag **II**

**aftershock** ['ɑːftəʃɒk] Nachbeben **VI U2**, 55

**afterwards** ['ɑːftəwədz] danach; hinterher **IV**

**again** [ə'gen] wieder; noch einmal; noch mal **I**

    over and over **again** [ˌəʊvər ən ˌəʊvər ə'gen] immer wieder **III**

**against** [ə'genst] gegen **II**

    **against** all odds [ə,genst ɔːl 'ɒdz] entgegen allen Erwartungen **III**

**age** [eɪdʒ] Alter; Zeitalter **III**

    Bronze **Age** ['brɒnz eɪdʒ] Bronzezeit (ca. 2200–800 v. Chr.) **III**

    golden **age** [ˌgəʊldn 'eɪdʒ] goldenes Zeitalter **III**

**aged** [eɪdʒd] im Alter von (**VI TS1**, 39)

travel **agency** ['trævl ˌeɪdʒnsi] Reisebüro **III**

**agent** ['eɪdʒnt] Agent/-in **VI U2**, 48

    travel **agent's** ['trævl ˌeɪdʒnts] Reisebüro **III**

**aggressive** [ə'gresɪv] aggressiv **II**

**ago** [ə'gəʊ] vor (zeitlich) **II**

**agony** aunt ['ægəni ˌɑːnt] Kummerkastentante **II**

to **agree** (on) [ə'griː] sich einigen (auf) **III**

    to **agree** (with) [ə'griː] einer Meinung sein (mit); zustimmen **II**

**agreement** [ə'griːmənt] Übereinstimmung; Einigkeit °**VI AC2**, 75

**agricultural** [ˌægrɪ'kʌltʃrl] landwirtschaftlich **VI U2**, 51

**agriculture** ['ægrɪkʌltʃə] Landwirtschaft; Agrikultur **VI U2**, 50

to **aim** to do sth [eɪm] anstreben; abzielen auf **VI TS1**, 38

**ain't** (= isn't/aren't) [eɪnt] ist nicht; sind nicht; hat/haben nicht **IV**

**air** [eə] Luft **III**

    **air** ambulance ['eər ˌæmbjələns] Rettungshubschrauber **V**

**air-conditioning** [ˌeəkən'dɪʃnɪŋ] Klimaanlage **IV**

**airline** ['eəlaɪn] Fluggesellschaft (**VI TS2**, 73)

**airplane** ['eəpleɪn] Flugzeug **V**

**airport** ['eəpɔːt] Flughafen **II**

**aka** [ˌeɪkeɪ'eɪ] alias **IV**

**alarm** [ə'lɑːm] Alarm **VI U1**, 19

    **alarm** clock [ə'lɑːm ˌklɒk] Wecker **II**

**alcohol** (no pl) ['ælkəhɒl] Alkohol **V**

**alien** ['eɪliən] Außerirdische/-r; außerirdisches Wesen **I**

**aligned** [ə'laɪnd] ausgerichtet **V**

**alive** [ə'laɪv] lebend; am Leben; lebendig **V**

**all** [ɔːl] alle/-s; ganz **I**

    after **all** [ˌɑːftər'ɔːl] doch; schließlich; immerhin **I**

    **all** but ['ɔːl bʌt] alle bis auf **VI U2**, 55

    **all** day ['ɔːl deɪ] den ganzen Tag **II**

    **all** night ['ɔːl naɪt] die ganze Nacht **I**

    **all** of them ['ɔːl əv ˌðem] alle **I**

    **all** of us ['ɔːl əv ˌʌs] wir alle **III**

    **all** over ['ɔːl 'əʊvə] überall (in) **I**

**all** the time [ɔːl ðə 'taɪm] die ganze Zeit **II**

    at **all** [ət 'ɔːl] überhaupt **I**

    to start **all** over again [stɑːt ɔːl 'əʊvər ə,gen] ganz von vorn beginnen **V**

bowling **alley** ['bəʊlɪŋ ˌæli] Bowlingbahn **I**

to **allow** [ə'laʊ] erlauben; gestatten **V**

    *to be **allowed** to (do sth) [bi ə'laʊd tə] dürfen **II**

**allowance** (AE) [ə'laʊəns] Taschengeld **V**

**all-rounder** [ɔːl'raʊndə] Alleskönner/-in; Multitalent **VI U1**, 9

**almost** ['ɔːlməʊst] fast; beinahe **II**

**alone** [ə'ləʊn] allein; ohne fremde Hilfe **I**

    *to leave sb **alone** [liːv ə'ləʊn] jmdn. in Ruhe lassen **IV**

**along** [ə'lɒŋ] entlang **I**

    *to sing **along** [sɪŋ ə'lɒŋ] mitsingen **III**

    **along** for the ride [ə,lɒŋ fə ðə 'raɪd] mit dabei **IV**

**aloud** [ə'laʊd] laut **V**

**alphabet** ['ælfəbet] Alphabet **I**

**alphabetical** [ˌælfə'betɪkl] alphabetisch **II**

**already** [ɔːl'redi] schon; bereits **I**

**also** ['ɔːlsəʊ] auch **II**

**although** [ɔːl'ðəʊ] obwohl **IV**

**always** ['ɔːlweɪz] immer; ständig **I**

**amazed** [ə'meɪzd] erstaunt; verblüfft **IV**

**amazing** [ə'meɪzɪŋ] unglaublich; toll; erstaunlich **II**

**ambulance** ['æmbjələns] Krankenwagen **III**

    air **ambulance** ['eər ˌæmbjələns] Rettungshubschrauber **V**

**American** [ə'merɪkən] Amerikanisch; amerikanisch; aus Amerika; Amerikaner/-in **II**

    Native **American** [ˌneɪtɪv ə'merɪkən] Ureinwohner/-in Amerikas; Indianer/-in; indianisch **IV**

**among** [ə'mʌŋ] unter; inmitten **III**

**amount** (of) [ə'maʊnt] Menge **IV**

**an** [ən] ein/-e **I**

to **analyse** ['ænlaɪz] analysieren **V**

**analysis** [ə'næləsɪs] Analyse; Untersuchung **V**

to **analyze** (AE) ['ænlaɪz] analysieren **IV**

**ancestor** ['ænsestə] Vorfahr/-in; Ahn/-in **V**

**ancient** ['eɪnʃnt] alt; altertümlich; antik **V**

**and** [ænd; ənd] und **I**

    **and** so on [ənd 'səʊ ˌɒn] und so weiter **VI TS1**, 37

**angel** ['eɪndʒl] Engel **IV**

**anger** (no pl) ['æŋgə] Zorn; Wut **III**

**angry** ['æŋgri] wütend; zornig; verärgert; böse **I**

    *to make sb **angry** [meɪk 'æŋgri] jmdn. wütend machen; jmdn. verärgern **V**

**anguish** ['æŋgwɪʃ] Qual; Leid (**VI U1**, 23)

**animal** ['ænɪməl] Tier **I**

    **animal** shelter ['ænɪml ˌʃeltə] Tierheim **III**

**animated** ['ænɪmeɪtɪd] Zeichentrick- **VI U2**, 49

**ankle** ['æŋkl] Fußgelenk; Fußknöchel **II**

to twist your **ankle** [ˌtwɪst jɔːr 'æŋkl] sich den Knöchel verrenken **II**

**annex** [ə'neks] Nebengebäude; Anbau (**VI U1**, 23)

**anniversary** [ˌænɪ'vɜːsri] Jubiläum; Jahrestag **V**

to **announce** [ə'naʊns] ankündigen; durchsagen **IV**

**announcement** [ə'naʊnsmənt] Ankündigung; Durchsage **III**

**annoyed** [ə'nɔɪd] verärgert **V**

**anonymity** [ˌænə'nɪməti] Anonymität **VI U2**, 63

**anonymous** [ən'ɒnɪməs] anonym **II**

**another** [ə'nʌðə] ein/-e andere/-r/-s; noch ein/-e; ein/-e andere/-r/-s **I**

**answer** ['ɑːnsə] Antwort **I**

    short **answer** [ˌʃɔːt 'ɑːnsə] Kurzantwort **I**

to **answer** ['ɑːnsə] antworten; beantworten **I**

    to **answer** the phone [ˌɑːnsə ðə 'fəʊn] einen Anruf entgegennehmen **I**

    **answering** machine ['ɑːnsrɪŋ məˌʃiːn] Anrufbeantworter **I**

**anthem** ['ænθəm] Hymne **III**

**anxiety** [əŋ'zaɪəti] Angst; Sorge; Besorgnis (**VI U2**, 61)

**any** ['eni] irgendein/-e/-er; irgendwelche **I**

    not **any** more [ˌnɒt eni 'mɔː] nicht mehr **I**

    not … **any** [nɒt … eni] kein/-e/-en **I**

not **anymore** (AE) [ˌnɒt eni'mɔː] nicht mehr **IV**

**anyone** else [ˌeniwʌn 'els] jemand anderes **II**

not … **anything** [ˌnɒt 'eniθɪŋ] nichts **I**

    **Anything** else? [ˌeniθɪŋ'els] Sonst noch etwas? **I**

**anyway** ['eniweɪ] trotzdem; jedenfalls; sowieso **II**

**anywhere** ['eniweə] irgendwo; überall (egal, wo) **II**

    just about **anywhere** [ˌdʒʌst əˌbaʊt 'eniweə] praktisch überall **IV**

**apart** [ə'pɑːt] auseinander; getrennt **V**

    **apart** from [ə'pɑːt frəm] abgesehen von; außer **V**

**apartheid** [ə'pɑːtaɪt] Apartheid **V**

**apartment** (AE) [ə'pɑːtmənt] Apartment; Wohnung **IV**

to **apologise** [ə'pɒlədʒaɪz] sich entschuldigen **III**

**apology** [ə'pɒlədʒi] Entschuldigung **VI U1**, 23

**app** [æp] App **II**

to **appear** [ə'pɪə] auftauchen; erscheinen **V**

**appearance** [ə'pɪərns] Erscheinung; Aussehen; Auftritt **V**

**applause** [ə'plɔːz] Applaus; Beifall (**VI U1**, 22)

**apple** ['æpl] Apfel **I**

**applicant** ['æplɪkənt] Bewerber/-in **VI U1**, 8

**application** [ˌæplɪ'keɪʃn] Bewerbung; Antrag **VI U1**, 8; Bewerbungs- °**VI U1**, 7

    **application** letter [ˌæplɪ'keɪʃn ˌletə] Bewerbungsschreiben **VI U1**, 8

to **apply** (to) [ə'plaɪ tə] gelten (für); zutreffen (auf) **V**; anwenden (auf) °**VI AC1**, 41
to **apply** (for) [ə'plaɪ fə] sich bewerben (um); beantragen **V**
to **apply** for [ə'plaɪ fə] fragen nach ⟨**VI U1**, 23⟩
**approach** [ə'prəʊtʃ] Herangehensweise; Vorgehensweise; Ansatz; Annäherung **IV**
**appropriate** [ə'prəʊpriət] angemessen **III**
to **approve** [ə'pru:v] anerkennen; gutheißen; genehmigen **VI U2**, 49
**April** ['eɪprəl] April **I**
**Arab** ['ærəb] arabisch **IV**
**architect** ['ɑ:kɪtekt] Architekt/-in **II**
**architecture** ['ɑ:kɪtektʃə] Architektur **V**
**area** ['eəriə] Areal; Gebiet; Fläche **II**
run **area** ['rʌn ˌeəriə] Gehege; Auslauf **III**
to **argue** ['ɑ:gju:] argumentieren; streiten **IV**; erörtern **V**
**argument** ['ɑ:gjəmənt] Auseinandersetzung; Streit; Argument **III**
**argumentative** [ˌɑ:gjə'mentətɪv] erörternd **V**
**argumentative** essay [ɑ:gjəˌmentətɪv ˌ'eseɪ] Erörterung **VI TS2**, 68
**arm** [ɑ:m] Arm **II**
**armchair** ['ɑ:mtʃeə] Sessel **V**
**army** ['ɑ:mi] Armee **V**
**aroma** [ə'rəʊmə] Duft ⟨**VI U2**, 61⟩
**around** [ə'raʊnd] um … herum; umher **I**
*to be **around** [ˌbi: ə'raʊnd] da sein; zusammen sein mit **IV**
*to find one's way **around** [ˌfaɪnd wʌnz ˌweɪ ə'raʊnd] sich zurechtfinden **IV**
*to show sb **around** (a place) [ˌʃəʊ ə'raʊnd] jmdn. (an einem Ort) herumführen **V**
to turn **around** [tɜ:n (ə)'raʊnd] (sich) umdrehen; wenden **II**
**around** [ə'raʊnd] ungefähr; etwa **VI TS1**, 35
to **arrange** [ə'reɪndʒ] arrangieren; anordnen **III**
to **arrest** [ə'rest] festnehmen; verhaften **II**
**arrival** [ə'raɪvl] Ankunft; Ankommende/-r; Neuzugang **IV**
**arrivals** hall [ə'raɪvlz ˌhɔ:l] Ankunftshalle **IV**
to **arrive** [ə'raɪv] ankommen **III**
**arrow** ['ærəʊ] Pfeil **III**
**Art** [ɑ:t] Kunstunterricht **I**
**art** [ɑ:t] Kunst **II**
clip **art** ['klɪp ɑ:t] Clipart; Grafik °**VI U2**, 58
**artichoke** ['ɑ:tɪtʃəʊk] Artischocke ⟨**VI U2**, 57⟩
**article** ['ɑ:tɪkl] Artikel; Bericht (in einer Zeitschrift, Zeitung) **II**
definite **article** [ˌdefɪnət 'ɑ:tɪkl] bestimmter Artikel °**VI U2**, 51
reference **article** ['refrns ˌɑ:tɪkl] Referenzartikel **III**
**artist** ['ɑ:tɪst] Künstler/-in **IV**
**artwork** ['ɑ:twɜ:k] Illustrationen; Bebilderung **V**

**as** [æz; əz] als **II**
**as** if [əz 'ɪf] als ob **III**
**as** [æz] während; indem **I**; wie **II**
**as** … **as** [əz … əz] so … wie **I**
**as** far **as** [əz 'fɑ:r ˌəz] soweit **VI TS2**, 69
**as** long **as** [əz 'lɒŋ ˌəz] solange **VI U2**, 49
**as** soon **as** [əz 'su:n ˌəz] sobald **II**
**as** with ['æz wɪð] wie (auch) bei ⟨**VI U2**, 57⟩
… **as** well **as** … [əz 'wel ˌəz] sowie; und (auch) **V**
**as** best **as** I can remember [əz ˌbest əz ˌaɪ kæn rɪ'membə] soweit ich mich erinnern kann ⟨**VI U2**, 61⟩
**as** [æz; əz] da; weil **V**
to **ask** [ɑ:sk] fragen; bitten **I**
**Ask** about … ['ɑ:sk əˌbaʊt] Frage/Fragt nach … **I**
to **ask** for ['ɑ:sk fə] fragen nach; bitten um **I**
*to be **asleep** [ˌbi: ə'sli:p] schlafen **II**
*to fall **asleep** [ˌfɔ:l ə'sli:p] einschlafen **I**
**aspect** ['æspekt] Aspekt; Gesichtspunkt **IV**
**aspiring** [ə'spaɪrɪŋ] aufstrebend **VI U2**, 46
**assault** [ə'sɔ:lt] Übergriff; Angriff; Tätlichkeit ⟨**VI U2**, 61⟩
**assembly** [ə'sembli] Versammlung; Morgenappell **II**
**assessment** [ə'sesmənt] Bewertung; Einschätzung; Beurteilung °**VI TS1**, 38
to **assign** [ə'saɪn] zuordnen; übertragen **VI U1**, 22
**assignment** [ə'saɪnmənt] Aufgabe; Auftrag; Mission **VI U1**, 22
**assistant** [ə'sɪstnt] Assistent/-in; Verkäufer/-in **II**
**assistant** counsellor [əˌsɪstnt 'kaʊnslə] Hilfsbetreuer/-in **VI U1**, 8
sales **assistant** ['seɪlz əˌsɪstnt] Verkäufer/-in **VI U1**, 9
to **associate** [ə'səʊʃieɪt] assoziieren; verbinden **VI U1**, 9
**association** [əˌsəʊʃi'eɪʃn] Verband; Organisation **V**
to **assume** [ə'sju:m] annehmen **VI AC1**, 41
**astronaut** ['æstrənɔ:t] Astronaut/-in **IV**
**at** [æt; ət] in; auf; bei; an; um (bei Uhrzeitangaben) **I**
**at** 7:30 [ət ˌsevn̩ 'θɜ:ti] um halb acht **I**
**at** all [ət ˌ'ɔ:l] überhaupt **I**
**at** all times [ˌət ˌɔ:l 'taɪmz] immer; jederzeit; stets **VI U1**, 8
**at** first [ət 'fɜ:st] zuerst; zunächst **II**
**at** home [ət 'həʊm] zu Hause **I**
**at** last [ət 'lɑ:st] endlich; schließlich **I**
**at** least [ət 'li:st] mindestens; wenigstens **II**
**at** the back of [ət ðə 'bæk ˌəv] hinten; am Ende; im hinteren Teil **II**
**at** the moment [ət ðə 'məʊmənt] im Moment; gerade **I**
**at** the same time [ət ðə ˌseɪm 'taɪm] zur selben Zeit; gleichzeitig **I**

**at** the scene [ət ðə 'si:n] vor Ort **V**
**at** the time [ˌət ðə 'taɪm] damals **IV**
**at** the weekend [ət ðə ˌwi:k'end] am Wochenende **I**
**athletics** (no pl) [æθ'letɪks] Leichtathletik **IV**
**atlas** ['ætləs] Atlas **II**
**atmosphere** ['ætməsfiə] Atmosphäre; Stimmung **II**
to **attach** [ə'tætʃ] anfügen; anhängen ⟨**VI U2**, 52⟩
**attachment** [ə'tætʃmənt] Anhang **VI U1**, 11
**attack** [ə'tæk] Angriff; Überfall **V**
to **attack** [ə'tæk] angreifen **III**
**attendant** [ə'tendnt] Aufseher/-in; Wärter/-in ⟨**VI U1**, 23⟩
flight **attendant** ['flaɪt əˌtendnt] Flugbegleiter/-in **IV**
**attention** [ə'tenʃn] Aufmerksamkeit; Beachtung **II**
to grab **attention** [ˌgræb ə'tenʃn] Aufmerksamkeit erregen **V**
*to pay **attention** to sb/sth [ˌpeɪ ə'tenʃn tʊ] jmdn./etw. beachten **II**
**attic** ['ætɪk] Dachboden **II**
**attitude** ['ætɪtju:d] Haltung; Einstellung **IV**
to **attract** [ə'trækt] anziehen **IV**
**attraction** [ə'trækʃn] Attraktion; Sehenswürdigkeit **II**; Anziehung; Anziehungskraft **VI U2**, 50
**attractive** [ə'træktɪv] attraktiv **IV**
**atypical** [eɪ'tɪpɪkl] atypisch ⟨**VI U2**, 60⟩
**au pair** [ˌəʊ'peə] Au-pair **VI U1**, 12
**audience** ['ɔ:diəns] Publikum **II**
**audio** ['ɔ:diəʊ] Audio-; Hör- **I**
**audio** tour ['ɔ:diəʊ ˌtʊə] Audioführung **II**
**audio-visual** effect [ˌɔ:diəʊvɪʒuəl ɪ'fekt] audiovisueller Effekt **II**
**audition** [ɔ:'dɪʃn] Vorsprechen; Vorsingen; Vortanzen **III**
**August** ['ɔ:gəst] August **I**
**aunt** [ɑ:nt] Tante **I**
agony **aunt** ['ægəni ˌɑ:nt] Kummerkastentante **II**
**auntie** ['ɑ:nti] Tantchen **IV**
**Aussie** (coll) ['ɒzi] Australier/-in; australisch (ugs.) **V**
**Australian** [ɒs'treɪliən] australisch; Australier/-in **III**
**author** ['ɔ:θə] Autor/-in **III**
**available** [ə'veɪləbl] erhältlich; verfügbar **IV**
*to be **available** [bi ə'veɪləbl] zur Verfügung stehen; abkömmlich sein **VI U1**, 8
**average** ['ævrɪdʒ] Durchschnitt; Durchschnitts- ⟨**VI TS1**, 39⟩
on **average** [ɒn ˌ'ævrɪdʒ] durchschnittlich; im Durchschnitt **VI U2**, 55
to **avoid** [ə'vɔɪd] vermeiden; meiden; aus dem Weg gehen **III**
**award** [ə'wɔ:d] Auszeichnung; Preis **II**
to be **aware** of sth [bi ə'weər ˌəv] sich etw. bewusst sein **IV**
**away** [ə'weɪ] weg **I**

\*to do **away** with sth [ˌduː ˌəˈweɪ wɪð] etw. abschaffen; etw. loswerden ⟨VITS2, 69⟩

\*to give **away** [ˌɡɪv ˌəˈweɪ] verteilen; verschenken; verraten; preisgeben **IV**

right **away** [ˌraɪt ˌəˈweɪ] sofort; gleich **I**

\*to run **away** [ˌrʌn ˌəˈweɪ] wegrennen **I**

straight **away** [ˌstreɪt ˌəˈweɪ] sofort; gleich **III**

\*to throw **away** [ˌθrəʊ ˌəˈweɪ] wegwerfen **I**

to turn **away** from sb/sth [ˌtɜːn ˌəˈweɪ frəm] sich von jmdm./etw. abwenden ⟨VI U2, 60⟩

**awesome** [ˈɔːsəm] super; spitze **IV**

**awful** [ˈɔːfl] schrecklich; furchtbar **I**

**awkward** [ˈɔːkwəd] peinlich; ungünstig; ungeschickt; unbeholfen **V**

**axe** [æks] Axt **III**

## B

**baby** [ˈbeɪbi] Baby; Säugling **I**

**babysitting** [ˈbeɪbɪsɪtɪŋ] Babysitting **V**

**back** [bæk] Rückseite; Rücken **III**; Ende; hinterer Bereich **V**

at the **back** of [ət ðə ˈbæk əv] hinten; am Ende; im hinteren Teil **II**

**back** to back [ˌbæk tʊ ˈbæk] Rücken an Rücken **I**

**back** [bæk] zurück **I**

\*to go right **back** to [ˌɡəʊ raɪt ˈbæk tə] zurückgehen auf **III**

\*to lean **back** [ˌliːn ˈbæk] sich zurücklehnen ⟨VI U1, 24⟩

to turn **back** [tɜːn ˈbæk] umkehren; zurückgehen **II**

**back** [bæk] damals **V**

**back** then [bæk ˈðen] damals **III**

**backache** [ˈbækeɪk] Rückenschmerzen; Rückenweh **II**

**background** [ˈbækɡraʊnd] Hintergrund **I**

**backing** [ˈbækɪŋ] Hintergrund-; Background- **III**

**backing** dancer [ˈbækɪŋ ˌdɑːnsə] Backgroundtänzer/-in **III**

**backpack** [ˈbækpæk] Rucksack **III**

**backseat** [ˈbæksiːt] Rücksitz **V**

**backstage** [bækˈsteɪdʒ] backstage; hinter der Bühne **VI U2, 48**

**backyard** [bækˈjɑːd] Garten; Hinterhof **III**

**bacon** [ˈbeɪkn] Schinkenspeck; Speck **I**

**bad** [bæd] schlecht; böse; schlimm (ugs.) **I**

\*to go **bad** [ˌɡəʊ ˈbæd] schiefgehen; schlecht werden; verderben **V**

Too **bad!** [ˌtuː ˈbæd] Zu dumm!; Schade! **I**

**badly-written** [ˈbædliˈrɪtn] schlecht geschrieben **IV**

**badminton** [ˈbædmɪntən] Badminton **I**

**bag** [bæɡ] Tasche; Tüte **I**

tea **bag** [ˈtiː bæɡ] Teebeutel **III**

**bagpipes** (pl) [ˈbæɡpaɪps] Dudelsack **III**

**baked** beans (pl) [ˌbeɪkt ˈbiːnz] weiße Bohnen in Tomatensoße **I**

**balance** [ˈbæləns] Gleichgewicht **VITS1**, 38

**ball** [bɔːl] Ball **I**

\*to keep the **ball** bouncing [ˌkiːp ðə bɔːl ˈbaʊntsɪŋ] hier: das Gespräch am Laufen halten **III**

**ballgame** [ˈbɔːlɡeɪm] Baseballspiel ⟨VI U2, 57⟩

to **ban** [bæn] bannen; verbieten; sperren **III**

**banana** [bəˈnɑːnə] Banane **I**

**band** [bænd] Band; Musikgruppe **III**

to **bang** [bæŋ] schlagen; knallen ⟨VI U2, 60⟩

**Bang!** [bæŋ] Peng! **II**

**bank** [bæŋk] Ufer **II**; Bank **IV**

word **bank** [ˈwɜːd ˌbæŋk] Wortsammlung **III**

**banner** [ˈbænə] Banner; Spruchband; Transparent **VI AC2, 74**

**bar** [bɑː] Bar **V**

**bar** graph [ˈbɑː ɡrɑːf] Säulendiagramm; Balkendiagramm **V**

chocolate **bar** [ˈtʃɒklət ˌbɑː] Schokoriegel **IV**

snack **bar** [ˈsnæk ˌbɑː] Café; Imbissstube **I**

**barbecue** [ˈbɑːbɪkjuː] Grillparty **V**

**barbie** (infml) (= barbecue) [ˈbɑːbi] Grillparty **V**

**bare** [beə] nackt; bloß **III**

**barefoot** [beəˈfʊt] barfuß ⟨VI U2, 61⟩

**bargain** [ˈbɑːɡɪn] Schnäppchen **I**

to **bark** [bɑːk] bellen **I**

to **base** on [ˈbeɪs ˌɒn] stützen auf **IV**

**baseball** [ˈbeɪsbɔːl] Baseball **IV**

**based** on [ˈbeɪst ˌɒn] basierend auf; beruhend auf **IV**

\*to be **based** [bi ˈbeɪst] ansässig sein **VI U2, 51**

**bashing** [ˈbæʃɪŋ] Prügel; Schelte ⟨VITS2, 68⟩

**basic** [ˈbeɪsɪk] grundlegend; Grund- **II**

**basically** [ˈbeɪsɪkli] eigentlich; grundsätzlich; im Grunde genommen **VITS2, 69**

**basics** (pl) [ˈbeɪsɪks] Grundlagen **III**

**basketball** [ˈbɑːskɪtbɔːl] Basketball **I**

**bat** [bæt] Schläger (Tischtennis; Baseball) **V**

**bath** [bɑːθ] Bad; Badewanne **I**

**baths** (pl) [bɑːθs] Badehaus; Therme **III**

**bathroom** [ˈbɑːθrʊm] Bad; Badezimmer **I**

**battery** [ˈbætri] Batterie; Akku **II**

**battle** [ˈbætl] Schlacht; Kampf **III**

**BC** (= before Christ) [biːˈsiː] vor Christus **III**

\*to **be** [biː] sein **I**

\*to **be** a team player [ˌbi ə ˈtiːm ˌpleɪə] gern im Team arbeiten **VI U1, 8**

\*to **be** able to (do sth) [bi ˈeɪbl tə] fähig sein zu; können; dürfen **II**

\*to **be** about [biː əˈbaʊt] sich handeln um **I**

\*to **be** about to do sth [bi əˈbaʊt tə] im Begriff sein, etw. zu tun **IV**

\*to **be** addictive [bi əˈdɪktɪv] süchtig machen ⟨VITS1, 39⟩

\*to **be** afraid (of) [bi əˈfreɪd əv] (sich) fürchten; Angst haben (vor) **IV**

\*to **be** allowed to (do sth) [bi əˈlaʊd tə] dürfen **II**

\*to **be** around [ˌbiː əˈraʊnd] da sein; zusammen sein mit **IV**

\*to **be** asleep [ˌbi əˈsliːp] schlafen **II**

\*to **be** available [bi əˈveɪləbl] zur Verfügung stehen; abkömmlich sein **VI U1, 8**

to **be** aware of sth [biˌəˈweər əv] sich etw. bewusst sein **IV**

\*to **be** based [bi ˈbeɪst] ansässig sein **VI U2, 51**

\*to **be** born [bi ˈbɔːn] geboren werden **III**

\*to **be** called [bi ˈkɔːld] heißen; genannt werden **III**

\*to **be** called to do sth [bi ˈkɔːld tə duː] auserwählt sein, etw. zu tun **III**

\*to **be** confronted with [bi kənˈfrʌntɪd wɪð] konfrontiert werden mit **VITS2, 71**

\*to **be** connected [bi kəˈnektɪd] zusammenhängen; in Zusammenhang stehen **IV**

\*to **be** considered (to be) sth [bi kənˈsɪdəd tə] als etw. gelten **IV**

\*to **be** crazy about [bi ˈkreɪzi əˌbaʊt] verrückt sein nach; abfahren auf **IV**

\*to **be** done with [bi ˈdʌn wɪð] fertig sein mit **IV**

to **be** entitled to sth [bi ɪnˈtaɪtld tə] berechtigt sein; ein Anrecht haben auf; Anspruch haben auf °**VI AC1, 41**

\*to **be** expected to (+ inf) [bi ɪkˈspektɪd tə] sollen **VI U1, 8**

\*to **be** fed up (with) [bi fed ˈʌp wɪð] sauer sein (auf); die Nase voll haben (von) **III**

\*to **be** gone [bi: ˈɡɒn] verschwunden sein; weg sein **II**

\*to **be** good at [bi: ˈɡʊd ət] gut sein in **I**

\*to **be** grounded [bi ˈɡraʊndɪd] Hausarrest haben **III**

\*to **be** hard on sb [bi ˈhɑːd ɒn] streng mit jmdm. sein **III**

\*to **be** homesick [bi ˈhəʊmsɪk] Heimweh haben **IV**

\*to **be** in [bi ˈɪn] dabei sein; mitmachen **II**

\*to **be** in a hurry [ˌbi ɪn ə ˈhʌri] es eilig haben; in Eile sein **V**

\*to **be** in charge (of) [bi ɪn ˈtʃɑːdʒ əv] die Verantwortung tragen (für); zuständig sein (für) **III**

\*to **be** in sb's shoes [ˌbi: ɪn sʌmbɒdɪz ˈʃuːz] an jmds. Stelle sein; in jmds. Haut stecken **III**

\*to **be** in the way [bi: ɪn ðə ˈweɪ] im Weg sein/stehen **I**

\*to **be** interested in [bi ˈɪntrəstɪd ɪn] interessiert sein an; sich interessieren für **II**

\*to **be** into [bi: ˈɪntə] mögen; stehen auf **I**

\*to **be** involved (in) [bi ɪnˈvɒlvd ɪn] beteiligt sein (an); involviert sein (in); engagiert sein (in) **V**

\*to **be** jealous (of) [bi: ˈdʒeləs] eifersüchtig sein (auf); neidisch sein (auf) **I** *to **be** known as [bi 'nəʊn‿əz] bekannt sein als **IV**

*to **be** late [bi: 'leɪt] zu spät dran sein; zu spät kommen **I**

*to **be** like [bi 'laɪk] sein **III**

*to **be** likely [bi 'laɪkli] wahrscheinlich sein **V**

*to **be** located [bi ləʊ'keɪtɪd] gelegen sein; liegen **IV**

*to **be** lucky [bi‿'lʌki] Glück haben **II**

*to **be** made of [bi 'meɪd‿əv] bestehen aus **III**

*to **be** made up of/from [bi meɪd‿'ʌp‿əv/frəm] zusammengesetzt sein aus; bestehen aus **V**

*to **be** obliged to (+ inf) [bi‿ə'blaɪdʒd tə] verpflichtet sein, etw. zu tun; müssen **VI U2**, 55

*to **be** on [bi‿'ɒn] an sein; laufen **II**; auf Sendung sein °**VI U2**, 57

*to **be** on fire [bi:‿ɒn 'faɪə] brennen **III**

*to **be** passionate about sth [bi 'pæʃnət ə‚baʊt] etw. leidenschaftlich gern tun; eine Leidenschaft für etw. haben; für etw. brennen **VI U1**, 8

*to **be** prejudiced against sb/sth [bi 'predʒədɪst ə‚genst] voreingenommen sein gegenüber jmdm./etw. **VI AC1**, 41

*to **be** related to [bi rɪ'leɪtɪd tə] verwandt sein mit **V**

*to **be** required to (+ inf) [bi rɪ'kwaɪəd tə] müssen **VI U2**, 55

*to **be** right [bi 'raɪt] recht haben **I**

*to **be** said to (+ inf) [bi 'sed tə] sollen; gelten als **VI U2**, 50

*to **be** scared (of) [bi: 'skeəd‿əv] Angst haben (vor) **I**

*to **be** set (in) [bi 'set ɪn] spielen (in); seinen Schauplatz haben (in) **IV**

*to **be** sick [bi 'sɪk] sich übergeben **IV**

*to **be** sorry [bi: 'sɒri] leid tun **I**

*to **be** stressed out [bi ‚strest 'aʊt] völlig gestresst sein **III**

*to **be** stuck [bi 'stʌk] festsitzen; feststecken; hängen bleiben **V**

*to **be** supposed to (+ inf) [bi sə'pəʊzd tə] sollen **VI U1**, 8

*to **be** surprised [bi sə'praɪzd] überrascht sein **II**

*to **be** suspended [bi sə'spendɪd] suspendiert werden; zeitweilig vom Unterricht ausgeschlossen werden **IV**

*to **be** swept out to sea [bi ‚swept‿aʊt tə 'si:] aufs offene Meer getrieben werden **V**

*to **be** tired of [bi 'taɪəd‿əv] es müde sein (zu); es leid sein (zu); es satt haben (zu) **IV**

*to **be** to (+ inf) ['bi tə] sollen **VI U2**, 55

*to **be** trapped [bi 'træpt] eingeschlossen sein; in der Falle sitzen **III**

*to **be** true to oneself [bi 'tru: tu wʌn‚self] sich selbst treu bleiben **V**

*to **be** unable to do sth [bi‚ʌn'eɪbl tə] unfähig sein, etw. zu tun; nicht in der Lage sein, etw. zu tun **VI TS1**, 35

*to **be** unlucky [bi:‚ʌn'lʌki] Pech haben **I**

*to **be** up to [bi‚'ʌp tə] vorhaben **II**

*to **be** used to (+ -ing) [bi 'ju:s tə] gewöhnt sein an; gewohnt sein **III**

*to **be** willing to do sth [bi 'wɪlɪŋ tə] gewillt sein, etw. zu tun; bereit sein, etw. zu tun **VI U2**, 54

*to **be** worried [bi 'wʌrid] beunruhigt sein; besorgt sein **II**

*to **be** worth [bi: 'wɜ:θ] wert sein **I**

*to **be** wrong [bi: 'rɒŋ] unrecht haben; sich irren **I**

**Be** careful! [bi: 'keəfl] Vorsicht!; Pass/Passt auf! **I**

Here you **are**. [‚hɪə ju‿'ɑ:] Bitte schön. **I**

How **are** you? [‚haʊ'ɑ: jə] Wie geht es dir?; Wie geht es euch?; Wie geht es Ihnen? **I**

How much **is/are** …? [‚haʊ 'mʌtʃ ɪz/ɑ:] Wie viel (kostet/kosten) …? **I**

I'**m** from … [‚aɪm frɒm] Ich bin aus … **I**

**Is** this how you (do) …? [ɪz 'ðɪs haʊ jʊ ‚du:] Machst du so …? **I**

**beach** [bi:tʃ] Strand **II**

**bead** of sweat [‚bi:d‿əv 'swet] Schweißperle ⟨**VI U2**, 62⟩

**bean** [bi:n] Bohne **VI U1**, 13

baked **beans** (pl) [‚beɪkt 'bi:nz] weiße Bohnen in Tomatensoße **I**

**bear** [beə] Bär **II**

grizzly **bear** ['grɪzli ‚beə] Grizzlybär **V**

**beat** [bi:t] Takt; Rhythmus **V**

*to **beat** [bi:t] schlagen; besiegen **II**

**beautiful** ['bju:tɪfl] schön; hübsch; wunderbar **II**

**because** [bɪ'kɒz] weil; da **I**

**because** of [bɪ'kɒz‿əv] wegen **II**

*to **become** [bɪ'kʌm] werden **II**

*to **become** extinct [bɪ‚kʌm ɪk'stɪŋkt] aussterben **III**

*to **become** friends [bɪ‚kʌm 'frendz] sich anfreunden; Freundschaft schließen **IV**

**bed** [bed] Bett **I**

*to go to **bed** [‚gəʊ tə 'bed] ins Bett gehen **I**

**bedroom** ['bedrʊm] Schlafzimmer **I**

**bee** [bi:] Biene **II**

**Beefeater** ['bi:ˌfi:tə] königlicher Leibgardist **II**

**before** [bɪ'fɔ:] vor (zeitlich); bevor **I**; schon einmal; vorher; zuvor **III**

*to **begin** [bɪ'gɪn] beginnen; anfangen **II**

**beginning** [bɪ'gɪnɪŋ] Anfang; Beginn **II**

to **behave** [bɪ'heɪv] sich benehmen; sich verhalten **III**

**behavior** (no pl) (AE) [bɪ'heɪvjə] Verhalten; Benehmen; Betragen **IV**

**behaviour** (no pl) [bɪ'heɪvjə] Verhalten; Benehmen; Betragen **IV**

**behind** [bɪ'haɪnd] hinter **I**

*to leave **behind** [‚li:v bɪ'haɪnd] zurücklassen **III**

**belief** [bɪ'li:f] Glaube; Überzeugung **VI AC2**, 75

**believable** [bɪ'li:vəbl] glaubwürdig **IV**

to **believe** [bɪ'li:v] glauben **I**

to **believe** in sb/sth [bɪ'li:v‿ɪn] an jmdn./etw. glauben **VI AC2**, 74

He couldn't **believe** his eyes. [hi ‚kʊdnt bɪ‚li:v hɪz‿'aɪz] Er traute seinen Augen nicht. **II**

**bell** [bel] Glocke **II**

saved by the **bell** [‚seɪvd baɪ ðə 'bel] noch mal Glück gehabt **III**

**belongings** (pl) [bɪ'lɒŋɪŋz] Habseligkeiten; Hab und Gut **V**

to **belong** (to) [bɪ'lɒŋ (tə)] gehören (zu) **II**

where I **belong** [‚weər aɪ bɪ'lɒŋ] wo ich hingehöre **V**

**below** [bɪ'ləʊ] unterhalb; unten **I**

**belt** [belt] Gürtel **III**

seat **belt** ['si:t belt] Sicherheitsgurt **V**

**bench** [benʃ] Bank; Sitzbank **III**

*to **bend** over [‚bend‿'əʊvə] sich vorbeugen; sich beugen über ⟨**VI U1**, 23⟩

**benefit** ['benɪfɪt] Vorteil; Nutzen; Unterstützung **IV**

**beside** [bɪ'saɪd] neben ⟨**VI U1**, 22⟩

**besides** [bɪ'saɪdz] außerdem; überdies ⟨**VI U2**, 60⟩

**besides** [bɪ'saɪdz] neben **III**

(the) **best** [best] (der/die/das) Beste **II**

to save the **best** for last [‚seɪv ðə ‚best fə 'lɑ:st] sich das Beste bis zum Schluss aufheben **IV**

**best** [best] beste/-r/-s; am besten **I**

as **best** as I can remember [əz ‚best əz‿aɪ kæn rɪ'membə] soweit ich mich erinnern kann ⟨**VI U2**, 61⟩

**Best** wishes [‚best 'wɪʃɪz] Viele Grüße; Herzliche Grüße **III**

the **best** … ever ['best … ‚evə] der/die/das beste … überhaupt **III**

*to **bet** [bet] wetten **VI TS2**, 70

**better** ['betə] besser; lieber **I**

You'd **better** … (= You had better) ['ju:d ‚betə] Du solltest lieber … **IV**

**between** [bɪ'twi:n] zwischen **I**

in **between** [‚ɪn bɪ'twi:n] dazwischen **III**

**beyond** [bi'ɒnd] jenseits; über … hinaus **VI AC1**, 40

**bicycle** motocross [‚baɪsɪkl 'məʊtəʊkrɒs] Fahrradmotocross **II**

**big** [bɪg] groß **I**

**big** deal [bɪg 'di:l] große Sache **IV**

**bighorn** sheep [‚bɪghɔ:n 'ʃi:p] Dickhornschaf **V**

**bike** [baɪk] Fahrrad **I**

mountain **biking** ['maʊntɪn ‚baɪkɪŋ] Mountainbikefahren **III**

**bilingual** [baɪ'lɪŋgwl] zweisprachig **II**

bill *(AE)* [bɪl] Geldschein; Rechnung **IV**

billboard [ˈbɪlbɔːd] Plakatwand **IV**

billion [ˈbɪliən] Milliarde **III**

billionaire [ˌbɪliəneə] Milliardär/-in **IV**

biographical [baɪəʊˈgræfɪkl] biografisch **III**

biological [ˌbaɪəˈlɒdʒɪkl] biologisch **VITS1**, 37

bird [bɜːd] Vogel **II**

birdwatching [ˈbɜːdˌwɒtʃɪŋ] Vogelbeobachtung **II**

date of birth [ˌdeɪt əv ˈbɜːθ] Geburtsdatum **IV**

birthday [ˈbɜːθdeɪ] Geburtstag **I**
  Happy **Birthday**! [ˈhæpi ˈbɜːθdeɪ] Alles Gute zum Geburtstag!; Herzlichen Glückwunsch zum Geburtstag! **I**

biscuit [ˈbɪskɪt] Keks **I**

bison [ˈbaɪsn], bison [ˈbaɪsn] *(pl)* Bison; Büffel **V**

bistro [ˈbiːstrəʊ] Bistro ⟨**VI U2**, 57⟩

a bit [ə ˈbɪt] ein bisschen; ein wenig **II**
  **bit** by bit [ˌbɪt baɪ ˈbɪt] Stück für Stück **IV**
  *to do one's **bit** [ˌduː ˈwʌnz ˈbɪt] seinen Teil beitragen **VI AC2**, 74

bitchy [ˈbɪtʃi] gehässig; gemein **V**

*to bite [baɪt] beißen **II**

bitter [ˈbɪtə] bitter **VI U1**, 13

bitterness *(no pl)* [ˈbɪtənəs] Bitterkeit; Verbitterung **V**

black [blæk] schwarz **I**
  **black** eye [blæk ˈaɪ] blaues Auge **V**
  *to go **black** [ˌgəʊ ˈblæk] schwarz werden **II**

to blend together [ˌblend təˈgeðə] ineinander verschmelzen ⟨**VI U2**, 61⟩

blind [blaɪnd] blind ⟨**VI AC1**, 40⟩

to blink [blɪŋk] blinzeln; zwinkern ⟨**VI U1**, 23⟩

block [blɒk] Block; Häuserblock **IV**
  building **block** [ˈbɪldɪŋ blɒk] Baustein **II**

to block [blɒk] blockieren; abblocken **II**

blog [blɒg] Blog; Internettagebuch **III**

blogger [ˈblɒgə] Blogger/-in **IV**

bloke *(fam)* [bləʊk] Typ *(ugs.)* **III**

blond [blɒnd] blond **III**

blood [blʌd] Blut **III**

bloody [ˈblʌdi] blutig ⟨**VITS2**, 70⟩

*to blow out [ˌbləʊ ˈaʊt] ausblasen; auspusten **I**

blue [bluː] blau **I**

blurred [blɜːd] verschwommen; verwischt **III**

BMX [ˌbiːemˈeks] BMX **II**

board [bɔːd] Brett; Tafel **III**
  tourist **board** [ˈtʊərɪst bɔːd] Touristeninformation **III**

boarding [ˈbɔːdɪŋ] Boarding **IV**
  **boarding** card [ˈbɔːdɪŋ ˌkaːd] Bordkarte **IV**

boat [bəʊt] Boot **I**

boating lake [ˈbəʊtɪŋ ˌleɪk] See zum Rudern **I**

body [ˈbɒdi] Körper **III**
  human **body** [ˌhjuːmən ˈbɒdi] menschlicher Körper **II**

bodybuilder [ˈbɒdiˌbɪldə] Bodybuilder/-in **VI U2**, 52

bodyguard [ˈbɒdigaːd] Bodyguard **IV**

bold [bəʊld] fett gedruckt **III**; fett ⟨**VI U1**, 7⟩

bone [bəʊn] Knochen **VI AC2**, 75

bonfire [ˈbɒnfaɪə] Lagerfeuer; Freudenfeuer **I**

to boo sb [buː] jmdn. ausbuhen ⟨**VITS2**, 68⟩

book [bʊk] Buch **I**
  exercise **book** [ˈeksəsaɪz ˌbʊk] Übungsheft **I**

to book [bʊk] buchen; reservieren **III**

boom [buːm] wirtschaftlicher Aufschwung; Boom; Hochkonjunktur **VI U2**, 50

to boom [buːm] dröhnen **III**; florieren; boomen **VI U2**, 50

boomtown [ˈbuːmtaʊn] schnell wachsende Stadt **V**

boot [buːt] Stiefel; Kofferraum **III**

border [ˈbɔːdə] Grenze **VI U2**, 50

bored [bɔːd] gelangweilt **I**

boredom [ˈbɔːdəm] Langeweile **VI U1**, 7

boring [ˈbɔːrɪŋ] langweilig **I**

*to be born [bi ˈbɔːn] geboren werden **III**

to borrow [ˈbɒrəʊ] (sich) ausleihen **II**

boss [bɒs] Boss; Chef **III**

bossy [ˈbɒsi] herrisch; rechthaberisch **III**

both [bəʊθ] beide **II**
  **both** … and … [ˈbəʊθ … ənd] sowohl … als auch … °**VI AC1**, 43

to bother [ˈbɒðə] stören; belästigen **IV**

bottle [ˈbɒtl] Flasche **I**

bottom [ˈbɒtəm] Boden; unterer Teil; Grund **V**

to bounce [baʊnts] springen; hüpfen **III**
  *to keep the ball **bouncing** [ˌkiːp ðə bɔːl ˈbaʊntsɪŋ] *hier:* das Gespräch am Laufen halten **III**

boundary [ˈbaʊndri] Grenze; Abgrenzung ⟨**VI U1**, 25⟩

bowl [bəʊl] Schale; Schälchen; Schüssel **I**
  to play **bowls** [ˌpleɪ ˈbəʊlz] Bowling spielen **III**

bowling alley [ˈbəʊlɪŋ ˌæli] Bowlingbahn **I**

box [bɒks] Box; Kasten; Schachtel; Kiste **I**
  **box** jellyfish [ˈbɒks ˌdʒelifɪʃ] Würfelqualle **V**
  phone **box** [ˈfəʊn ˌbɒks] Telefonzelle **IV**

boxing [ˈbɒksɪŋ] Boxen **II**
  round of **boxing** [ˌraʊnd əv ˈbɒksɪŋ] Boxrunde **II**

boy [bɔɪ] Junge **I**
  cabin **boy** [ˈkæbɪn ˌbɔɪ] Schiffsjunge **I**

boyfriend [ˈbɔɪfrend] Freund *(in einer Paarbeziehung)* **IV**

bracelet [ˈbreɪslət] Armband **I**

bracket [ˈbrækɪt] Klammer **III**

brain(s) [breɪn(z)] Gehirn; Verstand **V**

brain-dead [ˈbreɪnˌded] hirntot **V**

to brainstorm [ˈbreɪnstɔːm] Ideen sammeln **IV**

brand [brænd] Marke **IV**

brand-new [ˌbrændˈnjuː] brandneu **IV**

brave [breɪv] mutig; tapfer **I**

bread [bred] Brot **I**
  **bread** roll [ˈbred rəʊl] Brötchen **III**

break [breɪk] Pause **II**; Durchbruch **IV**
  half-term **break** [ˌhaːftɜːm ˈbreɪk] Halbjahresferien **I**
  lunch **break** [ˈlʌnʃbreɪk] Mittagspause **I**

*to break [breɪk] brechen; zerbrechen **I**
  *to **break** down [ˌbreɪk ˈdaʊn] zusammenbrechen **VITS2**, 68
  *to **break** into a song [breɪk ˌɪntʊ ə ˈsɒŋ] plötzlich anfangen zu singen **V**
  *to **break** sb's spirit [breɪk sʌmbədiz ˈspɪrɪt] jmdn. entmutigen ⟨**VITS2**, 69⟩

broken [ˈbrəʊkn] gebrochen; kaputt **I**

breakfast [ˈbrekfəst] Frühstück **I**
  *to have **breakfast** [ˌhæv ˈbrekfəst] frühstücken **I**

breath [breθ] Atem; Atemzug **III**
  *to take a **breath** [ˌteɪk ə ˈbreθ] Luft holen; Atem holen **III**
  Take a deep **breath**. [ˌteɪk ə ˌdiːp ˈbreθ] Atme(t) tief ein. **II**

to breathe [briːð] atmen **II**

breathtaking [ˈbreθˌteɪkɪŋ] atemberaubend **IV**

breezy [ˈbriːzi] unbeschwert; heiter ⟨**VI U1**, 7⟩

bridge [brɪdʒ] Brücke **II**

brief [briːf] kurz **VI U1**, 18

bright [braɪt] hell; leuchtend; strahlend **IV**

brilliant [ˈbrɪliənt] leuchtend ⟨**VI U1**, 25⟩

*to bring [brɪŋ] bringen; mitbringen **I**
  *to **bring** up [ˌbrɪŋ ˈʌp] zur Sprache bringen **VI AC1**, 42

on the brink of [ˌɒn ðə ˈbrɪŋk əv] am Rande von; kurz vor **III**

Brit [brɪt] Brite/Britin *(ugs.)* **IV**

British [ˈbrɪtɪʃ] britisch; Brite/Britin **I**

brochure [ˈbrəʊʃə] Broschüre; Prospekt **I**

broken [ˈbrəʊkn] gebrochen; kaputt **I**

Bronze Age [ˈbrɒnz eɪdʒ] Bronzezeit *(ca. 2200–800 v. Chr.)* **III**

brother [ˈbrʌðə] Bruder **I**

brown [braʊn] braun **I**

brownie [ˈbraʊni] Brownie ⟨**VI U2**, 60⟩

bubble [ˈbʌbl] Blase **VI AC2**, 75
  dot-com **bubble** [ˌdɒtkɒm ˈbʌbl] Internetblase; Dotcom-Blase **VI U2**, 50

buck *(AE) (coll)* [bʌk] Dollar ⟨**VI U1**, 7⟩

bucket [ˈbʌkɪt] Eimer **II**

Buddhist [ˈbʊdɪst] buddhistisch **V**

buddy *(infml)* [ˈbʌdi] Kumpel **VI U1**, 18

bugs *(pl)* [bʌgz] Ungeziefer **VI U2**, 54

*to build [bɪld] bauen **II**; aufbauen **III**
  *to **build** upon [ˌbɪld əˈpɒn] sich türmen auf ⟨**VI U1**, 24⟩

building [ˈbɪldɪŋ] Gebäude **I**

building block [ˈbɪldɪŋ blɒk] Baustein **II**

cyber bully [ˌsaɪbə ˈbʊli] *jemand, der andere in sozialen Netzwerken belästigt oder mobbt* **II**

**bullying** ['bʊliɪŋ] Mobbing ⟨**VITS1**, 39⟩
*****to give the bumps** [ˌgɪv ðə 'bʌmps] hochleben lassen **I**
goose **bumps** ['guːs ˌbʌmps] Gänsehaut ⟨**VIU2**, 62⟩
to **bump** [bʌmp] anstoßen; stoßen ⟨**VIU2**, 61⟩
to **bump** into sb [bʌmp 'ɪntə] jmdn. zufällig treffen; *hier:* jmdn. anrempeln **V**
a **bunch** of [ə ˌbʌnʃ əv] ein Haufen ⟨**VIU2**, 62⟩
**burger** ['bɜːgə] Hamburger **I**
*****to burn** [bɜːn] brennen; verbrennen **III**
*****to burn** down [bɜːn 'daʊn] abbrennen; niederbrennen **III**
*****to burst** [bɜːst] bersten; platzen **VIU2**, 50
**bus** [bʌs] Bus **I**
**bus** station ['bʌs ˌsteɪʃn] Busbahnhof **I**
**bush** [bʊʃ] Busch *(Buschlandschaft)*; Wildnis **III**; Busch; Strauch ⟨**VIU1**, 25⟩
**bushfire** ['bʊʃfaɪə] Buschfeuer **V**
**bushwalking** ['bʊʃˌwɔːkɪŋ] Buschwandern **V**
**business** ['bɪznɪs] Geschäft; Business **III**
**business** executive ['bɪznɪs ɪɡˌzekjətɪv] Geschäftsführer/-in; Manager/-in; gehobene Führungskraft **VIU1**, 9
**businessman** ['bɪznɪsmæn] Geschäftsmann **IV**
**busker** ['bʌskə] Straßenmusikant/-in **IV**
**busy** ['bɪzi] belebt; beschäftigt **I**
**but** [bʌt] aber **I**
not only … **but** (also) [nɒtˌəʊnli … bʌtˌ'ɔːlsəʊ] nicht nur … sondern (auch) **VIU1**, 16
all **but** ['ɔːl bʌt] alle bis auf **VIU2**, 55
**butter** ['bʌtə] Butter **III**
**button** ['bʌtn] Knopf **IV**
*****to buy** [baɪ] kaufen **I**
*****to buy** time [baɪ 'taɪm] Zeit gewinnen **V**
**buyer** ['baɪə] Käufer/-in **I**
**by** [baɪ] bei; neben; an; von **III**
**by** the river [baɪ ðə 'rɪvə] am Fluss **II**
**by** the time [baɪ ðə 'taɪm] bis *(zu dem Zeitpunkt)* **V**
*****to go by** [ˌgəʊ 'baɪ] vorbeigehen **VIU1**, 16
**by** any means [baɪ ˌeni 'miːnz] mit allen Mitteln **IV**
**by** (+ gerund) [baɪ] indem **V**
**by** (bike) [baɪ] mit *(dem Fahrrad)* **I**
**Bye!** [baɪ] Tschüss! **II**

## C

**cabin** ['kæbɪn] Kabine ⟨**VITS2**, 73⟩
**cabin** boy ['kæbɪn ˌbɔɪ] Schiffsjunge **I**
**cache** [kæʃ] Cache **III**
**cactus** ['kæktəs] Kaktus **IV**
**café** ['kæfeɪ] Café **I**
**cafeteria** [ˌkæfə'tɪəriə] Cafeteria **I**
**cake** [keɪk] Kuchen; Torte **I**
**calendar** ['kæləndə] Kalender **III**
**Californian** [ˌkælɪ'fɔːniən] kalifornisch; Kalifornier/-in **VIU2**, 50

(phone) **call** ['fəʊn ˌkɔːl] Anruf; Telefonanruf **I**
cattle **call** *(AE)* ['kætl ˌkɔːl] Vorspielen; Vorsingen **VIU2**, 46
to **call** [kɔːl] nennen; anrufen; rufen **I**
*****to be called** [bi 'kɔːld] heißen; genannt werden **III**
*****to be called** to do sth [bi 'kɔːld tə duː] auserwählt sein, etw. zu tun **III**
to **call** forward [ˌkɔːl 'fɔːwəd] nach vorn rufen ⟨**VIU1**, 22⟩
to **call** off [ˌkɔːl 'ɒf] abbrechen; absagen **V**
**caller** ['kɔːlə] Anrufer/-in **I**
**call-in** ['kɔːlɪn] *Sendung, bei der sich das Publikum telefonisch beteiligen kann* **III**
**calm** [kɑːm] Ruhe **V**
to **calm** down [ˌkɑːm 'daʊn] sich beruhigen **II**
**calm** [kɑːm] ruhig; friedlich **V**
**camel** ['kæml] Kamel **V**
**camel** racing ['kæml ˌreɪsɪŋ] Kamelrennen **II**
**camera** ['kæmrə] Fotoapparat; Kamera **II**
caught on **camera** [kɔːtˌɒn 'kæmrə] ertappt; mit der Kamera festgehalten **II**
**camp** [kæmp] Camp; Lager **V**
summer **camp** ['sʌmə kæmp] Sommerferienlager **II**
to **camp** [kæmp] campen; zelten **III**
to **campaign** (for) [kæm'peɪn fɔː] demonstrieren (für); aufmerksam machen (auf); sich engagieren (für) **III**
**camping** ['kæmpɪŋ] Camping; Zelten **II**
**can** [kæn] Dose; Büchse **I**
tin **can** ['tɪn kæn] Blechdose **III**
**can** [kæn; kən] können; dürfen **I**
**can't** [kɑːnt] kann nicht; können nicht **I**
**Canadian** [kə'neɪdiən] kanadisch; Kanadier/-in **IV**
**candidate** ['kændɪdət] Bewerber/-in; Kandidat/-in **VIU1**, 20
**candle** ['kændl] Kerze **I**
**candlelight** *(no pl)* ['kændlaɪt] Kerzenlicht **II**
**cannot** ['kænɒt] kann nicht; können nicht **II**
**canoe** [kə'nuː] Kanu **V**
**capital** ['kæpɪtl] Hauptstadt **II**
**capital** letter [ˌkæpɪtl 'letə] Großbuchstabe **I**
**captain** ['kæptɪn] Kapitän/-in; Mannschaftsführer/-in **I**
**caption** ['kæpʃn] Bildunterschrift; Untertitel **III**
to **capture** ['kæptʃə] ergreifen; einfangen **III**
**car** [kɑː] Auto **I**
motor **car** ['məʊtə ˌkɑː] Automobil **V**
**card** [kɑːd] Karte; Spielkarte **I**
boarding **card** ['bɔːdɪŋ ˌkɑːd] Bordkarte **IV**
prompt **card** ['prɒmpt kɑːd] Stichwortkarte; Rollenkarte **II**
**cardboard** ['kɑːdbɔːd] Pappe; Karton **V**
*****to take care** of sb [teɪk ˌkeəˈəv] sich um jmdn. kümmern; für jmdn. sorgen **III**

to **care** (about) ['keəˌˈbaʊt] wichtig nehmen; sich kümmern (um); sich interessieren (für) **II**
**career** [kə'rɪə] Beruf; Laufbahn; Karriere **III**
**careful** ['keəfl] vorsichtig; sorgfältig **II**
Be **careful!** [bi: 'keəfl] Vorsicht!; Pass/Passt auf! **I**
**caretaker** *(AE)* ['keəˌteɪkə] Pfleger/-in ⟨**VIU1**, 22⟩
**caretaking** ['keəˌteɪkɪŋ] Pflege ⟨**VIU1**, 22⟩
**carnival** ['kɑːnɪvl] Karneval **II**
**carpenter** ['kɑːpntə] Schreiner/-in; Zimmermann **VIU1**, 16
**carpet** ['kɑːpɪt] Teppich **II**
**carrot** ['kærət] Karotte; Möhre **I**
to **carry** ['kæri] tragen **III**
**cart** [kɑːt] Karren **IV**
**cartoon** [kɑː'tuːn] Cartoon; Zeichentrickfilm **III**
**cash** register ['kæʃ ˌredʒɪstə] Kasse ⟨**VIU2**, 60⟩
**cast** [kɑːst] Besetzung; Ensemble **V**
plaster **cast** ['plɑːstə kɑːst] Gipsverband **III**
**casting** ['kɑːstɪŋ] Casting; Rollenbesetzung **IV**
**castle** ['kɑːsl] Schloss; Burg **II**
**cat** [kæt] Katze **I**
*****to catch** [kætʃ] fangen **II**; mitbekommen *(ugs.)*; mitkriegen *(ugs.)* **III**; nehmen *(Zug, Bus)* **VIU2**, 48
*****to catch** an infection [ɪn'fekʃn] sich eine Infektion holen; sich einen Infekt holen **V**
*****to catch** oneself doing sth [kætʃ] sich (selbst) dabei ertappen, wie … **VIU1**, 14
**catchy** ['kætʃi] eingängig; einprägsam **III**
**category** ['kætəgri] Kategorie; Klasse **II**
**cattle** call *(AE)* ['kætl ˌkɔːl] Vorspielen; Vorsingen **VIU2**, 46
*****to get caught** [get 'kɔːt] erwischt werden; ertappt werden **IV**
**caught** on camera [kɔːtˌɒn 'kæmrə] ertappt; mit der Kamera festgehalten **II**
**cause** [kɔːz] Grund; Ursache **V**
to **cause** [kɔːz] verursachen **II**
to **cause** a stir [ˌkɔːzə 'stɜː] für Aufsehen sorgen **VIU2**, 46
**cave** [keɪv] Höhle **III**
**ceiling** ['siːlɪŋ] Zimmerdecke; Decke **V**
to **celebrate** ['seləbreɪt] feiern **I**
**celebration** [ˌselə'breɪʃn] Feier **V**
**celebrity** [sə'lebrəti] Prominente/-r; berühmte Person **III**
**cell** phone *(AE)* ['selfəʊn] Mobiltelefon; Handy **IV**
**Celt** [kelt] Kelte/Keltin **III**
**Celtic** ['keltɪk; 'seltɪk] keltisch **II**
**cent** [sent] Cent *(Währung)* **I**
**center** *(AE)* ['sentə] Zentrum; Center **IV**
**central** ['sentrl] zentral; Zentral- **II**
**centre** ['sentə] Zentrum; Center **I**

community **centre** [kəˈmjuːnəti ˌsentə] Gemeindezentrum **I**

leisure **centre** [ˈleʒə ˌsentə] Freizeitzentrum **I**

tourist information **centre** [ˌtʊərɪst ɪnfəˈmeɪʃn ˌsentə] Touristeninformation **I**

**centred** [ˈsentəd] zentriert **V**

**century** [ˈsenʃri] Jahrhundert **II**

**cereal** *(no pl)* [ˈsɪəriəl] Frühstückszerealie; Getreideprodukt *(z. B. Cornflakes oder Müsli)* **I**

**ceremony** [ˈserɪməni] Zeremonie **V**

**certain** [ˈsɜːtn] bestimmt; sicher; gewiss **V**

**certainly** [ˈsɜːtnli] sicherlich ⟨**VI TS2**, 73⟩

**chain** [tʃeɪn] Kette **V**

**chair** [tʃeə] Stuhl; Sessel **I**

to **chalk** sth up to experience [ˌtʃɔːk ʌp tə ɪkˈspɪəriəns] etw. als Erfahrung verbuchen **VI U2**, 46

**challenge** [ˈtʃælɪndʒ] Herausforderung **II**

to **challenge** [ˈtʃælɪndʒ] herausfordern **IV**

**champagne** [ʃæmˈpeɪn] Champagner ⟨**VI U1**, 6⟩

**champion** [ˈtʃæmpiən] Gewinner/-in; Sieger/-in; Champion **III**

**championship** [ˈtʃæmpiənʃip] Meisterschaft **IV**

**chance** [tʃɑːns] Chance; Gelegenheit; Möglichkeit **II**

**change** [tʃeɪndʒ] Änderung; Veränderung; Wechsel **III**; Münzgeld; Wechselgeld **IV**

climate **change** [ˈklaɪmət ˌtʃeɪndʒ] Klimawandel **VI U2**, 54

to **change** [tʃeɪndʒ] wechseln; (sich) ändern **II**

to **change** (onto) [tʃeɪndʒ (ˈɒntʊ)] umsteigen (in) **II**

to **change** one's mind [ˌtʃeɪndʒ wʌnz ˈmaɪnd] seine Meinung ändern **III**

Everything will have **changed**. [ˌevriθɪŋ wɪl hæv ˈtʃeɪndʒd] Alles wird sich geändert haben. **V**

**chant** [tʃɑːnt] Sprechgesang **II**

**chaos** [ˈkeɪɒs] Chaos; Durcheinander **III**

**chaotic** [keɪˈɒtɪk] chaotisch **V**

**chapter** [ˈtʃæptə] Kapitel **III**

**character** [ˈkærəktə] Charakter; Figur **I**

**character** trait [ˈkærəktə ˈtreɪt] Charaktereigenschaft °**VI U2**, 46

**characterisation** [ˌkærəktraɪˈzeɪʃn] Beschreibung; Personenbeschreibung; Charakterisierung **V**

**characteristic** [ˌkærəktəˈrɪstɪk] typisches Merkmal **IV**

*to be in **charge** (of) [bɪ ˌɪn ˈtʃɑːdʒ əv] die Verantwortung tragen (für); zuständig sein (für) **III**

**charity** [ˈtʃærɪti] Wohltätigkeitsverein; wohltätige Zwecke; Wohlfahrt **I**

**charity** shop [ˈtʃærɪti ʃɒp] Second-Hand-Laden **I**

**charm** [tʃɑːm] Zauberspruch ⟨**VI U2**, 60⟩

lucky **charm** [ˌlʌki ˈtʃɑːm] Glücksbringer; Talisman **I**

**chart** [tʃɑːt] Diagramm; Tabelle **V**

pie **chart** [ˈpaɪ ˌtʃɑːt] Kuchendiagramm; Tortendiagramm **V**

to **chase** [tʃeɪs] jagen; nachjagen **I**

**chat** [ˌtʃæt] Chat **III**

**chat** room [ˈtʃæt rʊm] Chatroom **II**

video **chat** [ˈvɪdiəʊ ˌtʃæt] Videochat **II**

to **chat** [tʃæt] plaudern; chatten *(sich online unterhalten)* **I**

**cheap** [tʃiːp] billig; preiswert **I**

to **cheat** [tʃiːt] mogeln; betrügen **IV**

**cheat** sheet [ˈtʃiːt ʃiːt] Spickzettel **IV**

**check** [tʃek] Scheck ⟨**VI U2**, 60⟩

to **check** [tʃek] überprüfen; prüfen; kontrollieren **I**

to **check** out *(coll)* [tʃek ˈaʊt] prüfen; abchecken; auschecken **III**

**checklist** [ˈtʃeklɪst] Checkliste **II**

**checkpoint** [ˈtʃekpɔɪnt] Kontrollpunkt **IV**

**cheek** [tʃiːk] Wange ⟨**VI U2**, 60⟩

**cheer** [tʃɪə] Jubel; Hurraruf **IV**

to **cheer** [tʃɪə] anfeuern; jubeln; zujubeln **II**

to **cheer** sb up [ˈtʃɪər ˈʌp] jmdn. aufheitern **III**

**Cheers!** [tʃɪəz] Danke! **III**

**cheese** [tʃiːz] Käse **I**

**chef** [ʃef] Koch; Küchenchef **VI U2**, 58

**chess** [tʃes] Schach **II**

**chest** [tʃest] Brust; Brustkorb **V**; Busen **VI TS2**, 71

**chewing** gum [ˈtʃuːɪŋ ˌɡʌm] Kaugummi **IV**

**chicken** [ˈtʃɪkɪn] Huhn; Hähnchen **I**

**chicken** tikka masala [ˌtʃɪkɪn ˌtɪkə məˈsɑːlə] *indisches Hühnchengericht* **I**

**Chief** Elder [ˌtʃiːf ˈeldə] Ratschef/-in; Ratsvorsitzende-r ⟨**VI U1**, 22⟩

**child, children** *(pl)* [ˈtʃaɪld; ˈtʃɪldrən] Kind **I**

**child** labor *(AE)* [ˌtʃaɪld ˈleɪbə] Kinderarbeit **IV**

**child** labour [ˌtʃaɪld ˈleɪbə] Kinderarbeit **V**

only **child** [ˈəʊnli ˌtʃaɪld] Einzelkind **I**

**childhood** [ˈtʃaɪldhʊd] Kindheit **V**

to **chill** out [tʃɪl ˈaʊt] chillen **III**

**chill** [tʃɪl] kalt ⟨**VI U1**, 7⟩

**chilly** [ˈtʃɪli] kühl; frisch ⟨**VI U2**, 60⟩

**chimney** [ˈtʃɪmni] Kamin; Schornstein **III**

**chin** [tʃɪn] Kinn ⟨**VI U2**, 60⟩

**Chinese** [tʃaɪˈniːz] Chinese/Chinesin; chinesisch; Chinesisch; aus China **V**

**chip** [tʃɪp] Chip **VI U2**, 51; Stückchen ⟨**VI U2**, 60⟩

**chips** *(pl) (BE)* [tʃɪps] Pommes frites **I**

**chocolate** [ˈtʃɒklət] Schokolade **I**

**chocolate** bar [ˈtʃɒklət ˌbɑː] Schokoriegel **IV**

**choice** [tʃɔɪs] Wahl; Auswahl **II**

*to make a **choice** [ˌmeɪk ə ˈtʃɔɪs] eine Wahl treffen **VI U1**, 26

*to **choose** [tʃuːz] auswählen; wählen **II**

to **chop** [tʃɒp] hacken; klein schneiden **VI U1**, 13

**chore** [tʃɔː] (lästige) Pflicht; Bürde **V**

**chorus** [ˈkɔːrəs] Refrain **III**

in **chorus** [ɪn ˈkɔːrəs] im Chor **IV**

clam **chowder** [ˌklæm ˈtʃaʊdə] Muschelsuppe **V**

**Christmas** [ˈkrɪsməs] Weihnachten **I**

to **chuckle** [ˈtʃʌkl] in sich hineinlachen ⟨**VI U1**, 26⟩

**church** [tʃɜːtʃ] Kirche **I**

**cinema** [ˈsɪnəmə] Kino **I**

**circle** [ˈsɜːkl] Kreis; Ring **I**

*to go round in **circles** [ɡəʊ ˌraʊnd ɪn ˈsɜːklz] sich im Kreis drehen **III**

**citizen** [ˈsɪtɪzn] Bürger/-in ⟨**VI U1**, 23⟩

**city** [ˈsɪti] Stadt; Großstadt **I**

**civil rights** *(pl)* [ˌsɪvl ˈraɪts] Bürgerrechte **V**

to **claim** [kleɪm] behaupten **IV**

**clam** chowder [ˌklæm ˈtʃaʊdə] Muschelsuppe **V**

to **clap** [klæp] klatschen **I**

**Clap** your hands. [ˌklæp jɔː ˈhændz] Klatsch/Klatscht in die Hände. **I**

**clarification** [ˌklærɪfɪˈkeɪʃn] Klärung; Klarstellung **IV**

**class** [klɑːs] Klasse; Schulklasse **I**; *hier:* Unterricht **II**

**class** display [ˈklɑːs dɪˌspleɪ] Ausstellung in der Klasse **I**

**class** poster [ˈklɑːs ˌpəʊstə] Klassenposter **I**

middle **class** [ˌmɪdl ˈklɑːs] Mittelschicht **V**

**classic** [ˈklæsɪk] Klassiker **V**

**classical** [ˈklæsɪkl] klassisch **IV**

**classmate** [ˈklɑːsmeɪt] Klassenkamerad/-in; Mitschüler/-in **I**

**classroom** [ˈklɑːsrʊm] Klassenzimmer **I**

adverbial **clause** [ədˌvɜːbiəl ˈklɔːz] Adverbialsatz **V**

contact **clause** [ˈkɒntækt ˌklɔːz] *Relativsatz ohne Relativpronomen* **II**

defining relative **clause** [dɪˌfaɪnɪŋ ˈrelətɪv ˌklɔːz] notwendiger Relativsatz **II**

if-**clause** [ˈɪf klɔːz] if-Satz **II**

main **clause** [ˈmeɪn ˌklɔːz] Hauptsatz **III**

non-defining relative **clause** [ˌnɒndɪfaɪnɪŋ ˈrelətɪv ˌklɔːz] nicht notwendiger Relativsatz **IV**

**clay** pipe [ˈkleɪ paɪp] Tonpfeife **II**

to **clean** [kliːn] säubern; reinigen **I**

to **clean** out [ˌkliːn ˈaʊt] ausräumen; entrümpeln **IV**

to **clean** up [ˌkliːn ˈʌp] aufräumen; sauber machen **V**

**clean** [kliːn] sauber **III**

to **clear** out [ˌklɪər ˈaʊt] ausräumen; entrümpeln **I**

**clear** [klɪə] klar; deutlich **I**

to **clench** [klenʃ] sich zusammenziehen ⟨**VI U2**, 62⟩

**clever** [ˈklevə] schlau; klug **II**

cliché [ˈkliːʃeɪ] Klischee **V**
click [klɪk] Klicken; Klick **II**
to **click** on [ˈklɪkˌɒn] anklicken **III**
cliff [klɪf] Klippe; Kliff **III**
climate [ˈklaɪmət] Klima **IV**
  **climate** change [ˈklaɪmət ˌtʃeɪndʒ] Klimawandel **VI U2**, 54
climatic [klaɪˈmætɪk] klimatisch **V**
climax [ˈklaɪmæks] Höhepunkt **III**
to **climb** [klaɪm] klettern; besteigen; steigen **I**
climbing [ˈklaɪmɪŋ] Klettern **II**
clip [klɪp] Clip; Ausschnitt **V**
  **clip** art [ˈklɪpˌɑːt] Clipart; Grafik °**VI U2**, 58
clique [kliːk] Clique **IV**
clock [klɒk] Uhr **I**
  alarm **clock** [əˈlɑːm ˌklɒk] Wecker **II**
  o'**clock** [əˈklɒk] Uhr *(Zeitangabe bei vollen Stunden)* **I**
to **clone** [kləʊn] klonen **III**
close [kləʊs] schmaler Durchgang **III**
to **close** [kləʊz] schließen; zumachen **I**
  to **close** down [ˌkləʊz ˈdaʊn] den Betrieb einstellen; schließen **VI U2**, 50
  to **close** oneself away from [ˌkləʊz əˈweɪ frəm] sich abschotten von **IV**
close [kləʊs] eng; knapp **I**; nahe **II**
  Look **closely** … [ˌlʊk ˈkləʊsli] Schau(t) genau … **II**
  That was **close**! [ˌðæt wəz ˈkləʊs] Das war knapp! **I**
closed [kləʊzd] geschlossen; zu **IV**
closet [ˈklɒzɪt] Schrank; Wandschrank **IV**
  walk-in **closet** [ˌwɔːkɪn ˈklɒzɪt] begehbarer Kleiderschrank **IV**
close-up [ˈkləʊsʌp] Nahaufnahme **II**
clothes *(pl)* [kləʊðz] Kleider; Kleidung **I**
clothing [ˈkləʊðɪŋ] Kleidung **IV**
  **clothing** drive [ˈkləʊðɪŋ ˌdraɪv] Kleidersammlung **IV**
cloud [klaʊd] Wolke **III**
  word **cloud** [ˈwɜːd ˌklaʊd] Wörterwolke **II**
cloudy [ˈklaʊdi] bedeckt; bewölkt **II**
clown [klaʊn] Clown **II**
club [klʌb] Klub; Verein; AG **I**
  Cooking **Club** [ˈkʊkɪŋ ˌklʌb] Koch-AG **I**
clue [kluː] Hinweis; Spur **II**
  *to have no **clue** [ˌhæv nəʊ ˈkluː] keine Ahnung haben **IV**
clumsy [ˈklʌmzi] ungeschickt; unbeholfen ⟨**VI U1**, 23⟩
cluster [ˈklʌstə] Bündel; Anhäufung **V**
coach [kəʊtʃ] Trainer/-in **I**; Reisebus **II**
coast [kəʊst] Küste **IV**
coastal path [ˌkəʊstl ˈpɑːθ] Küstenweg **III**
coastline [ˈkəʊstlaɪn] Küste; Küstenverlauf **III**
coat [kəʊt] Mantel **VI AC2**, 74
cocoa [ˈkəʊkəʊ] Kakao **VI U1**, 13
coconut [ˈkəʊkənʌt] Kokosnuss **II**
code [kəʊd] Code; Verschlüsselung **V**

dress **code** [ˈdres ˌkəʊd] Kleiderordnung; Bekleidungsvorschriften **IV**
coffee [ˈkɒfi] Kaffee **I**
cognitive [ˈkɒɡnətɪv] kognitiv **VI TS1**, 37
coin [kɔɪn] Münze **I**
coincidence [kəʊˈɪnsɪdns] Zufall **IV**
coke [kəʊk] Cola **I**
cold [kəʊld] Erkältung **II**
cold [kəʊld] kalt **II**
collage [kɒlˈɑːʒ] Collage **V**
to **collapse** [kəˈlæps] kollabieren; zusammenbrechen; einstürzen **VI U2**, 54
colleague [ˈkɒliːɡ] Kollege/Kollegin **VI U1**, 19
to **collect** [kəˈlekt] sammeln **I**
collection [kəˈlekʃn] Kollektion; Sammlung **II**
collective [kəˈlektɪv] gemeinsam; kollektiv ⟨**VI U1**, 23⟩
  **collective** noun [kəˈlektɪv] Sammelbegriff °**VI U2**, 53
college [ˈkɒlɪdʒ] Universität *(in den USA)* **V**
collocation [ˌkɒləˈkeɪʃn] Wortverbindung **II**
colonial [kəˈləʊniəl] kolonial; Kolonial- **V**
colonisation [ˌkɒlənaɪˈzeɪʃn] Kolonisierung; Kolonisation **V**
colonist [ˈkɒlənɪst] Siedler/-in; Kolonist/-in **IV**
to **colonize** *(AE)* [ˈkɒlənaɪz] kolonisieren **V**
colony [ˈkɒləni] Kolonie **II**
color *(AE)* [ˈkʌlə] Farbe ⟨**VI AC1**, 40⟩
colorful *(AE)* [ˈkʌləfl] farbenfroh; bunt **V**
colorless *(AE)* [ˈkʌlələs] farblos ⟨**VI U1**, 25⟩
colour [ˈkʌlə] Farbe **I**
  What **colour** is …? [ˌwɒt ˈkʌlər ɪz] Welche Farbe hat …? **I**
colourful [ˈkʌləfl] farbenfroh; bunt **I**
column [ˈkɒləm] Spalte **III**
combination [ˌkɒmbɪˈneɪʃn] Kombination; Verbindung **IV**
to **combine** [kəmˈbaɪn] kombinieren; verbinden **IV**
*to **come** [kʌm] kommen **I**
  *to **come** down [ˌkʌm ˈdaʊn] herunterkommen **I**
  *to **come** in [ˌkʌmˈɪn] hereinkommen **III**
  *to **come** out [ˌkʌmˈaʊt] sich outen **VI AC1**, 42
  *to **come** to one's mind [ˌkʌm tə wʌnz ˈmaɪnd] jmdm. in den Sinn kommen; jmdm. einfallen **V**
  *to **come** true [ˌkʌm ˈtruː] wahr werden; in Erfüllung gehen **IV**
  *to **come** up [ˌkʌmˈʌp] vorkommen **III**
  *to **come** up to [ˌkʌmˈʌp tə] zukommen auf **V**
  **Come** on! [ˌkʌmˈɒn] Komm schon!; Komm jetzt! **I**
comedian [kəˈmiːdiən] Komiker/-in; Comedian **II**
comedy [ˈkɒmədi] Komödie **III**
  **comedy** show [ˈkɒmədi ˌʃəʊ] Comedy Show **II**
to **comfort** [ˈkʌmfət] trösten; ermutigen **V**

comfortable [ˈkʌmftəbl] komfortabel; bequem **II**
comforting [ˈkʌmfətɪŋ] tröstlich; ermutigend **V**
comic [ˈkɒmɪk] Comicheft **II**
coming out [ˌkʌmɪŋˈaʊt] Coming-out **VI AC1**, 42
comma [ˈkɒmə] Komma **IV**
command [kəˈmɑːnd] Befehl **IV**
commanding [kəˈmɑːndɪŋ] gebieterisch; befehlend ⟨**VI U1**, 23⟩
comment [ˈkɒment] Kommentar **II**
to **comment** (on) [ˈkɒmentˌ(ɒn)] kommentieren **II**
commenting [ˈkɒmentɪŋ] kommentierend °**VI U1**, 11
commitment [kəˈmɪtmənt] Bindung; Verpflichtung; Engagement **VI U1**, 15
committee [kəˈmɪti] Komitee; Ausschuss **IV**
common [ˈkɒmən] gemeinsam; üblich; verbreitet; gängig **V**
  *to have in **common** [ˌhæv ɪn ˈkɒmən] gemeinsam haben **III**
to **communicate** [kəˈmjuːnɪkeɪt] kommunizieren; sich verständigen **II**
communication [kəˌmjuːnɪˈkeɪʃn] Kommunikation **II**
  **communications** network [kəˌmjuːnɪˈkeɪʃnz ˌnetwɜːk] Kommunikationsnetz; Nachrichtennetz **V**
community [kəˈmjuːnəti] Gemeinde; Gemeinschaft **V**
  **community** centre [kəˈmjuːnəti ˌsentə] Gemeindezentrum **I**
company [ˈkʌmpəni] Gesellschaft; Firma; Unternehmen **III**
  start-up **company** [ˈstɑːtʌp ˌkʌmpəni] Start-up(-Unternehmen); Unternehmensgründung **VI U2**, 50
  tour **company** [ˈtʊə ˌkʌmpəni] Reiseanbieter **IV**
comparative [kəmˈpærətɪv] Komparativ **II**
to **compare** (with/to) [kəmˈpeə] vergleichen (mit) **III**
comparison [kəmˈpærɪsn] Vergleich **II**
to **compel** [kəmˈpel] zwingen; veranlassen ⟨**VI U2**, 60⟩
to **compete** (with) [kəmˈpiːt] konkurrieren (mit); sich messen (mit); in Wettbewerb treten (mit) **III**
competition [ˌkɒmpəˈtɪʃn] Wettbewerb; Turnier **II**
  *to hold a **competition** [ˌhəʊld ə ˌkɒmpəˈtɪʃn] einen Wettbewerb durchführen **V**
competitive [kəmˈpetɪtɪv] leistungsorientiert; konkurrierend **III**
to **complain** [kəmˈpleɪn] sich beschweren; sich beklagen **IV**
to **complete** [kəmˈpliːt] fertigstellen; vervollständigen; vollenden **IV**

complete [kəmˈpliːt] vollständig; komplett; völlig **IV**

complicated [ˈkɒmplɪkeɪtɪd] kompliziert **IV**

compliment [ˈkɒmplɪmənt] Kompliment **V**

component [kəmˈpəʊnənt] Bestandteil; Komponente **VI U2**, 51

compound word [ˈkɒmpaʊnd wɜːd] Kompositum *(zusammengesetztes Wort)* **II**

comprehension [ˌkɒmprɪˈhenʃn] Verständnis; Verstehen **V**

comprehensive school [kɒmprɪˈhensɪv ˌskuːl] Gesamtschule **VI U1**, 10

to comprise [kəmˈpraɪz] umfassen; beinhalten; einschließen **VI U2**, 49

compromise [ˈkɒmprəmaɪz] Kompromiss **II**

to compromise [ˈkɒmprəmaɪz] Kompromisse eingehen **III**

compulsive [kəmˈpʌlsɪv] zwanghaft ⟨**VI TS1**, 39⟩

computer [kəmˈpjuːtə] Computer **I**

con [kɒn] Argument dagegen **II**
pros and cons *(pl)* [ˌprɒʊz ən ˈkɒnz] Argumente für und gegen etw.; Pro und Kontra °**VI U2**, 51

to concentrate [ˈkɒnsntreɪt] (sich) konzentrieren **IV**

concept [ˈkɒnsept] Vorstellung; Idee; Konzept **V**

concern [kənˈsɜːn] Sorge ⟨**VI TS1**, 39⟩

concert [ˈkɒnsət] Konzert **IV**

concise [kənˈsaɪs] präzise; kurz; prägnant **V**

to conclude [kənˈkluːd] enden; schließen; schlussfolgern **VI TS1**, 35

conclusion [kənˈkluːʒn] Schluss; Schlussfolgerung **V**

concrete [ˈkɒŋkriːt] Beton **IV**

concrete [ˈkɒŋkriːt] konkret **V**

conditional sentence [kənˌdɪʃnl ˈsentəns] Bedingungssatz **III**

to conduct [kənˈdʌkt] durchführen; ausführen **IV**

conference [ˈkɒnfrns] Konferenz; Tagung **IV**

confident [ˈkɒnfɪdnt] selbstsicher; selbstbewusst **II**

conflict [ˈkɒnflɪkt] Konflikt; Auseinandersetzung **V**

*to be confronted with [bi kənˈfrʌntɪd wɪð] konfrontiert werden mit **VI TS2**, 71

to confuse sb/sth with sb/sth [kənˈfjuːz] jmdn./etw. mit jmdm./etw. verwechseln °**VI TS1**, 38

confused [kənˈfjuːzd] verwirrt; wirr; konfus **III**

to connect (to) [kəˈnekt tə] verbinden (mit); vermitteln; anschließen **V**

*to be connected [bi kəˈnektɪd] zusammenhängen; in Zusammenhang stehen **II**

connection [kəˈnekʃn] Verbindung **III**

conscience [ˈkɒnʃns] Gewissen **IV**
guilty conscience [ˌgɪlti ˈkɒnʃns] Schuldbewusstsein; schlechtes Gewissen **V**

consecutive [kənˈsekjʊtɪv] aufeinanderfolgend; fortlaufend **IV**

consequence [ˈkɒnsɪkwəns] Konsequenz; Folge **IV**

conservation [ˌkɒnsəˈveɪʃn] Schutz; Erhaltung **VI U2**, 56

to consider [kənˈsɪdə] betrachten; erwägen **V**

*to be considered (to be) sth [bi kənˈsɪdəd tə] als etw. gelten **V**

to consist of [kənˈsɪst əv] bestehen aus **V**

conspiracy [kənˈspɪrəsi] Verschwörung **IV**

constant [ˈkɒnstənt] ständig; konstant; stetig; gleichmäßig **V**

construction [kənˈstrʌkʃn] Konstruktion **IV**
construction worker [kənˈstrʌkʃn ˌwɜːkə] Bauarbeiter/-in **VI U1**, 9

constructive [kənˈstrʌktɪv] konstruktiv **VI TS2**, 69

contact [ˈkɒntækt] Kontakt **II**
contact clause [ˈkɒntækt ˌklɔːz] *Relativsatz ohne Relativpronomen* **II**

to contain [kənˈteɪn] enthalten **IV**

container [kənˈteɪnə] Container; Behälter; Behältnis **VI U1**, 13

content [ˈkɒntent] Inhalt **IV**

contest [ˈkɒntest] Wettkampf; Wettbewerb **I**

contestant [kənˈtestnt] Kandidat/-in **VI TS2**, 68

context [ˈkɒntekst] Kontext; Zusammenhang **V**

continent [ˈkɒntɪnənt] Kontinent; Erdteil **IV**

to continue [kənˈtɪnjuː] fortfahren; andauern; weitermachen **III**; weitergehen **IV**

contrast [ˈkɒntrɑːst] Kontrast; Unterschied; Gegensatz **IV**

to contrast [kənˈtrɑːst] kontrastieren; gegenüberstellen **V**

to contribute to [kənˈtrɪbjuːt tə] beitragen zu ⟨**VI U2**, 56⟩

contribution [ˌkɒntrɪˈbjuːʃn] Beitrag; Beteiligung **VI U2**, 49

control [kənˈtrəʊl] Kontrolle **IV**

to control [kənˈtrəʊl] kontrollieren; steuern **IV**

controversial [ˌkɒntrəˈvɜːʃl] umstritten; kontrovers ⟨**VI TS2**, 73⟩

controversy [ˈkɒntrəvɜːsi] Kontroverse; Auseinandersetzung **VI U1**, 13

conversation [ˌkɒnvəˈseɪʃn] Konversation; Gespräch; Unterhaltung **I**
to hog a conversation [ˌhɒg ə kɒnvəˈseɪʃn] ein Gespräch für sich in Beschlag nehmen; ein Gespräch dominieren **III**

convict [ˈkɒnvɪkt] Sträfling **V**

to convince [kənˈvɪns] überzeugen **II**

convinced [kənˈvɪnst] überzeugt **IV**

convincing [kənˈvɪnsɪŋ] überzeugend **IV**

cook [kʊk] Koch/Köchin ⟨**VI U2**, 61⟩

to cook [kʊk] kochen **II**

cooker [ˈkʊkə] Herd **I**

cooking [ˈkʊkɪŋ] Kochen **I**
Cooking Club [ˈkʊkɪŋ ˌklʌb] Koch-AG **I**

*to leave it to cool [ˌliːv ɪt tə ˈkuːl] kalt stellen **I**

cool [kuːl] cool; super **I**; kühl **IV**

to coordinate [kəʊˈɔːdɪneɪt] koordinieren **VI U2**, 54

copper [ˈkɒpə] Kupfer **V**
copper-mining [ˈkɒpəˌmaɪnɪŋ] Kupferbergbau **V**

ad copy [ˈæd ˌkɒpi] Werbetext **IV**

to copy [ˈkɒpi] abschreiben; kopieren **I**

corn [kɔːn] Korn; Mais; Getreide **IV**

corner [ˈkɔːnə] Ecke **II**

Cornish [ˈkɔːnɪʃ] in Cornwall **III**

corporation [ˌkɔːpəˈreɪʃn] Konzern; Unternehmen **V**

to correct [kəˈrekt] verbessern; berichtigen; korrigieren ⟨**VI U1**, 26⟩
Correct … [kəˈrekt] Korrigiere/Korrigiert … **I**

correct [kəˈrekt] richtig; korrekt **I**

corridor [ˈkɒrɪdɔː] Gang; Flur; Korridor **IV**

cosmetics *(pl)* [kɒzˈmetɪks] Kosmetik **VI U1**, 13

*to cost [kɒst] kosten **I**

costume [ˈkɒstjuːm] Kostüm **I**

cougar [ˈkuːgə] Puma; Berglöwe **V**

cough [kɒf] Husten **II**

could [kʊd] könnte/-n **II**; konnte/-n **III**

student council [ˌstjuːdnt ˈkaʊnsl] Schülerrat **VI AC2**, 74

counsellor [ˈkaʊnslə] Betreuer/-in **VI U1**, 8
assistant counsellor [əˌsɪstnt ˈkaʊnslə] Hilfsbetreuer/-in **VI U1**, 8
senior counsellor [ˌsiːniə ˈkaʊnslə] leitender Betreuer/leitende Betreuerin; ranghohe/-r Minister/-in **VI U1**, 8

to count (on) [ˈkaʊnt ɒn] zählen (auf) **I**

counter [ˈkaʊntə] Theke ⟨**VI U2**, 60⟩; Zähler ⟨**VI U2**, 62⟩

counter [ˈkaʊntə] Gegen- °**VI TS2**, 69

country, countries *(pl)* [ˈkʌntri; ˈkʌntriz] Land **V**
in the country [ˌɪn ðə ˈkʌntri] auf dem Land **IV**

countryside [ˈkʌntrisaɪd] Land **III**

couple [ˈkʌpl] Paar **III**
a couple of [ə ˈkʌpl əv] ein paar **I**

course [kɔːs] Kurs **II**
of course [əv ˈkɔːs] natürlich; selbstverständlich **I**

court [kɔːt] Spielfeld **II**; Hof; Gericht; Gerichtshof **V**

cousin [ˈkʌzn] Cousin/Cousine **I**

cover [ˈkʌvə] Cover; Titelblatt **III**
cover version [ˈkʌvə ˌvɜːʃn] Coverversion **III**

to cover [ˈkʌvə] abdecken; bedecken; zudecken **III**

covered wagon [ˌkʌvəd ˈwægən] Planwagen **V**

cover-up [ˈkʌvərʌp] Vertuschung **IV**
cow [kaʊ] Kuh **III**
cowboy [ˈkaʊbɔɪ] Cowboy; Rinderhirte **IV**
crack [kræk] Knacken; Krachen **III**; Riss;
Spalt **VI U2**, 55
cracking [ˈkrækɪŋ] knackend; brechend **III**
craft [krɑːft] Handwerk; Gewerbe **VI U2**, 58
cramp [kræmp] Krampf **II**
crane [kreɪn] Kran **III**
total crap [ˌtəʊtl ˈkræp] völliger Quatsch
⟨**VI TS2**, 70⟩
to crash [kræʃ] abstürzen **II**; zusammen-
stoßen **III**; krachend herunterfallen
⟨**VI U2**, 60⟩
to crave [kreɪv] sich sehnen nach ⟨**VI U2**, 61⟩
craze [kreɪz] Manie; Fimmel; fixe Idee
⟨**VI U2**, 52⟩
crazy [ˈkreɪzi] verrückt **I**
*to be **crazy** about [bi ˈkreɪzi əˌbaʊt] verrückt sein nach; abfahren auf **IV**
*to go **crazy** [ˌgəʊ ˈkreɪzi] ausflippen;
durchdrehen; verrückt werden **II**
cream [kriːm] Creme; Sahne **I**
ice **cream** [ˌaɪs ˈkriːm] Eis; Eiscreme **I**
to create [kriˈeɪt] schaffen; erschaffen;
erfinden **I**
creative [kriˈeɪtɪv] kreativ **I**
creature [ˈkriːtʃə] Kreatur; Lebewesen;
Geschöpf **V**
credit [ˈkredɪt] Guthaben **II**
crew [kruː] Crew; Besatzung; Mannschaft;
Team **V**
cricket [ˈkrɪkɪt] Cricket **II**
crime [kraɪm] Verbrechen; Kriminalität **III**
criminal [ˈkrɪmɪnəl] Kriminelle/-r; Verbre-
cher/-in **III**
to cringe [krɪndʒ] schaudern; sich ducken **IV**
crisp (BE) [krɪsp] Kartoffelchip **I**
criterion [kraɪˈtɪəriən], criteria [kraɪˈtɪəriə]
(pl) Kriterium; Argument **III**
critical [ˈkrɪtɪkl] kritisch **IV**
to criticise [ˈkrɪtɪsaɪz] kritisieren **VI TS2**, 68
criticism [ˈkrɪtɪsɪzm] Kritik **VI TS1**, 34
crocodile [ˈkrɒkədaɪl] Krokodil **V**
to crop (a photo) [krɒp] (ein Foto) zurecht-
schneiden **III**
cross [krɒs] Kreuz **III**
to cross [krɒs] überqueren; kreuzen **II**; sich
kreuzen °**VI U2**, 53
*to keep your fingers **crossed** [ˌkiːp jɔː
ˌfɪŋgəz ˈkrɒst] die Daumen drücken **I**
crowd [kraʊd] Menschenmenge **II**
crowded [ˈkraʊdɪd] überfüllt **IV**
crown [kraʊn] Krone **III**
**crown** jewels [ˌkraʊn ˈdʒuːəlz] Kronjuwe-
len **II**
cruel [ˈkruːəl] grausam **III**
crushed [krʌʃt] eingequetscht; eingeklemmt
**IV**
to cry [kraɪ] schreien; rufen **II**; weinen **III**
CU (= See you) [ˈsiː juː] Bis dann!; Bis … **I**
cultivation [ˌkʌltɪˈveɪʃn] Anbau **VI U2**, 50

cultural [ˈkʌltʃrl] kulturell **IV**
culture [ˈkʌltʃə] Kultur **I**
Across **cultures** [əˌkrɒs ˈkʌltʃəz] Interkulturelles **I**
cup [kʌp] Tasse **III**
cupboard [ˈkʌbəd] Küchenschrank; Schrank **I**
curfew [ˈkɜːfjuː] Sperrstunde; Ausgangs-
sperre **IV**
curiosity [ˌkjʊəriˈɒsəti] Neugier **VI U1**, 7
curious [ˈkjʊəriəs] neugierig **VI U1**, 25
currency [ˈkʌrnsi] Währung **IV**
rip current [ˈrɪp ˌkʌrnt] Brandungsrückströmung **V**
currently [ˈkʌrntli] momentan **VI TS1**, 37
curry [ˈkʌri] Curry (Gewürz oder Gericht) **I**
custard [ˈkʌstəd] Vanillesoße; Vanillepud-
ding **I**
custom [ˈkʌstəm] Gewohnheit; Brauch;
Sitte **IV**
customer [ˈkʌstəmə] Kunde/Kundin **III**
customs (sg) [ˈkʌstəmz] Zoll **IV**
*to cut (off) [kʌt (ɒf)] schneiden; abschnei-
den **II**
*to cut down [ˌkʌt ˈdaʊn] fällen **VI U2**, 54
*to cut up [ˌkʌt ˈʌp] zerschneiden **IV**
cute [kjuːt] niedlich; süß **I**
CV (Curriculum Vitae) [ˌsiːˈviː] (kəˌrɪkjələm
ˈviːtaɪ) Lebenslauf **VI U1**, 8
cyber addiction [ˈsaɪbər əˌdɪkʃn] Internetsucht; Internetabhängigkeit ⟨**VI TS1**, 39⟩
**cyber** bully [ˌsaɪbə ˈbʊli] jemand, der
andere in sozialen Netzwerken belästigt
oder mobbt **V**
cycle [ˈsaɪkl] Zyklus; Kreislauf **VI TS1**, 37
to cycle [ˈsaɪkl] Fahrrad fahren **IV**
cycling [ˈsaɪklɪŋ] Radfahren **I**

## D

dad [dæd] Papa **I**
dam [dæm] Damm; Staumauer **V**
damage [ˈdæmɪdʒ] Schaden; Beschädigung
**VI U2**, 55
to damage [ˈdæmɪdʒ] schaden; beschädi-
gen **V**
dance [dɑːns] Tanz; Tanzveranstaltung **III**
to dance [dɑːns] tanzen **I**
to **dance** to [ˈdɑːns tə] tanzen zu **III**
dancer [ˈdɑːnsə] Tänzer/-in **II**
backing **dancer** [ˈbækɪŋ ˌdɑːnsə] Back-
groundtänzer/-in **III**
danger [ˈdeɪndʒə] Gefahr **III**
dangerous [ˈdeɪndʒrəs] gefährlich **I**
to dare [deə] wagen **V**
the dark [ðə ˈdɑːk] Dunkelheit **II**
dark [dɑːk] dunkel **II**
darkness [ˈdɑːknəs] Dunkelheit **III**
date [deɪt] Datum **I**; Verabredung; Date **IV**
**date** of birth [ˌdeɪt əv ˈbɜːθ] Geburtsdatum **IV**
to date [deɪt] ausgehen mit ⟨**VI AC1**, 40⟩
dating [ˈdeɪtɪŋ] Partnersuche; Daten **V**

daughter [ˈdɔːtə] Tochter **III**
day [deɪ] Tag **I**
all **day** [ˌɔːl ˈdeɪ] den ganzen Tag **II**
lucky **day** [ˌlʌki ˈdeɪ] Glückstag **VI U2**, 46
one **day** [wʌn ˈdeɪ] eines Tages **II**
*to take the **day** off [ˌteɪk ðə ˌdeɪ ˈɒf] sich
den Tag freinehmen **IV**
the other **day** [ðiˌʌðə ˈdeɪ] neulich **IV**
these **days** [ˌðiːz ˈdeɪz] zurzeit **III**; heutzutage ⟨**VI U2**, 61⟩
a (**day**/week/year) [ə ˈdeɪ/wiːk/jɪə] pro
(Tag/Woche/Jahr) **IV**
a **day** out in … [ə ˌdeɪ ˈaʊt ɪn] ein Tag
in … **II**
the next **day** [ðə ˌnekst ˈdeɪ] am nächsten
Tag **II**
G'**day**! (= Good day!) [gəˈdaɪ] Guten Tag.;
Hallo.; Hi. (Begrüßung in Australien) **V**
dead [ded] tot **II**
deadly [ˈdedli] tödlich **V**
deal [diːl] Abmachung; Übereinkunft; Handel; Geschäft **V**
big **deal** [bɪg ˈdiːl] große Sache **IV**
*to deal (with) [diːl] sich befassen mit;
umgehen mit **II**
dear [dɪə] Schatz ⟨**VI U2**, 62⟩
Oh **dear**! [əʊ ˈdɪə] Oje! **III**
Dear … [dɪə] Lieber …; Liebe … (Anrede in
Briefen) **I**
**Dear** Sir or Madam [dɪə ˌsɜːr ɔː ˈmædəm]
Sehr geehrte Dame, sehr geehrter Herr **III**
death [deθ] Tod **III**
to scare sb to **death** [ˌskeə tə ˈdeθ] jmdn.
zu Tode erschrecken **V**
debate [dɪˈbeɪt] Debatte **V**
decade [ˈdekeɪd] Jahrzehnt **VI U2**, 53
December [dɪˈsembə] Dezember **I**
to decide [dɪˈsaɪd] (sich) entscheiden **I**
decision [dɪˈsɪʒn] Entscheidung **III**
*to make a **decision** [ˌmeɪk ə dɪˈsɪʒn] eine
Entscheidung treffen **II**
deck [dek] Deck **I**
to declare [dɪˈkleə] erklären **V**
to decorate [ˈdekəreɪt] dekorieren; verzie-
ren; schmücken **I**
decorations (pl) [ˌdekəˈreɪʃnz] Dekoration;
Schmuck **I**
deep [diːp] tief **III**
**deep** fryer [ˌdiːp ˈfraɪə] Fritteuse **VI U2**, 58
to defeat [dɪˈfiːt] besiegen **III**
defining relative clause [dɪˈfaɪnɪŋ ˈrelətɪv
ˌklɔːz] notwendiger Relativsatz **II**
definite article [ˌdefɪnət ˈɑːtɪkl] bestimmter
Artikel °**VI U2**, 51
definitely [ˈdefɪnətli] bestimmt; definitiv;
eindeutig **I**
definition [ˌdefɪˈnɪʃn] Definition **III**
deforestation (no pl) [diːˌfɒrɪˈsteɪʃn] Abhol-
zung; Entwaldung ⟨**VI U2**, 56⟩
degree Fahrenheit (°F) [ˈfærnhaɪt] Grad
Fahrenheit **IV**

dehydration [ˌdiːhaɪˈdreɪʃn] Austrocknung **VI U2**, 54

delay [dɪˈleɪ] Verzögerung; Verspätung **IV**

delegate [ˈdelɪgət] Vertreter/-in; Delegierte/-r °**VI U2**, 59

to delete [dɪˈliːt] löschen **III**

delicious [dɪˈlɪʃəs] köstlich **IV**

to deliver [dɪˈlɪvə] liefern **V**

democracy [dɪˈmɒkrəsi] Demokratie **V**

democratic [ˌdeməˈkrætɪk] demokratisch **V**

to demonstrate [ˈdemənstreɪt] demonstrieren **IV**

dense [dens] dicht **IV**

to depart [dɪˈpɑːt] abfahren **III**

departure [dɪˈpɑːtʃə] Abflug; Abreise **IV**
departure lounge [dɪˈpɑːtʃə ˌlaʊndʒ] Abflughalle **IV**

to depend (on) [dɪˈpendˌ(ɒn)] abhängen von **III**

depressing [dɪˈpresɪŋ] deprimierend; bedrückend **IV**

deprivation [ˌdeprɪˈveɪʃn] Entbehrung; Entzug **VI TS1**, 37

deprived [dɪˈpraɪvd] beraubt; entzogen **VI TS1**, 37

to descend from [dɪˈsend frəm] abstammen von; herstammen von **V**

to describe [dɪˈskraɪb] beschreiben **I**

description [dɪˈskrɪpʃn] Beschreibung **II**

descriptive [dɪˈskrɪptɪv] beschreibend **V**

desert [ˈdezət] Wüste **IV**

to deserve [dɪˈzɜːv] verdienen **II**

design [dɪˈzaɪn] Design; Gestaltung; Entwurf **II**

to design [dɪˈzaɪn] entwerfen; gestalten **II**

designer [dɪˈzaɪnə] Designer/-in **III**
web designer [ˈweb dɪˌzaɪnə] Webdesigner **III**

desirable [dɪˈzaɪərəbl] wünschenswert; erstrebenswert **VI U1**, 7

desk [desk] Schalter **IV**; Schreibtisch **V**

desperate [ˈdesprət] verzweifelt; hoffnungslos; ausweglos **V**

destination [ˌdestɪˈneɪʃn] Ziel; Reiseziel **IV**

destiny [ˈdestini] Schicksal; Fügung; Vorsehung **VI U1**, 22

to destroy [dɪˈstrɔɪ] zerstören **V**

detail [ˈdiːteɪl] Detail; Einzelheit **II**

detective [dɪˈtektɪv] Detektiv/-in; Detektivgeschichte; Kriminalroman; Kriminalfilm; Krimi **III**
private detective [ˌpraɪvət dɪˈtektɪv] Privatdetektiv/-in **III**

detention [dɪˈtenʃn] Nachsitzen; Haft; Verhaftung **IV**

to determine [dɪˈtɜːmɪn] bestimmen; ermitteln **VI U1**, 22

determined [dɪˈtɜːmɪnd] (fest) entschlossen; entschieden; zielstrebig **V**

to develop [dɪˈveləp] (sich) entwickeln **V**

device [dɪˈvaɪs] Gerät; Vorrichtung **VI U2**, 51

devil [ˈdevl] Teufel **IV**

diagram [ˈdaɪəgræm] Diagramm **I**

dialect [ˈdaɪəlekt] Dialekt **III**

dialogue [ˈdaɪəlɒg] Dialog; Gespräch **I**

diamond [ˈdaɪəmənd] Diamant ⟨**VI U1**, 7⟩

diary [ˈdaɪəri] Tagebuch **III**
diary entry [ˈdaɪəri entri] Tagebucheintrag **III**
*to keep a diary [ˌkiːpˌə ˈdaɪəri] ein Tagebuch führen **V**

dice [daɪs] Würfel **II**
Roll two dice. [ˌrəʊlˌtuː ˈdaɪs] Würfle/Würfelt mit zwei Würfeln. **I**
throw the dice twice [ˌθrəʊ ðə daɪs ˈtwaɪs] würfle zweimal **II**

to dictate [dɪkˈteɪt] diktieren; vorschreiben **VI AC2**, 74

dictionary [ˈdɪkʃnri] Wörterbuch **I**

to die [daɪ] sterben **III**
It's to die for! [ˌɪts tə ˈdaɪ fɔː] Dafür könnte ich sterben!; Das ist unwiderstehlich! **V**

diet [daɪət] Diät ⟨**VI TS2**, 71⟩

difference [ˈdɪfrəns] Unterschied **I**
*to make a difference (to sth) [ˌmeɪkˌə ˈdɪfrəns] etw. verändern **VI AC2**, 74

different [ˈdɪfrnt] anders; unterschiedlich; verschieden **I**

difficult [ˈdɪfɪklt] schwierig **II**

difficulty [ˈdɪfɪklti] Schwierigkeit **V**

*to dig [dɪg] graben **II**

digital [ˈdɪdʒɪtl] digital ⟨**VI U2**, 62⟩

dilemma [daɪˈlemə] Dilemma; Zwickmühle **IV**

diner (AE) [ˈdaɪnə] einfaches Restaurant mit Theke und Tischen **IV**

dinner [ˈdɪnə] Abendessen **I**

dinosaur [ˈdaɪnəsɔː] Dinosaurier **II**

direct [dɪˈrekt] direkt **III**
direct speech [ˌdɪrekt ˈspiːtʃ] direkte Rede **IV**

direction [dɪˈrekʃn] Richtung **I**
stage direction [ˈsteɪdʒ dɪˌrekʃn] Regieanweisung **III**

director [dɪˈrektə] Regisseur/-in **IV**

dirt [dɜːt] Schmutz; Dreck **III**

dirty [ˈdɜːti] dreckig; schmutzig **II**

the disabled [ðə dɪˈseɪbld] Behinderte **VI U1**, 15

disadvantage [ˌdɪsədˈvɑːntɪdʒ] Nachteil **V**

to disagree [ˌdɪsəˈgriː] anderer Meinung sein; nicht einverstanden sein **III**

to disappear [ˌdɪsəˈpɪə] verschwinden **V**

disappointed [ˌdɪsəˈpɔɪntɪd] enttäuscht **I**

disappointing [ˌdɪsəˈpɔɪntɪŋ] enttäuschend **IV**

disaster [dɪˈzɑːstə] Desaster; Katastrophe; Unglück **V**

to disconnect [ˌdɪskəˈnekt] trennen; abschalten ⟨**VI TS1**, 39⟩

to discover [dɪˈskʌvə] entdecken **II**

discovery [dɪˈskʌvri] Entdeckung **III**

discrimination [dɪˌskrɪmɪˈneɪʃn] Diskriminierung **V**

to discuss [dɪˈskʌs] diskutieren **I**

discussion [dɪˈskʌʃn] Diskussion **II**

disease [dɪˈziːz] Krankheit **VI U2**, 54

disgusted [dɪsˈgʌstɪd] angeekelt; angewidert **V**

dish [dɪʃ] Gericht; Speise **IV**

dishes (pl) [ˈdɪʃɪz] Geschirr **V**
*to do the dishes [ˌduːˌðə ˈdɪʃɪz] den Abwasch machen **V**

dishonest [dɪˈsɒnɪst] unehrlich **IV**

dishwasher [ˈdɪʃwɒʃə] Spülmaschine **V**

to dislike [dɪsˈlaɪk] nicht mögen **IV**

dislikes (pl) [dɪsˈlaɪks] Abneigungen **IV**

to disobey [ˌdɪsəˈbeɪ] nicht gehorchen; ungehorsam sein **III**

display [dɪˈspleɪ] Ausstellung **II**; Ständer ⟨**VI U2**, 60⟩
class display [ˈklɑːs dɪspleɪ] Ausstellung in der Klasse **I**

disrespectful [ˌdɪsrɪˈspektfl] respektlos **V**

distance [ˈdɪstns] Distanz; Entfernung **II**

distant [ˈdɪstnt] entfernt; distanziert **VI U1**, 25

to distract [dɪˈstrækt] ablenken °**VI U2**, 58

district [ˈdɪstrɪkt] Distrikt; Bezirk **IV**

to disturb [dɪˈstɜːb] stören **V**

diversity [daɪˈvɜːsəti] Vielfalt; Verschiedenheit **VI AC1**, 41

to divide (up) [dɪˈvaɪd] aufteilen **III**

to divorce [dɪˈvɔːs] sich scheiden lassen ⟨**VI U2**, 60⟩

dizzy [ˈdɪzi] schwindelig **IV**

DJ [diːˈdʒeɪ] DJ; Discjockey **III**

*to do [duː] machen; tun **I**
*to be done with [bi ˈdʌn wɪð] fertig sein mit **IV**
*to do about [ˈduːˌəbaʊt] unternehmen wegen **II**
*to do away with sth [ˌduːˌəˈweɪ wɪð] etw. abschaffen; etw. loswerden ⟨**VI TS2**, 69⟩
*to do one's bit [ˌduːˌwʌnz ˈbɪt] seinen Teil beitragen **VI AC2**, 74
*to do our hair [ˌduːˌaʊə ˈheə] uns frisieren; unsere Haare machen **I**
*to do the dishes [ˌduː ðə ˈdɪʃɪz] den Abwasch machen **V**
*to do the shopping [ˌduː ðə ˈʃɒpɪŋ] Einkäufe machen; Besorgungen machen **III**
*to do well [ˌduː ˈwel] gute Leistungen erbringen **IV**
Don't worry! [ˌdəʊnt ˈwʌri] Keine Sorge! **I**
dos and don'ts [ˌduːz ənd ˈdəʊnts] Ge- und Verbote; was man tun und was man nicht tun sollte **III**
It wouldn't do me any good. [ˌɪt wʊdnt ˌduː mi: eni ˈgʊd] Es würde mir nichts nützen. **V**
We did it! [ˌwiː ˈdɪd ˌɪt] Wir haben es geschafft! **II**
You can do it! [ˌjuː kən ˈduː ˌɪt] Du schaffst es! **III**

doctor ['dɒktə] Arzt/Ärztin **II**

document ['dɒkjəmənt] Dokument °**VI U1**, 7

to document ['dɒkjəmənt] dokumentieren; festhalten ⟨**VI U2**, 61⟩

dog [dɒg] Hund **I**

to walk the **dog** [ˌwɔːk ðə 'dɒg] den Hund ausführen; mit dem Hund spazieren gehen **I**

I'm **dog-tired**. [ˌaɪm ˌdɒg'taɪəd] Ich bin hundemüde. **I**

dollar ['dɒlə] Dollar *(Währung)* **III**

dolphin ['dɒlfɪn] Delfin **III**

dominoes ['dɒmɪnəʊz] Domino **IV**

to donate [də'neɪt] spenden; stiften **IV**

door [dɔː] Tür **I**

French **doors** [ˌfrenʃ 'dɔːz] Terrassentür ⟨**VI U2**, 61⟩

front **door** [ˌfrʌnt 'dɔː] Haustür **II**

next **door** [ˌnekst 'dɔː] (von) nebenan **III**

doorbell ['dɔːbel] Türklingel **I**

dope [dəʊp] Rauschgift; Stoff ⟨**VI AC1**, 40⟩

dot-com bubble [ˌdɒtkɒm 'bʌbl] Internetblase; Dotcom-Blase **VI U2**, 50

double ['dʌbl] Doppel-; zweimal **IV**

doubt [daʊt] Zweifel **III**

down [daʊn] nach unten; herunter; hinunter **II**; nieder **IV**

*to break **down** [ˌbreɪk 'daʊn] zusammenbrechen **VI TS2**, 68

to close **down** [ˌkləʊz 'daʊn] den Betrieb einstellen; schließen **VI U2**, 50

*to come **down** [ˌkʌm 'daʊn] herunterkommen **I**

*to go **down** [ˌgəʊ 'daʊn] hinuntergehen; nach unten gehen; entlanggehen **I**

to note **down** [ˌnəʊt 'daʊn] notieren; aufschreiben **II**

to pull **down** [ˌpʊl 'daʊn] abreißen **III**

*to sit **down** [ˌsɪt 'daʊn] sich hinsetzen; sich setzen **I**

to slow **down** [ˌsləʊ 'daʊn] langsamer werden; bremsen **VI U1**, 25

to touch **down** [ˌtʌtʃ 'daʊn] landen **IV**

*to write **down** [ˌraɪt 'daʊn] aufschreiben **I**

downhill ['daʊnhɪl] bergab; abwärts ⟨**VI U1**, 24⟩

to download [daʊn'ləʊd] herunterladen *(aus dem Internet)* **II**

downriver [daʊn'rɪvə] flussabwärts; stromabwärts **V**

downstairs [daʊn'steəz] nach unten; im Untergeschoss; unten **II**

downtown *(AE)* [daʊn'taʊn] im Stadtzentrum **IV**

draft [drɑːft] Entwurf; Konzept **I**

drama ['drɑːmə] Theater; Drama **II**

dramatic [drə'mætɪk] dramatisch **II**

*to draw [drɔː] zeichnen **I**; ziehen **III**

*to **draw** the reader into the story/action [drɔː ðə ˌriːdə ɪntə ðə 'stɔːri/ˈækʃn] den Leser/die Leserin in die Geschichte/Handlung hineinziehen **III**

drawing ['drɔːɪŋ] Zeichnung **I**

dream [driːm] Traum **II**

*to dream [driːm] träumen **IV**

Dreaming ['driːmɪŋ] Traumzeit **V**

dress [dres] Kleid **III**

**dress** code ['dres ˌkəʊd] Kleiderordnung; Bekleidungsvorschriften **IV**

fancy **dress** ['fænsi dres] Verkleidung; Kostüm **II**

dresser ['dresə] Kommode ⟨**VI U2**, 61⟩

drink [drɪŋk] Getränk **I**

*to drink [drɪŋk] trinken **I**

drinking water ['drɪŋkɪŋ ˌwɔːtə] Trinkwasser **V**

drive [draɪv] Fahrt; Anfahrt; Autofahrt **IV**

clothing **drive** ['kləʊðɪŋ ˌdraɪv] Kleidersammlung **IV**

*to drive [draɪv] fahren **III**

*to **drive** off [draɪv 'ɒf] wegfahren **III**

driver ['draɪvə] Fahrer/-in **II**

drizzle ['drɪzl] Nieselregen **IV**

to drop [drɒp] fallen (lassen) **II**

to **drop** out (of) [drɒp 'aʊt əv] abbrechen **III**

to **drop** sb off [drɒp 'ɒf] jmdn. absetzen; jmdn. aussteigen lassen **V**

drop-off ['drɒpɒf] Abgabe **IV**

drought [draʊt] Dürre; Trockenheit **VI U2**, 50

to drown [draʊn] ertrinken; ertränken **III**

drum [drʌm] Trommel **V**

drums *(pl)* [drʌmz] Schlagzeug **III**

dry [draɪ] trocken **III**

dude *(coll)* [duːd] Mann; Alter *(ugs.)* **IV**

to dump [dʌmp] abladen **VI U1**, 13

during *(+ noun)* ['djʊərɪŋ] während *(+ Nomen)* **II**

dusty ['dʌsti] staubig **V**

duty ['djuːti] Pflicht ⟨**VI U1**, 23⟩

duty-free [ˌdjuːti'friː] zollfrei **IV**

DVD [ˌdiːviː'diː] DVD **I**

dwelling ['dwelɪŋ] Behausung; Wohnstätte ⟨**VI U1**, 23⟩

dystopia [dɪs'təʊpiə] Dystopie °**VI U1**, 27

dystopian [dɪs'təʊpiən] dystopisch °**VI U1**, 27

# E

e.g. (= for example) [ˌiː'dʒiː] z.B. *(= zum Beispiel)* **I**

each [iːtʃ] jede/-r/-s **I**

**each** other [iːtʃ'ʌðə] einander; sich; sich gegenseitig **I**

each [iːtʃ] pro Person; pro Stück **I**

ear [ɪə] Ohr **IV**

early ['ɜːli] früh **I**

this **early** [ˌðɪs ˌɜːli] so früh **III**

to earn [ɜːn] verdienen **I**

earth [ɜːθ] Erdboden; Erde; die Erde **II**

What on **earth** …? [ˌwɒt ˌɒn ˌɜːθ] Was um alles in der Welt …? **II**

earthquake ['ɜːθkweɪk] Erdbeben **VI TS1**, 34

east [iːst] Osten; Ost- **I**

Easter ['iːstə] Ostern **I**

eastern ['iːstn] östlich; Ost- **V**

easy ['iːzi] einfach; leicht **I**

easy-going [ˌiːzi'gəʊɪŋ] locker; unkompliziert **IV**

*to eat [iːt] essen; fressen **I**

eating ['iːtɪŋ] Essen; Ess- **VI U2**, 57

the ebb and flow [ˌði ˌeb ənd 'fləʊ] das Auf und Ab; die Höhen und Tiefen ⟨**VI TS1**, 37⟩

Eco ['iːkəʊ] Öko- **II**

economy [ɪ'kɒnəmi] Ökonomie; Wirtschaft **V**

edge of town [ˌedʒ əv 'taʊn] Stadtrand **V**

to edit ['edɪt] bearbeiten; überarbeiten °**VI TS1**, 38

to **edit** out [ˌedɪt 'aʊt] herausschneiden **III**

editor ['edɪtə] Herausgeber/-in; Redakteur/-in **VI TS2**, 68

letter to the **editor** [ˌletə tʊ ði 'edɪtə] Leserbrief **VI TS2**, 68

to educate ['edʒʊkeɪt] erziehen; bilden **V**

education *(no pl)* [edʒʊ'keɪʃn] Erziehung; Bildung **III**

effect [ɪ'fekt] Effekt; Wirkung **IV**

audio-visual **effect** [ˌɔːdiəʊvɪʒʊəl ɪ'fekt] audiovisueller Effekt **II**

special **effect** [ˌspeʃl ɪ'fekt] Spezialeffekt **IV**

effective [ɪ'fektɪv] effektiv; wirkungsvoll **IV**

effectiveness [ɪ'fektɪvnəs] Effektivität; Wirksamkeit **IV**

effort ['efət] Bemühung; Mühe **VI U2**, 46

egg [eg] Ei **I**

Egyptian [ɪ'dʒɪpʃn] Ägypter/-in; ägyptisch **IV**

eight [eɪt] acht **I**

either ['aɪðə; 'iːðə] beide(s) °**VI U1**, 9

**either** … or … ['aɪðə/'iːðə … ɔː] entweder … oder … **IV**

**either** of you ['aɪðər əv ˌjuː] einer von euch ⟨**VI U2**, 61⟩

not … **either** [nɒt … 'aɪðə; nɒt … 'iːðə] auch nicht **IV**

elder ['eldə] Älteste/-r **V**

Chief **Elder** [ˌtʃiːf 'eldə] Ratschef/-in; Ratsvorsitzende/-r ⟨**VI U1**, 22⟩

the elderly [ˌði 'eldəli] ältere Menschen; Senioren **VI U1**, 15

elderly ['eldəli] älter **III**

to elect [ɪ'lekt] wählen ⟨**VI U1**, 22⟩

election [ɪ'lekʃn] Wahl **V**

electric [ɪ'lektrɪk] elektrisch **III**

electrician [elɪk'trɪʃn] Elektriker/-in **III**

electricity [elɪk'trɪsəti] Elektrizität; Strom **III**

electrics [ɪ'lektrɪks] Elektrik **III**

electronic [elek'trɒnɪk] elektronisch **II**

elegant ['elɪgnt] elegant **V**

element ['elɪmənt] Element **III**

elephant ['elɪfənt] Elefant **III**

elevator *(AE)* ['elɪveɪtə] Aufzug; Lift **IV**

eleven [ɪ'levn] elf **I**

to eliminate [ɪ'lɪmɪneɪt] eliminieren; beseitigen ⟨**VI U1**, 27⟩

elk [elk] Elch **V**

**else** [els] andere/-r/-s; sonst noch **III**
  nobody **else** [ˈnəʊbədi els] niemand
  anderes **III**
  what **else** [ˌwɒtˈels] was sonst; was
  noch **I**
**elsewhere** [ˈelsweə] anderswo; woanders
  ⟨**VI U1**, 24⟩
**e-mail** [ˈiːmeɪl] E-Mail **I**
**to e-mail** [ˈiːmeɪl] mailen; per E-Mail
  schicken **II**
**to embarrass** [ɪmˈbærəs] in Verlegenheit
  bringen **VI AC1**, 43
**embarrassed** [ɪmˈbærəst] verlegen **II**
**embarrassing** [ɪmˈbærəsɪŋ] peinlich **II**
**emergency** [ɪˈmɜːdʒnsi] Notfall; Notlage;
  Notfall- **VI U2**, 54
**emotion** [ɪˈməʊʃn] Gefühl; Emotion **V**
**emotional** [ɪˈməʊʃnl] emotional; Gefühls- **III**
**emperor** [ˈemprə] Kaiser **III**
**emphasis** [ˈemfəsɪs] Betonung °**VI U1**, 19
**to emphasise** [ˈemfəsaɪz] betonen **VI U1**, 20
**empire** [ˈempaɪə] Reich; Kaiserreich **III**
**to employ** [ɪmˈplɔɪ] einstellen; anstellen;
  beschäftigen **V**
**employee** [ɪmˈplɔɪiː] Angestellte/-r; Mitar-
  beiter/-in; Arbeitnehmer/-in **V**
**employer** [ɪmˈplɔɪə] Arbeitgeber/-in **VI U1**, 9
**to empty** [ˈemti] leeren; ausräumen **V**
**empty** [ˈemti] leer **III**
**emu** [ˈiːmjuː] Emu **V**
**to enable** [ɪˈneɪbl] befähigen; ermöglichen
  ⟨**VI U2**, 52⟩
**enclosure** [ɪnˈkləʊʒə] Anlage; Beilage
  **VI U1**, 11
**to encourage** [ɪnˈkʌrɪdʒ] unterstützen;
  ermutigen **VI U1**, 8
**encyclopaedia** [ɪnˌsaɪkləˈpiːdiə] Enzyklopä-
  die; Lexikon **IV**
**end** [end] Ende; Schluss **I**
  in the **end** [ɪn ðiˈend] schließlich; zum
  Schluss **II**
**to end** [end] enden; beenden **II**
  to **end** up [ˌendˈʌp] enden; landen **II**
**ending** [ˈendɪŋ] Ende; Schluss (einer Geschichte) **I**
  happy **ending** [ˌhæpi ˈendɪŋ] Happy End
  **III**
**endless** [ˈendləs] endlos **IV**
**enemy** [ˈenəmi] Feind/-in **III**
**energy** [ˈenədʒi] Energie; Kraft **III**
search **engine** [ˈsɜːtʃˌendʒɪn] Suchmaschine
  **IV**
  steam **engine** [ˈstiːmˌendʒɪn] Dampfmaschine **III**
**engineer** [ˌendʒɪˈnɪə] Ingenieur/-in; Techni-
  ker/-in **IV**
**engineering** [ˌendʒɪˈnɪərɪŋ] Technik; Maschi-
  nenbau **VI U1**, 9
**English** [ˈɪŋglɪʃ] englisch; Englisch; aus
  England; Engländer/-in **I**
  **English**-speaking [ˈɪŋglɪʃˌspiːkɪŋ] englisch-
  sprachig **I**

I'm **English**. [aɪmˈɪŋglɪʃ] Ich bin Englän-
  der/-in. **I**
**to enjoy** [ɪnˈdʒɔɪ] genießen; sich freuen an **II**
  to **enjoy** oneself [ɪnˈdʒɔɪ] Spaß haben;
  sich amüsieren **III**
**enjoyable** [ɪnˈdʒɔɪəbl] angenehm; unterhaltsam **V**
**enlightenment** [ɪnˈlaɪtnmənt] Aufklärung;
  Erleuchtung **IV**
**enough** [ɪˈnʌf] genug; genügend **I**
**enslavement** [ɪnˈsleɪvmənt] Versklavung
  **VI TS1**, 35
**to enter** [ˈentə] hineingehen; betreten;
  eintreten; hier: mitmachen **II**
**to entertain** [ˌentəˈteɪn] unterhalten **IV**
**entertainer** [ˌentəˈteɪnə] Entertainer/-in;
  Unterhaltungskünstler/-in **IV**
**entertaining** [ˌentəˈteɪnɪŋ] unterhaltsam **IV**
**entertainment** (no pl) [ˌentəˈteɪnmənt]
  Unterhaltung **III**
**enthusiasm** [ɪnˈθjuːziæzm] Enthusiasmus;
  Begeisterung **IV**
**enthusiastic** [ɪnˌθjuːziˈæstɪk] enthusiastisch;
  begeistert **V**
**entire** [ɪnˈtaɪə] gesamt; ganz; komplett **V**
**entitled** [ɪnˈtaɪtld] mit dem Titel **VI TS1**, 35
  to be **entitled** to sth [bi ɪnˈtaɪtld tə]
  berechtigt sein; ein Anrecht haben auf;
  Anspruch haben auf °**VI AC1**, 41
**entrance** [ˈentrəns] Eingang; Eintritt **III**
**entrepreneur** [ˌɒntrəprəˈnɜː] Unternehmer/
  -in **VI U2**, 51
**entry** [ˈentri] Eintrag **III**; Beitrag; Einsen-
  dung **V**
  diary **entry** [ˈdaɪəri entri] Tagebucheintrag
  **III**
**envelope** [ˈenvələʊp] Umschlag; Briefum-
  schlag **V**
**environment** [ɪnˈvaɪrnmənt] Umwelt; Umgebung **III**
**environmental** [ɪnˌvaɪrnˈmentl] Umwelt-;
  umweltbedingt °**VI U2**, 45
**to envy** [ˈenvi] beneiden **V**
**epic** [ˈepɪk] episch; hier: geil **IV**
**equal** [ˈiːkwəl] gleich; gleichwertig **V**
**equipment** [ɪˈkwɪpmənt] Ausstattung;
  Ausrüstung **II**
**er** [ɜː] äh **I**
**era** [ˈɪərə] Ära; Zeitalter **IV**
**erosion** [ɪˈrəʊʒn] Erosion; Abtragung
  ⟨**VI U2**, 56⟩
**eruption** [ɪˈrʌpʃn] Ausbruch (Vulkan) **V**
**escalator** [ˈeskəleɪtə] Rolltreppe **I**
**escape** [ɪˈskeɪp] Flucht **III**
**to escape** (from) [ɪˈskeɪp frəm] fliehen;
  entfliehen; flüchten; entkommen **IV**
**especially** [ɪˈspeʃli] besonders; vor allem **V**
**essay** [ˈeseɪ] Essay **VI TS2**, 68
  argumentative **essay** [ɑːgjəˌmentətɪv
  ˈeseɪ] Erörterung **VI TS2**, 68
the **essentials** (pl) [ðiˌɪˈsenʃlz] das Wesentliche; die wichtigsten Punkte °**VI TS1**, 35

**to establish** [ɪˈstæblɪʃ] einführen **V**
**to estimate** [ˈestɪmeɪt] schätzen **IV**
**etc.** (= et cetera) [ɪtˈsetrə] usw. (= und so
  weiter) **II**
**ethnic** [ˈeθnɪk] ethnisch; Volks-; exotisch **IV**
**euro** [ˈjʊərəʊ] Euro (Währung) **I**
**European** [ˌjʊərəˈpiːən] Europäer/-in; euro-
  päisch; aus Europa **IV**
**to evaluate** [ɪˈvæljueɪt] evaluieren; auswer-
  ten; bewerten °**VI U1**, 8
peer **evaluation** [ˌpɪərˌɪˌvæljuˈeɪʃn] gegenseitige Beurteilung ⟨**VI AC1**, 43⟩
**even** [ˈiːvn] sogar; selbst **I**
  **even** though [ˌiːvn ˈðəʊ] auch wenn;
  obwohl **V**
**evening** [ˈiːvnɪŋ] Abend **I**
  in the **evenings** [ɪn ðiˈiːvnɪŋz] abends **I**
**event** [ɪˈvent] Ereignis; Veranstaltung **I**
**ever** [ˈevə] jemals **II**
  the best … **ever** [ˈbest … ˌevə] der/die/
  das beste … überhaupt **III**
**every** [ˈevri] jede/-r/-s **I**
**everybody** [ˈevribɒdi] jeder; alle **II**
**everyday** [ˈevrideɪ] alltäglich **III**
**everyone** [ˈevriwʌn] jeder; alle **I**
**everything** [ˈevriθɪŋ] alles **I**
  **Everything** will have changed. [ˌevriθɪŋ
  wɪl hæv ˈtʃeɪndʒd] Alles wird sich geändert haben. **V**
**everywhere** [ˈevriweə] überall **I**
**evidence** (no pl) [ˈevɪdns] Beweis; Beleg;
  Beweismaterial **VI TS1**, 37
**exact** [ɪgˈzækt] exakt; genau **VI U1**, 16
**to exaggerate** [ɪgˈzædʒəreɪt] übertreiben **IV**
**exaggerated** [ɪgˈzædʒəreɪtɪd] übertrieben **IV**
**exaggeration** [ɪgˌzædʒəˈreɪʃn] Übertreibung **V**
**exam** [ɪgˈzæm] Examen; Prüfung **II**
**examination** [ɪgˌzæmɪˈneɪʃn] Untersuchung;
  Prüfung **V**
**to examine** [ɪgˈzæmɪn] untersuchen; kontrollieren °**VI TS1**, 38
**example** [ɪgˈzɑːmpl] Beispiel **I**
  *to set a good **example** [setˌə ˌgʊd
  ɪgˈzɑːmpl] ein Vorbild sein **VI U1**, 8
  for **example** [fərˌɪgˈzɑːmpl] zum Beispiel
  **II**
**except** [ɪkˈsept] außer; bis auf **IV**
**exception** [ɪkˈsepʃn] Ausnahme **VI TS2**, 71
**excerpt** [ˈeksɜːpt] Auszug **IV**
**exchange** [ɪksˈtʃeɪndʒ] Austausch; Aus-
  tausch- **III**
  **exchange** student [ɪksˈtʃeɪndʒ ˌstjuːdnt]
  Austauschschüler/-in **III**
  student **exchange** [ˈstjuːdnt ɪksˌtʃeɪndʒ]
  Schüleraustausch **III**
**to exchange** [ɪksˈtʃeɪndʒ] austauschen **II**
**excited** [ɪkˈsaɪtɪd] aufgeregt; begeistert **I**
**excitement** (no pl) [ɪkˈsaɪtmənt] Aufregung
  **III**
**exciting** [ɪkˈsaɪtɪŋ] spannend; aufregend **I**
**Excuse** me … [ɪkˈskjuːz mi] Entschuldigung!; Entschuldigen Sie! **I**

**(business) executive** ['bɪznɪs ɪgˌzekjətɪv] Geschäftsführer/-in; Manager/-in; gehobene Führungskraft **VI U1**, 9

**to exempt from** [ɪg'zempt frəm] befreien von ⟨**VI U1**, 23⟩

**exercise** ['eksəsaɪz] Übung; Aufgabe **I**
    **exercise** book ['eksəsaɪz ˌbʊk] Übungsheft **I**

**exhausted** [ɪg'zɔːstɪd] erschöpft **VI U1**, 13

**exhausting** [ɪg'zɔːstɪŋ] anstrengend **V**

**exhilarating** [ɪg'zɪlɪreɪtɪŋ] berauschend; aufregend ⟨**VI U1**, 24⟩

**to exist** [ɪg'zɪst] existieren; bestehen **VI U2**, 50

**to expand** [ɪk'spænd] (sich) ausdehnen; erweitern **V**

**to expect** [ɪk'spekt] erwarten **III**
    *to be **expected** to (+ inf)* [bi ɪk'spektɪd tə] sollen **VI U1**, 8

**expectation** [ˌekspek'teɪʃn] Erwartung **IV**
    *to meet sb's **expectations*** [ˌmiːt sʌmbədɪz ˌekspek'teɪʃnz] jmds. Erwartungen erfüllen **V**

**expensive** [ɪk'spensɪv] teuer **I**

**experience** [ɪk'spɪəriəns] Erfahrung **II**
    to chalk sth up to **experience** [ˌtʃɔːk ʌp tə ɪk'spɪəriəns] etw. als Erfahrung verbuchen **VI U2**, 46

**to experience** [ɪk'spɪəriəns] erfahren; erleben **III**

**expert** ['ekspɜːt] Experte/Expertin **II**

**to explain** [ɪk'spleɪn] erklären **I**

**explanation** [ˌeksplə'neɪʃn] Erklärung; Erläuterung **V**

**to explode** [ɪk'spləʊd] explodieren **VI U2**, 46

**to explore** [ɪk'splɔː] auf Entdeckungsreise gehen; sich umschauen; erkunden; erforschen **I**

**explorer** [ɪk'splɔːrə] Forscher/-in; Forschungsreisende/-r; Entdecker/-in **VI U2**, 50

**export** ['ekspɔːt] Export; Ausfuhr **VI U1**, 13

**to export** [ɪk'spɔːt] exportieren; ausführen **VI U2**, 53

**to express** [ɪk'spres] ausdrücken **II**

**expression** [ɪk'spreʃn] Ausdruck; Wendung; Äußerung **II**
    facial **expression** [ˌfeɪʃl ɪk'spreʃn] Gesichtsausdruck **III**

**exterior** [ɪk'stɪəriə] Außen- **V**

*to become **extinct*** [bɪˌkʌm ɪk'stɪŋkt] aussterben **III**

**extinction** (no pl) [ɪks'tɪŋkʃn] Aussterben **III**

**extra** ['ekstrə] Statist/-in; Komparse/Komparsin **VI U2**, 46

**extra** ['ekstrə] extra; zusätzlich **I**

**extract** ['ekstrækt] Extrakt; Auszug; Exzerpt **V**

**extreme** [ɪk'striːm] extrem; radikal **IV**

**extremely** [ɪk'striːmli] sehr; äußerst **V**

**eye** [aɪ] Auge **II**
    black **eye** [blækˌaɪ] blaues Auge **V**

to raise one's **eyes** [ˌreɪz wʌnzˌaɪz] den Blick heben; aufblicken; hochblicken **V**

to roll one's **eyes** [ˌrəʊl wʌnzˌaɪz] die Augen verdrehen **III**

He couldn't believe his **eyes**. [hi ˌkʊdnt bɪˌliːv hɪzˌaɪz] Er traute seinen Augen nicht. **II**

**eye-catcher** ['aɪkætʃə] Blickfang; Hingucker **IV**

**eyewitness** ['aɪwɪtnəs] Augenzeuge/Augenzeugin **II**

## F

**fabric** (no pl) ['fæbrɪk] Stoff ⟨**VI U1**, 25⟩

**fabulous** ['fæbjələs] sagenhaft; fantastisch **IV**

**face** [feɪs] Gesicht **I**
    Put … **face** down. [pʊt ˌfeɪs 'daʊn] Lege/Legt … umgedreht hin. **I**

**to face** [feɪs] gegenüber stehen; konfrontiert werden mit **IV**; anblicken; sich zuwenden **V**
    Let's **face** it. [lets 'feɪsˌɪt] Machen wir uns doch nichts vor. **IV**

**face-to-face** [ˌfeɪstə'feɪs] von Angesicht zu Angesicht; Auge in Auge **V**

**facial** expression [ˌfeɪʃl ɪk'spreʃn] Gesichtsausdruck **III**

**fact** [fækt] Fakt; Tatsache **II**
    in **fact** [ɪn 'fækt] tatsächlich; eigentlich; genau genommen **V**

**factory** ['fæktri] Fabrik; Werk **III**

**factual** ['fæktʃʊəl] sachlich **III**
    **factual** text [ˌfæktʃʊəl 'tekst] Sachtext **III**

degree **Fahrenheit** (°F) ['færnhaɪt] Grad Fahrenheit **IV**

**to fail** sb [feɪl] jmdn. hängenlassen; jmdn. im Stich lassen **VI TS2**, 71
    to **fail** to do sth ['feɪl tə] versäumen, etw. zu tun; es nicht schaffen, etw. zu tun **IV**

street **fair** ['striːt feə] Straßenfest **VI AC1**, 41

**fair** [feə] gerecht; fair **I**
    **fair** play [feə 'pleɪ] Fairplay **III**

**to fake** [feɪk] vortäuschen; fälschen **II**

**fake** [feɪk] falsch; gefälscht **IV**

**fall** [fɔːl] Abnahme **VI TS1**, 37

*to **fall*** [fɔːl] fallen; hinfallen **I**
    *to **fall** asleep* [ˌfɔːlˌə'sliːp] einschlafen **I**
    *to **fall** down* [ˌfɔːlˌ'daʊn] stürzen; hinunterfallen **III**
    *to **fall** for* ['fɔːl fə] hereinfallen auf **IV**
    *to **fall** off* ['fɔːlˌ'ɒf] herunterfallen; hinunterfallen **II**
    *to **fall** over* [ˌfɔːlˌ'əʊvə] hinfallen; umkippen **V**

**fame** [feɪm] Ruhm **VI U2**, 63

*to get **familiar*** [ˌget fə'mɪliə] sich vertraut machen **V**

**family** ['fæmli] Familie **I**
    **family** tree ['fæmli ˌtriː] Stammbaum **I**
    host **family** ['həʊst ˌfæmli] Gastfamilie **III**

**famous** ['feɪməs] berühmt **I**

**fan** [fæn] Fan; Anhänger/-in **II**; Ventilator **V**

**fancy** dress ['fænsi dres] Verkleidung; Kostüm **II**

**fantastic** [fæn'tæstɪk] fantastisch; großartig **II**

**fantasy** ['fæntəsi] Fantasie; Traum- **I**; Fantasy **III**

**fanzine** [fæn'ziːn] Fanzeitschrift **II**

**FAQ** [ˌefeɪ'kjuː] Liste mit häufig gestellten Fragen **III**

**far** [fɑː] weit **II**
    as **far** as [əz 'fɑːrˌəz] soweit **VI TS2**, 69
    in the **far** west [ɪn ðə fɑː 'west] im äußersten Westen **III**
    so **far** [səʊ 'fɑː] bis jetzt **II**

**fare** [feə] Fahrpreis **III**

**farewell** [ˌfeə'wel] Abschied; Abschieds- **V**

**farm** [fɑːm] Farm; Bauernhof **I**

**to farm** [fɑːm] Landwirtschaft betreiben **V**

**farmer** ['fɑːmə] Farmer/-in; Landwirt/-in **II**

**fascinating** ['fæsɪneɪtɪŋ] faszinierend **III**

**fashion** ['fæʃn] Mode **II**

**fast** [fɑːst] schnell **I**
    **fast** food [ˌfɑːst'fuːd] Fastfood ⟨**VI U2**, 57⟩

**fate** [feɪt] Schicksal; Fügung; Vorsehung **V**

**father** ['fɑːðə] Vater **I**

in **favor** (of) (AE) [ɪn 'feɪvərˌəv] dafür; zugunsten (von) **V**

**favourite** ['feɪvrɪt] Favorit/-in; Günstling **III**

**favourite** ['feɪvrɪt] Lieblings- **I**

**fear** [fɪə] Angst; Furcht; Befürchtung **II**

**to fear** [fɪə] (sich) fürchten **V**

**fearful** ['fɪəfl] ängstlich **III**

**feather** ['feðə] Feder **III**

**feature** ['fiːtʃə] Eigenschaft; Merkmal **III**
    key **feature** [ˌkiː 'fiːtʃə] Hauptmerkmal **V**

**to feature** ['fiːtʃə] zeigen; aufweisen **III**

**February** ['februri] Februar **I**

*to be **fed up (with)*** [bi fedˌʌp wɪð] sauer sein (auf); die Nase voll haben (von) **III**

**federation** [ˌfedr'eɪʃn] Bundesstaat; Föderation **V**

**fee** [fiː] Gebühr **III**
    school **fees** (pl) ['skuːl fiːz] Schulgeld; Schulgebühren **III**

*to **feed*** [fiːd] füttern; ernähren **III**

**feedback** ['fiːdbæk] Feedback; Rückmeldung **II**

*to **feel*** [fiːl] fühlen; sich fühlen **I**
    *to **feel** left out* [ˌfiːl leftˌ'aʊt] sich ausgeschlossen fühlen **II**
    *to **feel** sick* [ˌfiːl 'sɪk] Übelkeit verspüren; sich schlecht fühlen **II**
    *to **feel** sorry for* [ˌfiːl 'sɒri fɔː] Mitleid haben mit; bedauern **III**

**feeling** ['fiːlɪŋ] Gefühl **II**

**fellow** ['feləʊ] Bursche; Kerl **V**

**female** ['fiːmeɪl] weiblich **VI U1**, 9

**ferry** ['feri] Fähre **IV**

**festival** ['festɪvl] Festival; Fest **I**

**to fetch** [fetʃ] holen; abholen **IV**

fever ['fiːvə] Fieber **II**

few [fjuː] wenige **II**

a **few** [ə 'fjuː] ein paar; wenige; einige **I**

fiction (no pl) ['fɪkʃn] Erzählliteratur; Erfindung; Prosa; Fiktion **III**

science **fiction** [ˌsaɪəns 'fɪkʃn] Science-Fiction (Zukunftsdichtung) **II**

fictional ['fɪkʃnl] fiktional; fiktiv; erdichtet **III**

field [fiːld] Feld; Spielfeld; Wiese; Weide; Acker **II**

fifteen [ˌfɪf'tiːn] fünfzehn **I**

fight [faɪt] Kampf; Streit **II**

*to **fight** [faɪt] kämpfen; (sich) streiten **II**

figure ['fɪgə] Figur; Gestalt **II**; Ziffer; Zahl **III**

wax **figure** ['wæks ˌfɪgə] Wachsfigur **II**

file [faɪl] Mappe; Datei; Sammlung °**VI U2**, 53

to **fill** [fɪl] (sich) füllen **III**

to **fill** in [fɪl ˈɪn] ausfüllen **II**

filling ['fɪlɪŋ] Füllung **IV**

film [fɪlm] Film **I**

**film** adaptation [ˌfɪlm ˌædæp'teɪʃn] Verfilmung °**VI U1**, 22

to **film** [fɪlm] filmen; drehen **III**

filmmaker ['fɪlmˌmeɪkə] Filmemacher/-in **I**

final ['faɪnl] endgültig **II**; letzte/-r/-s **III**

finally ['faɪnli] schließlich; endlich; zum Schluss; letztlich **II**

*to **find** [faɪnd] finden; herausfinden **I**

*to **find** one's way around [ˌfaɪnd wʌnz ˌweɪ əˈraʊnd] sich zurechtfinden **IV**

*to **find** out [ˌfaɪnd 'aʊt] herausfinden **I**

fine [faɪn] Geldstrafe; Bußgeld ⟨**VI TS2**, 73⟩

fine [faɪn] gut; in Ordnung; schön **I**

I'm **fine**. [ˌaɪm 'faɪn] Mir geht's gut. **I**

finger ['fɪŋɡə] Finger **I**

*to keep your **fingers** crossed [ˌkiːp jɔː ˌfɪŋɡəz 'krɒst] die Daumen drücken **I**

fingernail ['fɪŋɡəneɪl] Fingernagel **V**

finish line ['fɪnɪʃ ˌlaɪn] Ziellinie **II**

to **finish** ['fɪnɪʃ] beenden; enden; fertigstellen; aufhören **I**

finished ['fɪnɪʃt] fertig **II**

fire [faɪə] Feuer **III**

*to be on **fire** [ˌbiː ˌɒn 'faɪə] brennen **III**

firefighter ['faɪəˌfaɪtə] Feuerwehrmann/-frau **VI U1**, 9

fireworks (pl) ['faɪəwɜːks] Feuerwerk **I**

firm [fɜːm] fest ⟨**VI U1**, 23⟩

first [fɜːst] zuerst; als Erstes; erste/-r/-s **I**

at **first** [ət 'fɜːst] zuerst; zunächst **II**

**first** language [ˌfɜːst 'læŋɡwɪdʒ] Muttersprache **II**

**first** person narrator [ˌfɜːst ˌpɜːsn nəˈreɪtə] Ich-Erzähler/-in **III**

in the **first** place [ɪn ðə ˈfɜːst ˌpleɪs] überhaupt erst; von vornherein ⟨**VI TS2**, 69⟩

fish, fish (pl) [fɪʃ] Fisch **I**

fishing ['fɪʃɪŋ] Angeln; Fischen; Fischerei **III**

to **fit** [fɪt] passen **I**

to **fit** in [ˌfɪt ˈɪn] hineinpassen; sich einfügen **VI U1**, 22

*to get **fit** [ˌget 'fɪt] in Form kommen; fit werden **I**

fitness ['fɪtnəs] Fitness **VI U2**, 52

five [faɪv] fünf **I**

to **fix** [fɪks] reparieren; befestigen **II**

flag [flæɡ] Flagge; Fahne **III**

flair [fleə] Flair; Atmosphäre **II**

flame [fleɪm] Flamme **III**

flash [flæʃ] Blitz; Lichtblitz **III**

flashback ['flæʃbæk] Rückblende; Flashback **III**

flat [flæt] Wohnung **I**

flat [flæt] flach; platt **IV**

flavor (AE) ['fleɪvə] Geschmack; Aroma **IV**

flea market ['fliː ˌmɑːkɪt] Flohmarkt **I**

flight [flaɪt] Flug **III**

**flight** attendant ['flaɪt əˌtendnt] Flugbegleiter/-in **IV**

to **flip** [flɪp] blättern ⟨**VI U2**, 62⟩

flirty ['flɜːti] zum Flirten aufgelegt; kokett **V**

flood [flʌd] Flut; Hochwasser; Überschwemmung **VI U2**, 54

floor [flɔː] Fußboden **I**; Stockwerk **IV**

flour [flaʊə] Mehl **V**

the ebb and **flow** [ðiˌeb ənd 'fləʊ] das Auf und Ab; die Höhen und Tiefen ⟨**VI TS1**, 37⟩

to **flow** out [fləʊ ˈaʊt] hinausfließen **II**

flower ['flaʊə] Blume **II**

*to **fly** [flaɪ] fliegen **III**; hissen **IV**

flyer ['flaɪə] Flyer **I**

focus ['fəʊkəs] Blickpunkt; Schwerpunkt; Fokus **III**

out of **focus** [ˌaʊt əv 'fəʊkəs] unscharf **III**

to **focus** (on) ['fəʊkəs ˌɒn] sich konzentrieren (auf) **II**

focused ['fəʊkəst] zielgerichtet **VI U1**, 9

folder ['fəʊldə] Ordner; Mappe **I**

folks (infml) (pl) [fəʊks] Leute **V**

to **follow** ['fɒləʊ] folgen; hinterhergehen; befolgen **II**

follower ['fɒləʊə] Anhänger/-in; Follower/-in ⟨**VI U2**, 57⟩

the following [ðə 'fɒləʊɪŋ] folgende/-r/-s **III**

follow-up ['fɒləʊʌp] Fortsetzung; Folge- **IV**

font [fɒnt] Schriftart °**VI U2**, 58

food [fuːd] Essen; Lebensmittel **I**; Futter **III**

fast **food** [ˌfɑːst'fuːd] Fastfood ⟨**VI U2**, 57⟩

**food** stall ['fuːd stɔːl] Essensstand; Fressbude ⟨**VI U2**, 57⟩

foot [fʊt], **feet** [fiːt] (pl) Fuß (Längenmaß: 30,48 cm) **IV**

foot, feet (pl) [fʊt; fiːt] Fuß **I**

*to keep one's **feet** or hands still [ˌkiːp wʌnz: 'fiːtˌɔː 'hændz stɪl] die Beine und Hände ruhig halten **III**

on **foot** [ɒn 'fʊt] zu Fuß **II**

football ['fʊtbɔːl] Fußball **I**

for [fɔː; fə] für **I**; wegen **II**

**for** example [fər ɪgˈzɑːmpl] zum Beispiel **II**

**for** free [fə 'friː] umsonst; kostenlos **IV**

for (+ Zeitraum) [fɔː; fə] seit **III**

for ... [fɔː; fə] ... lang **II**

force [fɔːs] Kraft; Macht **IV**

to **force** [fɔːs] zwingen **VI U1**, 13

weather forecast ['weðə ˌfɔːkɑːst] Wettervorhersage **III**

foreground ['fɔːɡraʊnd] Vordergrund **IV**

foreign ['fɒrɪn] ausländisch; fremd **IV**

**foreign** language [ˌfɒrɪn 'læŋɡwɪdʒ] Fremdsprache **II**

forest ['fɒrɪst] Wald **II**

forever [fə'revə] für immer; ewig **II**

*to **forget** [fə'ɡet] vergessen **II**

*to **forgive** [fə'ɡɪv] vergeben; verzeihen **II**

fork [fɔːk] Gabel **III**

form [fɔːm] Form **I**; Formular **III**

negative **form** ['neɡətɪv ˌfɔːm] verneinte Form **I**

past **form** ['pɑːst fɔːm] Vergangenheitsform **II**

possessive **form** [pəˌsesɪv 'fɔːm] Possessivform **I**

short **form** ['ʃɔːt fɔːm] Kurzform **I**

to **form** [fɔːm] formen; bilden **II**

formal ['fɔːml] formal; formell; förmlich **II**

format ['fɔːmæt] Format **VI TS2**, 68

formatting ['fɔːmətɪŋ] Formatierung **V**

fortune ['fɔːtʃuːn] Vermögen; Reichtum **VI U2**, 50

forum ['fɔːrəm] Forum **II**

forward ['fɔːwəd] vorwärts **III**

to call **forward** [ˌkɔːl 'fɔːwəd] nach vorn rufen ⟨**VI U1**, 22⟩

*to lean **forward** [ˌliːn 'fɔːwəd] sich nach vorn lehnen **V**

to look **forward** to [ˌlʊk 'fɔːwəd tə] sich freuen auf **II**

foster ['fɒstə] Pflege- **V**

to **found** [faʊnd] gründen **III**

foundation [faʊn'deɪʃn] Stiftung; Gründung **V**

founder ['faʊndə] Gründer/-in **VI U2**, 49

water fountain ['wɔːtə ˌfaʊntɪn] Wasserspender **IV**

four [fɔː] vier **I**

four-letter word [ˌfɔːletə 'wɜːd] Schimpfwort ⟨**VI TS2**, 69⟩

fox [fɒks] Fuchs **II**

freeze frame ['friːz ˌfreɪm] Standbild **III**

to **free** [friː] befreien **VI AC1**, 40

free [friː] frei; kostenlos **I**

**free** time [friː 'taɪm] Freizeit **I**

for **free** [fə 'friː] umsonst; kostenlos **IV**

freedom (no pl) ['friːdəm] Freiheit; Unabhängigkeit **III**

freeway (AE) ['friːweɪ] Autobahn **IV**

*to **freeze** [friːz] erstarren ⟨**VI U2**, 62⟩

**freeze** frame ['friːz ˌfreɪm] Standbild **III**

freezer ['friːzə] Tiefkühlschrank **VI U2**, 58

French [frenʃ] französisch; Französisch **II**

**French** doors [ˌfrenʃ 'dɔːz] Terrassentür ⟨**VI U2**, 61⟩

frequent ['friːkwənt] häufig **VI TS2**, 68

**frequently** asked [ˌfriːkwəntliˈɑːskt] häufig gefragt I
**fresh** [freʃ] frisch I
**fresh-brewed** [ˈfreʃbruːd] frisch aufgebrüht ⟨VI U2, 61⟩
**Friday** [ˈfraɪdeɪ] Freitag I
**fridge** [frɪdʒ] Kühlschrank I
**fried** [fraɪd] gebraten *(in der Pfanne)* IV
**friend** [frend] Freund/-in I
  *to become **friends** [bɪˌkʌmˈfrendz] sich anfreunden; Freundschaft schließen IV
  *to make **friends** [ˌmeɪkˈfrendz] Freundschaft schließen II
  That's what **friends** are for. [ˌðæts wɒt ˈfrendzˌɑː ˌfɔː] Dafür sind Freunde da. I
**friendly** [ˈfrendli] freundlich; nett II
**friendship** [ˈfrendʃɪp] Freundschaft II
**frightened** [ˈfraɪtnd] verängstigt V
**frightening** [ˈfraɪtnɪŋ] furchterregend V
**fringe** [frɪndʒ] Rand-; Alternativ- III
**frolic** [ˈfrɒlɪk] Spaß ⟨VI U2, 61⟩
**from** [frɒm; frəm] aus; von I
  **from** the outside [ˌfrəm ðiˌaʊtˈsaɪd] von außen IV
  **from** … to [frəm … tə] von … bis I
  Where … **from**? [ˌweə … ˈfrɒm] Woher …? I
  **from** around the world [frɒm əˌraʊnd ðə ˈwɜːld] aus aller Welt III
**front** [frʌnt] Vorderseite; Front-; Vorder- III; Spitze; vorderer Bereich V
  **front** door [ˌfrʌntˈdɔː] Haustür II
  **front** yard *(AE)* [ˌfrʌntˈjɑːd] Vorgarten IV
  in **front** of [ɪnˈfrʌntˌəv] vor I
to **frown** [fraʊn] die Stirn runzeln V
**fruit** [fruːt] Frucht; Obst I
deep **fryer** [ˌdiːpˈfraɪə] Fritteuse VI U2, 58
**fulfilling** [fʊlˈfɪlɪŋ] erfüllend; befriedigend VI U1, 6
**full** [fʊl] ganz V
**full** (of) [fʊlˌəv] voll (von) I
  to talk with your mouth **full** [ˌtɔːk wɪð jɔː ˈmaʊθ fʊl] mit vollem Mund sprechen IV
**fun** [fʌn] Freude; Spaß I
  *to have **fun** [ˌhæv ˈfʌn] Spaß haben; sich amüsieren I
  *to make **fun** of [ˌmeɪk ˈfʌnˌəv] sich lustig machen über V
  It's **fun**. [ɪts ˈfʌn] Es macht Spaß. I
  No risk, no **fun**! [nəʊ ˌrɪsk nəʊ ˈfʌn] Wer nicht wagt, der nicht gewinnt. IV
**fun** [fʌn] lustig; witzig; fröhlich I
**function** [ˈfʌŋkʃn] Funktion IV
to **function** [ˈfʌŋkʃn] funktionieren °VI U1, 27
**funny** [ˈfʌni] lustig; witzig I; merkwürdig; komisch III
**fur** [fɜː] Fell; Pelz VI AC2, 74
**furniture** *(singular noun with plural meaning)* [ˈfɜːnɪtʃə] Möbel V
**further** [ˈfɜːðə] weiter (weg) III; weitere °VI U1, 14

**furthermore** [ˌfɜːðəˈmɔː] überdies; außerdem VI U1, 11
**fury** [ˈfjʊəri] Wut ⟨VI U2, 60⟩
**future** [ˈfjuːtʃə] Zukunft III
  **future** perfect [ˌfjuːtʃə ˈpɜːfɪkt] vollendetes Futur; Futur II °VI U2, 48
  **future** progressive [ˌfjuːtʃə prəˈɡresɪv] Verlaufsform der Zukunft °VI U2, 48
**future** [ˈfjuːtʃə] zukünftig IV

## G

**gadget** [ˈɡædʒɪt] Gerät; technische Spielerei III
**Gaelic** [ˈɡeɪlɪk] gälisch; Gälisch III
**gallery** walk [ˈɡælriˌwɔːk] Museumsrundgang; Vernissage I
**game** [ɡeɪm] Spiel I
  guessing **game** [ˈɡesɪŋ ˌɡeɪm] Ratespiel II
**gaming** [ˈɡeɪmɪŋ] Spielen; Zocken ⟨VI TS1, 39⟩
**gap** [ɡæp] Lücke; Spalt; Abstand I
  **gap** year [ˈɡæp ˌjɪə] *ein Jahr Auszeit (zwischen Schule und Ausbildung/Studium), das oft für einen freiwilligen ökologischen oder sozialen Dienst genutzt wird* VI U1, 15
**garage** [ˈɡærɑːʒ] Garage I
**garbage** *(AE)* [ˈɡɑːbɪdʒ] Müll; Abfall V
**garden** [ˈɡɑːdn] Garten I
**gardener** [ˈɡɑːdnə] Gärtner/-in ⟨VI U2, 61⟩
**gardening** [ˈɡɑːdnɪŋ] Gärtnern; Gartenarbeit ⟨VI U2, 57⟩
**garlic** [ˈɡɑːlɪk] Knoblauch IV
**gas** [ɡæs] Gas VI U2, 55
**gas(oline)** *(AE)* [ˈɡæsliːn] Benzin V
to **gasp** [ɡɑːsp] tief Luft holen; keuchen IV
**gate** [ɡeɪt] Gate; Flugsteig; Ausgang IV
**gay** [ɡeɪ] schwul; homosexuell; Schwuler; Homosexueller V
**GCSE** *(= General Certificate of Secondary Education)* [ˌdʒiːsiːesˈiː (ˌdʒenrl səˈtɪfɪkətˌəv ˌsekəndriˌedʒuˈkeɪʃn)] *allg. Abschluss der weiterführenden Schulen in GB* VI U1, 9
**GDP** [ˌdʒiːdiːˈpiː] BIP *(= Bruttoinlandsprodukt)* VI U2, 50
**geek** [ɡiːk] Außenseiter/-in IV
**gender** [ˈdʒendə] Geschlecht VI U1, 9
  **gender** stereotyping [ˈdʒendə ˌsteriəʊtaɪpɪŋ] geschlechtsspezifische Klischees VI U1, 9
**gene** [dʒiːn] Gen VI TS1, 37
**general** [ˈdʒenrl] General V
**general** [ˈdʒenrl] allgemein IV
  in **general** [ɪn ˈdʒenrl] im allgemeinen V
**generation** [dʒenəˈreɪʃn] Generation III
**generous** [ˈdʒenrəs] großzügig III
**genius** [ˈdʒiːniəs] Genie II
**genre** [ˈʒɑ̃ːnrə] Gattung III
**gentle** [ˈdʒentl] sanft; behutsam ⟨VI U1, 22⟩

**gentleman** [ˈdʒentlmən], **gentlemen** [ˈdʒentlmen] *(pl)* Gentleman; feiner Herr III
**geocaching** [ˈdʒiːəʊkæʃɪŋ] Geocaching III
**geography** [dʒiˈɒɡrəfi] Geografie; Erdkunde III
**German** [ˈdʒɜːmən] deutsch; Deutsch; aus Deutschland; Deutsche/-r I
**gerund** [ˈdʒernd] Gerundium IV
**gesture** [ˈdʒestʃə] Geste; Gebärde IV
*to **get** [ɡet] holen; bringen; bekommen; besorgen; kaufen I; werden III
  *to **get** a ride [ˌɡetˌə ˈraɪd] eine Mitfahrgelegenheit bekommen V
  *to **get** around [ˌɡetˌəˈraʊnd] *hier:* sich fortbewegen II
  *to **get** away with [ˌɡetˌəˈweɪ wɪð] davonkommen mit II
  *to **get** caught [ˌɡet ˈkɔːt] erwischt werden; ertappt werden IV
  *to **get** familiar [ˌɡet fəˈmɪliə] sich vertraut machen V
  *to **get** fit [ˌɡet ˈfɪt] in Form kommen; fit werden I
  *to **get** in [ˌɡetˈɪn] einsteigen IV
  *to **get** in the way [ˌɡetˌɪn ðə ˈweɪ] stören; im Weg stehen II
  *to **get** into [ˌɡetˈɪntə] einsteigen; hineingelangen I
  *to **get** into trouble [ˌɡetˌɪntə ˈtrʌbl] in Schwierigkeiten geraten IV
  *to **get** lost [ˌɡet ˈlɒst] verloren gehen; sich verirren II
  *to **get** off (a bus/train) [ˌɡetˈɒf] aussteigen (aus einem Bus/Zug) II
  *to **get** on (the bus) [ˌɡetˈɒn] einsteigen (in den Bus) III
  *to **get** on people's nerves [ˌɡetˌɒn ˌsʌmbɒdiz ˈnɜːvz] jemandem auf die Nerven gehen I
  *to **get** organised [ˌɡet ˈɔːɡənaɪzd] sich organisieren III
  *to **get** out of [ˌɡetˌaʊtˌəv] aussteigen II
  *to **get** ready [ˌɡet ˈredi] sich vorbereiten; sich fertig machen V
  *to **get** right [ˌɡet ˈraɪt] richtig beantworten III
  *to **get** started [ˌɡet ˈstɑːtɪd] anfangen II
  *to **get** sth out of one's head [ˌɡetˌaʊtˌəv ˌwʌnz ˈhed] etw. aus dem Kopf bekommen III
  *to **get** there [ˈɡet ˌðeə] hinkommen I
  *to **get** to [ˈɡet tə] kommen zu; kommen nach; erreichen I
  *to **get** to know [ˌɡet tə ˈnəʊ] kennenlernen III
  *to **get** up [ˌɡetˈʌp] aufstehen *(aus dem Bett)* I
  *to **get** used to sth [ˌɡet ˈjuːzd tə] sich an etw. gewöhnen IV
  *to **get** well [ˌɡet ˈwel] gesund werden V

had **gotten** off *(AE)* [hæd ˌgɒtn̩ˈɒf] waren ausgestiegen **V**

Time to **get** up! [taɪm tə ˌgetˈʌp] Es ist Zeit aufzustehen! **I**

**ghost** [gəʊst] Geist **II**

**giant** [dʒaɪənt] Riesen-; riesig **V**

**gift** [gɪft] Geschenk; Gabe **V**

**gig** [gɪg] Auftritt; Gig **III**

**gigantic** [dʒaɪˈgæntɪk] gigantisch; riesig **IV**

**girl** [gɜːl] Mädchen **I**

**girlfriend** [ˈgɜːlfrend] Freundin *(in einer Paarbeziehung)* **II**

**girlish** [ˈgɜːlɪʃ] mädchenhaft ⟨**VI U2**, 62⟩

**gist** [dʒɪst] das Wesentliche **II**

*to **give** [gɪv] geben; schenken **I**

  *to **give** a talk [gɪv ə ˈtɔːk] einen Vortrag halten **V**

  *to **give** away [gɪv əˈweɪ] verteilen; verschenken; verraten; preisgeben **IV**

  *to **give** sb a piggyback [gɪv ə ˈpɪgibæk] jmdn. Huckepack nehmen **IV**

  *to **give** sb funny looks [gɪv fʌni ˈlʊks] jmdn. schief anschauen **III**

  *to **give** thanks [ˌgɪv ˈθæŋks] danken **IV**

  *to **give** the bumps [ˌgɪv ðə ˈbʌmps] hochleben lassen **I**

  *to **give** up [gɪvˈʌp] aufgeben **III**

**giver** [ˈgɪvə] Geber/-in; Spender/-in **VI U1**, 22

**glacial** [ˈgleɪsiəl; ˈgleɪʃl] eisig; Gletscher- **V**

**glad** [glæd] froh **IV**

**glitz** and **glamor** *(AE) (no pl)* [glɪts n̩ ˈglæmə] Glanz und Glamour **VI U2**, 46

**glamorous** [ˈglæmrəs] glamourös **IV**

to **glance** at [ˈglɑːns ət] einen Blick werfen auf; blicken auf **V**

to **glare** at sb [gleə] jmdn. (zornig) anstarren ⟨**VI U2**, 60⟩

**glass** [glɑːs] Glas **I**

**glasses** *(pl)* [ˈglɑːsɪz] Brille **II**

to **gleam** [gliːm] glänzen; schimmern **V**

**glimpse** [glɪms] (kurzer/flüchtiger) Blick **V**

**glitz** and glamor *(AE) (no pl)* [glɪts n̩ ˈglæmə] Glanz und Glamour **VI U2**, 46

**global** [ˈgləʊbl] global; weltweit **VI AC2**, 74

**glossary** [ˈglɒsri] Glossar; Stichwortverzeichnis **IV**

**glove** [glʌv] Handschuh **I**

**gloved** [glʌvd] behandschuht ⟨**VI U2**, 60⟩

*to **go** [gəʊ] gehen; fahren **I**

  *to **go** *(+ adj)* [gəʊ] werden **V**

  *to **go** bad [gəʊ ˈbæd] schiefgehen; schlecht werden; verderben **V**

  *to **go** black [ˌgəʊ ˈblæk] schwarz werden **II**

  *to **go** by [ˌgəʊˈbaɪ] vorbeigehen **VI U1**, 16

  *to **go** crazy [gəʊ ˈkreɪzi] ausflippen; durchdrehen; verrückt werden **II**

  *to **go** down [gəʊ ˈdaʊn] hinuntergehen; nach unten gehen; entlanggehen **I**

  *to **go** for a walk [gəʊ fər ə ˈwɔːk] spazieren gehen **II**

  *to **go** off [gəʊˈɒf] weggehen **V**

  *to **go** on [gəʊˈɒn] weitergehen; weitermachen; weiterführen; fortfahren **I**

  *to **go** out [gəʊˈaʊt] ausgehen; hinausgehen **III**

  *to **go** over to [gəʊ ˈəʊvə tə] hinübergehen zu; zu jmdm. nach Hause gehen **II**

  *to **go** right back to [gəʊ raɪt ˈbæk tə] zurückgehen auf **III**

  *to **go** round in circles [gəʊ ˌraʊnd ɪn ˈsɜːklz] sich im Kreis drehen **III**

  *to **go** shopping [gəʊ ˈʃɒpɪŋ] einkaufen gehen **I**

  *to **go** swimming [ˌgəʊ ˈswɪmɪŋ] Schwimmen gehen **I**

  *to **go** to bed [gəʊ tə ˈbed] ins Bett gehen **I**

  *to **go** together [gəʊ təˈgeðə] zueinander passen; zueinander gehören **I**

  *to **go** with [ˈgəʊ wɪð] passen zu; gehören zu **I**

  *to **go** wrong [gəʊ ˈrɒŋ] schiefgehen **I**

  *to let **go** (of) [ˌlet ˈgəʊ (əv)] loslassen **II**

  **Go** on! [gəʊˈɒn] Los! **IV**

  *to be **gone** [bi ˈgɒn] verschwunden sein; weg sein **II**

  What's **going** on? [wɒts ˌgəʊɪŋˈɒn] Was ist los?; Was geht ab? **III**

**goal** [gəʊl] Tor; Ziel **I**

**goat** [gəʊt] Ziege **VI AC1**, 40

**gobbledygook** [ˈgɒbldiˌguːk] Kauderwelsch ⟨**VI U2**, 60⟩

the **gods** *(liter)* [ðə ˈgɒdz] die Götter *(literarisch)* **V**

**goddess** [ˈgɒdes] Göttin **IV**

**gold** [gəʊld] Gold **III**

  **Gold** Rush [ˈgəʊld ˌrʌʃ] Goldrausch **VI U2**, 50

**golden** [ˈgəʊldn] golden; Gold- **VI U2**, 50

  **golden** age [ˌgəʊldn ˈeɪdʒ] goldenes Zeitalter **III**

**golf** [gɒlf] Golf **III**

**gonna** (= going to) *(coll)* [ˈgɒnə] wird/werden **IV**

**good** [gʊd] gut **I**

  *to be **good** at [bi ˈgʊd ət] gut sein in **I**

  *to set a **good** example [set ə ˌgʊd ɪgˈzɑːmpl] ein Vorbild sein **VI U1**, 8

  **good** luck [ˌgʊd ˈlʌk] viel Glück **IV**

  **G'**day! *(= Good day!)* [gəˈdaɪ] Guten Tag.; Hallo.; Hi. *(Begrüßung in Australien)* **V**

  **Good** morning. [ˌgʊd ˈmɔːnɪŋ] Guten Morgen. **I**

  It wouldn't do me any **good**. [ɪt wʊdnt ˌduː mi eni ˈgʊd] Es würde mir nichts nützen. **V**

**goodbye** [gʊdˈbaɪ] auf Wiedersehen **I**

**goods** *(pl)* [gʊdz] Güter; Waren ⟨**VI U1**, 25⟩

**goose** bumps [ˈguːs ˌbʌmps] Gänsehaut ⟨**VI U2**, 62⟩

**gorge** scrambling [ˈgɔːdʒ ˌskræmblɪŋ] Schluchtenklettern **II**

**gossip** [ˈgɒsɪp] Klatsch; Tratsch; Gerede ⟨**VI U2**, 60⟩

**gotta** (= got to) *(coll)* [ˈgɒtə] muss/müssen ⟨**VI AC1**, 40⟩

**gotten** *(AE)* [ˈgɒtn] bekommen *(past participle von 'to get' in AE)*; geworden *(past participle von 'to get' in AE)* °**VI U2**, 46

to **govern** [ˈgʌvn] regeln; verwalten ⟨**VI U1**, 23⟩

**government** [ˈgʌvnmənt] Regierung **IV**

**governor** [ˈgʌvnə] Gouverneur/-in **VI U2**, 45

to **grab** [græb] greifen; ergreifen; schnappen **II**

  to **grab** attention [græb əˈtenʃn] Aufmerksamkeit erregen **V**

**grade** *(AE)* [greɪd] Note **IV**

8th-**grader** *(AE)* [ˈeɪθˌgreɪdə] Achtklässler/-in **IV**

**grammar** [ˈgræmə] Grammatik **II**

  **grammar** school [ˈgræmə ˌskuːl] Gymnasium **III**

**grandad** [ˈgrændæd] Opa **I**

great-great-**grandfather** [greɪtgreɪtˈgrænˌfɑːðə] Ururgroßvater **V**

**grandma** [ˈgrænmɑː] Oma **I**

**grandmother** [ˈgrænˌmʌðə] Großmutter **V**

**grandparents** *(pl)* [ˈgrænˌpeərənts] Großeltern **I**

**granny** [ˈgræni] Oma **I**

**grape** [greɪp] Traube **VI U2**, 53

**graph** [grɑːf] Diagramm; Schaubild **V**

  bar **graph** [ˈbɑː grɑːf] Säulendiagramm; Balkendiagramm **V**

  line **graph** [ˈlaɪn grɑːf] Kurvendiagramm **V**

**graphic** novel [ˈgræfɪk ˈnɒvl] Bildergeschichte; Comic **III**

to **grasp** [grɑːsp] erfassen; begreifen ⟨**VI U1**, 24⟩

**grass** [grɑːs] Gras **V**

**grassy** [ˈgrɑːsi] grasbewachsen ⟨**VI U2**, 61⟩

**grateful** [ˈgreɪtfl] dankbar **V**

**gratitude** [ˈgrætɪtjuːd] Dankbarkeit **III**

**gray** [greɪ] grau ⟨**VI U2**, 60⟩

**great** [greɪt] großartig; toll; super **I**

  **great** wheel [greɪt ˈwiːl] Riesenrad **V**

  **great**-great-grandfather [greɪtgreɪtˈgrænˌfɑːðə] Ururgroßvater **V**

**green** [griːn] grün **I**

**Greenwich** Mean Time *(= GMT)* [ˌgrenɪdʒ ˈmiːn ˌtaɪm] westeuropäische Zeit **I**

to **greet** [griːt] begrüßen; grüßen °**VI U1**, 19

**greeting** [ˈgriːtɪŋ] Gruß **I**

**grey** [greɪ] grau **I**

**grid** [grɪd] Gitter; Tabelle; Raster **I**

to **grin** [grɪn] grinsen **V**

**grizzly** bear [ˈgrɪzli ˌbeə] Grizzlybär **V**

**groan** [grəʊn] Stöhnen **IV**

to **groan** [grəʊn] stöhnen **IV**

**ground** [graʊnd] Boden; Erdboden **IV**

*to be **grounded** [bi ˈgraʊndɪd] Hausarrest haben **III**

**group** [gruːp] Gruppe; Klasse **I**

a **group** of three [ə ˌgruːpˌəv ˈθriː] eine Dreiergruppe **I**

tutor **group** [ˈtjuːtə ˌgruːp] Klasse (in einer englischen Schule) **I**

to **group** (around) [gruːp (əˈraʊnd)] gruppieren (um) **III**

**groupmate** [ˈgruːpmeɪt] Kamerad/Kameradin ⟨**VI U1**, 22⟩

*to **grow** [grəʊ] wachsen; anbauen; züchten **III**

  *to **grow** by [ˈgrəʊ baɪ] steigen um **V**

  *to **grow** up [grəʊ ˈʌp] aufwachsen; erwachsen werden **III**

**growth** [grəʊθ] Wachstum **V**

**guard** [gɑːd] Wache; Wächter/-in **II**

to **guard** [gɑːd] bewachen **VI U2**, 50

**guardian** [ˈgɑːdiən] Hüter/-in; Wächter/-in **V**

to **guess** [ges] raten; erraten; vermuten **I**; annehmen **IV**

  **guessing** game [ˈgesɪŋ ˌgeɪm] Ratespiel **II**

**guest** [gest] Gast **III**

**guesthouse** [ˈgesthaʊs] Gästehaus ⟨**VI U2**, 61⟩

**guide** [gaɪd] Führer/-in; Reiseführer **II**

to **guide** [gaɪd] führen; leiten **III**

**guidebook** [ˈgaɪdbʊk] Reiseführer **IV**

**guilty** [ˈgɪlti] schuldig **IV**

  **guilty** conscience [ˌgɪlti ˈkɒnʃns] Schuldbewusstsein; schlechtes Gewissen **V**

**guinea** pig [ˈgɪni ˌpɪg] Meerschweinchen **I**

**guitar** [gɪˈtɑː] Gitarre **IV**

chewing **gum** [ˈtʃuːɪŋ ˌgʌm] Kaugummi **IV**

**guy** [gaɪ] Typ; Kerl; (Pl.) Leute **II**

**gym**(nasium) [dʒɪm; dʒɪmˈneɪziəm] Turnhalle **IV**

## H

**habit** [ˈhæbɪt] Gewohnheit ⟨**VI TS1**, 39⟩

**haggis** [ˈhægɪs] Haggis (schottisches Gericht aus in einem Schafsmagen gekochten Schafsinnereien und Haferschrot) **III**

**hair** [heə] Haar(e) **I**

  *to do our **hair** [ˌduː ˌaʊə ˈheə] uns frisieren; unsere Haare machen **I**

**hairbrush** [ˈheəbrʌʃ] Haarbürste **III**

**half**, **halves** (pl) (of) [hɑːf; hɑːvz] die Hälfte **I**

  **half** an hour [ˌhɑːf ənˈaʊər] eine halbe Stunde **III**

**half** [hɑːf] halb **I**

  **half** past [ˌhɑːf ˈpɑːst] halb (bei Uhrzeitangaben) **I**

  **half**-sister [ˈhɑːfˌsɪstə] Halbschwester **I**

  **half**-term break [ˌhɑːftɜːm ˈbreɪk] Halbjahresferien **I**

*to meet **halfway** [ˌmiːt hɑːfˈweɪ] sich auf halbem Weg treffen **III**

**hall** [hɔːl] Halle; Saal **II**; Flur; Diele; Korridor **III**

  arrivals **hall** [əˈraɪvlz ˌhɔːl] Ankunftshalle **IV**

**hall** pass [ˈhɔːl pɑːs] Erlaubnis, sich während des Unterrichts auf dem Flur aufzuhalten **IV**

**hallway** [ˈhɔːlweɪ] Flur; Diele; Korridor **IV**

**ham** [hæm] Schinken **III**

**hammer** [ˈhæmə] Hammer **II**

**hand** [hænd] Hand **I**

  Clap your **hands**. [ˌklæp jɔː ˈhændz] Klatsch/Klatscht in die Hände. **I**

  On the one **hand** …, (but) on the other **hand** … [ɒn ðəˌwʌn ˌhænd … (bʌt) ɒn ðiˌʌðə ˌhænd …] Einerseits …, (aber) andererseits … **II**

to **hand** [hænd] reichen ⟨**VI U2**, 61⟩

**handout** [ˈhændaʊt] Informationsblatt; Arbeitsblatt **VI U2**, 58

*to **hang** on [ˌhæŋ ˈɒn] (einen Augenblick) warten **IV**

  *to **hang** out (with) (infml) [ˌhæŋ ˈaʊt wɪð] sich herumtreiben (mit); rumhängen (mit); sich treffen (mit) **III**

  *to **hang** up [ˌhæŋ ˈʌp] aufhängen **II**

to **happen** [ˈhæpn] geschehen; passieren **I**

**happiness** [ˈhæpɪnəs] Glück; Zufriedenheit; Fröhlichkeit **V**

**happy** [ˈhæpi] glücklich; froh; fröhlich **I**

  **happy** ending [ˌhæpi ˈendɪŋ] Happy End **III**

  **Happy** Birthday! [ˌhæpi ˈbɜːθdeɪ] Alles Gute zum Geburtstag!; Herzlichen Glückwunsch zum Geburtstag! **I**

to **harass** [ˈhærəs; həˈræs] belästigen; drangsalieren **VI U2**, 61

**harassment** [həˈræsmənt] Belästigung; Schikane **V**

**harbour** [ˈhɑːbə] Hafen **III**

**hard** [hɑːd] hart; schwer; schwierig; hier: stark **II**

  *to be **hard** on sb [bi ˈhɑːdˌɒn] streng mit jmdm. sein **III**

**hardly** [ˈhɑːdli] kaum **IV**

**hard**-working [ˌhɑːdˈwɜːkɪŋ] fleißig **VI U1**, 10

**harmless** [ˈhɑːmləs] harmlos; ungefährlich **V**

**harmony** [ˈhɑːməni] Harmonie °**VI U1**, 27

**harsh** [hɑːʃ] rau; hart **IV**

**harvest** [ˈhɑːvɪst] Ernte **IV**

to **harvest** [ˈhɑːvɪst] ernten **VI U1**, 13

**hat** [hæt] Hut **I**

to **hate** [heɪt] hassen; nicht mögen **II**

*to **have** [hæv] haben **I**

  *to **have** (a sweet) [hæv] (ein Bonbon) nehmen; (ein Bonbon) essen **I**

  *to **have** a look (at) [ˌhævˌə ˈlʊk] anschauen **II**

  *to **have** a point [ˌhævˌə ˈpɔɪnt] nicht ganz unrecht haben **III**

  *to **have** a voice [ˌhævˌə ˈvɔɪs] ein Mitspracherecht haben **VI AC2**, 74

  *to **have** breakfast [ˌhæv ˈbrekfəst] frühstücken **I**

  *to **have** fun [ˌhæv ˈfʌn] Spaß haben; sich amüsieren **I**

  *to **have** got [hæv ˈgɒt] besitzen; haben **I**

  *to **have** in common [ˌhævˌɪn ˈkɒmən] gemeinsam haben **II**

  *to **have** no clue [ˌhæv nəʊ ˈkluː] keine Ahnung haben **IV**

  *to **have** sth done [hæv] etw. machen lassen **V**

  *to **have** to [ˈhæv tə] müssen **II**

**hazard** [ˈhæzəd] Gefahr; Risiko °**VI U2**, 55

**he** [hiː] er **I**

**head** [hed] Kopf **I**

  *to get sth out of one's **head** [get ˌaʊtˌəv wʌnz ˈhed] etw. aus dem Kopf bekommen **III**

  **head** of state [ˌhedˌəv ˈsteɪt] Staatsoberhaupt **II**

  *to keep one's **head** above water [ˌkiːp wʌnz ˌhedˌəbʌv ˈwɔːtə] sich über Wasser halten **VI U2**, 46

  With a very big **head**! [ˌwɪð ə ˌveri bɪg ˈhed] Und ein Angeber! **II**

to **head** (for) [ˈhed fə] zusteuern auf **V**

to **head** out [ˌhed ˈaʊt] hinausgehen **V**

**headache** (no pl) [ˈhedeɪk] Kopfschmerzen; Kopfweh **II**

**heading** [ˈhedɪŋ] Überschrift; Titel **I**

**headline** [ˈhedlaɪn] Schlagzeile **III**

**headphones** (pl) [ˈhedfəʊnz] Kopfhörer **II**

**headquarters** (pl) [ˈhedˌkwɔːtəz] Zentrale; Hauptsitz **VI U2**, 45

**health** [helθ] Gesundheit **II**

**healthcare** [ˈhelθkeə] Gesundheitsversorgung **VI U1**, 9

**healthy** [ˈhelθi] gesund **I**

*to **hear** [hɪə] hören **I**

  I **hear** … [aɪ ˈhɪə] Ich habe gehört, dass … **I**

**heart** [hɑːt] Herz; hier: Zentrum **II**

  *to learn … by **heart** [ˌlɜːn baɪ ˈhɑːt] auswendig lernen **I**

**heat** (no pl) [hiːt] Hitze; Wärme **V**

**heating** [ˈhiːtɪŋ] Heizung **III**

  underfloor **heating** (no pl) [ˌʌndəflɔː ˈhiːtɪŋ] Fußbodenheizung **III**

**heavy** [ˈhevi] schwer; stark **III**

**hedgehog** [ˈhedʒhɒg] Igel **III**

high **heels** [ˈhaɪ hiːlz] Stöckelschuhe ⟨**VI TS2**, 73⟩

**heir** [eə] hier: Erbgut ⟨**VI AC1**, 40⟩

**helicopter** [ˈhelɪkɒptə] Helikopter; Hubschrauber **VI U2**, 54

Who the **hell** cares? [ˌhuː ðə hel ˈkeəz] Wen zum Teufel interessiert's? ⟨**VI TS2**, 70⟩

**Hello.** [helˈəʊ] Hallo. **I**

  *to say **hello** (to) [ˌseɪ helˈəʊ tə] grüßen; Grüße ausrichten (an) **I**

**help** [help] Hilfe **I**

to **help** [help] helfen **I**

  to **help** out [ˌhelp ˈaʊt] aushelfen **III**

  I can't **help** (+ -ing) [aɪ ˌkɑːnt ˈhelp] Ich kann nicht anders (als zu) … **V**

**helper** [ˈhelpə] Helfer/-in **VI U1**, 21

**helpful** ['helpfl] hilfsbereit; hilfreich **I**

**helpless** ['helpləs] hilflos **I**

**her** [hɜː] ihr/-e; sie **I**

**herb** [hɜːb] Kraut **IV**

**herd** [hɜːd] Herde; Rudel **V**

**here** [hɪə] hier **I**

right **here** [ˌraɪt 'hɪə] genau hier **II**

**Here** you are. [ˌhɪə juː 'ɑː] Bitte schön. **I**

**hero, heroes** (pl) ['hɪərəʊ, 'hɪərəʊz] Held **III**

**heroine** ['herəʊɪn] Heldin **III**

to **hesitate** ['hezɪteɪt] zögern **III**

**Hey!** [heɪ] Hi.; He!; Hallo. **I**

**Hi.** [haɪ] Hi.; Hallo. **I**

**hibernation** [ˌhaɪbə'neɪʃn] Winterschlaf **III**

*to **hide** [haɪd] (sich) verstecken **III**

**high** [haɪ] hoch; groß **II**

**high** heels ['haɪ hiːlz] Stöckelschuhe ⟨VI TS2, 73⟩

**high** school (AE) ['haɪ ˌskuːl] High School (weiterführende Schule in den USA, Oberstufe) **IV**

**high** tide ['haɪ ˌtaɪd] Flut **II**

the **high** street [ðə 'haɪ ˌstriːt] die Haupteinkaufsstraße **III**

**high-heeled** shoes [ˌhaɪ hiːld 'ʃuːz] Stöckelschuhe ⟨VI AC1, 40⟩

**high-level** [ˌhaɪ'levl] Spitzen-; auf höchster Ebene **VI TS2, 71**

**highlight** ['haɪlaɪt] Highlight; Höhepunkt **II**

**highly** ['haɪli] höchst- **IV**

**highway** (AE) ['haɪweɪ] Landstraße; Bundesautobahn (amerik.); Highway **V**

**hiking** ['haɪkɪŋ] Wandern **III**

**hill** [hɪl] Berg; Hügel **III**

**hillside** ['hɪlsaɪd] Hang **VI U2, 54**

**him** [hɪm] ihn; ihm **I**

**himself** [hɪm'self] er/sich (selbst); selber **II**

**Hindu** ['hɪnduː] Hindu; hinduistisch **V**

**hint** [hɪnt] Hinweis; Andeutung; Tipp **III**

**hip** [hɪp] hip; total in **V**

**hip-hop** ['hɪphɒp] Hip-Hop ⟨VI AC1, 40⟩

**his** [hɪz] sein/-e **I**

**Hispanic** [hɪ'spænɪk] lateinamerikanisch; Latino/Latina; Hispano-Amerikaner/-in **VI U2, 50**

**historian** [hɪ'stɔːriən] Historiker/-in **V**

**historic** [hɪ'stɒrɪk] historisch **III**

**historical** [hɪ'stɒrɪkl] historisch; geschichtlich **I**

**history** ['hɪstri] Geschichte **II**

living **history** show [ˌlɪvɪŋ 'hɪstəri ˌʃəʊ] Show, in der historischer Alltag nachgespielt wird **III**

recorded **history** [rɪˌkɔːdɪd 'hɪstri] hier: Aufzeichnung **VI U2, 55**

*to **hit** [hɪt] schlagen; treffen **I**

to **hitchhike** ['hɪtʃhaɪk] trampen; per Anhalter fahren **V**

**hitchhiker** ['hɪtʃhaɪkə] Tramper/-in **V**

**hitchhiking** ['hɪtʃhaɪkɪŋ] Trampen **V**

**hoax** [həʊks] Täuschung; Trick **IV**

**hobby, hobbies** (pl) ['hɒbi; 'hɒbiz] Hobby **I**

**hockey** ['hɒki] Hockey **II**

to **hog** a conversation [ˌhɒg ə kɒnvə'seɪʃn] ein Gespräch für sich in Beschlag nehmen; ein Gespräch dominieren **III**

*to **hold** [həʊld] halten; festhalten **I**

*to **hold** a competition [ˌhəʊld ə ˌkɒmpə'tɪʃn] einen Wettbewerb durchführen **V**

*to **hold** onto [həʊld 'ɒntə] (sich) festhalten an **III**

*to **hold** open [həʊld 'əʊpn] aufhalten **IV**

**hole** [həʊl] Loch **II**

**holiday** ['hɒlədeɪ] Urlaub; Feiertag **I**

**holidays** (pl) ['hɒlədeɪz] Ferien **I**

**home** [həʊm] Zuhause; Heim **I**

at **home** [ət 'həʊm] zu Hause **I**

**home** [həʊm] nach Hause **I**

**homeless** ['həʊmləs] obdachlos **IV**

the **homeless** [ðə 'həʊmləs] Obdachlose **VI U1**, 15

**homeless** shelter ['həʊmləs ˌʃeltə] Obdachlosenunterkunft **IV**

**homepage** ['həʊmpeɪdʒ] Homepage **I**

*to be **homesick** [bi 'həʊmsɪk] Heimweh haben **IV**

**hometown** ['həʊmtaʊn] Heimatstadt **IV**

**homework** ['həʊmwɜːk] Hausaufgabe(n) **I**

**honest** ['ɒnɪst] ehrlich **III**

**honey** ['hʌni] Honig **III**

**honor** (AE) ['ɒnə] Ehre **V**

in **honor** of (AE) [ɪn 'ɒnər ˌəv] zu Ehren **VI U2**, 49

to **honor** (AE) ['ɒnə] ehren; würdigen; auszeichnen **VI U1**, 22

to **hook** [hʊk] hier: fesseln **III**

to **hook** sb up with sb [hʊk ˌʌp wɪð] jmdn. mit jmdm. bekannt machen ⟨VI U2, 62⟩

**hope** [həʊp] Hoffnung **II**

to **hope** [həʊp] hoffen **I**

**hopeful** ['həʊpfl] hoffnungsvoll **I**

**hopefully** ['həʊpfli] hoffentlich **VI U1**, 11

**horn** [hɔːn] Horn **III**

**horrible** ['hɒrəbl] schrecklich; furchtbar **VI AC1**, 43

**horrified** ['hɒrɪfaɪd] entsetzt **I**

**horror** ['hɒrə] Horrorgeschichte; Horrorfilm; Horror **III**

**horse** [hɔːs] Pferd **I**

**hospital** ['hɒspɪtl] Hospital; Krankenhaus **II**

**host** [həʊst] Gastgeber/-in; Talkmaster **VI TS2**, 69

**host** family ['həʊst ˌfæmli] Gastfamilie **III**

to **host** [həʊst] ausrichten (Veranstaltung) **V**

**hostel** ['hɒstl] Herberge **IV**

youth **hostel** ['juːθ ˌhɒstl] Jugendherberge **V**

**hot** [hɒt] heiß **III**

**hotel** [həʊ'tel] Hotel **II**

**hotspot** ['hɒtspɒt] Hotspot; gefragter Ort **VI U2**, 52

**hour** [aʊə] Stunde **II**

half an **hour** [ˌhɑːf ən 'aʊər] eine halbe Stunde **III**

**house** [haʊs] Haus **I**

to move (**house**) [muːv (haʊs)] umziehen **III**

**household** ['haʊshəʊld] Haushalt **V**

**how** [haʊ] wie **I**

**How** many …? [ˌhaʊ 'meni] Wie viele …? **I**

**How** are you doing? [ˌhaʊ ˌɑː jə 'duːɪŋ] Wie geht es dir/euch/Ihnen? **V**

**How** are you? [ˌhaʊ 'ɑː jə] Wie geht es dir?; Wie geht es euch?; Wie geht es Ihnen? **I**

**How** much (is/are) …? [ˌhaʊ 'mʌtʃ ɪz/ɑː] Wie viel (kostet/kosten) …? **I**

**How** old are you? [haʊ ˌəʊld ə juː] Wie alt bist du?; Wie alt sind Sie? **I**

**How** to … ['haʊ tə] Wie man … **I**

Is this **how** you (do) …? [ɪz 'ðɪs haʊ jʊ ˌduː] Machst du so …? **I**

that's **how** [ðæts 'haʊ] so **II**

**however** [haʊ'evə] jedoch **IV**

to **hug** [hʌg] umarmen **I**

**huge** [hjuːdʒ] riesig; riesengroß; gewaltig **II**

to **hum** [hʌm] summen **II**

**human** ['hjuːmən] Mensch **IV**

**human** body [ˌhjuːmən 'bɒdi] menschlicher Körper **II**

**human** rights [ˌhjuːmən 'raɪts] Menschenrechte **V**

**Humanities** (pl) [hjuː'mænətiz] Sozialwissenschaften **II**

**humor** (no pl) (AE) ['hjuːmə] Humor; Stimmung **V**

**humour** (no pl) ['hjuːmə] Humor; Stimmung **III**

sense of **humour** (no pl) [ˌsens əv 'hjuːmə] Sinn für Humor **III**

**hundreds** of ['hʌndrədz əv] Hunderte (von) **III**

**hungry** ['hʌngri] hungrig **I**

to **hunt** [hʌnt] jagen **V**

*to be in a **hurry** [bi ˌɪn ə 'hʌri] es eilig haben; in Eile sein **V**

to **hurry** ['hʌri] eilen; sich beeilen **I**

*to **hurt** [hɜːt] verletzen; weh tun **II**

**hurt** [hɜːt] verletzt **II**

**husband** ['hʌzbənd] Ehemann **II**

**hydroplane** ['haɪdrəpleɪn] Gleitboot **V**

**hysterical** [hɪ'sterɪkl] hysterisch **V**

**I**

**I** [aɪ] ich **I**

**I** can't help (+ -ing) [aɪ ˌkɑːnt 'help] Ich kann nicht anders (als zu) … **V**

**I** don't know! [aɪ dəʊnt 'nəʊ] Ich weiß (es) nicht! **I**

**I** don't like … [aɪ 'dəʊnt laɪk] Ich mag … nicht.; Ich mache … nicht gern. **I**

**I** hear … [aɪ 'hɪə] Ich habe gehört, dass … **I**

I like … [aɪ ˈlaɪk] Mir gefällt …; Ich mag … I

I love you. [aɪ ˈlʌv ju] Ich liebe dich.; Ich mag dich. I

I love … [aɪ ˈlʌv] Ich liebe …; Ich mag … total gern. I

I'd like to … (= I would like to) [aɪd ˈlaɪk tə] Ich möchte …; Ich würde gern … I

I'd rather [aɪd ˈrɑːðə] ich würde lieber III

I'm (not) scared of … [ˌaɪm (nɒt) ˈskeəd‿əv] Ich habe (keine) Angst vor … I

I'm afraid … [ˌaɪm‿əˈfreɪd] Leider … IV

I'm dog-tired. [ˌaɪm ˌdɒgˈtaɪəd] Ich bin hundemüde. I

I'm English. [aɪm‿ˈɪŋglɪʃ] Ich bin Engländer/-in. I

I'm fine. [ˌaɪm ˈfaɪn] Mir geht's gut. I

I'm from … [ˌaɪm frɒm] Ich bin aus … I

I'm sorry! [ˌaɪm ˈsɒri] Tut mir leid! I

ice [aɪs] Eis I

ice cream [aɪs ˈkriːm] Eis; Eiscreme I

ice rink [ˈaɪs ˌrɪŋk] Eisbahn; Schlittschuhbahn I

icebreaker [ˈaɪsˌbreɪkə] Eisbrecher (Sätze, um mit jmdm. ins Gespräch zu kommen) IV

icon [ˈaɪkɒn] Ikone; Symbol V

icy [ˈaɪsi] eisig ⟨VI U2, 60⟩

idea [aɪˈdɪə] Idee; Einfall I

no idea [ˌnəʊ‿aɪˈdɪə] keine Ahnung II

ideal [aɪˈdɪəl] ideal VI U2, 50

to identify [aɪˈdentɪfaɪ] aufzeigen; identifizieren °VI AC1, 42

to identify with [aɪˈdentɪfaɪ wɪð] sich identifizieren mit III

identity [aɪˈdentəti] Identität II

idiot [ˈɪdiət] Idiot/-in II

i.e. [aɪˈiː] d.h. °VI TS1, 35

if [ɪf] wenn; falls; ob I

as if [əzˈɪf] als ob III

if-clause [ˈɪfˌklɔːz] if-Satz III

If I were you … [ˌɪf aɪ wɜː ˈjuː] Wenn ich du wäre … IV

to ignore [ɪgˈnɔː] ignorieren; außer Acht lassen III

ill [ɪl] krank III

illegal [ɪˈliːgl] illegal; unrechtmäßig; rechtswidrig III

illness [ˈɪlnəs] Krankheit V

to illustrate [ˈɪləstreɪt] veranschaulichen; darstellen; illustrieren V

image [ˈɪmɪdʒ] Bild; Abbildung IV

imaginary [ɪˈmædʒɪnri] erfunden; eingebildet V

imagination [ɪˌmædʒɪˈneɪʃn] Fantasie; Vorstellungskraft III; Einbildung ⟨VI U2, 62⟩

imaginative [ɪˈmædʒɪnətɪv] einfallsreich; fantasievoll III

to imagine [ɪˈmædʒɪn] sich (etwas) vorstellen I

immediately [ɪˈmiːdiətli] sofort; gleich IV

immense [ɪˈmens] riesig ⟨VI U1, 7⟩

immigrant [ˈɪmɪgrənt] Immigrant/-in; Einwanderer/-in IV

immigration [ˌɪmɪˈgreɪʃn] Immigration; Einwanderung; Einreise IV

immigration office [ˌɪmɪˈgreɪʃn ˌɒfɪs] Einwanderungsbehörde IV

impatient [ɪmˈpeɪʃnt] ungeduldig VI U1, 24

imperative [ɪmˈperətɪv] Imperativ; Befehlsform III

impolite [ˌɪmpˈlaɪt] unhöflich III

importance [ɪmˈpɔːtns] Bedeutung; Wichtigkeit V

important [ɪmˈpɔːtnt] wichtig I

impossible [ɪmˈpɒsəbl] unmöglich IV

impressed [ɪmˈprest] beeindruckt II

impression [ɪmˈpreʃn] Impression; Eindruck IV

to improve [ɪmˈpruːv] sich verbessern; verbessern I

improvement [ɪmˈpruːvmənt] Verbesserung IV

in [ɪn] in; im; rein; herein I

in addition to [ɪn‿əˈdɪʃn tə] neben; daneben; darüber hinaus V

in between [ˌɪn bɪˈtwiːn] dazwischen III

in chorus [ɪn ˈkɔːrəs] im Chor IV

in fact [ɪn ˈfækt] tatsächlich; eigentlich; genau genommen V

in favor (of) (AE) [ɪn ˈfeɪvər‿əv] dafür; zugunsten (von) V

in front of [ɪn ˈfrʌnt‿əv] vor I

in general [ɪn ˈdʒenrl] im allgemeinen V

in honor of (AE) [ɪn‿ˈɒnər‿əv] zu Ehren VI U2, 49

in need [ɪn ˈniːd] bedürftig; in Not II

in order to [ɪn‿ˈɔːdə tə] um … zu; mit der Absicht V

in particular [ɪn pəˈtɪkjələ] im besonderen VI TS1, 37

in secret [ɪn ˈsiːkrət] heimlich II

in spite of [ɪn ˈspaɪt‿əv] trotz V

in the country [ˌɪn ðə ˈkʌntri] auf dem Land IV

in the end [ɪn ðiˈˌend] schließlich; zum Schluss II

in the evenings [ɪn ðiˈiːvnɪŋz] abends I

in the first place [ɪn ðə ˈfɜːst ˌpleɪs] überhaupt erst; von vornherein ⟨VI TS2, 69⟩

in the mornings [ˌɪn ðə ˈmɔːnɪŋz] morgens; vormittags I

in the photo(s) [ˌɪn ðə ˈfəʊtəʊ(z)] auf dem Foto/den Fotos I

in the street [ɪn ðə ˈstriːt] in der Straße; auf der Straße I

inaccurate [ɪnˈækjərət] ungenau ⟨VI U1, 26⟩

incident [ˈɪnsɪdnt] Vorfall; Ereignis VI U2, 54

to include [ɪnˈkluːd] einschließen; beinhalten; aufnehmen; einbeziehen II

including [ɪnˈkluːdɪŋ] einschließlich; inklusive V

income [ˈɪnkʌm] Einkommen VI U2, 50

incomplete [ˌɪnkəmˈpliːt] unvollständig V

inconvenient [ˌɪnkənˈviːniənt] unbequem; lästig; ungünstig IV

increase [ˈɪnkriːs] Zunahme; Wachstum; Anstieg ⟨VI U2, 56⟩

to increase [ɪnˈkriːs] zunehmen; wachsen VI U2, 54

incredible [ɪnˈkredəbl] unglaublich V

in-crowd [ˈɪnkraʊd] Szene; die Angesagten; die Beliebten III

independence (no pl) [ˌɪndɪˈpendəns] Unabhängigkeit III

independent [ˌɪndɪˈpendənt] unabhängig III

Indian [ˈɪndiən] Inder/-in; indisch I; Indianer/-in; indianisch IV

to indicate [ˈɪndɪkeɪt] anzeigen; angeben ⟨VI U2, 62⟩

indigenous (fml) [ɪnˈdɪdʒɪnəs] einheimisch; heimisch V

indirect [ˈɪndɪrekt] indirekt IV

indirect speech [ˌɪndɪrekt ˈspiːtʃ] indirekte Rede IV

individual [ˌɪndɪˈvɪdʒuəl] Einzelperson; Einzelne/-r; Individuum IV

individual [ˌɪndɪˈvɪdʒuəl] individuell; einzeln II

indoors [ˌɪnˈdɔːz] im Inneren VI U2, 55

industry [ˈɪndəstri] Industrie; Branche; Gewerbe III

infection [ɪnˈfekʃn] Infektion; Infekt; Ansteckung V

*to catch an infection [ɪnˈfekʃn] sich eine Infektion holen; sich einen Infekt holen V

infinitive [ɪnˈfɪnətɪv] Infinitiv I

influence [ˈɪnfluəns] Einfluss V

to influence [ˈɪnfluəns] beeinflussen II

to inform [ɪnˈfɔːm] informieren V

informal [ɪnˈfɔːml] informell; zwanglos IV

information (no pl) [ˌɪnfəˈmeɪʃn] Information; Informationen I

informative [ɪnˈfɔːmətɪv] informativ IV

ingredient [ɪnˈgriːdiənt] Zutat III

injured [ˈɪndʒəd] verletzt VI TS1, 36

injury [ˈɪndʒəri] Verletzung II

inline skating [ˈɪnlaɪn ˌskeɪtɪŋ] Inlineskatefahren I

inner [ˈɪnə] innere/-r/-s; Innen- V

innocent [ˈɪnəsnt] unschuldig ⟨VI U2, 62⟩

innovation [ˌɪnəˈveɪʃn] Innovation; Neuerung V

innovative [ˈɪnəʊvətɪv; ˈɪnəvətɪv] innovativ; kreativ V

input [ˈɪnpʊt] Beitrag; Input °VI TS1, 36

insecure [ˌɪnsɪˈkjʊə] unsicher IV

on the inside [ɒn ðiˈˌɪnsaɪd] innen V

inside [ɪnˈsaɪd] innen; im Innern; hinein; nach drinnen; in; drin I

to insist (on) [ɪnˈsɪst ɒn] insistieren; bestehen auf VI U2, 61

to inspire [ɪnˈspaɪə] inspirieren; anregen IV

instant [ˈɪnstənt] Augenblick; Moment ⟨VI U1, 25⟩

instantly [ˈɪnstəntli] sofort V

**instead** [ɪn'sted] stattdessen III
  **instead** of [ɪn'sted ˌəv] statt; anstatt; an
  Stelle von IV
**instruction** [ɪn'strʌkʃn] Instruktion; Anwei-
  sung I
**instructor** [ɪn'strʌktə] Lehrer/-in; Betreuer/
  -in II
  surf **instructor** [ˌsɜ:f ɪn'strʌktə] Surflehrer/
  -in V
**instrument** ['ɪnstrəmənt] Instrument V
**insult** ['ɪnsʌlt] Beleidigung VI TS2, 68
to **insult** [ɪn'sʌlt] beleidigen VI TS2, 70
**insurance** [ɪn'ʃʊərns] Versicherung V
**intense** [ɪn'tens] intensiv; heftig V
**intention** [ɪn'tenʃn] Absicht; Intention
  °VI TS1, 38
**intentionally** [ɪn'tenʃnli] absichtlich
  ⟨VI U2, 62⟩
**interest** ['ɪntrəst] Interesse II
to **interest** ['ɪntrəst] (sich) interessieren II
*to be **interested** in [bi ˈɪntrəstɪd ˌɪn] interessiert sein an; sich interessieren für II
**interesting** ['ɪntrəstɪŋ] interessant I
**interior** [ɪn'tɪəriə] Inneres; Landesinneres V
**interior** [ɪn'tɪəriə] Innen- V
**international** [ˌɪntə'næʃnl] international I
**internet** ['ɪntənet] Internet I
to **interpret** [ɪn'tɜ:prɪt] interpretieren
  °VI TS1, 34
to **interrupt** [ˌɪntə'rʌpt] unterbrechen
  ⟨VI U1, 24⟩
**intersection** [ˌɪntə'sekʃn] Kreuzung IV
**interview** ['ɪntəvju:] Interview; Befragung I
  (job) **interview** ['dʒɒb ˌɪntəvju:] Vorstellungsgespräch VI U1, 11
to **interview** ['ɪntəvju:] interviewen; befra-
  gen I
**interviewee** [ˌɪntəvju'i:] Befragte/-r; Inter-
  viewte/-r IV
**interviewer** ['ɪntəvju:ə] Interviewer/-in;
  Befrager/-in IV
**into** ['ɪntə] in; in … hinein I
  *to be **into** [bi ˈɪntə] mögen; stehen auf I
**intransitive** [ɪn'trænsətɪv] intransitiv V
to **introduce** [ˌɪntrə'dju:s] einführen; einleiten IV; vorstellen V
**introduction** [ˌɪntrə'dʌkʃn] Einführung;
  Einleitung; Vorstellung II
to **invade** [ɪn'veɪd] einmarschieren (in);
  eindringen (in); überfallen III
to **invent** [ɪn'vent] erfinden III
**invention** [ɪn'venʃn] Erfindung III
**inventor** [ɪn'ventə] Erfinder/-in III
**inversion** [ɪn'vɜ:ʃn] Inversion °VI U1, 19
to **invert** [ɪn'vɜ:t] umdrehen °VI U1, 19
**investment** [ɪn'vesmənt] Einlage; Beteiligung; Investition VI U1, 18
**invisible** [ɪn'vɪzəbl] unsichtbar IV
**invitation** [ˌɪnvɪ'teɪʃn] Einladung I
to **invite** [ɪn'vaɪt] einladen I
to **involve** [ɪn'vɒlv] involvieren; einbeziehen;
  beteiligen IV

*to be **involved** (in) [bi ˌɪn'vɒlvd ˌɪn] beteiligt
  sein (an); involviert sein (in); engagiert
  sein (in) V
**involvement** [ɪn'vɒlvmənt] Engagement;
  Beteiligung VI U1, 15
**inward** ['ɪnwəd] ankommend III
**Irish** ['aɪrɪʃ] irisch; Irisch III
**ironic** [ˌaɪ'rɒnɪk] ironisch IV
**irregular** [ɪ'regjələ] unregelmäßig I
**irrelevant** [ɪ'reləvnt] irrelevant; nicht von
  Bedeutung VI TS1, 36
**irresponsible** [ˌɪrɪ'spɒnsəbl] unverantwort-
  lich; leichtsinnig VI TS2, 71
to **irritate** ['ɪrɪteɪt] verärgern; reizen V
**island** ['aɪlənd] Insel III
**issue** ['ɪʃu:; 'ɪsju:] Abneigung; Problem V
to **issue** ['ɪʃu:; 'ɪsju:] ausstellen; verhängen
  ⟨VI TS2, 73⟩
**it** [ɪt] es I
  *to make **it** ['meɪk ˌɪt] es schaffen IV
  **It** wouldn't do me any good. [ˌɪt wʊdnt
  ˌdu: mi ˌeni 'gʊd] Es würde mir nichts
  nützen. V
  **It's** fun. [ɪts 'fʌn] Es macht Spaß. I
  **It's** your turn. [ˌɪts 'jɔ: tɜ:n] Du bist dran. I
  **It's** …/They're … [ɪts/ðeə] Es kostet …/
  Sie kosten … I
  **It's** to die for! [ˌɪts tə 'daɪ fɔ:] Dafür könnte
  ich sterben!; Das ist unwiderstehlich! V
**IT** (= Information Technology) [ˌaɪ'ti:] Infor-
  matik; Informationstechnik III
**Italian** [ɪ'tæliən] Italiener/-in; italienisch;
  Italienisch; aus Italien V
**italics** [ɪ'tælɪks] Kursivschrift V
**item** ['aɪtəm] Gegenstand; Objekt IV
**its** [ɪts] sein/-e; ihr/-e I
**ivory** (no pl) ['aɪvri] Elfenbein III

## J

**jacket** ['dʒækɪt] Jacke III
**jam** [dʒæm] Marmelade; Konfitüre III
**January** ['dʒænjuri] Januar I
*to be **jealous** (of) [bi 'dʒeləs] eifersüchtig
  sein (auf); neidisch sein (auf) I
**jeans** (pl) [dʒi:nz] Jeans VI U2, 52
**jelly** ['dʒeli] Tortenguss; Götterspeise; Wa-
  ckelpudding; Gelee I
**jellyfish** ['dʒelifɪʃ] Qualle V
  box **jellyfish** ['bɒks ˌdʒelifɪʃ] Würfelqualle
  V
**jewel** ['dʒu:əl] Juwel; Edelstein III
  crown **jewels** [ˌkraʊn 'dʒu:əlz] Kronjuwe-
  len II
**jewellery** ['dʒu:əlri] Schmuck I
**jewelry** (AE) ['dʒu:əlri] Schmuck V
**Jewish** ['dʒu:ɪʃ] jüdisch IV
**job** [dʒɒb] Arbeit; Aufgabe; Job I
  (**job**) interview ['dʒɒb ˌɪntəvju:] Vorstellungsgespräch VI U1, 11
**job-related** ['dʒɒbrɪˌleɪtɪd] berufsbezogen
  °VI U1, 7

to **join** [dʒɔɪn] beitreten; sich anschließen;
  verbinden II
  to **join** in [dʒɔɪn ˌɪn] teilnehmen; mitmachen V
**joke** [dʒəʊk] Witz I
to **joke** [dʒəʊk] scherzen II
**journalist** ['dʒɜ:nlɪst] Journalist/-in VI TS1, 36
**journey** ['dʒɜ:ni] Reise; Fahrt III
to **judge** [dʒʌdʒ] beurteilen; bewerten III
**juggling** ['dʒʌglɪŋ] Jonglieren II
**juice** [dʒu:s] Saft I
**July** [dʒʊ'laɪ] Juli I
to **jump** [dʒʌmp] springen I
  to **jump** back [dʒʌmp 'bæk] zurücksprin-
  gen; hier: zurückschrecken II
  to **jump** the queue [dʒʌmp ðə 'kju:] sich
  vordrängeln I
**June** [dʒu:n] Juni I
**jungle** ['dʒʌŋgl] Dschungel IV
**junior** ['dʒu:niə] Junior; der/die Jüngere V
piece of **junk** [ˌpi:s ˌəv 'dʒʌŋk] Stück Schrott
  III
**jury** ['dʒʊəri] Jury; Preisgericht VI TS2, 68
**just** [dʒʌst] gerade; nur; einfach I
  **Just** a second … [ˌdʒʌst ə 'seknd] Einen
  Augenblick … V
  **just** about anywhere [ˌdʒʌst əˌbaʊt
  'eniweə] praktisch überall IV
  **just** in time [ˌdʒʌst ɪn 'taɪm] gerade
  rechtzeitig IV
**justice** ['dʒʌstɪs] Gerechtigkeit V
to **justify** ['dʒʌstɪfaɪ] rechtfertigen V

## K

**kangaroo** [ˌkæŋgr'u:] Känguru V
*to **keep** [ki:p] behalten; aufbewahren; halten I; weiter tun; immer wieder tun IV
  *to **keep** a diary [ˌki:p ə 'daɪəri] ein Tagebuch führen V
  *to **keep** away from [ˌki:p əˈweɪ frəm]
  (sich) fernhalten von III
  *to **keep** going [ki:p 'gəʊŋ] aufrechter-
  halten II
  *to **keep** in mind [ˌki:p ɪn 'maɪnd] beachten; im Gedächtnis behalten IV
  *to **keep** in touch [ˌki:p ɪn 'tʌtʃ] in Kontakt
  bleiben IV
  *to **keep** one's feet or hands still [ki:p
  wʌnz 'fi:t ɔ: 'hændz stɪl] die Beine und
  Hände ruhig halten III
  *to **keep** one's head above water [ki:p
  wʌnz ˌhed əbʌv 'wɔ:tə] sich über Wasser
  halten VI U2, 46
  *to **keep** out (of) [ki:p 'aʊt əv] draußen
  bleiben; draußen halten III
  *to **keep** the ball bouncing [ˌki:p ðə bɔ:l
  'baʊntsɪŋ] hier: das Gespräch am Laufen
  halten III
  *to **keep** up (with) [ki:p ˌʌp (wɪð)] mit-
  halten (mit); Schritt halten (mit) II

*to **keep** your fingers crossed [ˌkiːp jɔː ˌfɪŋɡəz 'krɒst] die Daumen drücken **I**

**key** [kiː] Schlüssel **II**
  **key** feature [ˌkiː 'fiːtʃə] Hauptmerkmal **V**
  **key** ring ['kiː ˌrɪŋ] Schlüsselbund; Schlüsselanhänger **III**
  **key** word ['kiː wɜːd] Stichwort; Schlüsselbegriff **I**

to **kick** [kɪk] schießen; treten **II**

**kid** [kɪd] Jugendliche/-r; Kind **IV**

to **kill** [kɪl] töten; umbringen **III**

**killer** ['kɪlə] Killer/-in **V**

**kilometre** (km) ['kɪləˌmiːtə; kɪ'lɒmɪtə] Kilometer **III**

**kilt** [kɪlt] Kilt; Schottenrock **III**

**kind** [kaɪnd] Art; Sorte **I**
  **kind** of ['kaɪnd əv] ziemlich **V**

**king** [kɪŋ] König **I**

**kiss** [kɪs] Kuss **VI AC1**, 41

to **kiss** [kɪs] (sich) küssen ⟨**VI U2**, 61⟩

**kitchen** ['kɪtʃɪn] Küche **I**

**kitty** litter ['kɪti ˌlɪtə] Katzenstreu **V**

**Kiwi** (infml) ['kiːwiː] Neuseeländer/-in **V**

**knife** [naɪf], **knives** [naɪvz] (pl) Messer **III**

**knight** [naɪt] Ritter **III**

**knob** [nɒb] Griff **II**

to **knock** [nɒk] stoßen; schlagen **V**

*to **know** [nəʊ] kennen; wissen **I**
  *to be **known** as [bi 'nəʊn əz] bekannt sein als **IV**
  *to get to **know** [ˌget tə 'nəʊ] kennenlernen **III**
  I don't **know**! [aɪ ˌdəʊnt 'nəʊ] Ich weiß (es) nicht! **I**
  You **know** how to … [juː 'nəʊ ˌhaʊ tə] Du weißt, wie man …; Ihr wisst, wie man … **I**

**know-it-all** ['nəʊɪtɔːl] Besserwisser/-in **VI U1**, 18

**knowledge** (no pl) ['nɒlɪdʒ] Wissen; Kenntnisse **V**

**koala** [kəʊ'ɑːlə] Koala **III**

**Korean** [kə'riːən] koreanisch; Koreanisch; Koreaner/-in **II**
  South **Korean** [ˌsaʊθ kə'riːən] Südkoreaner/-in; südkoreanisch; Südkoreanisch **II**

## L

**lab**(oratory) [læb; lə'bɒrətri] Labor **IV**

child **labor** (AE) [ˌtʃaɪld 'leɪbə] Kinderarbeit **IV**

**laboratory** [læb; lə'bɒrətri] Labor **IV**

child **labour** [ˌtʃaɪld 'leɪbə] Kinderarbeit **V**

**ladder** ['lædə] Leiter **II**

**lady** ['leɪdi] Lady; Dame **III**

**lady-in-waiting** [ˌleɪdiɪn'weɪtɪŋ] Hofdame **III**

**laid-back** [ˌleɪd'bæk] entspannt; locker **III**

**lake** [leɪk] See **I**
  boating **lake** ['bəʊtɪŋ ˌleɪk] See zum Rudern **I**

**lamb** [læm] Lamm; Lämmchen **I**

**lame** [leɪm] lahm; langweilig **V**

**land** [lænd] Land **I**

to **land** [lænd] landen **II**

**landing** ['lændɪŋ] Landung **IV**
  moon **landing** ['muːn ˌlændɪŋ] Mondlandung **IV**

**landscape** ['lændskeɪp] Landschaft **III**

**landscaped** ['lændskeɪpt] gepflegt ⟨**VI U1**, 25⟩

**landsurfing** ['lændsɜːfɪŋ] Landsurfen ⟨**VI U2**, 52⟩

**language** ['læŋgwɪdʒ] Sprache **I**
  first **language** [ˌfɜːst 'læŋgwɪdʒ] Muttersprache **II**
  foreign **language** [ˌfɒrɪn 'læŋgwɪdʒ] Fremdsprache **II**
  official **language** [əˌfɪʃl 'læŋgwɪdʒ] Amtssprache **II**

**laptop** ['læptɒp] Laptop **II**

**large** [lɑːdʒ] groß; riesig **II**

**lassi** ['lʌsi] Lassi **I**

to **last** [lɑːst] dauern; andauern; anhalten **VI U2**, 50

**last** [lɑːst] letzte/-r/-s **I**
  at **last** [ət 'lɑːst] endlich; schließlich **I**
  **last** name (AE) ['lɑːst neɪm] Nachname; Familienname **V**
  to save the best for **last** [ˌseɪv ðə ˌbest fə 'lɑːst] sich das Beste bis zum Schluss aufheben **IV**

**late** [leɪt] spät; zu spät **I**
  *to be **late** [bi 'leɪt] zu spät dran sein; zu spät kommen **I**

**later** ['leɪtə] später **I**

**latest** ['leɪtɪst] neueste/-r/-s **IV**

**Latin** ['lætɪn] Latein; lateinisch **V**

**Latino** [lə'tiːnəʊ] lateinamerikanisch **VI U2**, 53

**laugh** [lɑːf] Lachen **VI U1**, 25

to **laugh** [lɑːf] lachen **I**

**laughter** ['lɑːftə] Gelächter; Lachen **V**

**lavish** ['lævɪʃ] üppig; verschwenderisch **IV**

**law** [lɔː] Gesetz; Recht **VI U1**, 16

**lawn** [lɔːn] Rasen ⟨**VI U1**, 25⟩

*to **lay** [leɪ] legen **IV**

**layer** (of) ['leɪər əv] Schicht (aus); Lage (aus) **III**

**layout** ['leɪaʊt] Layout; Anordnung **III**

**lazy** ['leɪzi] faul **III**

**lead** part [liːd 'pɑːt] Hauptrolle **III**
  *to take the **lead** [ˌteɪk ðə 'liːd] die Führung übernehmen **VI AC2**, 75

*to **lead** [liːd] führen; anführen **III**
  *to **lead** off [liːd 'ɒf] wegführen **III**

**lead** [liːd] Haupt- **III**

**leader** ['liːdə] Führer/-in; Anführer/-in **V**

**lead-in** ['liːdɪn] Einführung; Einleitung **IV**

**leading** ['liːdɪŋ] führend **VI U2**, 50

**leaflet** ['liːflət] Broschüre; Informationsblatt; Prospekt **IV**

*to **lean** back [ˌliːn 'bæk] sich zurücklehnen ⟨**VI U1**, 24⟩

*to **lean** forward [ˌliːn 'fɔːwəd] sich nach vorn lehnen **V**

*to **learn** [lɜːn] lernen **I**
  *to **learn** about ['lɜːn əˌbaʊt] erfahren über **III**
  *to **learn** … by heart [lɜːn baɪ 'hɑːt] auswendig lernen **I**

at **least** [ət 'liːst] mindestens; wenigstens **II**

*to **leave** [liːv] verlassen; lassen; abfahren; losgehen **II**
  *to **leave** a message [ˌliːv ə 'mesɪdʒ] eine Nachricht hinterlassen **I**
  *to **leave** behind [liːv bɪ'haɪnd] zurücklassen **II**
  *to **leave** it to cool [liːv ɪt tə 'kuːl] kalt stellen **I**
  *to **leave** out [liːv 'aʊt] auslassen; weglassen **IV**
  *to **leave** sb alone [liːv əˈləʊn] jmdn. in Ruhe lassen **IV**
  *to **leave** space [liːv 'speɪs] Platz lassen **I**
  **Leave** that to me. [ˌliːv ðæt tə 'miː] Überlass das mir. **IV**

**left** [left] linke/-r/-s; links **I**
  on the **left** [ɒn ðə 'left] auf der linken Seite; links **I**

**left** [left] übrig **I**
  **left** over [left 'əʊvə] übrig **VI U1**, 16

**left-hand** ['lefthænd] linke/-r/-s **IV**

**leftovers** ['leftəʊvəz] Überbleibsel; Überreste **V**

**leg** [leg] Bein **II**

**legend** ['ledʒənd] Legende; Sage **III**

**legendary** ['ledʒəndri] legendär **V**

**leisure** ['leʒə] Freizeit; Freizeit- **I**
  **leisure** centre ['leʒə ˌsentə] Freizeitzentrum **I**

**lemon** ['lemən] Zitrone **II**

**lemonade** [ˌlemə'neɪd] Limonade **I**

*to **lend** ['lend tə] leihen; verleihen **III**

**length** [leŋθ] Länge **V**

zoom **lens** ['zuːm ˌlenz] Zoomobjektiv ⟨**VI U2**, 60⟩

**lesbian** ['lezbiən] lesbisch; Lesbe **VI AC1**, 42

**less** [les] weniger **III**
  to settle for **less** [ˌsetl fə 'les] sich mit weniger zufrieden geben **IV**

**lesson** ['lesn] Unterrichtsstunde; Schulstunde; Unterricht **I**

*to **let** [let] lassen **I**
  *to **let** go (of) [ˌlet 'gəʊ (əv)] loslassen **II**
  **Let**'s face it. [lets 'feɪs ɪt] Machen wir uns doch nichts vor. **IV**
  **Let**'s … [lets] Lass/Lasst uns … **I**

**letter** ['letə] Buchstabe **I**; Brief **II**
  application **letter** [ˌæplɪ'keɪʃn ˌletə] Bewerbungsschreiben **VI U1**, 8
  capital **letter** [ˌkæpɪtl 'letə] Großbuchstabe **I**
  **letter** to the editor [ˌletə tʊ ði 'edɪtə] Leserbrief **VI TS2**, 68

**level** ['levl] Niveau; Level **VI TS2**, 68

**liberty** [ˈlɪbəti] Freiheit **IV**
**library** [ˈlaɪbri] Bibliothek; Bücherei **III**
**lie** [laɪ] Lüge **III**
  white **lie** [ˌwaɪt ˈlaɪ] Notlüge **IV**
to **lie** [laɪ] lügen **II**
*to **lie** [laɪ] liegen **II**
**life**, **lives** (pl) [laɪf, laɪvz] Leben **II**
**lifeboat** [ˈlaɪfbəʊt] Rettungsboot **I**
**lifebuoy** [ˈlaɪfbɔɪ] Rettungsring **I**
**lifeguard** [ˈlaɪfɡɑːd] Rettungsschwimmer/
  -in **V**
**lifestyle** [ˈlaɪfstaɪl] Lebensstil; Lifestyle **III**
to **lift** [lɪft] heben; hochheben; anheben **IV**
**light** [laɪt] Licht; Lampe **II**
**light** [laɪt] leicht **III**
to **lighten** [ˈlaɪtn] aufhellen **III**
**lightning** (no pl) [ˈlaɪtnɪŋ] Blitz **II**
to **like** [laɪk] mögen; gern haben **I**
  would **like** [wʊd ˈlaɪk] würde-/st/-n/-t
  gern; hätte-/st/-n/-t gern **I**
  I don't **like** … [aɪ ˈdəʊnt laɪk] Ich mag …
  nicht.; Ich mache … nicht gern. **I**
  I **like** … [aɪ ˈlaɪk] Mir gefällt …; Ich
  mag … **I**
  I'd **like** to … (= I would like to) [aɪd ˈlaɪk
  tə] Ich möchte …; Ich würde gern … **I**
  Would you **like** …? [ˌwʊd jʊ ˈlaɪk]
  Möchtest du …?; Möchten Sie …?;
  Möchtet ihr …? **II**
**like** [laɪk] wie **I**
  *to be **like** [bi ˈlaɪk] sein **III**
  **like** that [laɪk ˈðæt] so **I**
  **like** this [laɪk ˈðɪs] so **I**
  What was it **like**? [ˌwɒt wɒz ɪt ˈlaɪk] Wie
  war es? **III**
*to be **likely** [bi ˈlaɪkli] wahrscheinlich sein **V**
**likes** (pl) [laɪks] Vorlieben **IV**
**limit** [ˈlɪmɪt] Limit; Grenze **III**
to **limit** to [ˈlɪmɪt tə] limitieren auf; begrenzen auf; beschränken auf **VI U1**, 18
**line** [laɪn] Zeile; Linie **I**
  finish **line** [ˈfɪnɪʃ ˌlaɪn] Ziellinie **II**
  **line** graph [ˈlaɪn ɡrɑːf] Kurvendiagramm **V**
  opening **line** [ˈəʊpnɪŋ ˌlaɪn] der erste
  Satz **III**
  poverty **line** [ˈpɒvəti ˌlaɪn] Armutsgrenze
  **VI U1**, 13
  *to stand in **line** (AE) [ˌstænd ɪn ˈlaɪn]
  anstehen; Schlange stehen; (sich) anstellen **IV**
  time **line** [ˈtaɪm ˌlaɪn] Zeitstrahl **I**
**lines** (pl) [laɪnz] Text **IV**
to **line** up [laɪn ˈʌp] (sich) aufstellen **III**
**link** [lɪŋk] Link; Verbindung **II**
to **link** [lɪŋk] verbinden **II**
  **linking** word [ˈlɪŋkɪŋ ˌwɜːd] Bindewort **I**
**linking** [ˈlɪŋkɪŋ] verbindend °**VI U1**, 11
**lion** [laɪən] Löwe **II**
**list** [lɪst] Liste **I**
to **list** [lɪst] auflisten; nennen **VI U1**, 9
to **listen** (to) [ˈlɪsn] zuhören; anhören **I**
  to **listen** for [ˈlɪsn fə] horchen auf **I**

**listener** [ˈlɪsənə] Zuhörer/-in **II**
**listening** [ˈlɪsnɪŋ] Hören **I**
**literature** [ˈlɪtrətʃə] Literatur **VI U1**, 27
**litre** (l) [ˈliːtə] Liter **III**
**litter** [ˈlɪtə] Müll; Abfall **V**
  kitty **litter** [ˈkɪti ˌlɪtə] Katzenstreu **V**
to **litter** [ˈlɪtə] verschmutzen; verunreinigen;
  Müll herumliegen lassen **IV**
**little** [ˈlɪtl] klein **I**; wenig **IV**
  a **little** [ə ˈlɪtl] ein wenig; etwas **I**
to **live** [lɪv] wohnen; leben **I**
  standard of **living** [ˌstændəd əv ˈlɪvɪŋ]
  Lebensstandard **IV**
**live** [laɪv] live **III**
**lively** [ˈlaɪvli] lebendig **II**
**living** room [ˈlɪvɪŋ rʊm] Wohnzimmer **I**
  *to make a **living** (from) [ˌmeɪk ə ˈlɪvɪŋ
  frəm] seinen Lebensunterhalt bestreiten
  (mit) **IV**
  **living** history show [ˌlɪvɪŋ ˈhɪstəri ˌʃəʊ]
  Show, in der historischer Alltag nachgespielt wird **III**
**lizard** [ˈlɪzəd] Echse; Eidechse **V**
to **load** [ləʊd] einräumen; laden **V**
**local** [ˈləʊkl] örtlich; lokal **III**
*to be **located** [bi ləʊˈkeɪtɪd] gelegen sein;
  liegen **IV**
**location** [ləʊˈkeɪʃn] Handlungsort; Lage;
  Standort **II**
**loch** [lɒx; lɒk] See (in Schottland) **III**
**locked** [lɒkt] abgeschlossen **II**
**locker** [ˈlɒkə] Schließfach; Spind **I**
**loft** [lɒft] Dachboden **I**
**logbook** [ˈlɒɡbʊk] Logbuch **IV**
**logic** [ˈlɒdʒɪk] Logik **III**
**logical** [ˈlɒdʒɪkl] logisch °**VI U2**, 59
**LOL** (= laughing out loud) [lɒl] LOL **II**
**Londoner** [ˈlʌndənə] Londoner/-in **I**
**lonely** [ˈləʊnli] einsam **I**
**long** [lɒŋ] lang **I**
  as **long** as [əz ˈlɒŋ əz] solange **VI U2**, 49
  **long** shot [ˈlɒŋ ˌʃɒt] Totale (Kameraeinstellung) **IV**
  no **longer** [nəʊ ˈlɒŋɡə] nicht länger; nicht
  mehr **V**
  (not) any **longer** [nɒt ˌeni ˈlɒŋɡə] (nicht)
  mehr; (nicht) länger **III**
**longhouse** [ˈlɒŋhaʊs] Langhaus **V**
**long-lasting** [ˈlɒŋlɑːstɪŋ] lang anhaltend **V**
**look** [lʊk] Blick **I**
  *to give sb funny **looks** [ˌɡɪv fʌni ˈlʊks]
  jmdn. schief anschauen **III**
  *to have a **look** (at) [ˌhæv ə ˈlʊk] anschau-
  en **II**
  *to take a **look** at [ˌteɪk ə ˈlʊk æt] einen
  Blick werfen auf **II**
to **look** [lʊk] schauen; sehen; aussehen **I**
  to **look** after [lʊkˈɑːftə] aufpassen auf;
  hüten; sich kümmern um **I**
  to **look** at [ˈlʊk ət] anschauen; ansehen **I**
  to **look** for [ˈlʊk fɔː] suchen nach **I**

  to **look** forward to [ˌlʊk ˈfɔːwəd tə] sich
  freuen auf **II**
  to **look** out [ˌlʊkˈaʊt] aufpassen **II**
  to **look** up [ˌlʊkˈʌp] nachschlagen; nachschauen **I**
  to **look** up to sb [ˌlʊkˈʌp tə] zu jmdm.
  aufschauen; jmdn. bewundern **VI TS2**, 71
  **Look** closely … [ˌlʊk ˈkləʊsli] Schau(t)
  genau … **II**
  what the man **looked** like [ˌwɒt ðə mæn
  ˈlʊkt laɪk] wie der Mann aussah **II**
**looks** (pl) [lʊks] Aussehen **III**
**loose** [luːs] locker; frei (**VI U2**, 61)
**lord** [lɔːd] Lord; Herr **III**
**lorry** [ˈlɒri] Lastwagen **IV**
*to **lose** [luːz] verlieren **II**
**loser** [ˈluːzə] Verlierer/-in; Loser/-in **V**
*to get **lost** [ˌɡet ˈlɒst] verloren gehen; sich
  verirren **III**
a **lot** [ə ˈlɒt] viel **I**
  a **lot** of [ə ˈlɒt əv] viel/-e; eine Menge **I**
  **lots** (of) [ˈlɒts əv] viel/-e; jede Menge **I**
**parking lot** [ˈpɑːkɪŋ ˌlɒt] Parkplatz **V**
**loud** [laʊd] laut **I**
  *to read/sing out **loud** [ˌriːd/sɪŋ aʊt ˈlaʊd]
  laut vorsingen **III**
**lounge** [laʊndʒ] Lounge; Aufenthaltsraum
  **VI U2**, 45
  departure **lounge** [dɪˈpɑːtʃə ˌlaʊndʒ]
  Abflughalle **IV**
**love** [lʌv] Liebe **III**
**Love** … [lʌv] Liebe Grüße; Herzliche Grüße
  (am Briefende) **I**
to **love** [lʌv] lieben; gern mögen **I**
  would **love** [wʊd ˈlʌv] würde-/st/-n/-t sehr
  gern; hätte-/st-/-n/-t sehr gern **I**
  I **love** you. [aɪ ˈlʌv ju] Ich liebe dich.; Ich
  mag dich. **I**
  I **love** … [aɪ ˈlʌv] Ich liebe …; Ich
  mag … total gern. **I**
**lovebirds** (pl) [ˈlʌvˌbɜːdz] Turteltauben **II**
**lovely** [ˈlʌvli] schön; hübsch **IV**
**lover** [ˈlʌvə] Freund/-in; Liebhaber/-in **V**
  nature **lover** [ˈneɪtʃə ˌlʌvə] Naturfreund/
  -in **V**
**low** [ləʊ] niedrig **II**
  **low** tide [ˈləʊ ˌtaɪd] Ebbe **II**
**luck** [lʌk] Glück **VI U2**, 46
  good **luck** [ˌɡʊd ˈlʌk] viel Glück **IV**
  What **luck**! [wɒt ˈlʌk] Was für ein Glück! **III**
**luckily** [ˈlʌkɪli] glücklicherweise **IV**
**lucky** … [ˈlʌki] … der/die Glückliche **I**
  *to be **lucky** [biˌˈlʌki] Glück haben **II**
  **lucky** charm [ˌlʌki ˈtʃɑːm] Glücksbringer;
  Talisman **I**
  **lucky** day [ˌlʌki ˈdeɪ] Glückstag **VI U2**, 46
**luggage** (no pl) [ˈlʌɡɪdʒ] Gepäck **IV**
**lunch** [lʌnʃ] Mittagessen **I**
  **lunch** break [ˈlʌnʃbreɪk] Mittagspause **I**
**lunchtime** [ˈlʌnʃtaɪm] Mittagszeit; Mittagspause **IV**

**lung** [lʌŋ] Lunge **IV**
   the **lungs** *(pl)* [ðə ˈlʌŋz] die Lunge **III**
**luxury** [ˈlʌkʃri] Luxus **IV**
(song) **lyrics** *(pl)* [sɒŋ ˈlɪrɪks] Liedtext **III**

## M

**Ma** [mɑː] Mama **V**
**ma'am** [mæm] gnädige Frau *(Anrede)*
   ⟨**VI U2**, 60⟩
**machete** [məˈʃeti] Machete; Buschmesser
   **VI U1**, 13
**machine** [məˈʃiːn] Automat; Maschine;
   Apparat; Gerät **I**
   answering **machine** [ˈɑːnsrɪŋ məˌʃiːn]
   Anrufbeantworter **I**
   vending **machine** [ˈvendɪŋ məˌʃiːn]
   Automat **IV**
   washing **machine** [ˈwɒʃɪŋ məˌʃiːn] Wasch-
   maschine **II**
**mad** [mæd] verrückt **II**; wütend **IV**
Dear Sir or **Madam** [dɪə ˌsɜːrˌɔː ˈmædəm]
   Sehr geehrte Dame, sehr geehrter Herr **III**
**made** up from [ˌmeɪdˌʌp frəm] zusammengesetzt aus **IV**
**magazine** [ˌmæɡəˈziːn] Zeitschrift **I**
**magic** [ˈmædʒɪk] Magie; Zauberei **IV**
**magical** [ˈmædʒɪkəl] magisch; Zauber- **III**
**mail** [meɪl] Post **V**
to **mail** [ˈiːmeɪl] mailen; per E-Mail schicken
   **II**
**main** [meɪn] Haupt- **I**
   **main** clause [ˈmeɪn ˌklɔːz] Hauptsatz **III**
**mainstream** [ˈmeɪnstriːm] Masse; Durchschnitt; Massen-; Durchschnitts- **VI AC1**, 41
**major** [ˈmeɪdʒə] wichtig; bedeutend; Haupt-
   **V**
**majority** [məˈdʒɒrəti] Mehrheit; Mehrzahl **V**
*to **make** [meɪk] machen; tun; bilden; *hier:*
   ergeben **I**; *hier:* lassen **V**
   *to be **made** of [bi ˈmeɪdˌəv] bestehen
   aus **III**
   *to be **made** up of/from [bi meɪdˌʌpˌ
   əv/frəm] zusammengesetzt sein aus;
   bestehen aus **V**
   *to **make** a choice [ˌmeɪkˌə ˈtʃɔɪs] eine
   Wahl treffen **VI U1**, 26
   *to **make** a decision [ˌmeɪkˌə dɪˈsɪʒn] eine
   Entscheidung treffen **II**
   *to **make** a difference (to sth) [ˌmeɪkˌə
   ˈdɪfrəns] etw. verändern **VI AC2**, 74
   *to **make** a living (from) [ˌmeɪkˌə ˈlɪvɪŋ
   frəm] seinen Lebensunterhalt bestreiten
   (mit) **IV**
   *to **make** a wish [ˌmeɪkˌə ˈwɪʃ] sich etwas
   wünschen **I**
   *to **make** friends [ˌmeɪk ˈfrendz] Freundschaft schließen **II**
   *to **make** fun of [ˌmeɪk ˈfʌnˌəv] sich lustig
   machen über **V**
   *to **make** it [ˈmeɪkˌɪt] es schaffen **IV**

   *to **make** money [ˌmeɪk ˈmʌni] Geld
   verdienen **I**
   *to **make** notes [ˌmeɪk ˈnəʊts] Notizen
   machen **I**
   *to **make** one's point [ˌmeɪk wʌnz ˈpɔɪnt]
   seinen Standpunkt deutlich machen
   **VI AC2**, 74
   *to **make** one's voice heard [ˌmeɪk wʌnz
   ˌvɔɪs ˈhɜːd] sich Gehör verschaffen
   **VI AC2**, 74
   *to **make** sb angry [meɪk ˈæŋɡri] jmdn.
   wütend machen; jmdn. verärgern **III**
   *to **make** sense [ˌmeɪk ˈsens] Sinn ergeben; einleuchten **IV**
   *to **make** somebody do something [meɪk]
   jmdn. dazu bringen, etw. zu tun **II**
   *to **make** sure [ˌmeɪk ˈʃɔː] sich versichern **I**
   *to **make** trouble [ˌmeɪk ˈtrʌbl] Ärger
   machen; in Schwierigkeiten bringen **I**
   *to **make** use of [meɪk ˈjuːzˌəv] benutzen;
   verwenden **IV**
**make-up** [ˈmeɪkʌp] Make-up **V**; Zusammensetzung °**VI U2**, 53
**male** [meɪl] männlich **VI U1**, 9
shopping **mall** [ˈʃɒpɪŋ ˌmɔːl] Einkaufszen-
   trum **V**
**man, men** *(pl)* [mæn; men] Mann **I**
   what the **man** looked like [ˌwɒt ðə mæn
   ˈlʊkt laɪk] wie der Mann aussah **II**
to **manage** (to do sth) [ˈmænɪdʒ tə] schaffen (etw. zu tun) **V**
**management** [ˈmænɪdʒmənt] Management
   ⟨**VI U2**, 61⟩
**manager** [ˈmænɪdʒə] Manager/-in **V**
**manga** [ˈmæŋɡə] Manga *(japanischer*
   *Comic)* **II**
**mango** [ˈmæŋɡəʊ] Mango **I**
**manners** *(pl)* [ˈmænəz] Manieren; Benehmen **IV**
**mansion** [ˈmænʃn] Herrenhaus; Villa
   ⟨**VI U2**, 62⟩
software **manual** [ˈsɒftweə ˌmænjuəl] Softwarehandbuch **III**
**many** [ˈmeni] viele **I**
   How **many** …? [ˌhaʊ ˈmeni] Wie viele …? **I**
**map** [mæp] Stadtplan; Landkarte **I**
   mind **map** [ˈmaɪnd mæp] Wörternetz
   *(eine Art Schaubild)* **I**
**marathon** [ˈmærəθn] Marathon **II**
**marble** [ˈmɑːbl] Marmor ⟨**VI U2**, 61⟩
**March** [mɑːtʃ] März **I**
**march** [mɑːtʃ] Marsch; Kundgebung
   **VI U1**, 14
to **march** [mɑːtʃ] marschieren **III**
**marine** stinger [məˌriːn ˈstɪŋə] Seewespe *(Würfelquallen-Art)* **V**
**mark** [mɑːk] Note **III**
**marked** [mɑːkt] markiert **IV**
**market** [ˈmɑːkɪt] Markt **I**
   flea **market** [ˈfliː ˌmɑːkɪt] Flohmarkt **I**
**marmalade** [ˈmɑːməleɪd] Marmelade aus
   Zitrusfrüchten **III**

to **marry** [ˈmæri] heiraten **III**
**mashed** potatoes *(pl)* [ˌmæʃt pəˈteɪtəʊz]
   Kartoffelpüree **III**
**mask** [mɑːsk] Maske **IV**
**mass** [mæs] Masse; Massen- **V**
   **mass** migration [ˌmæs maɪˈɡreɪʃn] Massenwanderung **V**
**masseur** [mæsˈɜː] Masseur ⟨**VI U2**, 61⟩
**massive** [ˈmæsɪv] riesig; massiv; *hier:* super
   **IV**
**master** [ˈmɑːstə] Herr/-in; Meister/-in **V**
   raven **master** [ˈreɪvn ˌmɑːstə] Herr der
   Raben **II**
**match** [mætʃ] Spiel; Match **II**
to **match** [mætʃ] zuordnen; passen zu;
   entsprechen **I**
**mate** [meɪt] Schiffsoffizier; Maat **I**; Kumpel
   **V**; Partner/-in **VI U1**, 26
**material** [məˈtɪəriəl] Material **II**
**material** [məˈtɪəriəl] materiell **VITS2**, 71
**materialistic** [məˌtɪəriəˈlɪstɪk] materialis-
   tisch **VI U1**, 6
**Maths** [mæθs] Mathematik; Mathe **II**
no **matter** [nəʊ ˈmætə] egal; ganz gleich **V**
   What's the **matter**? [ˌwɒts ðə ˈmætə] Was
   ist los?; Was hast du? **III**
to **matter** [ˈmætə] von Bedeutung sein; etw.
   ausmachen **VI U1**, 26
   It doesn't **matter**. [ɪt ˌdʌznt ˈmætə] Es ist
   egal. **III**
**mattress** [ˈmætrəs] Matratze ⟨**VI U2**, 61⟩
**May** [meɪ] Mai **I**
**may** [meɪ] (vielleicht) können; dürfen **II**
**maybe** [ˈmeɪbi] vielleicht **I**
**me** [miː] ich; mich; mir **I**
**meal** [miːl] Mahlzeit; Essen **II**
   ready **meal** [ˌredi ˈmiːl] Fertiggericht **I**
*to **mean** [miːn] bedeuten; meinen **II**
   (I) didn't **mean** to … [aɪ ˌdɪdnt ˈmiːn tə]
   Ich wollte nicht … **IV**
**mean** [miːn] gemein **IV**
**meaning** [ˈmiːnɪŋ] Bedeutung; Sinn **II**
**meaningful** [ˈmiːnɪŋfl] bedeutsam; wichtig
   **VI U1**, 6
by any **means** [baɪ ˌeni ˈmiːnz] mit allen
   Mitteln **IV**
**meat** *(no pl)* [miːt] Fleisch **III**
**mechanic** [məˈkænɪk] Mechaniker/-in;
   Mechatroniker/-in **II**
**media** [ˈmiːdiə] Medien **II**
   social **media** [ˌsəʊʃl ˈmiːdiə] soziale
   Netzwerke **IV**
**mediation** [ˌmiːdiˈeɪʃn] Sprachmittlung **I**
**medical** [ˈmedɪkl] medizinisch; ärztlich;
   Medizin- **V**
**medication** [ˌmedɪˈkeɪʃn] medizinische
   Behandlung; Medikamente ⟨**VI U1**, 23⟩
**medicine** *(no pl)* [ˈmedsn] Medizin; Medikamente **III**
   **medicine** people [ˈmedsn ˌpiːpl] Medizinmänner **V**
**medieval** [ˌmediˈiːvl] mittelalterlich **III**

**medium** ['miːdiəm] mittel; mittelgroß **IV**
  **medium** shot ['miːdiəm ʃɒt] Halbtotale (Kameraeinstellung) **IV**
*to **meet** [miːt] treffen; sich treffen **I**
  *to **meet** halfway [ˌmiːt hɑːf'weɪ] sich auf halbem Weg treffen **III**
  *to **meet** sb's expectations [ˌmiːt sʌmbədiz ˌekspek'teɪʃnz] jmds. Erwartungen erfüllen **V**
  *to **meet** up [ˌmiːt 'ʌp] sich treffen **IV**
  Nice to **meet** you. [ˌnaɪs tə 'miːt juː] Nett, dich/euch/Sie kennenzulernen. **V**
**melody** ['melədi] Melodie **III**
**melting** pot ['meltɪŋ ˌpɒt] Schmelztiegel **IV**
**member** ['membə] Mitglied **II**
**memorable** ['memrəbl] denkwürdig; unvergesslich ⟨VI U2, 48⟩
**memory** ['memri] Erinnerung; Gedächtnis **II**; Speicher ⟨VI U2, 62⟩
**mental** ['mentl] geistig ⟨VI TS1, 39⟩
**mention** ['menʃn] Erwähnung **V**
to **mention** ['menʃn] erwähnen **II**
**menu** ['menjuː] Speisekarte **IV**
**merchant** ['mɜːtʃənt] Kaufmann; Händler **II**
**mess** [mes] Unordnung; Durcheinander; Schweinerei **II**
to **mess** sth up [ˌmes 'ʌp] etw. durcheinanderbringen; etw. vergeigen **IV**
**message** ['mesɪdʒ] Botschaft; Nachricht **I**
  *to leave a **message** [ˌliːv ə 'mesɪdʒ] eine Nachricht hinterlassen **I**
  *to take a **message** [ˌteɪk ə 'mesɪdʒ] eine Nachricht entgegennehmen; jmdm. etw. ausrichten **I**
  text (**message**) ['tekst ˌmesɪdʒ] SMS; Kurznachricht **I**
**messy** ['mesi] unordentlich **III**
**metabolism** [mə'tæblɪzm] Stoffwechsel **VI TS1, 37**
**metal** ['metl] Metall **VI U2, 50**
**method** ['meθəd] Methode ⟨VI U1, 23⟩
**metre** ['miːtə] Meter **II**
**Mexican** ['meksɪkn] mexikanisch; Mexikanisch; aus Mexiko; Mexikaner/-in **VI U2, 45**
**microprocessor** ['maɪkrəprəʊsesə] Mikroprozessor **VI U2, 51**
**middle** ['mɪdl] Mitte **I**
  **middle** class [ˌmɪdl 'klɑːs] Mittelschicht **V**
  **middle** school (AE) ['mɪdl ˌskuːl] Mittelschule (weiterführende Schule in den USA, Mittelstufe) **IV**
  in the **middle** of nowhere [ɪn ðə ˌmɪdl əv 'nəʊweə] mitten im Nirgendwo **IV**
**midnight** ['mɪdnaɪt] Mitternacht **III**
**might** [maɪt] könnte/-n (vielleicht) **IV**
  It **might** as well be … [ɪt maɪt əs 'wel biː …] Es könnte/-n auch … sein. **III**
to **migrate** [maɪ'greɪt] wandern; umherziehen **V**
**migration** [maɪ'greɪʃn] Migration; Wanderung **V**

mass **migration** [ˌmæs maɪ'greɪʃn] Massenwanderung **V**
**mile** [maɪl] Meile (brit. Längenmaß) **II**
**milk** [mɪlk] Milch **II**
to **milk** [mɪlk] melken **III**
**million** ['mɪljən] Million **II**
  I've done this a **million** times before. [ˌaɪv dʌn ðɪs ə ˌmɪljən taɪmz bɪ'fɔː] Ich habe das schon eine Million Mal gemacht. **II**
**millionaire** [ˌmɪljə'neə] Millionär/-in **III**
**mind** [maɪnd] Geist; Verstand **III**
  to change one's **mind** [ˌtʃeɪndʒ wʌnz 'maɪnd] seine Meinung ändern **III**
  *to come to one's **mind** [ˌkʌm tə wʌnz 'maɪnd] jmdm. in den Sinn kommen; jmdm. einfallen **V**
  *to keep in **mind** [ˌkiːp ɪn 'maɪnd] beachten; im Gedächtnis behalten **IV**
  **mind** map ['maɪnd mæp] Wörternetz (eine Art Schaubild) **I**
  *to rise up in one's **mind** [raɪz ˌʌp ɪn wʌnz 'maɪnd] jmdm. in den Sinn kommen **III**
to **mind** [maɪnd] etwas dagegen haben; einem etwas ausmachen **IV**
  to **mind** sth [maɪnd] auf etw. aufpassen **IV**
**mine** [maɪn] Mine **III**
**mine** [maɪn] mein/-er/-e/-es **II**
**miner** ['maɪnə] Bergarbeiter/-in ⟨VI U2, 52⟩
**mini** [mɪni] Mini- **II**
**minimum** wage [ˌmɪnɪməm 'weɪdʒ] Mindestlohn **VI U2, 53**
**mining** ['maɪnɪŋ] Bergbau **III**
**minority** [maɪ'nɒrəti] Minderheit **V**
**minute** ['mɪnɪt] Minute **I**
**mirror** ['mɪrə] Spiegel **III**
**misery** (no pl) ['mɪzri] Elend; Jammer; Not **V**
**mismatch** ['mɪsmætʃ] Missverhältnis **VI TS1, 37**
**Miss** [mɪs] Fräulein (Anrede) **III**
to **miss** [mɪs] verpassen; versäumen **II**; vermissen **III**
**missing** ['mɪsɪŋ] fehlend; verschwunden **II**
  What is **missing**? [ˌwɒt ɪz 'mɪsɪŋ] Was fehlt? **I**
**mission** ['mɪʃn] Mission; Auftrag **IV**
**mistake** [mɪ'steɪk] Fehler **I**
**misunderstanding** [ˌmɪsʌndə'stændɪŋ] Missverständnis **III**
**misunderstood** [ˌmɪsʌndə'stʊd] missverstanden **III**
**mix** [mɪks] Mix **III**
to **mix** [mɪks] zusammenpassen **IV**
  to **mix** (up) [mɪks 'ʌp] mischen; vermischen **III**
**mixed** [mɪkst] gemischt **V**
**mixture** ['mɪkstʃə] Mischung ⟨VI U2, 60⟩
**mobile** ['məʊbaɪl] Handy; Mobiltelefon **II**
**modal** ['məʊdl] Modalverb **II**
**modal** ['məʊdl] Modal- **V**
quick-shot **mode** ['kwɪkʃɒt ˌməʊd] Serienaufnahmemodus ⟨VI U2, 60⟩

**model** ['mɒdl] Modell; Tonmodell; Model **I**
  role **model** ['rəʊl ˌmɒdl] Vorbild **VI TS2, 71**
**modelling** ['mɒdəlɪŋ] Modeln **III**
**modern** ['mɒdn] modern **II**
**mom** (AE) [mɒm] Mama **IV**
**moment** ['məʊmənt] Moment; Augenblick **II**
  at the **moment** [ət ðə 'məʊmənt] im Moment; gerade **I**
**mommy** (AE) ['mɒmi] Mami ⟨VI U2, 60⟩
**monarch** ['mɒnək] Monarch/-in **III**
**Monday** ['mʌndeɪ] Montag **I**
  on **Mondays** [ɒn 'mʌndeɪz] montags **I**
**money** ['mʌni] Geld **I**
  *to make **money** [ˌmeɪk 'mʌni] Geld verdienen **I**
  pocket **money** ['pɒkɪt ˌmʌni] Taschengeld **I**
  to raise **money** [ˌreɪz 'mʌni] Geld sammeln **II**
**monster** ['mɒnstə] Monster; Ungeheuer **I**
**montage** [mɒn'tɑːʒ] Montage **IV**
**month** [mʌnθ] Monat **II**
**monument** ['mɒnjəmənt] Monument; Denkmal **III**
**mood** [muːd] Stimmung; Laune **II**
**moon** [muːn] Mond **IV**
  **moon** landing ['muːn ˌlændɪŋ] Mondlandung **IV**
**moonlight** ['muːnlaɪt] Mondlicht **III**
**more** [mɔː] mehr; weitere **I**
  no **more** [ˌnəʊ 'mɔː] nicht mehr **IV**
  not any **more** [ˌnɒt eni 'mɔː] nicht mehr **I**
  **more** … than ['mɔː ðən] mehr … als **I**
**moreover** [mɔːr'əʊvə] überdies; außerdem **VI U1, 11**
**morning** ['mɔːnɪŋ] Morgen; Vormittag **I**
  in the **mornings** [ɪn ðə 'mɔːnɪŋz] morgens; vormittags **I**
  Good **morning**. [gʊd 'mɔːnɪŋ] Guten Morgen. **I**
(the) **most** [ðə 'məʊst] der/die/das meiste; die meisten **I**
**mostly** ['məʊstli] meistens; größtenteils; hauptsächlich **V**
**mother** ['mʌðə] Mutter **I**
**motion** ['məʊʃn] Bewegung °**VI U1, 14**
  **motion** picture [ˌməʊʃn 'pɪktʃə] Film; Spielfilm **V**
to **motivate** ['məʊtɪveɪt] motivieren **I**
**motivation** [ˌməʊtɪ'veɪʃn] Motivation; Beweggründe **IV**
**motive** ['məʊtɪv] Motiv; Beweggrund **IV**
bicycle **motocross** [ˌbaɪsɪkl 'məʊtəʊkrɒs] Fahrradmotocross **II**
**motor** car ['məʊtə ˌkɑː] Automobil **V**
**mountain** ['maʊntɪn] Berg **II**
  **mountain** biking ['maʊntɪn ˌbaɪkɪŋ] Mountainbikefahren **II**
**mountainous** ['maʊntɪnəs] bergig **IV**
**mouse** (sg), **mice** (pl) [maʊs; maɪs] Maus/Mäuse **I**

**mouth** [maʊθ] Mund **I**; Mündung **V**
to talk with your **mouth** full [ˌtɔːk wɪð jɔː ˈmaʊθ fʊl] mit vollem Mund sprechen **IV**
**move** [muːv] Bewegung **I**; Umzug **V**
on the **move** [ɒn ðə ˈmuːv] unterwegs **IV**
to **move** [muːv] (sich) bewegen **I**
to **move** (house) [muːv (haʊs)] umziehen **III**
to **move** in/into [muːvˈɪn/ˈɪntə] einziehen in **III**
**movement** [ˈmuːvmənt] Bewegung **V**
**movie** (AE) [ˈmuːvi] Film **IV**
**movie** theater (AE) [ˈmuːvi ˌθɪətə] Kino **IV**
**Mr** [ˈmɪstə] Herr (Anrede) **I**
**Mrs** [ˈmɪsɪz] Frau (Anrede) **I**
**much** [mʌtʃ] viel **I**
that **much** [ðæt ˈmʌtʃ] so viel **III**
**mud** [mʌd] Schlamm **II**
**muddy** [ˈmʌdi] schlammig **II**
**mudlark** [ˈmʌdlɑːk] jemand, der im Schlamm nach Sachen sucht, die er dann verkaufen kann **II**
**mudslide** [ˈmʌdslaɪd] Schlammlawine **VI U2**, 54
**muesli** [ˈmjuːzli] Müsli **III**
**mug** [mʌg] Becher **III**
**multi-** [ˌmʌlti] viel-; multi- ⟨**VI U2**, 56⟩
**multicultural** [ˌmʌltiˈkʌltʃrl] multikulturell **V**
**multi-ethnic** [ˌmʌltiˈeθnɪk] Vielvölker-; international **II**
**mum** [mʌm] Mama **I**
**mummy** [ˈmʌmi] Mama; Mami; Mutti **III**
**murder** [ˈmɜːdə] Mord **III**
to **murder** [ˈmɜːdə] ermorden; umbringen **V**
**muscle** [ˈmʌsl] Muskel ⟨**VI U1**, 26⟩
**muscle-packed** [ˈmʌslˌpækt] muskelbepackt ⟨**VI U2**, 52⟩
**muscular** [ˈmʌskjələ] muskulös **VI TS2**, 71
**museum** [mjuːˈziːəm] Museum **I**
**music** [ˈmjuːzɪk] Musik **I**
**musical** [ˈmjuːzɪkl] Musical **V**
**musical** [ˈmjuːzɪkl] musikalisch; Musik- **III**
**musician** [mjuːˈzɪʃn] Musiker/-in **II**
**Muslim** [ˈmʊzlɪm] Muslim/-in; muslimisch **V**
**must** [mʌst] müssen **I**
a **must** [ə ˈmʌst] ein Muss °**VI U1**, 10
**mustn't** [ˈmʌsnt] nicht dürfen **I**
to **mutter** [ˈmʌtə] murmeln **IV**
**my** [maɪ] mein/-e **I**
**My** favourite … [maɪ ˈfeɪvrɪt] Mein/e Lieblings … **I**
**My** name is … [maɪ ˈneɪmˌɪz] Ich heiße … **I**
**myself** [maɪˈself] ich/mir/mich (selbst); selber **II**
**mysterious** [mɪˈstɪəriəs] mysteriös; geheimnisvoll **III**
**mystery** [ˈmɪstri] Mysterium; Rätsel; Geheimnis **III**
**mythical** [mɪθɪkl] sagenhaft; sagenumwoben **IV**

# N

**naked** [ˈneɪkɪd] nackt **IV**
**name** [neɪm] Name **I**
last **name** (AE) [ˈlɑːst neɪm] Nachname; Familienname **V**
**name** day [ˈneɪm ˌdeɪ] Namenstag **I**
My **name** is … [maɪ ˈneɪmˌɪz] Ich heiße … **I**
What's your **name**? [ˌwɒts jə ˈneɪm] Wie heißt du?; Wie heißen Sie? **I**
to **name** [neɪm] nennen; benennen **I**
**narrative** perspective [ˌnærətɪv pəˈspektɪv] Erzählperspektive **III**
**narrative** technique [ˌnærətɪv tekˈniːk] Erzähltechnik **V**
**narrator** [nəˈreɪtə] Erzähler/-in **III**
first person **narrator** [ˌfɜːst ˌpɜːsn nəˈreɪtə] Ich-Erzähler/-in **III**
third person **narrator** [θɜːd ˌpɜːsn nəˈreɪtə] Er/Sie-Erzähler/-in **III**
**narrow** [ˈnærəʊ] eng; schmal **III**
**NASA** (= National Aeronautics and Space Administration) [ˈnæsə] NASA **IV**
**nasty** [ˈnɑːsti] garstig; gemein **II**
**nation** [ˈneɪʃn] Nation **V**
**national** [ˈnæʃnl] national; landesweit **V**
**national** park [ˌnæʃnl ˈpɑːk] Nationalpark; Naturpark **V**
**nationality** [ˌnæʃnˈæləti] Nationalität; Staatsangehörigkeit **VI U1**, 10
**native** [ˈneɪtɪv] einheimisch; eingeboren **V**
**Native** American [ˌneɪtɪv əˈmerɪkən] Ureinwohner/-in Amerikas; Indianer/-in; indianisch **IV**
**natural** [ˈnætʃrl] natürlich; Natur- **IV**
**nature** [ˈneɪtʃə] Natur **II**
**nature** lover [ˈneɪtʃə ˌlʌvə] Naturfreund/-in **V**
**near** [nɪə] nahe; in der Nähe von **I**
**nearby** [ˌnɪəˈbaɪ] in der Nähe **V**
**nearly** [ˈnɪəli] fast; annähernd **II**
not **necessarily** [ˌnɒt nesəˈserəli] nicht notwendigerweise; nicht unbedingt **IV**
**necessary** [ˈnesəsri] nötig; notwendig; erforderlich **IV**
**necessity** [nəˈsesəti] Notwendigkeit **V**
**necklace** [ˈnekləs] Halskette **III**
in **need** [ɪn ˈniːd] bedürftig; in Not **II**
There's no **need** to … [ˌðeəz nəʊ ˈniːd tə] Es gibt keinen Grund zu … **IV**
with special **needs** [wɪð ˌspeʃl ˈniːdz] behindert **II**
to **need** (to do) [niːd] (tun) müssen **I**
to **need** (to) [niːd] brauchen; benötigen **I**
**needn't** [ˈniːdnt] nicht brauchen; nicht müssen **I**
**needless** to say [ˌniːdləs tə ˈseɪ] natürlich; selbstverständlich **IV**
**negative** [ˈnegətɪv] negativ; verneint **III**
**negative** form [ˈnegətɪv ˌfɔːm] verneinte Form **I**

**neighborhood** (AE) [ˈneɪbəhʊd] Nachbarschaft **IV**
**neighbour** (BE) [ˈneɪbə] Nachbar/-in **I**
**neighbourhood** [ˈneɪbəhʊd] Nachbarschaft **III**
**nephew** [ˈnefjuː] Neffe **IV**
**nerd** [nɜːd] Nerd (Person, die intelligent, aber sozial unbeholfen ist) **IV**
*to get on people's **nerves** [ˌget ɒn ˌpiːplz ˈnɜːvz] jemandem auf die Nerven gehen **I**
**nervous** [ˈnɜːvəs] nervös; aufgeregt **II**
**net** [net] Netz **II**
to **net** off [net ˌɒf] durch ein Netz abtrennen **V**
**netball** [ˈnetbɔːl] Korbball **I**
**network** [ˈnetwɜːk] Netzwerk **V**
communications **network** [kəˌmjuːnɪˈkeɪʃnz ˌnetwɜːk] Kommunikationsnetz; Nachrichtennetz **V**
social **network** [ˌsəʊʃl ˈnetwɜːk] soziales Netzwerk **II**
**neutral** [ˈnjuːtrl] neutral °**VI TS2**, 72
**never** [ˈnevə] nie; niemals **I**
**nevertheless** [ˌnevəðəˈles] trotzdem; dennoch; nichtsdestoweniger **VI U1**, 11
**new** [njuː] neu **I**
**New Yorker** [ˌnjuː ˈjɔːkə] New Yorker/-in **IV**
**newchild** [ˈnjuːtʃaɪld], **newchildren** [ˈnjuːˌtʃɪldrən] (pl) hier: Baby ⟨**VI U1**, 26⟩
**newly-arrived** [ˌnjuːliˌəˈraɪvd] frisch angekommen **V**
**news** (sg) [njuːz] Nachrichten; Neuigkeiten **II**
**news** report [ˈnjuːz rɪˌpɔːt] Tatsachenbericht; Nachrichtenbeitrag; Meldung **III**
**newspaper** [ˈnjuːsˌpeɪpə] Zeitung **III**
**newsreader** [ˈnjuːsˌriːdə] Nachrichtensprecher/-in **I**
**next** [nekst] nächste/-r/-s; der/die Nächste(n) **I**
**next** door [nekst ˈdɔː] (von) nebenan **III**
**next** to [ˈnekst tə] neben **I**
the **next** day [ðə ˌnekst ˈdeɪ] am nächsten Tag **II**
**next** [nekst] als Nächstes **I**
**nice** [naɪs] nett; schön; lieb **I**
**Nice** to meet you. [ˌnaɪs tə ˈmiːt juː] Nett, dich/euch/Sie kennenzulernen. **V**
**nickname** [ˈnɪkneɪm] Spitzname **V**
**night** [naɪt] Nacht **I**
all **night** [ˌɔːl ˈnaɪt] die ganze Nacht **I**
**night** walk [ˈnaɪt wɔːk] Nachtwanderung **II**
**nightmare** [ˈnaɪtmeə] Alptraum **IV**
**nine** [naɪn] neun **I**
**niqab** [niˈkɒb] Niqab (Gesichtsschleier) **VI AC1**, 41
**2nite** (= tonight) [təˈnaɪt] heute Abend **I**
**no** [nəʊ] kein/-e **I**
**no** longer [nəʊ ˈlɒŋgə] nicht länger; nicht mehr **V**

**no** matter [nəʊ ˈmætə] egal; ganz gleich V

**no** more [nəʊ ˈmɔː] nicht mehr IV

**no** one [ˈnəʊ wʌn] niemand ⟨VI U1, 22⟩

**no** idea [ˌnəʊ aɪˈdɪə] keine Ahnung II

**no** sooner [nəʊ ˈsuːnə] kaum VI U1, 19

**no** wonder [ˌnəʊ ˈwʌndə] kein Wunder IV

**No** worries. [nəʊ ˈwʌriz] Kein Problem.; Gern geschehen. V

**no** [nəʊ] nein I

**nobody** [ˈnəʊbədi] niemand II

  **nobody** else [ˈnəʊbədi els] niemand anderes III

**nod** [nɒd] Nicken V

to **nod** [nɒd] nicken V

**noise** [nɔɪz] Lärm; Geräusch II

**noisy** [ˈnɔɪzi] laut III

**nomad** [ˈnəʊmæd] Nomade/Nomadin V

to **nominate** [ˈnɒmɪneɪt] nominieren; ernennen VI U2, 48

**nomination** [ˌnɒmɪˈneɪʃn] Nominierung; Ernennung VI U2, 49

**nominee** [ˌnɒmɪˈniː] vorgeschlagener Kandidat/vorgeschlagene Kandidatin VI U2, 49

**non-** [nɒn] nicht- II

  **non-defining** relative clause [ˌnɒndɪfaɪnɪŋ ˈrelətɪv ˌklɔːz] nicht notwendiger Relativsatz IV

**none** [nʌn] keine/-r/-s V

a sort of **nonstop** repetition [ə ˌsɔːt əv ˌnɒnstɒp ˌrepɪˈtɪʃn] eine Art Dauerschleife ⟨VI U2, 61⟩

**nope** (infml) [nəʊp] nee; nö IV

**normal** [ˈnɔːml] normal II

**normality** [nɔːˈmæləti] Normalität VI U2, 63

**normally** [ˈnɔːmli] normalerweise IV

**Norman** [ˈnɔːmən] Normanne/Normannin; normannisch III

**north** [nɔːθ] Norden; Nord- II; nördlich; im Norden III

**northern** [ˈnɔːðən] nördlich; Nord- VI U2, 50

**nose** [nəʊz] Nase II

**not** [nɒt] nicht I

  **not** any more [ˌnɒt eni ˈmɔː] nicht mehr I

  **not** anymore (AE) [ˌnɒt eniˈmɔː] nicht mehr IV

  **not** necessarily [ˌnɒt nesəˈserəli] nicht notwendigerweise; nicht unbedingt IV

  **not** only … but (also) [nɒt ˌəʊnli … bʌt ˌɔːlsəʊ] nicht nur … sondern (auch) VI U1, 16

  **not** until [nɒt ənˈtɪl] nicht bevor; erst um/ im IV

  **not** … any [nɒt … eni] kein/-e/-en I

  **not** … anything [ˌnɒt ˈeniθɪŋ] nichts I

  **not** … either [nɒt … ˈaɪðə; nɒt … ˈiːðə] auch nicht IV

  **not** … yet [nɒt ˈjet] noch nicht II

**notch** [nɒtʃ] hier: Klasse ⟨VI U1, 7⟩

**note** [nəʊt] Notiz; Anmerkung I

  *to make **notes** [ˌmeɪk ˈnəʊts] Notizen machen I

  *to take **notes** [teɪk ˈnəʊts] sich Notizen machen I

to **note** down [ˌnəʊt ˈdaʊn] notieren; aufschreiben II

**nothing** [ˈnʌθɪŋ] nichts I

to **notice** [ˈnəʊtɪs] bemerken; wahrnehmen II

**noticeboard** [ˈnəʊtɪsbɔːd] schwarzes Brett II

**noun** [naʊn] Nomen; Hauptwort I

  collective **noun** [kəˈlektɪv] Sammelbegriff °VI U2, 53

**novel** [ˈnɒvl] Roman III

  graphic **novel** [ˌgræfɪk ˈnɒvl] Bildergeschichte; Comic III

**November** [nəˈvembə] November I

**now** [naʊ] jetzt; nun I

  right **now** [ˌraɪt ˈnaʊ] jetzt gleich; sofort; gerade II

**nowhere** [ˈnəʊweə] nirgendwo; nirgendwohin III

  in the middle of **nowhere** [ɪn ðə ˌmɪdl əv ˈnəʊweə] mitten im Nirgendwo IV

**number** [ˈnʌmbə] Zahl; Nummer I

**nurse** [nɜːs] Krankenschwester; Krankenpfleger II

**nut** [nʌt] Nuss I

**nutrition** [njuːˈtrɪʃn] Ernährung ⟨VI U2, 57⟩

## O

**o'clock** [əˈklɒk] Uhr (Zeitangabe bei vollen Stunden) I

**oak** [əʊk] Eiche III

to **obey** [əˈbeɪ] gehorchen V

**object** [ˈɒbdʒɪkt] Objekt II; Gegenstand III

  **object** pronoun [ɒbdʒɪkt ˈprəʊnaʊn] Objektpronomen III

**objective** [əbˈdʒektɪv] objektiv VI TS1, 38

**objectivity** [ˌɒbdʒekˈtɪvəti] Objektivität ⟨VI TS1, 39⟩

*to be **obliged** to (+ inf) [bi əˈblaɪdʒd tə] verpflichtet sein, etw. zu tun; müssen VI U2, 55

to **observe** [əbˈzɜːv] beobachten; beachten; befolgen VI U2, 45

**obstacle** [ˈɒbstəkl] Hindernis VI U2, 59

**obvious** [ˈɒbviəs] offensichtlich IV

**occupation** [ˌɒkjəˈpeɪʃn] Beruf; Beschäftigung V

**October** [ɒkˈtəʊbə] Oktober I

against all **odds** [əˌgenst ɔːl ˈɒdz] entgegen allen Erwartungen III

**odd** [ɒd] seltsam; komisch IV

**of** [ɒv; əv] von I

  **of** course [əv ˈkɔːs] natürlich; selbstverständlich I

  **of** one's own [əv wʌnz ˈəʊn] eigen III

to drop sb **off** [drɒp ˈɒf] jmdn. absetzen; jmdn. aussteigen lassen V

*to take **off** [teɪk ˈɒf] abnehmen; herunternehmen; ausziehen I

*to take the day **off** [teɪk ðə ˌdeɪ ˈɒf] sich den Tag freinehmen IV

to turn **off** [tɜːnˌˈɒf] abschalten; ausschalten II

to **offend** [əˈfend] beleidigen; verletzen VI AC1, 43

special **offer** [ˌspeʃl ˈɒfə] Sonderangebot I

to **offer** [ˈɒfə] anbieten II

**office** [ˈɒfɪs] Büro I

  immigration **office** [ˌɪmɪˈgreɪʃn ˌɒfɪs] Einwanderungsbehörde IV

  ticket **office** [ˈtɪkɪt ˌɒfɪs] Kartenschalter III

police **officer** [pəˈliːs ˌɒfɪsə] Polizeibeamter; Polizist/-in II

**official** [əˈfɪʃl] Schiedsrichter/-in II; Beamte/-r IV

**official** [əˈfɪʃl] offiziell III

  **official** language [əˌfɪʃl ˈlæŋgwɪdʒ] Amtssprache II

**offline** [ˈɒflaɪn] offline II

**often** [ˈɒfn] oft; häufig I

**oh** [əʊ] null (bei Telefonnummern und Uhrzeitangaben) I

**Oh!** [əʊ] O! I

  **Oh** dear! [ˌəʊ ˈdɪə] Oje! III

**ointment** [ˈɔɪntmənt] Salbe II

**OK** [əʊˈkeɪ] o.k.; in Ordnung I

**okay** [əˈkeɪ] okay IV

**old** [əʊld] alt I

  the **old** [ðiˌˈəʊld] die Alten ⟨VI U1, 22⟩

  How **old** are you? [haʊˌˈəʊld ə juː] Wie alt bist du?; Wie alt sind Sie? I

**11-year-old** [ˌɪlevnˈjɪərəʊld] 11-Jährige/-r II

**old-timer** [ˌəʊldˈtaɪmə] alter Hase ⟨VI U2, 62⟩

**OMG!** (Oh my god!) [əʊ maɪ ˈgɒd] OMG! (Oh mein Gott!) IV

**on** [ɒn] auf; an; am; in; im I

  *to be **on** [bi ˈɒn] an sein; laufen II; auf Sendung sein °VI U2, 57

  **on** a shoestring [ɒn ə ˈʃuːstrɪŋ] für/mit wenig Geld IV

  **on** average [ɒn ˈævrɪdʒ] durchschnittlich; im Durchschnitt VI U2, 55

  **on** Mondays [ɒn ˈmʌndeɪz] montags I

  **on** my own [ɒn maɪ ˈəʊn] allein; für mich II

  **on** one's own [ɒn wʌnz ˈəʊn] allein; für sich V

  **on** the brink of [ɒn ðə ˈbrɪŋk əv] am Rande von; kurz vor III

  **on** the inside [ɒn ðiˈɪnsaɪd] innen V

  **on** the left [ɒn ðə ˈleft] auf der linken Seite; links I

  **on** the move [ɒn ðə ˈmuːv] unterwegs IV

  **on** the outside [ɒn ðiˈaʊtsaɪd] außen V

  **on** the right [ɒn ðə ˈraɪt] auf der rechten Seite; rechts I

  **on** time [ɒn ˈtaɪm] pünktlich II

  **on** top [ɒn ˈtɒp] oben; obendrauf I

  *to put **on** [pʊtˌˈɒn] anziehen III

  Come **on!** [kʌmˈɒn] Komm schon!; Komm jetzt! I

once [wʌns] einmal; einst **I**
one [wʌn] eins **I**
one (sg)/ones (pl) [wʌn/wʌnz] eine/-r/-s **II**
no **one** [ˈnəʊ wʌn] niemand ⟨**VI U1**, 22⟩
one-sided [ˌwʌnˈsaɪdɪd] einseitig **VI TS2**, 68
one-way ticket [ˈwʌnweɪ ˌtɪkɪt] einfache Fahrkarte **III**
online [ɒnˈlaɪn] online **II**
onlooker [ˈɒnˌlʊkə] Zuschauer/-in **V**
only [ˈəʊnli] einzige/-r/-s **II**
   **only** child [ˈəʊnli ˌtʃaɪld] Einzelkind **I**
only [ˈəʊnli] erst; bloß; nur **I**
   not **only** … but (also) [nɒt ˌəʊnli … bʌt ˈɔːlsəʊ] nicht nur … sondern (auch) **VI U1**, 16
onto [ˈɒntə] auf … hinauf **VI U1**, 13
Oops! [uːps] Hoppla!; Huch! **I**
to open [ˈəʊpn] öffnen; aufmachen **I**; hier: beginnen **III**; eröffnen **IV**
open [ˈəʊpn] offen; geöffnet; aufgeschlagen **I**
   *to hold **open** [ˌhəʊld ˈəʊpn] aufhalten **IV**
opening [ˈəʊpnɪŋ] Öffnung; Beginn **III**
   **opening** line [ˈəʊpnɪŋ ˌlaɪn] der erste Satz **III**
opinion [əˈpɪnjən] Meinung **II**
opportunity [ˌɒpəˈtjuːnəti] Chance; Gelegenheit; Möglichkeit **VI U1**, 8
opposite [ˈɒpəzɪt] Gegenteil °**VI U1**, 27
opposite [ˈɒpəzɪt] gegenüber; auf der anderen Seite von **I**
to oppress [əˈpres] unterdrücken **V**
optimistic [ˌɒptɪˈmɪstɪk] optimistisch **III**
option [ˈɒpʃn] Möglichkeit; Wahl; Option **III**
or [ɔː] oder **I**
   either … **or** … [ˈaɪðə/ˈiːðə … ɔː] entweder … oder … **IV**
oral [ˈɔːrl] mündlich **V**
orange [ˈɒrɪndʒ] Orange **I**
orange [ˈɒrɪndʒ] orange **I**
orca [ˈɔːkə] Schwertwal **V**
order [ˈɔːdə] Reihenfolge; Ordnung **I**; Befehl **III**
   in **order** to [ɪnˈɔːdə tə] um … zu; mit der Absicht **V**
   out of **order** [ˌaʊt əv ˈɔːdə] kaputt; außer Betrieb **IV**
   word **order** [ˈwɜːdˌɔːdə] Wortstellung; Satzstellung **I**
to order [ˈɔːdə] bestellen **IV**
ordinary [ˈɔːdnri] gewöhnlich; normal **VI U1**, 25
organisation [ˌɔːgnaɪˈzeɪʃn] Organisation **III**
to organise [ˈɔːgənaɪz] organisieren **I**
*to get organised [get ˈɔːgənaɪzd] sich organisieren **III**
organiser [ˈɔːgənaɪzə] Organisator/-in **VI U1**, 10
to organize (AE) [ˈɔːgənaɪz] organisieren **V**
orientation [ˌɔːriənˈteɪʃn] Orientierung; Orientierungs- **IV**

origin [ˈɒrɪdʒɪn] Ursprung; Herkunft; Abstammung **IV**
original [əˈrɪdʒnl] Original **III**
original [əˈrɪdʒnl] original; ursprünglich **III**
other [ˈʌðə] anders; andere/-r/-s; weitere **I**
   each **other** [ˌiːtʃˈʌðə] einander; sich; sich gegenseitig **I**
   the **others** [ðiˈʌðəz] die anderen **I**
   the **other** way around [ðiˈʌðə weɪ ˈraʊnd] andersrum; umgekehrt ⟨**VI U2**, 62⟩
otherwise [ˈʌðəwaɪz] sonst **IV**
Ouch! [aʊtʃ] Aua! **II**
ought to (+ inf) [ˈɔːt tə] sollen **VI U2**, 55
our [aʊə; ɑː] unser/-e **I**
out [aʊt] außerhalb; heraus; hinaus; nach draußen **I**
   to clean **out** [ˌkliːnˈaʊt] ausräumen; entrümpeln **IV**
   to clear **out** [ˌklɪərˈaʊt] ausräumen; entrümpeln **I**
   *to come **out** [ˌkʌmˈaʊt] sich outen **VI AC1**, 42
   to drop **out** (of) [ˌdrɒpˈaʊtˌəv] abbrechen **III**
   *to hang **out** (with) (infml) [ˌhæŋˈaʊt wɪð] sich herumtreiben (mit); rumhängen (mit); sich treffen (mit) **III**
   *to leave **out** [ˌliːvˈaʊt] auslassen; weglassen **IV**
   **out** and about [ˌaʊt ənˌəˈbaʊt] unterwegs **II**
   **out** of [ˈaʊtˌəv] aus … heraus **IV**
   **out** of focus [ˌaʊt əv ˈfəʊkəs] unscharf **III**
   **out** of order [ˌaʊt əv ˈɔːdə] kaputt; außer Betrieb **IV**
   to pick **out** [ˌpɪkˈaʊt] aussuchen; auswählen; heraushören; herausfiltern; herauslesen °**VI TS2**, 72
   to toss **out** [ˌtɒsˈaʊt] ausstoßen; hinauswerfen **V**
   to turn **out** to be [ˌtɜːnˈaʊt tə] sich herausstellen als °**VI U1**, 27
   a day **out** in … [əˌdeɪˈaʊt ɪn] ein Tag in … **II**
the outback [ði ˈaʊtbæk] Outback (australisches Hinterland) **V**
outcome [ˈaʊtkʌm] Ergebnis; Resultat **VI TS1**, 37
outdated [ˌaʊtˈdeɪtɪd] veraltet; überholt **VI TS2**, 71
outdoor [ˈaʊtdɔː] Freiluft-; Outdoor- **II**
outdoors [ˌaʊtˈdɔːz] im Freien **VI U2**, 55
   the **outdoors** [ði ˌaʊtˈdɔːz] die Natur **V**
outfit [ˈaʊtfɪt] Outfit; Kleidung **II**
outgoing [ˌaʊtˈgəʊɪŋ] kontaktfreudig **IV**
outlaw [ˈaʊtlɔː] Geächtete/-r; Gesetzlose/-r **III**
to outline [ˈaʊtlaɪn] skizzieren; umreißen °**VI U1**, 23
out-of-character [ˌaʊtəvˈkærəktə] ungewöhnlich **IV**
outrage [ˈaʊtreɪdʒ] Empörung ⟨**VI TS2**, 73⟩

from the outside [ˌfrəm ðiˌaʊtˈsaɪd] von außen **IV**
   on the **outside** [ˌɒn ðiˌaʊtsaɪd] außen **V**
outside [aʊtˈsaɪd] nach draußen; draußen; außerhalb **I**
   **outside** world [ˈaʊtsaɪd ˌwɜːld] Außenwelt **V**
outward [ˈaʊtwəd] abfahrend **III**
over [ˈəʊvə] hinüber; über **I**; vorüber; vorbei **II**
   *to bend **over** [ˌbendˈəʊvə] sich vorbeugen; sich beugen über ⟨**VI U1**, 23⟩
   *to go **over** to [ˌgəʊˈəʊvə tə] hinübergehen zu; zu jmdm. nach Hause gehen **II**
   **over** and **over** again [ˌəʊvərˌənˌəʊvər əˈgen] immer wieder **III**
   **over** to … [ˈəʊvə tə] weiter zu … **V**
   *to run **over** [ˌrʌnˈəʊvə] überfahren **V**
   *to win sb **over** [ˌwɪnˈəʊvə] jmdn. für sich gewinnen; jmdn. überzeugen **IV**
overall [ˌəʊvrˈɔːl] allgemein; Gesamt-; insgesamt **V**
*to overcome [ˌəʊvəˈkʌm] überwinden **VI U2**, 59
*to overdo [ˌəʊvəˈduː] übertreiben; zu weit gehen **IV**
to over-exaggerate [ˌəʊvərɪgˈzædʒreɪt] völlig übertreiben **V**
*to overhear [ˌəʊvəˈhɪə] belauschen; zufällig mit anhören **V**
to overlap [ˌəʊvəˈlæp] (sich) überlappen **IV**
overloaded [ˌəʊvəˈləʊdɪd] überladen **IV**
overnight [ˌəʊvəˈnaɪt] über Nacht **III**
to overreact [ˌəʊvəriˈækt] überreagieren **II**
overseas [ˌəʊvəˈsiːz] in Übersee; im Ausland **V**
to own [əʊn] besitzen **V**
own [əʊn] eigene/-r/-s **I**
   of one's **own** [əv wʌnzˈəʊn] eigen **III**
   on my **own** [ɒn maɪˈəʊn] allein; für mich **II**
   on one's **own** [ɒn wʌnzˈəʊn] allein; für sich **V**
owner [ˈəʊnə] Besitzer/-in **V**

## P

p.m. [piːˈem] nachmittags (Uhrzeit); abends (Uhrzeit) **I**
Pa [pɑː] Papa **V**
to pack [pæk] packen; einpacken **V**
   to **pack** up [ˈpækˌʌp] zusammenpacken **VI U2**, 46
to package [ˈpækɪdʒ] verpacken **V**
muscle-packed [ˈmʌslˌpækt] muskelbepackt ⟨**VI U2**, 52⟩
packet [ˈpækɪt] Päckchen; Paket; Packung **I**
to paddle [ˈpædl] paddeln **V**
paddleboard [ˈpædlbɔːd] Paddling Board (eine Art Surfbrett, auf dem man aufrecht stehend paddelt) **V**
page [peɪdʒ] Seite **I**

**pain** [peɪn] Schmerz **II**

to **paint** [peɪnt] anmalen; malen **I**

**painting** ['peɪntɪŋ] Malerei; Gemälde **II**

**pair** [peə] Paar **I**

  **pair** work ['peə ˌwɜːk] Partnerarbeit **II**

to **pair** [peə] Paare bilden **III**

  to **pair** up [peər ˌʌp] Paare bilden ⟨**VI TS2**, 73⟩

**pale** [peɪl] blass **V**

**palm tree** ['pɑːm ˌtriː] Palme **III**

**Pampers** ['pæmpəz] Windeln ⟨**VI U2**, 62⟩

**panel** ['pænl] Bild (eines Comics) **IV**; Gruppe; Team °**VI U1**, 21

to **panic** ['pænɪk] panisch werden **II**

**pants** (pl) [pænts] Hose ⟨**VI U2**, 52⟩

**paparazzo** [ˌpæprˈætsəʊ] Paparazzo ⟨**VI U2**, 61⟩

**paper** ['peɪpə] Papier **I**

  **piece** of paper [ˌpiːs ˌəv 'peɪpə] Stück Papier **I**

**papers** (pl) ['peɪpəz] Unterlagen; Papiere **V**

**paradise** ['pærədaɪs] Paradies **I**

**paragraph** ['pærəgrɑːf] Paragraf; Absatz **IV**

**parallel** ['pærəlel] Parallele **V**

to **paraphrase** ['pærəfreɪz] paraphrasieren; umschreiben **V**

**parcel** ['pɑːsl] Paket; Päckchen **I**

**parents** (pl) ['peərənts] Eltern **I**

**park** [pɑːk] Park **I**

  national **park** [ˌnæʃnl 'pɑːk] Nationalpark; Naturpark **V**

  RV **park** (AE) [ɑːˈviː ˌpɑːk] Campingplatz **VI U2**, 46

**parking** lot ['pɑːkɪŋ ˌlɒt] Parkplatz **V**

**parliament** ['pɑːləmənt] Parlament **V**

**part** [pɑːt] Teil; Stadtteil **I**; Rolle **III**

  lead **part** [liːd 'pɑːt] Hauptrolle **III**

  *to take **part** (in) [teɪk 'pɑːt (ɪn)] teilnehmen (an) **II**

**partially** sighted [ˌpɑːʃəli 'saɪtɪd] sehbehindert **II**

to **participate** [pɑːˈtɪsɪpeɪt] teilnehmen **II**

**participation** [pɑːˌtɪsɪˈpeɪʃn] Mitwirkung; Beteiligung **VI AC2**, 74

**participle** [pɑːˈtɪsɪpl] Partizip **V**

  past **participle** [ˌpɑːst pɑːˈtɪsɪpl] Partizip **II**

  present **participle** [ˌpreznt pɑːˈtɪsɪpl] Partizip Präsens **V**

**particular** [pəˈtɪkjələ] bestimmte/-r/-s **III**

  in **particular** [ˌɪn pəˈtɪkjələ] im besonderen **VI TS1**, 37

**particularly** [pəˈtɪkjələli] besonders **V**

**partner** ['pɑːtnə] Partner/-in **I**

**part-time** [ˌpɑːt'taɪm] Teilzeit-; Halbtags- **V**

**party** ['pɑːti] Party; Feier **I**; Partei **III**

hall **pass** ['hɔːl pɑːs] Erlaubnis, sich während des Unterrichts auf dem Flur aufzuhalten **IV**

to **pass** [pɑːs] zupassen; zuspielen **II**; durchgehen; vorbeigehen (an); passieren; bestehen **V**

  to **pass** (on) [ˌpɑːsˌ'ɒn] weitergeben **I**

**passenger** ['pæsndʒə] Passagier/-in; Fahrgast **IV**

  **passenger** seat ['pæsndʒə ˌsiːt] Beifahrersitz **V**

*to be **passionate** about sth [bi 'pæʃnət əˌbaʊt] etw. leidenschaftlich gern tun; eine Leidenschaft für etw. haben; für etw. brennen **VI U1**, 8

**passive** ['pæsɪv] Passiv **III**

  **passive** progressive [ˌpæsɪv prəˈgresɪv] Verlaufsform des Passivs **V**

**passive** ['pæsɪv] passiv **III**

**passport** ['pɑːspɔːt] Pass; Reisepass **IV**

**past** [pɑːst] Vergangenheit **II**

  **past** form ['pɑːst fɔːm] Vergangenheitsform **II**

  **past** participle [ˌpɑːst pɑːˈtɪsɪpl] Partizip **II**

  **past** perfect [ˌpɑːst 'pɜːfɪkt] Plusquamperfekt **III**

  **past** perfect progressive [ˌpɑːst ˌpɜːfɪkt prəˈgresɪv] Verlaufsform des Plusquamperfekts **IV**

  **past** progressive [ˌpɑːst prəˈgresɪv] Verlaufsform der Vergangenheit **II**

  simple **past** [ˌsɪmpl 'pɑːst] Vergangenheitsform **II**

**past** [pɑːst] letzte/-r/-s; vergangen °**VI U1**, 27

**past** [pɑːst] nach (bei Uhrzeitangaben); vorbei (an); vorüber (an) **I**

  half **past** [ˌhɑːf 'pɑːst] halb (bei Uhrzeitangaben) **I**

  quarter **past**/to ['kwɔːtə pɑːst/tə] Viertel nach/vor **I**

**pasta** ['pæstə] Pasta; Nudeln **I**

**pastry** ['peɪstri] Teig; Teigtasche **IV**

**path** [pɑːθ] Pfad; Weg **IV**

  coastal **path** [ˌkəʊstl 'pɑːθ] Küstenweg **III**

**patient** ['peɪʃnt] geduldig **VI U1**, 16

**pattern** ['pætn] Muster **III**

**pause** [pɔːz] Pause **III**

to **pause** [pɔːz] (eine kurze) Pause machen; innehalten ⟨**VI U1**, 24⟩

**pawn** shop ['pɔːn ʃɒp] Pfandhaus; Pfandleihe **III**

**pay** [peɪ] Lohn; Gehalt **VI U1**, 16

*to **pay** (for) [peɪ] bezahlen **I**

  *to **pay** attention to sb/sth [ˌpeɪ əˈtenʃn tʊ] jmdn./etw. beachten **III**

  That doesn't **pay** my rent. [ðət dʌznt ˌpeɪ maɪ 'rent] Davon kann ich meine Miete nicht bezahlen. **VI U2**, 53

**PC** (= Personal Computer) [piːˈsiː] PC **II**

**PE** (= Physical Education) [ˌpiːˈiː; ˌfɪzɪklˌedʒʊˈkeɪʃn] Sportunterricht **II**

**peace** [piːs] Frieden **V**

**peaceful** ['piːsfl] friedlich **V**

**peach** [piːtʃ] Pfirsich **III**

**peak** [piːk] Haupt-; Spitzen- **V**

**pedestrian** [pɪˈdestriən] Fußgänger/-in; Fußgänger- **VI AC1**, 41

**peer** evaluation [ˌpɪər ɪˌvæljuˈeɪʃn] gegenseitige Beurteilung ⟨**VI AC1**, 43⟩

**peer** pressure ['pɪə ˌpreʃə] Gruppenzwang **III**

to **peer** at ['pɪər ˌət] anschauen ⟨**VI U1**, 24⟩

to **peer-edit** ['pɪər ˌedɪt] gegenseitig kontrollieren **II**

**peer-editing** ['pɪər ˌedɪtɪŋ] gegenseitige Kontrolle °**VI TS1**, 36

**pen** [pen] Füller **I**

**penny, pence** (pl) ['peni; pens] Penny; Pence (brit. Währungseinheit) **I**

**pencil** ['pensl] Bleistift; Buntstift **I**

  **pencil**-case ['pensl ˌkeɪs] Federmäppchen; Mäppchen **I**

**penicillin** [ˌpenɪˈsɪlɪn] Penicillin **III**

**penny, pence** (pl) ['peni; pens] Penny; Pence (brit. Währungseinheit) **I**

**penthouse** ['penthaʊs] Penthouse; Wohnung mit Dachterrasse **IV**

**people** ['piːpl] Volk **V**

**people** (pl) ['piːpl] Leute; Menschen **I**

  medicine **people** ['medsn ˌpiːpl] Medizinmänner **V**

  **people** skills (pl) ['piːpl ˌskɪlz] soziale Kompetenz **VI U1**, 10

**per** [pɜː; pə] pro **III**

**percent** [pəˈsent], **percent** [pəˈsent] (pl) Prozent **V**

**perception** [pəˈsepʃn] Wahrnehmung °**VI U1**, 14

future **perfect** [ˌfjuːtʃə 'pɜːfɪkt] vollendetes Futur; Futur II °**VI U2**, 48

  past **perfect** [ˌpɑːst 'pɜːfɪkt] Plusquamperfekt **III**

  past **perfect** progressive [ˌpɑːst ˌpɜːfɪkt prəˈgresɪv] Verlaufsform des Plusquamperfekts **IV**

  present **perfect** [ˌpreznt 'pɜːfɪkt] das Perfekt **II**

  present **perfect** progressive [ˌpreznt ˌpɜːfɪkt prəˈgresɪv] Verlaufsform des Perfekts **III**

**perfect** ['pɜːfɪkt] perfekt; vollkommen **I**

**perfection** [pəˈfekʃn] Perfektion; Vollkommenheit **VI TS2**, 71

to **perform** [pəˈfɔːm] aufführen; auftreten **IV**

**performance** [pəˈfɔːməns] Aufführung; Vorstellung **IV**; Leistung **VI TS1**, 37

**perhaps** [pəˈhæps] vielleicht **III**

**period** ['pɪəriəd] Periode; Zeitspanne **III**

**period** (AE) ['pɪəriəd] Stunde; Unterrichtsstunde **IV**

**permanent** ['pɜːmnənt] permanent; dauerhaft **V**

**permission** [pəˈmɪʃn] Erlaubnis; Genehmigung **V**

to **permit** [pəˈmɪt] erlauben; genehmigen ⟨**VI U1**, 23⟩

to **persist** [pəˈsɪst] beharren ⟨**VI U2**, 60⟩

**persistent** [pəˈsɪstnt] hartnäckig; ausdauernd; beharrlich **VI U2**, 46

**person, people** (pl) ['pɜːsn; 'piːpl] Person; Mensch **I**

first **person** narrator [ˌfɜːst ˌpɜːsn nəˈreɪtə] Ich-Erzähler/-in **III**

third **person** narrator [θɜːd ˌpɜːsn nəˈreɪtə] Er/Sie-Erzähler/-in **III**

personal [ˈpɜːsnl] persönlich **I**

**personal** pronoun [ˌpɜːsnl ˈprəʊnaʊn] Personalpronomen °**VI TS2**, 69

personality [ˌpɜːsnˈæləti] Persönlichkeit **III**

perspective [pəˈspektɪv] Perspektive; Blickwinkel **II**

narrative **perspective** [ˌnærətɪv pəˈspektɪv] Erzählperspektive **III**

to persuade [pəˈsweɪd] überreden **II**

persuasive [pəˈsweɪsɪv] überzeugend **III**

pet [pet] Haustier **I**

petition [pəˈtɪʃn] Petition; Unterschriftenliste **VI AC2**, 74

phone [fəʊn] Telefon; Handy **I**

to answer the **phone** [ˌɑːnsə ðə ˈfəʊn] einen Anruf entgegennehmen **I**

cell **phone** (AE) [ˈselfəʊn] Mobiltelefon; Handy **IV**

**phone** box [ˈfəʊn bɒks] Telefonzelle **IV**

**phone** call [ˈfəʊn ˌkɔːl] Anruf; Telefonanruf **I**

rotary **phone** [ˈrəʊtri fəʊn] Telefon mit Wählscheibe **III**

to phone [fəʊn] anrufen; telefonieren **IV**

photo [ˈfəʊtəʊ] Foto; Fotografie **I**

in the **photo**(s) [ɪn ðə ˈfəʊtəʊ(z)] auf dem Foto/den Fotos **I**

**photo** shoot [ˈfəʊtəʊ ˌʃuːt] Fotoshooting; Fotoaufnahmen **III**

**photo** story [ˈfəʊtəʊ ˌstɔːri] Fotostory; Bildgeschichte **V**

*to take **photos** [ˌteɪk ˈfəʊtəʊz] fotografieren; Fotos machen **I**

to photobomb [ˈfəʊtəʊbɒm] ins Foto laufen **III**

to photograph [ˈfəʊtəɡrɑːf] fotografieren **VI U2**, 61

photographer [fəˈtɒɡrəfə] Fotograf/-in **III**

phrase [freɪz] Redewendung; Ausdruck; Satz **I**

set **phrase** [set ˈfreɪz] Floskel; feststehender Ausdruck °**VI TS1**, 38

Useful **phrases** [ˌjuːsfl ˈfreɪzɪz] nützliche Ausdrücke **I**

physical [ˈfɪzɪkl] physisch; körperlich **VI U1**, 13

piano [piˈænəʊ] Klavier; Piano **IV**

to pick [pɪk] auswählen; aussuchen **II**; pflücken **V**

to **pick** out [pɪk ˈaʊt] aussuchen; auswählen; heraushören; herausfiltern; herauslesen °**VI TS2**, 72

to **pick** up [pɪk ˈʌp] aufheben; mitnehmen; abholen **III**

picnic [ˈpɪknɪk] Picknick **I**

picture [ˈpɪktʃə] Bild; Foto **I**

motion **picture** [ˌməʊʃn ˈpɪktʃə] Film; Spielfilm **V**

*to see the bigger **picture** [ˌsiː ðə ˌbɪɡə ˈpɪktʃə] über den Tellerrand hinausschauen **V**

to picture [ˈpɪktʃə] sich vorstellen ⟨**VI U1**, 23⟩

pie [paɪ] Kuchen; Pastete **I**

**pie** chart [ˈpaɪ ˌtʃɑːt] Kuchendiagramm; Tortendiagramm **V**

piece [piːs] Stück **I**

**piece** of junk [ˌpiːs əv ˈdʒʌŋk] Stück Schrott **I**

pier [pɪə] Pier; Hafendamm **I**

pig [pɪɡ] Schwein **I**

guinea **pig** [ˈɡɪni ˌpɪɡ] Meerschweinchen **I**

*to give sb a **piggyback** [ɡɪv ə ˈpɪɡibæk] jmdn. Huckepack nehmen **IV**

Pilgrim [ˈpɪlɡrɪm] Pilger/-in **IV**

pill [pɪl] Pille; Tablette **II**

pilot [ˈpaɪlət] Pilot/-in **II**

pineapple [ˈpaɪnæpl] Ananas **III**

pink [pɪŋk] pink; rosa **I**

pioneer [ˌpaɪəˈnɪə] Pionier/-in **V**

pipe [paɪp] Rohr; Rohrleitung; Pfeife **II**

clay **pipe** [ˈkleɪ paɪp] Tonpfeife **II**

pitch [pɪtʃ] Spielfeld; Platz **II**

pizza [ˈpiːtsə] Pizza **I**

place [pleɪs] Ort; Stelle; Platz **I**

starting **place** [ˈstɑːtɪŋ pleɪs] Startpunkt **III**

*to take **place** [teɪk ˈpleɪs] stattfinden **I**

in the first **place** [ɪn ðə ˈfɜːst pleɪs] überhaupt erst; von vornherein ⟨**VI TS2**, 69⟩

to place [pleɪs] legen **III**; stellen; unterbringen **V**

placemat [ˈpleɪsmæt] Placemat; Platzdeckchen **I**

plan [plæn] Plan; Entwurf **I**

to plan [plæn] planen **I**

plane [pleɪn] Flugzeug **IV**

tanker **plane** [ˈtæŋkə ˌpleɪn] Tankflugzeug **VI U2**, 54

planet [ˈplænɪt] Planet **II**

planner [ˈplænə] Handbuch; Kalender **I**

route **planner** [ˈruːt ˌplænə] Routenplaner **IV**

plant [plɑːnt] Pflanze **III**

to plant [plɑːnt] pflanzen; anpflanzen **II**

plantation [plænˈteɪʃn] Plantage **VI U1**, 13

plaster cast [ˈplɑːstə kɑːst] Gipsverband **III**

plastic [ˈplæstɪk] Plastik; Kunststoff; Plastik- **VI U1**, 18

**plastic** surgery (no pl) [ˌplæstɪk ˈsɜːdʒəri] Schönheitschirurgie **V**

plate [pleɪt] Teller **III**

platform [ˈplætfɔːm] Plattform; Bahnsteig **III**

play [pleɪ] Theaterstück **III**

fair **play** [feə ˈpleɪ] Fairplay **III**

**play** on words [ˌpleɪ ɒn ˈwɜːdz] Wortspiel **III**

role **play** [ˈrəʊl pleɪ] Rollenspiel **I**

to play [pleɪ] spielen **I**

to **play** a trick (on) [ˌpleɪ ə ˈtrɪk ɒn] einen Streich spielen **I**

to **play** bowls [ˌpleɪ ˈbəʊlz] Bowling spielen **III**

player [ˈpleɪə] Spieler/-in; Mitspieler/-in **II**

*to be a team **player** [ˌbiː ə ˈtiːm ˌpleɪə] gern im Team arbeiten **VI U1**, 8

Please. [pliːz] Bitte. **I**

pleasure [ˈpleʒə] Freude; Vergnügen ⟨**VI U1**, 23⟩

plenty of [ˈplenti əv] eine Menge **VI TS1**, 38

plot [plɒt] Handlung **II**

plumber [ˈplʌmə] Installateur/-in; Klempner/-in **III**

plumbing [ˈplʌmɪŋ] Sanitärarbeit **III**

plural [ˈplʊərəl] Plural; Mehrzahl **I**

poaching (no pl) [ˈpəʊtʃɪŋ] Wilderei **III**

pocket [ˈpɒkɪt] Tasche; Hosentasche **III**

**pocket** money [ˈpɒkɪt ˌmʌni] Taschengeld **I**

a pocketful of [ə ˈpɒkɪtfl əv] Unmengen von/an **IV**

pod [pɒd] Hülse; Schote **VI U1**, 13

podcast [ˈpɒdkɑːst] Podcast **IV**

poem [ˈpəʊɪm] Gedicht **I**

point [pɔɪnt] Punkt; Zeitpunkt **II**

*to have a **point** [ˌhæv ə ˈpɔɪnt] nicht ganz unrecht haben **III**

*to make one's **point** [ˌmeɪk wʌnz ˈpɔɪnt] seinen Standpunkt deutlich machen **VI AC2**, 74

**point** of view [ˌpɔɪnt əv ˈvjuː] Standpunkt; Ansicht; Perspektive **II**

to the **point** [tə ðə ˈpɔɪnt] prägnant; treffend **III**

turning **point** [ˈtɜːnɪŋ ˌpɔɪnt] Wendepunkt **III**

I can't see the **point** of … [aɪ ˌkɑːnt siː ðə ˈpɔɪnt əv] Ich sehe keinen Sinn darin … **IV**

My **point** is … [maɪ ˈpɔɪnt ɪz] Was ich sagen will ist, … **VI TS2**, 69

to point at sb/sth [ˈpɔɪnt æt] mit dem Finger auf jmdn./etw. zeigen **IV**

to **point** out sth [ˌpɔɪnt ˈaʊt] hinweisen auf etw. **IV**

to **point** to [ˈpɔɪnt tə] deuten auf; hindeuten auf; zeigen auf **VI TS1**, 37

totem pole [ˈtəʊtəm ˌpəʊl] Totempfahl **V**

police [pəˈliːs] Polizei **II**

**police** officer [pəˈliːs ˌɒfɪsə] Polizeibeamter; Polizist/-in **II**

policy [ˈpɒləsi] Politik; politische Linie **V**

polite [pəˈlaɪt] höflich **I**

political [pəˈlɪtɪkl] politisch **IV**

politics (pl only) [ˈpɒlətɪks] Politik **VI U2**, 59

pollution [pəˈluːʃn] Verschmutzung **II**

pond [pɒnd] Teich **II**

pony [ˈpəʊni] Pony **I**

**pony** trekking [ˈpəʊni ˌtrekɪŋ] Ponyreiten im Gelände **III**

**swimming pool** ['swɪmɪŋ ˌpuːl] Swimming-pool; Schwimmbecken **III**

**poor** [pɔː; pʊə] arm **III**

the **poor** [ðə pʊə] die Armen **III**

soda **pop** (AE) ['səʊdə ˌpɒp] Limo **V**

**popular** ['pɒpjələ] beliebt; populär **I**

**populated** ['pɒpjəleɪtɪd] bevölkert; besiedelt **IV**

**population** [ˌpɒpjə'leɪʃn] Bevölkerung; Population **IV**

**pore** [pɔː] Pore ⟨**VI U2**, 62⟩

**pose** [pəʊz] Pose; Haltung **IV**

**position** [pə'zɪʃn] Stelle; Position **VI U1**, 8

**positive** ['pɒzətɪv] positiv **I**

**possessive** form [pə,sesɪv 'fɔːm] Possessiv-form **I**

**possibility** [ˌpɒsə'bɪləti] Möglichkeit **III**

**possible** ['pɒsəbl] möglich **I**

**post** [pəʊst] Post (Eintrag im Internet) **I**

to **post** [pəʊst] online stellen; posten **II**

**postcard** ['pəʊstkɑːd] Postkarte **III**

**poster** ['pəʊstə] Poster **I**

class **poster** ['klɑːs ˌpəʊstə] Klassenpos-ter **I**

**postman** ['pəʊstmən] Briefträger **II**

**pot** [pɒt] Topf **VI U2**, 45

melting **pot** ['meltɪŋ ˌpɒt] Schmelztiegel **IV**

**potato** [pə'teɪtəʊ], **potatoes** [pə'teɪtəʊz] (pl) Kartoffel **III**

mashed **potatoes** (pl) [ˌmæʃt pə'teɪtəʊz] Kartoffelpüree **III**

**pound** [paʊnd] Pfund (Maßeinheit) **IV**

**pound** (£) [paʊnd] Pfund (brit. Währungs-einheit) **I**

to **pour** [pɔː] einschenken; eingießen; schütten **I**

**poverty** ['pɒvəti] Armut **VI U1**, 13

**poverty** line ['pɒvəti ˌlaɪn] Armutsgrenze **VI U1**, 13

**power** [paʊə] Kraft; Macht; Stärke **III**

those in **power** [ˌðəʊz ɪn 'paʊə] die Re-gierenden; die Herrschenden **III**

**power** [paʊə] Strom; Elektrizität; Energie **V**

**power** cut ['paʊə ˌkʌt] Stromausfall **II**

**powerful** ['paʊəfl] stark; mächtig **III**

**practical** ['præktɪkl] praktisch **II**

**practice** ['præktɪs] Training; Übung **III**

to **practice** (AE) ['præktɪs] üben; ausüben; praktizieren; trainieren **IV**

to **practice** a religion [ˌpræktɪs ə rɪ'lɪdʒn] eine Religion ausüben **IV**

to **practise** ['præktɪs] üben; trainieren **I**

**practising** ['præktɪsɪŋ] Üben **I**

**prairie** ['preəri] Prärie **V**

to **pray** [preɪ] beten **III**

**precious** ['preʃəs] wertvoll; kostbar **VI U2**, 50

**prediction** [prɪ'dɪkʃn] Vorhersage; Voraus-sage **III**

to **prefer** [prɪ'fɜː] vorziehen **IV**

**preference** ['prefrns] Vorliebe **V**

**prehistoric** [ˌpriːhɪ'stɒrɪk] vorgeschichtlich **III**

**prejudice** ['predʒədɪs] Vorurteil **VI AC1**, 40

*to be **prejudiced** against sb/sth [bi 'predʒədɪst əˌgenst] voreingenommen sein gegenüber jmdm./etw. **VI AC1**, 41

**premiere** ['premieə] Premiere; Uraufführung **VI U2**, 46

**preparation** [ˌprepr'eɪʃn] Vorbereitung **V**

to **prepare** [prɪ'peə] vorbereiten; zuberei-ten **I**

**preposition** [ˌprepə'zɪʃn] Präposition **I**

**pre-reading** [ˌpriː'riːdɪŋ] vor dem Lesen **I**

**prescription** [prɪ'skrɪpʃn] Rezept (für Arznei-mittel) **II**

**present** ['preznt] Geschenk **I**; Gegenwart; Präsens **II**

**present** participle [ˌpreznt pɑː'tɪsɪpl] Partizip Präsens **V**

**present** perfect [ˌpreznt 'pɜːfɪkt] das Perfekt **II**

**present** perfect progressive [ˌpreznt ˌpɜːfɪkt prə'gresɪv] Verlaufsform des Perfekts **III**

**present** progressive [ˌpreznt prə'gresɪv] Verlaufsform des Präsens/der Gegen-wart **I**

simple **present** [ˌsɪmpl 'preznt] Gegen-wart; Präsens **I**

to **present** [prɪ'zent] präsentieren; vorstel-len **I**

to **present** sb with sth [prɪ'zent wɪð] jmdm. etw. bieten **VI TS2**, 71

**present** ['preznt] heutig; Gegenwarts- **III**

**presentation** [ˌpreznteɪʃn] Präsentation; Vortrag **I**

**presenter** [prɪ'zentə] Moderator/-in **I**

**president** ['prezɪdnt] Präsident/-in **IV**

to **press** [pres] drücken; pressen **II**

peer **pressure** ['pɪə ˌpreʃə] Gruppenzwang **III**

to **pretend** [prɪ'tend] vortäuschen; tun als ob **IV**

**pretty** ['prɪti] hübsch **III**

to **prevent** [prɪ'vent] verhindern; abhalten **V**

**pre-viewing** [ˌpriː'vjuːɪŋ] vor dem Ansehen °**VI AC1**, 42

**previous** ['priːviəs] früher; vorherig; vorher-gehend **V**

**price** [praɪs] Preis **I**

**primary** school ['praɪmri ˌskuːl] Grundschu-le **I**

**principal** (AE) ['prɪnsɪpl] Schulleiter/-in **IV**

to **print** [prɪnt] drucken °**VI U1**, 11

**print** [prɪnt] gedruckt; Druck- **II**

**printed** ['prɪntɪd] gedruckt ⟨**VI U1**, 23⟩

**priority** [praɪ'ɒrəti] Priorität; Vorrang **IV**

**prison** ['prɪzn] Gefängnis **II**

**privacy** ['prɪvəsi] Privatsphäre **VI AC1**, 41

**private** detective [ˌpraɪvət dɪ'tektɪv] Privat-detektiv/-in **III**

**prize** [praɪz] Preis; Gewinn **I**

**pro** [prəʊ] Argument dafür **II**

**pros** and cons (pl) [ˌprəʊz ən 'kɒnz] Argumente für und gegen etw.; Pro und Kontra °**VI U2**, 51

**probably** ['prɒbəbli] möglicherweise; wahr-scheinlich **II**

**problem** ['prɒbləm] Problem; Schwierig-keit **I**

**problematic** [ˌprɒblə'mætɪk] problematisch; schwierig **VI AC1**, 43

**process** ['prəʊses] Prozess °**VI U2**, 59

to **produce** [prə'djuːs] herstellen; produzie-ren **III**

**producer** [prə'djuːsə] Produzent/-in **VI U2**, 49

**product** ['prɒdʌkt] Produkt; Erzeugnis **IV**

**production** [prə'dʌkʃn] Produktion; Insze-nierung **IV**

**profession** [prə'feʃn] Beruf **VI U1**, 9

**professor** [prə'fesə] Professor/-in **VI TS1**, 37

**profile** ['prəʊfaɪl] Profil; Porträt **I**

to **profile** ['prəʊfaɪl] porträtieren ⟨**VI U2**, 61⟩

**program** (AE) ['prəʊgræm] Programm; Sendung **IV**

space **program** ['speɪs ˌprəʊgræm] Raum-fahrtprogramm **IV**

**programme** ['prəʊgræm] Programm; Sendung **II**

to **programme** ['prəʊgræm] programmieren °**VI U1**, 27

**progress** ['prəʊgres] Fortschritt **II**

future **progressive** [ˌfjuːtʃə prə'gresɪv] Ver-laufsform der Zukunft °**VI U2**, 48

passive **progressive** [ˌpæsɪv prə'gresɪv] Verlaufsform des Passivs **V**

past perfect **progressive** [ˌpɑːst ˌpɜːfɪkt prə'gresɪv] Verlaufsform des Plusquam-perfekts **IV**

past **progressive** [ˌpɑːst prə'gresɪv] Ver-laufsform der Vergangenheit **II**

present perfect **progressive** [ˌpreznt ˌpɜːfɪkt prə'gresɪv] Verlaufsform des Perfekts **III**

present **progressive** [ˌpreznt prə'gresɪv] Verlaufsform des Präsens/der Gegen-wart **I**

to **prohibit** [prə'hɪbɪt] untersagen; verbieten ⟨**VI U1**, 23⟩

**project** ['prɒdʒekt] Projekt **I**

to **promise** ['prɒmɪs] versprechen **III**

**prompt** [prɒmpt] Stichwort **III**

**prompt** card ['prɒmpt kɑːd] Stichwortkar-te; Rollenkarte **I**

**pronoun** ['prəʊnaʊn] Pronomen; Fürwort **IV**

object **pronoun** [ˌɒbdʒɪkt 'prəʊnaʊn] Objektpronomen **III**

reflexive **pronoun** [rɪˌfleksɪv 'prəʊnaʊn] Reflexivpronomen **III**

relative **pronoun** [ˌrelətɪv 'prəʊnaʊn] Rela-tivpronomen **II**

to **pronounce** [prə'naʊns] aussprechen **IV**

**pronunciation** [prəˌnʌnsi'eɪʃn] Aussprache **I**

**prop** [prɒp] Requisite **III**

**proper** ['prɒpə] richtig; ordentlich; angemessen **V**
**prospect** ['prɒspekt] Aussicht °**VI U2**, 51
**prostitute** ['prɒstɪtjuːt] Prostituierte
⟨**VI AC1**, 40⟩
**protagonist** [prəʊ'tægnɪst] Protagonist/-in;
Hauptfigur **IV**
to **protect** sb/sth (from) [prə'tekt frəm]
jmdn./etw. beschützen (vor) **V**
**protection** [prə'tekʃn] Schutz **VI AC2**, 74
**protest** ['prəʊtest] Protest **III**
to **protest** [prə'test] protestieren **V**
**protester** ['prəʊtestə] Protestierende/-r;
Demonstrant/-in **IV**
**proud** (of) ['praʊd_əv] stolz (auf) **II**
personal **pronoun** [ˌpɜːsnl 'prəʊnaʊn]
Personalpronomen °**VI TS2**, 69
to **provide** [prə'vaɪd] liefern; bereit stellen
**VI U1**, 13
**provocative** [prə'vɒkətɪv] provokativ; provo-
zierend **VI TS2**, 68
to **provoke** [prə'vəʊk] provozieren; hervor-
rufen **VI AC1**, 41
**psychological** [ˌsaɪkl'ɒdʒɪkl] psychologisch;
psychisch ⟨**VI U2**, 60⟩
**psychologist** [saɪ'kɒlədʒɪst] Psychologe/
Psychologin **VI TS2**, 69
the **public** [ðə 'pʌblɪk] die Öffentlichkeit **IV**
**public** ['pʌblɪk] öffentlich **II**
**public** transport (no pl) [ˌpʌblɪk
'trænspɔːt] öffentliche Verkehrsmittel **II**
**publication** [ˌpʌblɪ'keɪʃn] Veröffentlichung **V**
to **publish** ['pʌblɪʃ] veröffentlichen; publizie-
ren; verlegen **V**
**pudding** ['pʊdɪŋ] Pudding; Nachtisch **I**
to **pull** [pʊl] ziehen **I**
to **pull** down [ˌpʊl 'daʊn] abreißen **III**
**pumpkin** ['pʌmpkɪn] Kürbis ⟨**VI U1**, 25⟩
**punch** [pʌnʃ] Faustschlag; Boxhieb **V**
to **punch** [pʌnʃ] mit der Faust schlagen;
boxen **V**
**purple** ['pɜːpl] violett; lila **I**
**purpose** ['pɜːpəs] Ziel; Absicht; Zweck **IV**
to **pursue** [pə'sjuː] verfolgen **VI U2**, 46
to **push** [pʊʃ] stoßen; schieben; schubsen **II**
to **push** oneself ['pʊʃ wʌnˌself] sich alles
abverlangen; sich Mühe geben **III**
**pushy** ['pʊʃi] aufdringlich; penetrant;
aggressiv **IV**
*to **put** [pʊt] setzen; stellen; legen **I**
*to **put** on [pʊt_'ɒn] anziehen **III**
*to **put** through [pʊt_'θruː] verbinden **I**
*to **put** up [pʊt_'ʌp] aufstellen; errichten;
aufhängen **II**
**Put** … face down. [pʊt ˌfeɪs 'daʊn] Lege/
Legt … umgedreht hin. **I**
**puzzle** ['pʌzl] Rätsel; Puzzle **I**
**puzzled** ['pʌzld] verwirrt; verdutzt ⟨**VI U1**, 23⟩
**pyjamas** (pl) [pɪ'dʒɑːməz] Schlafanzug;
Pyjama **II**

## Q

**qualification** [ˌkwɒlɪfɪ'keɪʃn] Qualifikation;
Befähigung; Abschluss; Schulabschluss
**VI U1**, 8
**quality** ['kwɒləti] Qualität **I**
**quantity** ['kwɒntɪti] Menge; Quantität
**VI U1**, 13
**quarter** past/to ['kwɔːtə pɑːst/tə] Viertel
nach/vor **I**
**queen** [kwiːn] Königin **II**
**question** ['kwestʃən] Frage **I**
**question** tag ['kwestʃən ˌtæg] Frageanhängsel; Bestätigungsfrage **II**
to **question** ['kwestʃən] fragen; hinterfragen
**IV**
**questioning** ['kwestʃənɪŋ] fragend ⟨**VI U1**, 23⟩
**questionnaire** [ˌkwestʃə'neə] Fragebogen **III**
**queue** [kjuː] Schlange; Warteschlange **I**
to jump the **queue** [ˌdʒʌmp ðə 'kjuː] sich
vordrängeln **I**
**quick** [kwɪk] schnell **I**
**quickly** ['kwɪkli] schnell **II**
**quick-shot** mode ['kwɪkʃɒt ˌməʊd] Serienaufnahmemodus ⟨**VI U2**, 60⟩
**quiet** [kwaɪət] still; ruhig; leise **I**
**quill** [kwɪl] Federkiel **III**
**quite** [kwaɪt] ziemlich; ganz; völlig **IV**
**quiz** [kwɪz] Quiz; Rätsel **I**
**quotation** [kwə'təɪʃn] Zitat; Belegstelle **IV**
**quote** [kwəʊt] Zitat **II**
to **quote** [kwəʊt] zitieren **V**

## R

**rabbit** ['ræbɪt] Kaninchen **I**
**race** [reɪs] Wettlauf; Rennen **II**; Rasse
**VI AC1**, 41
to **race** [reɪs] laufen ⟨**VI U2**, 62⟩
**racial** ['reɪʃl] Rassen- **V**
camel **racing** ['kæml ˌreɪsɪŋ] Kamelrennen **II**
**racism** ['reɪsɪzm] Rassismus **V**
**racist** ['reɪsɪst] rassistisch; Rassist/-in **V**
**racquet** ['rækɪt] Schläger **II**
**radio** ['reɪdiəʊ] Radio **II**
**raffle** ['ræfl] Tombola **I**
**raft** [rɑːft] Floß **V**
rubber **raft** [ˌrʌbə 'rɑːft] Schlauchboot **V**
**rags** to riches [ˌrægz tə_'rɪtʃɪz] vom Tellerwäscher zum Millionär **IV**
**rain** [reɪn] Regen **IV**
acid **rain** [ˌæsɪd 'reɪn] saurer Regen
⟨**VI U2**, 56⟩
to **rain** [reɪn] regnen **II**
**rainbow** ['reɪnbəʊ] Regenbogen **III**
**raincoat** ['reɪnkəʊt] Regenmantel **III**
to **raise** [reɪz] wecken (Interesse); aufwer-
fen (Fragen) **VI U1**, 8
to **raise** money [ˌreɪz 'mʌni] Geld sammeln **II**
to **raise** one's eyes [ˌreɪz wʌnz_'aɪz] den
Blick heben; aufblicken; hochblicken **V**
**ranch** [rɑːntʃ; ræntʃ] Ranch **V**

**rap** [ræp] Rap **I**
to **rap** [ræp] rappen **I**
**rarely** ['reəli] selten **VI U1**, 16
**rat** [ræt] Ratte **I**
**rate** [reɪt] Rate ⟨**VI TS2**, 73⟩
to **rate** [reɪt] bewerten; einstufen **IV**
**rather** ['rɑːðə] ziemlich **V**
I'd **rather** [aɪd 'rɑːðə] ich würde lieber **III**
**rating** ['reɪtɪŋ] Kritik **III**
**raven** ['reɪvn] Rabe **II**
**raven** master ['reɪvn ˌmɑːstə] Herr der
Raben **II**
**RE** (= Religious Education) [ɑːr'iː; ˌrɪˌlɪdʒəs_
edʒʊ'keɪʃn] Religion (Schulfach) **II**
to **reach** [riːtʃ] erreichen; dran kommen **II**
to **reach** (for) ['riːtʃ fə] greifen (nach) **V**
to **react** [ri'ækt] reagieren **III**
**reaction** [ri'ækʃn] Reaktion **II**
*to **read** [riːd] lesen **I**
*to **read** out loud [ˌriːd aʊt 'laʊd] laut
vorsingen **III**
**reader** ['riːdə] Leser/-in **I**
*to draw the **reader** into the story/action
[ˌdrɔː ðə ˌriːdə ɪntə ðə 'stɔːri/ækʃn] den
Leser/die Leserin in die Geschichte/
Handlung hineinziehen **III**
**reading** ['riːdɪŋ] Lesen **I**
**ready** ['redi] fertig; bereit **II**
*to get **ready** [ˌget 'redi] sich vorbereiten;
sich fertig machen **V**
**ready** meal [ˌredi 'miːl] Fertiggericht **I**
**real** [rɪəl] echt; richtig; wirklich **II**
to **realise** ['rɪəlaɪz] erkennen; realisieren **III**
**realism** ['rɪəlɪzm] Realismus; Realitätssinn
**VI TS2**, 71
**realistic** [ˌrɪə'lɪstɪk] realistisch **II**
**reality** [ri'æləti] Realität; Wirklichkeit **V**
to **realize** (AE) ['rɪəlaɪz] erkennen; realisieren **IV**
**really** ['rɪəli] wirklich **I**
**reason** ['riːzn] Grund **II**; Vernunft; Verstand
**VI U2**, 45
**rebellion** [rɪ'beliən] Rebellion ⟨**VI U2**, 52⟩
*to **rebuild** [ˌriː'bɪld] wieder aufbauen **III**
to **recall** [rɪ'kɔːl] sich erinnern ⟨**VI U2**, 61⟩
to **receive** [rɪ'siːv] empfangen; erhalten;
bekommen **II**
**receiver** [rɪ'siːvə] Empfänger/-in; hier:
Hüter/-in **VI U1**, 23
**recent** ['riːsnt] kürzlich; neueste/-r/-s;
letzte/-r/-s **V**
**recently** ['riːsntli] kürzlich; neulich **IV**
**reception** [rɪ'sepʃn] Empfang **V**
**receptive** [rɪ'septɪv] empfänglich **IV**
**recipe** ['resɪpi] Rezept **III**
to **recite** [rɪ'saɪt] vortragen; rezitieren **III**
to **reckon** with ['rekn wɪð] rechnen mit
°**VI AC1**, 43
to **recognise** ['rekəgnaɪz] erkennen; anerkennen **VI TS1**, 39
to **recognize** (AE) ['rekəgnaɪz] erkennen;
anerkennen **V**

**recollection** [rekə'lekʃn] Erinnerung ⟨VI U1, 22⟩

to **record** [rɪ'kɔːd] aufnehmen; aufzeichnen II

**recorded** history [rɪˌkɔːdɪd 'hɪstri] *hier:* Aufzeichnung VI U2, 55

**recorder** [rɪ'kɔːdə] Flöte III

**recording** [rɪ'kɔːdɪŋ] Aufnahme; Aufzeichnung I

**recording** studio [rɪ'kɔːdɪŋ ˌstjuːdiəʊ] Aufnahmestudio; Tonstudio I

to **recruit** [rɪ'kruːt] rekrutieren; anwerben; einstellen VI TS1, 37

**recycling** [ˌriːˈsaɪklɪŋ] Recycling; Wiederaufbereitung II

**red** [red] rot I

**reduction** [rɪ'dʌkʃn] Reduzierung; Verminderung °VI TS1, 35

**redwood** (tree) ['redwʊd ˌtriː] Mammutbaum IV

to **reef** the sails [ˌriːf ðə 'seɪlz] die Segel einholen I

to **re-experience** [ˌriːɪk'spɪəriəns] noch einmal erleben ⟨VI U1, 24⟩

to **refer** to [rɪ'fɜː tə] sich beziehen auf IV

**reference** ['refrns] Referenz; Referenzschreiben VI U1, 10

**reference** (to sth) ['refrns tə] Anspielung (auf etw.); Erwähnung (von etw.); Bezugnahme (auf etw.) ⟨VI U1, 6⟩

**reference** article ['refrns ˌɑːtɪkl] Referenzartikel III

with **reference** to [wɪð 'refrns tə] bezugnehmend auf VI U1, 11

**referendum** [ˌrefr'endəm] Referendum; Volksentscheid III

to **reflect** [rɪ'flekt] wiederspiegeln; reflektieren V

**reflexive** [rɪ'fleksɪv] reflexiv; Reflexiv- III

**reflexive** pronoun [rɪˌfleksɪv 'prəʊnaʊn] Reflexivpronomen III

**refugee** [ˌrefjʊ'dʒiː] Flüchtling IV

**region** ['riːdʒn] Region; Gegend II

**register** ['redʒɪstə] Sprachebene; Register IV

cash **register** ['kæʃ ˌredʒɪstə] Kasse ⟨VI U2, 60⟩

**registration** [ˌredʒɪs'treɪʃn] Anwesenheitskontrolle II

**regular** ['regjələ] regelmäßig; gleichmäßig I; normal; üblich °VI U2, 58

to **regulate** ['regjəleɪt] regeln; regulieren VI U1, 22

**regulator** ['regjəleɪtə] Regulator/-in; Aufsicht führende Person IV

**rehearsal** [rɪ'hɜːsl] Probe V

to **rehearse** [rɪ'hɜːs] proben III

**reign** [reɪn] Herrschaft; Regierungszeit III

to **reign** [reɪn] herrschen; regieren III

**rejection** [rɪ'dʒektʃn] Ablehnung; Absage IV

*to be **related** to [bi rɪ'leɪtɪd tə] verwandt sein mit V

to **relate** to [rɪ'leɪt tə] Zugang finden zu III; nachvollziehen; sich identifizieren mit; verstehen VI TS1, 38

**relationship** [rɪ'leɪʃnʃɪp] Beziehung II

defining **relative** clause [dɪˌfaɪnɪŋ 'relətɪv ˌklɔːz] notwendiger Relativsatz II

non-defining **relative** clause [ˌnɒndɪfaɪnɪŋ 'relətɪv ˌklɔːz] nicht notwendiger Relativsatz IV

**relative** pronoun [ˌrelətɪv 'prəʊnaʊn] Relativpronomen II

to **relax** [rɪ'læks] sich entspannen; sich ausruhen; sich beruhigen II

**relaxed** [rɪ'lækst] entspannt; locker; gelassen VI U2, 46

**release** [rɪ'liːs] Freistellung; Entlassung ⟨VI U1, 23⟩

**relevant** ['reləvnt] relevant; von Bedeutung VI TS1, 38

**reliable** [rɪ'laɪəbl] verlässlich; zuverlässig; vertrauenswürdig IV

**relieved** [rɪ'liːvd] erleichtert V

**religion** [rɪ'lɪdʒn] Religion IV

to practice a **religion** [ˌpræktɪsˌə rɪ'lɪdʒn] eine Religion ausüben IV

**religious** [rɪ'lɪdʒəs] religiös; gläubig I

**reluctant** [rɪ'lʌktnt] widerstrebend; widerwillig V

to **rely** (on) [rɪ'laɪ ˌɒn] sich verlassen (auf); vertrauen (auf) III

to **remain** [rɪ'meɪn] bleiben VI U2, 50

to **remember** [rɪ'membə] sich erinnern (an); sich merken; denken an I

**Remember**? [rɪ'membə] Erinnerst du dich?; Erinnert ihr euch? I

as best as I can **remember** [əz ˌbest əz ˌaɪ kæn rɪ'membə] soweit ich mich erinnern kann ⟨VI U2, 61⟩

to **remind** (sb of sth/sb) [rɪ'maɪnd əv] (jmdn. an etw./jmdn.) erinnern III

to **remove** [rɪ'muːv] entfernen; abreißen V

to **renovate** ['renəveɪt] renovieren V

**rent** [rent] Miete VI U2, 53

That doesn't pay my **rent**. [ˌdət dʌznt ˌpeɪ maɪ 'rent] Davon kann ich meine Miete nicht bezahlen. VI U2, 53

to **rent** (out) [ˌrentˌ'aʊt] mieten III

to **repeat** [rɪ'piːt] wiederholen II

**repetition** [ˌrepɪ'tɪʃn] Wiederholung IV

a sort of nonstop **repetition** [ə ˌsɔːtˌəv ˌnɒnstɒp ˌrepɪ'tɪʃn] eine Art Dauerschleife ⟨VI U2, 61⟩

to **replace** (by/with) [rɪ'pleɪs] ersetzen (durch) V

**reply** [rɪ'plaɪ] Antwort; Erwiderung; Entgegnung I

to **reply** [rɪ'plaɪ] antworten; erwidern; entgegnen I

**report** [rɪ'pɔːt] Bericht; Meldung II

news **report** ['njuːz rɪˌpɔːt] Tatsachenbericht; Nachrichtenbeitrag; Meldung III

travel **report** [ˌtrævl rɪ'pɔːt] Reisebericht II

to **report** [rɪ'pɔːt] berichten; wiedergeben IV

**reporter** [rɪ'pɔːtə] Reporter/-in II

to **represent** [ˌreprɪ'zent] repräsentieren; darstellen; stehen für IV

**representative** [ˌreprɪ'zentətɪv] Repräsentant/-in; Stellvertreter/-in VI AC2, 75

**request** [rɪ'kwest] Bitte IV; Anfrage; Nachfrage VI U1, 10

to **require** [rɪ'kwaɪə] benötigen; erfordern V

*to be **required** to (+ inf) [bi rɪ'kwaɪəd tə] müssen VI U2, 55

*to **reread** [ˌriː'riːd] noch einmal lesen III

**rescue** ['reskjuː] Rettung II

to **rescue** ['reskjuː] retten III

**research** (no pl) [rɪ'sɜːtʃ] Recherche; Forschung; Untersuchung III

to **research** [rɪ'sɜːtʃ] recherchieren; erforschen; untersuchen V

**researcher** [rɪ'sɜːtʃə] Forscher/-in VI TS1, 37

**reservation** [ˌrezə'veɪʃn] Reservat V

**reserved** [rɪ'zɜːvd] reserviert; vorbehalten ⟨VI U1, 7⟩

**resident** ['rezɪdnt] Bewohner/-in; Einwohner/-in IV

**respect** [rɪ'spekt] Respekt IV

to **respect** [rɪ'spekt] respektieren V

**respectful** [rɪ'spektfl] respektvoll VI AC1, 41

to **respond** to [rɪ'spɒnd tə] reagieren auf; erwidern auf; antworten auf °VI TS2, 68

**response** [rɪ'spɒns] Antwort; Erwiderung; Rückmeldung IV

**responsibility** [rɪˌspɒnsə'bɪləti] Verantwortung; Aufgabe VI U1, 8

**responsible** [rɪs'pɒnsəbl] verantwortlich; verantwortungsvoll V

**rest** [rest] Rast; Ruhe °VI U1, 14

the **rest** [rest] der Rest I

to **rest** [rest] ausruhen; liegen ⟨VI U1, 24⟩

to **restate** [ˌriː'steɪt] noch einmal (mit anderen Worten) sagen °VI TS2, 72

**restaurant** ['restrɒnt] Restaurant; Gaststätte I

to **restrict** [rɪ'strɪkt] begrenzen; beschränken V

**restrictive** [rɪ'strɪktɪv] beschränkend; einengend V

**restroom** (AE) ['restrʊm] Toilette IV

**result** [rɪ'zʌlt] Ergebnis; Resultat II

to **result** in sth [rɪ'zʌltˌɪn] etw. ergeben; in etw. resultieren ⟨VI U2, 56⟩

**retail** ['riːteɪl] Einzelhandel V

*to **retell** [ˌriː'tel] nacherzählen; nochmals erzählen I

**return** ticket [rɪ'tɜːn ˌtɪkɪt] Hin- und Rückfahrkarte III

to **return** [rɪ'tɜːn] zurückkehren; zurückfahren III

to **reveal** [rɪ'viːl] offenbaren; aufdecken ⟨VI TS2, 73⟩

**review** [rɪ'vjuː] Kritik VI TS1, 34

to **review** [rɪ'vjuː] prüfen; durchsehen ⟨VI U2, 62⟩

to **revise** [rɪˈvaɪz] wiederholen **V**
**revision** [rɪˈvɪʒn] Wiederholung **II**
**reward** [rɪˈwɔːd] Belohnung; Preis **VI AC2**, 75
*to **rewrite** [ˌriːˈraɪt] umschreiben; neu schreiben **III**
**rhino** [ˈraɪnəʊ] Rhinozeros; Nashorn **III**
**rhyme** [raɪm] Reim **I**
  **rhyme** scheme [ˈraɪm skiːm] Reimschema **III**
to **rhyme** [raɪm] (sich) reimen **III**
**rhyming** [ˈraɪmɪŋ] sich reimend **III**
**rhythm** [ˈrɪðm] Rhythmus **I**
**rib** [rɪb] Rippe **V**
**rich** [rɪtʃ] reich **III**
  the **rich** [ðə rɪtʃ] die Reichen **III**
**riches** (pl) [ˈrɪtʃɪz] Reichtümer ⟨**VI U1**, 7⟩
  rags to **riches** [ˌrægz təˈrɪtʃɪz] vom Tellerwäscher zum Millionär **IV**
**ride** [raɪd] Fahrt; Ritt **IV**
  *to get a **ride** [ˌget ə ˈraɪd] eine Mitfahrgelegenheit bekommen **V**
  along for the **ride** [əˌlɒŋ fə ðə ˈraɪd] mit dabei **IV**
*to **ride** [raɪd] fahren; reiten **IV**
**rider** [ˈraɪdə] Reiter/-in; Fahrer/-in **V**
**rigging** [ˈrɪgɪŋ] Takelage **I**
**right** [raɪt] Recht **IV**
  civil **rights** (pl) [ˌsɪvl ˈraɪts] Bürgerrechte **V**
  human **rights** [ˌhjuːmən ˈraɪts] Menschenrechte **V**
**right** [raɪt] richtig; korrekt; rechts; rechte/-r/-s **I**
  *to be **right** [bi ˈraɪt] recht haben **I**
  *to get **right** [get ˈraɪt] richtig beantworten **III**
  on the **right** [ɒn ðə ˈraɪt] auf der rechten Seite; rechts **I**
**right** [raɪt] direkt **IV**; genau ⟨**VI U1**, 26⟩
  **right** away [ˌraɪt əˈweɪ] sofort; gleich **I**
  **right** here [ˌraɪt ˈhɪə] genau hier **II**
  **right** now [ˌraɪt ˈnaʊ] jetzt gleich; sofort; gerade **II**
**ring** [rɪŋ] Ring **III**
  key **ring** [ˈkiː ˌrɪŋ] Schlüsselbund; Schlüsselanhänger **III**
*to **ring** [rɪŋ] klingeln; läuten **I**; anrufen **IV**
**ice rink** [ˈaɪs ˌrɪŋk] Eisbahn; Schlittschuhbahn **I**
**rip current** [ˈrɪp ˌkʌrnt] Brandungsrückströmung **V**
**rise** [raɪz] Anstieg; Zunahme **VI TS1**, 37
*to **rise** [raɪz] steigen; sich erheben **III**; aufgehen (Sonne) **V**; aufstehen **VI TS1**, 37
  *to **rise** up in one's mind [raɪzˌʌp ɪn wʌnz ˈmaɪnd] jmdm. in den Sinn kommen **III**
**risk** [rɪsk] Gefahr; Risiko **V**
  *to take a **risk** [teɪk ə ˈrɪsk] ein Risiko eingehen **IV**
  No **risk**, no fun! [nəʊ ˌrɪsk nəʊ ˈfʌn] Wer nicht wagt, der nicht gewinnt. **IV**
to **risk** [rɪsk] riskieren **V**

**river** [ˈrɪvə] Fluss **I**
  by the **river** [baɪ ðə ˈrɪvə] am Fluss **II**
**riverbank** [ˈrɪvəbæŋk] Flussufer ⟨**VI U1**, 25⟩
**road** [rəʊd] Straße **II**
to **roar** [rɔː] dröhnen; brüllen; rauschen **III**
**roaring** [ˈrɔːrɪŋ] dröhnend; tosend; donnernd **III**
to **rob** [rɒb] ausrauben; rauben; berauben **V**
**robber** [ˈrɒbə] Räuber/-in **III**
**rock** [rɒk] Rock (Musik) **III**
  **rock** 'n' roll [ˌrɒkˌən ˈrəʊl] Rock 'n' Roll **II**
to **rock** [rɒk] schaukeln **IV**
**rocky** [ˈrɒki] felsig; steinig **III**
**role** [rəʊl] Rolle **I**
  **role** model [ˈrəʊl ˌmɒdl] Vorbild **VI TS2**, 71
  **role** play [ˈrəʊl ˌpleɪ] Rollenspiel **I**
  supporting **role** [səˈpɔːtɪŋ ˌrəʊl] Nebenrolle **V**
  to swap **roles** [ˌswɒp ˈrəʊlz] Rollen tauschen **I**
to **role-play** [ˈrəʊlpleɪ] ein Rollenspiel machen °**VI TS1**, 34
**bread roll** [ˈbred rəʊl] Brötchen **III**
**rock 'n' roll** [ˌrɒkˌən ˈrəʊl] Rock 'n' Roll **II**
to **roll** off [rəʊl] hinunterrollen; herunterrollen **II**
  to **roll** one's eyes [ˌrəʊl wʌnzˈaɪz] die Augen verdrehen **III**
  **Roll** two dice. [ˌrəʊl ˌtuː ˈdaɪs] Würfle/Würfelt mit zwei Würfeln. **I**
**roller skate** [ˈrəʊlə ˌskeɪt] Rollschuh; Rollschuh- ⟨**VI U2**, 52⟩
**Roman** [ˈrəʊmən] Römer/-in; römisch **II**
**romance** [rəˈmæns] Liebesgeschichte; Liebesfilm **II**
**Romanian** [rʊˈmeɪniən] Rumäne/Rumänin; rumänisch; Rumänisch **II**
**romantic** [rəˈmæntɪk] romantisch **V**
**roof** [ruːf] Dach **III**
**room** [ruːm; rʊm] Zimmer; Raum **I**
  chat **room** [ˈtʃæt rʊm] Chatroom **II**
  living **room** [ˈlɪvɪŋ rʊm] Wohnzimmer **I**
  side **room** [ˈsaɪd rʊm] Nebenraum **IV**
**roommate** [ˈruːmmeɪt] Zimmergenosse/Zimmergenossin **I**
**rope** [rəʊp] Seil **III**
**rotary phone** [ˈrəʊtri fəʊn] Telefon mit Wählscheibe **III**
**rough** [rʌf] rau; grob; uneben; holprig **V**
**round** [raʊnd] Runde **II**
  **round** of boxing [ˌraʊnd əv ˈbɒksɪŋ] Boxrunde **II**
  the **Round** Table [ðə ˌraʊnd ˈteɪbl] die Tafelrunde **III**
**round** [raʊnd] um … herum **II**
  *to go **round** in circles [gəʊ ˌraʊnd ɪn ˈsɜːklz] sich im Kreis drehen **III**
  to turn **round** [tɜːn ˌ(ə)ˈraʊnd] (sich) umdrehen; wenden **II**
**route** [ruːt] Strecke; Route **II**
  **route** planner [ˈruːt ˌplænə] Routenplaner **IV**

**routine** [ruːˈtiːn] Routine **IV**
**royal** [ˈrɔɪəl] königlich **I**
**rubber** [ˈrʌbə] Radiergummi **I**
  **rubber** raft [ˌrʌbə ˈrɑːft] Schlauchboot **V**
**rubbish** [ˈrʌbɪʃ] Müll; Gerümpel **I**
**rude** [ruːd] unhöflich; unverschämt **I**
**rudeness** [ˈruːdnəs] Unhöflichkeit; Unverschämtheit ⟨**VI U1**, 23⟩
**rug** [rʌg] Vorleger; Teppich **V**
**rugby** [ˈrʌgbi] Rugby **II**
to **ruin** [ˈruːɪn] ruinieren; zerstören **II**
**rule** [ruːl] Regel **I**
to **rule** [ruːl] herrschen; regieren **III**
**ruler** [ˈruːlə] Lineal **I**
**rumour** [ˈruːmə] Gerücht **VI AC1**, 43
**run** [rʌn] Rennen; Lauf **II**
  **run** area [ˈrʌn ˌeəriə] Gehege; Auslauf **III**
  salmon **run** [ˈsæmən ˌrʌn] Lachswanderung **V**
*to **run** [rʌn] rennen; laufen **I**; betreiben; leiten; führen **IV**
  *to **run** away [ˌrʌn əˈweɪ] wegrennen **I**
  *to **run** over [ˌrʌn ˈəʊvə] überfahren **V**
**runner** [ˈrʌnə] Läufer/-in **II**
**running** [ˈrʌnɪŋ] Laufen; Rennen **II**
**rural** [ˈrʊərl] ländlich **IV**
**rush** [rʌʃ] Rausch **VI U2**, 50; Eile ⟨**VI U2**, 62⟩
  Gold **Rush** [ˈgəʊld ˌrʌʃ] Goldrausch **VI U2**, 50
**Russian** [ˈrʌʃn] Russe/Russin; russisch; Russisch **V**
**RV park** (AE) [ˈɑːviː ˌpɑːk] Campingplatz **VI U2**, 46

## S

**sacred** [ˈseɪkrɪd] heilig **V**
**sad** [sæd] traurig **I**
**safari** [səˈfɑːri] Safari **V**
**safe** [seɪf] sicher; ungefährlich **II**
**safety** [ˈseɪfti] Sicherheit **V**
to reef the **sails** [ˌriːf ðə ˈseɪlz] die Segel einholen **I**
to **sail** [seɪl] segeln; umsegeln **III**
**sailboat** [ˈseɪlbəʊt] Segelboot **III**
**sailor** [ˈseɪlə] Seemann; Matrose **I**
**salad** [ˈsæləd] Salat **I**
**sale** [seɪl] Verkauf **II**
  **sales** assistant [ˈseɪlz əˌsɪstnt] Verkäufer/-in **VI U1**, 9
**salmon** [ˈsæmən], **salmon** [ˈsæmən] (pl) Lachs **V**
  **salmon** run [ˈsæmən ˌrʌn] Lachswanderung **V**
**saltie** (coll) [ˈsɔːlti] Salzwasserkrokodil **V**
**same**-sex [ˈseɪmˌseks] gleichgeschlechtlich **VI AC1**, 42
the **same** [ðə ˈseɪm] der-/die-/dasselbe; der/die/das gleiche **I**
  the **same** way as [ðə seɪm ˈweɪ æz] genauso wie **II**

**sameness** ['seɪmnəs] Gleichheit; Gleichförmigkeit **VI U1**, 25

**sample** ['sɑ:mpl] Probe; Muster **IV**

**sand** [sænd] Sand **V**

**sandal** ['sændl] Sandale **III**

**sandwich** ['sænwɪdʒ] Sandwich; belegtes Brot **I**

**sandy** ['sændi] sandig; Sand- **III**

**satellite** ['sætlaɪt] Satellit **V**

**satisfaction** [ˌsætɪsˈfækʃn] Zufriedenheit **VI U1**, 7

**satisfied** ['sætɪsfaɪd] zufrieden; befriedigt **VI U1**, 22

**Saturday** ['sætədeɪ] Samstag **I**

**sauce** [sɔ:s] Soße **III**

**sausage** ['sɒsɪdʒ] Wurst; Bratwurst **III**

to **save** [seɪv] retten; bergen **I**; sparen **III**
to **save** the best for last [ˌseɪv ðə ˌbest fə 'lɑ:st] sich das Beste bis zum Schluss aufheben **IV**
**saved** by the bell [ˌseɪvd baɪ ðə 'bel] noch mal Glück gehabt **III**

**sax** [sæks] Saxofon **I**

**saxophone** ['sæksəfəʊn] Saxofon **I**

*to **say** [seɪ] sagen; aufsagen; sprechen **I**
*to be **said** to (+ inf) [bi 'sed tə] sollen; gelten als **VI U2**, 50
needless to **say** [ni:dləs tə 'seɪ] natürlich; selbstverständlich **IV**
*to **say** hello (to) [seɪ hel'əʊ tə] grüßen; Grüße ausrichten (an) **I**

**saying** ['seɪɪŋ] Redensart; Sprichwort **III**

**scan** [skæn] Überfliegen ⟨**VI U2**, 60⟩

to **scan** [skæn] scannen; nach Details durchsuchen **I**

**scandal** ['skændl] Skandal **VI TS2**, 69

**scar** [skɑ:] Narbe **V**

to **scare** sb [skeə] jmdm. Angst machen; jmdn. erschrecken **V**
to **scare** sb to death [ˌskeə tə 'deθ] jmdn. zu Tode erschrecken **V**

**scared** [skeəd] verängstigt; ängstlich **IV**
*to be **scared** (of) [bi: 'skeəd ˌəv] Angst haben (vor) **I**

**scary** ['skeəri] unheimlich; gruselig; beängstigend **I**

**scene** [si:n] Szene **I**; Schauplatz **II**
acting a **scene** [ˌæktɪŋ ə 'si:n] eine Theaterszene spielen **I**
at the **scene** [ˌət ðə 'si:n] vor Ort **V**

**scenery** ['si:nri] Landschaft **IV**

**sceptical** ['skeptɪkl] skeptisch **IV**

**schedule** (AE) ['ʃedju:l; 'skedʒu:l] Stundenplan; Fahrplan; Terminkalender **IV**

rhyme **scheme** ['raɪm ski:m] Reimschema **III**

**school** [sku:l] Schule **I**
comprehensive **school** [kɒmprɪ'hensɪv ˌsku:l] Gesamtschule **VI U1**, 10
grammar **school** ['græmə ˌsku:l] Gymnasium **III**

high **school** (AE) ['haɪ ˌsku:l] High School (weiterführende Schule in den USA, Oberstufe) **IV**
middle **school** (AE) ['mɪdl ˌsku:l] Mittelschule (weiterführende Schule in den USA, Mittelstufe) **IV**
primary **school** ['praɪmri ˌsku:l] Grundschule **I**
**school** fees (pl) ['sku:l fi:z] Schulgeld; Schulgebühren **III**

**schoolbag** ['sku:lbæg] Schultasche **I**

**schoolwork** ['sku:lwɜ:k] Schularbeiten **IV**

**Science** [saɪəns] Naturwissenschaften **II**

**science** [saɪəns] Wissenschaft; Naturwissenschaft **IV**
**science** fiction [saɪəns 'fɪkʃn] Science-Fiction (Zukunftsdichtung) **II**

**scientific** [ˌsaɪən'tɪfɪk] wissenschaftlich; naturwissenschaftlich **VI TS1**, 38

**scientist** ['saɪəntɪst] Wissenschaftler/-in **III**

to **scoop up** [ˌsku:p ˌʌp] hochheben ⟨**VI U2**, 60⟩

**score** [skɔ:] Punktestand; Spielstand **II**

**scoreboard** ['skɔ:bɔ:d] Anzeigetafel ⟨**VI U2**, 57⟩

**Scot** [skɒt] Schotte/Schottin **III**

**Scottish** ['skɒtɪʃ] schottisch **III**

gorge **scrambling** ['gɔ:dʒ ˌskræmblɪŋ] Schluchtenklettern **II**

to **scream** [skri:m] schreien; kreischen **II**

**screen** [skri:n] Bildschirm ⟨**VI TS1**, 39⟩

**script** [skrɪpt] Drehbuch; Skript **III**

**scriptwriting** ['skrɪptˌraɪtɪŋ] Drehbuchschreiben **V**

**sculpture** ['skʌlptʃə] Skulptur **IV**

**sea** [si:] Meer **I**
*to be swept out to **sea** [bi ˌswept ˌaʊt tə 'si:] aufs offene Meer getrieben werden **V**

**seal** [si:l] Siegel **V**

**search** [sɜ:tʃ] Suche; Such- **II**
**search** engine ['sɜ:tʃ ˌendʒɪn] Suchmaschine **IV**

to **search** [sɜ:tʃ] durchsuchen ⟨**VI U1**, 24⟩
to **search** for ['sɜ:tʃ fə] suchen (nach) **IV**

**seashell** ['si:ʃel] Muschel **V**

**seasick** ['si:sɪk] seekrank **IV**

**season** ['si:zn] Saison; Jahreszeit **IV**

**seasonal** ['si:znl] saisonal; jahreszeitlich bedingt **VI U2**, 53

**seat** [si:t] Sitz; Sitzplatz **IV**
passenger **seat** ['pæsndʒə ˌsi:t] Beifahrersitz **V**
**seat** belt ['si:t belt] Sicherheitsgurt **V**

**second** ['seknd] Sekunde **V**
Just a **second** … [dʒʌst ə 'seknd] Einen Augenblick … **I**

**second** ['seknd] zweite/-r/-s **I**

**secondly** ['sekndli] zweitens **VI TS2**, 71

**secret** ['si:krət] Geheimnis **II**
in **secret** [ɪn 'si:krət] heimlich **II**

**secret** ['si:krət] geheim **III**

**section** ['sekʃn] Abschnitt; Paragraf **II**

**security** [sɪ'kjʊərəti] Sicherheit; Schutz; Wachdienst; Wach-; Sicherheits- **IV**

*to **see** [si:] sehen **I**
*to **see** the bigger picture [ˌsi: ðə ˌbɪgə 'pɪktʃə] über den Tellerrand hinausschauen **V**
**See** you! ['si: jə] Bis dann!; Bis … **I**
I can't **see** the point of … [aɪ ˌkɑ:nt si: ðə 'pɔɪnt ˌəv] Ich sehe keinen Sinn darin … **IV**
Wait and **see**! [ˌweɪt ˌənd 'si:] Warte ab! **I**

to **seem** [si:m] scheinen **III**

to **seep** [si:p] sickern ⟨**VI U2**, 62⟩

**segregation** [ˌsegrɪ'geɪʃn] Segregation; Trennung; Rassentrennung **V**

to **select** [sɪ'lekt] auswählen; aussuchen **VI U1**, 23

**selection** [sɪ'lekʃn] Auswahl; Auswahl- **VI U2**, 59

**self** [self], **selves** [selvz] (pl) das Selbst **III**

**self-confident** [self'kɒnfɪdnt] selbstsicher; selbstbewusst ⟨**VI U1**, 23⟩

**self-critical** ['self,krɪtɪkl] selbstkritisch **II**

**self-evaluation** [ˌselfɪˌvælju'eɪʃn] Selbsteinschätzung **I**

**selfie** ['selfi] Selfie **II**

**selfish** ['selfɪʃ] selbstsüchtig; egoistisch **VI U1**, 15

*to **sell** [sel] verkaufen **I**

**seller** ['selə] Verkäufer/-in (auf einem Flohmarkt) **I**

**semi-** ['semi] Halb- ⟨**VI U2**, 61⟩

*to **send** [send] schicken; senden **I**
*to **send** off [send 'ɒf] abschicken **III**

**senior** ['si:niə] älter **IV**
**senior** counsellor [ˌsi:niə 'kaʊnslə] leitender Betreuer/leitende Betreuerin; ranghohe/-r Minister/-in **VI U1**, 8

**sense** [sens] Sinn **III**
*to make **sense** [ˌmeɪk 'sens] Sinn ergeben; einleuchten **IV**
**sense** of humour (no pl) [sens ˌəv 'hju:mə] Sinn für Humor **III**

**sensible** ['sensɪbl] vernünftig **IV**

**sensitive** ['sensɪtɪv] sensibel; empfindsam; heikel **VI AC1**, 43

**sentence** ['sentəns] Satz **I**; Verurteilung; Strafmaß **V**
conditional **sentence** [kənˌdɪʃnl 'sentəns] Bedingungssatz **III**

to **separate** ['sepreɪt] (sich) trennen **IV**

**separate** ['seprət] separat; getrennt; verschieden **II**

**September** [sep'tembə] September **I**

**sequence** ['si:kwəns] Sequenz; Szene **III**; Abfolge; Reihenfolge **IV**

**serene** [sə'ri:n] ruhig; gelassen ⟨**VI U1**, 22⟩

**series** ['sɪəri:z], **series** ['sɪəri:z] (pl) Serie **III**

**serious** ['sɪəriəs] ernsthaft; ernst **I**

**seriousness** (no pl) ['sɪəriəsnəs] Ernst; Ernsthaftigkeit ⟨**VI U1**, 22⟩

to **serve** [sɜ:v] servieren; dienen; bedienen **V**

service ['sɜːvɪs] Service; Dienstleistung; Dienst **IV**

session ['seʃn] Sitzung; Stunde **VI U1, 24**

set [set] Umgebung; Rahmen; Aufnahmeort; Drehort **III**

    a set of [ə 'set əv] eine Liste von **III**

    set phrase [set 'freɪs] Floskel; feststehender Ausdruck °**VI TS1, 38**

\*to be set (in) [bi 'set ɪn] spielen (in); seinen Schauplatz haben (in) **V**

    \*to set a good example [set ə ˌgʊd ɪɡ'zɑːmpl] ein Vorbild sein **VI U1, 8**

    \*to set off [ˌset 'ɒf] hier: ein Feuerwerk zünden **III**

    \*to set the table [set ðə 'teɪbl] den Tisch decken **V**

    \*to set up [ˌset 'ʌp] einrichten; aufbauen **I**

setting ['setɪŋ] Schauplatz; Rahmen **II**

    account settings [ə'kaʊnt ˌsetɪŋz] Profileinstellungen **III**

to settle for less [ˌsetl fə 'les] sich mit weniger zufrieden geben **III**

settlement ['setlmənt] Siedlung **V**

settler ['setlə] Siedler/-in **V**

seven ['sevn] sieben **I**

several ['sevrl] einige; mehrere; verschiedene **II**

sex [seks] Geschlecht; Sexualität **VI TS2, 71**

    same-sex [ˌseɪm'seks] gleichgeschlechtlich **VI AC1, 42**

sexting ['sekstɪŋ] Versenden von Nacktfotos per Handy ⟨**VI TS1, 39**⟩

sexual ['sekʃʊəl] sexuell **V**

sexy ['seksi] sexy **V**

shade [ʃeɪd] Schattierung; Schatten ⟨**VI U1, 25**⟩

shadow ['ʃædəʊ] Schatten **III**

\*to shake [ʃeɪk] schütteln **V**

shaky ['ʃeɪki] zitternd; bebend ⟨**VI U1, 23**⟩

shall [ʃæl] sollen **VI U2, 55**

shallow ['ʃæləʊ] seicht; flach; oberflächlich ⟨**VI AC1, 40**⟩

shampoo [ʃæm'puː] Shampoo **IV**

shape [ʃeɪp] Form **IV**

to shape [ʃeɪp] formen **V**

to share [ʃeə] teilen **II**

shark [ʃɑːk] Hai **IV**

sharp [ʃɑːp] scharf; schneidend **III**

she [ʃiː] sie **I**

sheep, sheep (pl) [ʃiːp] Schaf **II**

    bighorn sheep [ˌbɪghɔːn 'ʃiːp] Dickhornschaf **V**

sheet [ʃiːt] Blatt **VI U1, 23**

    cheat sheet ['tʃiːt ʃiːt] Spickzettel **IV**

animal shelter ['ænɪml ˌʃeltə] Tierheim **III**

    homeless shelter ['həʊmləs ˌʃeltə] Obdachlosenunterkunft **V**

shift [ʃɪft] Verschiebung; Wechsel °**VI U2, 53**

to shift [ʃɪft] hin- und herrutschen ⟨**VI U1, 22**⟩

\*to shine [ʃaɪn] scheinen; glänzen **II**

shinty ['ʃɪnti] Shinty (eine Art Hockey) **III**

ship [ʃɪp] Schiff **I**

shipbuilding ['ʃɪpbɪldɪŋ] Schiffsbau **III**

shirt [ʃɜːt] Hemd; Shirt ⟨**VI TS2, 73**⟩

shock [ʃɒk] Schock **II**

shocked [ʃɒkt] schockiert; geschockt **IV**

shoe [ʃuː] Schuh **I**

    \*to be in sb's shoes [ˌbi: ɪn sʌmbɒdɪz 'ʃuːz] an jmds. Stelle sein; in jmds. Haut stecken **III**

    high-heeled shoes [ˌhaɪ hiːld 'ʃuːz] Stöckelschuhe ⟨**VI AC1, 40**⟩

on a shoestring [ˌɒn ə 'ʃuːstrɪŋ] für/mit wenig Geld **IV**

photo shoot ['fəʊtəʊ ˌʃuːt] Fotoshooting; Fotoaufnahmen **III**

\*to shoot (at) [ʃuːt (ət)] schießen (auf) **III**

\*to shoot [ʃuːt] drehen (Film) **VI U2, 46**

shop [ʃɒp] Geschäft; Laden **I**

    charity shop ['tʃærɪti ʃɒp] Second-Hand-Laden **I**

    pawn shop ['pɔːn ʃɒp] Pfandhaus; Pfandleihe **III**

to shop [ʃɒp] einkaufen; shoppen **IV**

shopper ['ʃɒpə] Käufer/-in **IV**

shopping ['ʃɒpɪŋ] Einkaufen; Einkäufe **I**

    \*to do the shopping [ˌduː ðə 'ʃɒpɪŋ] Einkäufe machen; Besorgungen machen **III**

    \*to go shopping [ˌgəʊ 'ʃɒpɪŋ] einkaufen gehen **I**

    shopping mall ['ʃɒpɪŋ ˌmɔːl] Einkaufszentrum **IV**

shore [ʃɔː] Ufer; Küste **II**

short [ʃɔːt] kurz **I**

    short answer [ˌʃɔːt 'ɑːnsə] Kurzantwort **I**

    short form ['ʃɔːt fɔːm] Kurzform **I**

shortage ['ʃɔːtɪdʒ] Knappheit; Mangel **VI U2, 50**

shorts (pl) [ʃɔːts] Shorts; kurze Hose **II**

shot [ʃɒt] Einstellung; Kameraeinstellung **II**; Aufnahme **III**

    long shot ['lɒŋ ʃɒt] Totale (Kameraeinstellung) **IV**

    medium shot ['miːdiəm ʃɒt] Halbtotale (Kameraeinstellung) **IV**

    wide shot ['waɪd ʃɒt] Totale (Kameraeinstellung) **V**

should [ʃʊd] sollte; solltest; sollten; solltet **II**

    shouldn't ['ʃʊdnt] sollte(n) nicht **II**

shoulder ['ʃəʊldə] Schulter **II**

to shout [ʃaʊt] schreien; rufen **I**

show [ʃəʊ] Show; Schau; Aufführung **II**

    comedy show ['kɒmədi ˌʃəʊ] Comedy Show **II**

    living history show [ˌlɪvɪŋ 'hɪstəri ʃəʊ] Show, in der historischer Alltag nachgespielt wird **III**

    talent show ['tælənt ˌʃəʊ] Talentwettbewerb **I**

to show [ʃəʊ] zeigen **I**

    to show off [ʃəʊ 'ɒf] angeben **II**

\*to show sb around (a place) [ˌʃəʊ ə'raʊnd] jmdn. (an einem Ort) herumführen **V**

to showcase one's talent [ˌʃəʊkeɪs wʌnz 'tælənt] sein Talent unter Beweis stellen **VI U2, 46**

shower ['ʃaʊə] Dusche **I**

show-off ['ʃəʊ ɒf] Angeber/-in **III**

to shrug (one's shoulders) [ʃrʌg] mit den Schultern zucken ⟨**VI U1, 25**⟩

to shuffle ['ʃʌfl] mischen **III**

shutter ['ʃʌtə] Fensterladen **IV**

    \*to slide the shutter [ˌslaɪd ðə 'ʃʌtə] die Blende einstellen ⟨**VI U2, 60**⟩

shy [ʃaɪ] schüchtern **II**

sick [sɪk] krank; unwohl **II**

    \*to be sick [bi 'sɪk] sich übergeben **IV**

    \*to feel sick [ˌfiːl 'sɪk] Übelkeit verspüren; sich schlecht fühlen **II**

side [saɪd] Seite **II**

    side room ['saɪd ˌrʊm] Nebenraum **IV**

sidewalk (AE) ['saɪdwɔːk] Gehweg; Gehsteig **IV**

sigh [saɪ] Seufzer ⟨**VI U1, 24**⟩

to sigh [saɪ] seufzen **V**

sight [saɪt] Sehenswürdigkeit; Anblick **II**; hier: Blick **III**

sighting ['saɪtɪŋ] Sichten **IV**

sightseeing ['saɪtsiːɪŋ] Sightseeing-; Besichtigungs- **II**

sign [saɪn] Zeichen; Schild **II**

to sign [saɪn] unterschreiben; unterzeichnen **IV**

signal ['sɪgnl] Signal; Empfang **III**

    signal word ['sɪgnəl ˌwɜːd] Signalwort **I**

signature ['sɪgnətʃə] Unterschrift **VI U1, 11**

significantly [sɪg'nɪfɪkəntli] auffallend; signifikant °**VI U2, 53**

silence (no pl) ['saɪləns] Stille; Schweigen; Ruhe **III**

silent ['saɪlənt] still; ruhig; schweigsam; stumm **III**

silicon ['sɪlɪkən] Silizium **VI U2, 51**

silly ['sɪli] Dummkopf **II**

silly ['sɪli] dumm; doof; albern **I**

silver ['sɪlvə] Silber **II**

similar ['sɪmɪlə] ähnlich **II**

similarity [ˌsɪmɪ'lærəti] Ähnlichkeit; Gemeinsamkeit **IV**

simple ['sɪmpl] einfach; simpel **III**

    simple past [ˌsɪmpl 'pɑːst] Vergangenheitsform **II**

    simple present [ˌsɪmpl 'preznt] Gegenwart; Präsens **I**

simply ['sɪmpli] einfach nur **IV**

since [sɪns] da **IV**

since (+ Zeitpunkt) [sɪns] seit; seitdem **III**

Yours sincerely [ˌjɔːz sɪn'sɪəli] Mit freundlichen Grüßen **VI U1, 11**

\*to sing [sɪŋ] singen **I**

    \*to sing along [ˌsɪŋ ə'lɒŋ] mitsingen **III**

*to **sing** out loud [ˌsɪŋ ˌaʊt 'laʊd] laut vorsingen **III**

**singer** ['sɪŋə] Sänger/-in **II**

to **single** out [ˌsɪŋɡl 'aʊt] herausgreifen; auswählen ⟨**VI U1**, 22⟩

**single** ['sɪŋɡl] einzeln; einzig; alleinstehend **IV**

**single** ticket ['sɪŋɡl ˌtɪkɪt] einfache Fahrkarte **III**

**singular** ['sɪŋɡjələ] Singular °**VI U2**, 53

**singular** ['sɪŋɡjələ] einzigartig ⟨**VI U1**, 22⟩

*to **sink** [sɪŋk] untergehen; sinken **III**

to **sip** [sɪp] schlürfen; schluckweise trinken ⟨**VI U2**, 61⟩

**sir** [sɜː] mein Herr (Anrede) **VI U1**, 24
   Dear **Sir** or Madam [dɪə ˌsɜːr ɔː 'mædəm] Sehr geehrte Dame, sehr geehrter Herr **III**

**sister** ['sɪstə] Schwester **I**
   half-**sister** ['hɑːfˌsɪstə] Halbschwester **I**

*to **sit** [sɪt] sitzen **I**
   *to **sit** down [ˌsɪt 'daʊn] sich hinsetzen; sich setzen **I**
   *to **sit** face to face [ˌsɪt feɪs tə ˌfeɪs] sich gegenüber sitzen **I**
   **Sit!** [sɪt] Sitz! (Befehl für Hunde); Platz! (Befehl für Hunde) **I**

**site** [saɪt] Website **II**; Ort; Gelände; Schauplatz **V**

**situation** [ˌsɪtjuˈeɪʃn] Situation **I**

**six** [sɪks] sechs **I**

**size** [saɪz] Größe; Kleidergröße **I**

roller **skate** ['rəʊlə ˌskeɪt] Rollschuh; Rollschuh- ⟨**VI U2**, 52⟩

to **skate** [skeɪt] Inlineskates fahren; Schlittschuh laufen **I**

**skateboard** ['skeɪtbɔːd] Skateboard **II**

**skateboarder** ['skeɪtbɔːdə] Skateboardfahrer/-in **VI U2**, 44

**skateboarding** ['skeɪtbɔːdɪŋ] Skateboardfahren **I**

**skatepark** ['skeɪtpɑːk] Skateboardanlage **VI U2**, 45

**skates** (pl) [skeɪts] Inlineskates; Rollschuhe; Schlittschuhe **I**

(inline) **skating** ['ɪnlaɪn ˌskeɪtɪŋ] Inlineskatefahren **I**

**skill** [skɪl] Fertigkeit; Geschick **I**
   people **skills** (pl) ['piːpl ˌskɪlz] soziale Kompetenz **VI U1**, 10

to **skim** [skɪm] überfliegen **II**

**skin** [skɪn] Haut; Fell **V**

**skinny** ['skɪni] dünn; mager **V**

to **skip** [skɪp] auslassen; schwänzen **IV**

**skirt** [skɜːt] Rock **III**

**sky** [skaɪ] Himmel **III**

**skyscraper** ['skaɪskreɪpə] Wolkenkratzer **IV**

to **slam** [slæm] niedermachen ⟨**VI TS2**, 73⟩

to **slap** [slæp] schlagen; einen Klaps geben ⟨**VI U2**, 60⟩

**slave** [sleɪv] Sklave/Sklavin **III**

**sled** [sled] Schlitten ⟨**VI U1**, 24⟩

**sleep** [sliːp] Schlaf **IV**

*to **sleep** [sliːp] schlafen **I**

**sleepingroom** ['sliːpɪŋrʊm] Schlafzimmer; Schlafraum ⟨**VI U1**, 23⟩

**sleepover** ['sliːpˌəʊvə] Übernachtung **I**

to **slice** [slaɪs] in Scheiben schneiden **I**

**slide** [slaɪd] Rutschbahn **I**; Folie °**VI U2**, 57
   water **slide** ['wɔːtə ˌslaɪd] Wasserrutsche **I**

*to **slide** the shutter [slaɪd ðə 'ʃʌtə] die Blende einstellen ⟨**VI U2**, 60⟩

**slight** [slaɪt] gering; leicht **VI U2**, 55

**slightly** ['slaɪtli] etwas; ein wenig ⟨**VI U2**, 60⟩

to **slip** into [slɪp 'ɪntə] schlüpfen in **IV**

**slogan** ['sləʊɡən] Slogan; Werbespruch **II**

time **slot** ['taɪm slɒt] Zeitfenster **II**

to **slow** down [sləʊ 'daʊn] langsamer werden; bremsen **VI U2**, 25

**slow** [sləʊ] langsam **I**
   to step into a story **slowly** [step ˌɪntʊ ə ˌstɔːri 'sləʊli] eine Geschichte langsam entwickeln **III**

**slum** [slʌm] Slum; Elendsviertel **V**

**small** [smɔːl] klein **I**
   **small** talk ['smɔːl ˌtɔːk] Smalltalk **III**

**smart** [smɑːt] schlau; klug; intelligent **III**

**smartcard** ['smɑːtkɑːd] Chipkarte **II**

**smartphone** ['smɑːtfəʊn] Smartphone **II**

to **smash** [smæʃ] zerschlagen; zerschmettern **IV**

**smell** [smel] Geruch; Duft; Gestank **VI U2**, 55

*to **smell** [smel] riechen; duften **III**

**smile** [smaɪl] Lächeln **I**

to **smile** [smaɪl] lächeln **I**

**smog** [smɒɡ] Smog ⟨**VI U2**, 56⟩

**smoke** [sməʊk] Rauch **III**

**smoky** ['sməʊki] verraucht **III**

to **smooth** [smuːð] glatt streichen ⟨**VI U1**, 22⟩

**smooth** [smuːð] glatt; weich; geschmeidig **VI U2**, 57

**smuggler** ['smʌɡlə] Schmuggler/-in **IV**

**snack** [snæk] Snack; Imbiss **I**
   **snack** bar ['snæk ˌbɑː] Café; Imbissstube **I**

**snake** [sneɪk] Schlange **V**

*to **sneak** [sniːk] schleichen; schmuggeln **IV**
   to **sneak** around [sniːk ə'raʊnd] herumschleichen **II**

to **snore** [snɔː] schnarchen **I**

**snow** [snəʊ] Schnee **III**
   **snow** tire (AE) ['snəʊ ˌtaɪə] Winterreifen **V**

**snow-capped** ['snəʊkæpt] schneebedeckt **V**

**so** [səʊ] so; also **I**
   **so** far [səʊ 'fɑː] bis jetzt **II**
   **so** is [ˌsəʊ ɪz] ebenso wie **III**
   **so** (that) [ˌsəʊ 'ðæt] damit; so dass **IV**

to **soak** up [səʊk 'ʌp] aufsaugen **III**

**soccer** (AE) ['sɒkə] Fußball **IV**

**social** ['səʊʃl] sozial; gesellschaftlich **IV**
   **social** media [ˌsəʊʃl 'miːdiə] soziale Netzwerke **IV**
   **social** network [ˌsəʊʃl 'netwɜːk] soziales Netzwerk **II**

**society** [sə'saɪəti] Verein; Gesellschaft **III**

**soda** pop (AE) ['səʊdə ˌpɒp] Limo **V**

**sofa** ['səʊfə] Sofa; Couch **I**

**soft** [sɒft] weich; sanft **V**

**software** ['sɒftweə] Software (Computerprogramme) **V**
   **software** manual ['sɒftweə ˌmænjuəl] Softwarehandbuch **III**

**soil** [sɔɪl] Erde; Boden **V**

**soldier** ['səʊldʒə] Soldat/-in **III**

**solution** [sə'luːʃn] Lösung **II**

to **solve** [sɒlv] lösen **III**

**Somali** [sə'mɑːli] Somali **IV**

**some** [sʌm; səm] einige; ein paar; etwas **I**

**somebody** ['sʌmbədi] jemand **I**

**someone** ['sʌmwʌn] jemand **II**

**something** ['sʌmθɪŋ] etwas **I**

**sometimes** ['sʌmtaɪmz] manchmal **I**

**somewhere** ['sʌmweə] irgendwo **II**

**son** [sʌn] Sohn **III**

**song** [sɒŋ] Song; Lied **I**
   *to break into a **song** [breɪk ˌɪntʊ ə 'sɒŋ] plötzlich anfangen zu singen **V**
   theme **song** ['θiːm sɒŋ] Titelmelodie **IV**

**soon** [suːn] bald **I**
   as **soon** as [əz 'suːn ˌəz] sobald **II**
   no **sooner** [nəʊ 'suːnə] kaum **VI U1**, 19

**Sorry!** ['sɒri] Entschuldigung!; Tut mir leid! **I**
   *to be **sorry** [bi: 'sɒri] leid tun **I**
   *to feel **sorry** for [ˌfiːl 'sɒri fɔː] Mitleid haben mit; bedauern **III**
   I'm **sorry!** [aɪm 'sɒri] Tut mir leid! **I**

a **sort** of nonstop repetition [ə ˌsɔːt əv ˌnɒnstɒp ˌrepɪ'tɪʃn] eine Art Dauerschleife ⟨**VI U2**, 61⟩

to **sort** [sɔːt] sortieren **V**
   to **sort** into [sɔːt 'ɪntʊ] einsortieren; sortieren nach **III**

**soul** [səʊl] Seele **V**
   You've got no **soul!** [juːv ˌɡɒt nəʊ 'səʊl] hier: Du hast kein Feingefühl! **V**

**sound** [saʊnd] Ton; Geräusch; Klang **I**

to **sound** [saʊnd] klingen **I**

**soundtrack** ['saʊndtræk] Soundtrack; Filmmusik **V**

**soup** [suːp] Suppe **IV**

**source** [sɔːs] Quelle **III**

**south** [saʊθ] Süden; Süd- **II**
   **South** Korean [ˌsaʊθ kə'riːən] Südkoreaner/-in; südkoreanisch; Südkoreanisch **II**

**southern** ['sʌðən] südlich; Süd- **V**

(the) **Southwest** [ˌsaʊθ'west] (der) Südwesten; im Südwesten; südwestlich **IV**

**souvenir** [ˌsuːvn'ɪə] Souvenir; Andenken **II**

**space** [speɪs] Raum; Fläche; Platz; Ort **II**
   *to leave **space** [liːv 'speɪs] Platz lassen **I**

**space** [speɪs] Weltraum; Weltall **IV**
   **space** program ['speɪs ˌprəʊɡræm] Raumfahrtprogramm **IV**

**spaceship** ['speɪsʃɪp] Raumschiff **II**

**Spanish** ['spænɪʃ] spanisch; Spanisch; die Spanier **III**

**sparkling** ['spɑːklɪŋ] glitzernd; funkelnd **V**

**sparse** [spɑːs] dünn; spärlich **IV**

*to **speak** [spi:k] sprechen **I**
 *to **speak** out (about sth) [ˌspi:k ˈaʊt] seine Meinung (über etw.) deutlich vertreten; sich (zu etw.) äußern **VI TS2**, 68
**speaker** [ˈspi:kə] Redner/-in; Sprecher/-in **I**
**speaking** [ˈspi:kɪŋ] Sprechen **I**
**spear** [spɪə] Speer **III**
**special** [ˈspeʃl] besonders; speziell **I**
 **special** effect [ˌspeʃl ɪˈfekt] Spezialeffekt **IV**
 **special** offer [ˌspeʃl ˈɒfə] Sonderangebot **I**
 with **special** needs [wɪð ˌspeʃl ˈni:dz] behindert **II**
to **specialize** in (AE) [ˈspeʃlaɪz ɪn] sich spezialisieren auf **VI U2**, 60
**specialty** (AE) [ˈspeʃlti] Spezialität; Besonderheit **IV**
**specific** [spəˈsɪfɪk] spezifisch; speziell **IV**
**spectacular** [spekˈtækjələ] spektakulär **III**
**spectator** [spekˈteɪtə] Zuschauer/-in ⟨**VI U2**, 57⟩
**speech** [spi:tʃ] Rede **III**
 direct **speech** [ˌdɪrekt ˈspi:tʃ] direkte Rede **IV**
 indirect **speech** [ˌɪndɪrekt ˈspi:tʃ] indirekte Rede **IV**
 **speech** bubble [ˈspi:tʃ ˌbʌbl] Sprechblase **I**
**speed** [spi:d] Geschwindigkeit **IV**
*to **spell** [spel] buchstabieren **I**
**spelling** [ˈspelɪŋ] Rechtschreibung **I**
*to **spend** [spend] ausgeben (Geld); verbringen (Zeit) **II**
to **spice** up [ˌspaɪs ˈʌp] aufpeppen **IV**
**spicy** [ˈspaɪsi] würzig; pikant **V**
**spider** [ˈspaɪdə] Spinne **III**
**spike** [spaɪk] Spitze; Stachel **IV**
*to **spill** [spɪl] verschütten; auslaufen **IV**
**spirit** [ˈspɪrɪt] Geist; Stimmung **V**
 *to break sb's **spirit** [ˌbreɪk sʌmbədiz ˈspɪrɪt] jmdn. entmutigen ⟨**VI TS2**, 69⟩
**spiritual** [ˈspɪrɪtjuəl] spirituell; geistig **V**
**spirituality** [ˌspɪrɪtʃuˈæləti] Spiritualität **V**
in **spite** of [ɪn ˈspaɪt əv] trotz **V**
**spoken** [ˈspəʊkn] gesprochen **II**
**spokesperson** [ˈspəʊksˌpɜ:sn] Sprecher/-in; PR-Sprecher/-in **V**
**sponge** [spʌndʒ] Rühr-; Biskuit- **I**
**spontaneous** [spɒnˈteɪniəs] spontan **III**
**spoon** [spu:n] Löffel **III**
**sport** [spɔ:t] Sport; Sportart **I**
**sporty** [ˈspɔ:ti] sportlich **VI TS2**, 71
**spot** [spɒt] Fleck; Ort **IV**
urban **sprawl** [ˌɜ:bn ˈsprɔ:l] Urbanisierung; Zersiedelung; Ausuferung des Stadtgebiets ⟨**VI U2**, 56⟩
to **spray-paint** [ˈspreɪpeɪnt] mit Farbe besprühen **VI AC2**, 74
*to **spread** [spred] (sich) verbreiten **VI AC1**, 43
**spring** [sprɪŋ] Frühling **III**
to **spy** on [ˈspaɪ ɒn] nachspionieren; bespitzeln °**VI U1**, 27

**square** [skweə] Quadrat; Quadrat- **V**
**squirrel** [ˈskwɪrəl] Eichhörnchen **I**
to **stack** [stæk] stapeln **VI U1**, 16
**stadium** [ˈsteɪdiəm] Stadion **II**
**staff** writer [ˈstɑ:f ˌraɪtə] festangestellter Journalist/festangestellte Journalistin ⟨**VI TS2**, 71⟩
**stage** [steɪdʒ] Bühne **III**
 **stage** direction [ˈsteɪdʒ dɪˌrekʃn] Regieanweisung **III**
to **stage** [steɪdʒ] aufführen; inszenieren **IV**
**stairs** (pl) [steəz] Treppe **III**
to **stalk** sb [stɔ:k] jmdn. stalken; jmdm. nachstellen **VI U2**, 61
food **stall** [ˈfu:d stɔ:l] Essensstand; Fressbude ⟨**VI U2**, 57⟩
*to **stand** [stænd] stehen **I**
 *to **stand** in line (AE) [ˌstænd ɪn ˈlaɪn] anstehen; Schlange stehen; (sich) anstellen **IV**
 *to **stand** in the way of sb/sth [ˌstænd ɪn ðə ˈweɪ əv] jmdm./etw. im Weg stehen **IV**
 *to **stand** out (from) [ˌstænd ˈaʊt] sich abheben (von); herausragen (aus) **VI U1**, 9
 *to **stand** up [ˌstænd ˈʌp] aufstehen (von einer Sitzgelegenheit) **I**
 *to **stand** up for sb/sth [ˌstænd ˈʌp fə] jmdn./etw. verteidigen; für jmdn./etw. einstehen **V**
**standard** [ˈstændəd] Standard °**VI U1**, 11
 **standard** of living [ˌstændəd əv ˈlɪvɪŋ] Lebensstandard **IV**
to **standardize** (AE) [ˈstændədaɪz] standardisieren; vereinheitlichen **VI U1**, 22
**standpoint** [ˈstændpɔɪnt] Standpunkt; Haltung °**VI TS2**, 72
**star** [stɑ:] Star; Stern **I**
to **stare** [steə] starren; anstarren **I**
**start** [stɑ:t] Anfang; Start **III**
to **start** [stɑ:t] anfangen; beginnen; starten **I**; hier: gründen **III**
 *to get **started** [ˌget ˈstɑ:tɪd] anfangen **II**
 to **start** all over again [ˌstɑ:t ɔ:l ˈəʊvər əˌgen] ganz von vorn beginnen **V**
 to **start** off [ˌstɑ:t ˈɒf] anfangen; beginnen; starten **V**
 **starting** place [ˈstɑ:tɪŋ pleɪs] Startpunkt **III**
**startled** [ˈstɑ:tld] alarmiert; verblüfft ⟨**VI U1**, 22⟩
**startling** [ˈstɑ:tlɪŋ] alarmierend; verblüffend ⟨**VI U1**, 23⟩
**start-up** company [ˈstɑ:tʌp ˌkʌmpəni] Start-up(-Unternehmen); Unternehmensgründung **VI U2**, 50
**state** [steɪt] Staat; Bundesstaat; Land **IV**
 head of **state** [ˌhed əv ˈsteɪt] Staatsoberhaupt **II**
to **state** [steɪt] darlegen; darstellen **V**; nennen °**VI U1**, 10
**statement** [ˈsteɪtmənt] Aussage; Behauptung; Erklärung **II**

**station** [ˈsteɪʃn] Haltestelle; Bahnhof; Station **I**; Sender **II**
 bus **station** [ˈbʌs ˌsteɪʃn] Busbahnhof **I**
**statistics** (pl) [stəˈtɪstɪks] Statistik **V**
**statue** [ˈstætʃu:] Statue; Standbild **IV**
to **stay** [steɪ] bleiben **I**; übernachten **III**
 to **stay** away from [ˌsteɪ əˈweɪ frəm] fernbleiben von; meiden **II**
 to **stay** in touch (with) [ˌsteɪ ɪn ˈtʌtʃ (wɪð)] in Kontakt bleiben (mit) **II**
 to **stay** with [ˈsteɪ wɪð] wohnen bei **II**
 **Stay** the way you are. [ˌsteɪ ðə weɪ ju ˈɑ:] Bleib wie du bist. **III**
**steady** [ˈstedi] kontinuierlich; unaufhörlich **IV**
**steak** [steɪk] Steak **I**
*to **steal** [sti:l] stehlen **II**
**steam** [sti:m] Dampf **III**
 **steam** engine [ˈsti:m ˌendʒɪn] Dampfmaschine **II**
**step** [step] Stufe; Schritt **I**
 **step**-by-**step** [ˌstepbaɪˈstep] Schritt-für-Schritt- **II**
to **step** [step] treten; steigen **IV**
 to **step** into a story slowly [step ˌɪntu ə ˌstɔ:ri ˈsləʊli] eine Geschichte langsam entwickeln **III**
**stepmum** [ˈstepmʌm] Stiefmutter **I**
**stereotype** [ˈsteriəʊtaɪp] Klischee; Stereotyp **VI U1**, 9
gender **stereotyping** [ˈdʒendə ˌsteriəʊtaɪpɪŋ] geschlechtsspezifische Klischees **VI U1**, 9
**steroid** [ˈsteroɪd] Steroide (Pl.) ⟨**VI TS2**, 71⟩
*to **stick** out [ˌstɪk ˈaʊt] hinausstrecken **V**
**still** [stɪl] Standbild **II**
**still** [stɪl] still **I**
 *to keep one's feet or hands **still** [ˌki:p wʌnz ˈfi:t ɔ: ˈhændz stɪl] die Beine und Hände ruhig halten **III**
**still** [stɪl] noch; immer noch **I**; dennoch **II**
*to **sting** [stɪŋ] stechen **III**
marine **stinger** [məˌri:n ˈstɪŋə] Seewespe (Würfelquallen-Art) **V**
**stir** [stɜ:] Bewegung; Erregung; Aufruhr ⟨**VI U1**, 22⟩
 to cause a **stir** [ˌkɔ:z ə ˈstɜ:] für Aufsehen sorgen **VI U2**, 46
**stomach** [ˈstʌmək] Magen; Bauch **II**
**stomachache** [ˈstʌməkeɪk] Bauchschmerzen; Bauchweh **II**
**stone** [stəʊn] Stein; Stein- **III**
**stop** [stɒp] Haltestelle; Halt **II**
to **stop** [stɒp] aufhören (mit); anhalten; stoppen **I**
 to **stop** sb from doing sth [ˈstɒp frəm] jmdn. davon abhalten, etw. zu tun **VI TS2**, 72
 **Stop** it! [ˈstɒp ɪt] Mach/Macht das aus!; Hör/Hört auf! **I**
**store** (AE) [stɔ:] Laden; Geschäft **IV**
**storm** [stɔ:m] Sturm **I**

story, stories (pl) ['stɔːri; 'stɔːriz] Story; Geschichte; Erzählung **I**
photo **story** ['fəʊtəʊ ˌstɔːri] Fotostory; Bildgeschichte **I**
to step into a **story** slowly [step ˌɪntʊ ə ˌstɔːri 'sləʊli] eine Geschichte langsam entwickeln **III**
storyline ['stɔːrilaɪn] Handlung **IV**
storyteller ['stɔːriˌtelə] Geschichtenerzähler/ -in **V**
straight [streɪt] gerade; direkt; geradewegs **IV**; heterosexuell **VI AC1**, 42
**straight** away [ˌstreɪt əˈweɪ] sofort; gleich **III**
**straight** on [streɪt ˈɒn] geradeaus **I**
to straighten up [ˌstreɪtn ˈʌp] aufräumen ⟨**VI U2**, 61⟩
strange [streɪndʒ] fremd; seltsam; merkwürdig **I**
stranger ['streɪndʒə] Fremde/-r **V**
strategy ['strætədʒi] Strategie **V**
strawberry ['strɔːbri] Erdbeere **VI U2**, 53
street [striːt] Straße (in der Stadt) **I**
in the **street** [ˌɪn ðə 'striːt] in der Straße; auf der Straße **I**
**street** fair ['striːt feə] Straßenfest **VI AC1**, 41
the high **street** [ðə ˈhaɪ ˌstriːt] die Haupteinkaufsstraße **III**
strength [streŋθ] Stärke; Kraft **V**
stress [stres] Betonung **III**
to stress [stres] betonen; hervorheben **III**
*to be stressed out [bi ˌstrest ˈaʊt] völlig gestresst sein **III**
strict [strɪkt] streng; strikt **III**
stripe [straɪp] Streifen **V**
to stroll [strəʊl] schlendern; bummeln; spazieren **VI U2**, 46
strong [strɒŋ] stark **II**
structure ['strʌktʃə] Struktur; Aufbau; Gliederung **III**
to structure ['strʌktʃə] strukturieren; gliedern **IV**
struggle ['strʌɡl] Anstrengung; Kampf **V**
to struggle ['strʌɡl] kämpfen; Mühe haben; ringen **V**
*to be stuck [bi 'stʌk] festsitzen; feststecken; hängen bleiben **V**
**stuck** in the middle of … [ˌstʌk ɪn ðə 'mɪdl əv] mitten in … stecken; feststecken in … **III**
student ['stjuːdnt] Schüler/-in; Student/-in **I**
exchange **student** [ɪksˈtʃeɪndʒ ˌstjuːdnt] Austauschschüler/-in **III**
**student** council [ˌstjuːdnt 'kaʊnsl] Schülerrat **VI AC2**, 74
**student** exchange ['stjuːdnt ɪksˌtʃeɪndʒ] Schüleraustausch **III**
studies (pl) ['stʌdiz] Studium; Lernen; Arbeit für die Schule **II**
studio ['stjuːdiəʊ] Studio; Atelier **IV**

recording **studio** [rɪˈkɔːdɪŋ ˌstjuːdiəʊ] Aufnahmestudio; Tonstudio **I**
study ['stʌdi] Studie; Untersuchung **VI TS1**, 37
to study ['stʌdi] studieren; lernen **III**
stuff [stʌf] Zeug **I**
stunt [stʌnt] Stunt **VI AC2**, 74
stupid ['stjuːpɪd] dumm; blöd **II**
style [staɪl] Stil **IV**
stylistic [staɪˈlɪstɪk] Stil-; stilistisch **IV**
subject ['sʌbdʒɪkt] Schulfach; Subjekt; Satzgegenstand **II**; Thema **III**
sub-point ['sʌbpɔɪnt] Unterpunkt °**VI U2**, 58
substance ['sʌbstns] Substanz; Gehalt **VI U2**, 58
substitute ['sʌbstɪtjuːt] Ersatz; Ersatz- **II**
suburb ['sʌbɜːb] Vorort **IV**
suburban [səˈbɜːbn] Vorstadt- **IV**
subway (AE) ['sʌbweɪ] U-Bahn **IV**
to succeed (in) [səkˈsiːd ɪn] Erfolg haben (in/bei/mit) **III**
success [səkˈses] Erfolg **III**
successful [səkˈsesfl] erfolgreich **III**
such [sʌtʃ] solch; solche/-r/-s **II**
It sucks. (slang) [ɪt 'sʌks] Das ist zum Kotzen. **IV**
sudden ['sʌdn] plötzlich ⟨**VI U1**, 22⟩
suddenly ['sʌdnli] plötzlich; auf einmal **I**
to sue sb for sth [suː] jmdn. wegen etw. verklagen ⟨**VI U2**, 61⟩
to suffer (from) ['sʌfə frəm] leiden (unter) **V**
sugar ['ʃʊɡə] Zucker **III**
to suggest [səˈdʒest] vorschlagen **IV**; andeuten; nahelegen **V**
suggestion [səˈdʒestʃn] Vorschlag; Anregung **I**
suit [suːt] Anzug; Kostüm **V**
to suit sb [suːt] (zu) jmdm. passen; jmdm. stehen **VI U1**, 19
suitable ['suːtəbl] geeignet; passend **VI U2**, 46
suitcase ['suːtkeɪs] Koffer **IV**
to sum up [ˌsʌm ˈʌp] zusammenfassen **II**
to summarize (AE) ['sʌmraɪz] zusammenfassen **V**
summary ['sʌmri] Zusammenfassung **IV**
summer ['sʌmə] Sommer **II**
**summer** camp ['sʌmə kæmp] Sommerferienlager **II**
summit ['sʌmɪt] Gipfel; Berggipfel **V**
sun [sʌn] Sonne **II**
Sunday ['sʌndeɪ] Sonntag **I**
sunflower ['sʌnflaʊə] Sonnenblume **III**
sunglasses (pl) ['sʌnˌɡlɑːsɪz] Sonnenbrille ⟨**VI U2**, 60⟩
sunny ['sʌni] sonnig **VI U2**, 50
sunset ['sʌnset] Sonnenuntergang **IV**
super ['suːpə] super **IV**
superhero ['suːpəˌhɪərəʊ] Superheld **V**
superlative [suːˈpɜːlətɪv] Superlativ **II**
supermarket ['suːpəˌmɑːkɪt] Supermarkt **I**

supermodel ['suːpəˌmɒdl] Topmodel ⟨**VI U2**, 60⟩
supernatural ['suːpəˌnætʃrl] übernatürlich **IV**
superpower ['suːpəˌpaʊə] Supermacht **II**
superstar ['suːpəˌstɑː] Superstar ⟨**VI U2**, 61⟩
to supply [səˈplaɪ] versorgen **III**
support (no pl) [səˈpɔːt] Unterstützung; Hilfe **V**
to support [səˈpɔːt] unterstützen **IV**
supporting [səˈpɔːtɪŋ] unterstützend °**VI TS2**, 69
**supporting** role [səˈpɔːtɪŋ ˌrəʊl] Nebenrolle **V**
*to be supposed to (+ inf) [bi səˈpəʊzd tə] sollen **VI U1**, 8
sure [ʃʊə; ʃɔː] sicher **I**
*to make sure [ˌmeɪk ˈʃɔː] sich versichern **I**
I'm (not) sure … [ˌaɪm nɒt ˈʃʊə] Ich bin mir (nicht) sicher … **III**
surf instructor [ˌsɜːf ɪnˈstrʌktə] Surflehrer/ -in **V**
surface ['sɜːfɪs] Oberfläche **IV**
surfer ['sɜːfə] Surfer/-in; Wellenreiter/-in ⟨**VI U2**, 52⟩
surfing ['sɜːfɪŋ] Surfen **III**
surgery ['sɜːdʒəri] Arztpraxis; Praxis; Praxisräume **I**
plastic **surgery** (no pl) [ˌplæstɪk 'sɜːdʒəri] Schönheitschirurgie **V**
surprise [səˈpraɪz] Überraschung **I**
to surprise [səˈpraɪz] überraschen **II**
*to be surprised [bi səˈpraɪzd] überrascht sein **II**
surprising [səˈpraɪzɪŋ] überraschend **II**
to surround [səˈraʊnd] umgeben; umringen **V**
surroundings (pl) [səˈraʊndɪŋz] Umgebung **V**
survey ['sɜːveɪ] Umfrage; Studie **I**
survival [səˈvaɪvl] Überleben **V**
to survive [səˈvaɪv] überleben **III**
survivor [səˈvaɪvə] Überlebende/-r **IV**
*to be suspended [bi səˈspendɪd] suspendiert werden; zeitweilig vom Unterricht ausgeschlossen werden **IV**
suspense [səˈspens] Spannung **III**
suspicious [səˈspɪʃəs] misstrauisch; argwöhnisch **IV**; verdächtig **V**
to swap [swɒp] tauschen **IV**
to **swap** roles [ˌswɒp 'rəʊlz] Rollen tauschen **I**
*to swear [sweə] schwören ⟨**VI U2**, 61⟩
bead of sweat [ˌbiːd əv 'swet] Schweißperle ⟨**VI U2**, 62⟩
sweatshirt ['swetʃɜːt] Sweatshirt **VI TS2**, 71
sweatshop ['swetʃɒp] Ausbeuterbetrieb **IV**
*to be swept out to sea [bi ˌswept aʊt tə 'siː] aufs offene Meer getrieben werden **V**
sweet [swiːt] süß **I**
sweets (pl) [swiːts] Süßigkeiten; Bonbons **I**
*to swim [swɪm] schwimmen **I**
swimming ['swɪmɪŋ] Schwimmen **I**

*to go **swimming** [ˌgəʊ ˈswɪmɪŋ] Schwimmen gehen **I**

**swimming** pool [ˈswɪmɪŋ ˌpuːl] Swimmingpool; Schwimmbecken **III**

**switch** [swɪtʃ] Schalter **III**

to **switch** [swɪtʃ] wechseln °**VI U1**, 27

to **switch** off [swɪtʃ ˈɒf] ausschalten **IV**

**syllable** [ˈsɪləbl] Silbe **III**

**symbol** [ˈsɪmbl] Symbol **II**

**symbolic** [sɪmˈbɒlɪk] symbolisch **V**

to **symbolize** (AE) [ˈsɪmbəlaɪz] symbolisieren **IV**

**system** [ˈsɪstəm] System **V**

## T

**table** [ˈteɪbl] Tisch **I**; Tabelle **V**

*to set the **table** [ˌset ðə ˈteɪbl] den Tisch decken **V**

the Round **Table** [ðə ˌraʊnd ˈteɪbl] die Tafelrunde **III**

**tablet** [ˈtæblət] Tablet **II**; Tafel **IV**

**tabloid** [ˈtæblɔɪd] Boulevardzeitung **VI U2**, 60

**taekwondo** [ˌtækwʌnˈduː] Taekwondo **II**

question **tag** [ˈkwestʃən ˌtæg] Frageanhängsel; Bestätigungsfrage **II**

**tail** [teɪl] Schwanz; Schweif **I**

*to **take** [teɪk] nehmen; mitnehmen; wegnehmen; bringen; mitbringen **I**; dauern; (Zeit) brauchen **II**

*to **take** a breath [ˌteɪk ə ˈbreθ] Luft holen; Atem holen **II**

*to **take** a look at [ˌteɪk ə ˈlʊk æt] einen Blick werfen auf **II**

*to **take** a message [ˌteɪk ə ˈmesɪdʒ] eine Nachricht entgegennehmen; jmdm. etw. ausrichten **I**

*to **take** a risk [ˌteɪk ə ˈrɪsk] ein Risiko eingehen **IV**

*to **take** a test [ˌteɪk ə ˈtest] einen Test machen **II**

*to **take** a vote [ˌteɪk ə ˈvəʊt] abstimmen **I**

*to **take** care of sb [ˌteɪk ˈkeər əv] sich um jmdn. kümmern; für jmdn. sorgen **III**

*to **take** notes [ˌteɪk ˈnəʊts] sich Notizen machen **I**

*to **take** off [ˌteɪk ˈɒf] abnehmen; herunternehmen; ausziehen **I**

*to **take** part (in) [ˌteɪk ˈpɑːt (ɪn)] teilnehmen (an) **II**

*to **take** photos [ˌteɪk ˈfəʊtəʊz] fotografieren; Fotos machen **I**

*to **take** place [ˌteɪk ˈpleɪs] stattfinden **I**

*to **take** sth the wrong way [ˌteɪk ðə rɒŋ ˈweɪ] etw. falsch auffassen; etw. in den falschen Hals bekommen **VI AC1**, 43

*to **take** the day off [ˌteɪk ðə ˌdeɪ ˈɒf] sich den Tag freinehmen **IV**

*to **take** the lead [ˌteɪk ðə ˈliːd] die Führung übernehmen **VI AC2**, 75

**Take** turns. [ˌteɪk ˈtɜːnz] Wechselt euch ab. **I**

**Take** a deep breath. [ˌteɪk ə ˌdiːp ˈbreθ] Atme(t) tief ein. **II**

**take-off** [ˈteɪk ˌɒf] Start; Abheben **IV**

**talent** [ˈtælənt] Talent **I**

to showcase one's **talent** [ˌʃəʊkeɪs wʌnz ˈtælənt] sein Talent unter Beweis stellen **VI U2**, 46

**talent** show [ˈtælənt ˌʃəʊ] Talentwettbewerb **I**

**talk** [tɔːk] Vortrag; Rede; Gespräch; Unterhaltung **IV**

*to give a **talk** [ˌgɪv ə ˈtɔːk] einen Vortrag halten **IV**

small **talk** [ˈsmɔːl ˌtɔːk] Smalltalk **III**

to **talk** [tɔːk] sprechen; reden **I**

to **talk** about … [ˈtɔːk əˌbaʊt] sprechen über; erzählen von **I**

to **talk** sb out of sth [ˌtɔːk ˈaʊt əv] jmdm. etw. ausreden °**VI U2**, 63

to **talk** to [ˈtɔːk tə] reden mit **I**

to **talk** with your mouth full [ˌtɔːk wɪð jɔː ˈmaʊθ fʊl] mit vollem Mund sprechen **IV**

**talker** [ˈtɔːkə] Sprecher/-in **III**

**talking** [ˈtɔːkɪŋ] Sprechen **I**

**tall** [tɔːl] groß; hoch **II**

**tanker** plane [ˈtæŋkə ˌpleɪn] Tankflugzeug **VI U2**, 54

to **tap** [tæp] antippen **II**

**target** [ˈtɑːgɪt] Ziel; Ziel- **IV**

**tartan** [ˈtɑːtn] Schottenkaro (bestimmtes Muster eines Clans); karierter Schottenstoff **III**

**task** [tɑːsk] Aufgabe; Auftrag **I**

to **taste** [teɪst] schmecken; probieren **III**

**tasteless** [ˈteɪstləs] geschmacklos (**VI TS2**, 73)

**tattoo** [tætˈuː] Tattoo; Tätowierung **III**

**tax** [tæks] Steuer; Abgabe **VI U1**, 16

**taxi** [ˈtæksi] Taxi **II**

**tea** [tiː] Tee **I**

**tea** bag [ˈtiː ˌbæg] Teebeutel **III**

*to **teach** [tiːtʃ] unterrichten; lehren; beibringen **I**

*to **teach** somebody a lesson [ˌtiːtʃ ə ˈlesn] jmdm. eine Lehre/Lektion erteilen **II**

**teacher** [ˈtiːtʃə] Lehrer/-in **I**

**team** [tiːm] Team; Gruppe **II**

*to be a **team** player [ˌbiː ə ˈtiːm ˌpleɪə] gern im Team arbeiten **VI U1**, 8

**tear** [tɪə] Träne **V**

to **tease** sb [tiːz] jmdn. aufziehen; jmdn. hänseln; jmdn. ärgern **III**

**tech** [tek] Technologie; Technik **IV**

**techie** [ˈteki] Technikfreak (**VI U2**, 61)

**technique** [tekˈniːk] Methode; Technik **IV**

narrative **technique** [ˌnærətɪv tekˈniːk] Erzähltechnik **V**

**Technology** [tekˈnɒlədʒi] Technik; Computerunterricht **II**

**technology** [tekˈnɒlədʒi] Technologie **II**

**teen** [tiːn] Jugend- **II**; Teenager; Jugendliche/-r **III**

**teenage** [ˈtiːneɪdʒ] jugendlich; Jugend- **IV**

**teenager** [ˈtiːnˌeɪdʒə] Teenager; Jugendliche/-r **I**

**telegraph** [ˈtelɪgrɑːf] Telegraf **V**

**telephone** [ˈtelɪfəʊn] Telefon **I**

*to **tell** [tel] erzählen; sagen; mitteilen **I**

**Tell** me about … [ˈtel miː əˌbaʊt] Erzähle mir von … **I**

**temperature** [ˈtemprətʃə] Temperatur **IV**

to **tempt** [tempt] in Versuchung führen; reizen **IV**

**temptation** [tempˈteɪʃn] Versuchung **IV**

**tempted** [ˈtemptɪd] in Versuchung gebracht **IV**

**tempting** [ˈtemptɪŋ] verführerisch **IV**

**ten** [ten] zehn **I**

**ten** times [ten ˈtaɪmz] zehnmal **I**

**tendency** [ˈtendənsi] Tendenz **VI U2**, 45

**tennis** [ˈtenɪs] Tennis **I**

**tense** [tens] Zeit; Zeitform (grammatisch) **II**

**term** [tɜːm] Begriff **IV**

**terrace** [ˈterɪs] Terrasse **V**

**terrible** [ˈterəbl] schrecklich; schlimm; furchtbar **V**

**territory** [ˈterɪtri] Gebiet; Revier; Territorium **V**

**test** [test] Test; Klassenarbeit; Prüfung **I**

*to take a **test** [ˌteɪk ə ˈtest] einen Test machen **II**

to **test** [test] testen; prüfen **III**

**testimonial** [ˌtestɪˈməʊniəl] Erfahrungsbericht **VI U1**, 8

**text** [tekst] Text **I**

factual **text** [ˌfæktʃʊəl ˈtekst] Sachtext **III**

**text** (message) [ˈtekst ˌmesɪdʒ] SMS; Kurznachricht **I**

wiki **(text)** [ˈwɪki ˌtekst] Wikitext **IV**

to **text** [tekst] eine SMS schicken **II**

**than** [ðæn] als (bei Vergleichen) **II**

more … **than** [ˈmɔː ðən] mehr … als **I**

*to give **thanks** [ˌgɪv ˈθæŋks] danken **IV**

to **thank** [θæŋk] danken **II**

**Thank** you. [ˈθæŋk ju] Danke. **I**

**thankful** [ˈθæŋkfl] dankbar **I**

**Thanks.** [θæŋks] Danke. **I**

**thanks** to [ˈθæŋks tə] dank; wegen **VI U2**, 54

**that** [ðæt] so (Betonung) **III**

**that** much [ðæt ˈmʌtʃ] so viel **III**

**that** [ðæt; ðət] dass **I**

so **(that)** [ˌsəʊ ˈðæt] damit; so dass **IV**

**that** [ðæt] das; jenes **I**

after **that** [ˌɑːftə ˈðæt] danach **I**

like **that** [laɪk ˈðæt] so **I**

**That** was close! [ˌðæt wəz ˈkləʊs] Das war knapp! **I**

**that** way [ˌðæt ˈweɪ] so; auf diese Weise **VI U2**, 46

**That's** … [ˌðæts] Das macht … **I**

**that's** how [ˌðæts ˈhaʊ] so **II**

**That**'s what friends are for. [ˌðæts wɒt 'frendz ˌɑː ˌfɔː] Dafür sind Freunde da. I
**that**'s why [ˌðæts 'waɪ] deshalb II
**that** [ðæt] der; dem; den; die; das *(Relativpronomen)* II
**the** [ðə; ði] der; die *(auch Pl.)*; das I
**the** others [ði ˌʌðəz] die anderen I
**the** same [ðə 'seɪm] der-/die-/dasselbe; der/die/das gleiche I
**the** … **the** [ðə … ðə] je … desto II
**theater** *(AE)* ['θɪətə] Theater IV
movie **theater** *(AE)* ['muːvi ˌθɪətə] Kino IV
**theatre** ['θɪətə] Theater I
**their** [ðeə] ihr/-e *(Pl.)* I
**them** [ðem] sie *(Pl.)*; ihnen I
**theme** [θiːm] Thema; Motto I
**theme** song ['θiːm sɒŋ] Titelmelodie IV
**then** [ðen] dann; danach I
back **then** [bæk 'ðen] damals III
**theory** ['θɪəri] Theorie IV
**therapist** ['θerəpɪst] Therapeut ⟨VI U2, 61⟩
**there** [ðeə] da; dort; dahin; dorthin I
**there** is/are [ðər ˌɪz/'ɑː] da ist/sind; es gibt I
**There**'s no need to … [ðeəz nəʊ 'niːd tə] Es gibt keinen Grund zu … IV
**therefore** ['ðeəfɔː] deshalb; deswegen; daher; somit VI U1, 11
**these** [ðiːz] diese (hier) I
**these** days [ˌðiːz 'deɪz] zurzeit III; heutzutage ⟨VI U2, 61⟩
**they** [ðeɪ] sie *(Pl.)* I
It's …/**They**'re … [ɪts/ðeə] Es kostet …/ Sie kosten … I
**thick** [θɪk] dick *(nicht für Personen)* III
**thing** [θɪŋ] Ding; Sache I
*to **think** [θɪŋk] denken; nachdenken; glauben I
*to **think** of ['θɪŋk ˌəv] halten von; denken über I; (sich) ausdenken; sich etwas einfallen lassen II
*to **think** up [θɪŋk ˌʌp] (sich) ausdenken; sich einfallen lassen IV
**third** [θɜːd] dritte/-r/-s I
**third** person narrator [ˌθɜːd ˌpɜːsn nəˈreɪtə] Er/Sie-Erzähler/-in III
**thirsty** ['θɜːsti] durstig III
**thirteen** [ˌθɜː'tiːn] dreizehn I
**this** [ðɪs] dies; diese/-r/-s I
**this** afternoon [ðɪs 'ɑːftənuːn] heute Nachmittag II
**this** early [ˌðɪs 'ɜːli] so früh III
**This** is … [ˈðɪs ɪz] Das (hier) ist … I
**thistle** ['θɪsl] Distel I
**those** [ðəʊz] diese dort; jene I
**those** in power [ˌðəʊz ɪn 'paʊə] die Regierenden; die Herrschenden III
**though** [ðəʊ] doch; jedoch; obwohl IV
even **though** [ˌiːvn 'ðəʊ] auch wenn; obwohl V
**thought** [θɔːt] Gedanke II

**thousands** of ['θaʊzndz ˌəv] tausende (von) I
**three** [θriː] drei I
**thrilled** [θrɪld] aufgeregt; außer sich vor Freude V
**thrilling** ['θrɪlɪŋ] aufregend V
**through** [θruː] durch I
**throughout** [θruˈaʊt] während; überall in VI U1, 22
*to **throw** (at) [θrəʊ] werfen (nach) I
*to **throw** away [θrəʊ əˈweɪ] wegwerfen I
**throw** the dice twice [ˌθrəʊ ðə daɪs 'twaɪs] würfle zweimal II
to **thud** [θʌd] pochen ⟨VI U2, 62⟩
**thumb** [θʌm] Daumen II
**thunder** *(no pl)* ['θʌndə] Donner II
**Thursday** ['θɜːzdeɪ] Donnerstag I
to **tick** [tɪk] abhaken II
**ticket** ['tɪkɪt] Los; Ticket; Eintrittskarte I; Fahrschein I
one-way **ticket** ['wʌnweɪ ˌtɪkɪt] einfache Fahrkarte III
return **ticket** [rɪ'tɜːn ˌtɪkɪt] Hin- und Rückfahrkarte III
single **ticket** ['sɪŋgl ˌtɪkɪt] einfache Fahrkarte III
**ticket** office ['tɪkɪt ˌɒfɪs] Kartenschalter III
high **tide** ['haɪ ˌtaɪd] Flut II
low **tide** ['ləʊ ˌtaɪd] Ebbe II
to **tidy** *(a room)* ['taɪdi] aufräumen; in Ordnung bringen I
to **tie** (to) ['taɪ tə] binden (an); fesseln (an) III
**tight** [taɪt] eng ⟨VI AC1, 40⟩
**till** [tɪl] bis I
**timber** ['tɪmbə] Holz; Bauholz V
**time** [taɪm] Zeit I; Mal II
all the **time** [ˌɔːl ðə 'taɪm] die ganze Zeit II
at all **times** [ˌət ɔːl 'taɪmz] immer; jederzeit; stets VI U1, 8
at the same **time** [ət ðə ˌseɪm 'taɪm] zur selben Zeit; gleichzeitig I
at the **time** [ˌət ðə 'taɪm] damals IV
*to buy **time** [ˌbaɪ 'taɪm] Zeit gewinnen V
by the **time** [ˌbaɪ ðə 'taɪm] bis *(zu dem Zeitpunkt)* V
free **time** [ˌfriː 'taɪm] Freizeit I
on **time** [ɒn 'taɪm] pünktlich II
ten **times** [ten 'taɪmz] zehnmal I
**time** line ['taɪm ˌlaɪn] Zeitstrahl I
**time** slot ['taɪm slɒt] Zeitfenster II
I can't wait till next **time**. [aɪ kɑːnt ˌweɪt tɪl nekst 'taɪm] Ich kann es bis zum nächsten Mal kaum erwarten. II
just in **time** [ˌdʒʌst ɪn 'taɪm] gerade rechtzeitig IV
**Time** to get up! [ˌtaɪm tə ˌget ˈʌp] Es ist Zeit aufzustehen! I
What **time**? [wɒt 'taɪm] Um wie viel Uhr? I
What's the **time**? [ˌwɒts ðə 'taɪm] Wie spät ist es?; Wie viel Uhr ist es? I

to **time** [taɪm] den richtigen Zeitpunkt wählen IV
**timetable** ['taɪmˌteɪbl] Stundenplan; Fahrplan I
**timing** ['taɪmɪŋ] Timing *(Wahl des richtigen Zeitpunkts)* °VI U2, 57
**tin** [tɪn] Zinn III
**tin** can ['tɪn kæn] Blechdose III
**tinned** [tɪnd] Dosen-; aus der Dose I
**tiny** ['taɪni] klein; winzig III
**tip** [tɪp] Tipp; Ratschlag I; Trinkgeld IV
to **tiptoe** ['tɪptəʊ] auf Zehenspitzen gehen II
**tire** *(AE)* [taɪə] Reifen V
snow **tire** *(AE)* ['snəʊ ˌtaɪə] Winterreifen V
**tired** [taɪəd] müde I
*to be **tired** of [bi ˈtaɪəd ˌəv] es müde sein (zu); es leid sein (zu); es satt haben (zu) IV
**title** ['taɪtl] Titel; Überschrift II
**to** [tʊ; tə] zu; nach; auf; in; vor *(bei Uhrzeitangaben)* I
from … **to** [frəm … tə] von … bis I
quarter past/**to** ['kwɔːtə pɑːst/tə] Viertel nach/vor I
**to** the point [tə ðə 'pɔɪnt] prägnant; treffend III
**toast** [təʊst] Toast I
to **toast** it up *(coll)* [ˌtəʊst ɪt ˈʌp] in Stimmung kommen *(auf einer Party)* ⟨VI U1, 7⟩
**tobacco** *(no pl)* [təˈbækəʊ] Tabak III
**today** [təˈdeɪ] heute I
**together** [təˈgeðə] zusammen; miteinander; gemeinsam I
**toilet** ['tɔɪlət] Toilette I
**tolerance** ['tɒlrns] Toleranz VI AC1, 40
**tolerant** ['tɒlrnt] tolerant IV
to **tolerate** ['tɒlreɪt] tolerieren; dulden VI TS2, 68
**tomato**, **tomatoes** *(pl)* [təˈmɑːtəʊ; təˈmɑːtəʊz] Tomate I
**tomorrow** [təˈmɒrəʊ] morgen I
**tone** [təʊn] Ton; Signalton IV
**tonight** [təˈnaɪt] heute Abend; heute Nacht IV
**too** [tuː] auch; zu I
**Too** bad! [ˌtuː ˈbæd] Zu dumm!; Schade! I
You **too**? [juː 'tuː] Du auch? I
**tool** [tuːl] Werkzeug; Gerät III
**toothbrush** ['tuːθbrʌʃ] Zahnbürste VI U1, 18
**toothpaste** ['tuːθpeɪst] Zahnpasta IV
**top** [tɒp] Spitze; oberer Teil; oberes Ende I
on **top** [ɒn 'tɒp] oben; obendrauf I
to **top** up [tɒpˈʌp] aufladen II
**top** [tɒp] Spitzen-; oberster; bester VI U1, 16
**topic** ['tɒpɪk] Thema II
to **topple** ['tɒpl] stürzen ⟨VI U2, 60⟩
**torch** [tɔːtʃ] Fackel; Taschenlampe II
to **toss** out [ˌtɒs ˈaʊt] ausstoßen; hinauswerfen V
**total** ['təʊtl] Summe; Gesamtmenge °VI U2, 58
a **total** of [ə ˈtəʊtl ˌəv] insgesamt V

total ['təʊtl] gesamt; Gesamt- V
    **total** crap [ˌtəʊtl 'kræp] völliger Quatsch
    ⟨**VI TS2**, 70⟩
totalitarian [təˌtælɪ'teəriən] totalitär
    °**VI U1**, 27
totally ['təʊtli] völlig; total IV
totem pole ['təʊtəm ˌpəʊl] Totempfahl V
\*to keep in **touch** [ˌkiːp ɪn 'tʌtʃ] in Kontakt
    bleiben IV
    to stay in **touch** (with) [ˌsteɪ ɪn 'tʌtʃ (wɪð)]
    in Kontakt bleiben (mit) II
to touch [tʌtʃ] berühren; antippen IV
    to **touch** down [tʌtʃ 'daʊn] landen IV
tour [tʊə] Tour; Fahrt; Rundgang II
    audio **tour** ['ɔːdiəʊ ˌtʊə] Audioführung II
    **tour** company ['tʊə ˌkʌmpəni] Reisean-
    bieter IV
tourism ['tʊərɪzm] Tourismus III
tourist ['tʊərɪst] Tourist/-in I
    **tourist** board ['tʊərɪst bɔːd] Touristenin-
    formation III
    **tourist** information centre [ˌtʊərɪst
    ɪnfə'meɪʃn ˌsentə] Touristeninformation I
toward [tə'wɔːd] in Richtung; auf … zu;
    darauf zu ⟨**VI U2**, 61⟩
towards [tə'wɔːdz] in Richtung; auf … zu;
    darauf zu II; gegenüber V
tower [taʊə] Turm III
town [taʊn] Stadt I
    edge of **town** [ˌedʒ əv 'taʊn] Stadtrand V
toy [tɔɪ] Spielzeug I
to trace [treɪs] verfolgen; nachspüren I
    to **trace** back [ˌtreɪs 'bæk] zurückverfolgen
    V
track [træk] Weg; Pfad; Spur; Fährte V
tractor ['træktə] Traktor IV
trade [treɪd] Handel **VI U1**, 13
to trade [treɪd] austauschen II
tradition [trə'dɪʃn] Tradition I
traditional [trə'dɪʃnl] traditionell III
traffic ['træfɪk] Verkehr IV
trail [treɪl] Weg; Pfad V
    walking **trail** ['wɔːkɪŋ treɪl] Wanderweg III
trailer (AE) ['treɪlə] Wohnwagen **VI U2**, 46
train [treɪn] Zug I
to train [treɪn] trainieren II
trainer ['treɪnə] Turnschuh III
training ['treɪnɪŋ] Ausbildung **VI U2**, 58
training ['treɪnɪŋ] Training II
character trait [ˌkærəktə 'treɪt] Charakter-
    eigenschaft °**VI U2**, 46
traitor ['treɪtə] Verräter/-in V
transition [træn'zɪʃn] Übergang **VI U2**, 57
transitive ['trænsətɪv] transitiv (ein Objekt
    nach sich ziehend) V
to translate [trænz'leɪt] übersetzen I
translation [trænz'leɪʃn] Übersetzung I
to transmit [trænz'mɪt] übertragen **VI U1**, 24
transport ['trænspɔːt] Verkehrsmittel;
    Transport III
    public **transport** (no pl) [ˌpʌblɪk
    'trænspɔːt] öffentliche Verkehrsmittel II

to transport [træn'spɔːt] transportieren;
    befördern IV
transportation (AE) [ˌtrænspɔː'teɪʃn] Trans-
    port V
\*to be trapped [bi 'træpt] eingeschlossen
    sein; in der Falle sitzen III
trash (AE) [træʃ] Abfall; Müll IV
travel ['trævl] (das) Reisen; Reise II
    **travel** agency ['trævlˌeɪdʒnsi] Reisebüro
    III
    **travel** agent's ['trævlˌeɪdʒnts] Reisebüro
    III
    **travel** report [ˌtrævl rɪ'pɔːt] Reisebericht II
to travel ['trævl] fahren; reisen II
traveler (AE) ['trævlə] Reisende/-r V
traveller ['trævlə] Reisende/-r IV
travelling (no pl) ['trævlɪŋ] (das) Reisen IV
treasure ['treʒə] Schatz II
treat [triːt] hier: Leckerli; Belohnung III
    It's my **treat**. [ɪts 'maɪ ˌtriːt] Das geht auf
    meine Rechnung. V
to treat [triːt] behandeln V
tree [triː] Baum I
    family **tree** ['fæmli ˌtriː] Stammbaum I
    palm **tree** ['pɑːm ˌtriː] Palme III
    redwood **tree** ['redwʊd ˌtriː] Mammut-
    baum IV
pony trekking ['pəʊni ˌtrekɪŋ] Ponyreiten im
    Gelände III
trend [trend] Trend; Entwicklung; Richtung
    **VI U2**, 52
trendsetting ['trendˌsetɪŋ] zukunftsweisend
    °**VI U2**, 52
trial [traɪəl] Qualifikation II
tribe [traɪb] Stamm; Volksstamm III
trick [trɪk] Trick; Streich I
    to play a **trick** (on) [ˌpleɪ ə 'trɪk ˌɒn] einen
    Streich spielen I
to trick [trɪk] austricksen; täuschen IV
tricky ['trɪki] schwierig; kompliziert **VI U1**, 20
trifle ['traɪfl] Trifle (englischer Nachtisch) I
trilogy ['trɪlədʒi] Trilogie °**VI U1**, 27
trip [trɪp] Trip; Reise; Ausflug; Fahrt II
trouble ['trʌbl] Ärger; Probleme; Schwierig-
    keiten II
    \*to get into **trouble** [ˌget ˌɪntə 'trʌbl] in
    Schwierigkeiten geraten IV
    \*to make **trouble** [ˌmeɪk 'trʌbl] Ärger
    machen; in Schwierigkeiten bringen I
troublemaker ['trʌblmeɪkə] Unruhestifter/
    -in IV
trousers (pl) ['traʊzəz] Hose III
trowel ['traʊəl] kleiner Spaten II
truck (AE) [trʌk] hier: Wagen IV; Truck;
    Lastwagen IV
truckload ['trʌkləʊd] Lastwagenladung IV
true [truː] wahr II
    \*to be **true** to oneself [bi 'truː tu wʌnˌself]
    sich selbst treu bleiben V
    \*to come **true** [ˌkʌm 'truː] wahr werden;
    in Erfüllung gehen IV
trunk (AE) [trʌŋk] Kofferraum IV

trust [trʌst] Vertrauen ⟨**VI U2**, 62⟩
to trust [trʌst] vertrauen III
truth [truːθ] Wahrheit IV
to try [traɪ] versuchen; probieren I
    to **try** on [traɪ ˈɒn] anprobieren II
    to **try** out [traɪ ˈaʊt] ausprobieren III
    **Try** … [traɪ] Versuch es mal mit …; Pro-
    bier mal … I
T-shirt ['tiːʃɜːt] T-Shirt I
tsunami [tsʊ'nɑːmi] Tsunami (durch Seebe-
    ben ausgelöste Flutwelle) ⟨**VI U2**, 56⟩
the Tube [ðə 'tjuːb] die Londoner U-Bahn II
Tudor ['tjuːdə] Tudor- III
Tuesday ['tjuːzdeɪ] Dienstag I
tune [tjuːn] Melodie III
tunic ['tjuːnɪk] Tunika; Kittel ⟨**VI U1**, 25⟩
tunnel ['tʌnl] Tunnel I
turbulent ['tɜːbjələnt] turbulent; aufgewühlt
    V
It's your **turn**. [ˌɪts 'jɔː tɜːn] Du bist dran. I
    Take **turns**. [ˌteɪk 'tɜːnz] Wechselt euch
    ab. I
    Your **turn**. ['jɔː tɜːn] Du bist dran. I
to turn [tɜːn] einbiegen; abbiegen I; drehen;
    (sich) umdrehen III
    to **turn** (a)round [tɜːn ˌ(ə)'raʊnd] (sich)
    umdrehen; wenden II
    to **turn** away from sb/sth [tɜːn ə'weɪ
    frəm] sich von jmdm./etw. abwenden
    ⟨**VI U2**, 60⟩
    to **turn** back [tɜːn 'bæk] umkehren;
    zurückgehen II
    to **turn** into [ˌtɜːn ˈɪntə] ändern in; um-
    wandeln in IV
    to **turn** off [ˌtɜːn ˈɒf] abschalten; ausschal-
    ten II
    to **turn** on [ˌtɜːn ˈɒn] einschalten V
    to **turn** out to be [tɜːn ˈaʊt tə] sich
    herausstellen als °**VI U1**, 27
    to **turn** to [ˈtɜːn tə] sich wenden an; sich
    zuwenden III
    **turning** point ['tɜːnɪŋ ˌpɔɪnt] Wendepunkt
    III
    It **turned** out that … [ɪt ˌtɜːnd ˈaʊt ðæt] Es
    stellte sich heraus, dass … IV
turned off [tɜːnd ˈɒf] abgetörnt V
tusk [tʌsk] Stoßzahn III
tutor ['tjuːtə] Klassenlehrer/-in I
    **tutor** group ['tjuːtə ˌgruːp] Klasse (in einer
    englischen Schule) I
tutorial [tjuː'tɔːriəl] Tutorium; Tutorial IV
TV [ˌtiː'viː] Fernsehen; Fernseher I
    to watch **TV** [ˌwɒtʃ tiː'viː] fernsehen I
tweet [twiːt] Nachricht auf Twitter V
twelve [twelv] zwölf I
twice [twaɪs] zweimal IV
twin [twɪn] Zwilling; Zwillings- III
to twist your ankle [ˌtwɪst jɔːr 'æŋkl] sich
    den Knöchel verrenken II
two [tuː] zwei I
    the **two** of them [ðə 'tuː əv ðəm] beide II

**two** of which [ˈtuː ˌəv wɪtʃ] zwei von ihnen **III**

**type** [taɪp] Typ; Art; Sorte **III**

**typical** [ˈtɪpɪkl] typisch **I**

**typically** [ˈtɪpɪkli] typisch **III**; typischerweise °**VI U1**, 27

**tyre** [taɪə] Reifen **V**

## U

**u** (= you) [juː; jə] du; Sie; ihr **I**

**UFO** [ˈjuːefˈəʊ] UFO **II**

**ugly** [ˈʌgli] hässlich **IV**

**umbrella** [ʌmˈbrelə] Regenschirm °**VI TS1**, 35

*to be **unable** to do sth [bi ˌʌnˈeɪbl tə] unfähig sein, etw. zu tun; nicht in der Lage sein, etw. zu tun **VI TS1**, 35

**unbelievable** [ˌʌnbɪˈliːvəbl] unglaublich; unglaubwürdig **V**

**uncle** [ˈʌŋkl] Onkel **I**

**uncomfortable** [ʌnˈkʌmftəbl] unwohl; unbehaglich; unbequem **V**

**under** [ˈʌndə] unter **I**

**underfloor** heating (no pl) [ˌʌndəflɔː ˈhiːtɪŋ] Fußbodenheizung **III**

**underground** [ˈʌndəgraʊnd] U-Bahn **II**

**underground** [ˈʌndəgraʊnd] unterirdisch **V**

to **underline** [ˌʌndəˈlaɪn] unterstreichen **III**

*to **understand** [ˌʌndəˈstænd] verstehen **I**

**understanding** [ˌʌndəˈstændɪŋ] Verständnis **II**

**understanding** [ˌʌndəˈstændɪŋ] verständnisvoll **V**

**undeveloped** [ˌʌndɪˈveləpt] unentwickelt; unausgereift **IV**

**unending** [ʌnˈendɪŋ] unendlich ⟨**VI U2**, 61⟩

**unexpected** [ˌʌnɪkˈspektɪd] unerwartet **IV**

**unfair** [ʌnˈfeə] unfair **II**

**unfamiliar** [ˌʌnfəˈmɪliə] nicht vertraut; unbekannt **III**

**unfortunately** [ʌnˈfɔːtʃnətli] leider; unglücklicherweise **VI U1**, 11

**unfriendly** [ʌnˈfrendli] unfreundlich **II**

**uniform** [ˈjuːnɪfɔːm] Uniform **I**

**unique** [juːˈniːk] einzigartig **V**

**uniqueness** [juːˈniːknəs] Einzigartigkeit °**VI U2**, 52

**unit** [ˈjuːnɪt] Lektion; Kapitel; Einheit **I**

**united** [juːˈnaɪtɪd] vereint; vereinigt **V**

**university** [juːnɪˈvɜːsəti] Universität **V**

the **unknown** [ði ʌnˈnəʊn] das Unbekannte **V**

**unless** [ənˈles] es sei denn, (dass) …; wenn nicht **V**

*to be **unlucky** [biː ʌnˈlʌki] Pech haben **I**

**unnecessary** [ʌnˈnesəsri] unnötig °**VI U2**, 58

**unofficial** [ˌʌnəˈfɪʃl] inoffiziell **III**

**unopened** [ʌnˈəʊpnd] ungeöffnet **V**

to **unpack** [ʌnˈpæk] auspacken **IV**

**unpredictable** [ˌʌnprɪˈdɪktəbl] unvorhersehbar ⟨**VI U1**, 25⟩

**unreal** [ʌnˈrɪəl] irreal **IV**

**unrealistic** [ˌʌnrɪəˈlɪstɪk] unrealistisch **IV**

**unrelated** to [ˌʌnrɪˈleɪtɪd tə] unzusammenhängend mit ⟨**VI U1**, 23⟩

**unsafe** [ʌnˈseɪf] unsicher; gefährlich ⟨**VI TS2**, 73⟩

**unsuccessful** [ˌʌnsəkˈsesfl] erfolglos; ergebnislos °**VI TS1**, 36

**unsure** [ʌnˈʃʊə] unsicher **IV**

**until** [ʌnˈtɪl] bis; erst wenn **II**

not **until** [ˌnɒt ˌənˈtɪl] nicht bevor; erst um/ im **IV**

**unusual** [ʌnˈjuːʒl] ungewöhnlich **VI U2**, 55

**unwillingly** [ʌnˈwɪlɪŋli] ungern; widerwillig **VI AC1**, 41

to **unwrap** [ʌnˈræp] auswickeln; auspacken **I**

**up** [ʌp] hinauf; nach oben **II**

*to cut **up** [kʌt ˌˈʌp] zerschneiden **IV**

to end **up** [end ˌˈʌp] enden; landen **II**

*to get **up** [get ˌˈʌp] aufstehen (aus dem Bett) **I**

*to give **up** [gɪv ˌˈʌp] aufgeben **III**

to look **up** [lʊk ˌˈʌp] nachschlagen; nachschauen **I**

to look **up** to sb [lʊk ˌˈʌp tə] zu jmdm. aufschauen; jmdn. bewundern **VI TS2**, 71

**up** to [ˈʌp tə] bis zu **V**

What's **up**? [wɒts ˌˈʌp] Was ist los? **III**

*to build **upon** [ˌbɪld əˈpɒn] sich türmen auf ⟨**VI U1**, 24⟩

**upright** [ˈʌpraɪt] aufrecht **V**

*to **upset** [ʌpˈset] aus der Fassung bringen **III**

**upset** [ʌpˈset] aufgebracht; bestürzt **II**

**upstairs** [ʌpˈsteəz] nach oben; im Obergeschoss; oben **II**

**up-to-date** [ˌʌptəˈdeɪt] modern; zeitgemäß; aktuell **IV**

**urban** [ˈɜːbn] städtisch; Stadt- **IV**

**urban** sprawl [ˈɜːbn ˈsprɔːl] Urbanisierung; Zersiedelung; Ausuferung des Stadtgebiets ⟨**VI U2**, 56⟩

**urbanization** [ˌɜːbnaɪˈzeɪʃn] Urbanisierung; Verstädterung ⟨**VI U2**, 56⟩

to **urge** sb to do sth [ɜːdʒ] jmdn. zu etw. drängen **VI U2**, 50

**us** [ʌs] uns **I**

**US** [juːˈes] US-amerikanisch **IV**

**use** [juːs] Verwendung; Gebrauch; Nutzen **IV**

*to make **use** of [meɪk ˈjuːz ˌəv] benutzen; verwenden **IV**

to **use** [juːz] benutzen; verwenden; gebrauchen **I**

*to be **used** to (+ -ing) [bi ˈjuːs tə] gewöhnt sein an; gewohnt sein **III**

*to get **used** to sth [get ˈjuːzd tə] sich an etw. gewöhnen **V**

**used** to (+ infinitive) [ˈjuːst tə] pflegte(n) zu; tat(en) früher **V**

**useful** [ˈjuːsfl] nützlich; hilfreich **I**

**Useful** phrases [ˈjuːsfl ˈfreɪsɪz] nützliche Ausdrücke **I**

**useless** [ˈjuːsləs] nutzlos **IV**

**usual** [ˈjuːʒl] üblich **III**

**usually** [ˈjuːʒli] normalerweise; gewöhnlich; meistens **I**

**utopia** [juːˈtəʊpiə] Utopie °**VI U1**, 27

## V

**vacation** (AE) [vəˈkeɪʃn] Ferien; Urlaub **IV**

to **vacuum** [ˈvækjuːm] staubsaugen **V**

**valley** [ˈvæli] Tal **V**

**valuable** [ˈvæljuəbl] wertvoll **VI AC2**, 75

**value** [ˈvæljuː] Wert **V**

**variety** (of) [vəˈraɪətɪ əv] Vielzahl (an); Vielfalt (von) **V**

**various** [ˈveəriəs] verschieden; verschiedenartig **VI AC1**, 40

**vegetable** [ˈvedʒtəbl] Gemüse **III**

**vegetarian** [ˌvedʒɪˈteəriən] Vegetarier/-in **III**

**vegetarian** [ˌvedʒɪˈteəriən] vegetarisch **III**

**vending** machine [ˈvendɪŋ məˌʃiːn] Automat **IV**

**verb** [vɜːb] Verb **I**

**verse** [vɜːs] Vers; Strophe **III**

**version** [ˈvɜːʃn] Version **III**

cover **version** [ˈkʌvə ˌvɜːʃn] Coverversion **III**

**versus** (vs.) [ˈvɜːsəs] gegen **III**

**very** [ˈveri] sehr **I**

**very** much [ˌveri ˈmʌtʃ] sehr **I**

**vet** [vet] Tierarzt/Tierärztin **I**

**victim** [ˈvɪktɪm] Opfer **V**

**Victorian** [vɪkˈtɔːriən] viktorianisch; Viktorianer/-in **III**

**video** [ˈvɪdiəʊ] Video **II**

**video** chat [ˈvɪdiəʊ ˌtʃæt] Videochat **II**

**view** [vjuː] Aussicht; Sicht; Ausblick; Blick **II**; Ansicht; Einstellung; Standpunkt **V**

point of **view** [ˌpɔɪnt əv ˈvjuː] Standpunkt; Ansicht; Perspektive **II**

to **view** [vjuː] ansehen; anschauen **V**

**viewer** [ˈvjuːə] Zuschauer/-in **II**; Display (Kamera) **VI U2**, 62

**viewing** [ˈvjuːɪŋ] Hör-/Sehverstehen **I**

**village** [ˈvɪlɪdʒ] Dorf **I**

**villain** [ˈvɪlən] Bösewicht **III**

**violence** (no pl) [ˈvaɪələns] Gewalt **III**

**violent** [ˈvaɪələnt] gewaltsam; gewalttätig; brutal **III**

**VIP** (very important person) [ˌviːaɪˈpiː] VIP; Promi ⟨**VI U1**, 7⟩

**visa** [ˈviːzə], **visas** [ˈviːzəz] (pl) Visum, Visa (Pl.); Einreisebewilligung **IV**

**visit** [ˈvɪzɪt] Besuch **I**

to **visit** [ˈvɪzɪt] besichtigen; besuchen **I**

**visitor** [ˈvɪzɪtə] Besucher/-in **I**

**visual** [ˈvɪʒuəl] Bild **IV**

**visual** [ˈvɪʒuəl] visuell; optisch **V**

**vitamin** [ˈvɪtəmɪn] Vitamin **III**

**vocabulary** [vəˈkæbjəlri] Vokabular; Wortschatz **I**

**voice** [vɔɪs] Stimme **I**

*to have a **voice** [ˌhæv ə 'vɔɪs] ein Mitspracherecht haben **VI AC2**, 74
*to make one's **voice** heard [ˌmeɪk wʌnz
ˌvɔɪs 'hɜːd] sich Gehör verschaffen
**VI AC2**, 74
**volcano** [vɒl'keɪnəʊ], **volcanoes**
[vɒl'keɪnəʊz] (pl) Vulkan **V**
**volleyball** ['vɒlibɔːl] Volleyball **I**
**volunteer** [ˌvɒlən'tɪə] Freiwillige/-r; freiwillig; Ehrenamtliche/-r; ehrenamtlich
**VI U1**, 15
to **volunteer** [ˌvɒlən'tɪə] eine ehrenamtliche
Tätigkeit übernehmen **VI U1**, 15
**vote** [vəʊt] Abstimmung; Stimme; Wahl
**VI AC2**, 74
*to take a **vote** [ˌteɪk ə 'vəʊt] abstimmen **I**
to **vote** [vəʊt] abstimmen; wählen **I**
**vulgar** ['vʌlgə] vulgär; gewöhnlich **VI AC1**, 43

# W

**wage** [weɪdʒ] Lohn **VI U1**, 16
minimum **wage** [ˌmɪnɪməm 'weɪdʒ] Mindestlohn **VI U2**, 53
**wagon** ['wægən] Wagen; Waggon; Planwagen; Karren **V**
covered **wagon** [ˌkʌvəd 'wægən] Planwagen **V**
to **wait** (for) [weɪt] warten (auf) **I**
I can't **wait** till next time. [aɪ kɑːnt ˌweɪt
tɪl nekst 'taɪm] Ich kann es bis zum
nächsten Mal kaum erwarten. **II**
**Wait** and see! [ˌweɪt ənd 'siː] Warte ab! **I**
**waiter** ['weɪtə] Kellner/-in; Bedienung **V**
*to **wake** up [ˌweɪk 'ʌp] aufwachen; aufwe-
cken **III**
**walk** [wɔːk] Gang **V**
gallery **walk** ['gælri ˌwɔːk] Museumsrundgang; Vernissage **I**
*to go for a **walk** [ˌgəʊ fər ə 'wɔːk] spazieren gehen **II**
night **walk** ['naɪt wɔːk] Nachtwanderung
**II**
to **walk** [wɔːk] gehen; laufen **I**
to **walk** the dog [ˌwɔːk ðə 'dɒg] den Hund
ausführen; mit dem Hund spazieren
gehen **I**
**walk-in** closet [ˌwɔːkɪn 'klɒzɪt] begehbarer
Kleiderschrank **IV**
**walking** ['wɔːkɪŋ] Wandern **II**
**walking** trail ['wɔːkɪŋ treɪl] Wanderweg **III**
**wall** [wɔːl] Wand; Mauer **I**; Online-Pinnwand
**III**
to **wander** ['wɒndə] gehen ⟨**VI U2**, 61⟩
**wanna** (= want to) (infml) ['wɒnə] will/
wollen ⟨**VI TS2**, 70⟩
**wannabe** (infml) ['wɒnəbi] Möchtegern;
Möchtegern- **VI U2**, 46
to **want** (to) ['wɒnt tə] wollen; mögen **I**
**wanted** ['wɒntɪd] gesucht **V**
**war** [wɔː] Krieg **IV**
**wardrobe** ['wɔːdrəʊb] Kleiderschrank **I**

to **warm** up [ˌwɔːm 'ʌp] aufwärmen; sich
aufwärmen **I**
**warm** [wɔːm] warm **III**
**warm-up** ['wɔːm ʌp] Aufwärmübung **I**
to **warn** [wɔːn] warnen **IV**
**warrior** ['wɒriə] Krieger **III**
to **wash** [wɒʃ] waschen; sich waschen **I**
to **wash** up [ˌwɒʃ 'ʌp] angespült werden **II**
**washing** machine ['wɒʃɪŋ məˌʃiːn] Wasch-
maschine **II**
**waste** [weɪst] Verschwendung **IV**
to **waste** [weɪst] verschwenden **II**
**wasteful** ['weɪstfl] verschwenderisch **IV**
to **watch** [wɒtʃ] beobachten; (sich) ansehen;
zuschauen **I**
to **watch** TV [ˌwɒtʃ tiː'viː] fernsehen **I**
**water** ['wɔːtə] Wasser **I**
drinking **water** ['drɪŋkɪŋ ˌwɔːtə] Trinkwasser **V**
**water** fountain ['wɔːtə ˌfaʊntɪn] Wasserspender **IV**
**water** slide ['wɔːtə ˌslaɪd] Wasserrutsche **I**
**waterfront** ['wɔːtəfrʌnt] Hafenviertel; Ufer **V**
**wave** [weɪv] Welle **I**
to **wave** [weɪv] winken; schwenken **V**
**wax** [wæks] Wachs **II**
**wax** figure ['wæks ˌfɪgə] Wachsfigur **II**
**way** [weɪ] Weg; Art und Weise **I**
*to be in the **way** [biː ɪn ðə 'weɪ] im Weg
sein/stehen **I**
*to find one's **way** around [ˌfaɪnd wʌnz
ˌweɪ ə'raʊnd] sich zurechtfinden **IV**
*to get in the **way** [ˌget ɪn ðə 'weɪ] stören;
im Weg stehen **II**
*to take sth the wrong **way** [ˌteɪk ðə rɒŋ
'weɪ] etw. falsch auffassen; etw. in den
falschen Hals bekommen **VI AC1**, 43
in other **ways** [ɪn ˌʌðə weɪz] auf andere
Weise **II**
that **way** [ˌðæt 'weɪ] so; auf diese Weise
**VI U2**, 46
the other **way** around [ðiː ˌʌðə weɪ 'raʊnd]
andersrum; umgekehrt ⟨**VI U2**, 62⟩
the same **way** as [ðə seɪm 'weɪ æz]
genauso wie **II**
**way** [weɪ] lange ⟨**VI U2**, 60⟩
**we** [wiː; wi] wir **I**
**We**'re from … ['wɪə frəm] Wir sind
aus … **I**
**weak** [wiːk] schwach **IV**
**weakness** ['wiːknəs] Schwäche **VI U1**, 9
**wealth** [welθ] Reichtum; Vermögen **VI U2**, 50
**wealthy** ['welθi] wohlhabend; reich **IV**
**weapon** ['wepən] Waffe **III**
*to **wear** [weə] anhaben; tragen (Kleidung) **I**
**weather** ['weðə] Wetter **I**
**weather** forecast ['weðə ˌfɔːkɑːst] Wettervorhersage **III**
**web** [web] Netz; Spinnennetz **III**
**web** designer ['web dɪˌzaɪnə] Webdesigner **III**

**website** ['websaɪt] Website; Internetauf-
tritt **I**
**wedding** ['wedɪŋ] Hochzeit **I**
**Wednesday** ['wenzdeɪ] Mittwoch **I**
**week** [wiːk] Woche **I**
**weekday** ['wiːkdeɪ] Wochentag **II**
**weekend** [ˌwiːk'end] Wochenende **I**
at the **weekend** [ət ðə ˌwiːk'end] am
Wochenende **I**
to **weigh** [weɪ] wiegen **III**
**weight** [weɪt] Gewicht **III**
**weighted** ['weɪtɪd] beladen; belastet
⟨**VI U1**, 24⟩
**weird** [wɪəd] merkwürdig; seltsam; sonder-
bar **II**
**Welcome!** ['welkəm] Willkommen! **II**
to **welcome** ['welkəm] willkommen heißen
**II**
You're **welcome**. [jɔː 'welkəm] Bitte schön.;
Nichts zu danken.; Gern geschehen. **I**
*to do **well** [duː 'wel] gute Leistungen
erbringen **V**
*to get **well** [get 'wel] gesund werden **V**
**well**-developed [ˌweldɪ'veləpt] gut entwi-
ckelt; ausgereift **IV**
**well**-known [ˌwel'nəʊn] (wohl) bekannt
**VI TS1**, 37
**well**-suited (to doing sth) [ˌwel'suːtɪd]
geeignet (für/um zu); passend (für)
**VI TS1**, 37
**well**-written [ˌwel'rɪtn] gut geschrieben **IV**
… as **well** as … [əz 'wel əz] sowie; und
(auch) **V**
**well** [wel] tja; nun **I**
**Welsh** [welʃ] walisisch; Walisisch; Waliser/
-in **II**
**west** [west] Westen; West- **I**
in the far **west** [ɪn ðə fɑː 'west] im äußers-
ten Westen **III**
**western** ['westən] westlich; West- **V**
**wet** [wet] nass **II**
**whale** [weɪl] Wal **V**
**what** [wɒt] was; welche/-r/-s; was für ein **I**
**What** a … ['wɒt ə] Was für ein/-e … **IV**
**What** about … ? ['wɒt əbaʊt] Wie wär's
mit …?; Was ist mit …? **I**
**What** are …? ['wɒt ɑː] Welche … sind
es? **I**
**What** colour is …? [ˌwɒt 'kʌlər ɪz] Welche
Farbe hat …? **I**
**what** else [ˌwɒt 'els] was sonst; was noch **I**
**What** is missing? [ˌwɒt ɪz 'mɪsɪŋ] Was
fehlt? **I**
**What** is … about? [ˌwɒt ɪz … ə'baʊt]
Worum geht es in/im …? **I**
**what** it's all about [ˌwɒt ɪts ɔːl ə'baʊt]
worum es geht **VI U2**, 46
**what** it's like [ˌwɒt ɪts 'laɪk] wie das ist **II**
**What** luck! [ˌwɒt 'lʌk] Was für ein Glück! **III**
**What** on earth …? [ˌwɒt ˌɒn 'ɜːθ] Was um
alles in der Welt …? **II**

**what** the man looked like [ˌwɒt ðə mæn ˈlʊkt laɪk] wie der Mann aussah **II**

**What** time? [wɒt ˈtaɪm] Um wie viel Uhr? **I**

**what** to … [ˈwɒt tə] was man … **I**

**What** was it like? [ˌwɒt wɒz ɪt ˈlaɪk] Wie war es? **III**

**What**'s that? [wɒts ˈðæt] Was ist das? **I**

**What**'s up? [ˌwɒts ˈʌp] Was ist los? **III**

**What**'s your favourite …? [ˈwɒts jə ˌfeɪvrɪt] Was ist dein/-e Lieblings…? **I**

**What**'s your name? [ˌwɒts jə ˈneɪm] Wie heißt du?; Wie heißen Sie? **I**

**What**'s going on? [wɒts ˌgəʊɪŋ ˈɒn] Was ist los?; Was geht ab? **III**

**what**'s more [ˌwɒts ˈmɔ:] außerdem; überdies **V**

**What**'s the matter? [ˌwɒts ðə ˈmætə] Was ist los?; Was hast du? **III**

**What**'s the time? [ˌwɒts ðə ˈtaɪm] Wie spät ist es?; Wie viel Uhr ist es? **I**

**whatever** [wɒtˈevə] wie auch immer; egal (was/welche) **IV**

**wheat** [wi:t] Weizen **IV**

**wheel** [wi:l] Rad; Steuerrad; Steuer **I**

great **wheel** [ˌgreɪt ˈwi:l] Riesenrad **V**

to **wheel** around [ˌwi:l əˈraʊnd] herumwirbeln ⟨**VI U2**, 60⟩

**wheelchair** [ˈwi:ltʃeə] Rollstuhl **II**

**when** [wen] wenn; wann; als **I**

**whenever** [wenˈevə] wann immer; jedes Mal, wenn; so oft **II**

**where** [weə] wo; wohin **I**

**Where** … from? [ˌweə … ˈfrɒm] Woher …? **I**

**where** I belong [ˌweər aɪ bɪˈlɒŋ] wo ich hingehöre **IV**

… **where** to go. [ˌweə tə ˈgəʊ] … wohin ich gehen kann. **II**

I go **wherever** the wind takes me. [aɪ ˌgəʊ weəˌrevə ðə wɪnd ˈteɪks mi:] Ich lasse mich treiben. **IV**

**whether** [ˈweðə] ob **IV**

**which** [wɪtʃ] welche/-r/-s **I**

**which** [wɪtʃ] der; die; das; dem; den (Relativpronomen) **II**

a **while** [ə ˈwaɪl] eine Weile **II**

**while** [waɪl] während **I**

to **whine** [waɪn] quengeln ⟨**VI U2**, 60⟩

to **whip** [wɪp] schlagen **I**

**whisky** [ˈwɪski] Whisky **III**

to **whisper** [ˈwɪspə] flüstern **I**

**white** [waɪt] weiß **I**

**white** lie [ˌwaɪt ˈlaɪ] Notlüge **IV**

**who** [hu:] wer; wem; wen **I**

**Who** … for? [ˌhu: ˈfɔ:] Für wen …? **I**

**Who** is it? [ˌhu: ˈɪz ɪt] Wer ist es? **I**

**Who** the hell cares? [ˌhu: ðə hel ˈkeəz] Wen zum Teufel interessiert's? ⟨**VI TS2**, 70⟩

**Who**'s in? [hu:z ˈɪn] Wer macht mit?; Wer ist dabei? **II**

**who** [hu:] der; dem; den; die (Relativpronomen) **II**

**whole** [həʊl] ganz **I**

**whom** [hu:m] wem; wen **IV**

**whoosh** [wʊʃ] wusch **I**

**whose** [hu:z] wessen **IV**

**whose** [hu:z] dessen; deren (Relativpronomen) **II**

**why** [waɪ] warum **I**

that's **why** [ðæts ˈwaɪ] deshalb **II**

**wide** [waɪd] breit; weit; ausgedehnt **III**

**wide** shot [ˈwaɪd ʃɒt] Totale (Kameraeinstellung) **V**

**wide-brimmed** [ˈwaɪdbrɪmd] breitkrempig ⟨**VI U2**, 60⟩

**widespread** [ˈwaɪdspred] weit verbreitet **V**

**wife**, **wives** (pl) [waɪf, waɪvz] Ehefrau **II**

**wifi** [ˈwaɪfaɪ] WLAN **IV**

**wiki** (text) [ˈwɪki ˌtekst] Wikitext **IV**

**wild** [waɪld] wild **III**

**wilderness** [ˈwɪldənəs] Wildnis **V**

**wildfire** [ˈwaɪldfaɪə] Flächenbrand **VI U2**, 54

**wildlife** [ˈwaɪldlaɪf] Tierwelt (in freier Wildbahn) **V**

**will** [wɪl] werden (futurisch) **III**

\*to be **willing** to do sth [bi ˈwɪlɪŋ tə] gewillt sein, etw. zu tun; bereit sein, etw. zu tun **VI U2**, 54

**willingly** [ˈwɪlɪŋli] gern; freiwillig **VI AC1**, 41

**win** [wɪn] Sieg °**VI U2**, 58

\*to **win** [wɪn] gewinnen; siegen **I**

\*to **win** sb over [ˌwɪn ˈəʊvə] jmdn. für sich gewinnen; jmdn. überzeugen **IV**

**wind** [wɪnd] Wind **III**

I go wherever the **wind** takes me. [aɪ ˌgəʊ weəˌrevə ðə wɪnd ˈteɪks mi:] Ich lasse mich treiben. **IV**

**window** [ˈwɪndəʊ] Fenster **I**

**windsurfing** [ˈwɪndsɜ:fɪŋ] Windsurfen **III**

**wine** [waɪn] Wein **I**

**winner** [ˈwɪnə] Gewinner/-in; Sieger/-in **I**

**winter** [ˈwɪntə] Winter **III**

**wisdom** (no pl) [ˈwɪzdəm] Weisheit; Klugheit **VI U1**, 16

**wish** [wɪʃ] Wunsch **I**

\*to make a **wish** [ˌmeɪk ə ˈwɪʃ] sich etwas wünschen **I**

Best **wishes** [ˌbest ˈwɪʃɪz] Viele Grüße; Herzliche Grüße **III**

to **wish** [wɪʃ] (sich) wünschen **IV**

**with** [wɪð] mit; bei **I**

as **with** [ˈæz wɪð] wie (auch) bei ⟨**VI U2**, 57⟩

**within** [wɪˈðɪn] innerhalb **IV**

**without** [wɪˈðaʊt] ohne **I**

**witness** [ˈwɪtnəs] Zeuge/Zeugin **II**

**wizard** [ˈwɪzəd] Zauberer **III**

**wobbly** [ˈwɒbli] wackelig **II**

**wolf** [wʊlf], **wolves** [wʊlvz] (pl) Wolf **V**

**woman**, **women** (pl) [ˈwʊmən; ˈwɪmɪn] Frau **I**

no **wonder** [ˌnəʊ ˈwʌndə] kein Wunder **IV**

to **wonder** [ˈwʌndə] sich Gedanken machen; sich fragen **V**

**wonderful** [ˈwʌndəfl] wunderbar **II**

**wood** [wʊd] Wald; Wäldchen; Holz **III**

**wooded** [ˈwʊdɪd] bewaldet **V**

**wooden** [ˈwʊdn] hölzern; aus Holz **III**

**Woof!** [wʊf] Wau! **I**

**word** [wɜ:d] Wort **I**

compound **word** [ˈkɒmpaʊnd wɜ:d] Kompositum (zusammengesetztes Wort) **II**

four-letter **word** [ˌfɔ:letə ˈwɜ:d] Schimpfwort ⟨**VI TS2**, 69⟩

key **word** [ˈki: wɜ:d] Stichwort; Schlüsselbegriff **I**

linking **word** [ˈlɪŋkɪŋ ˌwɜ:d] Bindewort **I**

play on **words** [ˌpleɪ ɒn ˈwɜ:dz] Wortspiel **III**

signal **word** [ˈsɪgnəl ˌwɜ:d] Signalwort **I**

**word** bank [ˈwɜ:d ˌbæŋk] Wortsammlung **III**

**word** cloud [ˈwɜ:d ˌklaʊd] Wörterwolke **II**

**word** order [ˈwɜ:dˌ ɔ:də] Wortstellung; Satzstellung **I**

**word**-building [ˈwɜ:dˌbɪldɪŋ] Wortbildung **II**

**work** [wɜ:k] Arbeit **I**

pair **work** [ˈpeə wɜ:k] Partnerarbeit **II**

to **work** [wɜ:k] arbeiten **I**; funktionieren **II**

to **work** out [ˌwɜ:k ˈaʊt] herausfinden; ausarbeiten **II**; funktionieren; klappen **III**

**workbook** [ˈwɜ:kbʊk] Arbeitsheft; Übungsheft **IV**

**worker** [ˈwɜ:kə] Arbeiter/-in **VI U1**, 9

construction **worker** [kənˈstrʌkʃn ˌwɜ:kə] Bauarbeiter/-in **VI U1**, 9

**workshop** [ˈwɜ:kʃɒp] Workshop **I**

**world** [wɜ:ld] Erde; Welt **I**

outside **world** [ˈaʊtsaɪd ˌwɜ:ld] Außenwelt **V**

from around the **world** [frɒm əˌraʊnd ðə ˈwɜ:ld] aus aller Welt **III**

**worldwide** [ˌwɜ:ldˈwaɪd] weltweit **VI U2**, 50

**worm** [wɜ:m] Wurm **I**

**worried** [ˈwʌrid] beunruhigt; besorgt **III**

\*to be **worried** [bi ˈwʌrid] beunruhigt sein; besorgt sein **II**

No **worries**. [ˌnəʊ ˈwʌriz] Kein Problem.; Gern geschehen. **III**

to **worry** [ˈwʌri] sich Sorgen machen **II**

Don't **worry**! [dəʊnt ˈwʌri] Keine Sorge! **I**

the **worst** [ðə ˈwɜ:st] der/die/das schlimmste; der/die/das schlechteste **II**

\*to be **worth** [bi: ˈwɜ:θ] wert sein **I**

**would** [wʊd] würde/-st/-n/-t **III**

**would** like [wʊd ˈlaɪk] würde/-st/-n/-t gern; hätte/-st/-n/-t gern **I**

**would** love [wʊd ˈlʌv] würde/-st/-n/-t sehr gern; hätte/-st-/-n/-t sehr gern **I**

**Would** you like …? [ˌwʊd jʊ ˈlaɪk] Möchtest du …?; Möchten Sie …?; Möchtet ihr …? **II**

**wounded** [ˈwu:ndɪd] verwundet; verletzt **III**

**Wow!** [waʊ] Wow! **I**

to **wrap** [ræp] einwickeln; einpacken **I**

**wrapping** [ˈræpɪŋ] Verpackung; Hülle **I**

to **wreck** [rek] zerstören ⟨VI U2, 62)
**wrist** [rɪst] Handgelenk II
*to **write** [raɪt] schreiben I
  *to **write** down [ˌraɪt ˈdaʊn] aufschreiben I
**writer** [ˈraɪtə] Autor/-in; Verfasser/-in III
  staff **writer** [ˈstɑːf ˌraɪtə] festangestellter Journalist/festangestellte Journalistin ⟨VI TS2, 71)
**writing** [ˈraɪtɪŋ] Schreiben I
**wrong** [rɒŋ] falsch I
  *to be **wrong** [bi: ˈrɒŋ] unrecht haben; sich irren I
  *to go **wrong** [ɡəʊ ˈrɒŋ] schiefgehen I

## X

**XOXO** [ˌhʌɡzˌən ˈkɪsɪz] Umarmungen und Küsse *(am Ende von E-Mails und SMS)* I

## Y

to **yank** [jæŋk] zerren (an) ⟨VI U2, 60)
**yard** [jɑːd] Garten; Hof IV
  front **yard** *(AE)* [ˌfrʌnt ˈjɑːd] Vorgarten IV
**yeah** *(infml)* [jeə] ja I
**year** [jɪə] Jahr; Schuljahr I
  gap **year** [ˈɡæp ˌjɪə] *ein Jahr Auszeit (zwischen Schule und Ausbildung/Studium), das oft für einen freiwilligen ökologischen oder sozialen Dienst genutzt wird* VI U1, 15
11-**year**-old [ˌɪˌlevnˈjɪərəʊld] 11-Jährige/-r II
18-**year**-old [eɪtiːn ˈjɪərˌʊəʊld] 18-jährig II
**yearbook** [ˈjɪəbʊk] Jahrbuch II
**yellow** [ˈjeləʊ] gelb I
**yes** [jes] ja I
**yesterday** [ˈjestədeɪ] gestern II
**yet** [jet] schon; noch II; doch; und trotzdem; und dennoch IV
  not … **yet** [nɒt ˈjet] noch nicht II
**yoghurt** [ˈjɒɡət] Joghurt I
**you** [juː; jə] du; ihr; Sie I
  **You** too? [ju ˈtuː] Du auch? I
  **You**'d better … (= You had better) [ˈjuːd ˌbetə] Du solltest lieber … IV
  **You**'re welcome. [jɔː ˈwelkəm] Bitte schön.; Nichts zu danken.; Gern geschehen. I
**young** [jʌŋ] jung I
**your** [jɔː; jə] dein/-e; euer/eure; Ihr/-e I
  What's **your** name? [wɒts jə ˈneɪm] Wie heißt du?; Wie heißen Sie? I
  **Your** turn. [ˈjɔː tɜːn] Du bist dran. I
**yours** [jɔːz] dein/-er/-e/-es; eure/-r/-s; Ihr/-e II
  **Yours** … [jɔːz] Viele Grüße … *(am Ende von Briefen und Mails)* II
  **Yours** sincerely [jɔːz sɪnˈsɪəli] Mit freundlichen Grüßen VI U1, 11
**yourself** [jɔːˈself] du/dir/dich/Sie/sich (selbst); selber I
**yourselves** [jɔːˈselvz] ihr/euch/Sie/sich (selbst); selber III

**youth** [juːθ] Jugend IV
  **youth** hostel [ˈjuːθ ˌhɒstl] Jugendherberge V

## Z

**zero** [ˈzɪərəʊ] null I
**zone** [zəʊn] Zone IV
**zoo** [zuː] Zoo; Tierpark II
**zoom** lens [ˈzuːm lenz] Zoomobjektiv ⟨VI U2, 60)
to **zoom** in (on) [zuːmˌ ˈɪn ɒn] heranzoomen (auf) III
**zucchini** [zʊˈkiːni] Zucchini ⟨VI U2, 57)

## Boys' names

**Abdoulaye** [ˌabdʊˈlɛ] VI U1, 13
**Alex** [ˈælɪks] VI U2, 46
**Ali** [ˈɑːli] V
**Amir** [ɑːˈmiːr] II
**Arnold** [ˈɑːnld] V
**Arthur** [ˈɑːθə] V
**Austin** [ˈɒstɪn] IV
**Ben** [ben] I
**Benjamin** [ˈbendʒəmɪn] VI U1, 23
**Bill** [bɪl] V
**Bob** [bɒb] I
**Brad** [bræd] III
**Brodie** [ˈbrəʊdi] IV
**Callum** [ˈkæləm] IV
**Carlos** [ˈkɑːlɒs] V
**Charlie** [ˈtʃɑːli] V
**Clayton** [ˈkleɪtn] V
**Clifton** [ˈklɪftən] V
**Connor** [ˈkɒnə] ⟨VI U2, 60)
**Damian** [ˈdeɪmiən] I
**Dan** [dæn] VI U1, 18
**Daniel** [ˈdænjəl] IV
**Dave** [deɪv] I
**David** [ˈdeɪvɪd] I
**Dennis** [ˈdenɪs] V
**Desmond** [ˈdezmənd] I
**Diego** [diˈeɪɡəʊ] IV
**Ed** [ed] II
**Eddie** [ˈedi] IV
**Erik** [ˈerɪk] V
**Ethan** [ˈiːθn] III
**Finn** [fɪn] III
**Frank** [fræŋk] II
**Gabriel** [ˈɡeɪbriəl] ⟨VI U1, 26)
**Gordy** [ˈɡɔːdi] V
**Harrison** [ˈhærɪsn] IV
**Henry** [ˈhenri] I
**Jack** [dʒæk] I
**Jake** [dʒeɪk] V
**James** [dʒeɪmz] II
**Jamie** [ˈdʒeɪmi] I
**Jay** [dʒeɪ] I
**Jim** [dʒɪm] III
**John** [dʒɒn] II
**Jonas** [ˈdʒəʊnəs] VI U1, 22

**Jonathan** [ˈdʒɒnəθn] VI TS1, 37
**Josh** [dʒɒʃ] IV
**Lawrence** [ˈlɔːrəns] IV
**Lee** [liː] V
**Liam** [ˈliːəm] VI AC1, 42
**Luke** [luːk] I
**Mario** [ˈmæriəʊ] III
**Mark** [mɑːk] IV
**Marley** [ˈmɑːli] II
**Marlon** [ˈmɑːlən] IV
**Matt** [mæt] III
**Matthew** [ˈmæθjuː] V
**Max** [mæks] III
**Mick** [mɪk] II
**Mike** [maɪk] II
**Moses** [ˈməʊzɪz] V
**Moshe** [ˈmɒʃə] V
**Nasim** [ˈneɪzɪm] ⟨VI U2, 60)
**Nathan** [ˈneɪθn] II
**Nick** [nɪk] II
**Paul** [pɔːl] VI TS1, 37
**Peter** [ˈpiːtə] II
**Phil** [fɪl] VI U1, 20
**Rick** [rɪk] III
**Rob** [rɒb] IV
**Russell** [ˈrʌsl] VI TS1, 37
**Ryan** [raɪən] VI U1, 9
**Scott** [skɒt] IV
**Sean** [ʃɔːn] III
**Shahid** [ʃɑːˈhiːd] I
**Shane** [ʃɑːn] VI TS2, 69
**Simon** [ˈsaɪmən] IV
**Steve** [stiːv] I
**Stuart** [ˈstuːət] III
**Thomas** [ˈtɒməs] III
**Tim** [tɪm] IV
**Todd** [tɒd] ⟨VI U2, 62)
**Tony** [ˈtəʊni] I
**Tristan** [ˈtrɪstən] IV
**Tyler** [ˈtaɪlə] I
**Wesley** [ˈwezli] IV
**Will** [wɪl] II
**Zach** [zæk] V

## Girls' names

**Abbie** [ˈæbi] V
**Adriana** [ˌeɪdriˈɑːnə] VI U2, 53
**Alice** [ˈælɪs] II
**Alicia** [əˈlɪsiə; əˈlɪʃə] I
**Alva** [ˈælvə] III
**Amber** [ˈæmbə] I
**Amy** [ˈeɪmi] VI U1, 18
**Anna** [ˈænə] I
**Anne** [æn] I
**Anne-Marie** [ˌænməˈriː] ⟨VI U2, 62)
**Annie** [ˈæni] II
**Anya** [ˈænjə] IV
**Ashley** [ˈæʃli] IV
**Ava** [ˈɑːvə] V
**Carla** [ˈkɑːlə] ⟨VI U2, 62)
**Carol** [ˈkærəl] I

Carrie [ˈkæri] V
Cassie [ˈkæsi] VI U1, 16
Ceri [ˈkeri] II
Christine [krɪˈstiːn] IV
Cindy [ˈsɪndi] V
Claire [ˈkleə] I
Courtney [ˈkɔːtni] VI U1, 20
Daphne [ˈdæfni] ⟨VI U2, 61⟩
Eileen [aɪˈliːn] V
Ella [ˈelə] VI U1, 9
Emily [ˈemɪli] I
Emma [ˈemə] VI U1, 18
Erin [ˈɪərɪn] ⟨VI TS1, 39⟩
Eva [ˈiːvə] IV
Fiona [fiˈəʊnə] V
Frances [ˈfrɑːnsɪs] I
Gwen [gwen] II
Haley [ˈheɪli] IV
Harriet [ˈhæriət] V
Helen [ˈhelɪn] III
Holly [ˈhɒli] I
Irina [ɪˈriːnə] I
Ivy [ˈaɪvi] III
Janie [ˈdʒeɪni] IV
Jean [dʒiːn] III
Jenna [ˈdʒenə] V
Jenny [ˈdʒeni] IV
Jessica [ˈdʒesɪkə] IV
Judith [ˈdʒuːdɪθ] III
Julie [ˈdʒuːli] I
June [dʒuːn] IV
Kate [keɪt] II
Kelly [ˈkeli] IV
Kim [kɪm] V
Kirsty [ˈkɜːsti] III
Lara [ˈlɑːrə] VI TS2, 68
Laura [ˈlɔːrə] I
Lauren [ˈlɔːrən] II
Leanne [liˈæn] IV
Libby [ˈlɪbi] V
Lilly [ˈlɪli] V
Lou [luː] I
Lucy [ˈluːsi] I
Madison [ˈmædɪsn] IV
Maisie [ˈmeɪzi] II
Margaret [ˈmɑːgrət] III
Maria [məˈriːə] ⟨VI U2, 61⟩
Martha [ˈmɑːθə] VI U1, 8
Mary [ˈmeəri] II
Megan [ˈmegən] III
Meredith [ˈmerədɪθ] IV
Mila [ˈmiːlə] I
Mina [ˈmiːnə] II
Nancy [ˈnænsi] IV
Ninja [ˈnɪndʒə] VI U2, 47
Nisha [ˈnɪʃə] VI TS2, 68
Olivia [ɒlˈɪviə] I
Penelope [pəˈneləpi] V
Penny [ˈpeni] V
Pia [ˈpiːə] I
Pippa [ˈpɪpə] ⟨VI TS2, 73⟩
Polly [ˈpɒli] II

Rebecca [rɪˈbekə] V
Rita [ˈriːtə] IV
Rose [rəʊz] I
Rosie [ˈrəʊzi] V
Ruby [ˈruːbi] II
Rylee [ˈraɪli] IV
Saanvi [ˈsɑːnvi] VI U1, 20
Sally [ˈsæli] I
Sarah [ˈseərə] IV
Selena [səˈliːnə] V
Sophie [ˈsəʊfi] IV
Stella [ˈstelə] VI TS2, 70
Sue [suː] V
Susan [ˈsuːzn] V
Tamara [təˈmɑːrə] III
Tanya [ˈtɑːnjə] V
Tatiana [ˌtætiˈɑːnə] ⟨VI U2, 60⟩
Tina [ˈtiːnə] III
Violet [ˈvaɪələt] III
Vivien [ˈvɪvjən] III
Willow [ˈwɪləʊ] ⟨VI U2, 61⟩

## Surnames

Ashton [ˈæʃtən] II
Azad [əˈzɑːd] I
Blanchard [ˈblænʃəd] IV
Campbell [ˈkæmbl] ⟨VI TS2, 73⟩
Carter [ˈkɑːtə] V
Cotter [ˈkɒtə] ⟨VI TS1, 39⟩
Dolan [ˈdəʊlən] VI TS2, 69
Eaton [ˈiːtən] VI TS2, 69
Elliot [ˈeliət] I
Ford [fɔːd] IV
Forester [ˈfɒrɪstə] V
Foster [ˈfɒstə] VI TS1, 37
Fox [fɒks] VI TS2, 70
Francis [ˈfrɑːnsɪs] III
Fraser [ˈfreɪzə] I
Frazee [ˈfreɪziː] ⟨VI U2, 60⟩
Fuller [ˈfʊlə] V
Green [griːn] I
Harris [ˈhærɪs] V
Hartley [ˈhɑːtli] VI U1, 13
Henry [ˈhenri] V
Jameson [ˈdʒeɪmsn] V
Jones [dʒəʊnz] IV
Karp [kɑːp] III
Kelley [ˈkeli] VI TS1, 37
King [kɪŋ] III
Kumani [kuˈmɑːni] VI TS2, 68
Lee [liː] ⟨VI TS2, 73⟩
Lewis [ˈluːɪs] VI U1, 10
Llewellyn [luˈelɪn] ⟨VI TS1, 39⟩
Maldini [mɔːlˈdiːni] VI TS2, 68
McDonald [məkˈdɒnld] V
Miller [ˈmɪlə] III
Morse [mɔːs] V
Nicholls [ˈnɪkəlz] III
Parker [ˈpɑːkə] II
Philipp [ˈfɪlɪp] V
Preston [ˈprestən] I

Pulsford [ˈpʌlsfɔːd] III
Ramirez [rəˈmɪərez] VI U2, 54
Reid [riːd] V
Richardson [ˈrɪtʃədsn] I
Ross [rɒs] VI U1, 8
Shaw [ʃɔː] VI TS2, 71
Strasser [ˈstræsə] ⟨VI U2, 62⟩
Swindon [ˈswɪndən] I
Thompson [ˈtɒmsən] II
Twine [twaɪn] ⟨VI U2, 61⟩
Vail [veɪl] V
Walker [ˈwɔːkə] I
Watney [ˈwɒtni] IV
Webb [web] VI TS1, 37
Woodruff [ˈwʊdrʌf] IV
Wright [raɪt] II

## Place names

Abengourou [aˌbɛngʊˈruː] VI U1, 13
Aberdeen [ˌæbəˈdiːn] Stadt in Schottland III
Birmingham [ˈbɜːmɪŋəm] III
Boston [ˈbɒstn] Stadt in den USA IV
Brighton [ˈbraɪtn] VI U1, 10
Bristol [ˈbrɪstl] III
Broadway [ˈbrɔːdweɪ] Straße in NYC IV
Brooklyn [ˈbrʊklɪn] Stadtteil von New York IV
Camden Market [ˈkæmdən ˌmɑːkɪt] II
Chester [ˈtʃestə] VI U1, 11
Chicago [ʃɪˈkɑːgəʊ] Stadt in den USA IV
Cologne [kəˈləʊn] Köln I
Covent Garden [ˌkɒvnt ˈgɑːdn] II
Cracow [ˈkrækɒv; ˈkrɑːkaʊ] Krakau I
Dover [ˈdəʊvə] englische Küstenstadt am Ärmelkanal I
Dunstan [ˈdʌnstən] VI U1, 10
Edinburgh [ˈedɪnbrə] III
Florence [ˈflɒrns] Florenz VI TS1, 34
Glasgow [ˈglɑːzgəʊ] Stadt in Schottland III
Heathrow [ˌhiːθˈrəʊ] Flughafen in London IV
Hollywood [ˈhɒliwʊd] II
Houston [ˈhjuːstn] Stadt in den USA IV
Hyde Park [ˌhaɪd ˈpɑːk] II
Isle of Man [ˌaɪl əv ˈmæn] III
Larksdale Rise [ˌlɑːksdeɪl ˈraɪz] VI U1, 11
Leeds [liːdz] Stadt in Nordengland VI TS2, 71
Liverpool [ˈlɪvəpuːl] I
London [ˈlʌndən] I
Los Angeles (LA) [lɒsˌˈændʒɪliːz (elˈeɪ)] US-amerikan. Stadt VI U2, 46
Manhattan [mænˈhætn] Stadtteil von New York IV
Melbourne [ˈmelbən] Stadt in Australien V
Miami [maɪˈæmi] Stadt in den USA V
Mud Springs [ˌmʌd ˈsprɪŋs] Ort in Kalifornien VI U2, 50
New Delhi [njuː ˈdeli] V
New York [ˌnjuː ˈjɔːk] III
Nottingham [ˈnɒtɪŋəm] III
Oxford [ˈɒksfəd] englische Universitätsstadt VI TS1, 37

Perth [pɜ:θ] *Stadt in Australien* **V**

Philadelphia [ˌfɪləˈdelfiə] *Stadt in den USA* **IV**

Pretoria [prɪˈtɔ:riə] *Stadt in Südafrika* **V**

Radford [ˈrædfəd] **VI TS2**, 69

Salinas [seɪˈlaɪnəs] *Stadt in Kalifornien* **VI U2**, 45

San Francisco [ˌsæn frənˈsɪskəʊ] *Stadt in den USA* **VI U2**, 51

Santa Monica [ˌsæntə ˈmɒnɪkə] **VI U2**, 52

Seattle [siˈætl] **V**

Silicon Valley [ˌsɪlɪkən ˈvæli] *bedeutender Standort der IT- und High-Tech-Industrie* **VI U2**, 45

Stratford-upon-Avon [ˌstrætfədəpɒnˈeɪvn] *Geburtsort Shakespeares* **III**

Sydney [ˈsɪdni] *Stadt in Australien* **V**

Vancouver [vænˈku:və] *Stadt in Kanada* **V**

Venice [ˈvenɪs] *Stadtteil von Los Angeles* **VI U2**, 45

Washington, D.C. [ˌwɒʃɪŋtən ˌdi:ˈsi:] *Hauptstadt der USA* **IV**

Wimbledon [ˈwɪmbldən] **I**

York [jɔ:k] *Stadt im Norden Englands* ⟨**VI TS2**, 73⟩

## Geographical names

Africa [ˈæfrɪkə] Afrika **III**

Alabama [ˌæləˈbæmə] *US-amerik. Bundesstaat* **IV**

America [əˈmerɪkə] **II**

Antarctica [ænˈtɑ:ktɪkə] Antarktis **V**

Arizona [ˌærɪˈzəʊnə] *US-Bundesstaat* **IV**

Asia [ˈeɪʒə] Asien **V**

Atlantic Ocean [ətˌlæntɪk ˈəʊʃn] Atlantischer Ozean **III**

Australia [ɒsˈtreɪliə] Australien **II**

Austria [ˈɔ:striə] Österreich **II**

Ayers Rock [ˌeəz ˈrɒk] Ayers Rock (*= Uluru, heiliger Berg der Aborigines*) **V**

Bangladesh [ˌbæŋɡləˈdeʃ] Bangladesch **IV**

Bavaria [bəˈveəriə] Bayern **VI U1**, 12

Big Sur [ˌbɪɡ ˈsɜ:] *Küstenstreifen in Kalifornien* **VI U2**, 45

Brazil [brəˈzɪl] Brasilien **VI U2**, 50

Britain [ˈbrɪtn] Großbritannien **I**

British Columbia [ˌbrɪtɪʃ kəˈlʌmbiə] *kanadische Provinz* **V**

British Empire [ˌbrɪtɪʃ ˈempaɪə] *britisches Königreich* **II**

British Isles [ˌbrɪtɪʃ ˈaɪlz] Britische Inseln **III**

California [ˌkælɪˈfɔ:niə] Kalifornien (*US-amerik. Bundesstaat*) **IV**

Canada [ˈkænədə] Kanada **I**

China [ˈtʃaɪnə] China **I**

Cornwall [ˈkɔ:nwɔ:l] **III**

Cuba [ˈkju:bə] Kuba **IV**

Egypt [ˈi:dʒɪpt] Ägypten **IV**

England [ˈɪŋɡlənd] England **I**

Europe [ˈjʊərəp] Europa **V**

European Union (EU) [ˌjʊərəpiən ˈju:njən (i:ju:)] Europäische Union **II**

Florida [ˈflɒrɪdə] *US-amerikan. Bundesstaat* ⟨**VI TS2**, 73⟩

France [frɑ:ns] Frankreich **II**

Germany [ˈdʒɜ:məni] Deutschland **I**

Great Britain (GB) [ˌɡreɪt ˈbrɪtn] Großbritannien **III**

India [ˈɪndiə] Indien **II**

Iraq [ɪˈrɑ:k] Irak **V**

Ireland [ˈaɪələnd] Irland **V**

Israel [ˈɪzreɪl] Israel **V**

Italy [ˈɪtəli] Italien **II**

Ivory Coast [ˌaɪvri ˈkəʊst] Elfenbeinküste **VI U1**, 13

Japan [dʒəˈpæn] Japan **VI U2**, 50

Kenya [ˈkenjə] Kenia **IV**

Latin America [ˌlætɪn əˈmerɪkə] Lateinamerika **IV**

Loch Ness [ˌlɒx ˈnes; ˌlɒk ˈnes] *See in Schottland* **III**

Maryland [ˈmeərɪlænd] *US-amerik. Bundesstaat* **V**

Mexico [ˈmeksɪkəʊ] Mexiko **V**

(the) Midwest [ˌmɪdˈwest] (der) Mittlere Westen **IV**

Milwaukee [mɪlˈwɔ:ki] *US-amerik. Bundesstaat* **V**

Missouri [mɪˈzʊəri] *US-amerik. Bundesstaat* **V**

Montana [mɒnˈtænə] *US-amerik. Bundesstaat* **V**

New Jersey [ˌnju: ˈdʒɜ:zi] *US-amerik. Bundesstaat* **V**

New Mexico [ˌnju: ˈmeksɪkəʊ] *US-amerik. Bundesstaat* **IV**

New Zealand [ˌnju: ˈzi:lənd] Neuseeland **V**

North Sea [ˌnɔ:θ ˈsi:] Nordsee **III**

Northern Ireland [ˌnɔ:ðn ˈaɪələnd] Nordirland **III**

Oregon [ˈɒrɪɡən] *US-amerik. Bundesstaat* **V**

Oxfordshire [ˈɒksfədʃə] **VI TS2**, 69

the Pacific Northwest [ðə pəˌsɪfɪk nɔ:θˈwest] Pazifischer Nordwesten **IV**

Pennsylvania [ˌpensɪlˈveɪniə] *US-amerik. Bundesstaat* **V**

Poland [ˈpəʊlənd] Polen **I**

Queensland [ˈkwi:nzlənd] *Staat in Australien* **V**

Republic of Ireland [rɪˌpʌblɪk əv ˈaɪələnd] Republik Irland **III**

the Rockies (= the Rocky Mountains) [ðə ˈrɒkiz] *Gebirge in the USA* **IV**

Russia [ˈrʌʃə] Russland **IV**

Scandinavia [ˌskændɪˈneɪviə] Skandinavien **III**

Scotland [ˈskɒtlənd] Schottland **III**

Somalia [səˈmɑ:liə] Somalia **IV**

South Africa [ˌsaʊθ ˈæfrɪkə] Südafrika **II**

Soviet Union [ˌsəʊviət ˈju:njən] Sowjetunion **IV**

Spain [speɪn] Spanien **II**

Sweden [ˈswi:dn] Schweden **IV**

Thailand [ˈtaɪlænd] Thailand ⟨**VI TS2**, 73⟩

Thames [temz] **I**

Uluru [u:ˈlu:ru:] Uluru (= Ayers Rock, heiliger Berg der Aborigines) **V**

United Kingdom (UK) [ju:ˈkeɪ] Vereinigtes Königreich von Großbritannien und Nordirland **I**

the US (= the United States) [ðə ju:ˈes] die USA (= die Vereinigten Staaten) **IV**

USA (United States of America) [ˌju:esˈeɪ (juːˌnaɪtɪd ˌsteɪts əv əˈmerɪkə)] USA (Vereinigte Staaten von Amerika) **II**

Vietnam [ˌvjetˈnæm] Vietnam **V**

Virginia [vəˈdʒɪnjə] *US-amerik. Bundesstaat* **V**

Wales [weɪlz] **II**

Washington State [ˌwɒʃɪŋtən ˈsteɪt] *US-Bundesstaat* **IV**

Wisconsin [wɪˈskɒnsɪn] *US-amerik. Bundesstaat* **IV**

Wyoming [waɪˈəʊmɪŋ] *US-amerik. Bundesstaat* **V**

## Other names

1984 [ˌnaɪntiˈneɪtiˈfɔ:] *Buchtitel* **VI U1**, 27

Allegro [əˈleɡrəʊ] **VI U1**, 18

Arminder Singh Dhillon [ˌɑ:mɪndə ˌsɪŋ drˈlɒn] *britischer Erfinder* **VI U1**, 18

the BBC [ðə ˌbi:bi:ˈsi:] *britische Rundfunkanstalt* **VI TS1**, 37

Big Ben [ˌbɪɡ ˈben] **II**

Bixby Bridge [ˌbɪksbi ˈbrɪdʒ] *Stahlbeton-Bogenbrücke in Kalifornien* **VI U2**, 45

Bollywood [ˈbɒliwʊd] Bollywood (*indische Filmindustrie: Bombay + Hollywood*) **V**

Brian Malarkey [ˌbraɪən məˈlɑ:ki] **VI U2**, 58

Buckingham Palace [ˌbʌkɪŋəm ˈpælɪs] **II**

Cafazine [ˌkæfəˈzi:n] *Name eines Cafés* ⟨**VI U2**, 60⟩

Capital City Academy (CCA) [ˌkæpɪtl ˌsɪti əˈkædəmi] *Schule in London* ⟨**VI TS1**, 39⟩

Census Bureau [ˈsensəs ˌbjʊərəʊ] *US-amerik. Bundesbehörde für Volkszählung* **V**

Central Plaza [ˌsentrl ˈplɑ:zə] ⟨**VI U1**, 25⟩

Childwise [ˈtʃaɪldwaɪz] *Forschungsinstitut* ⟨**VI TS1**, 39⟩

Cisco Systems [ˌsɪskəʊ ˈsɪstəmz] *US-amerikan. Unternehmen aus der Telekommunikationsbranche* **VI U2**, 51

Daily News [ˌdeɪli ˈnju:z] *Name einer Tageszeitung* **VI TS1**, 35

Dragons' Den [ˌdræɡnz ˈden] **VI U1**, 18

El Dorado [ˌel dəˈrɑ:dəʊ] **VI U2**, 50

En Vogue [en ˈvəʊɡ] *Bandname* **VI AC1**, 40

Giants [ˈdʒaɪənts] *Name eines Baseballteams* **VI U2**, 57

Hollywood Boulevard [ˌhɒliwʊd ˈbu:ləvɑ:d] *Straße in Los Angeles* **VI U2**, 44 the **Houses of Parliament** [ðə ˌhaʊzɪzˌəv ˈpɑːləmənt] *britisches Parlamentsgebäude* **II**

**The Hunger Games** [ðə ˈhʌŋgə ˌgeɪmz] *Buchtitel* **VI U1**, 27

**Independence Day** [ˌɪndɪˈpendəns ˌdeɪ] *amerikanischer Unabhängigkeitstag* **IV**

**Industrial Revolution** [ɪnˌdʌstrɪəl revlˈuːʃn] *die industrielle Revolution* **III**

**Jackie Robinson** [ˌdʒæki ˈrɒbɪnsn] *US-amerik. Baseballspieler* **VI U2**, 58

**New York Weekly** [ˌnjuː ˈjɔːk ˈwiːkli] *US-Wochenzeitung* ⟨**VI U2**, 60⟩

**Ne-Yo** [ˈniːjəʊ] *US-amerik. Sänger* ⟨**VI U1**, 7⟩

**Nikon** [ˈnɪkɒn] *finnisches Technologieunternehmen* ⟨**VI U2**, 60⟩

**OG** [əʊˈdʒiː] **IV**

**Oracle** [ˈɒrəkl] *US-amerikan. Soft- und Hardwarehersteller* **VI U2**, 51

**Orlando Cepeda** [ɔːˌlændəʊ səˈpiːdə] *US-amerik. Baseballspieler* **VI U2**, 58

**Oz** *(coll)* [ɒz] *Oz (Spitzname für Australien)* **V**

**Pledge of Allegiance** [ˌpledʒ ˌəv əˈliːdʒns] *Treueeid auf die amerikanische Flagge* **IV**

**Redhatch Road** [ˌredhætʃ ˈrəʊd] **VI U1**, 10

**Revolutionary War** [revlˌuːʃnri ˈwɔː] *Amerikanischer Unabhängigkeitskrieg* **V**

**Statue of Liberty** [ˌstætʃuːˌəv ˈlɪbəti] *Freiheitsstatue* **IV**

**Supreme Court** [suːˌpriːm ˈkɔːt] *Oberster Gerichtshof* **V**

**Thanksgiving** [ˌθæŋksˈgɪvɪŋ] *amerik. Erntedankfest* **IV**

**The Real Housewives of Orange County** [ˌðə rɪəl ˌhaʊswaɪvzˌəv ˌɒrɪndʒ ˈkaʊnti] *Name einer Fernsehsendung* **VI U2**, 58

**The Taste** [ðə ˈteɪst] *Name einer Fernsehsendung* **VI U2**, 58

**Thirsty Merc** [ˌθɜːsti ˈmɜːk] *australische Band* ⟨**VI U1**, 7⟩

**Top Chef** [ˌtɒp ˈʃef] *Name einer Kochsendung* **VI U2**, 58

**Top Chef Masters** [ˌtɒp ʃef ˈmɑːstəz] *Name einer Kochsendung* **VI U2**, 58

**Vine Street** [ˈvaɪn striːt] *Straße in Los Angeles* **VI U2**, 49

**Walk of Fame** [ˌwɔːkˌəv ˈfeɪm] **VI U2**, 49

**Whiteleaf** [ˈwaɪtliːf] **VI U1**, 10

**Wikipedia** [ˌwɪkɪˈpiːdiə] **VI U2**, 58

the **World Series** [ˌwɜːld ˈsɪəriːz] *jährliches Endspiel zwischen den Gewinnern der beiden großen Baseballligen in den USA* **VI U2**, 58

**World War I** [ˌwɜːld ˌwɔː ˈwʌn] *Erster Weltkrieg* **V**

**World War II** [ˌwɜːld ˌwɔː ˈtuː] *Zweiter Weltkrieg* **II**

**Yosemite National Park** [jəʊˌsemɪti ˌnæʃnl ˈpɑːk] **VI U2**, 55

## Famous names

**Alison Lurie** [ˌælɪsn ˈlʊəri] *US-amerik. Schriftstellerin* **VI U2**, 45

**Annie Leibovitz** [ˌæni ˈliːbəvɪts] *bekannte Fotografin* ⟨**VI U2**, 62⟩

**Arnold Schwarzenegger** [ˌɑːnld ˈʃwɔːtsnegə] *38. Gouverneur Kaliforniens (2003–2011)* **VI U2**, 45

**Bobby Slayton** [ˌbɒbi ˈsleɪtən] *US-amerik. Schauspieler* **VI U2**, 45

**Carl Laemmle** [ˌkɑːl ˈlæmlə] *Gründer der Universal Studios* **VI U2**, 49

**Christopher Columbus** [ˌkrɪstəfə kəˈlʌmbəs] **V**

**Edward Abbey** [ˌedwəd ˈæbi] *US-amerik. Schriftsteller* **VI U2**, 45

**Elizabeth I** [ɪˌlɪzəbəθ ðə ˈfɜːst] **II**

**Franklin D. Roosevelt** [ˌfræŋklɪn diː ˈrəʊzəvelt] *32. Präsident der USA* **V**

**George Orwell** [ˌdʒɔːdʒ ˈɔːwel] *englischer Schriftsteller* **VI U1**, 27

**George Washington** [ˌdʒɔːdʒ ˈwɒʃɪŋtən] *1. Präsident der USA* **V**

**Henry VIII** [ˌhenri ði ˈeɪtθ] *Heinrich VIII.* **III**

**Jacob Davis** [ˌdʒeɪkəb ˈdeɪvɪz] *US-amerik. Schneider* **VI U2**, 52

**Jimmy Carter** [ˌdʒɪmi ˈkɑːtə] *39. Präsident der USA* **VI U2**, 45

**John F. Kennedy** (JFK) [ˌdʒɒnˌef ˈkenədi; dʒeɪˌef keɪ] *35. Präsident der USA* **IV**

**Levi Strauss** [ˌliːvaɪ ˈstraʊs] *Erfinder der Jeans* **VI U2**, 52

**Lois Lowry** [ˌləʊɪs ˈlaʊri] *US-amerik. Schriftstellerin* ⟨**VI U1**, 26⟩

**Lyndon B. Johnson** [ˌlɪndn biː ˈdʒɒnsn] *36. Präsident der USA* **V**

**Mark Twain** [ˌmɑːk ˈtweɪn] *US-amerik. Schriftsteller* **VI U2**, 51

**Nelson Mandela** [ˌnelsn mænˈdelə] *1. südafrikan. Präsident nach Abschaffung der Apartheid* **V**

**Pink** [pɪŋk] *US-amerik. Sängerin* **VI U2**, 45

**Suzanne Collins** [suːˌzæn ˈkɒlɪnz] *US-amerik. Schriftstellerin* **VI U1**, 27

**Thomas Jefferson** [ˌtɒməs ˈdʒefəsn] *3. Präsident der USA* **V**

**William Shakespeare** [ˌwɪljəm ˈʃeɪkspɪə] *englischer Dramatiker (1564–1616)* **III**

> **Tip**
>
> Die Wörter und Ausdrücke auf diesen Seiten musst du nicht auswendig lernen. Aber in vielen Situationen im Klassenzimmer wirst du sie nützlich finden!

## Vocabulary for instructions and activities

(Die mit * gekennzeichneten Begriffe werden im Fachlehrplan von mindestens einem Bundesland als Operatoren definiert. Die Verwendung der geforderten Operatoren in *Green Line* beginnt in Band 1 und wird Band für Band ausgebaut.)

| | |
|---|---|
| Act (out) one of the scenes / the dialogues. | Spiele eine der Szenen / die Dialoge vor. |
| Add more words / ideas. | Füge weitere Wörter / Ideen hinzu. |
| ***Analyse** the text. | Analysiere den Text. |
| Ask your partner questions. | Stelle deinem Partner / deiner Partnerin Fragen. |
| Answer your partner's questions. | Beantworte die Fragen deines Partners / deiner Partnerin. |
| ***Characterise** the protagonist. | Charakterisiere die Hauptfigur. |
| Choose a character / one of the situations / options. | Wähle eine Figur / eine der Situationen / Optionen aus. |
| ***Comment** on the statistics. | Kommentiere die Statistik. |
| ***Compare** English and German. | Vergleiche das Englische und das Deutsche. |
| Complete the answers. | Vervollständige die Antworten. |
| ***Contrast** the situation of the two teenagers. | Stelle die Situation der beiden Teenager einander gegenüber. |
| Copy the grid / the mind map. | Schreibe die Tabelle / die Mindmap ab. |
| Correct the wrong sentences. | Korrigiere die falschen Sätze. |
| ***Describe** what you see / how it makes you feel. | Beschreibe, was du siehst / wie du dich dabei fühlst. |
| ***Discuss** different ideas. | Diskutiert verschiedene Ideen. |
| Divide up into two groups. | Teilt euch in zwei Gruppen auf. |
| ***Evaluate** the advert. | Bewerte die Anzeige. |
| ***Examine** the author's intention. | Untersuche die Absicht des Autors. |
| Exchange your flyers / questions. | Tauscht eure Flyer / Fragen untereinander aus. |
| ***Explain** your answer. / Explain why. | Erkläre deine Antwort. / Erkläre warum. |
| Fill in the grid / the form. | Fülle die Tabelle / das Formular aus. |
| Finish your brochure. | Mache deine Broschüre fertig. |
| Form expert groups. | Bildet Expertengruppen. |
| Get organised. | Organisiert euch. |
| Give reasons / examples. | Nenne Gründe / Beispiele. |
| Give feedback. | Gib ein Feedback. |

| | |
|---|---|
| Guess the new words. | Errate die neuen Wörter. |
| ***Illustrate** the main points of the text. | Veranschauliche die Hauptpunkte des Textes. |
| Improve your text / part of the report. | Verbessere deinen Text / deinen Teil des Berichts. |
| ***Interpret** the information. | Interpretiere die Informationen. |
| ***Justify** your answer. | Begründe deine Antwort. |
| Listen to the sentences / the dialogue. | Höre dir die Sätze / den Dialog an. |
| ***Look up** the words. | Schlage die Wörter nach. |
| Make a poster / a grid / a mind map / notes. | Fertige ein Poster / eine Tabelle / eine Mindmap / Notizen an. |
| ***Match** the sentence parts. | Ordne die Satzteile einander zu. |
| Note down what is missing. | Notiere, was fehlt. |
| ***Outline** the Information given in the text. | Skizziere die im Text enthaltenen Informationen. |
| Practise your scenes / the dialogues. | Übe deine Szenen / die Dialoge. |
| ***Point out** what you find interesting. | Lege dar, was du interessant findest. |
| ***Present** the information from your text. | Präsentiere die Informationen aus deinem Text. |
| Put in the correct forms. | Setze die richtigen Formen ein. |
| Put the verbs in the right / correct form. | Bringe die Verben in die richtige Form. |
| Read your text aloud. / Read your text out loud. | Lies deinen Text laut vor. |
| Record your final report / dialogue. | Nehmt euren fertigen Bericht / Dialog auf. |
| Repeat the sentences / the dialogues. | Wiederhole die Sätze / die Dialoge. |
| ***Report** what the people say. | Berichte, was die Leute sagen. |
| Scan the text for details. | Suche den Text nach Details ab. |
| Share the information with your partner. | Teile die Informationen mit deinem Partner / deiner Partnerin. |
| ***Show** what the letter is about. | Zeige, worum es in dem Brief geht. |
| Skim the text for the gist. | Überfliege den Text und finde die wichtigsten Aussagen. |
| ***State** your reaction to the story. | Lege deine Reaktion auf die Geschichte dar. |
| ***Sum up / Summarise** what happens in the story. | Fasse zusammen, was in der Geschichte passiert. |
| Swap roles. | Tauscht die Rollen. |
| Take notes. | Mache dir Notizen. |
| Take turns. | Wechselt euch ab. |
| ***Talk** with / to your partner (about …). | Sprich mit deinem Partner / deiner Partnerin (über …). |
| ***Tell** your partner about your experiences. | Erzähle deinem Partner / deiner Partnerin von deinen Erfahrungen. |
| Think about different problems. | Denke über verschiedene Probleme nach. |
| ***Translate** the words / sentences. | Übersetze die Wörter / Sätze. |
| Underline the words that change. | Unterstreiche die Wörter, die sich ändern. |
| Use the ideas / the vocabulary. | Verwende die Ideen / die Vokabeln. |
| Work with a partner or in a group. | Arbeite mit einem Partner / einer Partnerin oder in einer Gruppe. |
| ***Write** dialogues / a short text / a reply / a summary. | Schreibe Dialoge / einen kurzen Text / eine Antwort / eine Zusammenfassung. |
| Write about your friends. | Schreibe über deine Freunde. |
| Write down your ideas / key words. | Schreibe deine Ideen / Schlüsselwörter auf. |

**Find more online:**
5qu7af

■ ■ ■ Grundform, *simple past* und *past participle* sind identisch
■ ■ ● Grundform unterscheidet sich vom *simple past* und *past participle*
■ ● ■ Grundform und *past participle* sind identisch, nur das *simple past* hat eine andere Form
■ ● ▲ Grundform, *simple past* und *past participle* haben alle eine andere Form

| ■ Grundform | ■ simple past | ■ past participle | Deutsch |
|---|---|---|---|
| bet [bet] | bet [bet] | bet [bet] | wetten |
| burst [bɜːst] | burst [bɜːst] | burst [bɜːst] | bersten; platzen |
| cost [kɒst] | cost [kɒst] | cost [kɒst] | kosten |
| cut [kʌt] | cut [kʌt] | cut [kʌt] | schneiden |
| hit [hɪt] | hit [hɪt] | hit [hɪt] | schlagen, treffen |
| hurt [hɜːt] | hurt [hɜːt] | hurt [hɜːt] | verletzen, sich weh tun |
| let [let] | let [let] | let [let] | lassen |
| put [pʊt] | put [pʊt] | put [pʊt] | legen, setzen, stellen |
| spread [spred] | spread [spred] | spread [spred] | (sich) verbreiten |

| ■ Grundform | ● simple past | ● past participle | Deutsch |
|---|---|---|---|
| bring [brɪŋ] | brought [brɔːt] | brought [brɔːt] | (mit)bringen |
| build [bɪld] | built [bɪlt] | built [bɪlt] | bauen |
| burn [bɜːn] | burnt [bɜːnt] / burned [bɜːnd] | burnt [bɜːnt] / burned [bɜːnd] | (ver)brennen |
| buy [baɪ] | bought [bɔːt] | bought [bɔːt] | kaufen |
| catch [kætʃ] | caught [kɔːt] | caught [kɔːt] | fangen; mitbekommen |
| dream [driːm] | dreamt [dremt] / dreamed [driːmd] | dreamt [dremt] / dreamed [driːmd] | träumen |
| feel [fiːl] | felt [felt] | felt [felt] | fühlen |
| find [faɪnd] | found [faʊnd] | found [faʊnd] | finden |
| get [get] | got [gɒt] | got [gɒt] / gotten ['gɒtn] | bekommen; werden |
| hang [hæŋ] | hung [hʌŋ] | hung [hʌŋ] | hängen |
| have [hæv] | had [hæd] | had [hæd] | haben |
| hear [hɪə] | heard [hɜːd] | heard [hɜːd] | hören |
| hold [həʊld] | held [held] | held [held] | halten |
| keep [kiːp] | kept [kept] | kept [kept] | (auf)bewahren, behalten |
| lead [liːd] | led [led] | led [led] | (an)führen |
| lean [liːn] | leant [lent] / leaned [liːnd] | leant [lent] / leaned [liːnd] | (sich) lehnen |
| learn [lɜːn] | learnt [lɜːnt] / learned [lɜːnd] | learnt [lɜːnt] / learned [lɜːnd] | lernen |
| leave [liːv] | left [left] | left [left] | (ver)lassen |
| lend [lend] | lent [lent] | lent [lent] | (ver)leihen |
| make [meɪk] | made [meɪd] | made [meɪd] | machen, tun |
| meet [miːt] | met [met] | met [met] | treffen |
| pay [peɪ] | paid [peɪd] | paid [peɪd] | (be)zahlen |
| read [riːd] | read [red] | read [red] | lesen |
| say [seɪ] | said [sed] | said [sed] | sagen |
| sell [sel] | sold [səʊld] | sold [səʊld] | verkaufen |
| send [send] | sent [sent] | sent [sent] | senden, verschicken |
| shoot [ʃuːt] | shot [ʃɒt] | shot [ʃɒt] | schießen (auf) |
| sit [sɪt] | sat [sæt] | sat [sæt] | sitzen |
| sleep [sliːp] | slept [slept] | slept [slept] | schlafen |
| smell [smel] | smelt [smelt] | smelt [smelt] | riechen, duften |

| | | | |
|---|---|---|---|
| spell [spel] | spelt [spelt] | spelt [spelt] | buchstabieren |
| spend [spend] | spent [spent] | spent [spent] | ausgeben, verbringen |
| spill [spɪl] | spilt [spɪlt] | spilt [spɪlt] | verschütten, auslaufen |
| stand (up) [stænd] | stood (up) [stʊd] | stood (up) [stʊd] | (auf)stehen |
| sting [stɪŋ] | stung [stʌŋ] | stung [stʌŋ] | stechen |
| teach [ti:tʃ] | taught [tɔ:t] | taught [tɔ:t] | lehren, unterrichten |
| tell [tel] | told [təʊld] | told [təʊld] | erzählen |
| think [θɪŋk] | thought [θɔ:t] | thought [θɔ:t] | (nach)denken, glauben |
| understand [ˌʌndəˈstænd] | understood [ˌʌndəˈstʊd] | understood [ˌʌndəˈstʊd] | verstehen |
| win [wɪn] | won [wʌn] | won [wʌn] | gewinnen, siegen |

| ■ Grundform | ● simple past | ■ past participle | Deutsch |
|---|---|---|---|
| become [bɪˈkʌm] | became [bɪˈkeɪm] | become [bɪˈkʌm] | werden |
| come [kʌm] | came [keɪm] | come [kʌm] | kommen |
| run [rʌn] | ran [ræn] | run [rʌn] | laufen, rennen |

| ■ Grundform | ● simple past | ▲ past participle | Deutsch |
|---|---|---|---|
| be [bi:] | was / were [wɒz / wɜ:] | been [bi:n] | sein |
| blow (out) [bləʊ] | blew [blu:] | blown [bləʊn] | (aus)blasen, (aus)pusten |
| break [breɪk] | broke [brəʊk] | broken [ˈbrəʊkn] | (zer)brechen, kaputt machen |
| choose [tʃu:z] | chose [tʃəʊz] | chosen [tʃəʊzn] | (aus)wählen |
| do [du:] | did [dɪd] | done [dʌn] | machen, tun |
| draw [drɔ:] | drew [dru:] | drawn [drɔ:n] | zeichnen |
| drink [drɪŋk] | drank [dræŋk] | drunk [drʌŋk] | trinken |
| drive [draɪv] | drove [drəʊv] | driven [ˈdrɪvn] | fahren |
| eat [i:t] | ate [et] | eaten [i:tn] | essen |
| fall [fɔ:l] | fell [fel] | fallen [ˈfɔ:lən] | fallen |
| fly [flaɪ] | flew [flu:] | flown [fləʊn] | fliegen |
| forget [fəˈget] | forgot [fəˈgɒt] | forgotten [fəˈgɒtn] | vergessen |
| give [gɪv] | gave [geɪv] | given [ˈgɪvn] | geben |
| go [gəʊ] | went [went] | gone [gɒn] | gehen, fahren |
| grow [grəʊ] | grew [gru:] | grown [grəʊn] | wachsen; anbauen |
| know [nəʊ] | knew [nju:] | known [nəʊn] | kennen, wissen |
| ring [rɪŋ] | rang [ræŋ] | rung [rʌŋ] | klingeln; anrufen |
| rise [raɪz] | rose [rəʊz] | risen [ˈrɪzn] | steigen, sich erheben |
| see [si:] | saw [sɔ:] | seen [si:n] | sehen |
| shake [ʃeɪk] | shook [ʃʊk] | shaken [ˈʃeɪkn] | schütteln |
| show [ʃəʊ] | showed [ʃəʊd] | shown [ʃəʊn] | zeigen |
| sing [sɪŋ] | sang [sæŋ] | sung [sʌŋ] | singen |
| sink [sɪŋk] | sank [sæŋk] | sunk [sʌŋk] | sinken, untergehen |
| speak [spi:k] | spoke [spəʊk] | spoken [ˈspəʊkn] | sprechen |
| swim [swɪm] | swam [swæm] | swum [swʌm] | schwimmen |
| take [teɪk] | took [tʊk] | taken [ˈteɪkn] | nehmen |
| throw [θrəʊ] | threw [θru:] | thrown [θrəʊn] | werfen |
| wake up [ˌweɪkˈʌp] | woke up [ˌwəʊkˈʌp] | woken up [ˌwəʊknˈʌp] | aufwachen; aufwecken |
| wear [weə] | wore [wɔ:] | worn [wɔ:n] | anhaben, tragen |
| write [raɪt] | wrote [rəʊt] | written [ˈrɪtn] | schreiben |

# Grammar solutions

## Unit 1

### G1  How to sound more formal

1. Being a camp counsellor gives you an opportunity to lead groups, take on responsibility and to build your self-confidence. **Moreover**, it looks great on your CV. – Tom
2. **Personally**, I think that working as an assistant camp counsellor at a summer camp is the best experience any teenager can have. – Jane
3. It was really hard work. **In fact**, it was **probably** the hardest job I've ever had to do! – Brian
4. Spending 24 hours a day with a group of active young kids can be exhausting. **Nevertheless**, I wouldn't have missed the experience for the world. – Sarah
5. You don't have to be crazy to work as a camp counsellor, but it helps! It was the most amazing job I've ever had and I had a fantastic time. **Hopefully**, I can go back for more next year! – Marco

### G2  I watched the kids ...

1. He always arrives really late for work and then he leaves early. Yesterday I saw him **arrive** at 9:30, **hang** his jacket on the chair, then **leave** again.
2. He prefers magazines to company reports. Today I noticed him **reading** a car magazine.
3. And he makes a lot of personal phone calls. This morning I was walking past his office when I heard him **telling** somebody all about his last holiday.
4. He also takes other people's equipment without asking. Yesterday I watched him **pick up** a pen from his colleague's desk, quickly **put** it into his pocket and then **walk away**.
5. Our boss isn't happy with him. As I was walking past her office today, I could hear her **shouting** at him.

### G3  They arrived feeling exhausted

After a busy morning at work yesterday, I decided to spend my lunch break relaxing on the beach. But as I **lay reading** quietly, I soon **found myself wondering** if I had made the right choice. There weren't many people on the beach, just a few dog-walkers and two girls who were chatting quietly nearby as they **sat eating** ice creams. Then suddenly a large dog **came running** towards the two girls. He was barking loudly and the girls were scared. So they began to scream. When that didn't help, they threw stones. A moment later, the dog's owner **arrived shouting** angrily at the two girls. Then he **caught me watching** the drama, so he started shouting at me too! I **came hoping** for some peace on the beach. I **left thinking** the world had gone crazy!

### G4  The Words-of-Wisdom Wall

I was walking past the pet shop, **which** I often do on my way into town, when I noticed a job advert in the window. They were looking for a student **who** could help them on Saturdays. It seemed the perfect job for me, so I went in. The shop manager, **who** was really busy, quickly explained everything **(that)** I needed to know and then offered me the position. I liked the other people **who** worked there and I liked the job. But it was *hard*. When the shop was full of people, **which** it usually was, it was difficult to find time to take a break. And the money **(that)** I earned wasn't enough for the hours **(which)** I had to put in. – Dan

### G5  Not only was it super cold, but ...

**No way should people** be allowed to use mobile phones in public places. **Not only do they** make lots of noise, **but** they also force others to listen to their private conversations. Yesterday a woman on my bus talked non-stop. **Hardly had she** finished one call **when** she started again. **Never have I** heard such silly, unnecessary conversations! I was glad when she got off the bus. **Only then was I** able to read my book in peace.

### G6  I do remember how it feels ...

1. I'm surprised. I do look really good in grey!
2. I do hope that you get the job.
3. So you did meet Tom yesterday!
4. You're right. The milk does taste strange.
5. I do know what you mean, but that isn't true / you're wrong.
6. Do let me know if I can bring you some more coffee.
7. She's heard so many good things about you and really does want to meet you!
8. Good evening, I'm glad you could come! Please do come in, the others are already here.
9. Mr Braxton, you do know that one should / that you should never be late for a job interview, but nevertheless you were late / you arrived late / you came late.
10. You didn't really enjoy yourself at the party. – No, I did enjoy myself. I just had to leave early.

## Unit 2

### G7  It starts at 8:00 but we're meeting at 6:00

Ella:  What **are you doing** tomorrow?
Mia:  I'm **meeting** my cousin at the new shopping mall. It **opens** tomorrow at 10:00. Why don't you come with us?
Ella:  That sounds like a great idea. How **are you getting** there?
Mia:  By bus or by subway. I haven't decided yet. The bus is cheaper but it **leaves** earlier and it **takes** a lot longer.
Ella:  I've got a better idea. My brother **is driving** into town tomorrow morning. I'm sure he won't mind taking us with him. But let me ask him first what time he **is going**.

### G8  What will Alex be doing by the time he's 30?

On Monday morning Alex **will be meeting** his agent. In the afternoon he**'ll be writing** a movie review for the internet. On Tuesday he**'ll be going** to an audition. On Wednesday he**'ll be interviewing** stars at a movie premiere on Hollywood Boulevard. On Thursday he**'ll be visiting** his buddy Dave. And on Friday his parents **will be coming** for the weekend so he**'ll be picking** them up from the airport.

### G9  What will Alex have done by the time he's 30?

I really hope that by the time people read my blog I**'ll have gotten** my big break and that I**'ll be living** my dream. In six months' time, I'm sure I**'ll have become** a star and the reporters **will be wanting** to interview me. Then of course I'll be friendly and polite, but I'll tell them never to call me before 11:00 because I **won't have got up** by then. I**'ll still be sleeping**.

### G10 California in the world

Sorry I didn't send you an e-mail earlier, but I was tired after all **the** fun we had at **the** movie premiere last night. When I got up, it was already 10:30. Then after (–) breakfast, I had to learn all about **the** history of California for **a** test on Wednesday. That took about **an** hour and **a** half. And I haven't even started to learn about **the** economy or **the** different landscapes yet. No, I haven't gone back to (–) college. **The** test is for a job with **the** Tourist Office. If I pass, I'll soon be able to work as **a** tour guide

two or three times **a** week in-between my auditions. But I've already heard it's pretty difficult and (–) most people have to take it at least twice, so I'm not very hopeful. I haven't found (–) fame as **an** actor yet. But I can honestly say that I've found (–) happiness. L.A. is such **a** fantastic city and I just love **the** excitement of living here. For me, it's simply **the** most exciting city in **the** US.

### G11  Should we be worried?

a)  1.  If Mrs. Kent is late today, we **are to** wait for her in the hall.    2.  Have you been to the new restaurant in West Street? It **is supposed to / is said to** be very good.    3.  The plane landed early. It **was supposed to** land at 8:30.    4.  If Lisa isn't feeling better soon, I think she **should / ought to** see a doctor.    5.  Are you hungry? **Shall** I make us a sandwich?    6.  We can take cell phones to school but we **aren't supposed** to use them in class.

b)  1.  We've got plenty of time. We **needn't / don't need to** hurry.    2.  It's not going to rain today, so we **won't need to** take an umbrella.    3.  There were no trains or buses to the village, so I **was forced to** take a taxi.    4.  There's no food in the cupboard. I**'ll need to** go shopping today.    5.  Sometimes we **must / are forced to** make difficult decisions. We have no choice.    6.  **Are** firefighters **obliged to / required to** rescue animals?

# Unit solutions

## Unit 1, Introduction → page 6, ex. 1c

*Explain if one of the photos below or the photo on p. 6 comes closer to your 'good life'.*

A

B

# A look at some career statistics

## The UK's best-paying jobs

The UK Office for National Statistics publishes yearly rankings[1] of average salaries in nearly 350 professions. Here are some of the top jobs, followed by others further down the list. (For comparison: In parts of London, renting a small flat can easily cost £25,000 a year.)

| Rank | English job title | German job title | Salary |
|---|---|---|---|
| 1 | chief executive / senior official | Geschäftsführer/-in; Firmenchef/-in | £ 118,065 |
| 2 | broker | Börsenmakler/-in | 116,104 |
| 3 | pilot | Pilot/-in | 86,342 |
| 4 | marketing / sales manager | Marketingleiter/-in; Vertriebsleiter/-in | 82,360 |
| 5 | financial institution manager | Direktor/-in eines Geldinstituts / einer Versicherung | 77,387 |
| 7 | air traffic controller | Fluglotse/-lotsin | 75,060 |
| 9 | medical practitioner (doctor) | Arzt / Ärztin | 72,315 |
| 10 | IT manager | IT-Experte / Expertin | 66,733 |
| 92 | secondary education teacher | Lehrer/-in Sekundarstufe I | 33,665 |
| 123 | web design professional | Webdesigner/-in | 30,339 |
| 135 | office manager | Büroleiter/-in; Chefsekretär/-in | 29,588 |
| 155 | business associate / professional | Bürokaufmann/-frau | 28,274 |
| 266 | secretary / personal assistant | Sekretär/-in; Assistent/-in | 19,295 |
| 291 | chef | Koch / Köchin | 17,531 |
| 339 | fitness instructor | Fitnesstrainer/-in | 11,054 |

Source: UK Office for National Statistics (2016)

## An alternative ranking: The UK's most satisfying[2] jobs

A study conducted by the Cabinet Office of the Prime Minister, however, shows that the most satisfying jobs aren't always those that pay the best:

| Rank | English job title | German job title | Salary |
|---|---|---|---|
| 1 | clergy member | Amtsträger/-in einer Kirche | £ 20,568 |
| 2 | chief executive / senior official | Geschäftsführer/-in; Firmenchef/-in | 118,065 |
| 3 | manager / proprietor in agriculture | Leiter/-in; Eigentümer/-in in der Agrarwirtschaft | 31,721 |
| 4 | secretary | Sekretär/-in | 19,295 |
| 5 | quality assurance professional | Experte / Expertin für Qualitätskontrolle | 42,898 |

Source: Cabinet Office (2014)

### Surprising facts
- The world average for women in high management positions is just 24%. Japan is near the bottom of the list at just 9%, the UK comes in at 20%, while Russia tops the list at 43%.
- In English, a 'manager' can be just about anything: a powerful businessperson who earns millions, or a person who runs a small shop.
- In the US, if your employer hands you a 'pink slip', it means you're losing your job. (A 'slip' is a piece of paper.)

**1 ranking** [ˈræŋkɪŋ] Rangliste | **2 satisfying** [ˈsætɪsfaɪɪŋ] zufriedenstellend; befriedigend

# Contrasts: San Francisco and Los Angeles

San Francisco, the Bay, the Golden Gate Bridge

Typical beach scene in Santa Monica, L.A.

## SAN FRANCISCO

**Population:** 860,000 (metro[1]: 4.6 million)
**Area:** 232 sq. mi (600 km²)
**Economic profile:** Long history as trade mecca (major port, railroad terminus); SF and nearby San José (= Silicon Valley) together form world capital of the IT / tech industry; tourism; wine country
**Important historical dates:**
- **Gold Rush:** Massive wealth discovered in the Bay Area, starting in 1849
- **Earthquake of 1906:** 80 % of city destroyed
- **'Summer of Love', 1967:** Heart of the world's alternative 'hippie' youth movement

## LOS ANGELES

**Population:** 3.9 million (metro: 13 million)
**Area:** 503 sq. mi (1,302 km²)
**Economic profile:** World capital of the entertainment industry (film, TV & music); massive suburban sprawl[2] due to booming economy and year-round good weather; tourism; trendsetter in fitness, lifestyle
**Important historical dates:**
- Host city for **Summer Olympics** in 1932, 1984
- Violent, large-scale **race riots** in 1965, 1992
- The first ARPANET transmission was sent from the University of California in 1969; the **internet** was born.

At first glance, California's two most famous cities couldn't be more different. Up in Northern California, there's San Francisco with its historical Victorian architecture, its lively downtown, and its liberal tradition as a mecca for alternative lifestyles. And of course it also has a 'nerdy' reputation as the world's capital of IT / tech innovation. Then there's L.A., in Southern California, where the huge and powerful entertainment industry gives the city a sexy, glamorous, body-conscious[3] image as a place to be. But 'city' isn't really the right term here: L.A. is more like a collection of endless communities with no real centre for city life.

But a second glance might reveal that the two cities are just two sides of the same coin: Both are a magnet for Americans and foreigners who want to live their own 'California dream' in places of great natural beauty, with strong economies, and with residents who love the relaxed, freetime-oriented lifestyle that California invented.

**Surprising facts**
- It's about 200 km from one end of metropolitan L.A. to the other – the same distance as from Frankfurt to Stuttgart.
- The weather in San Francisco can get very cool in summer: First-time tourists are often surprised to find they need a jacket in July or August.

---

**1 metro** ['metrəʊ] Großraum- | **2 sprawl** [sprɔːl] Ausdehnung | **3 body-conscious** ['bɒdi ˌkɒnʃəs] körperbewusst

# The UK Parliament today

## House of Commons

One elected Member of Parliament (MP) for each of about 650 constituencies. Each MP has to be elected directly by the voters of a constituency. The candidate with the most votes in each constituency becomes its MP.

## House of Lords

About 800 non-elected members. Most are appointed; about 90 members, however, are hereditary peers. There is now a strong movement in the House of Commons to allow only elected Lords (except the Law Lords).

### The Sovereign
represents the country as Head of State

appoints

### The Cabinet
governs/decides policies
**Prime Minister**
Ministers

Archbishops, bishops and life peers appointed by Sovereign on recommendation of Prime Minister

need confidence of

can dissolve

### House of Lords
about 800 Lords; mostly appointed

### House of Commons
about 650 MPs; make laws

can delay legislation

The people

elect a government for a maximum period of five years. The candidate who polls the most votes in a constituency is elected Member of Parliament in the House of Commons.

# A history of Parliament

 **1**

John, who became King of England in 1199, was unsuccessful in war. He lost most of his land in France. He asked his barons to give him more money, but they refused. When he tried to make them pay heavy taxes, they rebelled. In 1215 they formed an army, captured London and forced John to sign a treaty. It was called Magna Carta and is one of the most important documents in English history.

 **2**

Most people at that time were not rich barons and churchmen, but poor peasants working on the barons' land. Magna Carta did not mention them. But the document was important because it did limit the king's power. Also, it formed the basis for the first Parliament, which was called by Edward I in 1295. This became known as the Model Parliament because it had so many of the features of later Parliaments.

 **3**

King James II became king in 1685. He tried to rule alone, so Parliament invited James's daughter Mary and her Dutch husband William of Orange to come to England as King and Queen. Nobody wanted to fight for James, so it was a Glorious (and Bloodless) Revolution. William and Mary had to sign a document called the Bill Of Rights (1689), which made sure that Parliament was more important than the monarch.

**Important articles from Magna Carta**

- The English Church shall be free to choose its own bishops.
- No special taxes can be created unless the barons meet and agree to them.
- Freemen should only be imprisoned if they have had a proper trial.
- The barons shall choose 25 representatives to check that the king does not break these rules.

**The Lords**
- Barons
- Bishops
- Abbots

**The King**
- Parliament only met when the king wanted it to.
- Parliament could not tell the king what to do, but it could stop taxes if it disagreed with them.

**The Commons**
Representatives of the
- towns/boroughs
- knights

**Bill of Rights**
- Parliament, not the monarch, passes laws and decides on taxes.
- Parliament keeps a check on the army.
- MPs have absolute freedom of speech.

# The American government today

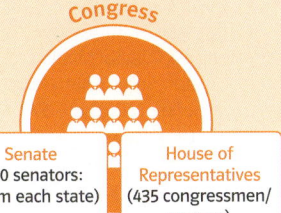

## Congress

| Senate (100 senators: 2 from each state) | House of Representatives (435 congressmen/women) |

- can impeach and remove the president.
- may ignore the president's veto.
- The Senate approves the appointment of members of the Supreme Court.
- The Senate approves treaties made by the president.

## The President

- controls foreign policy and makes treaties.
- may veto laws made by Congress.
- can recommend laws.
- appoints members of the Supreme Court; confirmation by the Senate is required.

## The Supreme Court

- watches over the Constitution and interprets the laws.
- can call laws made by Congress unconstitutional.
- can call the president's decisions unconstitutional.

### The people

- elect a president for four years, indirectly through the Electoral College
- elect senators for six years.
- elect one third of representatives every two years.

# The American Constitution and the Bill of Rights

The War of Independence from Britain ('American Revolutionary War') ended in 1783 with an American victory. On September 17, 1787, delegates from the original 13 colonies signed the new Constitution of The United States.

In 1791 the Bill of Rights was added to the Constitution. This guaranteed:

**Freedom of assembly**
- Freedom to hold public meetings.
- Meetings must be peaceful and obey local laws.

**Freedom of religion**
- Freedom of worship.
- Freedom to belong to any religion, or to none.
- No official state religion is allowed.

**Freedom of the press**
- Freedom to print books, newspapers, and magazines.
- No one may print lies that harm other citizens ('libel').

**Freedom of speech**
- Freedom to express ideas and opinions.
- No one may use this freedom to tell lies in order to harm or to injure other citizens ('slander').

**The Constitution represents two basic beliefs:**
- The individual is important and must be free.
- The people have the right to choose the officials of the government (government by 'consent of the governed').

**Freedom of petition**
- Freedom to encourage the government to pass laws.
- Freedom to ask the government to take certain actions.

**Freedom and security of citizens**
- No unlawful search may be made of homes.
- Citizens may carry guns for self-defence.

**Rights to equal justice**
All persons accused of a crime must be treated fairly and equally in a court of law.

## Bild- und Textquellen

**Bildquellen:**

**U1** Getty Images (Blend Images), München; **U2** iStockphoto (ekash), Calgary, Alberta; **2.1** iStockphoto (sturti), Calgary, Alberta; **3.1** shutterstock (De Visu), New York, NY; **5.1** shutterstock (oneinchpunch), New York, NY; **6.1** shutterstock (View Apart), New York, NY; **8.1** Getty Images (E+/kali9), München; **9.1** shutterstock (Monkey Business Images), New York, NY; **10.1** shutterstock (suicidecrew), New York, NY; **10.1** shutterstock (suicidecrew), New York, NY; **12.1** AIFS in Bonn, Bonn; **13.1** laif (Daniel Rosenthal), Köln; **13.2** Getty Images (2011 Manfredi Caracausi/Moment), München; **15.1** iStockphoto (RapidEye), Calgary, Alberta; **15.2** Getty Images (Klaus Vedfelt/DigitalVision), München; **15.3** shutterstock (SpeedKingz), New York, NY; **15.4** Getty Images (Universal Images Group), München; **15.5** iStockphoto (asiseeit), Calgary, Alberta; **15.6** iStockphoto (FatCamera), Calgary, Alberta; **16.1** iStockphoto (sturti), Calgary, Alberta; **16.2** shutterstock (StockLite), New York, NY; **16.3** shutterstock (Nejron Photo), New York, NY; **17.1** shutterstock (Ema Woo), New York, NY; **18.1** Bulls Press (SWNS.com), Frankfurt; **20.1** Fosseway Films, London; **20.2** Fosseway Films, London; **20.3** Fosseway Films, London; **22.1** Hüter der Erinnerung (The Giver), USA 2014, Regie: Phillip Noyce (c) Interfoto (NG Collection), München; **25.1** Hüter der Erinnerung (The Giver), USA 2014, Regie: Phillip Noyce (c) Interfoto (NG Collection), München; **26.1** Hüter der Erinnerung (The Giver), USA 2014, Regie: Phillip Noyce (c) Interfoto (NG Collection), München; **27.1** Cover aus der Reihe Young Adult Literature: Klett English Editions, ISBN 978-3-12-578140-5, © Ernst Klett Sprachen GmbH, Stuttgart 1998; **28.1** Masterfile, Düsseldorf; **30.1** Thinkstock (monkeybusinessimages), München; **30.2** Savage Chickens; **32.1** Masterfile, Düsseldorf; **33.1** Getty Images (Patrick Aventurier), München; **34.1** iStockphoto (georgeclerk), Calgary, Alberta; **37.1** shutterstock (Sabphoto), New York, NY; **39.1** shutterstock (pim pic), New York, NY; **40.1** www.CartoonStock.com (Reynolds, Dan), Bath; **40.2** Getty Images (ABC Photo Archives/ABC via Getty Images; EN VOGUE), München; **41.1** shutterstock (De Visu), New York, NY; **41.2** Getty Images (2003 Ulrich Baumgarten), München; **41.3** iStockphoto (svetikd), Calgary, Alberta; **42.1** Fosseway Films, London; **42.2** Fosseway Films, London; **42.3** Fosseway Films, London; **43.1** Fosseway Films, London; **43.2** Fosseway Films, London; **44.1** shutterstock (Sean Pavone), New York, NY; **45.1** shutterstock (Maks Ershov), New York, NY; **45.2** shutterstock (littleny), New York, NY; **45.3** Alamy stock photo (inga spence), Abingdon, Oxon; **45.4** Getty Images (Corbis News), München; **46.1** Alamy stock photo (Sunshine Pics), Abingdon, Oxon; **49.1** Getty Images (Bettmann), München; **49.2** Klett-Archiv-RF-HF, Stuttgart; **50.1** Klett-Archiv-RF-HF, Stuttgart; **50.2** Dream Maker Software (RF), Colorado; **50.3** Geoatlas, Hendaye; **50.4** Klett-Archiv-RF-HF, Stuttgart; **50.5** Dream Maker Software (RF), Colorado; **50.6** Thinkstock (flowgraph), München; **50.7** Geoatlas, Hendaye; **50.8** Geoatlas, Hendaye; **50.9** Klett-Archiv-RF-HF, Stuttgart; **50.10** Klett-Archiv-RF-HF, Stuttgart;

**52.1** iStockphoto (tomprout), Calgary, Alberta; **52.2** Klett-Archiv-RF-HF, Stuttgart; **53.1** iStockphoto (rightdx), Calgary, Alberta; **54.1** shutterstock (Digital Media Pro), New York, NY; **55.1** shutterstock (Joseph Sohm), New York, NY; **56.1** Getty Images (Moment Mobile), München; **57.1** Klett-Archiv-RF-HF, Stuttgart; **57.2** Getty Images (Major League Baseball), München; **58.1** Getty Images (Greg Gayne/NBC/NBCU Photo Bank), München; **59.1** shutterstock (oneinchpunch), New York, NY; **65.1** iStockphoto (LauriPatterson), Calgary, Alberta; **67.1** shutterstock (s_bukley), New York, NY; **67.2** laif (Polaris), Köln; **67.3** shutterstock (Kathy Hutchins), New York, NY; **68.1** Getty Images (Stefania D'Alessandro), München; **71.1** iStockphoto (RapidEye), Calgary, Alberta; **73.1** shutterstock (Monkey Business Images), New York, NY; **73.2** Getty Images (Westend61), München; **73.3** Alamy stock photo (Ray Evans), Abingdon, Oxon; **75.1** Fosseway Films, London; **75.2** Fosseway Films, London; **75.3** Fosseway Films, London; **77.1** shutterstock (Uber Images), New York, NY; **77.2** Ullstein Bild GmbH, Berlin; **78.1** Getty Images (Westend61), München; **79.1** iStockphoto (Stolk), Calgary, Alberta; **80.1** shutterstock (Arina P Habich), New York, NY; **83.1** Alamy stock photo (Kumar Sriskandan), Abingdon, Oxon; **84.1** Getty Images (ROBYN BECK/AFP), München; **85.1** iStockphoto (MOF), Calgary, Alberta; **87.1** shutterstock (Spectral-Design), New York, NY; **87.2** Alamy stock photo (Juice Images), Abingdon, Oxon; **95.1** Thinkstock (Tom Ackerman), München; **96.1** iStockphoto (clu), Calgary, Alberta; **99.1** PONS GmbH, Stuttgart; **101.1** shutterstock (oliveromg), New York, NY; **108.1** Getty Images (DigitalVision), München; **109.1** Getty Images (E+/BraunS), München; **109.2** shutterstock (Phoenixns), New York, NY; **109.3** shutterstock (Monkey Business Images), New York, NY; **110.1** shutterstock (Syda Productions), New York, NY; **114.1** shutterstock (Ingus Kruklitis), New York, NY; **117.1** iStockphoto (subman), Calgary, Alberta; **117.2** shutterstock (Dobo Kristian), New York, NY; **124.1** shutterstock (FashionStock.com), New York, NY; **124.2** iStockphoto (RapidEye), Calgary, Alberta; **128.1** shutterstock (Hadrian), New York, NY; **132.1** iStockphoto (SoumenNath), Calgary, Alberta; **136.1** shutterstock (Galina Barskaya), New York, NY; **136.2** shutterstock (Vic Labadie), New York, NY; **140.1** shutterstock (granata1111), New York, NY; **140.2** shutterstock (suicidecrew), New York, NY; **140.3** shutterstock (ValeStock), New York, NY; **140.4** shutterstock (Chris Jenner), New York, NY; **194.1** Thinkstock (Creatas Images), München; **199.1** shutterstock (Dean Drobot), New York, NY; **199.2** shutterstock (Dean Drobot), New York, NY; **200.1** Getty Images (E+/RoBeDeRo), München; **201.1** iStockphoto (shelbyorme), Calgary, Alberta; **201.2** iStockphoto (oscity), Calgary, Alberta; **202.1** Kessler-Medien, Saarbrücken; **203.1** MEV Verlag GmbH, Augsburg; **203.2** MEV Verlag GmbH, Augsburg; **203.3** Getty Images RF (Photodisc), München; **203.4** creativ collection Verlag GmbH, Freiburg

**Textquellen:**

**7.1** Song: Champagne Life, Text: Gough, David Dorohn / SMITH, SHAFFER, Verlag: EMI Blackwood Music Inc / Pen in the ground publishing / Universal Music Z-Tunes EMI Music Publishing Germany GmbH, Berlin / Musik Edition Discoton GmbH, Berlin; **7.2** Song: The good life, Text: Hume, Jon Cobbe/Thistlethwayte, Rai Paul, Verlag: Sony ATV Music Publishing Australia P/L Sony / ATV Music Publishing (Germany) GmbH, Berlin; **9** By Richard Garner, The Independent, London, August 23, 2012; **12** Timo S, www.aifs.de; **22-23** Excerpt from THE GIVER by Lois Lowry. Copyright © 1993 by Lois Lowry. Reprinted by permission of Houghton Mifflin Harcourt Publishing Company. All rights reserved.; **33** By Marleen, earthlink e.V., München, 2016; **37** By Jonathan Webb, BBC News, September 8, 2015, www.bbc.com, © 2015 BBC, London; **39** Copyright Guardian News & Media Ltd 2015; **40** Song: Free your mind, Text: FOSTER, DENZIL DELANO / Levert, Gerald Edward / MC Elroy, Thomas Craig, Verlag: Two Tuff Enuff Publishing / Willesden Music Inc EMI Music Publishing Germany GmbH, Berlin / Imagem Music GmbH, Berlin; **49** Stadt Bremerhaven, 2014; **52** Deutsche Welle, 2012; **60–62** From FAMOUS by Todd Strasser. Copyright © 2011 by Todd Strasser. Reprinted with the permission of Simon & Schuster Books for Young Readers, an imprint of Simon & Schuster Children's Publishing Division. All rights reserved.

**Sollte es in einem Einzelfall nicht gelungen sein, den korrekten Rechteinhaber ausfindig zu machen, so werden berechtigte Ansprüche selbstverständlich im Rahmen der üblichen Regelungen abgegolten.**

Alaska
(U.S.)

Aleutian Is.
(U.S.)

CANADA

UNITED
KINGDO

IRELAND

UNITED STATES
OF AMERICA

Channel Is.
(U.K.)

Gibraltar (U.K.)

Hawaiian
Islands
(U.S.)

Bermuda
(U.K.)

BAHAMAS

Turks and Caicos Is. (U.K.)

Virgin Is. (U.K./U.S.)

Cayman Is.
(U.K.)

Anguilla (U.K.)

BELIZE

JAMAICA

ANTIGUA AND BARBUDA

Puerto
Rico (U.S.)

DOMINICA

ST. CHRISTOPHER AND NEVIS

ST. LUCIA

Montserrat (U.K.)

BARBADOS

GRENADA

ST. VINCENT AND GRENADINES

TRINIDAD AND TOBAGO

GAMBIA

NIGER

SIERRA LEONE

GUYANA

LIBERIA

GHANA

CAMER

Palmyra Is.
(U.S.)

Howland Is.
(U.S.)

Jarvis Is.
(U.S.)

Ascension
(U.K.)

KIRIBATI

TUVALU

Tokelau Is. (N.Z.)

WESTERN
SAMOA

American
Samoa
(U.S.)

Cook Is.
(N.Z.)

Saint Helena
(U.K.)

NA

TONGA

Pitcairn Is
(U.K.)

Tristan da Cunha
(U.K.)

Gough Is.
(U.K.)

Falkland Is./
Malvinas (U.K.)

**NAME**  Countries in which English is the / an official language   Independent Commonwealth

YPRUS

PAKISTAN

INDIA

BANGLADESH

HONG KONG

SUDAN

ERITREA

SOUTH SUDAN

NDA

KENYA

A

TANZANIA

SEYCHELLES

BIA

MALAWI

ZIMBABWE

ANA

SWAZILAND

LESOTHO

TH ICA

MALDIVES

SRI LANKA

Laccadive Is. (Ind.)

Andaman Is. (Ind.)

PHILIPPINES

MALAYSIA

BRUNEI

SINGAPORE

PALAU

MICRONESIA

NORTHERN MARIANAS

Guam (U.S.)

MARSHALL ISLANDS

KIRIBATI

NAURU

SOLOMON ISLANDS

TUVALU

PAPUA NEW GUINEA

VANUATU

FIJI

Aleutian Is. (U.S.)

Midway Is. (U.S.)

Wake Is. (U.S.)

Chagos Is. (U.K)

Diego Garcia (U.K.)

MAURITIUS

Cocos Is. (Austl.)

Christmas Is (Austl.)

AUSTRALIA

Lord Howe Is. (Austl.)

Norfolk Is. (Austl.)

Kermadec Is. (N.Z.)

NEW ZEALAND

Prince Edward Is. (S.Afr.)

McDonald Is. (Austl.)

Auckland Is. (N.Z.)

Macquarie Is (Austl.)

Bounty Is (N.Z.)

Antipodes Is. (N.Z.)

Chatham Is. (N.Z.)

ne   Dependent territories of Commonwealth states (in brackets)      SCALE 1 : 88,000,000

# CALIFORNIA

OREGON

IDAHO

*Goose Lake*

*Upper Lake*

Redwood
National
Park

USA

▲ *Lassen Peak*
10,457 ft (3,187 m)

Redding

*Pyramid Lake*

*C o a s t   R a n g e s*

*S a c r a m e n t o   C e n t r a l*

*S i e r r a*

NEVADA

*Lake Tahoe*

Napa
Valley

Sacramento

*S a n   J o a q u i n*

Yosemite National Park

*Mono Lake*

San Francisco

Silicon Valley

San Jose

*N e v a d a*

Salinas

Mount Whitney ▲
14,505 ft (4,421 m)

*Death Valley*
-282 ft (-86 m)

*Pacific
Ocean*

*B i g   S u r*

*V a l l e y*

CALIFORNIA

Mojave Desert

CALIFORNIA REPUBLIC

Malibu

Santa Monica

Venice

Los Angeles

HOLLYWOOD

Palm Springs

*C o l o r a d o*

ARIZONA

*Salton Sea*

San Diego

MEXICO

ALASKA
Denali ▲
CANADA

CANADA

Seattle
Portland
WASHINGTON

OREGON

ROCKY

MONTANA

NORTH DAKOTA

SOUTH DAKOTA

WYOMING

IDAHO

NEBRASKA

San Francisco

NEVADA

UTAH

Mountains

Denver

COLORADO

CALIFORNIA

KA

Las Vegas

HOLLYWOOD

Los Angeles
San Diego

Pacific Ocean

ARIZONA

Phoenix

NEW MEXICO

OKLAH

TEXAS

HAWAII

MEXICO